HUMAN PERFORMANCE, SITUATION AWARENESS AND AUTOMATION:
CURRENT RESEARCH AND TRENDS

HPSAA II
Volume I

Human Performance, Situation Awareness and Automation: Current Research and Trends

Edited by:

Dennis A. Vincenzi, Ph.D.
Department of Human Factors and Systems
Embry-Riddle Aeronautical University
600 S. Clyde Morris Blvd.
Daytona Beach, FL 32114
dennis.vincenzi@erau.edu

Mustapha Mouloua, Ph.D.
Department of Psychology
University of Central Florida
4000 Central Florida Blvd
Orlando, FL 32816
mouloua@pegasus.cc.ucf.edu

Peter A. Hancock, Ph.D.
Department of Psychology
University of Central Florida
4000 Central Florida Blvd
Orlando, FL 32816
phancock@pegasus.cc.ucf.edu

 Routledge
Taylor & Francis Group

LONDON AND NEW YORK

HUMAN PERFORMANCE, SITUATION AWARENESS AND AUTOMATION:
CURRENT RESEARCH AND TRENDS

HPSAA II
Volume I

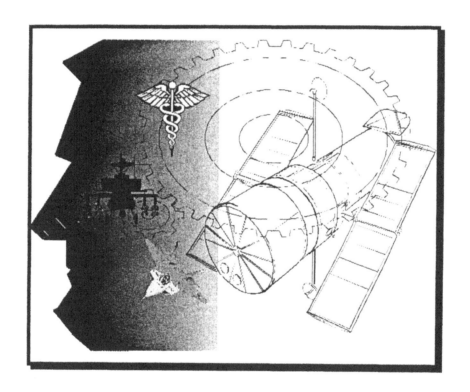

Edited by:

Dennis A. Vincenzi
Mustapha Mouloua
Peter A. Hancock

Proceedings of the Second Human Performance, Situation Awareness and Automation Conference (HPSAA II), held in Daytona Beach, FL, March 22 – 25, 2004.

Conference Chairs:

Dennis A. Vincenzi, Conference Chair, Embry-Riddle Aeronautical University
Mustapha Mouloua, Conference Co-Chair, University of Central Florida

Scientific Program Committee:

Prof. Jean Bresson, *Ecole Nationale De L'Aviation Civile (ENAC)*
John E. Deaton, *Florida Institute of Technology*
Mica R. Endsley, *SA Technologies*
Peter A. Hancock, *University of Central Florida*
David Kaber, *North Carolina State University*
Anthony Majoros, *The Boeing Company*
Prof. Regis Mollard, *Université René Descartes-Paris*
Raja Parasuraman, *The Catholic University of America*
Mark Scerbo, *Old Dominion University*
John Wise, *Honeywell International*

Technical Editing and Graphic Design by:

Dennis A. Vincenzi
Ryan Wasson

Department of Human Factors and Systems
Embry-Riddle Aeronautical University
600 S. Clyde Morris Blvd.
Daytona Beach, FL 32114

FOREWORD

In the era which followed the second world-war, human-machine interaction was dominated by the questions of movement control and movement accuracy as luminaries such as Craik, Crossman, McRuer, Baron and their respective colleagues fought to generate analog solutions to problems fundamentally framed as questions about analog machines. As pointed out in his admirable keynote paper (Moray, this volume), the challenge was often understood as a complex of demands but even within such multi-tasking environments, the continuous control problem was the one that thrust itself predominantly to the fore. Significant and successful efforts to address such challenges were indeed forthcoming just as the necessity of this aspect of human-machine interaction began to wane. Not merely because of the digital revolution, but also the very fact that these continuous control problems themselves were open to successful resolution left them vulnerable to the engineering community who rightfully sought to solve soluble problems.

As with all technical leaps, in solving a range of problems, such successes create a vista of others. In our science, this transition was observed in the content composition of scientific conferences. The once vibrant 'Annual Manual' Conference dissolved, not so much as with a bang (bang) as with a whimper. There being no fundamental vacuum in human endeavors, the translated problem was resurrected through the wonderful insights of individuals such as Sheridan and Moray who understood that the issue of control had been removed one level to a supervisory one, in which the actions of the operator were much more sporadic and intermittent with all the issues of dissociation, memory capacity, mental workload, and vigilance that this remove engendered. Of course, there had previously been rudimentary process control systems but now this form of interaction was thrust to the fore. For almost a decade, such work was the topic of workshops and sporadic meetings as the associated issues resolved themselves and the technical systems of this form were designed, fabricated, operated, and decimated.

It was a ground swell of understanding, largely championed by Charles Billings that found formalized expression in the first meeting in the present series, conceived and convened by Raja Parasuraman and Mustapha Mouloua. In 1994 they hosted the inaugural Conference in Rockville, Maryland with the paradoxical title, 'Human Performance in Automated Systems.' While the general perception of automation involves machine response with no human intervention, that Conference rapidly established that the human involvement, although further removed from the site of activity, nevertheless continued to exert a crucial influence over operations, even if this influence was only evident at the design stage. A strong motivation for holding this first meeting was the growing realization that automation was pervasive in virtually all walks of life, a trend which continues today and still acts as a stimulus for the series of meetings that have taken place subsequently.

From Cocoa Beach, Florida in 1996 through Norfolk, Virginia in 1998 we have seen research presentations on human interaction with automated systems in domains as diverse as transportation, medicine, manufacturing engineering, aerospace operations consumer products, and now consumer software. In 2000, the Conference on Automation joined forces with a partner group on situation awareness (SA) with a highly successful first combined meeting in Savannah, Georgia. The situation awareness group itself had a history of successful meetings, again in both Georgia and Florida. In keeping with the increasing emphasis on a move from immediate manual control to remote, periodic interaction, the ascending complexity of systems demands that one be aware of a large range of environmental and task-based stimulation in order to match what is done with what has to be done. Thus SA and automation-based interaction fall naturally together and the present Conference is the second incarnation of this most fruitful union.

The efforts evident in the present conference are captured by a number of themes. Moray in his keynote implores us not to forget the hard won knowledge of the past, protesting that the success of quantitative modeling of skill-based behavior can well form a template for successful quantitative modeling of both rule-based and knowledge-based behavior. His admonitions should receive deserved attention. There is also a small but growing recognition that affective facets of performance and detailed individual differences in operator's attitudes and capacities are issues with which we must now grapple. Primarily, we still seek unified models, theories, taxonomies and descriptions to characterize what is a dispersed domain of interaction but one in which we continue to seek and explicate core issues. There is indeed still much for us to accomplish, although where this will occur under the same banner title, or whether there will again be a technology-driven and societally-driven metamorphosis, only the future will tell. As we move inexorably further into the 21st Century, further diversification of the applications of automation will evidently continue, the revolution in genetic technology being an obvious coming example. Given the pervasive nature of this form of human-machine interaction, it is vital that we apply the lessons of the past to map a future for the symbiotic relationship between humans and the artifacts we create. It is as part of this on-going endeavor that the present volume is offered.

Peter A. Hancock, Ph.D., *University of Central Florida*
Dennis A. Vincenzi, Ph.D., *Embry-Riddle Aeronautical University*
Mustapha Mouloua, Ph.D., *University of Central Florida*

ACKNOWLEDGEMENTS

As with any successful effort, there is never one single individual, organization or agency that is totally responsible for that success. Such is the case with this conference. Many individuals contributed countless hours toward the organization and successful execution of this conference, and many organizations provided critical funding to support this conference. It is with great pleasure that I attempt to recognize their efforts and express heartfelt thanks for all their hard work.

I would like to thank the following persons for devoting their time and effort to make important contributions to the organization of the Human Performance, Situation Awareness and Automation Conference II (HPSAA II):

- Susan Vincenzi
- Ryan Wasson

Susan Vincenzi planned the conference food menus and assisted in the planning and organization of many logistical details of the conference ranging from delivery of equipment to listing and purchasing of necessary supplies for the conference. Ryan Wasson was largely responsible for the technical editing of all papers submitted for publication in the proceedings. He contributed many hours of tireless effort to make the papers and proceedings as uniform and consistent as possible. His assistance prior to and during the conference was much needed and greatly appreciated.

I would like to thank the scientific committee for their comments and suggestions during the process of organizing the meeting. Their help and guidance in this regard was invaluable. The scientific committee included Mustapha Mouloua, Jean Bresson, John Deaton, Mica Endsley, Peter Hancock, David Kaber, Anthony Majoros, Regis Mollard, Raja Parasuraman, Mark Scerbo and John Wise.

I would like to offer special thanks to the conference co-chair, Mustapha Mouloua, for his unending enthusiasm and contributions toward organization and marketing of the conference.

Finally, I would like to thank all our sponsors, without whose generous support, this conference would not have been possible. The support provided by the different sponsors ranged from manpower and supplies to major monetary contributions that funded various operational aspects of the conference that included but were not limited to funding for guest speakers, travel expenses, student support, printing of programs, and printing of proceedings to provide a permanent record for dissemination of information throughout the scientific community. The conference sponsors are:

- The National Aeronautics and Space Administration (NASA) Langley Research Center (LaRC)
- The Office of Naval Research (ONR)
- The U.S. Army Medical Research Acquisition Activity (USAMRAA)
- The Defense Advanced Research Projects Agency (DARPA)
- CHI Systems, Inc.
- Human Solutions, Inc.
- Interface Analysis Associates
- Embry-Riddle Aeronautical University
- The University of Central Florida
- Florida Institute of Technology

My sincerest thanks go out to all these individuals and organizations for their support in making this conference a great success.

Dennis A. Vincenzi, Ph.D.
Conference Chair
Embry-Riddle Aeronautical University

TABLE OF CONTENTS

CONFERENCE KEYNOTE ADDRESS

TECHNICAL PAPERS

SITUATION AWARENESS

AIR TRAFFIC CONTROL

DECISION MAKING

DRIVER PERFORMANCE AND DISTRACTION

CONFERENCE KEYNOTE ADDRESS

Où sont les neiges d'antan?[1]

Written by:

Neville Moray
Magagnosc, France
moray2@wanadoo.fr

Presented by:

Thomas B. Sheridan
Massachusetts Institute of Technology

---

[1] "Where are the snows of yesteryear?". François Villon. 1450.

ABSTRACT

Starting from an examination of two modern papers, about situation awareness and about allocation of function in human-machine systems, this paper examines the requirements for a quantitative predictive model of rule-based behaviour. It shows that much relevant empirical evidence exists in papers of 30 to 40 years ago, and that there has been convergence both of theory and data. It offers tentative guidelines towards the development of a predictive model.

INTRODUCTION: SITUATION AWARENESS AND AUTOMATION

It is well-known that elderly people are incapable of transferring new material from working to long term memory, but are adept at recalling material from the past. In the spirit of that observation I thought that I would take the one or two (fairly) recent papers, and use the remote past to illuminate the work that respected scientists and researchers are currently doing. The two modern papers that I would like to examine are Endsley, (1995), and Parasuraman, Sheridan, and Wickens, (2000).

I want to examine these papers because the results of a recent straw poll of over 100 people, inquiring as to which papers they thought were historically the most important human/factors ergonomics papers, surprised me, and made me wonder what had happened to HF models. Top of the poll was Bainbridge (1983), and equal second were Miller (1956), and Rasmussen, (1983). It is curious that there were no candidate papers from "classical" industrial ergonomics (even when deliberately requested) and very few votes for classical engineering candidate papers.

The lack of engineering papers is particularly surprising. People seem to have been thinking mainly of advanced human-machine systems when asked about their opinions of HF/ergonomics (I take it that the words mean the same thing), but there was almost no support for papers on control theory. Yet control theory is the one area where there has been quite exceptional success in theory based practical applications. It provides almost the only area in which we have developed not just good descriptive models, not just an ability to perform strong analysis of system performance, but also are able to predict, even in advance of prototypes, whether a machine will be usable by operators. Why have people forgotten its achievements so soon?

I think perhaps the vote suggests the following:

1. A shift from skill-based behaviour (SBB) to automation, with an increasing emphasis on rule-based-behaviour (RBB) and knowledge-based behaviour (KBB), (Rasmussen, 1983.).
2. A mature recognition of the importance of limits due to inherent psychological mechanisms such as memory, channel capacity, etc. (the Miller paper). (In modern work this is called "bounded rationality".)
3. Increasing interest in automation and the impact of system complexity.

The two papers which I have taken as the starting point of this talk reflect such conclusions. Perhaps control theory has lost its influence because it was traditionally concerned with SBB, and with the increasing interest in complex continuous processes with extensive automation on the one hand, and with automated and robotic discrete manufacturing on the other, there is less interest in SBB. As Tom Sheridan once remarked, it is ironic that just as we really learned how to model manual control it began to disappear. Even aviation seldom requires SBB: for an extreme example see the recent paper in Ergonomics in Design (Cummings 2004.), and of course the Airbus series of aircraft. Even so, it is remarkable that the influence of classical and optimal control theory seems to have disappeared from human factors and ergonomics literature. Why, for example, did the Annual Manual meetings cease? Is this meeting their successor? If so, where are the computational and *predictive* models? And, (what I find very worrying), why are there so few references in our literature to engineering journals, such as *Automatica, IEEE Transactions on Systems Science and Cybernetics,* and other places where engineers are describing their approaches to human-machine system design and modeling?

IN SEARCH OF PREDICTIVE MODELS

One reason for the success of control theory was the tight coupling between human and machine in manual control systems. The highly practised human became a component (even if adaptive one which could, on occasion, switch into RBB or KBB). The result was a highly quantitative and predictive set of models (McRuer and Krendel, 1959; McRuer and Jex,1967; Young, 1973). The least developed aspect was adaptive control, although there were many good papers , (e.g. Young, L. 1969; Crossman & Cooke, 1974).and a particularly fine book by Kelley (1968) that pretty well sank without trace and is almost never referenced in modern papers. If we are now all so interested in advanced, automated human-machine systems, why have has no equivalent predictive models appeared for RBB and KBB?

In what follows, when I speak of "predictive" models I am looking for more than ordinal prediction. Models should say more than, "If you make it like this it will be better than if you make it like that."; rather, one would like them to say, "This is what will happen in the next five seconds." I think that the intense interest in "situation awareness" (SA), is a reflection of a desire for such models.

Table 1 lists some of the reasons we have not seen any predictive models arise to supplement control theory.

TABLE 1.
WHY HAVE NO NEW PREDICTIVE MODELS FOLLOWED CONTROL THEORY?

- The loss of contact with engineering has led people to avoid models tightly coupled to the dynamics of the systems and environments.
- A zeitgeist developed in the 1980s that rejected mathematical models in favour of a deeper psychological understanding of the operators' cognitive processes. But almost no predictive models have resulted.
- In modern systems the coupling between human and machine is much looser. (It was loose even for very slow manual control processes and was never developed for discrete manufacturing. See papers in Edwards and Lees (1974) for discrete intervention in the case of slow process control.)
- The coupling changed from physical causality to logical and semantic relationships (Rasmussen, 1986).
- The operators' role changed from controller to supervisor and intervener.
- Operators' actions afforded by the systems became ever less analog, and less depended on physical strength and skill. (Interfaces intervened between operator actions and provided digital control of the systems.)
- As human-machine systems (HMS) become ever more complex and larger, teams, rather than individuals control them, and modeling team behaviour seems at first sight very different from modeling individual behaviour.

If we are to develop new predictive models, two things are needed: a return to a detailed interest in models that capture system dynamics, and a way to describe the coupling between operators and the new machines. Reading recent papers suggests that implicitly people recognize the need to improve coupling. Table 2 lists some work that supports this contention.

TABLE 2.
EVIDENCE OF INTEREST IN IMPROVING HUMAN MACHINE COUPLING

1. The emphasis on Situation Awareness.
2. The discussion of the design of automation by Parasuraman, Sheridan and Wickens (2000).
3. Klein's work on Recognition Primed Decisions
4. Wood's notion of "visual momentum".
5. The ideas of Rasmussen and Vicente about "ecological" displays and controls.

It is clear that a predictive model at the level of RBB and KBB will not be a purely quantitative mathematical model in the way that control theory was for SBB. In that respect Bainbridge was right to challenge control theory as a general model for process control (Bainbridge, 1981; Montmollin & De Keyser, 1985.). But while a mathematical model may not be possible, a *computational* model that includes quantitative components is surely a desirable goal, and the need for a mixed model is evident if we look closely at Endsley's account of SA.

In fact, there are several models that have tried to extend the exact modelling of SBB that was achieved by control theory to RBB and KBB, even though not necessarily while thinking in those terms:

1. SOAR
2. ACT*-R
3. PROCRU

and there are also some specialized models such as those of Hollnagel and Cacciabue (Cacciabue, Cojazzi, Hollnagel, & Mancini, 1992; Cacciabue, P.C., DeCortis, F., Drozdowicz, B., Masson, M., & Nordvik, J-P. 1992; Hollnagel, 2003);Roth, Woods & Pople, 1992; and Baron. Fehrer, Pew, and Horwitz, 1986.

The first two have been applied to modeling "real" behaviour to some extent, although SOAR and ACT*-R have seldom been used to model real time activities particularly where satisficing under time pressure rather than optimal decision making is required. (I use "ACT*-R" to cover all the recent versions.) It is particularly to be regretted that PROCRU was not further developed, because it included optimal control theory for SBB, and was reaching for the ability that SOAR and ACT*-R have to deal with semantics, logical reasoning, and other aspects of the psychological mechanisms that support complex psychological operations.

A look at Endsley's account (Endsley, 1995) of situation awareness emphasises the need for complex computational models. It is ostensibly a paper about SA, but could equally well have been published as an introductory chapter in a text on cognitive psychology: it is about *everything*, perception, attention, working memory, long-term memory, decision making, and so on. This is not really surprising, because SA is not really the name of a particular psychological function. It is a shorthand description for, "keeping track of what is going on around you in a complex, dynamic environment." Obviously, one needs to use all one's cognitive (and for that matter motivational and emotional) abilities for such a task. Equally, the aim of efficient SA is to keep the operator tightly coupled to the dynamics of the environment.

Often one thinks of automation as loosening the coupling between operators and the task, so as to lighten their loads, but it is clear that Parasuraman et al. (2000) do not think that. Indeed all the best researchers on automation, including Parasuraman et al., Woods, Hollnagel, Rasmussen, Vicente, Bainbridge, etc., point out that the major problem with automation is the desire to reduce the load on operators coupled with its inability to keep them tightly in the loop. In the classical description of Supervisory Control, (Sheridan, 1978), the flow chart of closed loop supervisory control makes this quite clear (Figure 1).

The main thrust of Parasuraman et al. (2000) is to make this coupling strong but flexible. In the supervisory control part of Figure 1 the block called "human operator transfer function" conceals a great deal. It is clear in earlier discussions of adaptive control (such as Young ,1969; and Kelley, 1968), that the block actually contains what amounts to Endsley's model of dynamic cognition, because the operator has to assess the situation, make plans, decide how to act, and if necessary intervene, as Sheridan (1978) described. Parasuraman et al.'s analysis of automation in essence disassembles the flow chart of cognition into sub-functions and proposes that automation be allocated to these different sub-functions as required to optimize the coupling of human operators to the task. On some occasions it may be most effective to substitute machine sensing and perception for that of humans, on other occasions to substitute machine planning or decisions making, and on others control or action. (And of course there is always the possibility of automating two or more sub-functions simultaneously.)

One reason to try to develop a computational predictive model is that there is a large measure of agreement about what should be in such a model, and how to link it to decisions about automation. In addition to the well-known block diagrams of Endsley and of Wickens, there are the descriptions of human machine interaction in Roth, Woods & Pople (1992), Rasmussen, (1984, 1995), and Bainbridge (1991), and less well known ones such as Hess (1987), Hollnagel, (2003), and Cacciabue et al.(1992). There is even considerable agreement between those developed by the engineering human factors community and SOAR or ACT*-R. Here, for example, is a quotation from Hess (1987):

"(The internal model is) a volatile internal spatial/temporal representation of the environment which the human is assumed to possess and use while interacting with complex dynamic systems."

Hess goes on to suggest that in a multi-dimensional world the operator chooses a frame within which to stay, using time-driven planning, and that time scales change as O moves up or down the hierarchy of representation. It all sounds very like a synthesis of what Endsley would later describe and what Rasmussen had already discussed.

Surely the time has come to try for an overall computational synthesis. Roth et al. (1992) were well on the way to such a model, as indeed were the developers of PROCRU (Baron, Muralidharan, Lancrafty, & Zacharias, 1980; Baron et al., 1986). Sanderson and I, in the early 1990s, got as far as writing pseudo-code for Rasmussen's ladder, although we never completed it (Sanderson, 1991). (See Figure 2.)

Looking at that pseudo-code today, it appears to contain many productions rather like a first pass at a model of SA. (See particularly Productions 2, 3, and 4). Productions 6, 13, and 14 on the other hand might be relevant to deciding what part of the processing might be allocated to automation.

Let us look a bit more closely at some ways that a computational model of SA and function allocation might be tied together, and implemented as a computational model.

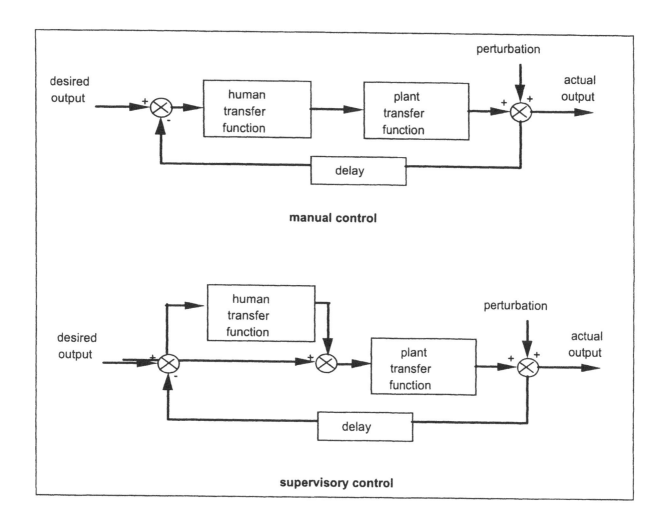

Figure 1. Manual and supervisory control

5

MODEL CONVERGENCE IN THE LITERATURE

Suppose that we want to decide whether, for some task, it is reasonable to expect operators to monitor the dynamic environment, or whether that task should be allocated to automation. Let us start by looking at Endsley's definition of SA. According to her it is

> "the perception of the elements in the environment within a certain volume of time and space, the comprehension of their meaning, and the projection of their status into the near future.".
>
> (Endsley, 1995.)

1.   if state = Alert then ...
   p(response$_i$) = f(alert type, environmental invariance, practice, response mapping, etc.)
   ... then carry out response$_i$

2.   if state = Alert and response not carried out
   then set goal = Observe information and data

3.   if goal = Observe information and data then ...
   data = f(data available, scanning habits, current scheduling policy, hypotheses,
                   incoming events, time to observe, etc.)
   ... then Data = {d$_1$, d$_2$, ... }

4.   if goal = Identify state then ...
   state = f(observability, data observed, diagnosticity of data, operator knowledge,
                   familiarity, likelihood, time, etc.)
   ... then State = s$_i$

5.   if goal = Determine state consequences and State = s$_i$ then ...
   state consequences = f(system mental model, performance goal, etc.)
   ... then State consequences = {sc$_1$, sc$_2$, ... , uncertain}

6.   if goal = Evaluate performance criteria then ...
   performance goal = f(organizational knowledge, etc.)
   ... then Performance goal = {g$_1$, g$_2$, ... }

    .
    .
    .

13.   if goal = Choose criterion and Criterion = c$_i$
    then set goal = Define policy: operationalize criterion

14.   if Criterion = c$_i$ and goal = Define policy: operationalize criterion then ...
    policy = f(criterion c$_i$, memory of criterion-policy mappings, momentary system configuration, policy
                    feasibility, display/technological constraints, time available, etc.)
    ...then Policy = p$_i$.

Figure 2. Pseudo-code for Rasmussen's Decision Ladder.

Why is this difficult for people? And why is it hard to model RBB and KBB in "a certain volume of time and space"?

It is not just the "volume" of time and space that is the problem. It is the rate at which events occur (constraints caused by limited time and the dynamics of the environment) and the quantity of information to be processed (the complexity of space, or rather, of things that exist in space). I am reminded of Simon's famous remark that it is the complexity of the environment rather than the complexity of the mind wherein complexity lies.

Effective SA requires operators to simplify the environment so that observations can be handled by limited memory, and at a rate within the capacity of limited attention. There is a considerable amount of empirical and theoretical work on how people simplify the complexity of their environments, and by so doing gain time to handle the rate of events. If we can understand how people do this, we will be in a better position to decide what aspect of their task to automate, what version of Parasuraman et al.'s (2003) array of automation to implement. We might begin by considering the spectrum of task times described by Sanderson and Fisher (1994). (See Figure 3.)

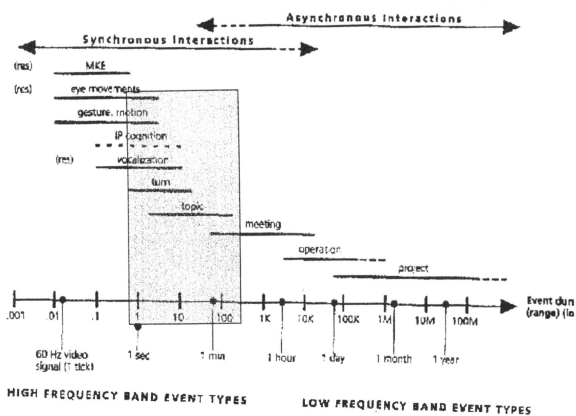

Figure 3: A spectrum of durations of event classes (Sanderson and Fisher, 1994).

I have overlain Sanderson's spectrum with a window that marks the region where I would expect people to have little difficulty in handling information in real time. If events occur faster than this, then operators will need assistance to update their SA, and if events occur very much more slowly, they will have difficulty in integrating the information to obtain an overall picture due to loss of information from working memory. Of course if the environment which they are observing is very complex, (high dimensional), even a low event rate for individual parts of it may cause too high an event rate to allow O to maintain SA. It is important to consider very large and slow process such as process control as well as high bandwidth systems such as high performance aircraft. Both ends of the spectrum are important and cause problems for the human operator.

Consider some more of the characteristics of SA as described by Endsley. SA is a dynamic description of the status of the environment and the human-machine system during a functionally important window.

"There is evidence that an integrated picture of the current situation may be matched to prototypical situations in memory... (a theory of SA) should explain dynamic goal selection, attention to appropriate critical cues, expectancies, regarding future states of the situation, and the tie between situation awareness and typical actions."

(Endsley, 1995.)

Wherever we look at Endsley's description of SA, we find that workers in other contexts have said similar things. That is most encouraging. The next three figures, 4, 5, and 6 are Figures 1, 2, and 4 from Endsley's 1995 paper.

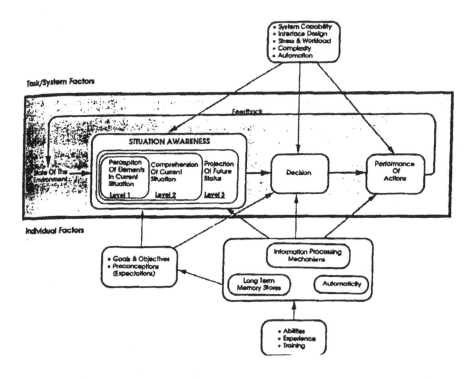

Figure 4. Endsley's model of Situation Awareness

For example, the contents of the SA box in her Figure 1 could easily map onto the hierarchy of information processing described in Rasmussen's "ladder" (Rasmussen, 1984.), and her description of "best match" categorization in SA recognition onto Reason's account of pattern matching in his discussion of the origins of human error (Reason, 1990). Her discussion of perception and the role of expectation is closely related to what one would find in the theory of signal detection. Her "space" can be related to the ecological problem spaces of Rasmussen and Vicente (1989), as can her discussion of display design. And if I may be allowed to cite some of my own work on mental models, there is a striking similarity between the contents of the SA box in her Figure 1 and my conclusions of how mental models are used to guide monitoring (Figure 7).

The most interesting thing about these similarities is that they have come about serendipitously, because the researchers involved were working on different problems. The convergence is remarkable, and Endsley's account of SA serves as an excellent convergence point.

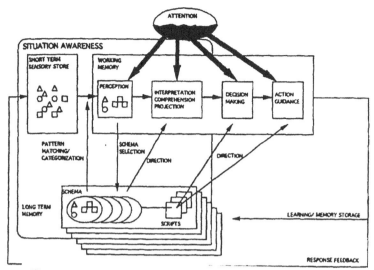

Figure 5. Endsley's model of information processing

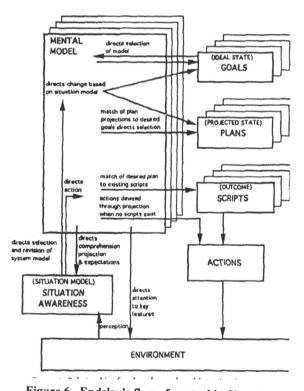

Figure 6. Endsley's flow of control in Situation Awareness

9

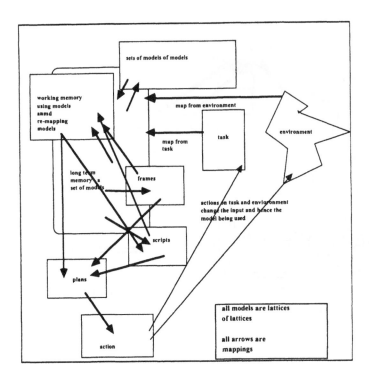

Figure 7. Moray's mental model information flow chart

HOW DO THEY DO IT? REDUCING COMPLEXITY

When we look at the immense complexity of the environments in which expert operators manage to maintain good SA, their performance is really quite remarkable. If we look back at the literature of the last 50 years we find that expert operators seem to manage remarkably well in situations that on a superficial analysis of the bandwidth and complexity of the environment would seem nearly impossible. Given that they are often probably forced to use RBB and KBB, which are known to be very demanding of cognitive skills, how are they doing it? Before looking at some of this empirical evidence, let us consider how in general complexity can be handled.

One way is decompose the environment into groupings of elements, within each group of which there is a strong mutual causal interaction and coherence, and between which there is little. We can think of this as looking at a complex body in terms of its "organs" or "molecules", rather than its "atoms". There are several suggestions as to how this might be done. Recently Yufik and Sheridan (1991); Yufik, Y. M., Sheridan, T. B., & Venda, V. F. 1992; proposed a way to build mental models with just this property. And somewhat earlier (Moray ,1986), I offered a less sophisticated account of the same topic. These papers show how the detection of coupling among variables would allow an observer to reduce the amount of processing needed to keep track of the state of the environment, at very little cost in accuracy. (We shall see later that Beishon (1974) thought that empirical evidence from process control supported this kind of behaviour in ovenmen.) The degree of re-composition of information (from "atoms" to molecules to organs, etc.) would depend on discovering the natural decomposition of the environment, and reasons to think that it is one of the main differences between a neophyte and an expert (Canas, Quesada, Antoli, & Fajarda, 2003). Furthermore, there has been extensive discussion of how to decompose a large system into its natural components even if one does not understand initially how it is put together. (See for example, the little known papers by Conant, 1976). Rasmussen (personal communication, 1993) has suggested that causal models (as distinct from mathematical descriptive models) should be based on decomposing a system into objects and its behaviour into events, rather than simply treating all variables alike as individual entities, and probably the findings of McKinney and Davis (2003) on the use of training for crisis management reflects this.

One consequences for this approach to SA and operator mental modeling would be that automation might be designed both to encourage such skills in the operators and direct their attention to appropriate levels of "molecules", and also, equally importantly, to keep track of the finer details so that if unforeseen events or system failures occur, the automation can support a return to more detailed examination of state space when that is needed. Note that this is what Rasmussen, Vicente, Woods and other "ecological system" designers recommend, namely information at appropriate levels for the particular cognitive operations form moment to moment. By knowing how the operators mentally decompose the system, strong hints about the design of support for "visual momentum" will be found.

Let us return to the question of timing. Sanderson's spectrum is but one way to view the rate limitation on cognition. I would like to draw your attention to two others. The first is quantitative. Forty years ago, Wohl, (1961; also 1982), reported very interesting data about the times it took people to repair radar sets. Data from Wohl (1982) are shown in Figure 8.

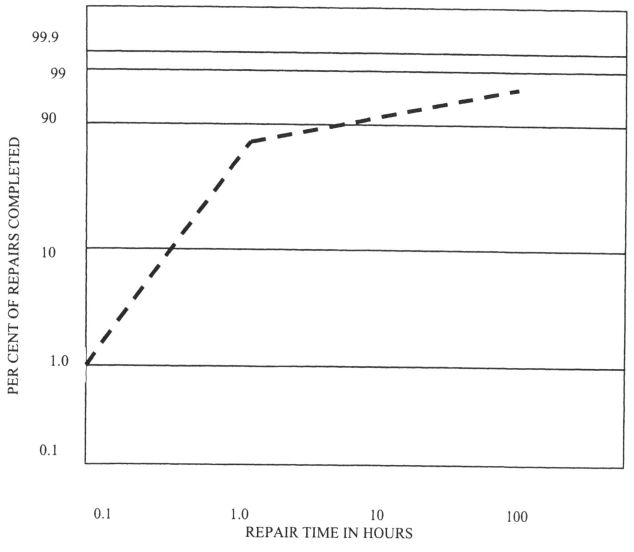

Figure 8. The proportion of radar set faults diagnosed and repaired as a function of time since work on them began. (After Wohl, 1982.)

11

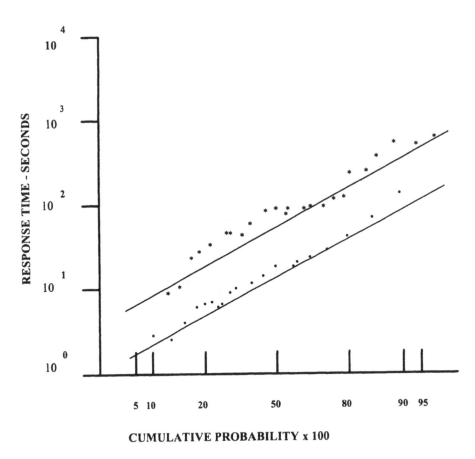

Figure 9. Cumulative probability of response related to time since incident. (After Beare et al 1984.)

Wohl discusses the shape of this plot in terms that today sound similar to the distinction between RBB and KBB. The steep initial slope, in which as time passes the repair men are more and more likely to reach a solution, seems to occur while they using a "test according to well known rules" strategy (RBB). If this finally fails, they are forced to try to think of new things to do (KBB), and from then on the slope of the curve (on a Weibull plot) is less than 45^0, meaning that it is less and less likely that they will find the solution. (A practical conclusion would be, "After an hour, throw it away and buy a new one.") What I particularly want to draw your attention to is the first part of the curve, when the operators are drawing on their deeply learned set of pattern matching rules. In this case about 90% of work on this task is completed in an hour. Consider now another, closely related curve (Beare, A. N., Dorris, R. E., Bovell, C. R., Crowe, D. S., and Kozinsky, E. J.,(1984). Here it is not a Weibull plot, but a log-normal time-reliability curve (Figure 9).

In this study, although the environment is quite different (a high fidelity nuclear power plant simulator,) these curves closely resemble the first part of Wohl's curve. They also resemble nearly two dozen others plotted by Beare et al. for a variety of diagnostic tasks in a nuclear power plant. (Note that they are plotted in an unusual way, the independent variable being on the ordinate, and the dependent variable on the abscissa, unlike Wohl's data and most others that have used this kind of plot. In Beare et al.'s version a flatter slop is a faster slope.) Much simpler systems show similar curves, as do the data in Wohl (1961), but they are flatter, i.e. approach completion faster.

Such curves could be used to calibrate the success of automation intervention. They provide an estimate of what can be expected from the general population of operators. If working with automation lowers the slope, then automation is assisting diagnosis. In Beare et al. there is also a feature that suggests that the operators are simplifying the environment. The upper curve in each case is based on field data for operators' responses to real faults in the plant: the lower curve is based on responses to simulations of the same faults. In all but one of Beare et al.'s plots the curves are linear and parallel, the curves for the simulated data being almost exactly one log unit lower than the field data, that is, ten times faster. An obvious explanation is that operators in the simulator are excluding a large range of events that are possible in the real world but are not believed to be plausible in a (limited duration but

12

very expensive) simulator training session. In all the published curves that I know of data are pooled over different operators and different occasions. They are not based on repeated trials by one operator. That is, at present these curves represent a normal distribution of (probably Rule Based) talent over the population of operators. If anyone is looking for a simple but interesting Ph.D. project, they could look at the extent to which plots such as these are similar to those from single operators performing a task many times. (The implications, as reports like to say, "is left as an exercise for the reader".)

These plots are another way of describing the boundaries of rate of information processing in complex environments, that is, defining the envelope within which SA can be effectively performed. I would like to consider one more way of representing rate limits and that is by the use of Minkowski diagrams, one of which is shown in Figure 10.

The original Minkowski diagram was invented (Minkowski, 1909) to represent the implications of the fact that nothing can travel faster than light, and what is represented is spacetime, not space and time. The "world line" represents the history of an entity. At the intersection P(0,0) ("here and now") there are some parts of the universe whose state is hidden from the entity because there has not been time for information traveling at the speed of light to reach it. Similarly there are regions of the future that the entity cannot causally affect because there will not be time for any control signal to reach them, limited again by the speed of light. Here I will use a "pseudo-Minkowski" space to discuss the constraints on keeping SA and intervention up to date. (Peter Hancock (personal communication) has independently suggested using these diagrams.)

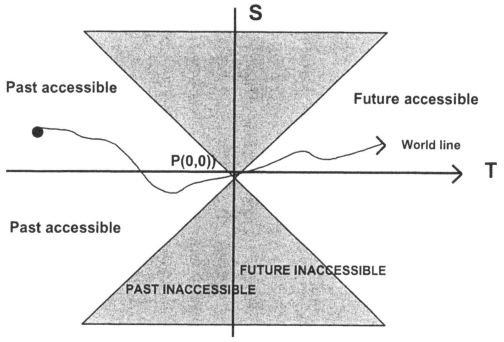

Figure 10.   **Minkowski Space-Time Diagram**

Figure 10 shows such a diagram adapted to our purposes. At the "here and now" is our operator, O. The vertical direction is a dimension representing a set of facts about the system state. The horizontal axis is real time. O's knowledge of what has happened in the environment is limited by the time it takes to access information about it. For example, the slope of the accessible/inaccessible boundary on the left of "Now" will depend on how fast attention can be switched, how fast eyes can be moved, how fast the interface can deliver state information from sensors, and so on. To the right of "Now" is O's ability to affect the world causally in the near future. The slope in general will be different from that prior to now, because the time it takes to perform actions, which depends on the biodynamics of muscles, on the speed with which sensors act, on how long it takes to call up screens with icons for actions, etc., will be different from the rate of sensing the environment.

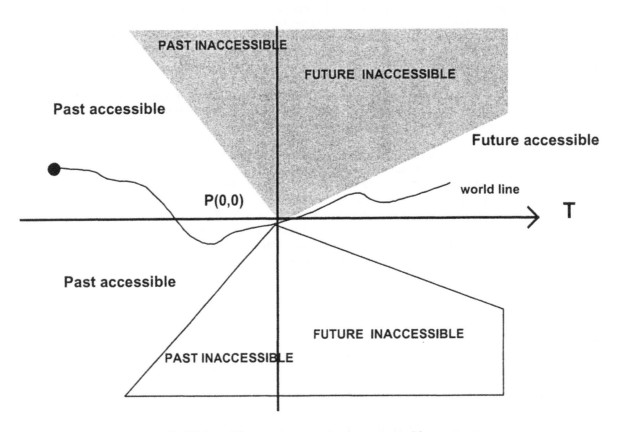

Figure 11. A pseudo Minkowski space for assessing human-machine systems

The problem for O in maintaining effective SA is clear in such a diagram. The properties of the human-machine system and the properties of the environment outwith that system determine the slopes of the Minkowski space, and hence what is in principle accessible, either for updating O's information about the state of the world, or for affecting its future. The task for automation is also clear: it is to make the slopes of the accessible/inaccessible boundaries as steep as possible, thus reducing the inaccessible regions. If we were able to determine the actual structure of the real information space, and the slopes of the boundaries, we could, for example, decide whether to put effort into the input or the output side of the system (the sensing or acting automation in Parasuraman et al.'s formulation). In Figure 11 it is clear that above all, automation is needed on the output side.

Just for fun, in Figure 12 we can represent the effect of predictor displays or fast time models, whether mental or automated. They are valuable because they let us know the future *in the inaccessible regions.*

I find this representation interesting and stimulating, but I have to admit a small weakness. I think that one could define the slopes of the boundaries for specific aspects of a task, using what we know about eye movements, Card et al.'s (1983) Model Human Processor, and a direct examination of a particular interface. But I have completely failed, despite some fairly vigorous efforts, to discover a general metric for the space as a whole, or even really to be satisfied that I understand what the notion of vertical "distance" really is as a property of the human-machine system and the environment outwith it.. Again, I am happy to leave that problem to the reader.

That is probably enough speculation about theory and the future. I now want to remind you of how much is already known about SA and how operators become coupled to their environment at the RBB and KBB levels. When we have reviewed the empirical data, we will be able to see what a tightly coupled RBB system would be like, and hence how a computational predictive model may be developed.

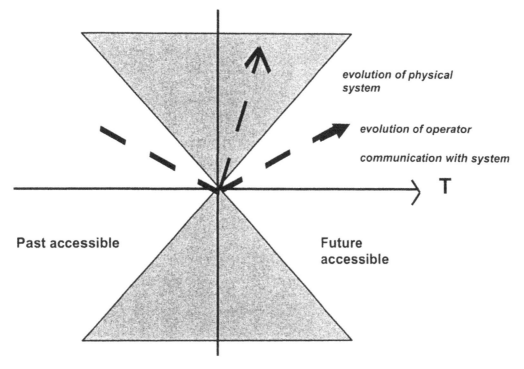

Figure 12. Minkowski Space-time Diagram with operator knowledge and model of process

ON TO THE PAST: SOME EARLY EMPIRICAL WORK

As many of you will know, Europeans view the recent American enthusiasm for the study of naturalistic decision making with a slightly ironic eye, since there is a long-standing tradition of field work in human industrial decision making in Europe that is at least fifty years old. I want to draw on some of that early work to support the claims by Endsley and others concerning the characteristics of SA.

As long ago as 1960, Crossman was describing supervisory control, and the effects of automation in steel, chemical and petroleum industries. In his paper on "Automation and Skill" there are diagrams that anticipate Sheridan (1978) and show the flow of information in manual and "automatic" control. Here are some quotations from his work (Crossman, 1960).

"Analytic study suggests that a specific control skill comprises five components:

1) *Sensing* - the ability to detect the signs and indications such as "noises, smells and appearance, which indicate how the plant is running.

2) *Perceiving* - the ability to interpret these signs and the instrument readings in relation to one another, and to infer what is happening.

3) *Prediction* – of what is likely to happen in a given situation of the controls are left alone.

4) *Familiarity with the controls* – knowing what means can be use to influence the process, what their effects are, and how they interact with others.

5) *Decision* – the ability to select the control action most likely to achieve the desired result in the given circumstances or to avert unfavourable developments when they threaten."

15

The last item, decisions, can be carried out in several ways.

i.   "The operator may follow a 'rule of thumb' – doing what has always been done in a given situation, or what worked last time; but this allows little flexibility.

ii. He may use a 'mental model' or idea of the process, on which he can try out the different possible control actions in his imagination and pick the best bet. A good operator seems to 'feel' his way into the process, becoming *intuitively* aware of what is going on and what to do about it.

iii. The operator may use a logical approach and consciously reason out the meaning of things, analyze the situation, and come to a *rational* decision.

On the whole, discussions with operators have suggested that the first, or 'rule of thumb', methods is common among the less good operators, and the second, or 'intuitive', method is often characteristic of the better ones.

In another of his papers he discussed strategies of monitoring and sampling behaviour, both for the demands made by the dynamics of the process being controlled, and also in regard to the use by O of mental models (Crossman, Cooke and Beishon, 1974.) In particular he drew attention to the fact that the Sampling Theorem was an effective model for a limit on sampling, but that it needed to be modified by cognitive factors, to produce what Crossman called "the effective bandwidth" of the task:

"The more normal use of human vision evidently is to create and maintain an internal image, map or model of the environment, from which information can be extracted to determine future action."

"Conclusions from field and laboratory studies

1. The operator's basic minimum rate of sampling in the two process tasks studied was determined from the system bandwidth as predicted by Sender's application of the Shannon-Wiener sampling theorem, provided that account is taken of the allowed error tolerance by calculating an 'effective bandwidth'.

2. However, a much more detailed analysis of factors n contributing to the operator's uncertainty, its rate of growth over time, and the cost attached to sampling is needed to give an even moderately accurate estimates of sampling rate in the various circumstances encountered when they rose above the minimum.

3. The problem of sampling could not be divorced from the more general problem of control, which in turn raised questions of the required accuracy, cost of error, operator's knowledge of system structure, degree, type, and predictability of disturbance, and effects of response lag.

4. While forgetting was not positively identified as a cause of increased sampling rate, the data were consistent with this possibility.

5. The data suggest the following empirical generalizations about sampling behaviour which agree fairly well with predictions from the uncertainty analysis given above.

a. When a variable is at its desired value and the system is correctly adjusted so that there is no residual drift due to small errors of control setting, the 'background' sampling rate is determined by the highest frequency component of random disturbance that has an *amplitude great enough to cause excursions exceeding the allowed tolerance.* This is the 'effective bandwidth' which the system presents to input noise.

b. When a variable is within the specified range but the system is not quite correctly adjusted so that it tends to drift off, sampling rate is determined by the rate of drift, and rises *when the variable is near either of the limits of its tolerance range.*

c. When a variable is outside its tolerance band and the operator is making large stepwise control changes in an attempt to correct it, *a sample is taken after each control change at a time when the response is expected to have reached some 80% of its final value << about 2 time constants>>* ... (this rule) only applies when the operator is uncertain of the precise effect of control changes.

d. Sampling rate rises when whenever general observation of the system or its surroundings shows that anything unusual may be happening, even though it is not known to be relevant to the particular variable sampled.

e. Operators may estimate the rate of change of a variable either by prolonged observation during one sample, or by remembering its value at one sample and comparing it with the next. In general they do not attempt to estimate higher derivatives.

He also commented on the need to mix quantitative and qualitative analysis, anticipating the ideas of De Keyser (1981) on what she called "informal information":

"The analyst should note that not only quantities expressed in numerical form are variables, but also factors assessed subjectively such as state of a firebed or the turbulence of a liquid. The following five factors normally govern the sampling rate of a given variable:

1. Its (true) bandwidth – roughly speaking the speed with which the system can permit the variable to change.
2. The amplitude of any random disturbance or *noise* which may affect it.
3. Its *tolerance* the latitude for variation about a desired value which is permissible without incurring a penalty.
4. *Predictability* ...operators can often forecast future system state changes from known patterns of behaviour or from auxiliary information.
5. *Control calibration* ...sampling rate is increased whenever the operator makes control adjustments because a variable's response to changes in a relevant control setting is imperfectly predictable."

Perhaps the most remarkable of the early work is that of Iosif (1968a,b; 1969a,b) performed in Rumania, using the crews of manually controlled fossil-fuel power stations, refineries and simulators. This work is based on *nearly 700 hours of observations of skilled operators* and how they scanned the instrument panels during process control to maintain knowledge of the system state, in other words how they maintained situation awareness. His conclusions are as follows. The monitoring strategy is a function both of subjective factors and of the physical characteristics of the process (the environment). The monitoring strategy depends on the operator having a deep understanding of the technical process, and on the attitudes adopted, and the latter particular include the degree of "prudence" of the operators (Os), (Iosif specifically mentions confidence and Os' decision criterion,) and on the degree to which Os anticipates disturbances. Iosif actually derives a statistic "ε" which is a measure of "prudence". This statistic depends non-linearly on the frequency of disturbances, and depends also both on the technical characteristics of the plant and on individual differences, and seems to relate also to how long it takes Os to notice that a disturbance has occurred. Anticipation of disturbances is very important and is also a function of the frequency of disturbances. (This ability of Os to anticipate disturbances, and then to use the instrumentation not to inform them that a disturbance has occurred but to confirm their anticipation is again very reminiscent of some of the observations by De Keyser (1981, 1987) some 15 years later in Belgium.) What is important is the way Os use mental causal models to anticipate the evolution of the process. This means that even for rare disturbances, they tend to be looking in the right place when the disturbance actually occurs. In Endsley's terms, SA permits prediction, and monitoring is not a stochastic process, but one driven by a recognition of system state and a prediction of its future value.

Iosif's description of his operators is strikingly similar to the optimal control model, in which observations are made to establish the state vector of the controlled process, related to a model of the process in the Kalman filter, and from moment to moment choose either the past history embodied in the model, or the recent observations, to minimise the error of their estimate. Iosif claims that Os make strategically appropriate observations because they have a mental model of the frequencies of disturbances, and in addition use current observations to understand the evolution of the process. They also make use of observations on one variable to predict the values of causally related (tightly coupled) variables which they then do not need to observe.

"The ability to anticipate is the result of a deep understanding of these correlations, leading to a prompt detection of variations, observations of values that signal certain effects."

This of course is another way of reducing the complexity of the system: as I suggested earlier Os are using the values of observations on one part of a "molecule" to predict other parts of the same molecule without observing them, as I suggested in Moray (1976)). Iosif also notes, as did De Keyser (op. cit.) that operator use information from other members of the team, from telephone conversations, etc., to supplement the "official" information displayed on the console.

Iosif also performed some studies in a process control simulator. He found that the vast majority of fault diagnoses required only the initial hypothesis or a hypothesis revised on the basis of operator "deep causal knowledge". He was able to understand about 80% of the diagnoses made. In about 70% of diagnoses the first hypothesis was correct, or deep causal knowledge led to a rapid revision of the hypothesis. Only about 6% used guesswork and only 1.5% failed to diagnose the disturbance.

Compare this with Endsley (1995):

"There is evidence that an integrated picture of the current situation may be matched to prototypical situations in memory."

"...(SA) should explain dynamic goal selection, attention to appropriate critical cues, expectancies regarding future states of the situation, and the time between situation awareness and typical actions"

"...(SA) is the perception of elements in the environment within a volume of time and space, the comprehension of their meaning, and the projection of their status in the near future."

Iosif's data could almost have been designed to support Endsley's description, although anticipating the notion of SA by 30 years. I commend his papers to your attention. They deserve to be far better known. Some of his results are shown in Figures 13 – 17.

And as we have seen, many of Crossman's observations from the 1960s support Endsley's proposals (Crossman, 1960; 1964).

There is a great deal of empirical data that should be regarded as the fundamental data for any discussions of these problems. An outstanding source book for much of this work is *The Human Operator In Process Control* (Edwards and Lees, 1974). To give you an idea of the richness of these data, Lees (1974) in that book cites 135 references specifically to the behaviour of the human operator in process control, and in another book by Edwards and Lees they list more than 2000 studies of process control!

Another place of where Endsley's discussion of SA resembles earlier work is her discussion of the role of expectation in perception . This could be fitted into to the framework of the Theory of Signal Detection (TSD), and her discussion of the way in which Os use a "best match" categorization of observations on the environment is very similar to James Reason's "pattern matching" hypothesis in his discussion of human error. Her discussion of display design (p. 51.) and her notion of the "space" to which SA is relevant would fit very well with Vicente's discussions of ecological displays, and in general her ideas of system design anticipate those of Parasuraman et al. (2000) on automation. The SA box in her Figure 1 could contain something very similar to a Rasmussen "Decision Ladder". It is even worth perhaps going back to the work on perceptual learning and concept formation in the 1950s, such as that of Gibson and Gibson (1955) to understand how Os assemble the perceptual information for SA, although of course the early work will need to be re-interpreted for our current context.

Let me make plain that I am not criticizing Endsley for lack of originality. Far from it. As she herself says, she is trying to synthesize previous work, and her paper is masterly in that respect. Indeed since I first read it I have thought that it is the only paper that does justice to the complexity of SA. I want to emphasise how much we know, and suggest that if there is so much agreement among major researchers, surely we could move from analysis to a predictive model, and hence to more powerful support for decisions about automation and allocation of function.

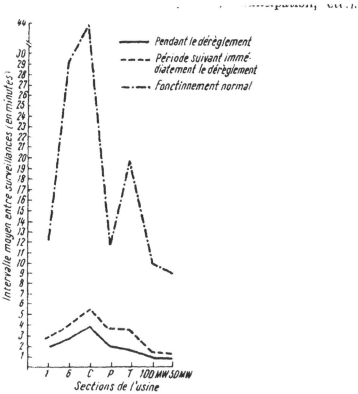

Graphique 7. — Fréquence d'observation des situations du processus technologique à un moment donné.

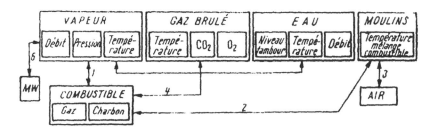

Figure 13. Intervals between successive monitoring as a function of the subsystem and whether an abnormal disturbance has occurred. (Iosif, 1968)

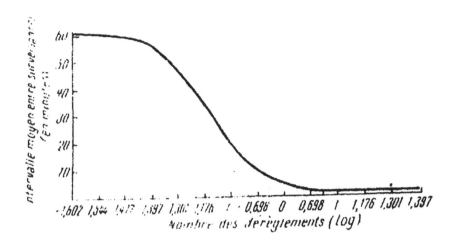

Figure 14 Interval between observations as a function of log(number of disturbances. (Iosif, 1968)

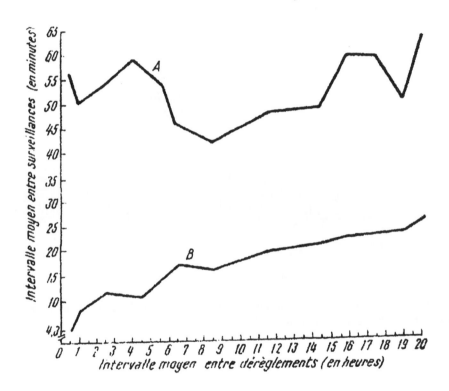

Figure 15 Mean intervals (in minutes) between observations as a function of intervals (in hours) between disturbances. Curve A an unimportant variable. Curve B a critical variable. (Iosif, 1968)

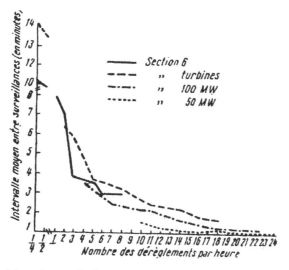

Figure 16 Mean intervals (in minutes) between observations as a function of mean intervals (in hours) of disturbances for different plant (Iosif, 1968).

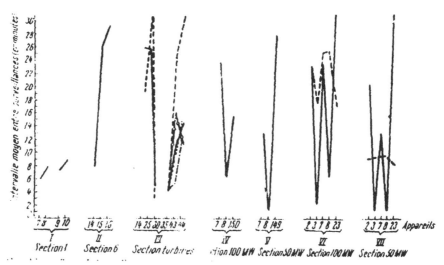

Figure 17. Mean interval (in minutes) between observations on groups of variables that are strongly correlated. (Iosif, 1968.)

I think there are two central functions in SA, from which others follow, (1) a monitoring strategy, and (2) recognizing the state of the system based on the resulting observations. What do we know about these functions that could be used to develop a computational model?

21

MODELS OF STRATEGIC MONITORING.

In the case of monitoring there is almost an *embarras de richesse* Moray (1986) reviewed nearly a dozen models for monitoring, and since then others have appeared. From what Iosif and Endsley have said about SA monitoring, it is clear that simple stochastic model such as that of Senders (1964) will not be appropriate. We require at least a model that responds to an observation that the value of the variable is near to a limit by increasing the probability that another sample will be taken soon after. There are several such models, such as those by Senders, Elkind, Grignetti and Smallwood (1965); Carbonell (1966), Sheridan (1970), and Moray, Richards and Low (1980). There are abundant empirical data going back to Crossman et al..(1974) and even to the work of Fitts 55 (!) years ago (Jones, Milton and Fitts, 1949). However, we need a model that contains more of a semantic component. Iosif found that people made use of the structure of their mental causal models and of the correlation among the values of groups of variables, and Rasmussen and Batstone (1989) suggest that people actively probe the boundaries of system performance, deliberately allowing systems to reach constraint boundaries to learn how to handle the dynamics of the system:

"Proposition 16. Designers should carefully consider that humans are boundary seeking and that their reliability depends on the opportunity to touch the boundary to loss of control and to learn to cope with recovery.". . .

Proposition 20. Before you consider to support (sic) operators by solving their problems through predictive situation analysis, make sure they have available the information about:

1) actual system state
2) design basis and intended function
3) boundaries around acceptable performance and problem
4) available resources for action.

Consider that the information is structurally related and that integrated symbolic displays can be based on primary data."

(Report to World Bank,1989)

Endsley also speaks of pilots and other operators pushing at the boundaries of performance.

Sometimes reliance on correlations among variables may lead to cognitive tunnel vision (which incidentally was reported over 50 years ago by Russell Davis (1948) in the context of prolonged attention in pilots). Endsley makes the point that in automated systems SA (the knowledge of current system state) decreases. This is almost a matter of logic rather than an empirical fact: if the environment is less observable at an appropriate bandwidth, then its state will be less accurately identified – unless the automation is arranged so that O can predict unsampled values on the basis of correlation and causal modeling.

One model that could be looked at more closely uses queuing theory, (Senders and Posner, 1976). But still to my way of thinking it is too close to a purely stochastic model. Certainly we need something that is sensitive to system bandwidth. When Endsley speaks of SA being concerned with a certain volume of time and space, we can see the space as being the number of sources of information (either in terms of the instruments on a control panel, or as the number of locations in the environment in which a significant event may occur when flying at attack aircraft). The volume of time is of course directly related to the bandwidth of the system, (or rather, as Crossman says, the "effective bandwidth" (Crossman et al., 1974). That in turn depends on where in Sanderson's spectrum our task is located, which in turn (for a task such as flying an aircraft) depends on what maneuvers the pilot chooses to make, and how fast he or she flies. For a very high frequency of events SA must be updated very rapidly. For very low frequencies updating at infrequent intervals is sufficient providing that the correct variables are sampled and memory adequate. Iosif was dealing with a low frequency system, where some significant events occurred at intervals of several hours, and it is desirable to extend the concepts out into the ultra-low-frequency (ULF) region of project management, thus generalizing a model into the realm of "organizational accidents" (Reason, 1997).

A very interesting sampling model, which appears never to have been developed beyond its original definition, is that due to Milgram (1983). Its great advantage is that in addition to covering high dimensional multivariate displays Milgram claims that it can be related to the perception of patterns, citing Wewerinke (1980).

Based as it is in optimal control theory, Milgram's model is attractive for two further reasons. The first is that the covariance matrix at the heart of the model is a natural representation of coupling between variables, and hence of the dependence on correlations to reduce complexity; and secondly because it naturally leads to a consideration of what action to take in response to an observation (and hence to the updating of the system state estimate). This is important because as we have seen, Crossman and his co-workers found that scan patterns were affected by the discriminability of signals (signal/noise ratio, as Senders, 1964 predicted) and also by the actions taken by operators (as Iosif also found). Following the adjustment of a control which forced a variable to a new value, Crossman found that the next look at the value of adjusted variable tended to be when it had reached about 80% of its final value. Crossman noted that the bandwidth of a process control system, which seems at first sight to be toward the right hand end of Sanderson's spectrum, is realty higher: what he called "the effective bandwidth" was the highest frequency of random fluctuation that had a peak amplitude that could exceed the tolerance band of the process. This again relates to Iosif's discussion of the effect of frequency of disturbances. Moray and Synnock and Sims (1973) on the other hand, in a task where the bandwidth depended on the velocity generated chosen by O (roughly, a laboratory equivalent of driving at a self-selected rate along a twisty road) found that observers sampled at fixed intervals, apparently as a function of forgetting (see also Moray, Richards and Low, 1980 for a further discussion of forgetting-driven sampling; and Senders (1983) on monitoring while driving. and Moray and Inagaki, 2002 for a recent attempt to formulate a general model.

To sum up this section, we need a model of strategic sampling that can encompass not just bandwidth and tolerance threshold, but is sensitive to effective bandwidth, memory liability, correlations (that represent causal coupling) among variables, relative values of different variables, control actions and their effects, and can handle *patterns* of variable values as its effective input. Milgram's model seems to me very promising. It could handle both SBB and RBB if we knew how operators use the patterns of information they construct from sampling. Like all the sampling models it is quantitative. What is remarkable, when one looks back to at the literature of the 1960s and 1970s is the very large number of quantitative models that have been proposed. I must plead guilty myself for joining in the lemming-like tendency to rush down theoretical slopes into the conceptual sea without sufficient attention to what has already been achieved (see, e.g., and Moray and Inagaki,). There is really no excuse for not stopping, drawing breath, and reviewing what they all have in common.

HOW IS KNOWLEDGE REPRESENTED IN SA?

We now come to the second topic which I want to look at in the light of old data, namely the nature of operators' knowledge. Obviously Os acquire the values of variables, be they environmental or on control panels, as a series of sequential perceptions. But we have seen good reason from the empirical and theoretical literature to believe that they are not stored in that way. Forty five years ago Miller (1956) spoke of "chunking" in short term memory, and, as we saw, Yufik & Sheridan (1991), Yufik et al. (1992) , and Moray (1986) have all discussed possible ways that the complex knowledge might be simplified in long-term memory. At the same time there is widespread agreement among people who have studied workers in complex processes that reasoning (KBB) is rare. Rather, Os most commonly use RBB, that is to say, "IF (state X) THEN (action Y)" rules. (Rasmussen, 1984; Woods, 1984, 1991; Wohl, 1982;). When we look at the old empirical literature there is strong support for this. We will examine two studies.

The first is by Beishon, (1969) who studied the control of bakers' ovens in an industrial bakery. The task was complex. What we might call embryonic cakes, loaves and buns entered an oven in batches, but as a continuous process, and had to be baked for different times, and at different temperatures, without waiting to cool down or heat up the oven between batches. O had to use an extensive knowledge of different kinds of dough, the effect of the size of the loaves, etc., temperatures, composition of the mix of products, etc., and observations from moment to moment of the oven temperature, to determine the time of baking and the changes in the heater settings. Beishon's conclusion was that his Os did not work these out, but used a large mental look-up table. That is, the signals for control formed a complex pattern, what we could call the left hand side of the "IF...THEN... " rule. As with Crossman, I will quote extensively from his report:

23

Only about 11% of the time is spent on control and inspection activity, but a large proportion of the time spent on "manual" activities (e.g. cleanup) is spent thinking about the process.

(It is possible to identify some of the ovenman's) Recognizable routines:
1.　　recognition of cake type and classification as to normal/abnormal
2.　　Oven allocation
3.　　Oven adjustment
4.　　entry of cakes into oven when conditions are appropriate
5.　　check or sample
6.　　feedback/adjustment
7.　　new item (baked according to trial and error if not previously known)
8.　　Abnormal item (needs ad hoc operations to deal with them

The existence of baking time and burner pattern information, and the way in which the ovenman can produce it when asked, suggests that he has a number of look-up tables in memory stores to which he has ready access. Further study of these has been made and the following tables appear to be present:

1　Facts about the preferred times and temperatures for all the usual cake-types.
2　Facts about the degree of tolerance each cake-type has for departures from the preferred baking conditions. (this will give information about the need for sampling when cakes have traveled some way down the oven.)
3　Facts about the burner patterns which will achieve the temperature profiles obtained from (1q) above.
4　Methods or procedures for getting the oven to change from one temperature state to another; this includes information about the times taken for various changes.
5　Expectancies concerning the kinds of cakes which will arrive for baking and also the time of day when they are likely to come.
6　Methods or procedures for adjusting baking conditions to correct specific fault conditions which are detected on inspection of the partially, or completely, baked items.

(If we try to simulate the ovenman's behaviour, we find we need):

1.　A main procedure
2.　That is subject to interrupts, which may be caused by external triggers or internal triggers.
3.　External triggers are things like the arrival of new batches for baking.
4.　Internal when, e.g. he interrupts what he is doing to look through the inspection ports.
5.　Jumps from one completed routine to another are not so obvious – there is behaviour which appears not to be related to ongoing system state. It seems to be due to anticipation, and the reason for its occurrence is not obvious until some time later when the anticipation is fulfilled.

(The ovenman seems to play a "rule-book game" (which describes rule based behaviour such as that invoked by Rasmussen,)
"A key concept underlying this rule book system is the assumption that human operators categorize continuous, and to some extent discontinuous, variables into a limited number of categories…(if so) *the state of the system* at any one point in time can be described in terms of a bounded space in a multi-dimensional *system space*. For example, if a system had only two variables, say temperature and humidity, and these were categorized into three classes, the system as seen by the observer would be in one of nine possible system states which form a two-dimensional; matrix or array. It is possible to construct a multi-dimensional space which represents his view of the oven system. The system will not always be of the same 'volume' in multidimensional space. This concept of the system space with its separate states is important because without it the ovenman is faced with an infinite, or almost infinite, number of conditions or states in which the oven system could be. It is unlikely that the ovenman will carry an actual multi-dimensional system space for the complete system in his head, more likely there will be a

large number of two- and three-dimensional subsystem spaces available. The position is probably even more complicated since the categorizations used by humans are not fixed in time and immediate past experience can change the category structure as adaptation level studies show."
Note the emphasis on reducing the size of the problem, as we discussed earlier.

An even more impressive study is that by Dutton and Starbuck, (1971). They studied the ability of an experienced operator, "Charlie", to predict the time it would take to fulfill orders on a weaving machine (Figure 18). They made objective measures of his behaviour, and also interviewed him over several months and used protocol analysis. From the objective measures they were able to develop a quantitative equation that described how he performed his task. The task seemed at first sight almost impossible, given the combinatorial complexity of the situation. It sounds however as though Charlie would please Gary Klein, for he seems not to have spent time puzzling over the problem quantitatively, but to have recognized almost at once what the answer was to the scheduling problems. In the protocols Charlie was able to describe how he thought he performed the task, and again, the conclusion to which Dutton and Starbuck came was that he used a very large mental pattern look-up table.

Dutton and Starbuck developed the following quantitative equation to describe Charlie's behaviour:

$T = aR + (b + gW)L$
where
$T =$ The sum of the times for the segments scheduled
$R =$ The number of "ripper set-ups" used
$W =$ The weight per square yard of the cloth
$L =$ The length in yards of the material to be produced
$a =$ Time required for "set-up"
$b + gW =$ time per yard produced
They also developed a model based on what Charlie told them of how he worked:
$T = L/S$ (1)
where
$S = f(A, \text{type of cloth, texture, properties of material})$ (2)
and
$S =$ speed measured in yards/hour
$A =$ mean length of a "rip"
(Note that $S = 1/(a/A + b + gW)$ even if Charlie was unaware of the fact.)

Dutton and Starbuck comment, "Charlie thus uses two non-linear relations, of which one is quite complex, in order to construct a simple linear relation." This latter is then used to schedule the task.

Relation (1) seems to be a description of a mental model rather than a true equation, and (2) is effectively a very large multidimensional look-up table, with between 2000 and 5000 entries. As we noted earlier, even very large lookup tables as components of mental models is probably less demanding from the point of view of mental workload than performing mental calculations. Charlie seems to be using a combination of RBB (the look-up table) and KBB (reasoning), based on a mental model or models built up by long experience, and which enables him to finesse the need for direct complex calculation." (Moray,1999).

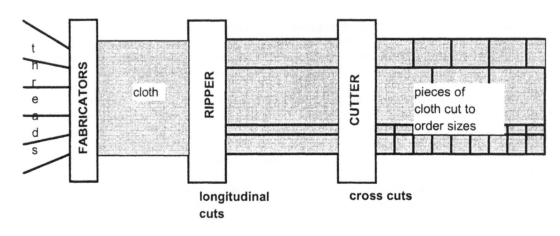

VARIABLES	CHARACTERISTICS	RANGE OF VALUES
FABRICATORS	1 general, 1 specialised	1 - 2
MEASURES OF SCHEDULES	length of material requested (yards)	15 - 24 000
TYPES OF CLOTH		1 - 5
PROPERTIES OF CLOTH		1 - 500
WIDTH OF CLOTH	measured by number of fibres	21 - 45
CHANGES OF WIDTH	number of different fibres	0 - 30
CHARACTERISTICS OF ORDERS FROM CLIENTS		1 - 50
SPEED OF PROCESS PROCESSUS	yards per hour	600 - 2400
DURATION OF PRODUCTION RUN	estimation of remaining material to be cut	0.5 - 24 hrs

Figure 18. Characteristics of Charlie's run-time estimator (after Dutton and Starbuck, 1971.)

It is also well-known that nuclear power plant operators claim to perform diagnosis by recognizing the patterns of illuminated alarm tiles in the control room, and of course, the work of Klein on "naturalistic decision making" , and Reason's analysis of human error (the GEMS model) all emphasize how frequently operators rely on patterns to make state estimates, even if, (as Endsley says) they have to opt for an imperfect match with memory.

TOWARD A QUANTITATIVE PREDICTIVE MODEL OF SA

Let me finally return to the question of a computational model that could combine a representation of Situation Assessment as suggested by Endsley and allocation of function in line with the suggestions of Parasuraman, Sheridan and Wickens (2000). We start with a classical closed control loop, but now the error signal is both represented and used at the level of Rule Based Behaviour (Figure 19.)

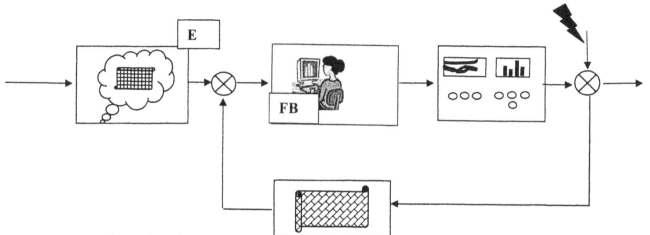

Figure 19. A first pass at a closed loop block diagram for Rule-Based Behaviour.

The basic notion is that instead calculating the error signal as a simple difference from the value of the required output, what is compared is the operator's expected pattern in the mental look-up table in long term memory (E) and the pattern in working memory constructed from the recent inputs obtained from monitoring the environment (FB), subject to chunking and prediction. Rasmussen (1993) suggests that in complex systems the error signal is a form of pattern matching; and of course Endsley in her model of SA says,

> "There is evidence that an integrated picture of the current situation may be matched to a prototypical situation in memory"

> (Endsley, 1995.)

> "The more normal use of human vision evidently is to create and maintain an internal image, map or model of the environment, from which information can be extracted to determine future action."

> (Crossman et al., 1974.)

There will not be a perfect match, because the environment is dynamic, because not all values of the environment will be sampled, because the correlations among the variables will be imperfect, and because working memory is fallible.

The degree of pattern matching determines what next happens:

(Case 1) a (more or less perfect match) leads to no action, and a default monitoring strategy.
(Case 2) an imperfect match with variables within their normal range indicates the need for more sampling to update the state estimate;
(Case 3) an imperfect match with some variables at or over their tolerance threshold indicates a need for intervention (followed by more sampling as per Crossman's findings).

Pattern matching could be performed by any of the available AI techniques. The expected values of the patterns should take into account the "chunking" of information and the way in which past sampling of the task has built up the mental model, including knowledge of correlations among variables, etc.. If it is found that Case 2 continues, then automation should be invoked to improve the presentation of information. This might be done by helping O to better schedule monitoring; or it might require the automation to take into account the way in which the system is naturally decomposed, or how O in fact decomposes it, to change the nature of the display. As Woods (1991) suggested, since situation assessment is contextual, displays should match the particular context, and this should assist in recognition-based decisions, thus speeding up O's response:

> "...representational form is defined in terms of how data on the state and behavior of the system is MAPPED into the syntax and dynamics of visual form in order to produce information transfer."

This would require the perceptual and decision-making aspects of automation (Parasuraman et al., 2000), and would also support better "visual momentum" (Woods, 1984) and improve "cognitive coupling" (Fitter and Syme, 1980).

If despite operator intervention in Case 3 it is found that Case 3 persists, then automation should be asked to intervene on the action side. Other possibilities are left for the reader. The point of departure for programming might be Sanderson's pseudo-code, with monitoring algorithms based on Milgram's model since it includes implicitly the possibility for representing patterns in the form of the Kalman filter. Thus part of the model could be used to request automation to take over or enhance the monitoring strategy. As I think about this I increasingly regret the fact that PROCRU was not developed, because I think I am describing something rather similar.

CONCLUSION

I have tried in this paper to do three things. First, I have tried to show that there is a very large degree of agreement, albeit expressed in different languages and in different contexts, in research on situation assessment, allocation of function, and more generally about cognition as applied to the analysis of how operators monitor and control dynamic systems. Therefore, rather than generating yet more models, the time has come, surely, to synthesize this knowledge into a "modal model".

Second, I have tried to show that while the elegance of the classical and optimal control models of Skill-Based behaviour cannot be expected, it may well be possible to produce a computational predictive model for the moment to moment prediction of behaviour in monitoring, situation assessment, and control, including interaction with automation. It will predict where O looks and what O then does. It will not be easy, and may well require the kind of effort that has been put into SOAR and ACT*-R and PROCRU. But it would be worth the effort.

Finally, and I think most importantly, I want to ask you not to forget the past. For some reason psychology, whether pure or applied, seems to have a poor memory for what has already been discovered. Unlike the physical sciences, there is a tendency to re-do research using different language, rather than building progressively on the details on past work. The late Paul Kolers once told me that he thought this was because we do not have a strong notation to describe what we do. Whatever the reason, it is wasteful, and also, to my mind, disrespectful to our predecessors. Excellent empirical work, deeply relevant to today's concerns, has existed for thirty, forty, and even more than fifty years[2], but the original empirical studies appear to have been forgotten. It would, I think, be worth your while to dig them up. There are still people who know where these papers are to be found, even when they are in unpublished research reports, quite apart from books and journals, and a study such as Iosif's based on nearly 700 hours of observations would save at least a year or two of anyone's research time and money. And if work is reported in French, German or Japanese, most universities will have people competent in those languages. Perhaps such people are not in engineering or psychology departments, but many is the impoverished humanities professor or graduate student who would be happy to translate for you at a cost that would be a fraction of replicating the work of Iosif or Crossman. If we have to stand on the shoulders of giants to see further than others, we had better remember where we have buried the giants.

REFERENCES

Bainbridge, L. 1983. The ironies of automation. Automatica, 19(6) 775 -779.

Bainbridge, L. 1981. Mathematical equations or processing routines? In J.Rasmussen and W.B.Rouse (eds), Human Detection and Diagnosis of System Failures, New York: Plenum Press. 259-286.

Bainbridge, L. 1991. Mental models in cognitive skill: the example of industrial process operation. In A. Rutherford and Y. Rogers, Models in the mind. London: Academic Press.

Baron, S. Muralidharan, R., Lancrafty, R. & Zacharias, G. 1980 PROCRU: a model for analyzing crew procedures in approach to landing. Technical Report No. 4374. Cambridge, MA: Bolt, Bernanek and Newman, Inc.

Baron, S., Fehrer, R., Pew, R. and Horwitz, P. 1986. Approach to modelling supervisory control of a nuclear power plant. NUREG/CR-2988. Washington, DC: Nuclear Regulatory Commission.

Beare, A. N., Dorris, R. E., Bovell, C. R., Crowe, D. S., and Kozinsky, E. J. 1984. A Simulator-Based Study of Human Errors in Nuclear Power Plant Control Room Tasks. NUREG/CR-3309. U.S. Nuclear Regulatory Commission, Washington, D.C.

Beishon, R. J. 1969 An analysis and simulation of an operator's behaviour in controlling continuous baking ovens. In F. Bresson and M. de Montmollin (eds.) The simulation of human behaviour. Paris Dunod. Re-printed in E. Edwards and F.Lees (eds.), The Human Operator in Process Control, London: Taylor and Francis. 79 - 90.

Cacciabue, P.C., Cojazzi, G., Hollnagel, E. & Mancini, S. 1992. Analysis and modelling of pilot-airplane interaction by an integrated simulation approach. Proceedings of IFAC, Delft, Holland.

Cacciabue, P.C., DeCortis, F., Drozdowicz, B., Masson, M., & Nordvik, J-P. (1992) COSIMO: a cognitive simulation model of human decision making and behavior in accident management of complex plants. IEEE Transactions on Systems, Man, and Cybernetics, SMC-22(5),1058-1074

Carbonell, J. R. (1966). A queuing model for many-instrument visual sampling. IEEE Transactions on Human Factors in Electronics, HFE-7, 157-164.

Card, S.K., Moran, T.P., and Newell, A. 1983. The psychology of human-computer interaction. Hillsdale, N.J.: Lawrence Erlbaum Associates.

Canas, J. J., Quesada, J. F., Antoli, A., & Fajarda, I. 2003. Cognitive flexibility and adaptability to environmental changes in dynamic complex problem-solving task. Ergonomics, 46(5), 482 – 501.

Conant, R.C. 1976. Laws of information that govern systems, IEEE Transactions on Systems, Science and Cybernetics, SMC-6, 240-255.

Crossman, E. R. F. W. 1960 Automation and Skill. London: Her Majesty's Stationary Office. (Reprinted in Edwards, E. and Lees, F. (eds.) 1974. The human operator in process control. London: Taylor and Francis. 1 – 24.)

Crossman, E. R. F. W. 1964. Visual attention and the sampling of displayed information in process control. Technical report HFT-64-11(T). department of Industrial Engineering, University of California at Berkeley.

Crossman, E. R. F. W. & Cooke, F. W. 1974..; Manual control of slow response systems. In The human operator in process control, E. Edwards and F. Lees, Eds. London: Taylor & Francis. 51-66.

Crossman, E. R. F. W. , Cooke, J. E., and Beishon, R. J. Visual attention and the sampling of displayed information in process control. In The human operator in process control, E. Edwards and F. Lees, Eds. London: Taylor & Francis 25–50.

Cummings M. 2004 Display design in the F/A-18 Hornet. Ergonomics in design, 11(4),16-19

De Keyser, V. 1981. La fiabilité humaine dans les processus continus, les centrales thermo-électriques et nucléaires. Technical Report 720-ECI-2651-C-(0) GCE -DGXII, CERI, Bruxelles.

De Keyser, V., De Cortis, F., Housiaux, A. & Van Daele, A. (1987) Les Communications Hommes-Machines dans les Systèmes Complexes. Appendice, Technical Report Contrat No. 8, Actions Nationales de Recherche En Soutien A Fast. Université de Liège, Belgium.

Dutton, J. M., and Starbuck, W. 1971. Finding Charlie's run-time Estimator. In J. M. Dutton and W. Starbuck (eds.). Computer Simulation of Human Behavior. New York: Wiley.

Edwards, E. & Lees, F., (eds.) 1974. The human operator in process control London: Taylor & Francis

Endsley, M. R. 1995. Towards a theory of situation awareness in dynamic systems. Human Factors, 37(1), 32 – 64

Fitter. M., & Sime, M. 1980. Responsibility and shared decision making. In H. T. Smith and T. R. G. Green (eds.) Human Interaction with Computers. London" Academic Press.

Gibson, J. J. and Gibson, E. J. 1955. Perceptual learning: differentiation or enrichment? Psychological Review, 62(1), 32 – 41.

Hess, R. 1987. A qualitative model of human interaction with complex dynamic systems. IEEE Transactions on Systems, Man and Cybernetics, SMC-17(1) 33-50.

Hollnagel, E. 2003. The ECOM model. Personal communication. erik.hollnagel@telia.com

Iosif, G. 1968. La stratégie dans la surveillance des tableaux de commande. I. Quelques facteurs déterminants de caractère objectif. Revue Roumanien de Science Social-Psychologique, 12, 147-161.

Iosif, G. 1969a. La stratégie dans la surveillance des tableaux de commande. I. Quelques facteurs déterminants de caractère subjectif. Revue Roumanien de Science Social-Psychologique, 13, 29-41.

Iosif, G. 1969b. Influence de la correlation fonctionelle sur parametres technologiques. Revue Roumanien de Science Social-Psychologique, 13, 105-110

Iosif, G. 1969c. Some relevant main problems of the control panels monitoring activity. Studia Psychologica, XI(4), 293-299.

Iosif, G. 1972. Le diagnostique des incidents par les opérateurs de centrals thermiques. Le Travail Humain, 35(1), 37-48.

Iosif, G. 1975. Diagnosis functions in thermo power station operators. Revue Roumanien Sciences Sociales – Serie de Psychologie, 19(2), 179-197.

Jones, R. E., Milton, J. L.,& Fitts, P. M. 1949. Eye fixations of aircraft pilots, I. A review of prior eye-movement studies and a description of a technique for recording the frequency, duration and sequences of eye-fixations during instrument flight. USAF Technical Report No. 5837. Wright {Patterson Air Force Base, Dayton Ohio.

Kelley, C. 1968. Automatic and manual control, NY: Wiley.

Lees, F. 1974. Research on the process operator. In Edwards, E. & Lees, F., (eds.) 1974. The human operator in process control London: Taylor & Francis

McKinney, E. H. & Davis, J. 2003. effects of deliberate practice on crisis decision performance. Human Factors, 45(3), 436 – 444.

McRuer, D. T., & Krendel, E. S. 1959. The Human Operator as a Servo System Element. Journal of the Franklin Institute, Vol. 267, Nos. 5 & 6,.;

McRuer, D. T., & Jex, H. R. 1967. A review of quasi-linear pilot models IEEE Transactions on Human Factors in electronics, HFE-3, 231-249.;

Milgram, P. 1983. A multivariate autoregressive display monitoring model. Report No. NLR MP 83033 U, National Aerospace Laboratory NLR, The Netherlands.

Miller G A (1956) The magical number seven, plus or minus two: some limits on our capacity for processing information. Psychological Review, 63, 81 – 9,

Minkowski, H. 1909. Raum end Zeit. Physiche Zeitschrift, 20, 104 –111.

Montmollin, M., & De Keyser, V. 1985. Expert logic vs. operator logic. In, Johannsen, G., Mancini, G., and Martensen, S. (eds.) Analysis, design, and Evaluation of MMS. Confeence Report from CEC-ISPRA., Italy

Moray, N., "Attention, Control, and Sampling Behavior," Monitoring Behavior and Supervisory Control," (eds., T. Sheridan, and G. Johannsen) Plenum Press, 221-245, 1976.

Moray, N., 1986. "Modeling Cognitive Activities: Limitations in Relation to Computer Aids," In E. Hollnagel, G. Mancini, and D. Woods(eds.) Intelligent Decision Support in Process Environments Springer-Verlag, Berlin, 273-292.

Moray, N., 1986 Monitoring Behavior and Supervisory Control, In K. Boff, L. Kaufmann, and J. Beatty Handbook of Perception and Human Performance, (eds.,) Wiley,. Ch. 45.

Moray, N. 1989. A lattice theory approach to the structure of mental models. Philosophical Transactions of the Royal Society of London, series B, 327, 447-593.

Moray, N. 1998. Mental models in theory and practice. Proceedings of Attention and Performance XVII, Beit Oren, Israel. July.

Moray, N. 1999. The cognitive psychology and cognitive engineering of industrial systems. In F. T. Durso (ed.). Handbook of Applied Cognition. Chichester, UK: John Wiley and Sons. 209-246.

Moray, N., M. Richards, and J. Low, The Behaviour of Fighter Controllers, Contract Report, Ministry of Defense, London, 1980.

Moray, N., G. Synnock, and A. Sims, 1973 Tracking a static display, IEEE Transactions on Systems, Man and Cybernetics, SMC-2, 518-521,.

Parasuraman, R., Sheridan, T. B., & Wickens, C. D. 2000. A model for types and levels of human interaction with automation. IEEE Transactions on Systems, Man, and Cybernetics – Part A. Systems and Humans, 30(3), 286-297.

Rasmussen, J. (1983). Skills, rules, and knowledge; signals, signs, and symbols, and other distinctions in human performance models. IEEE Transactions on Systems, Man, and Cybernetics, SMC-13, 257-266.

Rasmussen, J. 1986. Information processing and human-machine interaction: an approach to cognitive engineering. Amsterdam: North-Holland.

Rasmussen, J., and Batstone, R. 1989. Why do complex organizational systems fail? Summary proceedings of a cross-disciplinary workshop in "Safety Control and Risk Management. Washington, D.C.: World Bank.

Rasmussen, J. 1993. Modelling adaptive systems. Unpublished report from Riso National Laboratory.

Rasmussen, J., Pederesen, A-M., & Goodstein, L. (1995). Cognitive Engineering: concepts and applications. New York: Wiley.

Rasmussen, J. & Vicente, K. 1989. Coping with human errors through system design: implications for ecological interface design. International Journal of Man-Machine Studies, 31, 517-534.

Reason, J. 1990, Human error, Cambridge: Cambridge University Press.

Reason, J. 1997. Managing risks of organizational accidents. Ashgate Gower.

Roth, E. M., Woods, D. D. & Pople, H. E. 1992. Cognitive simulation as a tool for cognitive task analysis. Ergonomics, 35(10) 1113 – 1198.

Russell Davis, D. 1948. Pilot error: some laboratory experiments. Air Ministry A.P. 3139A. London: His Majesty's Stationary Office. 1-39

Sanderson, P.M. 1991. Towards the model human scheduler. International Jounral of Human Factors in Manufacturing, 1, 195 -215.

Sanderson, P. M. & Fisher, C. 1994. Exploratory sequential data analysis: foundations. Human-Computer Interaction, 9(3-4), 251 – 318.

Senders, J. W., Elkind, J. I., Grignetti, M. C. & Smallwood, R. (1965) An investigation of the visual sampling behavior of human observers. Technical Report NASA-3860. Cmbridge, Mass: Bolt, Beranek, and Newman, Inc.

Senders. J. W. 1964. The human operator as a monitor and controller of multi-degree of freedom systems. IEEE Transactions on Human Factors in Electronics, HFE-5, 2-5.

Senders, J. W. 1983. Visual Sampling Processes. Katholieke Hogeschool Tilburg, Netherlands. (also published by Lawrence Earlbaum Associates.)

Senders and Posner, 1976. A queuing model of monitoring and supervisory behavior. In Sheridan, T. B. & Johannsen, G. (eds.) Monitoring Behavior and Supervisory Control, New York: Plenum Press. 245-259

Sheridan, T. B. 1978. Towards a general model of Supervisory Control. In. T. B. Sheridan and G. Johannsen (eds.), Monitoring Behavior and Supervisory Control, New York: Plenum Press. 271-282.

Sheridan, T. B. 1970. On how often the supervisor should sample. IEEE Transactions on Systems Science and Cybernetics. SSC-6(2), 142-145.

Wewerinke, P. 1980. Visual scene perception in manual control. Journal of Cybernetics and Information Science, 3(1), 3-26.

Wohl, J. G. 1961. Research data on maintainability. IEEE Transactions on Human Factors in electronics, HFE-2(20), 87 – 92.

Wohl, J. G. 1982. Maintainability prediction revisited: diagnostic behavior, system complexity, and repair time. IEEE Transactions on Systems, Man and Cybernetics, SMC-12, 241-250

Woods, D. D. 1991. Overview of representational aiding. Technical report, Cognitive Engineering Research Laboratory, Ohio State University.

Woods, D. D. 1984. Visual momentum. International Journal of Man-Machine Studies, 21, 229 – 244.

Young, L. R.. 1969. On adaptive manual control. IEEE Transactions on Man-Machine Systems, MMS-10, 292-331.

Young, L.R. 1973. Human control capabilities. In J. F. Parker, Jr. & V. R. West. (eds). Bioastronautics Data Book. Washington, D.C. National Aeronautics and Space Administration.

Yufik, Y. M., & Sheridan, T. B. 1991. A technique to assess the cognitive complexity of man-machine interface. Report to US Army and NASA-Ames Research Centre.

Yufik, Y. M., Sheridan, T. B., & Venda, V. F. 1992. Knowledge measurement, cognitive complexity, and cybernetics of mutual man-machine adaptation. In C. V. Negoita (ed.) Cybernetics and Applied Systems. New Yor:k: Marcel Decker, Inc. 187 – 237.

FOOTNOTE

2. For an example of an excellent early field study, see Bryan, W. L. & Harter, N. 1898. Studies in the physiology and psychology of the telegraphic language. *Psychological Review, 4*, 27-53 ***This work was done one hundred and six (106) years ago!***

SITUATION AWARENESS

SITUATION AWARENESS:
AN ACTOR NETWORK THEORY PERSPECTIVE

Anthony J. Masys
University of Leicester, UK

ABSTRACT

Maintaining a high level of Situation Awareness (SA) is considered one of the most essential elements for safe and effective flight operations. In a study of accidents among major air carriers, 88% of those involving human error could be attributed to problems associated with situation awareness, similarly problems with SA were found to be the leading casual factor in a review of military aviation mishaps (Endsley, 1999). Given the problems and consequences associated with human error in aviation, current strategies to address SA often focus on aircraft systems design and training programs in order to improve the efficacy and safety of flight operations. In complex domains such as aviation, situation awareness is inherently distributed over multiple people and groups and over human and machine agents. Sociology offers an interesting approach to looking at the socio-technical elements of systems through the application of Actor Network Theory (ANT). "By advocating a seamless web composed of actors, the Actor Network approach dissolves the dichotomous relationship between humans and machines and society and technology into a non-anthropocentric framework" (Sommerville, 1997). It facilitates the perspective that looks at the inter-connectedness of the heterogeneous elements characterized by the technological and non-technological (human, social, organizational) elements. "Complex systems cannot be understood by studying parts in isolation. The very essence of the system lies in the interaction between parts and the overall behaviour that emerges from the interactions" (Ottino, 2003). This paper introduces ANT as an approach to examining situation awareness in aviation and proposes the perspective that situation awareness is a systemic attribute, a construct resident within a network of heterogeneous elements.

Keywords: Actor Network Theory; Situation Awareness; Human Error

INTRODUCTION

Maintaining SA is a fundamental requirement in operating complex socio-technical systems such as those found in aviation, medicine, and nuclear industry. In fact, the challenges associated with the introduction of new technology are one of the main factors that contributed to the growth in interest in SA (Endsley, 2000). The hegemony of the cognitive approach within the field of Human Factors is being enriched by innovative applications from sociology such as symbolic interactionism, ethnomethodology, cultural-historical theory and phenomenology. These perspectives encourage us to re-examine the ontological and epistemological foundations of the traditional paradigm (Bannon, 1998). Actor Network Theory (ANT) facilitates a systemic perspective of SA in complex domains such as aviation. The ontological perspective of ANT enables an analysis of the spatial and temporal dimensions of complex socio-technical systems. It suggests that to understand SA in complex systems is to look at the relationality inherent within the network of heterogeneous elements. Building on the foundation of Situation Awareness as proposed by Endsley (1999), Actor Network Theory (ANT) is introduced as a systemic approach providing an ontological framework that shows the complex interconnectivity of heterogeneous elements characterized by the technological and non-technological (human, social, organizational) that contribute to the development and maintenance of SA.

Situation Awareness

Operating complex systems requires a high level of decision-making, and performance that is predicated on achieving and maintaining a certain level of SA. To address the consequences associated with human error resulting from poor situation awareness, a significant amount of research and contributions have been made to the understanding and modeling of SA by researchers such as Endsley (2000). The cognitive approach to SA, dominant within the literature, has facilitated the conceptualization of models using such frameworks as Information Processing theory (Wickens: 1992) and the applications from a Mental Models perspective (Endsley, 2000). Applications of these models and others exist throughout a wide range of complex systems. Of particular interest is the SA associated with complex socio-technical systems such as aviation. "Clearly understanding SA in the aviation environment rest on a clear elucidation of its elements (at each of the three levels of SA), identifying which things the aircrew needs to perceive, understand and project" (Endsley,1999).

Actor Network Theory

ANT is an approach to structuring and explaining the links between society and technology and focuses on the way the technological and non-technological (human, social, organizational) elements link together to form a seamless web. Originating from the study of technology, ANT "itself can be transferred into a sociological tool of analysis. It enlarges the methodological range of the social sciences and facilitates the understanding of technological development. From the start technical, scientific, social, economic or political considerations are inextricably bound up (heterogeneity and complexity)" (Bijker,1987). The application of Actor Network Theory terms and concepts have worked their way into organization theory, geography, medical anthropology and psychology (Brown,1999). Through its application, both human and machine (non-human) elements are treated in a symmetrical manner. The strength of ANT rests on its ability to analyze situations where it is difficult to separate humans and non-humans, and in which the actors have variable forms and competencies (Callon,1999). A fundamentally relationary worldview, "ANT builds explicitly on semiotics, where objects are seen as simply relational contingencies."(Law,1999)

Fundamental concepts of ANT are the conceptualization of the Actor and the Network.

Latour describes the actor in ANT as "a semiotic definition – an actant – that is, something that acts or to which activity is granted by others" (Noe and Alroe,2003). The notion of an actor- actant- "is not linked to the quality of the entity as such, but to the quality of the entity in the frame of the network into which the entity is mobilised:...For the semiotic approach tells us that entities achieve their form as a consequence of the relations in which they are located. But this means that it also tells us that they are performed in, by, and through those relations." (Law, 1999)

The heterogeneous elements that make up the network are not fixed but are defined in relation to the other elements in the system. The network, from an ANT perspective may not have the characteristics idealized by the technical perspective. "An Actor network may have no compulsory paths, no strategically positioned nodes."(Latour,1998)

Fundamental processes within ANT are inscription and translation. Inscription refers to the way technical artifacts embody patterns of use: Technical objects thus simultaneously embody and measure a set of relations between heterogeneous elements.

Consider the human factors of cockpit design:

> In such a translation, or design, process, the designer works out a scenario for how the system will be used. This scenario is inscribed into the system. The inscription includes programs of action for the users, and it defines roles to be played by users and the system. In doing this, she is also making implicit or explicit assumptions about what competencies are required by the users as well as the system. In ANT terminology, she delegates roles and competencies to the components of the socio-technical network, including users as well as the components of the system (Latour 1991). By inscribing programs of actions into a piece of technology, the technology becomes an actor imposing its inscribed program of action on its users.
> The inscribed patterns of use may not succeed because the actual use deviates from it. Rather than following its assigned program of action, a user may use the system in an unanticipated way, she may follow an anti-program (Latour 1991). When studying the use of technical artifacts one necessarily shifts back and forth "between the designer's projected user and the real user" in order to describe this dynamic negotiation process of design (Akrich 1992, p. 209). (www.ifi.uio.no)

The process of translation has been described as pivotal in any analysis of how different elements in an actor network interact (Somerville,1997). Translation rests on the idea that actors within a network will try to enroll (manipulate or force) the other actors into positions that suit their purposes. When an actor's strategy is successful and it has organized other actors for its own benefit it can be said to have translated them. Automation is one such factor that organizes the other actors, such as pilots, to perform in a monitoring role vice an active role. The relational effect of automation resonates throughout the aviation industry including not only the cockpit and flight crew but also the Air Traffic Control (ATC) services as discussed in detail in Endsley (1999).

From an ANT perspective, the translation and inscription that is resident within a system such as an avionics system (including the designs, motivations and organizational strategies) reverberate throughout the network of heterogeneous elements. These effects can have positive and negative consequences during flight operations and thereby become contributing or precipitating factors for human error through the degradation of SA, a construct of the actor network.

Discussion

ANT, through its processes of translation and inscription, facilitates a methodology that looks at the external artifacts as actors and relational effects within the network. This highlights the key focus areas for discussion:

- Actors ⇒ Heterogeneous elements
- Relationality
- Networks
- Systems Design

Actors ⇒ Heterogeneous elements

Recall that the notion of an actor- actant- "is not linked to the quality of the entity as such, but to the quality of the entity in the frame of the network into which the entity is mobilised" (Law, 1999).

An actor is defined by its relationality within the network. For example, a Global Positioning Satellite (GPS) unit should not be seen as an entity in itself but rather is identified by its functionality within the network where it is performed on and performs as a heterogeneous element. It ceases to be a GPS system when it is not connected to its functional network. By itself, where someone sees an object, the ANT perspective facilitates the perception of the GPS as itself a network of heterogeneous elements comprised of such elements as the supporting systems, power sources, engineers, designers, and military infrastructure that supports the integrated GPS. The socio-technical nature of the GPS system, for example, becomes evident from the ANT perspective. It can therefore only participate in the SA construct through its relationary connection to the other heterogeneous elements of the network. The functional and dysfunctional relations between the GPS system and the other actors permeate beyond the 'local' and are resident within a 'system space' characterized by spatial and temporal heterogeneity. Thus, the actors (human or nonhuman) are defined by their relationality. Their participation in the SA construct is a function of the inscription and translation processes.

Relationality

The nature of relational effects between the actors in an actor network characterizes the SA. These relational effects cross-spatial and temporal dimensions thereby allowing ANT to work in a 'system space'. In terms of a loss of SA, the system space responds to the question about where things went wrong by delocalizing these geographically. Instead, location is treated as a reference of links and relations in a system (Law,2000).

The attributes of particular elements in the system, any particular node in the network, are entirely defined in relation to other elements in the system, to other nodes in the network (Law,2000). From this perspective, SA is not resident in any actor (human or technical) but is rather an attribute of the network. For example, when engineers work, they are typically involved in designing and building projects that have both technical and social content and implications (Law, Callon, 1988). Technical manuals or designs for nuclear power stations imply conclusions about the proper structure of society, the nature of social roles, and how these roles should be distributed (Law,Callon,1988). A similar argument can be made for the aviation industry. Aviation is governed by technical design parameters, standard operating procedures, rules and regulations. These factors imply conclusions about the nature of social roles and distribution of them within the aviation industry. It includes a network of actors from the engineering design team to the pilots and maintenance team. All have relational effects that permeate the network. We have to understand the content of the engineering work because it is in this content that the technical and the social are simultaneously shaped (Law,Callon,1988). Automation and cockpit design is just one example. The social is interconnected with the technical and thus cannot be separated from it. The causes of the loss of SA require analysis and cannot be deduced from the fact of that failure or accident. -"to talk systems is to talk of relations and relational effects" (Law,2000). The relations are subject to the inscription and translations that are resident within the system. Dysfunctional inscription and translations result in dysfunctional relations and relational effects that can precipitate an accident (Law,2000).

Airspeed, an element of SA, is a function of the network of heterogeneous elements. "Pilots continually are reading, writing, reconstituting and reconstructing the meaning and the organization of both the internal and the external representations of the speeds" (Hutchins,1988). The socio-technical network represented by the heterogeneous materials facilitates the SA construct. A weak or dysfunctional relation between the elements, be they in the design, training, organizational or cultural aspects can result in the degradation of SA and hence the propensity towards an aviation accident.

The social dimension of aviation in terms of design, organizational goals involves designs on who will use it, how they will use it and the processes to facilitate its use. From an organizational stand point it will involve the definition of roles of the users and their relational connectivity, which includes authority, command, span of control and influence. "The inscription of processes and roles on the technology does not mean that the human actors and social institutions will use the network according to the inscription. There may be a mismatch between the technical network and the actor network which results in unintended use, misuse or none-use." (McBride,www.cse.dmu.ac.uk) -"to talk systems is to talk of relations and relational effects" (Law,2000).

As a systemic attribute, SA is designed into an avionic system (human and technical) through the processes of inscription and translation. A contributing element of the SA construct are the engineering staff addressing technical and social requirements in addition to the underlying social fabric of political, economic and cultural elements. The relational effects between the design team and aircrew transcend temporal and spatial scales. SA is therefore not restricted to the purview of the pilot or aircrew but is formed in a network of heterogeneous elements. The integrity of the SA construct can be affected by dysfunctional relations such that "an apparently stable set of relations can be dissolved" like the Ladbroke Grove disaster (Law, 2000). Similarly, "adding complexity to the relations which make up a system in order to strengthen those relations may actually dissolve those relations in practice" (Law,2000). Callon describes dynamic imbalance as a quality of the Actor Network because actors in a system are functionally related. Changes in one or more cause imbalances or reverse salients in the advancing system front. (Bijker,1987)

Network

Just as "the capacity to be strategic cannot be assigned to a human actor within a network but should be described as the effect of the association of a heterogeneous network (corporate manager + fax + secretary +...)" (Gomart, Hennion,1999) so to we can conceptualize SA as a construct of a heterogeneous network of relations.
SA is socio-technical construct and is constituted within an interactive and complex matrix of social, technical, economic and political relations. These are not only captured in the operation of an aviation asset but also in its development and its construction.

The complex aetiology of SA arises from the complexity inherent within the relational elements. The network topology of ANT is characterized by the heterogeneous spatial and temporal scales such that time and space are folded so that the past and distant are made intrinsically relevant (Brown,Capdevila,1999).
"The individual actant becomes enrolled in these specific territorializations through the work of the refrain that folds time so that what occurred last week may become distant than that which occurred hundreds of years ago."(Brown,Capdevila,1999) The relationality reflected and contributing to this spatial and temporal heterogeneity facilitates the network topology and as such defines the SA construct.

System design

System design is an integral part of the SA construct. Endsley (1999) writes:

> "While a lack of information can certainly be seen as a problem for SA, too much information poses an equal problem. A major factor in creating a challenge for SA is the complexity of the many systems that must be operated. There has been an explosion of avionics systems, flight management systems and other technologies on the flight deck that have greatly increased the complexity of the systems aircrew must operate. System complexity can negatively effect both pilot workload and SA through an increase in the number of system components to be managed, a high degree of interaction between these components and an increase in the dynamics or rate of change of the components."

As a systemic attribute, SA is defined and affected by the heterogeneous elements and relational nature inherent within the network. Dysfunctional network relations can lead to a breakdown of the SA attribute as articulated by Endsley (1999): " SA may also be negatively impacted by the automation of tasks as it is frequently designed to put the aircrew 'out of the loop". This out of the loop phenomenon is a system characteristic and can be considered a result of a dysfunctional inscription and translation of the elements within the network.

Reports indicate that the probability of human failure in monitoring automation increases when devices behave reasonably but incorrectly, and when operators are simply not alert to the state of automation (Endsley,1996). The inscription of automated systems has a relational effect concerning degree of trust in, reliance on and confidence of the system. A dysfunctional inscription can be described as an erosion of the relational effects and thereby affect the stability of the overall network. The inscription of passive participation in systems and the translation associated with that inhibit the development of effective SA.

CONCLUSION

The human element in an aviation accident is well documented within the flight safety reports. "An analysis of human error in different domains shows that much of it is not due to poor decision making, but poor situation awareness." (Endsley,1999) Consequently, a thorough understanding of the relationship between the social and the technical contained within human error in complex systems is crucial for understanding the systemic nature of SA. "Complex systems cannot be understood by studying parts in isolation. The very essence of the system lies in the interaction between parts and the overall behaviour that emerges from the interactions."(Ottino,2003) The tight coupling exhibited on the different temporal and spatial scales by the actors in the systemic construct of Situation Awareness, emphasizes the need for new paradigms in systems analysis. ANT facilitates this analysis by not only looking at the mapping of interactions between individuals but also by looking at following the actors in order to map the way in which they define and distribute roles, and mobilize or invent others to play these roles. Such roles may be social, political, technical or bureaucratic in nature; the objects that are mobilized to fill them are also heterogeneous and may take the form of people, organizations, and machines. The network metaphor is a way of underlying the simultaneously social and technical character of aviation accidents (Law,Callon,1988). From a cognitive perspective, "SA in the aviation setting is challenged by the limitations of human attention and working memory."(Endsley,1999) From the ANT perspective, SA is reflected in the relationality inherent within the network characterized by the interconnectivity of the heterogeneous elements and is challenged by the nature of the inscription and translation processes. SA is an evolving dynamic construct that is dependent on the dynamic nature of the actor network. This conceptualization defines SA as a systemic attribute resident within a network of heterogeneous elements.

REFERENCES

Bannon, L.J. (1998) CSCW: Towards a Social Ergonomics. Presented at the RTO Human Factors and Medicine Panel (HFM) Symposium, Edinburgh, UK, 20-22 April 1998. Published in RTO MP-4.

Bijker, W.E., Hughes, T.P., Pinch, T.J. (1987) The Social construction of technological systems: New directions in the sociology and history of technology. MIT.

Brown, S., and Capdevila, R. (1999) Perpetuum mobile: substance, force and the sociology of translation. Published in Law, J and Hassard, J. Actor Network Theory and After. Blackwell Publishers, Oxford, UK.

Callon, M. (1999) Actor-Network theory-the market test. Published in Law, J and Hassard, J. Actor Network Theory and After. Blackwell Publishers, Oxford, UK.

Endsley, M.R. (1999) Situation Awareness in Aviation Systems. In Garland, D.J., Wise, J.A. and Hopkin. V.D. (Eds) (1999) Handbook of Aviation Human Factors. Mahwah, NJ: Lawrence Eribaum Associates.

Endsley, M.R. (2000) Theoretical Underpinnings of situation awareness: A critical review. In Endsley, M.R. and Garland, D.J. (Eds) (2000) Situation Awareness Analysis and Measurement. Mahwah, NJ: Lawrence Erlbaum Associates.

Endsley, M.R. (1999) Situation Awareness and Human Error: Designing to Support Human Performance. Proceedings of the High Consequence Systems Surety Conference-Albuquerque, NM.

Endsley, M.R. (1996) Automation and Situation Awareness. In R. Parasuraman & M. Mouloua (Eds), Automation and human performance: Theory and applications (pp. 163-181). Mahwah, NJ: Lawrence Erlbaum.

Gomart, E. and Hennion, A. (1999) A sociology of attachment: music, amateurs, drug users. Published in Law,J and Hassard,J. Actor Network Theory and After. Blackwell Publishers, Oxford,UK.

Hutchins, E. (1988) How a cockpit Remembers Its Speed. Cognitive Science (19), 265-288.

Latour, B. (1998) On Actor Network Theory: A few Clarifications. http://www.mystae.com/streams/science/box9.html

Law, J. (1999) After ANT: complexity, naming and topology. In: Law, J. & Hassard,J. (eds) Actor-Network Theory and after. England. Oxford: Blackwell Publisher.

Law,J. Networks,Relations, Cyborgs: on the Social Study of technology. Published by the Centre for Science Studies and the Department of Sociology, Lancaster University at http://www.comp.lancs.ac.uk/sociology/soc042jl.html

Law, J. (2000) Ladbroke Grove, Or How to Think about Failing Systems. Published by the Centre for Science Studies and the Department of Sociology, Lancaster University at http://www.comp.lancs.ac.uk/sociology/soc055jl.html,

Law, J., Callon, M. (1988) Engineering and Sociology in a Military Aircraft Project: A Network Analysis of Technological Change. Social Problems, Vol. 35, No. 3, June 1988.

McBride, N. Using Actor-Network Theory to predict the organizational success of a communications network. http://www.cse.dmu.ac.uk/~nkm/WTCPAP.html

Noe, E. Nad Alroe, H. Combining Luhmann and Actor-Network Theory to see Farm Enterprises as Self-organizing Systems. To be presented at: The Opening of Systems Theory" in Copenhagen May 23-25 2003. http://asp.cbs.dk/ccc/NoeElroe.pdf

Ottino, J. (2003) Complex Systems. AIChE Journal. Vol.49, No. 2. February 2003, pg 292-299.

Somerville, I. Actor Network Theory: A useful paradigm for the analysis of the UK cable/ on-line sociotechnical ensemble? http://hsb/baylor.edu/eamsower/ais.ac.97/papers/somervil.html
www.ifi.uio.no/~oleha/Publications/bok.6.html

SITUATION AWARENESS, THE ABSTRACTION HIERARCHY AND THE DESIGN OF USER INTERFACES OF COMMAND AND CONTROL DECISION SUPPORT SYSTEMS

Runar Olafsen and Karsten Bråthen

FFI (Norwegian Defence Research Establishment), Norway

ABSTRACT

This paper combines the theory of situation awareness (SA) with ecological psychology and ecological interface design (EID), especially the abstraction hierarchy (AH), and identifies design principles for military command and control decision support systems (C2DSS) user interfaces. First, level 2 SA information should be presented directly. Second, the user interface should enable all modes of processing, perceptive, intuitive and deliberate, by making information at different abstraction levels available. These principles guided the design of the user interface presented. The results indicate that the design principles and the use of AH seem feasible for deciding the information content of military C2DSS user interfaces.

Keywords: Situation awareness; Abstraction Hierarchy; Command and Control; Decision Support System; User interface

INTRODUCTION

New concepts of military operations such as network-centric warfare (NCW) have emerged with the development and diffusion of information and communication technologies. The basic assumption in NCW is that networking of sensors, decision-makers and shooters will increase combat power, improve the SA of decision-makers, speed of command, lead to a higher tempo, increased effectiveness and efficiency of operations (Alberts et al., 2001). Decision-makers need to achieve a high level of SA as a basis for their decisions, and act relatively faster then their opponents. These claims may be contradictory and decision-makers need to make trade-offs between these. In addition, they do so in dynamic and complex situations on the basis of inadequate information, with high stakes, under time pressure and other features targeted by the field of naturalistic decision-making (Klein, 1998).

One of the functions of military C2DSS is to provide relevant information supporting decision-makers in achieving appropriate levels of SA. In short, SA is knowledge about what is going on. Many failures in decision-making and choice of actions in complex dynamic contexts are due to failures in SA (Endsley, 2003). SA is the key determent of decision-making in complex and dynamic contexts. To support SA is thereby to support decision-making.

Sharing information does not necessary lead to improved SA. First, relevant information need to be distributed to the right decision-makers at the right time. Second, information needs to be presented in the right form supporting decision-makers to achieve and maintain appropriate levels of SA. In the design of C2DSS user interfaces, this concerns the *content* of the information and the *form* in which the information is presented. The EID framework includes two conceptual tools, the AH and the skills, rules, and knowledge (SRK) taxonomy, that concern the content and the form of information presented on user interfaces (Vicente & Rasmussen, 1992).

We have used the AH in the design of a C2DSS user interface. The purpose of the user interface is to support decision-makers in achieving and maintaining appropriate SA The design of the user interface is based on theories of SA (Endsley, 1995; 2003), ecological psychology (Gibson, 1979), and EID (Vicente & Rasmussen, 1990; 1992). The first section of this paper describes and discusses the theoretical background for the design. The second section presents other studies on C2DSS for supporting SA. Finally, the last section presents the user interface of our application, its status, and future work.

The purpose of the paper is to contribute to the understanding of the design of C2DSS user interfaces supporting decision-makers in complex and dynamic contexts. The aim is to narrow the gap between theory and practice. The point of departure is Endsley's (1995) model of SA in dynamic decision-making.

PERSPECTIVES ON SITUATION AWARENESS

Endsley's (1995) model for SA in dynamic decision-making identifies three levels of SA. Level 1 SA is achieved by perceiving the status, attributes and dynamics of relevant elements (data and cues) in the situation. Then these elements are combined to a more holistic comprehension of their meaning in relation to current goals (level 2 SA). Finally, level 3 SA enables decision-makers to anticipate and predict possible developments of the current situation into future events (Endsley, 2003).

Higher levels of SA build upon the lower levels and are thereby not achievable unless awareness on the lower levels exists. This is consistent with the linearity inherent in the *information processing paradigm*. Accordingly, human information processing starts from the pickup of data through the senses. The perception process converts data into information. *Meaning* of information is added through cognitive processes, i.e. the matching of information with mental models, schemata and/or scripts.

Ecological psychology opposes the information processing paradigm and advocates a close link between perception, knowledge and behaviour (e.g. Niesser, 1976; Gibson, 1979, Vicente & Rasmussen, 1990). Humans and the environment are complementary and part of the same system. Perception is a continuous act registering persistence and change (i.e. events) of things in the environment. In addition, "perceiving is knowing". Comprehension of situations does not necessary involve cognitive processing. *Meaning* and *value* of things and events is in the environment available through direct perception of information and affordances. *Affordances* are properties of things and events with reference to an observer and closely linked to behaviour. Affordances point to what things and events mean to us, what we can do with them and they to us, if we want to approach them, avoid them, or change them (Gibson, 1979).

Kahneman (2003) differentiate between intuitive and deliberate processes in addition to perceptual processing. *Intuitive processing* resembles perceptual processing except for that it involves conceptual representations in addition to perceptual representations. Intuitive processing is fast, effortless and works in parallel. *Deliberate processing* (reasoning) uses conceptual representations, is slow, takes effort, work in serial, and is controlled. People tend to prefer intuitive processing rather than deliberate processing in problem-solving activities (Kahneman, 2003; Vicente & Rasmussen, 1992; Klein, 1998).

In sum, this means that decision-makers can achieve higher levels of SA through direct perception of information and affordances. User interfaces may support comprehension (level 2 SA) by enabling intuitive processing. A design goal of C2DSS user interfaces is to present relevant level 2 SA information directly, in an actionable form (Endsley, 2003). EID and the use of AH in particular can reveal information and affordances supporting the SA of decision-makers in complex and dynamic settings (Vicente, 2002).

EID AND THE ABSTRACTION HIERARCHY

EID is a theoretical framework for designing user interfaces for complex sociotechnical systems and has been applied to a variety of domains like process control, aviation, and command and control. The framework concerns the design of interfaces assisting in coping with unfamiliar and unanticipated events, which are relevant for decision-makers in military command and control (Vicente & Rasmussen, 1992).

The *AH* concern the information content and structure of the user interface. According to Vicente & Rasmussen (1992) the AH is a psychological relevant way of describing complex work domains and serves as an externalisation of a mental model of the work domain. The AH consist of five different levels of abstraction (see table 1). Each level represents the work domain, but on different abstraction levels. The lower levels (physical form, physical function) concern physical aspects. The higher abstract levels (generalised function, abstract function and functional purpose) concern functional aspects (Rasmussen, 1983).

The *SRK taxonomy* is basically a description of modes in which humans process information. Humans interpret information according to processing mode. A match between processing mode and information form is most efficient. If there is a mismatch, the information needs to be transformed into the appropriate form, which demands cognitive effort and thereby decreases performance.

The basic design goals of EID are to enable processing at all levels and to not force processing at a higher level than necessary. Processing at the lower levels (skill-based behaviour and rule-based behaviour) is most efficient. This is similar to perceptual and intuitive processing, as described by Kahneman (2003). However, in novel situations the user interface must enable problem solving and deliberate reasoning (knowledge-based processing). To do so, users need access to information on different levels of abstractions.

DESIGNING C2DSS USER INTERFACES

Military command and control concern information about human intentions in addition to physical aspects. There are some studies concerning the applicability of EID to intentional systems, like military command and control (e.g. Chalmers, 2003; Treurniet et al., 1999; Vicente, 2002). As far as we know, empirical data and experimental testing are still insufficient. However, Treurniet et al. (1999) found that the AH can be used to include information not included in current C2DSS.

Often, C2DSS user interfaces present data/information supporting the perceptual part of SA, i.e. level 1 SA. In the AH, this correspond to the physical form and physical function levels (Treurniet et al., 1999). A reason for this is that abstract information on opponent units is harder to achieve. A consequence is that decision-makers to a larger extent need to employ deliberate reasoning to achieve level 2 SA. When possible, the user interfaces should seek to enable intuitive processing by presenting the more abstract level 2 SA information directly, keeping the users "in the loop" (Endsley, 2003). The user interfaces should also facilitate deliberate reasoning, e.g. in novel situations, by making information at the different abstraction levels available (Vicente, 2002).

We have used these principles in the design of a C2DSS user interface. By presenting the design, we aim to show how these particular principles and the AH have been put into practice.

A C2DSS USER INTERFACE

The C2DSS user interface is part of a military command and control information system (C2IS) demonstrator developed for experimentation. Among other things, the demonstrator is used for experimentation on the production and distribution of a shared situation picture (Hansen, Mevassvik & Bråthen, 2003). A modified version of the AH developed by Treurniet et al. (1999) for tactical maritime command and control guided the design of the information content of the user interface (Table 1).

Table 1. An abstraction hierarchy for joint command and control (based on Rasmussen 1983; Treurniet et al., 1999)

Abstraction level	Command and control analogy	Typical aspects and examples
Functional purpose	Mission	Intent, e.g. ground target attack...
Abstract function	Functional cooperation of entities	Roles, e.g. reconnaissance, surveillance...
Generalised function	Tasks, behavioural patterns	Activities, e.g. searching, acquiring target data, battle damage assessment (BDA)...
Physical function	Dynamic behaviour	Kinematics, course, speed, sensor activation...
Physical form	Track, entity, target	Attributes, e.g. environment, allegiance, position, ID, classification...

The user interface includes a representation of a joint situation picture. Information about and representations of friendly, neutral and opposing entities are presented on top of a geographical map. Available information on different abstraction levels is presented, enabling users to focus on the level of interest. Like many other C2DSS user interfaces, graphical symbols and text represent level 1 SA information. In addition, the user interface presents available abstract information concerning level 2 SA by including information of tasks, roles, and mission. So far, this information is presented to the users as text adjacent to the graphical representations of the units.

Figure 1 shows the user interface in a simulated ground target attack mission. The symbols represent the allegiance, environment, position and classification of the units, including velocity vectors and track histories. The colour of the text separates the different abstraction levels. The symbols and the text in *white* correspond to attributes and dynamics of entities (physical form and physical function). *Yellow* text corresponds to tasks (generalised function), *orange* to role in co-operation (abstract function) and *red* to the overall mission of the operation (functional purpose).

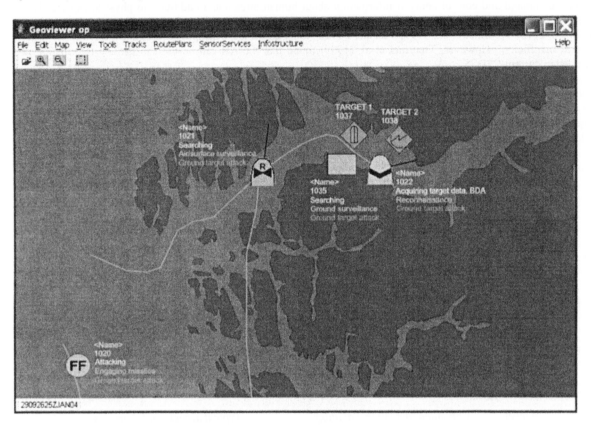

Figure 1. The C2DSS user interface in a simulated ground target attack mission.

DISCUSION

As Treuniet et al. (1999), we found the AH useful in determine the content of the information presented on the C2DSS user interface. The physical levels in the AH correspond to level 1 SA information, whereas the abstract levels correspond to level 2 SA information.

In the example presented in Figure 1, the abstract information concerned own units. In a military command and control context, it is especially hard to acquire abstract information concerning opponents. This may involve advanced data fusion and/or humans generating and entering the information into the C2DSS manually. In addition this will require representations of uncertainty, because the information typically is hypothetical.

The example given represents the current status of the ongoing work. So far, the use of AH is promising, but we need to continue to develop the user interface design by testing different solutions. Future work will concern the *content* by improving and expanding the AH to other situations, and the *form* in which the information is presented. Moving from textual to graphical representations will presumably lessen the cognitive effort of the users, given that they have the appropriate training and experience.

CONCLUSION

In this paper, we have combined the theory of SA with ecological psychology and the EID, especially AH, and identified some design principles for C2DSS user interfaces. First, level 2 SA information should be presented directly. Second, the user interface should enable all modes of processing, perceptive, intuitive and deliberate, by making information at the different abstraction levels available to users. These principles guided the design of the user interface presented. The results indicate that the design principles and the use of AH seem feasible for deciding the information content of the user interface.

This is a first step in our work using theories of SA in complex dynamic contexts, ecological psychology and EID in the design of C2DSS user interfaces for supporting the SA of decision-makers in military operations.

REFERENCES

Alberts, D.S., Garstka, J.J., Hayes, R.E., & Signori, D.A. (2001). Understanding InformationAge Warfare (2nd ed.). USA: CCRP Publication Series.

Chalmers, B. (2003). Supporting threat response management in a tactical naval environment. Proceedings of the 8th International Command and Control Research and Technology Symposium, National Defence University, Washington DC, USA, June 17-19.

Endsley, M.R. (1995). Towards a theory of situation awareness in dynamic systems,Human Factors, 37(1), 23-64.

Endsley, M. R. (2003). Designing for Situation Awareness: An Approach to User-Centered Design. London & New York: Taylor & Francis.

Gibson, J. (1979). The Ecological Approach to Visual Perception. Boston: Houghton Mifflin.

Hansen, B. J., Mevassvik, O. M., & Bråthen, K. (2003). A demonstrator for command andcontrol information system technology experimentation. Proceedings of the 8thInternational Command and Control Research and Technology Symposium, NationalDefence University, Washington DC, USA, June 17-19.

Kahneman, D. (2003). A perspective on judgement and choice. Mapping bounded rationality. American Psychologist, 58(9), 697-720.

Klein, G. (1998). Sources of Power: How People Make Decisions. Cambridge, MA: MITPress.

Neisser, U. (1976). Cognition and Reality. San Francisco: Freeman.

Rasmussen, J. (1983). Skills, rules, and knowledge; signals, signs, and symbols, and otherdistinctions in human performance models. IEEE Transactions on Systems, Man, andCybernetics, 13(3), 257-266.

Treurnitet W, van Delft J, Paradis S (1999). Tactical information abstraction framework inmaritime command and control. Paper presented at the RTO SAS Symposium, Issy les Moulineaux, France, January 12-14.

Vicente, K.J. (2002). Ecological interface design: Progress and challenges. Human Factors,44(1), 62-78.

Vicente, K.J., & Rasmussen, J. (1990). The ecology of human-machine systems II:Mediating "direct perception" in complex work domains. Ecological Psychology, 2(2),207-249.

Vicente, K.J., & Rasmussen, J. (1992). Ecological interface design: Theoretical foundations.IEEE Transactions on Systems, Man, and Cybernetics, 22(4), 589-606.

Wong, W.B.L., Sallis, P.J., & O'Hare, D. (1998). The ecological approach to interfacedesign: Applying the abstraction hierarchy to intentional domains. Proceedings of the8th Australian Conference on Computer-Human Interaction OzCHI'98, 144-150.

SITUATION AWARENESS IN MILITARY COMMAND AND CONTROL (C4I) SYSTEMS: THE DEVELOPMENT OF A TOOL TO MEASURE SA IN C4I SYSTEMS AND BATTLEFIELD ENVIRONMENTS. STAGE 1: SA METHODS REVIEW

Paul Salmon, Prof Neville Stanton, Dr Guy Walker & Dr Damian Green
Defence Technology Centre for Human Factors Integration (DTC HFI), London

ABSTRACT

To date, few specific techniques for the assessment of situation awareness (SA) in C4i (command, control, computers and communication) and battlefield environments have been developed, tested and validated in the human factors literature. A methods review was conducted in order to assess the potential usage of existing approaches to the measurement and assessment of SA during the design and evaluation process of a novel C4i system. A set of criteria were used in order to establish which of the methods were the most suitable for use in the design and evaluation of C4i systems. Furthermore, the output of the analysis is designed to act as a methods manual, aiding practitioners in the use of the SA assessment techniques reviewed. The following paper describes the purpose and process of the methods review, and offers conclusions regarding the approach to the measurement and assessment of SA in C4i environments.

Keywords: Situation Awareness, Measurement, Command and Control, military, methods review.

SA and the military

Research into the achievement and maintenance of SA in military command and control and infantry battlefield environments has become one of the most important challenges facing the human factors community. The importance of such research cannot be underestimated, where catastrophic consequences are typically associated with a loss of or poor SA. Endsley et al (2000) emphasise the importance of SA as a critical determinant of success in combat situations. SA in command and control and battlefield situations is one of the most important requirements of infantry commanders and soldiers. Infantry commander's must have a clear understanding of the ongoing situation, including a knowledge of own troops (location, condition, tactics, morale, casualties etc), enemy troops (location, goals, tactics, equipment, number etc), mission goals, terrain, time constraints, and of course civilians (location, number, safety etc) (Endsley et al 2000). The soldiers on the ground must also possess an accurate understanding of the situation, including factors such as the enemy (location, number, tactics, weaponry, future actions etc), their own unit or team, civilians etc. Often the onus in such dynamic, information rich environments falls onto technology to enhance SA. Technology that gives an advantage over the enemy is a huge asset in the age of the high-tech battlefield.

New technology, design concepts and training procedures developed to enhance military personnel's achievement and maintenance of SA require rigid and valid scientific testing in order to evaluate their effect on SA. According to Endsley et al (2000) the U.S Army research Institute is currently developing models and measures of SA for infantry operations. Matthews et al (2000) report the first attempt to define SA requirements for military operations in urbanised terrain (MOUT) and also test techniques for assessing SA in MOUT exercises. Matthews & Beal (2002) describe the testing of an SA assessment technique in military field training exercises and McGuinness & Ebbage (2000) report the testing of a technique developed for the assessment of SA in command and control environments. In other domains where an assessment of SA is required, it is often the case that an existing SA assessment technique is re-developed for the domain in question e.g. SAGAT-TRACON (Endsley & Kiris 1995) is a development of SAGAT for the air traffic control domain. However, the assessment of SA in C4i environments may not be so simple. The tasks undertaken in command and control situations are typically team-based tasks whereby task critical information is dispersed across a number of team-members. Indeed, it is envisaged that the proposed C4i system may include gold (command centre), silver (mobile command units) and bronze (foot soldier) command levels. In order to assess the effectiveness of the system, an assessment of SA is required simultaneously at each of the command levels. Also of significance to C4i environments is the distributed cognition approach to SA (Artman & Garbis 1988), which suggests that SA resides not only in the individuals operating the system, but also in artefacts used within the system, such as displays, computers and wearable technology. Artman & Garbis (1988) argue that the current models of SA ignore coordinated team

44

effort and that the future of SA requires that distributed cognition be further investigated. This approach to SA also poses further questions regarding the current measurement of SA in distributed systems, such as C4i systems. How SA is measured and exactly what is measured in these systems requires further investigation.

SA measurement and assessment

The provision of valid and reliable methods for assessing SA is crucial during system design and evaluation. Endsley (1995) suggests that SA measures are necessary in order to evaluate the effect of new technologies and training interventions upon SA, to examine factors that affect SA, to evaluate the effectiveness of processes and strategies for acquiring SA and in investigating the nature of SA itself. The goal of the C4i system is to facilitate the development and achievement of accurate and complete SA to all members of the military team, from command (gold, silver and bronze) down to foot soldier level. Therefore, the assessment of overall team and individual team-member SA is a necessary provision throughout the C4i design process. Any design concepts require continuous testing as to the level of SA that they provide and the effects upon individual and team SA that they have. It goes without saying that the end-design should offer at least a more complete and accurate level of SA to its users than existing systems do. Designers need to be made aware of the effect of novel design concepts on end-user SA. Therefore, accurate, valid and reliable SA assessment techniques are required.

There are a number of different approaches to the assessment of SA available to the human factors (HF) practitioner. For the purposes of this methods review, the following categories of SA measurement technique were proposed.

1) On-line Freeze techniques – involve the administration of SA related queries on-line, during a freeze of the simulated task under analysis.
2) Real-time probe techniques – involve the administration of SA related queries on-line, but with no freeze of the task under analysis.
3) Self-rating techniques – administered post-trial, involves participants providing a subjective rating of their SA via a rating scale.
4) Observer rating techniques – involve a subject matter expert (SME) observing the task under analysis and providing an assessment of participant SA.
5) Questionnaire techniques – involve the administration of SA related questionnaires post-trial, in order to gain a measure of participant SA.

In total, twelve SA assessment techniques were chosen for review (presented in table 1). The techniques were chosen after a review of the appropriate literature.

Table 1. SA techniques chosen for review

Method	Type	Author/Source
CARS – Crew Awareness Rating Scales	Self-Rating	McGuinness & Foy (2000)
MARS – Mission Awareness Rating Scales	Self-Rating	Matthews & Beal (2002)
SABARS – Situation Awareness Behavioural Rating Scales	Observer-Rating	Matthews & Beal (2002)
SACRI – Situation Awareness Control Room Inventory	On-line freeze	Hogg et al (1995)
SAGAT – Situation Awareness Global Assessment Technique	On-line freeze	Endsley (1995b)
SALSA	On-line freeze	Hauss & Eyferth (2003)
SASHA_L SASHA_Q	Real-time probe Questionnaire	Jeannot, Kelly & Thompson (2003)
SARS – Situation Awareness Rating Scales	Self-rating	Waag & Houck (1994)
SART – Situation Awareness Rating Technique	Self-rating	Taylor (1990)
SA-SWORD – Situation Awareness Subjective Workload Dominance	Self-rating	Vidulich & Hughes (1991)
SPAM – Situation Present Assessment method	Real-time probe	Durso et al (1998)

45

Methods Review

The twelve SA assessment techniques were then analysed using the set of pre-determined criteria outlined in table 2. The criteria were designed not only to establish which of the methods were suitable for use in the design of C4i systems, but also to aid the HF practitioner in the selection and use of the appropriate method(s). The output of the analysis is designed to act as a methods manual, aiding practitioners in the use of the HF design techniques reviewed. A summary of the methods review is presented in table 3.

Table 2. SA methods review criteria (Source: Stanton et al In Press)

Criteria	Description
Name and acronym	The name of the technique and its associated acronym
Author(s), affiliations(s) and address(es)	The names, affiliations and addresses of the authors are provided to assist with citation and help in using the method
Background and applications	This section introduces the method, its origins and development, the domain of application of the method and also application areas that it has been used in.
Domain of application	Describes the domain that the technique was originally developed and applied in.
Procedure and advice	This section describes the procedure for applying the method as well as general points of expert advice.
Flowchart	A flowchart is provided, depicting the methods procedure.
Advantages	Lists the advantages associated with using the method in the design and evaluation of C4i systems.
Disadvantages	Lists the disadvantages associated with using the method in the design and evaluation of C4i systems.
Example	An example, or examples, of the application of the method are provided to show the methods output.
Related methods	Any closely related methods are listed, including contributory and similar methods.
Approximate training and application times	Estimates of the training and application times are provided to give the reader an idea of the commitment.
Reliability and Validity	Any evidence on the reliability or validity of the method are cited
Tools needed	Describes any additional tools required when using the method.
Bibliography	A bibliography lists recommended further reading on the method and the surrounding topic area.

CONCLUSIONS

It is clear from the review that there is scope for further investigation into the measurement of SA in C4i environments. Existing techniques are limited in that they are tailored specifically to assess individual SA. In terms of the type of technique used, it appears that a combination of an on-line freeze probe technique (e.g. SAGAT) and a post-trial self rating technique (e.g. SARS), along with the performance of the task(s) under analysis may be a suitable way of assessing SA in a C4i environment. According to the literature, SAGAT is currently the most widely used and validated approach to the assessment of SA. Freeze techniques are attractive due to their objectivity, direct nature and their appropriateness for use in simulated environments. Whilst self-rating techniques suffer from a number of problems associated with collecting SA data post-trial (e.g. SA correlated with performance, participants forgetting low SA periods of the task, participants not being aware of missing SA etc) it is felt that their use in the assessment of SA in C4i should not be discounted. It seems that a multiple measure approach, similar to that seen in the assessment of workload, may be appropriate, and that the use of a specific C4i SA self-rating technique would be useful. Such a technique could be used in conjunction with an on-line freeze technique in order to offer a more comprehensive assessment of SA. The exact nature of the technique remains unclear, and a number of difficulties are apparent. Firstly, the dispersed nature of command and control environments in terms of geographical location (e.g. command centre, foot soldiers) means that incorporating a simulation freeze may prove very difficult. Whilst it may be easy to test the C4i command centre interface by freezing the appropriate screens and displays, to simultaneously freeze the situation 'in the field' (i.e. foot soldiers

Table 3. Summary of SA methods review

Method	Type of method	Domain	SME's required	Training time	Application time	Tools needed	Validation studies	Advantages	Disadvantages
CARS	Self rating technique	Military (infantry operations)	No	Low	Med	Pen and paper	Yes 2	1) Developed for use in infantry environments. 2) Less intrusive than on-line techniques. 3) Quick, easy to use requiring little training.	1) Construct validity questionable. 2) Limited evidence of use and validation. 3) Possible correlation with performance.
MARS	Self rating technique	Military (infantry operations)	No	Low	Med	Pen and paper	Yes 2	1) Developed for use in infantry environments. 2) Less intrusive than on-line techniques. 3) Quick, easy to use requiring little training.	1) Construct validity questionable. 2) Limited evidence of use and validation. 3) Possible correlation with performance.
SABARS	Observer rating	Military (infantry operations)	Yes	High	Med	Pen and paper	Yes 2	1) SABARS behaviours generated from infantry SA requirements exercise. 2) Non-intrusive.	1) SME's required. 2) The presence of observers may influence participant behaviour. 3) Access to field settings required.
SACRI	Freeze on-line probe technique	Nuclear Power	No	Low	Med	Simulator Computer	Yes 1	1) Removes problems associated with collecting SA data post-trial.	1) Requires expensive simulators. 2) Intrusive to primary task.
SAGAT	Freeze on-line probe technique	Aviation (military)	No	Low	Med	Simulator Computer	Yes 10+	1) Widely used in a number of domains. 2) Subject to numerous validation studies. 3) Removes problems associated with collecting SA data post-trial.	1) Requires expensive simulators. 2) Intrusive to primary task. 3) Substantial work is required to develop appropriate queries.
SALSA	Freeze on-line probe technique	ATC	No	Low	Med	Simulator Computer	Yes 1	1) Removes problems associated with collecting SA data post-trial e.g. correlation with performance, forgetting etc.	1) Requires expensive simulators. 2) Intrusive to primary task. 3) Limited use and validation.
SASHA	Real-time probe technique Post-trial quest	ATC	Yes	High	Med	Simulator Computer Telephone Pen and paper	No	1) Offers two techniques for the assessment of SA.	1) Construct validity questionable. 2) Generation of appropriate SA queries places great burden upon analyst/SME. 3) Limited evidence of use or validation studies.
SARS	Self rating technique	Aviation (military)	No	Low	Low	Pen and paper	Yes 1	1) Quick and easy to use, requires little training 2) Non-intrusive to primary task.	1) Problems of gathering SA data post-trial e.g. correlation with performance, forgetting low SA. 2) Limited use and validation evidence.
SART	Self rating technique	Aviation (military)	No	Low	Low	Pen and paper	Yes 10+	1) Quick and easy to administer. Also low cost. 2) Generic – can be used in other domains. 3) Widely used in a number of domains.	1) Correlation between performance and reported SA. 2) Participants are not aware of their low SA. 3) Construct validity is questionable.
SA-SWORD	Paired comparison technique	Aviation	No	Low	Low	Pen and paper	Yes 2	1) Easy to learn and use. Also low cost. 2) Generic – can be used in other domains. 3) Useful when comparing two designs.	1) Post-trial administration – correlation with performance, forgetting etc. 2) Limited use and validation evidence. 3) Does not provide a measure of SA.
SPAM	Real-time probe technique	ATC	Yes	High	Low	Simulator Computer Telephone	Yes 4	1) No freeze required.	1) Low construct validity. 2) Limited use and validation. 3) Participants may be unable to verbalise spatial representations.

47

equipment displays) may prove very difficult, if not impossible. Secondly, significant work is required in conducting an SA requirements analysis in C4i systems and in generating the appropriate SA queries. Consequently, this would form the next stage in the development of a freeze type C4i SA measurement tool. Thirdly, an assessment of both individual and overall team SA is required. One possible approach to the assessment of individual and team SA may be the use of an on-line freeze technique, accompanied with a self-rating technique whereby participants are asked to rate their own SA and then to rate the level of SA possessed by the team as a whole and also by other individual team members. A similar approach has been used in the assessment of team workload, using the NASA-TLX (Hart & Staveland 1988), where individual team members are asked to rate their own workload using the NASA-TLX and then to give a subjective estimation of the team's overall workload using a modified version of the TLX (Bowers & Jentsch In Press). Finally, the distributed cognition approach to SA raises new questions surrounding the assessment of SA, and represents a challenge to the human factors community regarding the measurement of SA in distributed systems. Exactly what is measured and how it is measured fall under scrutiny, and further investigation into this approach to describing SA is required.

Acknowledgements: This work from the Human Factors Integration Defence Technology Centre was part-funded by the Human Sciences Domain of the UK Ministry of Defence Scientific Research Programme.

REFERENCES

Artman, H., & Garbis, C. (1988). Situation Awareness as Distributed Cognition. In T. Green, L. Bannon, C. Warren, J. Buckley (Eds.) Cognition and cooperation. Proceedings of the 9th conference of cognitive ergonomics. (pp. 151-156). Limerick, Ireland.

Bowers, C. A., & Jentsch, F. (In Press). Team Workload. In N. A. Stanton, A. Hedge, K, Brookhuis, E. Salas, & H. Hendrick. (In Press). (eds) Handbook of Human Factors methods. UK, Taylor and Francis.

Durso, F.T., Hackworth, C.A., Truitt, T., Crutchfield, J., Manning, C.A. (1998). Situation awareness as a predictor of performance in en route air traffic controllers. Air Traffic Quarterly, 6, 1-20.

Endsley, M. R. (1995). Measurement of Situation Awareness in Dynamic Systems, Human Factors, Vol. 37, pp65-84

Endsley, M. R., & Kiris, E. O. (1995) Situation awareness global assessment technique (SAGAT) TRACON air traffic control version user guide. Lubbock, Texas Tech University.

Endsley, M. R., Holder, L. D., Leibricht, B. L., Garland, D. J., Wampler, R. L., & Matthews, M. D. (2000). Modelling and Measuring Situation Awareness in the infantry operational environment. Research report 1753. Alexandria, VA: US Army Research Institute.

Hart, S. G., & Staveland, L. E. (1988) Development of a multi-dimensional workload rating scale: Results of empirical and theoretical research. In P. A. Hancock & N. Meshkati (Eds.), Human Mental Workload. Amsterdam. The Netherlands. Elsevier.

Hauss, Y. & Eyferth, K. (2003). Securing future ATM-concepts' safety by measuring situation awareness in ATC. Aerospace Science and Technology.

Hogg, D. N., Folleso, K., Strand-Volden, F., & Torralba, B. (1995). Development of a situation awareness measure to evaluate advanced alarm systems in nuclear power plant control rooms. Ergonomics, Vol 38 (11), pp 2394-2413.

Jeannott, E., Kelly, C., Thompson, D. (2003). The development of Situation Awareness measures in ATM systems. EATMP report. HRS/HSP-005-REP-01.

Matthews, M. D. & Beal, S. A. (2002). Assessing Situation Awareness in Field Training Exercises. U.S. Army Research Institute for the Behavioural and Social Sciences. Research Report 1795.

Matthews, M. D., Pleban, R. J., Endsley, M. R., & Strater, L. D. (2000). Measures of Infantry Situation Awareness for a Virtual MOUT Environment. Proceedings of the Human Performance, Situation Awareness and Automation: User Centred Design for the New Millennium Conference.

McGuinness, B. & Foy, L. (2000). A subjective measure of SA: the Crew Awareness Rating Scale (CARS). Presented at the Human Performance, Situational Awareness and Automation Conference, Savannah, Georgia, 16-19 Oct 2000.

McGuinness, B. & Ebbage, L. (2000). Assessing Human Factors in Command and Control: Workload and Situational Awareness Metrics.

Stanton, N. A., Hedge, A., Brookhuis, K., Salas, E., & Hendrick, H. (In Press) (eds) Handbook of Human Factors and Ergonomics methods. UK, Taylor and Francis.

Taylor, R. M. (1990). Situational Awareness Rating Technique (SART): The development of a tool for aircrew systems design. In Situational Awareness in Aerospace Operations (AGARD-CP-478) pp3/1 –3/17, Neuilly Sur Seine, France: NATO-AGARD.

Vidulich, M. A., & Hughes, E. R. (1991). Testing a subjective metric of situation awareness. Proceedings of the Human Factors Society 35th Annual meeting. Pg 1307 – 1311.

Waag, W. L., & Houck, M. R (1994). Tools for assessing situational awareness in an operational fighter environment. Aviation, Space and Environmental Medicine. 65(5) A13

INTENTION-REPRESENTED ECOLOGICAL INTERFACE DESIGN FOR SUPPORTING COLLABORATION WITH AUTOMATION: SITUATION AWARENESS AND CONTROL IN INEXPERIENCED SCENARIOS

Hiroshi Furukawa, Hiroyuki Nakatani and Toshiyuki Inagaki
University of Tsukuba, Japan

ABSTRACT

Human operators faced with an unexpected situation can take effective actions if they aware constraints in work space of a human-machine system (HMS). This paper describes a design concept of Ecological Interface Design (EID) display indicating information about intention of automation. Aim of this interface is aiding operators to comprehend means and goals used by automated controllers and the significance of them in achievement of a top goal of the HMS. An experiment was performed to examine the efficacy of the intention-represented EID in supporting operators using a partially-automated process control simulation. The results show that the performance was significantly higher with the proposed EID than with a standard EID. The proposed interface has ability to support operators in essential tasks for operations of HMSs, which are assessment of tasks of automated controllers, awareness of goals of the controllers, prediction of control actions by the controllers, prediction of system behaviors, decision making and action planning, and also knowledge-based operations in inexperienced situations.

Keywords: Intention of Automation; Ecological Interface Design; Human-Automation Collaboration; Inexperienced Events

INTRODUCTION

Operator's awareness of operational constraints in work space is a key factor for improving total performance of human-machine systems (HMS) especially in unexpected situations, where rules, procedures, or empirical knowledge of the operator may not be any longer efficacious. Maintaining awareness of automation is one of the general requirements for the improvement. However, current HMSs may not always meet this requirement (Sheridan, 2000, Billings, 1997, Parasuraman & Riley, 1997).

A main goal of this study is development of a design concept of human-machine interface (HMI) that can prevent two critical cases resulting from operator's misunderstanding about intention of automation, i.e., its goal and means. The first case is where human operator fails to achieve his/her goal because of operational constraints induced by automation. The goal may be incompatible with that of an automated controller, or the means intended to use by the operator may be unavailable because a controller had been using it for another purpose. This is a typical case for automation-induced surprise (Sarter, Woods & Billings, 1997). Another target case is where an operator conflicts with the achievement of an indispensable goal allocated to an automated controller. If an operator disengaged the controller to achieve his/her own goals, the results of this local-goal or selfish control might be catastrophic disasters.

If operators can understand intention of automation quantitatively and qualitatively, it is expected that they can select proper means to achieve his or her goals, which does not harm but pursue the top goal of a human-machine system. However, it must be inappropriate to provide information about detailed mechanisms of automation under rigid time constraints (Sheridan, 2000).

Authors have proposed a design concept of HMI providing information about intention of automation, Intention-Represented Ecological Interface Design (Furukawa & Inagaki, 2001). Information about the intention is identified using the Abstraction-Decomposition Space (ADS) (Rasmussen, 1986). An ADS is a framework for representing functional structures of work in a HMS, which describes hierarchical relationships between a top goal and physical components with multiple viewpoints, such as abstraction and aggregation. Since operator's comprehension of the functional states based on the ADS is an essential view for the work, a system-centered view is necessary for operators to control a HMS, comprehend system states, make operational plans, and execute the plans appropriately in abnormal or unanticipated conditions (Miller & Vicente, 2001). Ecological Interface Design (EID) is a design concept, in which the ADS of a target system is represented to allow operators to comprehend states of the functions intuitively (Vicente and Rasmussen, 1990, 1992, Vicente, 2002). The HMI is designed to support operators to have a system-centered view. This can be thought of as the externalization of the operator's mental model of the system onto the HMI (Rasmussen and Pejtersen, 1995). In the proposed intention-represented

HMI design concept, the EID display was used as the basic framework to implement the identified information about the automation's intention into an interface display.

Our previous study shows that participant's performance in state comprehension and decision making heavily depended on the strategies that they used (Furukawa & Parasuraman, 2003). Some participants controlled only responsible tasks as one of controllers and completely left some tasks to the highly-capable automated controllers. The others supervised the automated controllers and intervened in the tasks at some situations, and used the information about intentions of the automated controllers. The performance in the state comprehension test of the latter was significantly higher than that of the former.

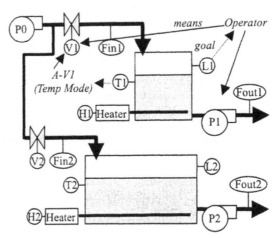

Figure 1. A target system: a heated water supply plant.

In this study, the efficacy of the Intention-Represented EID was examined using participants with a system-centered view in experienced situations and inexperienced scenarios. In the training phase of this study, participants were trained to have a system- centered view, namely monitoring the whole functions of work and taking necessary actions to achieve the top goal of the system.

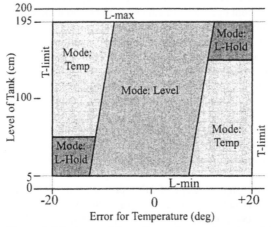

Figure 2. Mode transition of an automated system A-V.

METHOD

An experiment was conducted to examine the efficacy of the intention-represented EID in supporting operators. Participants performed a partially-automated process control simulation with the intention-represented EID and with a standard EID without the indication. The scenarios included situations that had been experienced before as well as unexpected events.

Process Control Simulation

This study used a heated water supply plant (Figure 1), which was a simplified and automated version of the DURESS process control simulation (Vicente and Rasmussen, 1990, 1992). A top goal of this plant is a supply of water with demanded temperatures and flow rates to a customer. Demands of temperatures (T1&T2) and outflow rates (Fout1&2) are indicated through HMI periodically, every thirty seconds. As penalties, a profit of a task is reduced with high rates for errors in temperatures and outflow rates, and with much lower rates for levels of the reservoirs.

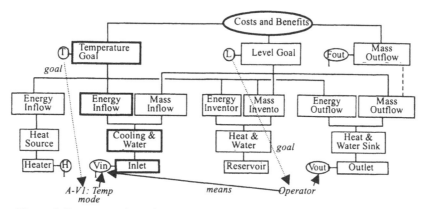

Figure 3. Representation of automation's and an operator's intention on the framework of Abstraction-Decomposition Space. (ADS is based on an example in Vicente & Rasmussen, 1990)

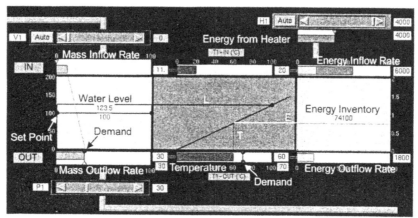

Figure 4. A means-ends representation of a reservoir based on an EID form proposed by Vicente.

51

To answer demands on outflow rates, operators must change settings of the outflow pumps in manual. There were two automated controllers for each line. A controller A-H used a heater to adjust temperatures of water to demand values. A controller A-V for an inlet valve had three different modes, which was hard for participants to recognize (Figure 2). In a mode Level, the system adjusts water level in the reservoir (L1/L2) to a set point (100cm). The mode changes to "Temp" when error of temperature gets larger than a preset threshold, and the automated system adjusts the temperature to a demand value. If current temperature is higher than a demand value, inlet flow rate will be increased automatically. Therefore, level of reservoir becomes higher, even if the level is higher than the set point. In a mode L-Hold, the system tries to hold the current level of the reservoir, not to exceed safety level limit; L-max (195cm) or L-min (5cm). When error of the temperature gets more or less then 20 degrees, P1/P2 stops automatically for safety of a customer (T-limit). Temperatures are crucial parameters because of these safety limits.

Implementation

Figure 3 describes the ADS of a line in the target plant. A goal of the A-V in Temp mode is to keep the temperature of water in the reservoir at a specified value. Means are several functions connected to the goal. Means used by automated controllers can be described in the framework of ADS, which are emphasized with heavy-lined boxes in Figure 3. A central idea of a design concept, Intention-Represented EID, is that information about the means and their relations with goals must be in the HMI.

For investigation of the proposed concept, HMI was implemented using MATLAB (language of technical computing, The MathWorks, Inc.) on a personal computer (19" display). Current states of automated controllers were indicated by several panels; auto/manual and their modes.

An HMI based on EID was implemented without automation's intention (Figure 4). The left part showed mass balance between mass inflow rate, level of water and mass outflow rate, and the right part described energy balance between inflow rate, inventory and outflow rate of energy. The center part represented relationships between temperature of the reservoir (T), water level (L) and energy inventory (E) (Vicente & Rasmussen, 1990, 1992).

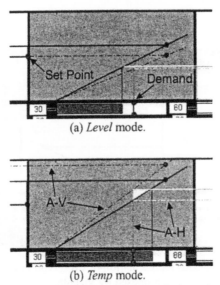

(a) *Level* mode.

(b) *Temp* mode.

Figure 5. The representation forms for intention
of automation in different modes.

The center part of a HMI with automation's intention is described in Figure 5. These forms were automatically changed according to a mode of A-V. Dotted lines in Level mode (a) represented a goal state of automated controllers, where A-H tried to keep T at the demand value, and L for A-V. In Temp mode (b), intention of A-V was indicated by dotted lines. They represented a goal state of A-V, supposing that the energy inventory does not change from current mount. In the same way, intention of A-H was represented with another dotted lines, supposing that the level of water remains stationary.

Participants

The experiment used sixteen paid participants (under-graduate and graduate students). All participants reported that they had normal or corrected to normal vision and hearing. They were asked to learn behaviors and a physical model of the target plant, and to master skills for controlling the plant using an operator's manual book and through controlling the plant actually. Their strategies were identified based on data collected by interviews and eye-movement recording. Twelve participants were selected to attend the main experiment, who supervised the system with the system-centered view.

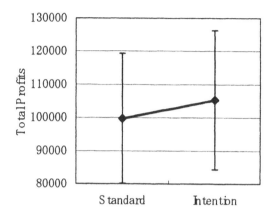

Figure 6. Total profit of the participants with the standard EID and the intention-represented EID

Procedure

The twelve participants were randomly divided into two groups of six. The order of using the HMI was counterbalanced across the participants.

Six scenarios were prepared, and all was performed in random order in each round with one of the EID displays. Each scenario includes a large change in both or one of demands on temperature and an outflow rate at a reservoir. Scenarios #1 to #4 were selected from scenarios used in the training phase. The efficacy of the HMI during well-trained situations was examined with data of these scenarios. Scenarios #5 and #6 were new for the participants, and participants had to use detailed and deep knowledge about the system and the automated controllers to operate the HMS in the conditions.

RESULTS

A repeated measures ANOVA test shows that the total profit of the participants was significantly higher with the intention-represented EID than with a standard EID ($F(1,11)=5.43$, $p=.040*$). Figure 6 shows the means and standard deviations in the conditions as a function of the types of EID.

The results of the ANOVA tests on the performances with the proposed EID and the standard EID under different conditions of the scenarios and the types of the performance were summarized in Table 1. The benefit of the intention-represented EID mostly emerged in improvement of performance related to operations on the water level of the Reservoir 1 (L1) and in the inexperienced scenarios (#5 and #6).

Table 1. Conditions where the performance was significantly better with the intention-represented EID than with a standard EID (p-values are given as results of the ANOVA tests).

	Profit	Penalty								
		Water Level	L1	L2	Temp.	T1	T2	Outlet Flow	P1	P2
Total (#1 - #6)	.040*	.049*	.050*	-	-	-	-	-	-	-
#1	-	-	-	-	-	-	-	-	-	-
#2	-	-	-	-	-	-	-	-	-	-
#3	-	-	-	-	-	-	-	-	-	-
#4	.039*	-	-	-	-	-	-	-	-	-
Inexperienced (#5 and #6)	.045*									
#5	-	-	.040*	-	-	-	-	-	-	-
#6	-	-	-	-	.005**	.025*	-	-	-	-

*: <.05, **: <.01, -: no significant differences, gray: the tests were not conducted.

DISCUSSION

These findings indicate that the Intention-Represented EID has the efficacy in supporting participant's operation even in inexperienced conditions. To reveal the actual strategies used and the use of the intention information during the operations, analyses on the data from participant's interviews and eye-movement recording were performed. In the following section, the reasons for the improvement in operations related to the water level of Reservoir 1 and at the inexperienced situations are discussed.

Mode and Goal Awareness

Since the volume of the Reservoir 1 is much smaller than that of Reservoir 2, the difficulty in adjustment of L1 by changing the inlet flow rate was much laborious than L2. When the A-V took long to settle the levels, participants might improve the situations by manual operations. Therefore, proper assessment of the states of A-V in proper time was a key factor for getting high profits.

While operating in such situation with the standard EID, the participants had to read the temperature to identify whether A-V was having difficulties in trying to settle the water level in Level mode, or to control the temperate by changing the inlet flow rate in Temp mode. On the other hand, the participants could perceive the current goal of the automated controller quantitatively and directly from the intention-represented EID. This case shows that the intention information is critical for rapid operators' assessment on the state of the automation, and the efficacy of the proposed HMI to support operators for their mode and goal awareness.

Operations Based on State Prediction

Another type of the improvement related to L1 was due to the participants' rapid and accurate prediction of the system state when they were supported by the proposed EID. Participant's awareness of goal level set by the automated controller was significant for getting high performance at Reservoir 1, since assessment of the necessity of manual control on L1 was a critical decision when the mode had changed from Temp to Level mode. It was confirmed that participants could aware the future state of L1 quantitatively when they used the intention-represented EID. However, it was difficult for them to predict the state without it. The accurate prediction of states that would be achieved by automation was indispensable for appropriate human-automation collaboration in this context.

Knowledge-Based Operations in Inexperienced Situations

In the inexperienced scenarios #5 and #6, operators had to take knowledge-based operations to settle the state of the plant. The two inlet lines to the reservoirs are branches of a single main line. Therefore, the actual flow rate of the inlet line was lower than the demand of the A-V when the total of the flow rates of the lines exceeded the maximum rate for the main line. Since the controlling algorithms of the controllers are independent of each other, the automated controllers could not achieve the own goals simultaneously. To achieve the level demands for the two reservoirs, manual control by operators was necessary. Even the participants were instructed in advance that the actual flow rates might be limited to be much lower than the demand due to the constraint, some participants misunderstood the reason of the fluctuation of the temperature when they used the standard EID. However, all the participants could aware the situation appropriately and take appropriate actions with the intention-represented EID. This must be empirical evidence that the proposed EID has an efficacy in supporting operators to understand the constraints in the HMS, and to make operating plans to achieve system goals which are feasible in the situations.

CONCLUSION

This study examined the efficacy of the Intention-Represented EID design concept in tasks of state comprehension, decision making and operational actions in process control. The results indicate that the proposed HMI has ability to support operators in essential tasks for appropriate operations of HMS, which are assessment of automated controller's tasks, awareness of goals of the controllers, prediction of control actions by the controllers, prediction of system behaviors, decision making and action planning, and also knowledge-based operations in unexpected or inexperienced situations.

REFERECES

Billings, C. E. (1997). Aviation automation, the search for a human-centered approach, LEA.

Furukawa, H. and Inagaki, T. (2001). "A Graphical Interface Design for Supporting Human-Machine Cooperation: Representing Automation's Intention by Means-Ends Relations," Proc. of 8th IFAC/IFIP/IFORS/IED Symposium on Analysis, Design, and Evaluation of Human-Machine Systems, pp. 651-656.

Furukawa, H. and Parasuraman, R. (2003). "Supporting system-centered view of operators through ecological interface design: Two experiments on human-centered automation," Proc. Human Factors and Ergonomics Society 47th Annual Meeting, pp.567-571.

Miller, C. A. and Vicente, K. J. (2001). "Comparison of display requirements generated via hierarchical task and abstraction-decomposition space analysis techniques," International Journal of Cognitive Ergonomics, 5(3), pp.335-355.

Parasuraman, R. and Riley, V. (1997). "Humans and automation: use, misuse, disuse, abuse," Human Factors, 39(2), Sheridan, T. B. (2000). HCI in supervisory control: twelve dilemmas. In P. F. Elzer, et al. (eds.), Human Error and System Design and Management. Springer, pp.1-12.

Rasmussen, J. (1986). Information processing and human-machine interaction, Elsevier Science Publishing.

Rasmussen, J. and Pejtersen, A. M. (1995). Virtual ecology of work. In J. M. Flach, P. A. Hancock, J. Caird, and K. J. Vicente (eds.), Global Perspectives on the ecology of human-machine systems. Lawrence Erlbaum Associates, pp. 121-156.

Sarter, N. B., Woods, D. D., and Billings, C. E. (1997). Automation surprises. In G. Salvendy (ed), Handbook of Human Factors and Ergonomics. John Wiley & Sons, pp. 1926-1943.

Vicente, K. J. (2002). "Ecological Interface Design: Progress and Challenges," Human Factors, 44(1), 62-78.

Vicente, K. J. and Rasmussen, J. (1990). "The ecology of human-machine systems II: Mediating direct perception in complex work domains," Ecological Psychology, 2, 207-249.

Vicente, K. J. and Rasmussen, J. (1992). "Ecological interface design: Theoretical foundations," IEEE Transactions on Systems, Man, and Cybernetics, 22(4), 589-606.

INTEGRATING SAGAT INTO HUMAN PERFORMANCE MODELS

Christopher C. Plott
Micro Analysis & Design

Mica R. Endsley and Laura D. Strater
SA Technologies

ABSTRACT

Over the last decade a number of methods for empirically assessing individual and team situation awareness in simulator and operational environments have been developed and applied. The Situation Awareness Global Assessment Technique (SAGAT) has been used across a number of operational contexts for empirically assessing situation awareness. The results of these applications have shown that SAGAT is both theoretically sound and provides a valid method for assessing situation awareness. During the same period, simulation models of human performance for assessing and predicting individual and team performance times, accuracies, and workload were also developed and applied across a wide variety of contexts. In particular, several efforts have demonstrated the predictive validity of task network models of human performance. Measures of situation awareness have only recently begun to be incorporated into these types of human performance models. In this paper, we describe a method for incorporating the SAGAT scoring system into task network models of human performance. In addition, we provide a discussion of the benefits of exploring the dynamics of the situation awareness measures through the exercising of the human performance models.

Keywords: Situation awareness; SAGAT; Human performance modeling

INTRODUCTION

Methods of assessing situation awareness (SA) and reflecting human performance in simulation models are both providing considerable insights to human-systems interaction. Integrating SA into human performance models can extend both capabilities. In this paper, we describe an initial effort for integrating a specific SA assessment approach, SAGAT, into task network models of human performance. We describe how it can be done, issues in applying the approach, and the potential benefits. We begin with a brief background of the methodologies.

Situation Awareness Global Assessment Technique (SAGAT)

The Situation Awareness Global Assessment Technique (SAGAT), is a global tool developed to assess SA across all of its elements based on a comprehensive assessment of operator SA requirements (Endsley, 1987, 1988, 1990b) . As a global measure, SAGAT includes queries about all operator SA requirements, including Level 1 (perception of data), Level 2 (comprehension of meaning) and Level 3 (projection of the near future) components. This includes a consideration of system functioning and status as well as relevant features of the external environment. The approach minimizes possible biasing of attention, as subjects cannot prepare for the queries in advance since they could be queried over almost every aspect of the situation to which they would normally attend.

Using SAGAT, subjects report the values of key parameters relevant to maintaining overall situation awareness and to critical decisions they need to make at a given point in time. To allow queries from a comprehensive array of SA requirements, presentation of SAGAT queries is conducted during a temporary halt in the action or simulation. These reported parameter values are then compared to the actual values, and if they are within predefined tolerance ranges they are scored as correct. Otherwise, they are scored as incorrect. These scores are averaged for each query across all times sampled, so that an average score can be calculated for friendly location, or predicted enemy action, for example. In addition, the scores can also be rolled up into an overall SA score, however, this measure has limited utility due to the multivariate nature of the SA construct.

The SAGAT technique has thus far been shown to have a high degree of validity for measuring SA. SAGAT has been shown to have predictive validity, with SAGAT scores indicative of pilot performance in a combat simulation (Endsley, 1990a). Content validity was also established, showing the queries used to be relevant to SA in a fighter aircraft domain (Endsley, 1990b). Empirical validity has been demonstrated through several studies which have shown that a temporary freeze in the simulation to collect SAGAT data did not impact performance and that such data could be collected for up to 5 or 6 minutes during a freeze without running into memory decay problems (Endsley, 1990b, 1995). A certain degree of measurement reliability has been demonstrated in a study that found high reliability of SAGAT scores for four individuals who participated in two sets of simulation trials (Endsley & Bolstad, 1994)

Human Performance Modeling

Over the past 15 years, a set of tools has emerged for modeling human performance in complex systems that are based on the concept of task network modeling (Laughery et al, 2000). These tools involve the functional decomposition of human (and other system component) activity into a network form. Then, through the addition of information such as function time, accuracy, resource requirements, and functional interdependencies, a computer simulation of the system can be constructed that allows the prediction of crew performance, utilization, and areas of potential risk. Additionally, factors such as fatigue, cognitive workload, and other performance-shaping factors can be explored using this approach.

Task network modeling is an approach to modeling human performance in complex systems that has evolved for several reasons. First, it is a reasonable means for extending the staple of the analysis of manned systems – the task and function analysis. Task analyses organized by task sequence are the basis for the task network model. Second, in addition to complex operator models, task network models can interact with sophisticated models of other system hardware and software to create a closed-loop representation of the human/machine system allowing the prediction of system dynamics. Third, task network models can be built into computer simulations using commercial discrete-event simulation packages, so the technology is there to support it. Finally, task network modeling has been demonstrated to provide reasonable input to many types of human/system design issues.

With a task network model, the analysts can examine a design (e.g., control panel redesign) and address questions such as "How much longer will it take to perform this procedure?" and "Will there be an increase in the error rate?" or "Will I need to add more people?" Furthermore, given a task network model of an operator in an existing or conceived system, the model can be modified to address human centered design questions by making changes to the model such as:

- Modifying task times based on changes in the time required to access and use a new display
- Modifying task times and accuracies based upon changes in the content and format of displays
- Changing task sequence, eliminating tasks, and/or adding tasks based upon changes in procedures
- Changing allocation of tasks and ensuing task sequence based upon reallocation of tasks among operators or automated systems
- Changing task time and accuracies based upon stressors such as sleep loss or drug effects

The above list is not intended as a definitive list of all the ways that these models may be used to study design or operations concepts, but should illustrate how these models can be used to address design and operational issues.

There are many descriptions of the use of task network modeling to support the human-system integration process in military and commercial systems including ships (Scott-Nash et al, 2000), aircraft (Laughery et al, 1986), ground-based vehicles (Lockett et al, 1990), command and control systems (Archer et al, 1999), and many others. Work is underway at MA&D to integrate cognitive modeling using ACT-R (Anderson & Lebiere, 1998) with task network modeling so that cognitive process modeling can be part of system evaluation. In addition, task network models representing the human-in-the-loop have been successfully linked to other simulations including war-gaming simulations (Peters et al, 2002), anthropometric manikin simulators (Plott et al, 2003), and aircraft flight simulators (Hoagland et al, 2000).

Modeling Situation Awareness

Measures of situation awareness have only recently begun to be included in task network models. SA problems, however, have been found to be behind as much as 88% of human error (Endsley, 1995). Making this linkage, therefore, is essential for robustly representing human behavior in human performance models. It is also important that measures of SA used in the human performance models are consistent with, and can be compared to, those used in operational or other empirical environments.

Archer et al (2000) developed a representation of SA based in "information driven decision making" architecture that reflected SA based on what elements of information the operator has been presented with and "how fresh" that information may be to the operator. Engh et al (1997) included a simple short-term memory scheme into their models to reflect SA, and found reasonably good relationships between the predictions and the results of in-simulator assessments using a technique called SACRI (Hogg et al, 1994), which is similar to SAGAT.

METHOD

While the results of the efforts discussed above are promising, for this effort we chose to integrate the SAGAT approach into human performance models. SAGAT provides a straightforward scoring approach that can be readily integrated into task network human performance models. The SAGAT approach can be incorporated into task network models of human performance by: 1) modeling the actual changes in the parameter values over the course of a simulated scenario; 2) identifying tasks or other events where the operator updates their knowledge of parameter values; 3) selecting points in the model to apply the SAGAT scoring, and 4) integrating the operating knowledge updates and SAGAT scoring into the model.

For demonstration purposes, we integrated SAGAT into models originally developed for the Air Warfare Coordinator position for a future ship design. We first identified the tasks where the operator's SA would be updated. These are highlighted in the network diagram shown in Figure 1.

To reflect the Air Warfare Coordinator's current SA, we added "operator stored" variables for each of the parameters identified as important for maintaining SA to the model. In this case, the parameters for each track (e.g., friendly aircraft, hostile aircraft, missiles) the Air Warfare Coordinator should be monitoring are critical for maintaining SA. These basically reflect the operator's current "memory" of the variables from the last time that they were updated. In each of the tasks identified as opportunities for SA updates, we incorporated a function for setting the "stored" values to the current value for the parameters. As the model runs, we capture the difference between the "operator stored" values and the actual values for the parameters.

As the values are compared, they are also scored using the SAGAT scheme. A function compares the stored values to the current actual values, determines if they are within the tolerance limits, and assigns a 1 to those that are, and a 0 to those that are not. For numerical values the tolerance limit was set to +/- 5%. This is a typical range, but could vary based on the sensitivity of the actual parameters or policy decisions. Non-numerical parameters (e.g., hostile intent) were evaluated as true or false. The scores are then totaled up for each track. A SAGAT score is then be computed for each track, and the entire set of active tracks can be rolled up to compute the overall SA score. The Figure 2 illustrates the total SA score for relevant track parameters over the course of a scenario.

DISCUSSION

When implementing a scheme such as SAGAT into a human performance model there are several important considerations to take into account. These factors should be fully considered during the design of the model and the collection of data to support it. First, SAGAT uses a large number of parameters to compute the SA score. If this full range of parameters is not considered within the model, the SA scores may become distorted since the score is computed as a percentage. Second, the timing and rate of changes in these parameters is also important to reflect in the model since they can significantly affect changes in the SA score. For example, when representing a hostile aircraft, the full set of key parameters (e.g., bearing, speed, distance, intent) should be included and should change in accordance with expected maneuvers and doctrine. One approach for representing changes in parameters used by Archer et al (2000) was to represent changes in information quality based on initial quality and the volatility of the information over time to create decay functions for the parameters. When available, linking to other simulations that generate the changes (e.g., flight simulators, war-gaming simulations) is also effective. Finally, it is important to consider how operator memory and human errors are represented in the model. In the demonstration model we built,

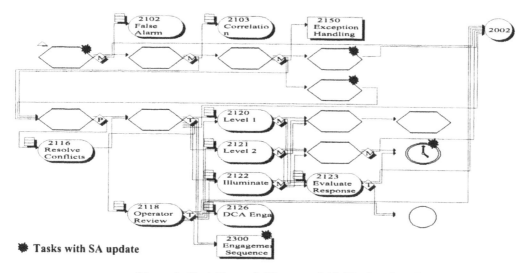

Figure 1. Task Network Diagram of Air Warfare Coordinator Tasks

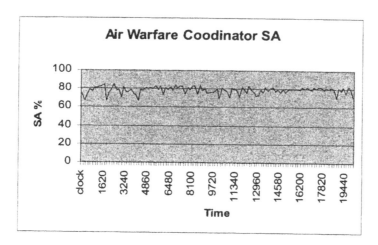

Figure 2. Sample Model Output – Operator SA for Track Parameters

"perfect memory" and no processing errors were assumed. This reflects best-case SA given the structure of the tasks and the environmental conditions. For example, Engh et al (1997) included a simple short-term memory scheme into their models to reflect SA, while the work of Anderson & Lebiere (1998) reflects a much more robust representation of human information processing and memory. Error data estimates from human reliability analysis tables (Kirwan, 1994) or available empirical data could also be incorporated into the models to reflect errors in perceiving, storing, or recalling the values of the parameters.

Once a model has been developed it provides several benefits that complement empirical data collection. First, the sampling of the SA scores can be done more frequently and selectively than in empirical environments. This enables the identification of key scenario events or time frames that impact the SA scores. This information can guide empirical data collection or identify potential design problems early on. The models can also be used to perform sensitivity analyses to help determine things such as the demand levels where the SA scores start to deteriorate or the relative impacts of changes operator numbers or the introduction of automation. The models can also be used to assess interactions between SA and other human performance parameters such as cognitive workload or fatigue.

ACKNOWLEDGEMENTS

The work presented in this paper was sponsored by the Naval Surface Warfare Center, Dahlgren Division (NSWCDD) and conducted under SBIR Phase I topic N03-060, Methods & Metrics to Measure the Impact of Knowledge Superiority Technologies on the Warfighter, contract N00178-03-C-1068.

REFERENCES

Anderson, J. & Lebiere, C. (1998). The Atomic Components of Thought. Mahwah, NJ: Lawrence Earlbaum Associates, Publishers.

Archer, S., Knapp, B., Archer R. and Walters, B. (1999). "Innovative Approaches to Modeling—An Application in Missile Defense." Paper presented at the Society for Computer Simulation Conference.

Archer, S., Warwick, W. and Oster, A. (2000). "Current Efforts to Model Human Decision Making in a Military Environment," Paper presented at the Advanced Simulation Technologies Conference, Washington DC.

Endsley, M. R. (1987). SAGAT: A methodology for the measurement of situation awareness (No. NOR DOC 87-83). Hawthorne, CA: Northrop Corporation.

Endsley, M. R. (1988). Situation Awareness Global Assessment Technique (SAGAT). Proceedings of the National Aerospace and Electronics Conference (NAECON) (pp. 789-795). New York: IEEE.

Endsley, M. R. (1990a). Predictive utility of an objective measure of situation awareness. Proceedings of the Human Factors Society 34th Annual Meeting (pp. 41-45). Santa Monica, CA: Human Factors Society.

Endsley, M. R. (1990b). Situation awareness in dynamic human decision making: Theory and measurement (doctoral dissertation). Los Angeles, CA: University of Southern California.

Endsley, M. R. (1995). Measurement of situation awareness in dynamic systems. Human Factors, 37(1), 65-84.

Endsley, M. R., & Bolstad, C. A. (1994). Individual differences in pilot situation awareness. International Journal of Aviation Psychology, 4(3), 241-264.

Engh, T., Yow, A., and Laughery, K. R. (1997). Task Network Modeling of Operator Interaction with an Alarm System. Proceedings of the Sixth Conference on Human Factors and Power Plants sponsored by IEEE, June 8-12, 1997, Orlando, FL.

Hogg, D. N., Folleso, K., Torralba, B., and Volden, F. S. (1995) "Development of a Situation Awareness Measure to Evaluate Advanced Alarm Systems in Nuclear Power Plant Control Rooms." Ergonomics. 38(11), pp. 2394-2413.

Hoagland, D.G., Martin, E.A., Brett, B.E., Doyal, J.A., LaVine, N.D., Sargent, R.A. (2000) "The Combat Automation Requirements (CART) Program: Results and Lesson Learned from Recent Testing of Advanced Human Performance Models Interacting with DoD Constructive Simulations," Fall 2000 Simulation Interoperability Workshop, Orlando, FL.

Kirwan, B. (1994). A Guide to Practical Human Reliability Assessment. Bristol, PA : Talylor Francis.

Laughery, K.R., Drews, C., and Archer, R., (1986). A Micro Saint Simulation Analyzing Operator Workload in a Future Attack Helicopter. In Proceedings of NAECON Meeting, Dayton, Ohio, May 1986.

Laughery, R. Scott-Nash, S. Wetteland, C. and Dahn, D. (2000) Task network modeling as the basis for crew optimization on ships. Human Factors in Ship Design.

Lockett, J.F., Plocher, T., and Dahl (now Archer), S.G., "Crew Reduction in Armored Vehicles Ergonomic Study (CRAVES)", Proceedings of the Ergonomics Society's 1990 Annual Conference, pg 264-269, 1990.

Peters, S.D., LaVine, N.D., Napravnik, L. (2002) "Composable Behaviors in an Entity Based Simulation," Spring 2002 Simulation Interoperability Workshop, Orlando, FL.

Plott, B., Hamilton, A., Laughery, R. "Linking Human Performance and Anthropometric Models Through an Open Architecture," Society for Automotive Engineers, Digital Human Modeling for Design and Engineering Proceedings, June 2003.

Scott-Nash, S., Carolan, T., Humenick, C., Lorenzen, C., and Pharmer, J, (2000). "The Application of a Validated Performance Model to Predict Future Military System Capability." In the proceedings of the 2000 Interservice Industry Training Systems Conference, Orlando, Florida.

SPATIAL AUDIO DISPLAY CONCEPTS SUPPORTING SITUATION AWARENESS FOR OPERATORS OF UNMANNED AERIAL VEHICLES

Brian D. Simpson, Robert S. Bolia, Mark H. Draper
Air Force Research Laboratory

ABSTRACT

Unmanned aerial vehicle (UAV) control, whether by direct teleoperation or supervisory techniques, requires a high level of situation awareness (SA). At present, this awareness is formed and maintained by means of visual displays and monaural auditory warnings. Research on binaural hearing suggests that humans use the auditory modality for both the development and maintenance of SA in natural environments. It is reasonable to assume, then, that this capacity can be leveraged in UAV operational environments through the use of spatial audio display technology. The purpose of this paper is to suggest spatial audio display concepts that may enhance SA for UAV operators. This will be accomplished by examining potential deficits in SA at each level of Endsley's model (1988; 1995a) and proposing particular display concepts that might reduce these deficits. Implications for SA research on spatial audio displays will also be addressed.

Keywords: Situation Awareness, Spatial Audio Displays, Presence, Unmanned Aerial Vehicles

INTRODUCTION

Unmanned aerial vehicles (UAVs) will play an increasing role in future military operations due to their inherent advantages over manned aircraft. These vehicles are particularly well-suited for specific air operations that, for traditional manned aircraft, would be extremely complicated, exceedingly dangerous, or even impossible to accomplish. For example, UAVs can be sent on extremely long-duration, high-altitude missions in which they can essentially "park" themselves over enemy installations in order to continuously monitor activity and hence limit the enemy's ability to develop surprise operations. Such operational persistence is impossible to achieve with a human pilot in the cockpit. Additionally, because UAVs are operated from sites that are remote from harm's way, they reduce the risk of crew injury, capture, or loss of life. Lastly, UAVs have the potential for considerable reduction in overall lifecycle costs resulting from lower production and operational expenses.

The task of operating a teleoperated UAV is quite different from that of piloting a traditional manned aircraft. Much of the visual information about the surrounding environment that is directly available to the pilot of a traditional aircraft is likely to be either absent, distorted, or delayed for the operator of a UAV. So, too, will be vestibular information about the gravitational forces acting on the aircraft, ambient auditory information that would ordinarily indicate such things as the status of the engines, and haptic feedback from control devices. Moreover, because of the difficulties in maintaining a reliable datalink in actual operational settings, there are often problems related to noise, variations in available bandwidth (leading to potentially long/variable delays), and intermittent and unpredictable datalink dropouts. Because of these and other limitations, many current UAVs are limited to ISR (intelligence, surveillance, and reconnaissance) operations.

Among the most demanding of current and future missions are combat operations, and Unmanned Combat Aerial Vehicles (UCAVs) are now being designed for this purpose. These aircraft will be utilized in especially complex and dynamic operations where wider performance envelopes are necessary to carry out critical maneuvers on very short time scales. Given that the deleterious effects of datalink delays and degradations are magnified as the remote environment becomes more dynamic and complex, the vision for future UAVs/UCAVs includes the transition from manual to supervisory control. Additionally, future concepts of operations will require a change in the ratio of the number of operators to the number of vehicles from many-to-one to one-to-many, further reducing the level of engagement of a particular operator in the direct control of a particular vehicle. Therefore, critical to the success of these UAV and UCAV operations will be the ability to provide the appropriate information to the operators in order to support adequate situation awareness.

Situation awareness (SA) may be generally conceived of as knowledge of those factors in one's surroundings that are meaningful and relevant to achieving some set of goals. The relation to tasks that are goal-driven implies that SA is by nature domain specific. That is, the elements necessary for achieving sufficient SA for a fighter pilot differ from those required by an air battle manager or a UAV operator (Vidulich, Bolia, & Nelson, *in press*). The domain specificity in SA has implications for its understanding and measurement, as well as for the design of interfaces to support it. Nevertheless, Endsley has suggested a definition of SA that appears to be useful across domains: "the perception of the elements in the environment within a volume of time and space, the comprehension of their meaning and the projection of their status in the near future" (Endsley, 1988, p. 97). From this, Endsley suggests that SA may be more formally broken down into three component levels that can be independently addressed, studied, and measured. They are: *Level 1 SA*, which refers to the perception of elements in an environment within a particular volume of time and space; *Level 2 SA*, which pertains to the comprehension of the meaning of these elements; and *Level 3 SA*, which is concerned with the projection of the status of the elements in the near future. Although SA has been directly linked to most aspects of a mission and is generally considered to be critical for good operator performance, Endsley cautions that SA must be considered separately from the decision-making and the performance stages.

Maintaining effective SA is a primary challenge in the development of displays and controls for operators in any complex environment, but may be particularly challenging for the designer of interfaces for remotely piloted vehicles. A pilot operating within a complex environment can directly perceive elements in the real world and may rapidly develop an understanding of the problem space by gleaning ambient information from peripheral elements including weather, terrain, and other vehicles in the airspace; he or she can maintain some level of understanding of the general vehicle status from displays in the cockpit, the auditory environment, and other crew members. However, many of these real-world cues are not as readily available to the operator of a UAV. Providing sufficient information to support effective SA for a geographically separated UAV operator presents a unique challenge to the interface designer.

Currently, UAV operator interfaces emphasize the presentation of information through visual displays. While often the most appropriate means for information conveyance, such systems run the risk of overloading the visual information processing capacity of the operator. The integration of multimodal displays affords the potential to offload the visual channel where appropriate. The inherent redundancy of information presentation in such displays provides safeguards against undetected or unrecognized operationally meaningful information while also allowing for synergistic relations to occur for the conveyance of higher-order information.

Auditory display technologies, in particular, have shown great promise both as an information-bearing channel in isolation and as a component of an overall multimodal display system. Human auditory perception excels in exactly those areas most critical for information transfer in complex settings. Audition serves as an early warning system - sound is inherently interpreted with respect to its signaling or warning significance. For example, loud sounds with brisk onsets are interpreted as exceedingly urgent and may cause a startle response; sirens or warning tones may signal an event in the environment that may require more consideration. Note also that neural transmission in the auditory system processing is substantially faster than transmission in the visual system, making it ideal for the display of time-critical warnings (Mowbray & Gebhard, 1969). The auditory system also plays a fundamental role in verbal communication, which is in many cases the most direct, efficient, and unambiguous means of information transfer. What is inherently appealing about these characteristics of the auditory system is that they are attention-demanding and serve to make the individual aware of elements in the situation. Moreover, the auditory system provides this information independent of the location of the event, for the auditory system monitors the environment in 4π steradians at all times – even when one is sleeping. Thus, critical to supporting situation awareness, information can be obtained about events in the environment even when they occur outside of the operator's visual field of view.

Although auditory displays do exist in most operational interfaces, they are rudimentary at best, and fail to leverage the natural spatial auditory processing capabilities of humans. That is, the ability of humans to determine the location of a sound source, and moreover to monitor events at multiple locations simultaneously, have not been fully exploited. Spatial auditory display technologies take advantage of the properties of the binaural auditory system by recreating and presenting to an operator the spatial information that would naturally be available in a "real-world" listening environment. Such displays are intuitive and thus impose no additional demands on the information processing capacity of the operator.

Previous research suggests that performance on communication tasks and visual search tasks is vastly improved with spatial audio displays (Bolia & Nelson, 2003). Furthermore, several researchers have considered the implications of spatial audio displays for situation awareness in aerospace applications (McKinley, Ericson, & D'Angelo, 1994; Parker, Smith, Stephan, Martin, & McAnally, *in press*; Veltman & Oving, 1999). Potential applications include spatialized communication channels, navigation aids, target cueing, and threat warnings.

If one considers the types of SA-related errors that occur in aviation mishaps within the context of the UAV operator environment, it is clear that spatial audio may offer significant utility at each level of SA. Endsley's (1995b) SA Error Taxonomy describes several reasons that SA may break down within operational settings. Level 1 SA errors have been shown to account for 76% of aviation mishaps that are attributed to human error (Jones and

Endsley, 1996). These errors could occur as a result of the lack of availability of required data, or a failure of the system to present available data. Errors might also occur because the data are provided to the operator but are difficult to detect or are merely not observed, not attended to, misperceived, or forgotten by the operator. Spatial auditory displays would likely benefit the operator in each of these situations.

Because audition serves as an early warning system and is uniquely designed to monitor all locations simultaneously, presenting information over spatial audio displays would greatly reduce the chance of critical information going undetected. The auditory system is exquisitely sensitive to change, even when it occurs outside of the focus of attention (Wenzel, 1994). Changes associated with onsets (e.g., the introduction of new elements into a display) and offsets (e.g., the removal of an existing element from a display) are particularly well-detected by the auditory system and are often impossible to ignore, thus driving the allocation of attention. Several authors have in fact suggested that the spatial auditory system evolved specifically to regulate gaze. Supporting this hypothesis, spatial auditory displays have been shown to reduce visual target acquisition/identification times by a factor of 2-5 in very simple visual scenes; much greater benefits occurred as the complexity of the visual scene increased (Bolia, D'Angelo, & McKinley, 1999). As a result, spatial audio cueing might be especially useful to UAV operators who are tasked with finding ground targets in the remote environment through control of a maneuverable UAV camera.

Additionally, the monitoring of multiple sources of information will be critical for maintaining SA in future UAV systems. The auditory system is capable of segregating multiple simultaneous sounds into different streams that relate to different environmental variables (Bregman, 1990), and one cue for segregation is space (Brungart, Ericson, & Simpson, 2002). Moreover, the system has the ability to relegate some sounds to the background (leave them "unattended") yet still monitor them, maintaining some level of spatial and semantic awareness about them. This may also help to overcome the problems of inhibition of memory due to high task loading. Systematic misperceptions may be overcome through redundant coding. Providing auditory information that is consistent with, and covaries with, visual information is not only unambiguous, but is consistent with operator expectancies, thus providing a more natural, intuitive interface. This may have display implications for operators who must simultaneously monitor multiple UAVs or UCAVs.

Much of the research done on monitoring multiple auditory channels has involved the use of spatial audio to improve speech intelligibility and reduce workload for operators listening to multiple radios or intercom channels. This could be useful to UAV operators who often engage in verbal communications with a variety of distributed team members, not only for its potential to improve communications effectiveness, but also because spatial awareness of talker location would provide the operators with an additional cue to the identity of the talker based on a predetermined mapping of communications channels. This may portend enhancements of both Level 1 and Level 2 SA.

The appropriate comprehension and development of mental models necessary for achieving Level 2 SA may also be supported by an auditory environment in which the operator may be immersed and experience a sense of presence (i.e., "being there"). Support for this comes from the work of Ramsdell (1978), who suggested that one function of the auditory system is to connect one to the real world on a primitive level utilizing the incidental sounds that serve to make up the auditory "background." This work was based on reports from suddenly-deafened individuals who reported that the world seemed "dead" and "(un)coupled", that "it was almost impossible to believe in the passage of time ...couldn't hear a clock tick" (p.503). Ramsdell distinguished this level of auditory perception from that of communication and warning, which are more obvious and overt functions of the auditory system, and suggested that this primitive level of perception is critical for a sense of "connectedness" to the world. Gilkey and Weisenberger (1995) likened the experience of suddenly-deafened individuals to that of the user of a virtual environment with an impoverished auditory display. Perceptually rich virtual auditory environments are believed to lead to a strong sense of presence (Gilkey, Simpson, and Weisenberger, 2001). Although the link between presence and task performance is less clear (Welch, 2000) than that believed to exist between SA and performance, it has been suggested that this is due in part to the lack of a robust measure of presence and/or the use of gross performance metrics that may not be sensitive to issues regarding how the interface is actually being used (Kalawsky, 2000), and thus how the sense of presence may contribute to that usage. The sense of presence is concomitant with an engagement on the part of the operator, and this may be critical when the operator takes on a supervisory role over semi-autonomous UAVs. In this situation, there exists the potential that the operator will 'fall out' of the control loop and may have difficulty reentering when necessary. Immersion in the virtual environment (i.e., the UAV operator interface) may facilitate intuitive interaction and ensure that the operator remains engaged in the mission even if not directly flying the vehicle.

Finally, the support of Level 3 SA may be assisted by an auditory display that is spatially, spectrally, and temporally dynamic. Information about the current and future states of highly-dimensional environments may be related via auditory information in a way that is engaging and intuitive. Operators may discern overall relationships and trends in order to better predict future states (see Kramer, 1994). Auditory motion perception can be used to demonstrate trajectories of elements in the environment and are particularly compelling when used in conjunction with analogous visual displays for predicting future states, allowing the UAV operator to "fly several seconds ahead of the aircraft." This temporal aspect of SA may be particularly well-supported by a spatial audio display.

There are a number of unexplored applications for spatial audio that have the potential to enhance situation awareness for UAV operators. The need to monitor multiple simultaneous environments (e.g., the virtual operational environment and the real-world environment in which the operator station is located) may be supported by signal processing techniques employing room acoustics models to make the two categories of display elements appear to originate from different "rooms." An auditory environment that is slaved to the UAV camera may allow the operator to unambiguously center a visual target in a complex visual scene that would otherwise be difficult to find. Spatial audio displays can lead to a level of realism that as yet cannot be achieved in visual displays. Thus, they contribute substantially to a sense of presence and task engagement that could potentially improve overall operator performance. Finally, auditory displays are extremely low-cost and easily implemented when compared to their visual counterpart. Future research is planned to more fully examine these applications of spatial audio supporting SA in the UAV operator environment.

REFERENCES

Bolia, R. S., D'Angelo, W. R., & McKinley, R. L. (1999). Aurally-aided visual search in three-dimensional space. Human Factors, 41, 664-669.

Bolia, R. S., & Nelson, W. T. (2003). Spatial audio displays for target acquisition and speech communications. In L. J. Hettinger & M. W. Haas (Eds.) Virtual and adaptive environments: applications, implications, and human performance issues (pp.187-197). Mahwah, NJ: Lawrence Erlbaum Associates, Inc.

Bregman, A. S. (1990). Auditory scene analysis. Cambridge, MA: MIT Press.

Brungart, D. S., Ericson, M. A., & Simpson, B. D. (2002). Design considerations for improving the effectiveness of multitalker speech displays. Proceedings of ICAD 2002 (pp. 424-430). International Community for Auditory Display.

Endsley, M. R. (1988). Design and evaluation for situation awareness enhancement. Proceedings of the Human Factors Society 32nd Annual Meeting (pp. 97-101). Santa Monica, CA: Human Factors Society.

Endsley, M. R. (1995a). Towards a theory of situation awareness. Human Factors, 37, 32-64.

Endsley, M. R. (1995b). A taxonomy of situation awareness errors. In R. Fuller, N. Johnston, & N. McDonald (Eds.) Human factors in aviation (pp. 287-292). Aldershot, England:Ashgate Publishing Ltd.

Gilkey, R. H., Simpson, B. D., & Weisenberger, J. M. (2001). Creating Auditory Presence. Proceedings of the HCI 2001 International Conference, New Orleans, USA. 609-613.

Gilkey, R. H., & Weisenberger, J. M. (1995). The sense of presence for the suddenly deafened adult. Presence, 4, 357-363.

Kalawsky, R. S. (2000). The validity of presence as a reliable human performance metric in immersive environments. Proceedings of the 3rd International Workshop on Presence, Delft, The Netherlands.

Kramer, G.. (1994). An introduction to auditory display. In G. Kramer (Ed.), Auditory display: Sonification, audification, and auditory interfaces (pp. 1-77). Reading, MA: Addison-Wesley.

Jones, D. G., & Endsley, M. R. (1996). Sources of situation awareness errors in aviation. Aviation, Space, and Environmental Medicine, 67, 507-512.

McKinley, R. L., Ericson, M. A., & D'Angelo, W. R. (1994). Three-dimensional auditory displays: Development, applications, and performance. Aviation, Space, and Environmental Medicine, 65, 31-38.

Mowbray, G. H., & Gebhard, J. W. (1961). Man's senses as informational channels. In W. W. Sinaiko (Ed.) Human Factors in the Design and Use of Control Systems. New York: Dover, pp.115-149.

Parker, S. P. A., Smith, S. E., Stephan, K. L., Martin, R. L., & McAnally, K. I. (in press). Effects of supplementing head-down displays with 3-D audio during visual target acquisition. International Journal of Aviation Psychology.

Ramsdell, R.S. (1978). The psychology of the hard-of-hearing and the deafened adult. In H. Davis & S. R. Silverman (Eds.), Hearing and deafness (4th ed., pp. 499-510). New York: Holt, Rinehart & Winston.

Veltman, J.A., & Oving, A.B. (1999). 3-D sound in the cockpit to enhance situation awareness (Report TM-99-A061). Soesterberg, The Netherlands: TNO Human Factors.

Vidulich, M. A., Bolia, R. S., & Nelson, W. T. (in press). Technology, organization, and collaborative situation awareness in air battle management: Historical and theoretical perspectives. In S. Banbury & S. Tremblay

(Eds.), <u>A cognitive approach to situation awareness: Theory, measures, and application</u>. Aldershot, UK: Ashgate Publishing Ltd.

Welch, R.B. (2000). How can we determine if the sense of presence affects task performance? <u>Presence: Teleoperators and Virtual Environments</u> 9, 574.577.

Wenzel, E. M. (1994). Spatial sound and sonification. In G. Kramer (Ed.), <u>Auditory display: Sonification, audification, and auditory interfaces</u> (pp. 127-150). Reading, MA: Addison-Wesley.

COCKPIT SYSTEM SITUATIONAL AWARENESS MODELING TOOL

John Keller and Dr. Christian Lebiere
Micro Analysis & Design, Inc.

Capt. Rick Shay
Double Black Aviation Technology LLC

Dr. Kara Latorella
NASA Langley Research Center

ABSTRACT

This project explored the possibility of predicting pilot situational awareness (SA) using human performance modeling techniques for the purpose of evaluating developing cockpit systems. The Improved Performance Research Integration Tool (IMPRINT) was combined with the Adaptive Control of Thought-Rational (ACT-R) cognitive modeling architecture to produce a tool that can model both the discrete tasks of pilots and the cognitive processes associated with SA. The techniques for using this tool to predict SA were demonstrated using the newly developed Aviation Weather Information (AWIN) system. By providing an SA prediction tool to cockpit system designers, cockpit concepts can be assessed early in the design process while providing a cost-effective complement to the traditional pilot-in-the-loop experiments and data collection techniques.

Keywords: Human Performance Modeling, Situational Awareness, ACT-R, IMPRINT, AWIN

INTRODUCTION

Currently, pilot SA can be measured objectively using existing techniques for current systems or prototypes of future systems. However, these techniques can only be applied to systems mature enough that it is often too late to make fundamental design changes. By providing an SA prediction tool to cockpit system designers, cockpit concepts can be assessed early in the design process while providing a cost-effective complement to the traditional pilot-in-the-loop experiments and data collection techniques. Allowing modeling predictions of SA early in the design also helps designers understand the trade-offs between candidate designs and better explore the design space in response to environmental and operator scenario conditions. Finally, modeling techniques provide insights not only into what went wrong but also into how, leading to direct suggestions on how to alter the design to remedy the problems.

The goal of this work was to determine if the combination of a discrete event simulation tool and a cognitive modeling tool could be used to predict the SA of pilot's during the use of a new cockpit system. We used IMPRINT to execute a weather scenario based on the sequence of weather cues a pilot would encounter while using the AWIN system. ACT-R dynamically simulated the activation levels of each chunk determined by subsymbolic processes such as memory decay, cue priming and rehearsal over the course of the scenario. The pilot's SA was based on the activation levels of the chucks of weather information that determine their availability for cognitive processing (Keller et al 2003).

IMPRINT

IMPRINT is a discrete event simulation tool that consists of a set of automated aids to assist analysts in conducting human performance analyses. It assists a user in estimating the likely performance of a new system by facilitating the construction of flow models that describe the scenario, the environment, and the goals that must be accomplished. Users build these models by breaking down the goals into a network of functions. Each of the functions is then further broken down into a network consisting of other functions and tasks. Then, a user estimates the time it will take to perform each task and the likelihood that it will be performed accurately. By executing a simulation model multiple times, you can study the range of results that occur. The tool has been used successfully to predict human performance in complex and dynamic operational environments. However, it does not include an embedded model of cognitive or psychological processes. Rather, it relies on the modeler to specify and implement these constructs.

ACT-R

ACT-R is a cognitive architecture that can be used to model a wide range of human cognition. It has been used to model tasks as simple as memory retrieval (Anderson, Bothell, Lebiere & Matessa, 1998) and visual search (Anderson, Matessa & Lebiere, 1997) to tasks as complex as learning physics (Salvucci & Anderson, 2001) and designing psychology experiments (Schunn & Anderson, 1998). It predicts what happens cognitively every few hundred milliseconds in performance of a task. As such, it is situated at a level of aggregation considerably above basic brain processes but considerably below significant tasks like air-traffic control.

The information flow in the ACT-R cognitive architecture is composed of asynchronous modules communicating with a central production module through associated buffers that can hold only a limited amount of information (Figure 1). The perceptual and motor modules extract information from the environment in a plausibly limited manner, e.g. only one item can be attended to at a time, actions and shifts of attention take time, etc. The declarative module holds facts and information in long-term memory. The goal module holds the current context, which is composed of the system's intention together with associated information. The central production system is composed of productions, or condition-action rules, that test the current state of the modules through their associated buffers and requests actions from these modules using the same buffers.

ACT-R also has a subsymbolic level in which continuously varying quantities are processed, often in parallel, to produce much of the qualitative structure of human cognition. These subsymbolic quantities participate in neural-like activation processes that determine the speed and success of access to chunks in declarative memory as well as the conflict resolution among production rules.

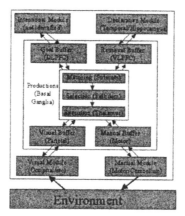

Figure 1. The overall flow of control in ACT-R

Because ACT-R and IMPRINT were targeted at different behavioral levels, they perfectly complement each other. IMPRINT is focused on the task level, how high-level functions break down into smaller-scale tasks and the logic by which those tasks follow each other to accomplish those functions. ACT-R is targeted at the "atomic" level of thought, the individual cognitive, perceptual and motor acts that take place at the sub-second level. Goals in ACT-R correspond directly to tasks in IMPRINT, providing a natural integration level. Certain tasks in an IMPRINT task network can be implemented as ACT-R models, combining the cognitive accuracy of a cognitive architecture with the tractability and ease of design of task networks.

AWIN

We chose an early prototype of the Aviation Weather Information (AWIN) system as the candidate cockpit system. AWIN is a hand-held tool (Figure 2) that provides weather information to general aviation pilots to support strategic flight planning for hazardous weather avoidance. It presents a graphical map overlaid with NEXRAD mosaic, METAR graphics (showing ceiling and visibility category), as well as textual information. The system gives the user options for how the information is displayed, a range of levels of details through which the user can zoom and an aircraft icon that shows their current position in real time. The tool allows pilots to strategically plan their flight paths in order to avoid bad weather.

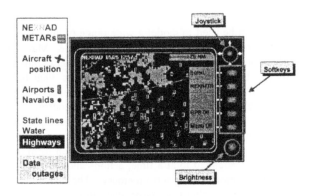

Figure 2. AWIN interface description

METHODS

A recent flight test of AWIN used a prototype system developed by Bendix-King to assess general aviation pilots' weather decision making and included the collection of SA data during the flight tests (NASA website). During the flights, several test subject pilots had access to different types of weather information that included audio weather reports, visual cues and the AWIN system. At specified periods during the flight the pilots were asked to plot the position of the weather cell nearest to their position. In this way, the testers were able to evaluate the weather SA of the pilots across the different types of weather source information.

We created a sequence of weather cues based on data from one of these flights in order to provide a scenario for the model. Table 1 shows the first few events of the scenario timeline. The 'New Nexrad' events represent the periodic updating of the weather maps to the AWIN unit. The 'HIWAS Weather Report' event represents one of the audio weather reports available to the pilots. The 'Position Report' event represents the pilot test task of plotting their exact position based on information from the flight crew. The 'SA Questionnaire' events represent the points during the flight when the test subjects were asked to report their weather SA. Finally, the 'Take off role' event represents the actually beginning of the flight. The full scenario covers approximately 1 hour and includes 12 Nexrad events, 3 audio weather events, 3 position reports and 6 SA questionnaire periods.

Table 1. Weather scenario event list and timeline example

Start time	Interval	Event
18:33:16	0:00:00	New Nexrad 1
18:34:00	0:00:44	Take off role
18:37:17	0:03:17	New Nexrad 2
18:43:17	0:06:00	New Nexrad 3
18:49:30	0:06:13	Position Report 1
18:53:40	0:04:10	SA Questionnaire 1
18:57:48	0:04:08	HIWAS Weather Report
19:01:48	0:04:00	SA Questionnaire 2
19:03:37	0:01:49	New Nexrad 4

Each event includes data relevant to the pilot. The 'Position Report' data included the latitude and longitude of the aircraft for the current time period. Each of the audio weather reports contains the latitude and longitude of locations referenced relative to serious weather. For example, for an audio report indicating that there was a thunderstorm 30 miles north east of Charleston, the event would include the location of the referenced city, the indicated distance and a bearing of 45 degrees. The Nexrad events represent the data available through the AWIN system. It includes the latitude and longitude of the aircraft since the location is given on the AWIN display and the relative distance and bearing to the several of the nearest weather cells.

IMPRINT Model

We used IMPRINT to execute the weather scenario. Figure 3 shows the IMPRINT network diagram for the AWIN weather SA model. The nodes of the diagram are connected by lines that represent the sequence in which the nodes are executed when the model is run. The data from each weather event is stored within the IMPRINT model and is used to either effect the network diagram or is passed to the ACT-R model as weather cues. One entity is generated for each report and is used to reference the associated data. When the model is executed, node 5 schedules all of the report entities that will traverse the network diagram based on the scenario timeline. Each entity in turn will execute one of nodes 8 through 13 depending on what type of event the entity represents. Each of these nodes advances the simulation clock by the amount of time it took for that event to occur. For each entity, node 4 transmits the scenario cue data associated with that entity to the ACT-R model.

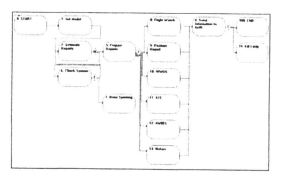

Figure 3. IMPRINT network diagram for AWIN model

ACT-R Model

For the purposes of this project, we focused on SA associated with understanding the situation based on the understanding of the cues commonly referred to as Level 2 SA. As such, the cognitive model is focused on the tasks of encoding and retrieving spatial weather information. It assumes that the human pilots knew how to process audio report information and how to manipulate the AWIN system to extract the needed weather information. Thus we didn't explicitly model the perceptual/motor processes that would have provided an accurate picture of SA Level 1. According to the position reports, pilots seemed to have an excellent awareness of the current position of the aircraft. Weather patterns, on the other hand, moved slowly and no questions were explicitly asked about projecting their future positions. Thus we didn't try to represent the SA Level 3 expert knowledge that might have been used to perform position corrections.

The ACT-R model is composed of a number of unit tasks consisting of a type of goal, together with the associated production rules to solve that goal. The goals include encoding of weather information and retrieving the location of weather patterns. The first two tasks in the model concern the encoding of spatial weather information. Audio weather information was typically given with reference to a fixed landmark, e.g. "Weather front 60 miles N.N.E. of Wilmington". Therefore, the weather pattern position was encoded in a single chunk as a bearing and distance relative to the stated landmark. Representing visual information, such as that provided by NEXRAD maps, is somewhat more complex. Representational constraints that limit the size of chunks prevent us from representing a map, or even a part of it, as a single chunk. Instead, each weather pattern is encoded using a redundant set of chunks, each representing its position relative to a given landmark. Landmarks are selected to favor those nearer the weather pattern. Each relative position is encoded as bearing and distance from the landmark, with noise added to represent estimation error in encoding (Figure 4).

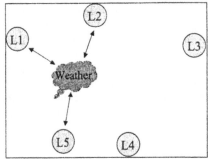

Figure 4. Encoding of a weather pattern position relative to nearby landmarks

RESULTS

The task of answering the SA questionnaire involves retrieving all known weather patterns. For any given pattern, that means retrieving the chunk encoding its position relative to a landmark, then retrieving the chunks encoding the landmark's position as well as the aircraft's current position, and then using those pieces of information to infer the weather pattern's relative position to the aircraft. When all the weather patterns have been retrieved and their relative position to the aircraft determined, the pattern with the shortest distance to the aircraft is matched and returned as the closest one. The SA picture provided could include drawing each weather pattern retrieved or simply the closest one as requested in the SA questionnaire. The probability of retrieving any information about the position of a weather pattern as a function of time elapsed since encoding and of the number of encodings. The probability decreases sharply with time as a function of the decay of activation captured by the base-level learning equation. In addition, multiple model executions generate a measure of the error in recalling the position of a weather pattern as a function of number of encodings for a number of different conditions.

DISCUSSION

The methodology and results demonstrated in this effort provide an effective process for modeling operator SA. The ACT-R cognitive model performs the same task as the human pilots and makes predictions that can be matched directly with human data (latency response, probability recall, magnitude and distribution of positional error, etc). Thus observable performance and situation awareness are a function of the same underlying cognitive and perceptual mechanisms. The same cognitive model can also make workload predictions (Lebiere, 2001), and thus capture possible SA-workload tradeoffs, since more information presented might improve SA at the expense of a higher workload. A quantitative computational model can generate all those performance measures, which can be used to cross-validate the model along multiple scales. The degree of modeling can be adjusted to focus on different levels of SA, e.g. by including a detailed model of the manipulation of the AWIN tool. The impact of design decisions can then be assessed by having the model interact with the same system design used for human pilots.

CONCLUSIONS

The ability to create model-based predictions of SA has a wide range of benefits not only within the cockpit system development community but for the development of any system designed to provide information to human operators in high workload or risk environments. Although additional research and development is required, this work has demonstrated that currently existing human performance modeling tools can be used to predict the SA provided by a cockpit system.

REFERENCES

Anderson, J. R.; Bothell, D., Lebiere, C., & Matessa, M. (1998). An integrated theory of list memory. Journal of Memory and Language, 38, 341-380.

Anderson, J. R., Matessa, M., & Lebiere, C. (1997). ACT-R: A theory of higher level cognition and its relation to visual attention. Human Computer Interaction, 12, 439-462.

Chamberlain, J. P., & Latorella, K. A. (2001). Convective Weather Detection by General Aviation Pilots With Conventional and Data-Linked Graphical Weather Information Sources, In <u>Proceedings of the 20th Digital Avionics Systems Conference</u>.

Keller, J., Lebiere, C., & Shay, R. (2003). Cockpit System Situational Awareness Modeling Tool, Phase I SBIR Final Report, NASA Contract NAS1-03013.

Lebiere, C. (2001). A theory-based model of cognitive workload and its applications. In <u>Proceedings of the 2001 Interservice/Industry Training, Simulation and Education Conference (I/ITSEC 2001</u>). Arlignton, VA: NDIA.

Salvucci, D. D., & Anderson, J. R. (2001). Integrating analogical mapping and general problem solving: The path-mapping theory. Cognitive Science, 25, 67-110.

Schunn, C. & Anderson, J. R. (1998). Scientific discovery. In J. R. Anderson, & C. Lebiere (Eds.). The atomic components of thought, 255-296. Mahwah, NJ: Erlbaum.

DEVELOPMENT OF A METRIC FOR COLLABORATIVE SITUATION AWARENESS

Elizabeth R. Redden , Linda R. Elliott, Daniel D. Turner
Army Research Laboratory

Cynthia L. Blackwell
SBCCOM-Natick Soldier Center

ABSTRACT

Situation Awareness (SA) measurement has primarily focused on individual SA. Here, we conceptualize measurement of collaborative SA (CSA) that models the three levels of SA among team members, and the communication necessary for effective comprehension and projection in the leader. Perceptual information must be effectively distributed to the leader, to enable quick calculated decisions on a dynamic battlefield. Several PC-based 3-D infantry vignettes were developed to replicate a mission in a military urban terrain site. Three-person teams played the roles of an infantry squad leader and two subordinate team leaders, who in turn led PC-based "synthetic" team members. Measures of SA were drawn at the squad leader and at the subordinate team leader level, based on knowledge of critical cues. In addition, the structure of communication patterns was predicted to affect leader SA. This paper reports methodology, plans, and preliminary results within this program of investigation.

Keywords: Team Situation Awareness; Collaborative Situation Awareness; Infantry

INTRODUCTION

The study of situation awareness (SA) originated with issues related to aircraft pilot performance where pilots often referred to the term in an operational sense (Endsley, 1988) and grew to more complex, cognitive based theory (Endsley, 1993). This perspective has since expanded to consider SA in teams, in terms of shared mental models, team communication, overlapping knowledge, and complementary knowledge structures (e.g., Cannon-Bowers et al., 1991; Cooke, 2000; Entin & Serfaty, 1999; Klein, 2000; Salas et al, 1995). These approaches have contributed much to clarification of issues and concepts.

However, it has become clear that issues are multifaceted and more shared knowledge is not necessarily better, particularly in complex, dynamic, and interdependent situations. In this paper, we focus on hierarchical team structures, where leaders must coordinate, decide, and perform quickly. Here, the emphasis is on collaborative situation awareness (CSA). CSA is needed for the leader to make quick calculated decisions on a dynamic battlefield, using data that is collected from many sources, including individual soldiers.

This emphasis on the leader as the central component in CSA, led ARL-HRED to develop a CSA metric that follows Schwartz's (1990) proposal that team SA is moderated by leaders in hierarchical teams. This observation is also inherent in other theories of team decision-making performance (Hollenbeck et al., 1995). In this study, individual SA has more emphasis on awareness of perceptual cues, which must be communicated to the leader. CSA is measured through leader comprehension of the situation and projection of a future course of action. The process leading up to CSA maps the perception and communication of cues.

For this investigation of CSA, we used PC-based gaming simulation scenarios based on an actual military operations in urban terrain (MOUT) site at an Army infantry training center. Previously, most studies of infantry SA were performed in the field (French et al., in press; Redden et al., in press; Redden, 2002; Redden & Blackwell, 2001a, 2001b). PC-based investigation of SA of infantry soldiers poses a more complex challenge than that of display-driven operators (e.g., C2 operators). Infantry soldiers gain and verify information from an array of cues, such as verbal and radio communications, terrain, and other tactile and environmental cues. They must process map information, then recognize their location as they navigate along planned routes. It is one thing to maintain and build SA of friendly and opposing forces (OpFor) given a "godseye" display, and another to do so when at ground level.

Advancements in PC-based videogames now offer fairly realistic 3-D immersive gaming contexts, including some that focus on infantry tasks and tactics. Thus, this type of platform was chosen for this initial investigation of CSA. The goals in this study were to (a) design MOUT scenarios to elicit realistic communications and tactics, (b) develop script-based assessment of team member and team leader SA at the three levels of SA, (c) manipulate communication structures, and (d) assess the degree to which individual SA and communication structures affect the SA of the leader. The effects of manipulations will be assessed through measurement of CSA. Measurement is discussed in more detail in the "measures" section.

METHOD

Participants

Participants will be enlisted infantry soldiers drawn from the Officer Candidate School, the Airborne School, and the US Marine Corp assigned to Fort Benning, Georgia. Extensive demographic, cognitive ability, training, and experience data will be collected.

MATERIALS

The Research platform is a commercial-off-the-shelf videogame that provides infantry squad-based counter-terror scenarios (Tom Clancy's Rainbow Six Ravenshield). The platform allows flexibility in mission planning, and computer-based synthetic soldiers that can obey friendly squad leaders. It also provides synthetic opposing forces.

Operational relevance was achieved through several means. First, a Ravenshield map was programmed that produced a replication of the McKenna MOUT site at Fort Benning, Georgia. This allows the possibility of further validation of results using a field exercise using the same terrain and building configurations. Figure 1 displays the map, the objective (end point), and route options.

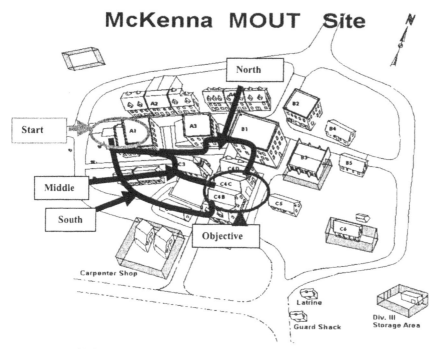

Figure 1. Ravenshield MOUT Map, Objective, and Route Options.

Three scenarios were developed to elicit similar task demand. While Ravenshield scenarios do not have physical fidelity, they have been scaled to capture essential job-related decisions and tasks (content fidelity), relative to research goals, at the appropriate level of cognitive difficulty and yield measures (construct fidelity) that are theoretically grounded (Elliott et al, in press; Elliott et al., 2001). In each, the mission objective is to secure and clear an objective building from enemy combatants, while minimizing friendly and civilian casualties. Information cues are presented that make one route more effective than the others. For example, in one scenario there are obstacles (e.g., concertina wire) and enemy snipers. Enemy sniper location is cued by text or visual identification once in range. Table 1 provides script information for roles in one scenario event.

Table 1. Script For Single Scenario Event.

Squad Leader	Squad Members	Platoon Leader/WC	OpFor/COB*
Attack from building A1, west end, to C4A and C4B 1st and 2nd floors. Find and rescue the COB. Engage OpFor as necessary	Status: Tm A: One member has gunshot wound to the inner thigh, not incapacitating.	Mission: Clear 1st and 2nd floors of C4A and C4B simultaneously, look for and rescue civilians, perform reconnaissance for follow-on force, eliminate any OpFor	1 OpFor move from outside (Westside) to room 2 1st floor, C4A. 1 OpFor move from outside (Westside) to room 3 1st floor, C4B. 1 OpFor room 4 1st floor, C4A.
Give Platoon Leader short plan of attack.	All other members are 100%.	encountered, and be prepared to hold and defend south end of building C4.	2 COB move from outside (Westside) to room 3 1st floor, C4A.
Designate Tm A to attack Bldg C4A and Tm B to attack Bldg C4B.	Tm B: Two new guys with limited training.	My location is: helipad west of building A1.	1 OpFor room 1, C4B 2nd floor 1 OpFor room 4, C4B 2nd floor 2 COBs room 7, C4B 2nd floor 1 OpFor room 2, C4A 2nd floor

* OpFor: Opposing Forces / COB: Civilians on Battlefield

DESIGN

The overall experimental design has three equivalent scenarios, crossed with three types of communication structure and two types of information cues. We crossed the levels of scenarios to negate any effect due to differences in scenarios. Communication structure was manipulated three ways. Participants work in three-person teams, a squad leader and two team leaders. One structure allows all participants to communicate freely. A second structure has communication between each team leader and squad leader (but no communication among team leaders). The third structure has no communication among participants. Information cues provide participants information regarding such mission critical information as location of the OpFor. The cues also have implications for optimal route selection.

MEASURES

Events are scripted where information cues were provided through environmental and visual cues. Assessment of SA is consistent with Endsley's (1993) framework of perception, comprehension, and projection, with regard to levels of comprehension of information cues. Questions are crafted to be consistent with one of Endsley's three levels of SA and are administered at the conclusion of the short vignette. A question to document perception might ask if some cue or event was noticed. A question to ascertain comprehension might ask about the implication of two perception cues. A projection question might ask about future plans arising from the information. See Table 2 for examples.

Table 2. Sample SA questions for each level of SA.

Question	Type of SA Question
1. What route did you select to your objective and why? a. North of Church to building C4 b. Between Church and Building C1 and C2 to C4 c. South of C1 and C2 to C4 And why? _____	Projection
2. Are there any OpFor, other than those on the objective, which can observe or place effective fires on your likely avenues of approach? a. Yes from the south b. Yes, from the north c. Yes, from building B1 d. Yes, from building at north end of street e. No d. Other (Specify) _____	Comprehension
3. Were there any obstacles between your starting position and objective? a. Yes, between A1&C1 and C2&C1 b. Yes, north of Church and C1&C2 c. Yes, between C2-C4A d. Yes, between church & C4B e. No f. Other (Specify) _____	Perception
4. Were there any reports of receiving hostile fire in your initial attack from other than your objective? a. Yes, in building B1 b. Yes, woodline south of McKenna c. Yes, woodline each of McKenna d. No e. Other (Specify) _____	Perception

Table 2 provides examples of questions designed to assess knowledge of information cues, for each role (Squad Leader, Team Leader A, Team Leader B) and for each level of SA (perception, comprehension, and projection).

For this study, questions were developed systematically to distinguish the levels of SA through measurement, a process not often reported in the literature. When the levels are so distinguished, we can then ascertain the degree to which correct projection is dependent on comprehension and perception. While it is logical to assume that projection is indeed dependent on the prior processes, there is also a counter-argument that experts may project correctly without consciously processing all perception cues.

For this effort, we assume that lack of perception and comprehension will lead to less accurate projection, with regard to route selection. Use of this model enables more diagnostic interpretation of SA measures. If perception does indeed lead to better projection, an implication is that SA can be enhanced through better provision of cues. On the other hand, if correct perception or comprehension does not lead to more accurate projection, this may infer a need for more training or complex decision aiding, to enable participants to more effectively interpret cues.

RESULTS

Data collection is ongoing. Some refinements in scenario structure and information cue content were made after initial runs. A total of about 30 teams will participate.

DISCUSSION

This paper described the conceptualization and measurement approach to CSA. It offers a systematic approach, based on Endsley's three levels of SA that models the effects of communication among team members on the level and type of SA in the leader. It also reflects the quantitative modeling approach of Hollenbeck's Multilevel theory (MLT) of hierarchical team decision making, particularly in teams with distributed information or expertise. CSA is distinguished from MLT in that it distinguishes the levels of SA. Figure 2 describes the constructs and relationships conceptualized in CSA. Perceptual awareness measured at the team leader level and the degree to which team leader information is communicated to the squad leader is expected to mediate the degree of SA comprehension and projection of the leader.

Team Leaders   **Squad Leader**

Figure 2. Collaborative SA Model.

This model will be tested using hierarchical regression analyses.

REFERENCES

Cannon-Bowers, J.A. and Salas, E. (1991). Cognitive Psychology and Team Training: Shared Mental Models of Complex Systems. Bulletin Human Actors Society, 33, 1-4.

Cooke, N. J., Salas, E., Cannon-Bowers, J. A., &Stout, R. (2000). Measuring team knowledge. HumanFactors, 42, 151-173.

Elliott, L. R., Dalrymple, M. A., Schiflett, S. G., & Miller, J. C. (In Press). Scaling Scenarios: Development and Application to C4ISR Sustained Operations Research. In S. Schiflett, L. Elliott, E. Salas, & M. Coovert (Eds.) Scaled Worlds: Development, Validation, and Applications. Ashgate Publishing Limited, Surrey, England.

Elliott, L. R., Dalrymple, M. A., Regian, J. W., Schiflett, S. (2001). Scaling Scenarios for Synthetic Task Environments: Issues Related to Fidelity and Validity. Proceedings of the Human Factors and Ergonomics Society 45th Annual Meeting (pp 377-381). Minneapolis, MN: Human Factors Society.

Endsley, M. R. (1988). Design and evaluation for situation awareness enhancement. Proceedings of the Human Factors Society 32nd Annual Meeting (pp. 97-101). Santa Monica, CA: Human Factors Society.

Endsley, M. R. (1993). Situation Awareness in Dynamic Human Decision Making: Theory. In R. D. Gilson, D. J. Garland, & J. M. Koonce (Eds.), Situational Awareness in Complex Systems. Daytona Beach: Embry-Riddle Aeronautical University Press.

Entin, E.E. and Serfaty, D. (1999). Adaptive team coordination. Journal of Human Factors, Vol. 41, No.2, pp. 321-325.

French, H. T., Matthews, M., & Redden, E. (In press). Infantry Situation Awareness. In Simon Banbury and Sébastien Tremblay (Eds.) A cognitive approach to Situation Awareness: Theory, Measurement and Application. Ashgate Publishing Limited, Aldershot, England.

Hollenbeck, J.R., Ilgen, D.R. Sego, D., Hedlund, J., Major, D.A., and Phillips, J. (1995). The multi-level theory of team decision-making: Decision performance in teams incorporating distributed expertise. Journal of Applied Psychology, 80, 292-316.

Klein, G. (2000). Cognitive Task Analysis of Teams. In J. Schraagen, S. Chipman, & V. Shalin (Eds.) <u>Cognitive Task Analysis</u>. Mahwah, NJ: Lawrence Erlbaum.

Redden, E. S. (2002). <u>Virtual Environment Study of Mission-Based Critical Information Requirements (ARL-TR-2636).</u> Adelphi, MD: Army Research Laboratory.

Redden, E. S. & Blackwell, C. L. (2001a). Measurement of Situation Awareness in Free-play Exercises. In <u>Proceedings of the Human Performance, Situation Awareness and Automation Conference</u>, Savannah, Georgia.

Redden, E. S. & Blackwell, C. L. (2001b). <u>Situation Awareness and Communication Experiment for Military Operations in Urban Terrain - Experiment I. (ARL TR-2583).</u> Adelphi, MD: Army Research Laboratory.

Redden, E.S., Sheehy, J.B., & Bjorkman, E.A. (in press). The study and measurement of human performance by military service laboratories. In J.W. Ness, V. Tepe, & D. Ritzer (Eds.), <u>The Science and Simulation of Human Performance</u>. Dayton, OH: Human Systems Information Analysis Center.

Salas, E., Prince, C., Baker, D.P. & Shresta, L. (1995). Situation Awareness in Team Performance: Implications for Measurement and Training. <u>Human Factors, 37</u>, 123-136.

Schwartz, D. (1990). Training for situational awareness. <u>Houston, TX: Flight Safety International</u>.

MEASURING AND PREDICTING SA IN C4I; DEVELOPMENT AND TESTING OF A REFINED SA MEASUREMENT TECHNIQUE, AND A NEW CONCEPT FOR SA PREDICTION.

Dr Guy H. Walker, Prof Neville A. Stanton, Paul Salmon, & Dr Damian Green
Brunel University, BIT Lab, School of Engineering and Design,

ABSTRACT

The methods to be reported in this paper are being developed to meet the prototyping needs of new military C4i (Command Control Communications and Computers) systems. Part 1 of this paper presents a concept for a structured means to predict SA. The concept is based on integrating existing methods to enable the SA present in the system to be compared with the SA required by the task. Part 2 of this paper reports on several methodological enhancements to existing SA measurement techniques. Having made the comparison between system and task SA the aim is to more objectively measure individual SA resulting from any match or miss-match. Between them the refined approaches could help to predict prominent sources of potential SA errors before new C4i systems are built, and to accurately measure resultant SA once they are.

Keywords: SA Measurement, SA Prediction, Analytical Prototyping.

INTRODUCTION

This paper presents two new approaches for the measurement and prediction of Situation Awareness (SA) in the design of military C4i (Command, Control, Communication, and Computers) systems using virtual environments. Three existing mainstream SA methods have been identified, all of which offer to measure SA. These are SART (Situational Awareness Rating Technique), SAGAT (Situation Awareness Global Assessment Technique) and SACRI (Situational Awareness Control Room Inventory).

SART is a self-report questionnaire probing 10 dimensions. The main difficulty with SART is meta-cognitive. That is to say there is a question concerning the ability of individuals to subjectively rate SA that they may not even be in receipt of. SAGAT and SACRI on the other hand utilise a probe recall method. The logic of the approach is undeniably strong, but it is argued that it is not strong enough to justify the claim that the methods are an 'objective' means to measure SA as both claim (Endsley & Garland, 2000; Hogg et al., 1995). If measurement is defined as the process of converting observations into quantities through theory, then objectivity is achieved when; *"within the range of objects for which the measuring instrument is intended, its function* [is] *independent of the object of measurement"* (Thurstone, 1928, p. 547), and, the results are independent from the conditions in which the measurement took place. It is unlikely that *any* method in behavioural science could meet these criteria in full. It is these issues that suggest a number of methodological improvements to SA measurement that are presented in Part 2 of this paper. Part 1 on the other hand is concerned with SA prediction, and the issues here are much more easily stated; there simply are no established or mainstream methods for SA prediction. In answer to this a structured concept for SA prediction is proposed.

Part 1 - Predicting SA

Scope

Existing methods are able to inform the practitioner about what tasks are being performed, in what temporal order they need to be performed in and what information requirements support the task(s). On the system side, methods exist to inform the practitioner of what state the system is in. It seems possible that based on integrating these existing methods a highly structured comparison can then be made between what information is provided by the system versus the information required by the task. Taking a systemic view of SA, information is understood as supporting knowledge related to specific topics within the system (Stanton et al., 2004). The prediction method therefore accesses SA present (or absent) in the C4i system and the straightforward comparison based on this could enable at least some potential SA problems to be identified and addressed before it needs to be built.

PROCEDURE

Step 1 – Construct a Hierarchical Task Analysis (HTA)

The first stage is to model the actual or proposed interaction using HTA.

Step 2 – Subject the HTA to a Critical Path Analysis (CPA)

CPA is a project management tool, but in this application can be used to calculate the combination of tasks that effect the time taken to complete the task most. A refinement offered by Baber and Mellor (2001) is to not only consider time as the main critical path variable, but to also consider modality. Two tasks sharing the same modality must be performed in series. The result is that CPA enables a logical, temporal description of the task sequence.

Step 3 – Perform a requirements analysis

After performing the CPA it is then possible to systematically elicit the information required to support the tasks at the appropriate time at which the tasks occur. The question is simply what information does the operator require in order for the task to be performed successfully. This process is similar to that embodied within SAGAT, but discreet information requirements can be obtained by pursuing a task level as opposed to sub-goal level analysis.

Step 4 – Model the system using TAFEI

Task Analysis For Error Identification (TAFEI) is a method that enables errors with system use to be predicted by modelling the interaction between user and system (Baber & Stanton, 1994). TAFEI makes the assumption that actions are constrained by the state of the system at any particular point in the interaction, and that the system offers information to the user about its functionality. The CPA enables the TAFEI state space diagrams to be mapped onto the interaction timeline, and for the information offered by the system to be compared with the information required by the tasks, as illustrated below. It is then possible for the practitioner to make use of the TAFEI transition matrix to assess situations in which although system and task information may be matched, the system will nevertheless allow illegal transactions to take place. In such situations the potential for SA failures in the user part of the system could be increased, and for the users perception of system state to become uncoupled from the actual system state. A structured means to perform and represent this stage of the analysis is currently under development.

Sample Results

In the analysis, when the task does not receive the information it requires to support SA it scores 0, when it does, it scores 1, when no information is required by the task at that time the score is –1. The graph represents where potential failures in information provided versus information required are occurring. At these points the attainment of SA could be at risk. The method allows the practitioner to target specific areas of the user/system interaction to help mitigate this risk before a system needs to be built. The figure above presents the analysis for a single task, but using a spreadsheet the method can expand to easily capture and present a whole task analysis. This could enable a whole system to be analytically prototyped based on information requirements and SA.

Part 2 - Measuring SA

Concomitant with a concept for predicting SA before a system is necessarily built is a means to test those predictions by measuring SA after a system is built. The prediction concept in Part 1 provides insight into SA residing in the C4i system, whereas Part 2 of this paper moves on to consider ways to measure the SA residing in the individual. Of the three available methods SAGAT and SACRI can be identified as the more rigorous approaches. However, there are three main requirements in order to answer fundamental concerns about objectivity;

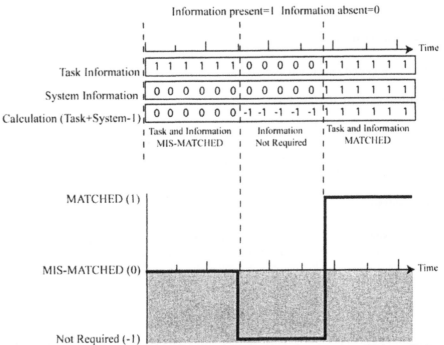

Figure 1 – Calculation data table and visual output of SA prediction concept.

First, a revised SA measurement method requires set procedures to systematically assess the objective, publicly observable state of the world that is to be compared with the participants SA of that world. The aim would be to place less reliance on the agreement between expert judges (and therefore subjectivity) that is found within both SAGAT and SACRI.

Second, in the case of both existing methods the constructs being measured can be regarded as multi-dimensional. For example, a determination as to *"Which aircraft is your highest priority threat"* (Endsley & Garland, 2000) invokes a complex cognitive appraisal of events that is argued by Annett (2002) as being unavoidably subjective. One strategy to answer these concerns is to pursue a more atomistic level of analysis, focusing on the *information* required to support discreet tasks. Bell and Lyon (2000) propose that *"All aspects of momentary SA are eventually reducible to some form of [..] information in working memory"* (p.42).

Third, a further potential confound within both SAGAT and SACRI is the use of parametric statistics to compare constructs that are measured along rating scales. It is argued that rating scales are merely ordinal, and therefore violate the assumptions underpinning the use of these tests (Lodge, 1980). A revised method would overcome these concerns through the use of non-parametric tests.

A method based on these concepts still cannot be regarded as truly objective, but it would provide a highly systematic set of procedures and controls, provide a form of valid quantitative structure, and offer improved accuracy, transferability and validity.

METHOD

Step – 1

Frame the experimental design in terms of Signal Detection Theory (SDT). For example, conceptually the null condition can be regarded as the noise condition, and subsequent changes to the null condition (in the form of information additions) can be regarded as signal trials.

Step – 2

Run the probe recall trials. This requires the participant to rate their confidence as to the presence or absence of specific information in the scenario. At any given pause the objective, publicly observable and measurable state of the simulation is known. The underlying logic of SAGAT remains in their being a comparison between *subjective* confidence ratings and the actually existing *objective* state of the scenario. This comparison provides the basis for a measure of sensitivity derived through the use of SDT.

Step – 3

Perform the sensitivity analysis. This involves organising the participant responses into a taxonomy of Hit, Miss, False Alarm and Correct Rejections. The Hit and False Alarm rates supplied by the observer responses can then be converted into proportions of the actually existing signal/noise events. A correction factor is applied to the data prior to computing the sensitivity measure d-prime (d') (McNicol, 1972).

Sample Results

Higher d' values are associated with more 'Hits', therefore more accurate ratings concerning information actually present in the scenario, therefore implying better SA (or at least level 1 SA). Presented below are some results gained through using this method in a dynamic task activity. The shaded area represents the sensitivity level achieved in the baseline (noise) condition. Conditions 1, 5 and 7 offer significantly better SA than the baseline condition, whereas Condition 3 appears to offer worse SA.

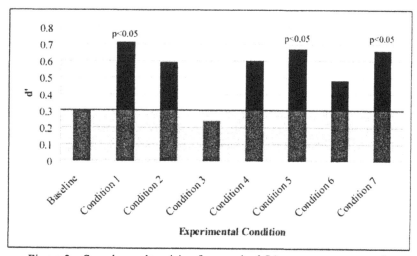

Figure 2 – Sample results arising from revised SA measurement procedure.

Statistical Tests on d' vs. Experimental Condition

Non-parametric procedures are employed primarily because rating scales cannot be considered as continuous data as assumed within parametric tests. In practice, two further advantages were discovered;

1. Non-parametric tests enable the full data set to be used and avoid a number of problems in accounting for outliers and variability in the data.
2. Parametric tests are based on comparing the mean d' across individuals across experimental conditions. This places d' in error (Ingleby, 1968). Non-parametric tests use ranking procedures and therefore avoid this problem.

Post hoc testing for the Friedman procedure involves the Dunns test, and allows multiple pair-wise comparisons to be made. Finally, the effect size observed in the experiment can also be calculated using R_{phi} in order to provide an approximate numerical measure of association between independent and dependant variables. Given the transformations made to the data this final calculation provides a good feel for the effect that the independent variable may have on resulting SA.

DISCUSSION

Part 1

Currently there are no mainstream methods available to the practitioner in order for them to easily predict SA. The method concept presented above offers one simple and pragmatic way to meet this need. Disadvantages are that the approach is based on error free normative performance, which in turn means that unpredictable aspects of performance and SA may not be captured. Similarly, time data for task and system performance may not be readily available or else be difficult to calculate. Despite these potential disadvantages, and in the absence of any alternative, the method still succeeds in being able to identify potentially important SA problems before the expense of a physical prototype is incurred.

Part 2

It should be clear that SAGAT and SACRI are not an objective means to measure SA. The main issues are the degree of subjectivity involved in the determination of the objective state of the scenario during probe recall freeze events; the multi-dimensionality of probe items; and the lack of a formal quantitative structure. The revised method answers these concerns by focusing on information actually present versus information required. This in turn helps to provide uni-dimensional constructs to be measured using SDT and structured measures of sensitivity. Sensitivity has the advantage that it is a publicly observable psychophysical attribute measured in physical units, is separate from the object of measurement and largely independent from the conditions in which the measurement took place. Whilst readily admitting to not being fundamentally objective, the revised method is an improvement that succeeds in offering better measurement accuracy and transferability.

To conclude, these two concepts for SA prediction and measurement are intended to fulfil the goal of HFI in the design of C4i systems using virtual environments. The concepts are also an example of method integration, helping to provide a coherent set of procedures for practitioners, rather than yet more methods.

Acknowledgements: This work from the Human Factors Integration Defence Technology Centre was part-funded by the Human Sciences Domain of the UK Ministry of Defence Scientific Research Programme.

REFERENCES

Annett, J. (2002). Subjective rating scales: Science or art? Unpublished manuscript, University of Warwick at Coventry.

Baber, C. and Mellor, B.A. (2001) Modelling multimodal human-computer interaction using critical path analysis. International Journal of Human Computer Studies, 54, 613-636.

Baber, C. & Stanton, N. A. (1994). Task analysis for error identification: a methodology for designing error-tolerant consumer products. Ergonomics, 37, 1923-1941.

Bell , H. H., & Lyon, D. R. (2000). Using observer ratings to assess situation awareness, In M. R. Endsley (ed.). Situation awareness analysis and measurement. Mahwah, NJ: Lawrence Erlbaum Associates.

Endsley, M. R. & Garland, D. J. (Eds.). (2000). Situation awareness analysis and measurement. New Jersey: Lawrence Erlbaum Associates.

Hogg, D. N., Folleso, K., Strand-Volden, F., & Torralba, B. (1995). Development of a situation awareness measure to evaluate advanced alarm systems in nuclear power plant control rooms. Ergonomics, 38(11), 2394-2413.

Ingleby, J. D. (1968). Decision-making processes in human perception and memory. Unpublished Ph.D. thesis: University of Cambridge.

Jones, D. G., & Endsley, M. R. (1996). Sources of situation awareness errors in aviation. Aviation, Space, and Environmental Medicine, 67, (6), 507-512.

Lodge, M. (1980). Magnitude Scaling. London: Sage

McNicol, D. (1972). A primer of signal detection theory. London: George Allen & Unwin Ltd.

Stanton, N., Baber, C., Walker, G., Salmon, P., & Green, D. (2004). Toward a theory of agent-based systemic situational awareness. Submission to HPSAA II, Daytona, FL.

Thurstone, L. L. (1928). Attitudes can be measured. American Journal of Sociology, 33, 529-544.

TOWARD A THEORY OF AGENT-BASED SYSTEMIC SITUATIONAL AWARENESS

Guy Walker, Paul Salmon and Damian Green
Brunel University, UK

Neville Stanton, Chris Baber
University of Birmingham, UK

ABSTRACT

The purpose of this paper is to propose foundations for a systemic theory of situation awareness based on the analysis of interactions between agents (i.e., both human and artefact) in subsystems. This approach may help promote a better understanding of technology-mediated interaction in systems, as well as helping in the formulation of hypotheses and predictions concerning shared situation awareness. It is proposed that agents within a system each hold their own situational awareness which may be very different from (although compatible with) other agents. It is argued that we should not hope for, or indeed want, sharing of this awareness, as different system agents have different purposes. This view marks situational awareness as a dynamic and collaborative process that binds agents together on tasks on a moment-by-moment basis. Implications of this viewpoint for development of a new theory of situational awareness are offered.

Keywords: agents, systems, theory, dynamic, driving, shared SA, teams

Three contemporary theories of SA

Contemporary theories of situation awareness (SA), tend to focus on the individual actor, for example the embedded-interactive model (Smith & Hancock, 1995; Adams et al, 1995), the cognitive sub-functions model (Bedney & Miester, 1999) and the three-level model (Endsley, 1995). The embedded-interactive model offers a good explanation of the dynamic aspects of situational awareness, such as how momentary knowledge is updated and how the search for information from the world is conducted. This view focuses on the interaction of the person with the world. The cognitive sub-functions model is good for considering how underlying cognitive functions might interact. This view focuses on the information processing activities within the mind. The three-level model is good at describing the types of data that SA activities might produce. This latter model indicates types of SA measures that might be taken (i.e., perception of elements, comprehension, and projection), whereas the embedded-interactive model might argue for data on the status of the world, and the cognitive sub-functions model would require data on the individual. All three models are underpinned by general models of human information processing in individuals.

Team SA

As was pointed out earlier, most of the initial research on situational awareness focused on the individual. More recently, this research has begun to consider situational awareness in teams. For example, Kaber & Endsley (1998) have argued for research on shared situational awareness, where team members have similar SA requirements. To date, most of the team SA research seems to have highlighted the need for a shared understanding (Salas et al, 1995; Jentsch et al, 1999). We have found that there are occasions when team members have different goals and therefore their SA requirements may be different. We make this point with reference to two case studies from our own research. The first case study involves the fire (F), police (P), and hospital (H) dealing with a child that has broken into a remote farm and come into contact with hazardous material. The second case study involves an analysis of the information requirements of team members in an energy distribution company in the UK.

In the first study, Baber et al (2004) observed an exercise on the Hazardous Materials course at the Fire Service Training College in the UK. The incident management comprise five phases: initiate response to incident (1), perform initial incident assessment (2), chemical identification (3), chemical assessment (4), and resolve incident (5). From Baber et al's analysis, it is possible to see that the information that could be drawn upon during the incident becomes available to the performers at different phases during the unfolding of the incident. Thus, the fire-fighters (F) are not aware that the child has respiratory problems until around phase 4, or that the farm is deserted until well into phase 3, i.e. until arrival at the scene. With this knowledge, the definition of response is made easier, the question of which Personal Protective Equipment to wear can be solved and the search strategy simplified. Thus, Situation Awareness, from a system perspective, can be viewed as the sum of knowledge relating to specific topics within the system. The challenge in incident management becomes one of ensuring that the appropriate agents have access to appropriate knowledge of topics at the right time.

Table one. SA during the five phases of Hazardous Materials management

SA Topic	Phase 1	Phase 2	Phase 3	Phase 4	Phase 5
Break-in	P				
Respiratory		H P		F	
Material		F			F H
Culprit's story		P			
Remote farm	P	F			
Farm = deserted		P	F		
Powder ID					F H

In the second study, Stanton et al (2004) explored the idea of mapping levels of task abstraction (LOTA) onto the roles of control room engineers in an energy distribution company. The idea of mapping LOTA on to trouble-shooting tasks in Rasmussen's (1986) original proposals for describing work in socio-technical systems has been further explored by Vicente (1999), who shows how the LOTA together with a systems representation can be used to illustrate the decision space that people traverse when solving problems. Despite the fact that the examples tend to present the work of a single person, one can imagine this being extended to a team or group of people working together. In the latter case the decision space will be traversed by a number of individuals. Stanton et al (2004) argued that people only occupy part of this decision space, depending upon their role. An illustration of the decision space in an energy distribution company is shown in table two (the roles of the PSM, EME, SSE, TME, RDE, RME, GDE, TDE and RE are not described, to protect the anonymity of the company). The darker the cell the greater the proportion of activity at that LOTA.

Table two. The decision space for the energy distribution team.

ABSTRACTION LEVEL	PSM	EME	SSE	TME	NDE	RME	GDE	TDE	RE
Functional Purpose	■	▧	▧						
Abstract Function	▧	■	■	▧					
Generalised Function	■	■	■	■	■	■	▧	■	▧
Physical Function	▧	▧	▧	▧	▧	▧	■	▧	■
Physical Form					■	▧	■	■	■

As table two shows, the decision space for the PSM, EME and SSE is in the top left of the diagram. The decision space for the TME, NDE and RME is in the middle of the diagram. The decision space for the GDE, TDE and RE is at the bottom right of the diagram. Thus the trajectory is similar to that proposed by Vicente (1999), but this decision space is for a team rather than an individual. The degree of overlap of the decision spaces might prove to be an effective measure of team coordination and cohesiveness. Certainly gaps in the decision space might prove problematic, as indeed might too much overlap. Gaps would require someone to identify that part of the decision space requires traversing whereas too much overlap would mean that responsibility for the decision space was ambiguous

Taken together, these two studies suggest two important findings. First, different collaborative teams could have different types of SA depending upon their goals and activities (as did the hospital, police and fire service). Second, different levels within the same team might have different types of SA depending upon the level in the system they are working at (as did the PSM, PME and RE for example). Both of these findings call for a theory of SA that is modelled around the idea of interacting team members having compatible, but not identical SA. This might best be illustrated in a simple thought experiment based on motorway (freeway) driving.

Thought experiment #1: Situationally aware drivers

The concept of situational awareness offers an explanation of how the driver manages to combine longer-term goals (such as driving to a destination) with shorter-term goals (such as avoiding collisions) in real-time (Sukthankar, 1997). Drivers are required to keep track of a number of critical variables in a dynamic and changeable environment, such as: their route, their position, their speed, the position and speed of other vehicles, road and weather conditions, and the behaviour of their own vehicle. Drivers also need to be able to predict how these variables will change in the near future, in order to anticipate how to adapt their own driving. Research has suggested that poor situational awareness is a greater cause of accidents than excessive speed or improper driving technique (Gugerty, 1997).

Situationally aware drivers manage to communicate their intentions to other drivers (and anticipate the intentions of other drivers) without verbal coordination, as they drive along motorways (freeways) at high speeds. This is partly due to the constraints of the system and the conventions of road use, and partly due to compatible, but non-identical, forms of SA. No one driver will have that same SA as any other driver; each will be unique. The information relevant to each driver will be disposed differently for every driver – driver A has driver B behind him, whereas driver B has driver A ahead of him. The compatible, and behaviourally interacting, SA enables the loosely coupled ground transportation system to function effectively. Degradation of SA in any one driver may be compensated for by other drivers. Thus the system is both dynamic and flexible. This is another important proposition for our theory, and requires that we consider the contribution made by the systems perspective in more detail.

The systems perspective

Researchers such as Hollnagel (1993) and Hancock (1997) have made powerful arguments for the system's perspective in analysing human-machine interaction. The hierarchical and heterachical relationships and interactions between structures and functions at different levels have certainly served human factors researchers well in the past (Singleton, 1989). In a review of contemporary team work research, Paris et al (2000) found that most theories, models and taxonomies comprise a tripartite input-process-output approach from general systems theory. This seems to be a useful distinction for the development of a predictive model. Indeed the systems theoretic approach would enable different levels of description appropriate to the nature of the prediction being offered. Example of possible input, process and output variables are suggested in table three.

Table three. Examples of Input, Process and Output (IPO) Variables

Input	Process	Output
Organizational	Exchange of information	Time
Environment	Interactions	Error
Task design	Communication	Workload
Team composition	Adaptation	Situation awareness

These IPO variables are similar to those found by Stanton and Ashleigh (2000) in a review of the team work literature and an observational study team working in a modern human supervisory control room. The systems framework offers the possibility of analysing interactions and relationships at many different levels and focusing of specific interactions within sub-systems. Recent research has suggested that technical aspects of the system are part of the joint cognitive system (Hollnagel, 1993). Research into trust and technology suggests that there are shared traits between interpersonal trust and technological trust (Muir, 1994; Muir & Moray, 1996). Ashleigh & Stanton (2001) have show that those shared traits included emotive constructs (i.e., confidence, respect, commitment and teamwork), cognitive constructs (e.g., understanding, ability, and expectancy), and behavioural constructs (e.g., reliability, performance and communication). The authors report that the people they interviewed did not distinguish between human or non-human agents when using these constructs. The idea of collaborative human and non-human SA agents seems to be a useful concept to carry forward into our theory. Again we could illustrate the idea in a simple thought experiment based on (semi) automated motorway (freeway) driving.

Thought experiment #2: Situationally aware cars

Walker et al (2001) present a technology road map that suggests situationally aware cars could become a commercial reality within 15 years. Handling management systems could detect, via G-sensors and inputs from the active yaw system, the type of road that the vehicle is travelling on. Algorithms, or even neural networks, within the engine management and active yaw control systems deduce driving style the driver is adopting. The traffic information and GPS navigation system could help the driver select routes that maximise the efficiency with which the road network can be used. Behind the scenes, the engine management systems could optimise ignition and valve timing in order to promote fuel efficiency. Collision avoidance technology could help keep the car in lane and, in the event of an unavoidable collision, apply emergency braking and brace the driver for impact. All of these activities could be performed without any explicit communication with the driver, who concentrates on getting to his or her destination.

Extending our first thought experiment, we could imagine the driver progressingalong the motorway whilst being largely unaware of the vehicle's own SA capability. Contemporary technologies are capable of merging video and radar data to detect the intended path of the vehicle, position in lane, together with the trajectories of other vehicles. This data can be integrated to identify the current status of the driving environment (such as cut-in's by other vehicles, e.g., level 2 SA) and anticipate the future (such as identify potential collisions, e.g., level 3 SA). The design of the vehicle may be such that these outcomes are only communicated to the driver at the point when he or she needs to intervene. Thus the human and non-human elements of the system co-exist only passing information when it is appropriate to do so. The technology could allow these systems to communicate between vehicles, so that potential collisions are resolved without drivers ever knowing that they were possible. Furthermore, as the vehicle becomes sufficiently 'smart' to have its own SA, there arises the issue of whether it can progress without knowledge of the driver's SA. For example, the driver is approaching a junction (and the vehicle has detected both the junction and an oncoming car) and receive indication, e.g., via flashed headlights, from an oncoming car to signal that space is available to pull out. The car, having no awareness of the exchange between drivers, might determine that the action of pulling out violates its rules and seek to prevent the driver action. Of course, the issue of decision-priority is important is such systems. However, for this paper, the point of this thought experiment is to demonstrate how agents within a system will work with their own SA and that this may lead to conflict which requires resolution.

Propositions for the development of a theory of Systemic SA

On the basis of the evidence presented in this paper, we feel that it is possible to propose a set of tenets that could form the basis of a systemic theory of SA. These propositions are as follows:

a. SA held by human and non-human agents
b. Multiple views on SA of the same scene for different agents
c. Non-overlapping and overlapping SA depends on agent's goals
d. Communication between agents may be non-verbal behaviour, customs and practice (but this may pose problems for non-native system users)
e. SA holds loosely-coupled systems together
f. An agent may compensate for degradation in SA in another agent

The challenge for now is to develop measures and evidence that will enable us to substantiate this theory. In particular, our work focuses on the question of how best to describe SA at a system's level and how communication between agents within a system can support effective performance.

Acknowledgements: This work from the Human Factors Integration Defence Technology Centre was part-funded by the Human Sciences Domain of the UK Ministry of Defence Scientific Research Programme.

REFERENCES

Adams, M.J., Tenney, Y.J. and Pew, R.W., 1995, Situation awareness and the cognitive management of complex systems, Human Factors 37, 85-104

Ashleigh, M.J. & Stanton, N.A. 2001, Trust: key elements in human supervisory control domains, Cognition, Work & Technology, 3, 92-100.

Baber, C.; Walker, G.; Salmon, P. and Stanton, N. A. (2004) Observation Study Conducted at the Fire Service Training College. Human Factors Integration - Defence Technology Centre Report.

Bedny, G. & Meister, D. 1999 Theory Of Activity And Situation Awareness International Journal of Cognitive Ergonomics 3, 63-72

Endlsey M. R. 1995, Toward a theory of situation awareness in dynamic systems, Human Factors, 37, 32-64

Jentsch, F., Barnett, J. & Bowers C. A. 1999, Who is flying this plane anyway? What mishaps tell us about crew member role assignment and air crew situation awareness. Human Factors, 41, 1-14

Hollnagel, E. 1993, Human Reliability Analysis – Context and Control. London: Academic Press.

Kaber D. B. & Endsley M. R. 1997, Out-of-the-loop performance problems and the use of intermediate levels of automation for improved control system functioning and safety, Process Safety 16, 126-131

Muir, B. M. 1994, Trust in automation: Part 1. Theoretical issues in the study of trust and human intervention in automated systems. Ergonomics, 37, 1905-1922.

Muir, B. M. & Moray, N. 1996, Trust in automation: Part 2. Experimental studies of trust and human intervention in process control simulation. Ergonomics, 39, 429-460.

Rasmussen, J. 1986, Information Processing and Human Machine Interaction. New York: North-Holland.

Salas, E., Prince, C. & Baker D. P. 1995, Situation awareness in team performance – implications for measurement and training, Human Factors 37, 123-136

Smith, K. & Hancock, P. A. 1995, Situation awareness is adaptive, externally directed consciousness, Human Factors 37, 137-148

Stanton, N. A. & Ashleigh, M. (2000) A field study of team working in a new human supervisory control system. Ergonomics 43, 1190-1209.

Singeton, T. 1989, The Mind at Work. Cambridge: Cambridge University Press.

Stanton, N. A.; Ashleigh, M. J.; Roberts, A, D. and Xu, F. 2004, Levels of abstraction in human supervisory control teams. Submitted to Computers, Technology and Work

Vicente, K. 1999, Cognitive Work Analysis. Mahwah, NJ: Lawrence Erlbaum Associates.

Walker, G. H., Stanton, N.A., and Young, M.S. 2001, Where is computing driving cars? A technology trajectory of vehicle design. International Journal of Human Computer Interaction, 13, 203-229.

DYNAMIC MONITORING OF TRAFFIC FLOW:
The Driver's Situation Awareness

Xianjun Sam Zheng, George W. McConkie, and Yu-chi Tai
University of Illinois at Urbana-Champaign

ABSTRACT

A study was conducted to explore the potential of a new research method, the Change Blindness Paradigm, for investigating one aspect of drivers' situation awareness: their mental representation of nearby vehicles on the roadway. As 13 experienced drivers drove in a high-fidelity, single-monitor driving simulator, occasionally the location of a vehicle in the road ahead or one of its properties (its color or type) would suddenly change. Sometimes, in a blocked design, the change occurred during a brief (150 ms) blanking of the screen and sometimes there was no blank. Blanking the screen eliminates local stimulus cues that normally accompany change, so detection must be based on memory. All changes were well detected in the No-blank condition. In the Blank condition, detection of location change was near zero, while detection of color and identity change remained quite good. We argue that vehicle location is coarsely represented in drivers' memory, and that this, together with vehicle features, is used to visually monitor more fine-grained location information.

Keywords: Driving, Situation Awareness, Mental Representation, Change Detection

INTRODUCTION

When driving, people must be aware of a number of aspects of their situation, including their speed and lane position, the activities and locations of other vehicles, traffic regulation signs, landforms and road characteristics, and indicators suggesting potential hazards. These are constantly changing, so the current state must be visually monitored by drivers. Previous research (Gugerty, 1997) has shown that drivers retain explicit awareness of up to five nearby vehicles. The present experiment uses the change detection research method (e.g., Pringle, Irwin, Kramer, & Atchley, 2001; Rensink, O'Regan & Clark, 1997) to further investigate what aspects of the driver's environment are being represented in memory. As such, it is a study of change detection in a dynamic stimulus environment.

Wallis & Bülthoff (2000) conducted change detection studies using simple simulated or photographic short dynamic driving scenes containing several off-road objects (i.e., bench, box, ball, etc.). These objects changed color, orientation, position or presence (appear and disappear) during repetitive 1/3 sec display blanking periods. Detection of changes varied with task (driving or not), object and type of change. On average changes in color and presence were detected better than those in position and orientation. Results were similar for simulated and photographic stimuli.

In the current study, participants were driving in a simulator and occasionally the screen would blank for 150 ms. On some occasions when the image returned to the screen, the location, color or identity of a moving or parked vehicle ahead was different than it had been previously. The location change involved moving the vehicle nearer or farther away by 10% or 30%. The changes occurred to vehicles that were either about 30 or 60 meters away, which corresponded to about 2.24 sec or 4.47 sec of driving time at 30 mph, the specified driving speed. The participants were instructed to press a button on their steering wheel whenever they detected something change in this manner. In order to make sure that the changes used were perceptible, in some driving episodes the same changes were made without blanking the screen.

METHOD

Participants drove in a high-fidelity, PC-based driving simulator. Five visual information channels were displayed on one 21-inch KDS monitor (1024 x 768 pixels; 60 Hz refresh rate): windshield view, speedometer, and left, right and center rear-view mirrors (see Figure 1 for an example). Twelve driving scenarios were created using DriveSafety's HyperDrive Authoring Suite™ Version 1.4.1. Each scenario was about 3 miles long and required about 6 min to drive at the specified speed of 30 mph. All were four-lane urban roads with two lanes in each direction separated by a low barricade. Lanes in each direction were separated by a broken white line, and there was a parking lane and sidewalk on each side of the roadway.

Participants

Thirteen adults (3 females, 10 males; age 20-32 years, mean 26) from University of Illinois, all with valid driver's licenses and at least two years of driving experience (mean 5.7 years; mean annual driving distance, 6,650 miles) were paid to serve as participants. All had normal or corrected-to-normal vision.

Critical Locations and Experimental Conditions

Thirty-two critical locations were identified in each scenario. On average a critical location was encountered every 10 sec during driving assuming a 30 mph speed. Experimental manipulations occurred at these locations. Over 90% of the time there was more than one vehicle on the road ahead at the critical location, and there could be as many as 6.

On half the scenarios, the screen was blanked (replaced with a homogeneous grey screen) for 150 ms when a critical location was reached; on the other half of the scenarios, the specified changes occurred without any blanking of the screen (No-blank condition).

A display change always involved a change in a vehicle ahead of the driver. This vehicle was either 30 (Near) or 60 m (Far) ahead, and was either moving in one of the two lanes ahead (Moving condition) or was not moving and was in the parking lane to the right (Parked condition). The specified vehicle either moved to a new location (Location condition), changed color (Color condition; change between red, green, blue or white), changed identity (Identity condition; change between compact car, SUV, pickup truck or van), or made no change (Control condition). Vehicles in the Location condition were moved either 10% or 30% of their distance from the driver's vehicle (Displacement size), either closer or farther away (Displacement direction).

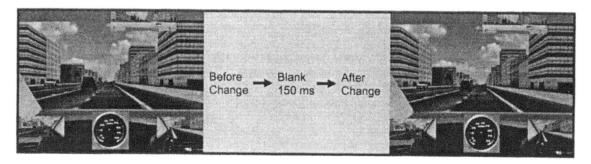

Figure 1. This Figure shows the five visual-channel driving display using HyperDrive software and a display change example: The three images arranged horizontally show the display immediately before a blank, the grey blanking screen, and the display immediately after returning. The change illustrated is 30% location displacement (a moving vehicle at 30m is displaced 30% farther away).

Design and Procedure

The experiment used a 2 (Blank/No-blank) x 2 (Parked/Moving) x 2 (Near/Far) x 4 (Color/Identity/Location/Control) design, with the Location condition expanded into a 2 (Displacement size) x 2 (Displacement direction) design. This produced 56 conditions, with each driver tested 6 times in each. Each participant drove six of the scenarios in the Blank condition and six in the No-blank condition, alternating in blocks of three, with the assignment of condition to scenario varying across drivers according to a Latin square; other conditions were all tested within scenarios with the order randomized separately for each scenario.

After being instructed in the nature of the change detection task, participants were seated in the simulator. They received speed control practice, and then practiced driving with the No-blank and Blank display conditions. At this point, participants were assigned to a condition sequence, beginning the actual experiment with three scenarios in the Blank or No-blank condition, three in the other condition, and a repeat of this sequence, as specified by the design. The entire experiment took about 1 hr and 45 min to complete.

RESULTS

The proportion of display changes that were detected (Hits) in each condition was calculated, as well as the likelihood of pressing the button in the control (no change) condition (False Alarms). From the Hit and False Alarm data, a d' score was calculated for each condition for each subject using different False Alarm values for the Blank and No-blank conditions. The d' score indicates the distance between assumed noise and signal-plus-noise distributions, thus indicating the participants' sensitivities to the different types of stimulus changes. Large values indicate greater sensitivity.

A 2 (Blank/No-blank) x 2 (Near/Far) x 2 (Parked/Moving) x 2 (Displacement Size) x 2 (Displacement Direction) ANOVA showed no significant effect of Direction (F(1,12) = 0.14; p=.909) nor did it enter into any significant interaction. Therefore, the data were collapsed across Displacement Direction and new d' values were calculated for each experimental condition for each subject.

Detecting Location Changes in the No-blank and Blank Condition

A 2 (Near/Far) x 2 (Parked/Moving) x 2 (Displacement Size) ANOVA test was performed on data from the No-blank condition. In the No-blank condition, the d' values are consistently very high (see Figure 2 (a)), indicating high sensitivity to these display changes. Detection was affected by all three variables: changes in nearer vehicles were more detectable than in farther vehicles (F(1, 12) = 8.639, p = .012), changes in moving vehicles more detectable than in parked (F(1, 12) =18.211, p = .001), and larger displacements were more detectable than smaller (F(1, 12)= 19.092, p = .001). Two interactions (Location x Status, F(1, 12)= 34.744, p<.0005; Location x Status x Displacement Size, F(1, 12)= 10.858, p =.006) appear to be due to one condition: detection is much poorer for the smallest displacement, when applied to parked, distant vehicles (see Figure 2 (a)).

A similar ANOVA test was conducted with d' data from the Blank condition. Here the mean d' values are near zero (see Figure 2(b)), indicating essentially no sensitivity to these changes in location. A significant effect for Parked/Moving conditions (moving > parked, F(1, 12)= 9.158, p = .011) and two interactions (Location x Displacement Size, F(1, 12)= 8.224, p = .014 ; Status x Displacement Size, F(1, 12)= 8.801, p = .012) all appear to be primarily due to a high value in one cell: the Far, Moving, 30% Displacement condition has a mean d' of 1.05, which is above all the other 7 conditions included in this analysis and the only value that is significantly different from zero. It seems odd that displacements of more distant vehicles should be detected better than of closer vehicles.

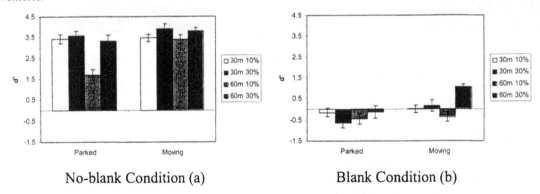

No-blank Condition (a)   Blank Condition (b)

Figure 2. Mean d' (± SE) for detection of different displacement size changes at different locations in No-blank Condition (a) and Blank Condition (b) (Location x Status x Displacement Interaction).

Detecting Location, Color and Identity Changes

Figure 3 presents the Blank/No-blank x Change Type interaction (F (3, 36)
= 26.956, p <.0005), indicating that location displacements were poorly detected in the Blank condition, but well detected in the No-blank condition, as noted above; in contrast, changes in color and identity were detected well in both conditions. This is the primary finding from this analysis and is discussed further below.

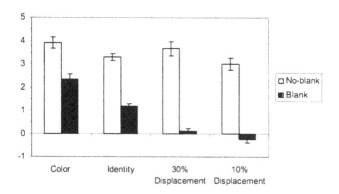

Figure 3. Mean d' (± SE) for detection of different types of change in Blank and No-blank conditions (Blank/No-blank x Change Type Interaction).

DISCUSSION

The No-blank condition results indicate that all of the stimulus manipulations were very perceptible (d' values in the 3.0 and 4.0 range; hit rates of 70% and 80%), though there is evidence that the drivers were not monitoring parked vehicles, particularly those at a distance, as effectively as moving vehicles.

As in other studies of change blindness (Rensink et al., 1997), the results are quite different when changes occur during a blanking period. Whereas stimulus change in the No-blank condition can be detected perceptually on the basis of local stimulus motion, in the Blank condition this local motion is hidden by a global change and detection requires the involvement of retained information. Thus, detection of all types of change is high in the No-blank condition; but in the Blank condition, the detection performance was much poorer, showing a change blindness effect. However, the blank affected the detection to different changes differently. Detection of vehicle color and type remained quite good, indicating that drivers are attending to nearby vehicles and that this information is being maintained in their mental representations. In contrast, the detection of changes in vehicle location was detected very poorly, in most cases at the level of False Alarms. Apparently the mental representation of the locations of vehicles, moving or parked, is very coarse.

We suggest that vehicle location, while being very important to the driving task, is encoded in memory in a more coarse and qualitative manner than was measured in the current study. For example, location may be coded only in terms of a few rough distance categories (perhaps near, medium and far distant), which lane the vehicle is in, and the general direction and velocity of motion. When a finer-grained representation is required, this is obtained through visual input. This represents a compromise position between those who argue for a rather complete memory representation of viewed scenes (e.g., Standing, Conezio, & Haber, 1970) and those who argue that this is not necessary because the information is available in the visual stimulus array and, hence, readily accessible visually (e.g., O'Regan & Noë, 2001). This compromise position proposes that observers represent in memory those aspects of the stimulus array that are needed in order to readily orient their visual systems to the regions or objects where more fine-grained information can be obtained. Apparently drivers' memory representation of location is coarser than 30% of object distance. Further research is needed to test this proposal.

Another surprising finding is that displacement direction has no effect; we expected that displacements bringing a vehicle closer to a driver would be more salient since that signals a potential for danger. This result indicates one basis for the prevalence of rear-end collisions (Brown, Lee, & McGehee, 2001). Since distance is coarsely represented, a driver is unlikely to detect that a vehicle ahead is slowing, based on a reduced distance observed on two discrete samples (for example, looking at a vehicle before and after a glance at some other object). Apparently, vehicle slowing is generally visually detected from continuous changes in flow fields.

Finally, this study indicates that the change blindness paradigm is useful for investigating one aspect of drivers' situational awareness: i.e., what information about the surrounding environment is being represented in memory.

ACKNOWLEDGEMENTS

This research was supported by a grant from General Motors to the second author. The simulator was set up by Braden Kowitz as part of the Integrated Systems Laboratory at Beckman Institute, directed by Hank Kaczmarski.

REFERENCES

Brown, T. L., Lee, J. D., & McGehee, D. V. (2001). Human performance models and rear-end collision avoidance algorithms. Human Factors, 43(3), 462-482.

Gugerty, L. J. (1997). Situation awareness during driving: Explicit and implicit knowledge in dynamic spatial memory. Journal of Experimental Psychology: Applied, 3(1), 42-66.

Lamy, D., & Tsal, Y. (2000). Object features, object locations, and object files: Which does selective attention activate and when? Journal of Experimental Psychology: Human Perception & Performance, 26(4), 1387-1400.

O'Regan, J. K., & Noë, A. (2001). A sensorimotor account of vision and visual consciousness. Behavioral and Brain Sciences, 24(5), 939-1011.

Pringle, H. L., Irwin, D. E., Kramer, A. F., & Atchley, P. (2001). The role of attentional breadth in perceptual change detection. Psychonomic Bulletin & Review, 8(1), 89-95.

Rensink, R. A., O'Regan, J. K., & Clark, J. J. (1997). To see or not to see: The need for attention to perceive changes in scenes. Psychological Science, 8(5), 368-373.

Standing, L., Conezio, J., & Haber, R. N. (1970). Perception and memory for pictures: Single-trial learning of 2500 visual stimuli. Psychonomic Science, 19(2), 73-74.

Wallis, G., & Bülthoff, H. (2000). What's scene and not seen: Influences of movement and task upon what we see. Visual Cognition, 7(1-3), 175-190.

SITUATIONAL AWARENESS AND USABILITY
WITH AN AUTOMATED TASK MANAGEMENT SYSTEM

James A. Pharmer
Navair Orlando Training Systems Division

Melissa D. Weaver
Basic Commerce and Industries (BCI), Inc.

ABSTRACT

One approach to reducing the operators required to man future Navy surface combatants is the use of task-managed systems. These systems process incoming information and provide recommended courses of action to operators. This paper discusses the results of an experiment to investigate the feasibility of applying task management techniques to support manning reduction in the context of air defense warfare. Situational awareness (SA) and usability evaluations were conducted with a prototype design and realistic warfighting scenario. The task management application, the methods used for the determination of SA, and the investigation results are discussed, as well as results from the usability evaluation. Overall, operators may have had some difficulties in gaining higher-level SA when using the task manager. Based on operator feedback, one of the most promising features for simplified task management support was a Gantt chart display that provided operators with a general timeline of recommended tasks as well as a history of actions taken.

Keywords: task management; automation; situational awareness; usability

INTRODUCTION

The United States Navy has placed a strong emphasis on the goals of manning reduction and the development of tools to support the fewer warfighters in performing increasingly complex tasks. Previously reported findings within this program of research have demonstrated that a human-centered design approach to the development of a prototype air defense warfare interface could support a 50% manning reduction with marked improvements in performance indicating better operator SA (Freeman, Campbell, & Hildebrand, 2000 and Pharmer, Campbell, & Hildebrand, 2001). Another approach to meeting manning reduction goals is the addition of a task management system, which processes incoming information and provides recommended courses of action to operators. This research was conducted to evaluate the usability and performance impacts of a prototype automated task management system that focused on air warfare. The concept tested was designed and prototyped based on lessons learned and usability test results from previous research (Osga, Van Orden, Campbell, Kellmeyer, & Lulue, 2002). The testing approach, experimental plan, tactical scenario, and control data set were based on previous experimentation (Freeman, Campbell, & Hildebrand, 2000 and Pharmer, Campbell, & Hildebrand, 2001).

Two issues are consistently identified in the literature as potential pitfalls to developing these types of decision support tools. First, given that decision support tools remove the operator to some degree from the nuts and bolts of the decision making process, there is a real danger that these operators may lose some SA. Second, careful attention must be paid to the usability of these systems to ensure high levels of operator performance without undue workload, memory, and SA burdens.

METHOD

Two interfaces were developed and utilized in the test. The basic interface followed a human-centered design approach and included what were considered low-cost/risk improvements to the current version. In comparison, the automated task management interface included additional task management support and consisted of three primary components: the Task Manager primary user interface, the Tactical Situation (TACSIT) Task List (TTL), and the Response Planning Manager (RPM). The Task Manager primary user interface tries to assist the operators in completing their jobs by initiating tasks based upon operator pre-programmed rules. When operators select the system-initiated tasks, appropriate information sets are provided to enable informed decisions about how to proceed. The TTL provides quick access to the highest priority tasks within each task group. The RPM is a Gantt chart display where operators can look for a general timeline of track-appropriate tasks as well as a history of what has been done by themselves or other team members concerning the track. The bars in the chart can also be used as another method to access the tasks.

Six intact combat watch teams of five each were tested in each automation support condition. Subject matter expert (SME) raters provided by the Aegis Training and Readiness Center conducted all data collection at the Integrated Command Environment Human Performance Laboratory at NAVSEA Dahlgren. Each team performed the same realistic air defense warfare scenario consisting of two 45-minute segments, a lower difficulty segment followed by a higher difficulty segment. At the end of each of these segments was a 'coast' period during which participants were asked to fill out pencil-and-paper measures. An event-based measurement approach was utilized which centered on critical events associated with 25 of the air contacts. The validity of this measurement approach has been demonstrated in prior Navy research (Johnston, Cannon-Bowers, & Smith-Jentsch, 1995). During the scenario, the SME evaluators assessed each watchstander on the timeliness and accuracy of performing critical actions utilizing a handheld computer version of the Air Warfare Team Performance Index (Dwyer, 1992). Upon completion of the scenario performance testing, teams participated in debrief interviews.

Situational Awareness

Endsley (1988) has provided one of the most widely used and accepted definitions of the SA construct. By this definition, SA can be decomposed into a three-level hierarchy where perception (Level I) involves the recognition of relevant cues in the environment, comprehension (Level II) involves interpretation of these cues in forming an understanding of the significance of those cues as part of the bigger picture, and projection (Level III) involves predicting future actions of those elements in the environment in the near future.

Traditionally, SA measurement has been performed through the use of probes or queries inserted into a 'paused' scenario. Due to limitations in the training software in an earlier condition of this investigation, it was not possible to 'pause' the scenario. However, the scenario design allowed for questionnaires probing 'contacts of interest' to be administered during the two 'coast' periods in the middle and at the end of the scenario. Further, indirect queries were made through embedding questions into the typical communications between the operators and the 'supervisory' role players. These direct and indirect probes provided a subjective means of observing whether operators viewed specific tracks in the scenario as 'contacts of interest'. However, for a contact in the scenario to be of interest to the operators, it must have had some characteristic, which called attention to it. Thus, the probes in this investigation were realistically only capturing Level I SA. Deeper analyses of the task performance measures were necessary to determine whether the task management would yield higher-level SA. Performance-based inferences would determine not only whether or not the operators perceived the contacts in the scenario but whether they responded appropriately to them, uncovering whether or not they comprehended the intent of those contacts (Level II), and planned appropriately for potential future threat (Level III).

Usability

In addition to SA evaluations, usability assessments of the task management support were also conducted to help interpret the performance results and determine which features of the interface were beneficial and which needed improvement. Usability data was collected from a variety sources including post-experimental team interviews, automated button press logging, and analysis of over-the-shoulder videos of the one of the watchstander positions.

RESULTS AND DISCUSSION

Situational Awareness

As expected, the indirect and direct probes of the participants yielded some information as to whether or not operators recognized specific tracks in the scenario as 'contacts of interest'. Analyses of the probe data did show that the critical tracks in the scenario were indeed recognized. Operators reported these tracks to 'role players' flawlessly, as would be expected given the extensive training that they receive to qualify for their positions in the combat information center. However, analysis of the performance data indicated that operators may have had some difficulties in gaining higher-level SA when using the task manager. There were substantial inefficiencies in the way that teams using the task manager allocated physical resources to identify and prepare to defend against threats. For example, within the scenario, operators were presented with a forced choice between responding to two contacts of interest. One contact was an imminent threat or 'critical contact of interest' while the other contact was somewhat less threatening based on factors such as flight profile. Teams with higher levels of SA were expected to recognize the differences between these tracks and either commit aircraft to visually identify the threatening contact, cover the aircraft with weapons, or 'lock on' with radar.

While the working hypothesis for this investigation was that the task manager would support better SA, as evidenced by better allocation of these limited resources to the most threatening targets, the performance data did not support the expected gains. One potential reason for this apparent lack of improved SA may, at least in part, be explained by the post-scenario interviews. At least one participant reported reverting to a strategy of clearing tasks from the task manager during periods of high workload without fully considering the tactical relevance of the contacts. While this comment is only anecdotal in nature, it does lead to further empirical questions that should be investigated before significant resources are committed to incorporating task managers across the fleet. The task management system developed to support performance and SA for this study focused on air defense warfare, a highly demanding and event-driven domain. Although the results of the current study did not show SA benefits, there may be domains where task management may indeed show returns on the investment into this technology. Only careful consideration of the human in the design process, through empirical testing and usability testing can determine whether task management can support SA in these domains.

Usability

Overall, subjective feedback gathered from the participants during debrief sessions indicated that they liked the automated task management concept. The three topics that will be discussed further include task sorting, task icon location, and use of a task timeline chart.

During development of the task management interface, much consideration was given to the question of how the tasks should be re-sorted over time. Automatic sorting would reduce operator workload, but there was a concern that having the tasks move around as the operator is working may be distracting or frustrating. In addition, the operators would not be able to use task location as a trigger, such as planning to do a task in a certain location next. Simple mockups were created and tested with a few subjects and it appeared that manual sorting was preferable, thus it was selected for the test with a visual cue for the participants indicating when items should be re-sorted. However, both subjective and video analysis results indicate that participants did not consistently perform the manual task sorting. Based on video analysis, the median number of times the operator sorted was only 1.5. The watchstander that was videotaped is one of the busiest positions and the addition of workload from the task management tool, such as having to manually sort, may have been too much. During the debrief interviews, the participants noted that they often forgot to sort and suggested this functionality be automatic.

Participants were asked whether they preferred selecting task icons from the lower Task Manager screen or on the TACSIT Task List. In general, operators seemed to favor the TTL because it did not require them to look as far away from their main display and thus better-supported continuous SA. However, a few operators did choose the Task Manager screen due to fact that it tended to show all their tasks in one place. Some participants also indicated that they utilized both options in a combination approach. A strong preference for the TTL shortcuts was demonstrated with post-experimental video analysis. The median number of uses was 3.5 for the Task Manager method and 126.5 for the TACSIT Task List (p<0.001). Given that tasks were not being frequently re-sorted, the TTL may have been incorrectly presenting the highest priority tasks thereby negatively impacting operator performance and SA.

The Response Planning Manger was also positively received by most of the participants. The RPM provides both a way to access tasks and view a track's task history, including what actions have been performed, when, and by whom. Certain watchstanders who need to monitor the status of actions related to all tracks seemed to use it frequently. Other watchstanders used it as a history of what they or others on the team had done. In addition, features such as the RPM and tabs that allowed participants to see the tasks of other team members can support the development of shared SA across team members. This was noted in particular during the debrief interviews as a feature that participants believe helped reduce communications on the internal team circuit. As a representation of suggested tasks over time and a method for accessing them, the RPM may be a way to provide task management support that will require less operator attention but will be available to be used when needed. Unfortunately, automatic data logging was not available to determine RPM use objectively and it was difficult to assess reliably from the video analysis. Thus, the only data available were comments from the post-experiment interviews. It is recommended that future experimentation examine this feature in greater detail and include objective data collection.

CONCLUSION

The SA data collection using combined results from probes and task measures indicated that operators had some difficulties in gaining higher-level SA when using the task manager. In some cases, the teams with the task manager were less likely to make tactically sound decisions. It is speculated that during periods of high workload operators reverted to a strategy of clearing tasks from the task manager without fully considering the tactical relevance of the contacts. In addition, although participants favored shortcut access to tasks next to their main displays over the complete task manager screen, there is a concern that the combination of these displays may begin to overload the operators with information or drive the completion of tasks without enhancing SA.

Although results indicated that the complete task management system might not be required for this type of scenario, the response-planning manager (RPM) was a promising feature and may be worth considering as a simplified form of task management support. The RPM is a Gantt chart display where operators can look for a general timeline of track-appropriate tasks as well as a history of actions taken. Participants in particular called out the RPM as a feature that reduced the communications required among the team and supported the development of team SA. Further research with this feature is recommended.

ACKNOWLEDGEMENTS

This work was funded by the Office of Naval Research (ONR) and supported by the Naval Sea Systems Command Dahlgren Integrated Command Environment (ICE) Human Performance Lab in Dahlgren, VA. We are indebted those Navy members who served as participants and administrators (Aegis Training and Readiness Center) in the experiments described above. The opinions expressed here are the authors' and do not necessarily reflect the views of the U.S. Navy or the Department of Defense.

REFERENCES

Dwyer, D. J. (1992). An index for measuring naval team performance. Proceedings of the Human Factors Society 36th Annual Meeting. Santa Monica, CA: Human Factors and Ergonomics Society, 1356-1360.

Endsley, M. R. (1988). Design and evaluation for situation awareness enhancement. Proceedings of the Human Factors Society 32nd Annual Meeting. Santa Monica, CA: Human Factors Society, 99-101.

Freeman, T. J., Campbell, G. E., & Hildebrand, G. A. (2000). Measuring the impact of advanced technologies and reorganization in a CIC environment. Proceedings of the Human Factors and Ergonomics Society 44th Annual Meeting. Santa Monica, CA: Human Factors and Ergonomics Society, 642-645.

Johnston, J. H., Cannon-Bowers, J. A. & Smith-Jentsch, K. A. (1995). Event based performance measurement system for shipboard command teams. Proceedings of the 1st International Symposium on Command and Control Research and Technology. Washington, D. C.: The Center for Advanced Command and Technology, 274-276.

Osga, G., Van Orden, K., Campbell, N., Kellmeyer, D., & Lulue, D. (2002). Design and Evaluation of Warfighter Task Support Methods in a Multi-Modal Watchstation (Tech. Rep. No. 1874). San Diego, CA: SPAWAR Systems Center (SSC).

Pharmer, J. A., Campbell. G. E., & Hildebrand, G. A. (2001). Report on the ONR/SC-21 Science and Technology Manning Affordability Initiative Aegis Comparison Study MMWS Build-1 Results. Orlando, FL: Naval Air Warfare Training Center.

THE GLOBAL IMPLICIT MEASURE (GIM): CONCEPT AND EXPERIENCE

Robert L. Shaw
NTI, Inc.

Bart J. Brickman and Lawrence J. Hettinger
Northrop Grumman Information Technology

ABSTRACT

The two most common approaches to the measurement of situation awareness (SA) in today's practice are the memory-probe and secondary-task techniques. Both these approaches suffer from the same limitations: they are intrusive and the act of SA measurement actually risks altering that SA. The Global Implicit Measure (GIM) concept was developed to avoid these weaknesses, and to provide a means of SA measurement applicable to real-time human-engineering problems.

The GIM is a performance-based technique that assesses quantitatively and implicitly the SA of a test subject in real time during the performance of a complex task. This paper describes the theoretical constructs and the first practical application of this technique. The GIM concept provides a powerful research tool for assessing SA in complex simulated scenarios, either *post hoc* or in real time, and may provide the basis for practical automated adaptive control techniques.

Keywords: Situation Awareness; Human Performance Measurement; Implicit Measures

INTRODUCTION

The two most common approaches to the measurement of situation awareness (SA) in today's practice are the memory-probe and secondary-task techniques. Both these approaches suffer from the same limitations: they are intrusive and the act of SA measurement actually risks altering that SA. The GIM concept was developed to avoid these weaknesses, and to provide a means of SA measurement applicable to real-time human-engineering problems (Vidulich, M.A., 2000).

The GIM is a performance-based technique that attempts to assess quantitatively and implicitly the SA of a test subject in real time during the performance of a complex task. This paper describes the theoretical constructs and the practical application of this technique as developed during the performance of the *Vista Warrior* program conducted at the Air Force Research Laboratory Human Effectiveness Directorate (AFRL/HEC) at Wright-Patterson AFB, OH. The *Vista WarrioR* program provided a highly realistic simulated air-combat mission capability within which to explore human-system performance. The GIM technique was employed in part to assess the validity, usefulness, and effectiveness of this concept for the purposes of evaluating new fighter cockpit interface designs, and to provide potential inputs to adaptive control algorithms. GIM scoring was supplemented by more conventional quantitative and qualitative SA and workload measurement techniques for thoroughness and comparison purposes (Brickman, B.J., *et al*, 1995).

GIM scoring, as implemented for *Vista Warrior*, was accomplished by multiple computer algorithms that assigned a score to the pilot test subject according to his/her actions during a simulated air-combat mission. The algorithms monitored multiple aspects of the subjects' performance and compared pilot actions with those prescribed by the "Rules of Engagement" (ROE) provided prior to the mission. These "rules" detailed the procedures and tactics to be employed during the mission in response to virtually any given situation. Experienced pilot test subjects were trained extensively so that they were intimately familiar and proficient with these rules. Subsequently, when the subject adhered to the prescribed rules during the mission, the inference was made that he/she correctly perceived and interpreted the current situation. GIM scores, therefore, theoretically provided a real-time implicit measure of SA.

There are several inherent advantages to the GIM concept when compared with most current widely used techniques. Primary among these is that GIM is transparent to the test subject, lacking the intrusiveness of many standard approaches. Task performance is not interrupted for memory probes that tend to break the subject's train of thought and cue him/her to aspects of the mission situation that they may not otherwise have considered. GIM is also objective and real-time, without reliance on a subject's short-, or long-term memory. This real-time attribute may also allow GIM to facilitate applications like adaptive control/display techniques (Vidulich, M.A., 2003). One of the disadvantages of GIM as currently implemented is a relatively high workload requirement for test developers and researchers, as multiple interface-, and scenario-specific GIM scoring algorithms must be developed and tested. Another possible negative is that, since ground truth must be well defined for accurate scoring, GIM may be more useful in research environments than in operational applications.

METHOD

The *Vista Warrior* test program was conducted in the Fusion Interfaces for Tactical Environments Laboratory (FITE Lab) facilities of AFRL/HEC at Wright-Patterson AFB. These facilities were designed for the purpose of investigating the human-factors aspects of new display technologies as they relate to the fighter cockpit. The objective of *Vista Warrior* was to develop and evaluate the effectiveness of various display techniques with a view toward improving the fighter pilot's performance in the air-to-air tactical environment.

The evaluation strategy was to present experienced fighter pilots with two simulated fighter cockpits, one ("Conventional") representative of today's typical controls and displays, and the other ("Candidate") which employs a number of unconventional display technologies, methods, and techniques intended to improve the pilot's interface with his aircraft and its systems. One of the primary display techniques being evaluated was a large-format color "big-picture" display that combined flight reference, radar, and threat data on a single head-down display. Numerous simulated air-combat scenarios were performed employing each cockpit design, measurements were taken, and pilot impressions were recorded to assess the impact and effectiveness of each Candidate display technique.

Facilities

The FITE Lab cockpit includes a simulated F-16 shell, and is fitted with an F-16C throttle and side-stick controller. This is a fixed-base simulator situated in a small cubical enclosure measuring approximately 12 ft on a side. Out-the-Window (OTW) views of ground features, other aircraft, etc., are projected on three walls and the ceiling. All system controls accessible to the pilot are situated on the stick and throttle. Most controls not relevant to the air-combat task are automated or eliminated. The simulation was controlled from computer terminals located in an adjacent area. Computing power for the simulation and all the displays is provided by a number of personal computers (PCs). Displays available, in addition to the OTW projection, included a Head-Down Display (HDD), a Head-Up Display (HUD), a Helmet Mounted Display (HMD), a 3-D sound system, and a haptic (tactile) display system. Also integral to the system were two Auxiliary Terminals manned by "threat" pilots. These terminals supplemented the capability of the FITE Lab to generate "computerized" threats, providing additional realism to simulated air-combat scenarios. Aircraft flight models, weapons and sensor models, were virtually identical for both cockpit designs to be evaluated, as well as for the manned threats.

Scenario

The mission chosen was a single-ship fighter Defensive Counter-Air (DCA) scenario in which the evaluation cockpit represented a fighter assigned to protect an airfield from enemy air attack. The defending fighter was initiated at the designated Combat Air Patrol (CAP) point, and the test subject was instructed to defend the airfield from attack by a flight of four automated enemy bombers (Su-24s) escorted by a pair of manned threat fighters (MiG-29s). There were no active ground threats or friendly cooperating forces assigned or simulated, although there was an automated "friendly" F-15 fighter placed randomly in the scenario as a distraction for both the test subject and the enemy forces. Additionally, a simulated "neutral" civilian airliner was also introduced on a random basis during the scenario (Vidulich, M. and McMillan, G., 2000).

The test subjects were instructed to follow specified procedures and tactics, called Rules of Engagement (ROE),
which were considerably more restrictive than would normally be the case for traditional ROE. This ensured standardized tactics and procedures to aid in the goal of evaluating cockpit displays and controls. The test subjects were instructed to remain in a prescribed CAP pattern at a specified airspeed and altitude until "Commit Criteria"

were met. These Commit Criteria required at least one of the enemy bombers to be inside the designated threat sector, or an enemy fighter to be located inside the threat sector with a "hot" (closing) aspect. When the test subject identified these criteria, he/she was instructed to leave the CAP pattern and attack the offending aircraft. In the event that Commit Criteria were met by multiple threat aircraft, a priority order was assigned. Specific intercept and weapons-employment tactics were provided by the ROE, depending on the range, altitude, and aspect of the priority target. The goal was to destroy the enemy fighter-bombers as top priority unless the enemy fighters became a threat, then the most threatening enemy fighter became the priority. Four Defensive Conditions (DEFCONs 1 through 4) were defined, based on the priority threat fighter's range, aspect, and weapons and radar status. Specific offensive and/or defensive tactics were to be followed, depending on the prevailing DEFCON.

Each mission was sub-divided into four phases: CAP, Intercept, Egress, and Safe. Any DEFCON was possible during any mission segment except CAP. The mission was initiated in the CAP phase, which ended with the satisfaction of Commit Criteria. During the CAP phase the test subject was to fly the designated CAP parameters while searching for enemy aircraft in an attempt to identify when Commit Criteria were attained. Intercept phase commenced with the satisfaction of Commit Criteria. The test subject's primary goal during the Intercept phase was to destroy all the enemy fighter-bombers while avoiding destruction by the threat fighters. The Intercept phase terminated with either the destruction of all enemy fighter-bombers, destruction of the defending fighter, expenditure of all weapons by the defending fighter, or upon the defending fighter reaching a designated critical fuel state. When any of these conditions was met, the Intercept phase terminated and the Egress phase commenced. During the Egress phase the primary goal of the defending fighter was to return to the designated "Safe Area" within 20 NM of the airfield as quickly as possible at a designated altitude. The Egress phase ended and the Safe phase began when this goal was achieved. The Safe phase ended when the test subject called "Knock It Off" from within the Safe Area. The mission was also terminated whenever the test subject called Knock It Off or the defending fighter was destroyed, either by hostile action or by crashing, regardless of mission phase. Although this scenario was outwardly simple, it proved to be deceptively difficult to accomplish successfully, even by experienced fighter pilots, thereby providing a demanding environment for assessment of the performance of test subjects and the comparison of cockpit displays and controls.

Subjects

Eighteen highly experienced military pilots (aged 30 to 48 years) from the United States, France, and Great Britain participated in the experiment. The subjects reported total flight experience that ranged from 1,720 hours to 4,808 hours, with a mean of 2,980 hours (Brickman, B. J., et al, 1999). Eleven of the participants reported significant experience piloting Fighter type aircraft (with mean Fighter experience of 1,353 hours). These pilots reported experience in several aircraft types including F-4, F-14, F-16, F-15, Jaguar, Mirage, Rafale, and Tornado.

Experimental Design

The two crew station interface designs (Candidate , Conventional) were combined factorially with three initial threat altitudes (low, medium, and high) to provide six unique start points for the mission scenario. These conditions were manipulated within subjects; thus, every pilot performed the evaluation using both crewstations, in each of the three possible starting locations. The presentation sequence of the conditions was counterbalanced to guard against order effects.

GIM Development

An experienced fighter-pilot subject matter expert (SME) identified twenty Measures of Performance (MOPs) for real-time GIM scoring, and developed and validated the GIM scoring algorithms for each. Throughout the mission, a number of MOPs were monitored and recorded to assess the performance of the test subject on a continuing basis. These MOPs included flight conditions (e.g., airspeed, altitude, course, etc.) and switch/control positions (e.g., radar control selections, chaff/flare dispensing, weapons selections and firing, speedbrake actuation, etc.). The detailed ROE prescribed the proper condition for each of these MOPs for every possible situation, depending on mission phase and DEFCON. The number of MOPs scored at any time ranged from 10 to 19, depending on mission phase and DEFCON (Vidulich, M. and McMillan, G., 2000). The test subjects' compliance with the ROE, therefore, represented an implicit indication of his/her understanding of the current tactical situation, i.e., SA.

For each mission phase and DEFCON, computerized scoring algorithms were developed. These algorithms were designed to generate a raw score of "1" when the correct condition existed for a given MOP, and zero when an incorrect condition existed. A score of "-1" was assigned when the MOP was not relevant to the given situation and when an incorrect condition was the result of another higher-priority error. This latter convention was intended to avoid penalizing the score multiple times for a single error. After the scoring algorithms had assigned raw scores to the MOPs, weights were assigned to each MOP according to SME assessment of the importance of that MOP for each tactical situation. Weights were assigned to be "relative," rather than absolute, and adjusted so that the sum of all weights for each mission phase/DEFCON was 100 to avoid biasing the scores for any given condition. Whenever the scoring algorithms generated a "no score" (-1) raw score for a given MOP under certain conditions, it was not evaluated and no weight was applied. This necessitated devising a "dynamic weighting" scheme to adjust the relative weights so that the sum of the weights for each phase always equaled 100 for normalization. A Phase Score was generated for each mission phase/DEFCON by multiplying the raw scores (0 or 1) for each MOP by its assigned weight, and summing the result. A perfect Phase Score would, therefore, always be 100.

An assumption was made that the highest of the eight Phase Scores should correspond to the "true phase," (i.e., the actual phase based on ground truth) if the test subject possessed a valid understanding of the tactical situation. Since the subject's assessment of the existing phase was critical to performance of the mission according to the prescribed ROE, a "bonus" was given when this condition existed (i.e., when the highest Phase Score corresponded to the true phase). A formula was developed for a Global SA (GSA) score, based on the highest Phase Score with the bonus applied if applicable.

GIM scoring was performed continuously at a 5-Hz rate, and the results were provided on a computer monitor which came to be called the "GIM-o-Meter." This display, which was accessible to the test subjects and the instructor during training but not during actual data collection, provided real-time digital raw scores for each MOP, as well as digital and bar graphs of all eight Phase Scores and the GSA. The GIM-o-Meter was found to be invaluable for validation of the GIM scoring algorithms during development and for test subject feedback during training.

RESULTS

GIM Situation Awareness Scoring and Analysis

To date, GIM scoring and analysis has been completed for the CAP phase of the simulated Air Defense mission. A comparison of the mean GIM SA scores by crewstation configuration for the CAP phase is presented in Figure 1. It can be seen that the general trends in SA scores were very similar between cockpits. An analysis of individual missions shows an initial rise in SA scores early in the mission due to a "cockpit setup" period, during which the pilots checked the displays and flight conditions and configured the crewstation as required by the ROE. Following this initial period the pilots had to fly the outbound ("hot") leg of the CAP pattern straight-and-level at the required altitude and airspeed. The GIM SA scores were high throughout this relatively easy portion of the mission.

A sharp drop in GIM SA scores (approximately frame 200) following this plateau appears to be almost entirely due to lost awareness of the vertical coverage requirements for the radar. The ROE specified radar coverage from the ground to 50,000 MSL at the border of the threat sector at all times while in the CAP. It is apparent that the subjects simply placed the radar elevation control on one setting (detent) and did not adjust it as the distance to the threat sector boundary decreased on the outbound leg of the CAP.

Following this drop in SA scores there is another brief plateau until the fighter reached the 30-NM turn point at the hot end of the CAP pattern (approximately frame 300). At this point SA scores began to decrease gradually due to occasional late turns and deviations from the prescribed altitude and airspeed. This is not surprising, since pilot workload increases substantially during such maneuvers. It may also reflect pilot attention being diverted to assessing radar contacts, which often began to appear near the turn point or during the turn itself.

The drop in scores generally ceased at about frame 400, as the turn from the outbound to inbound leg of the CAP was completed and workload decreased. This was followed (about frame 450) by another rapid rise in scores as distance to the threat sector boundary increased during the inbound (cold) leg of the CAP, followed by a gradual rise in SA scores after the turn from inbound to outbound legs of the CAP. The CAP phase typically ended during the second outbound leg of the CAP pattern when threat aircraft began to cross the outer boundary of the threat sector, requiring interception by the primary fighter.

Figure 2 reveals only minor differences between the two crewstations, most likely due the nature of the requirements of the CAP phase. The CAP phase required little more than basic instrument flying skills for which pilots tended to use the HUD almost exclusively. The two HUD formats were essentially identical (with one minor difference) during this period, so the lack of significant differences in performance is not surprising. Greater differences would be expected during the more difficult dynamic segments of the mission such as the Intercept, Weapons Deployment, and Defensive Maneuvering phases. In fact, the GIM scores for the two crewstations did begin to dissociate near the end of the CAP Phase (approximately frame 480), as the pilots transitioned from the CAP to the more demanding Intercept phase. The analysis of the remaining mission segments is underway in order to further examine these results (Brickman, B. J., et al, 1999).

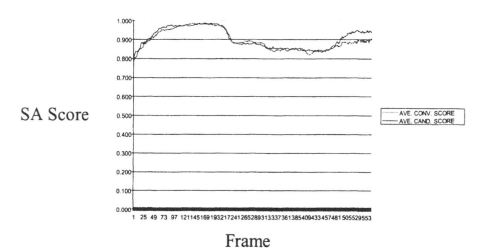

Figure 1. CAP Phase Mean GIM Situation Awareness Scores by Crewstation.

Subjective Situation Awareness Ratings

The 13-D Cognitive Compatibility-Situation Awareness Rating Technique (13-D CC-SART) was completed at the conclusion of the final session for each pilot. This technique enabled the determination of a mean subjective situation awareness rating, for each crew station configuration. A 2 (crew station configuration) x 4 (mission phase) x 13 (rating dimension) repeated measures ANOVA was performed on the data. The ANOVA revealed a statistically significant main effect for crew station configuration, $F (1,17) = 7.514$, $p < .01$. An examination of the means revealed that pilots rated SA significantly higher for the candidate crew station (mean of 5.235) than for the conventional crew station (mean of 4.727).

DISCUSSION

The initial results of the Global Implicit Measurement technique presented here are limited in scope, reflecting the results of the GIM scoring algorithms only for the CAP phase of the air defense mission. As such, any inferences based on these results must remain guarded. The GIM SA scores did appear to accurately track with the changing demands on the pilot throughout the CAP phase.

The analysis thus far, however, has yielded no substantial difference in GIM SA scores between the two alternative crewstation configurations. This is most probably due to the nature of the tasks demanded in the CAP phase. The CAP phase required little more than basic instrument flying skills and the primary instrument used in this task (HUD) was nearly identical in both Conventional and Candidate crewstations. However, as the pilots began to transition from the CAP phase to the more demanding intercept phase, there does appear to be an increasing dissociation in GIM SA scores between the two crewstations (Brickman, B. J., et al, 1999). At this point, consistently higher mean scores were seen for the Candidate crewstation. Furthermore, examination of 13 D CC-SART situation awareness data showed significantly higher SA scores were achieved with the Candidate crewstation over the Conventional crewstation over the course of the entire mission. Perhaps this suggests that the differences in SA seen in the GIM data near the end of the CAP phase continue throughout the more demanding portions of the mission (Intercept and Weapons Deployment). Analysis of the later more challenging mission phases must be finished before any conclusions may be made, although initial results seem promising.

The potential for a real time, non-invasive, assessment of pilot SA may provide important inputs to advanced interface design and possibly to the development of dynamically adaptive interface systems. Due to the resolution of the scoring algorithms, the GIM technique may be suitable for use in evaluating differences in SA due to alternative interface design concepts. If the GIM technique is able to identify why SA was higher using one interface design as compared to another, it would provide valuable input to the iterative design of complex crewstations.

In addition, the GIM technique may also be applied to the development of dynamically adaptive crewstations (e.g., crewstations that automatically adjust displays and/or controls based on the environment, the tactical situation, or the behavior of the pilot). However, the need for known "objective ground truth" may limit the effectiveness of GIM in an operational environment. For example, uncertainty in ground truth due to the fog of war would effect GIM scoring and thus impact any adaptive interface system based on GIM data. GIM becomes much more effective to the extent that fog-of-war is a non-factor. For this reason, GIM data might be used with greater success when applied to dynamically adaptive interfaces in more controlled research efforts, or in learning environments such as flight and weapons systems training simulators.

CONCLUSION

There are several inherent advantages to the GIM concept when compared with most current widely used techniques. Primary among these is that GIM is transparent to the test subject, lacking the intrusiveness of many standard approaches. The mission is not interrupted for memory probes that tend to break the subject's train of thought and cue him/her to aspects of the mission situation that may not otherwise have been considered. GIM is also objective and real-time, without reliance on a subject's short-, or long-term memory. This real-time attribute may also allow GIM to facilitate applications like adaptive control/display techniques. For interface design applications the GIM technique can be very powerful as a diagnostic tool, as well as for scoring SA. Since performance in multiple areas is recorded, it is a relatively simple matter to determine the MOPs that contribute most negatively to the performance of an interface design, so that upgrade efforts can be focused in the most promising areas. One of the disadvantages of GIM as currently implemented is a relatively high workload requirement for test developers and researchers, as multiple interface-, and scenario-specific GIM scoring algorithms must be developed and tested. Another possible negative is that, since ground truth must be well defined for accurate scoring, GIM may be more useful in research and simulated training environments than in operational applications.

REFERENCES

Brickman, B.J., *et al* (1995). An assessment of situation awareness in an air combat simulation: The Global Implicit Measurement Approach. In D.J. Garland, & M.R. Endsley (Eds.), <u>Experimental analysis and measurement of situation awareness</u>: Proceedings of an International Conference (pp. 339-344). Daytona Beach, FL: Embry-Riddle Aeronautical University Press.

Brickman, B. J., *et al* (1999). The Global Implicit Measurement of situation awareness: Implications for design and adaptive interface technologies. In M.W. Scerbo and M. Mouloua (Eds.) <u>Automation technology and human performance: Current research and trends,</u> (Lawrence Erlbaum Associates, Mahwah, NJ), 160-164.

Vidulich, M.A. (2000). The role of scope as a feature of situation awareness metrics. In Garland, D.J. and Endsley, M.R. (Eds.). <u>Experimental analysis and measurement of situation awareness,</u> (Embry-Riddle Aeronautical University Press, Daytona Beach, FL), 69-74.

Vidulich, M.A. (2003). Mental workload and situation awareness: Essential concepts for aviation psychology practice. In Pamela S. Tsang & Michael A. Vidulich (Eds.), <u>Principles and practice of aviation psychology,</u> ((Lawrence Erlbaum Associates, Mahwah, NJ), 115-146.

Vidulich, M. and McMillan, G. (2000). The Global Implicit Measure: Evaluation of metrics for cockpit adaptation. In P.T McCabe, M.A. Hanson, & SA. Robertson (Eds.), <u>Contemporary ergonomics 2000</u> *(pp.* 75-80). London: Taylor & Francis.

LONG-CYCLE, DISTRIBUTED SITUATION AWARENESS AND THE AVOIDANCE OF DISASTERS

Carys Siemieniuch, Murray Sinclair
Loughborough University, United Kingdom

ABSTRACT

This paper considers the characteristics of long-cycle situation awareness in those industries where the plant may be in place for decades, and where the potential for disaster exists for all that time. The main characteristics affecting long-term situation awareness are firstly, the rate of change to the process, secondly the pressures for greater efficiency from the plant as competitors make improvements, thirdly the inevitable changes in personnel within the plant which will occur, and fourthly the cultural changes which will take place over that period. Through all of these changes, the integrity of the plant must be maintained, and those people designated as responsible for the safe operation of the plant must be able to identify any drift from safe operation of the plant. The paper discusses structural issues for civilian high-reliability organisations capable of delivering this behaviour.

Keywords: process ownership; high reliability organizations; drift to disaster; organizational design; human factors

INTRODUCTION

Rasmussen (1997; 2000) and Amalberti (1999), discuss the drift of a process away from the safe working envelope for the process, over an extended period of time (i.e. decades). Examples of this drift are the explosion of the Union Carbide pesticides plant at Bhopal in India, and the destruction of the Piper Alpha oil platform in the North Sea. In both of these cases, there were plenty of warning signs that indicated that the facility was drifting from its safe operating envelope (the 'drift to disaster'– see for example the websites at http://www.bhopal.com/, http://www.owlnet.rice.edu/~conway/piper/, and Rasmussen (1997).

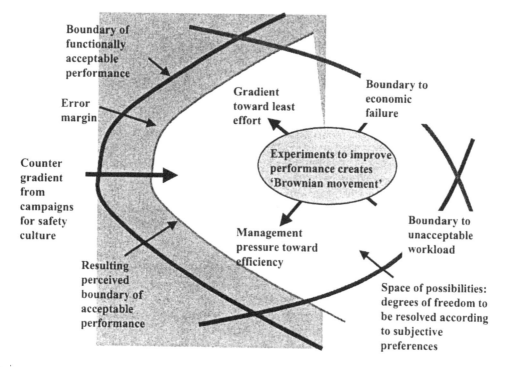

Fig. 1 Rasmussesen's 'drift to disaster' diagram (redrawn). The safe envelope is in the middle; the drift is to the left, where disaster lurks.

There are several characteristics of organisations over this period of time which create dangers for a process:

- Changes in their competitive environments, affecting the goals and performance of the organisation. Typically, these changes involve 'down-sizing', or requiring process plants to handle more complex or more evolved products, usually by upgrading or patching the old plant, rather than by re-design.
- Changes in personnel over time, leading to a loss of historical knowledge about the process. Natural change, due to retirements, are one cause of loss of knowledge; downsizing is a more potent, immediate cause. Typically, downsizing means that middle-aged members of staff and those close to retirement suffer the worst of the retrenchment, and these are the holders of most of the corporate memory.
- Different people make decisions affecting the process; these people usually do not have comprehensive knowledge of the process, and where individuals do have good knowledge of aspects of the process, these may not overlap much with other decision makers. This issue is discussed well by (Turner and Kynaston-Reeves 1968; Turner 1978)
- Different groups are responsible for design, operation and maintenance, and communication among them is not always sufficient, nor is it timely, and nor is it accurate. The Challenger and Columbia disasters stand in testimony to this.
  Since we cannot change the external drivers, it is these characteristics we must address. Currently, these are addressed by:
- process audits at infrequent times, often at the behest of insurance companies and executed by external bodies,
- safety campaigns from time to time, and
- assignment of operational safety to operational management and technological safety to maintenance management.

Significant gains in safety have resulted; however, these approaches may be insufficient with the rise in legal importance of good governance (see, for example, http://www.icgn.org/documents/globalcorpgov.htm).

DISASTERS, CORPORATE GOVERNANCE AND 'HIGH RELIABILITY ORGANISATIONS'

If there is one consistency among the investigations of disasters, it is that either the necessary systems and procedures (for training, auditing, safety management, etc.) were not in place, (e.g. Bhopal) or that they were in place but their operation was of insufficient quality (e.g. Challenger and Columbia). Both of these issues are issues of corporate governance, and we discuss this briefly.

The notion of corporate governance suffers from too many different definitions, depending on the background discipline of the definer. We have adopted the version offered by the Organisation for Economic Co-operation and Development (OECD), insofar as it seems to contain most other versions that have been put forward:

"Corporate governance is the system by which business corporations are directed and controlled. The corporate governance structure specifies the distribution of rights and responsibilities among different participants in the corporation, such as, the board, managers, shareholders and other stakeholders, and spells out the rules and procedures for making decisions on corporate affairs. By doing this, it also provides the structure through which the company objectives are set, and the means of attaining those objectives and monitoring performance" (OECD 1999)

This definition includes both the internal and external affairs of the organisation; it implies the need for risk management; it embraces the whole organisation; and, although it is well-hidden within this definition, it does imply that the adequacy and quality of organisational processes are significant aspects of good corporate governance – it is difficult to see how this could be delivered without these two aspects.

It follows fairly swiftly, from consideration of these points, that the organisation would have to pay co-ordinated attention to all of the following, as components of corporate governance:

- Structure (e.g. allocation of responsibility and authority; autonomy)
- Infrastructure (e.g. IT&T networks; security; access)
- Resources (e.g. time, money, people, knowledge & skills, equipment, and the distribution of these)
- Leadership (e.g. commitment to goals, support, clarity of communications)
- Culture (e.g. trust, willingness to learn, tolerance & retrieval of 'errors')
- Policies (e.g. resource management, change management, safety culture, suppliers, customers)
- People (e.g. selection, training, appraisal, knowledge, commitment)
- Processes (e.g. maturity, simplicity, metrication, controllability)
- Technology (e.g. maturity, deployment, utilisation, replacement)
- Knowledge (e.g. formal, tacit; organisational configuration; lifecycle)

One further aspect is also well-hidden in the definition. Given that the organisation operates within a dynamic context, there is the need to take a life-cycle view of the organisation and its processes, and this introduces the need for long-term situation awareness, particularly when one considers that the OECD has said that 'the half-life of most worker skills in 3.5 years" (OECD 1998), the Commission of the European Union issued a report stating that "80% of all technology will be replaced in the next decade" (Gavigan 1999), and over that decade, about 25% of the people in the organisation will leave. The danger here is that disasters can have historical causes, from decisions made a decade ago, for a more simple process, by people no longer present in the organisation, These issues indicate the need for organisations to have well-embedded processes for self-awareness, self-renewal, and knowledge lifecycle management.

One way in which these issues could be addressed is by the creation and maintenance of 'High Reliability Organisations' (e.g. Roberts and Bea 2001; Weick, Sutcliffe et al. 1999) where reliability refers to the avoidance of disasters in particular, but also includes accidents and other unwanted events. In Weick's elegant expression, it is concerned with maintenance of the 'dynamic non-event'. This is an approach less concerned with the philosophy and management of 'errors' (slips, lapses, mistakes, violations) and more concerned with the philosophy of organisational support for humans in situation control (adjustments, compensations, recoveries and improvisations). As (Reason 2000) has expressed it, the management of errors is concerned with reducing human variability, whereas HRO theory recognises human variability as a protection for a system in a dynamic, uncertain world. Sullivan & Beach (2003), following Roberts & Bea (2001), have outlined some of the organisational requirements for HROs; however, they have not indicated how these might be instantiated, and, particularly, have not discussed the need for continuity of learning and wisdom, both of which are human attributes, It will be noted that the literature in general is very sparse regarding 'wisdom management'.

Hence, we now need to consider how continuity and wisdom can be provided within the organisation, and how these can be expressed effectively for long-term control. One way in which this could be accomplished is by the notion of Process Ownership, and we turn to this next.

PROCESS OWNERSHIP

First, we define a 'Process', for the purposes of this paper:
- A Process has customers
- The Process is made up of activities which create value for the customer
- A Process is instantiated by the allocation of goals, resources, responsibilities, and authority, and by the acceptance of appropriate metrics for measuring the performance of the process

Process Ownership was introduced in the 1990s (e.g. Hammer 1996), with the notion of value chains. This early conception saw the role of the Process Owner more as an operational role than as a governance role. If, however, the role is re-defined to place emphasis on the latter, we may have better control over the drift to disaster. The intention here is that the process is 'owned' by a given individual, who 'leases' the process to a process manager who is responsible for the day-to-day operation of the process. For example, the process might be owned by a Manufacturing Systems Engineer with instantiations of the process located in Daytona, China and France operated by local managers and operators. The Process Owner's responsibilities may be defined as:
- documenting the process as 'best current practice'.
- maintaining the integrity of the capability within the process (tools, procedures, skills, and the health and safety of its stakeholders).
- authorising improvements to the process, to ensure it continues to be 'best current practice'.
- ensuring that process changes do not have bad effects on related processes (and *vice versa*).
- Supporting the change process for making process improvements.
- Authorising physical instantiations of the process in a given geographic location, and ensuring that any changes necessary for the process to fit the local context do not harm the integrity of the process
- Ensuring that the process metrics are properly used, and the results are made accessible.
- The Process Owner thus becomes distinct from the Process Manager, who is responsible for process performance goals. The Process Owner now maintains corporate governance over the process, and is the repository of process knowledge and process history, both of which are fundamental to continued process safety as discussed above.

The advantages of this approach are:
- it focusses management attention on the prime assets of the organisation – its knowledge, and the efficient deployment and utilisation of that knowledge.
- it engenders a focus on strategic considerations
- it provides a basis for a thorough understanding of process capabilities with their related safety issues within the enterprise
- it presents a coherent structure for good governance for safety, and for the maintenance of any 'safety cases', as demanded by regulatory authorities;
- it provides a built-in bias against the slow 'drift to danger' identified by Rasmussen and others (though it does not eliminate it).

The disadvantages are:
- the role will become ineffective unless the Process Owner is supported and resourced from the highest levels of the organisation, especially with regard to sufficient time to execute the role properly, and to have sufficient authority to stop the process should the Process Owner have cause for alarm about the state of the process in a given instantiation.
- Process Owners will be unable to perform their roles effectively unless the organisation has reached a high level of process maturity
- it divorces direct responsibility for process integrity from process performance.
- there will be differences between the goals for Process Owners and Process Managers/Operators, with the potential for considerable conflict.
- Where a process consists of many sub-processes, each with a process owner, it is possible that conflict will occur between the sub-process owners, leading to delays in innovation and capability acquisition.
- the inevitable creation of an hierarchy of roles for process ownership may be seen to be an exercise in over-staffing, to be resisted fiercely in the interests of profit and efficiency
- the pool of people competent to undertake the role in a given organisation appears to be small (see, for example, the list of components of corporate governance outlined above); the pool of those capable of giving training and acting as experts in process ownership appears to be much, much smaller.

Nevertheless, this approach seems to offer a means of addressing the drift to disaster problem, which is not particularly evident in current organisational scenarios. It also appears that companies are gradually moving towards this approach (unfortunately, this is not the stuff of experiments), and it is hoped that case evidence may follow in the next decade.

REFERENCES

Amalberti, R. (2001). "The paradoxes of almost totally safe transportation systems." Safety Science (in press).

Gavigan, J. P. (1999). The learning imperative for Europe's aging workforce. Seville, Institute for Prospective Technological Studies FUT1E386, World Trade Centre, Isla de la Cartuja, Seville, Spain.

Hammer, M. (1996). Beyond re-engineering, Harper Collins.

OECD (1998). Policy implications of ageing societies. Paris, Organisation for Economic Co-operation & Development: OECD Working Papers Vol VI, no 21.

OECD (1999). Principles of Corporate Governance. Paris, Organisation for Economic Co-operation and Development.

Rasmussen, J. (1997). "Risk management in a dynamic society: a modelling problem." Safety Science 27: 183-213.

Rasmussen, J. (2000). "Human factors in a dynamic information society: where are we heading?" Ergonomics 43(7): 869-879.

,Reason J. (2000). "Human error: models and management." British Medical Journal 320: 768-770.

Roberts, K. H. and R. Bea (2001). "When Systems Fail." Organizational Dynamics 29(3): 179-191.

Turner, B. and T. Kynaston-Reeves (1968). The concept of Temporal Disjunctive Information. Private Communication.

Turner, B. A. (1978). Man-made disasters, Wykeham Publications.

Sullivan, J. and R. Beach (2003). Understanding System Development and Operation in High Reliability Organizations: a conceptual model. The Security Conference, Las Vegas, USA. http://www.information-institute.org/security/1stConf/default.htm

APPLYING SITUATION AWARENESS THEORY TO OBSERVER/TRAINERS FOR THE JOINT TASK FORCE

Beth Blickensderfer
Embry-Riddle Aeronautical University

Charles E. Burgdorf, John Burns
Sonalysts, Inc.

ABSTRACT

Recent research in joint military training (Burns et al, 2003) has revealed a potential domain for situation awareness research and practice: the observers and trainers of the military Joint Task Force Headquarters (JTF HQ). A Joint Task Force is composed of a headquarters and military forces from two or more of the armed services. It is established, normally on a short term or temporary basis, to accomplish a specific mission. The size of the Joint Task Force is tailored to its mission. It could involve large scale combat operations or smaller scale humanitarian or disaster relief missions such as occurred in south Florida during Hurricane Andrew. The Commander of the Joint Task Force (CJTF) normally works for a senior military commander such as the commander of a unified or combatant command. The JTF HQ members generate the orders, plans, and reports that direct the entire military operation.

A principal method for training the Joint Task Force is a "wargame." In such a wargame, a simulation model represents a theater of operations and requires the JTF HQ to function as it would under actual operational conditions. As the JTF HQ conducts its mission, a diverse group of training and control personnel support the training exercise. Among this group, "observer/trainers" act as facilitators for the training audience by observing, assessing, and coaching its performance. The task of Observer/Trainers (O/Ts) is cognitively complex. The O/Ts must unobtrusively observe the JTF HQ, develop and maintain complete situation awareness of both the events in the simulation and the strategy and actions that the JTF HQ employs. They assess organizational structure and examine documents and products that the JTF HQ produces. They evaluate performance and provide real-time instructional feedback as appropriate.

The activities of the observer/trainers follow the three phases or levels of SA described in Endsley (1995): perception, comprehension, and projection of the future. In terms of perception, the O/Ts listen to conversations among the JTF HQ personnel and observe actions that these personnel make. In terms of comprehension, the O/Ts use the data that they gather to develop an understanding of, among other things: 1) the JTF HQ personnel's understanding of how the particular JTF that they are a part of operates (e.g., who talks to whom, hierarchy of decision making, roles and responsibilities, communication and coordination patterns, etc.), and 2) how much the respective members understand about the JTF operation and what the JTF staff members should be doing. Finally, in terms of projection of the future, the O/Ts must predict the results of actions the JTF HQ personnel take. Based on their projections of results, if the O/Ts observe a JTF staffer begin to take action(s) which will lead to a chain of events culminating with trouble in the mission, the O/T decides whether to intervene or allow the chain of events to occur.

The purpose of this paper is to discuss the JTF training environment in respect to SA theory. To accomplish this we will first define and describe the JTF training environment. Next, we will apply the Endsley (1995) model of situation awareness in dynamic decision making, and provide examples from the domain. Finally, we will present suggestions for future research in this domain.

Keywords: Situational Awareness, Training, Decision Making, Joint Task Force

INTRODUCTION

The US Military has used the "wargaming" method in one form or another for centuries to analyze and train its forces in the art of war/military art. The last twenty years have yielded advances in computer technology that have moved the military away from the set piece games of World Wars I and II eras and towards sophisticated virtual constructs of the battlespace (i.e., the areas of interest to and influenced by operational commanders). One training audience for which use of these simulations is essential is the Joint Task Force. Key to the effectiveness of these simulations is use of "Observer/Trainers" (O/Ts) who observe, assess, and coach the training audience's performance. A recent cognitive task analysis in this area (Burns, et al., 2003) noted that situational awareness (SA) is one key aspect of Observer/Trainer (O/T) performance. The Burns et al. work, however, did not fully address the issue of situation awareness. The purpose of this paper is to describe and discuss the joint task force training environment in respect to situation awareness of the O/Ts. To accomplish this, the paper first describes the joint task force training environment. Next, it describes the job of O/Ts in light of Endsley's (1995) model of situation awareness. Finally, it delineates areas for further research and development.

Training the Joint Task Force Headquarters (JTF HQ)

A Joint Task Force (JTF) is composed of personnel from two or more of the armed services (Air Force, Army, Navy, Marines). The JTF HQ is composed of a commander and staff who proportionately represent the service makeup of the forces it will direct and control. The headquarters is responsible for leading joint military forces to accomplish a specified mission. The commander and staff analyze the mission, develop a concept of operations that will accomplish the mission, and identify the forces necessary to accomplish the mission. They generate the orders, plans, and reports that direct the entire campaign or separate operation. The military currently trains JTF HQ via various virtual and constructive simulations. These simulations portray operational environments such as an entire theater of operations. The simulations provide a backdrop and context for the JTF HQ to operate as it would in the actual operational environment and are often in the form of wargames. A wargame takes place over several days to a few weeks. The tasks of the JTF HQ require complex skills, as the tasks are centered around gleaning information from command, control, communications, computers, intelligence, surveillance, & reconnaissance (C4ISR) systems and making plans and decisions. The nature of the command and control tasks and team environment introduces a number of challenges for scenario development, data collection for feedback, and feedback processes.

Observer/Trainers (O/Ts)

In the training model employed at the US Joint Forces Command's Joint Warfighting Center, the Observer/Trainers (O/Ts) play a crucial role in addressing some of the JTF HQ training challenges. As the JTF HQ operates to accomplish its mission, a group of instructors called "observer/trainers" (O/Ts) observe, assess, and coach their performance. The O/Ts must unobtrusively observe the JTF, develop and maintain complete understanding and awareness of the events in the simulation, the training audience's understanding of the scenario, and the strategy that the JTF HQ is employing to accomplish its mission. Finally, the O/Ts must provide real-time instructional feedback as appropriate. Thus, a major component of the O/Ts performance is to develop and maintain situation awareness (SA) of both the simulation and the training audience and then make instructional decisions based largely on their SA. As SA seems to be of such significance to this task, it is important to consider and understand the elements involved in this specific domain. The next section will apply the Endsley (1995) model of SA to the O/T task.

SITUATION AWARENESS IN O/TS

Endsley's (1995) model of situation awareness is shown in figure 1. Looking at the center of the model, the situation awareness construct is divided into three levels. Level 1 is the perception of elements in the current situation. Level 2 is the comprehension of the current situation, and Level 3 is the projection of future status. Moving to the top of figure 1, one major influence on the perception of elements, and SA itself, is the task or system. Similarly, the bottom of figure 1 depicts "individual factors" which also influence perception of elements in the environment, and SA. Finally, looking again at the center of the model, the level of SA achieved, the influence of task/system characteristics, and individual factors all influence any decision that is made and, in turn, any subsequent performance of actions.

The next paragraphs provide a more detailed description of the model with respect to the O/T domain.

Level 1: Perception. Endsley (1995) describes the first step in achieving SA to "perceive the status, attributes, and dynamics of relevant elements in the environment." For the O/Ts this means perceiving data regarding both the scenario (e.g., events that have occurred, events yet to occur, and events currently underway-- the location, type, number, capabilities, and dynamics of the friendly and opposing forces, etc.) and the training audience's performance (e.g., various types of knowledge, planning behaviors, team skills, and etc.). The data comes from a variety of sources including video tele-conferences, Powerpoint briefings, operation orders, phone calls, meetings, emails, web page bulletin boards and email via a variety of computer networks.

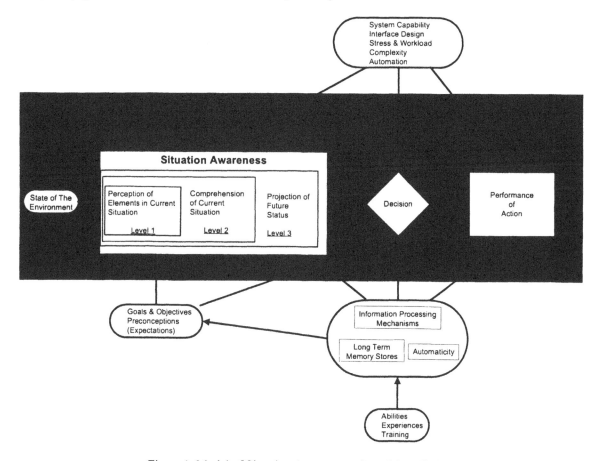

Figure 1. Model of Situation Awareness adapted from Endsley (1995)

As shown in Figure 1, the task/system itself has considerable influence on how the elements in the environment are perceived. Thus, it is important to consider how such characteristics influence the O/T task. As noted, O/Ts gather input from a variety of electronic sources and the training audience itself (the JTF HQ). O/Ts must collect the input by observing displays, listening to the training audience members, observing their actions, and examining any products they produced. Differences in display/interface design and differences in communication styles and personality of JTF HQ members can influence the data the O/T gathers from the environment. Also depicted in figure 1 are "individual factors" which influence perception. For O/Ts examples include: prior experience in JTF operations, prior training in instructional techniques, information processing mechanisms, the individual's goals and objectives, expectations of what will happen in the exercise, and knowledge of training objectives. Individual differences on each of these factors can influence how each individual O/T perceives incoming data.

Level 2: Comprehension. The next step is comprehension of the elements perceived. It is in this stage that each O/T synthesizes the data gathered in Level 1 to develop an understanding of multiple facets of the training environment including: 1) the JTF HQ personnel's understanding of how the particular organization they are a part of operates (e.g., who talks to whom, hierarchy of decision making, roles and responsibilities, communication and coordination patterns, etc.), and 2) the scenario itself. Indeed with the sheer amount of information available (some of which may be conflicting) it is not surprising that just making sense of it all is a tremendous cognitive load. To facilitate this process, the O/Ts have regular group meetings during the exercise where they integrate and discuss their observations and ensure that they have an accurate understanding of the situation.

Level 3: Projection. The last level of SA is projection of future status. In this stage, the O/Ts must take their understanding of the training audience's mode of operation and predict the results of actions (or inactions) that the JTF HQ personnel take (or fail to take). For example, in deciding to move forces into a desert area, an O/T realized that the JTF HQ did not take action to ensure that adequate water supplies would arrive at the correct time. Based on the lack of water for the troops, the O/T predicted impediments to the operation.

Decisions and Actions. Looking again at the center of the model, the level of SA achieved, the influence of task/system characteristics, and individual factors all influence any decision that the O/T makes relative to performance assessment and instructional action. Consider an O/T who observes a JTF HQ staff member begin to take action(s) that will lead to a chain of events culminating with trouble in the mission. Based on his prediction of what will happen, the O/T decides whether to intervene or to allow the chain of events to occur. Examples of interventions include giving corrective feedback (providing specific prescriptive guidance as to what a training audience member should do), using a "Socratic" / questioning process with the training audience member to help guide them down a more effective path, or doing nothing and allowing the training audience to see the results of the mistake. If the O/T does not have accurate SA, it is unlikely that he would make an effective instructional decision. That is, poor SA can lead to misinterpretation of the training audience's actions on the part of the O/Ts. Negative training can result via O/Ts giving inappropriate feedback or no feedback when, in fact, feedback is called for.

Another example of a decision and action based on the O/T's SA revolves around the input that O/Ts provide regarding future scenario events for an already in progress training session (i.e., from the master scenario event list). Accurate SA allows the O/Ts to predict performance of the training audience and whether future events will be problematic/ineffective for training (e.g., a mistake by the training audience on "Event 3" will make "Event 6" a moot point). The O/Ts suggest adding events, deleting events, or other changes to better tailor the scenario to fit the training audience's training needs. Without accurate SA and interventions to change events, the training session will be less effective.

A third example of the influence of SA on O/Ts decisions and actions has to do with O/Ts needing to maintain SA to enable themselves to be in the right place at the right time to observe specific behaviors and actions of the training audience. Based on what actions they anticipate the training audience to take and when they expect these actions to occur, the O/Ts ensure that they are in the right place at the right time to observe and provide feedback. Once again, inaccurate predictions results in missed training opportunities for the training audience (i.e., O/T won't be there to observe performance and provide coaching/feedback).

In sum, a number of examples from the O/T tasks seem to fit the Endsley (1995) model of SA. Next, research and development needs will be discussed.

RESEARCH AND DEVELOPMENT NEEDS

In terms of progressing the knowledge of SA in this domain, as well as offering tools to help the O/Ts perform their job, research and development needs are varied. Ideally, the first step would be to develop measures of effectiveness with respect to the O/Ts' ability to achieve situational awareness. Examining the degree to which previously developed measures (e.g., pilots, nuclear power plants) are applicable and valid is one potential route. Since O/Ts are far from the only instructors who need to develop SA of their students' understanding, it is likely that tools developed for this purpose could be tailored to and applicable to numerous other instructional settings as well.

In addition, tools that help O/Ts achieve SA quickly and to maintain their SA easily are of interest. The benefit is clear: the fewer cognitive resources that the O/Ts must devote to developing and maintaining SA, the more cognitive resources that O/Ts could devote to instruction. With the current system, it is likely that learning opportunities exist that go unaddressed especially in complex, large scale training events when O/Ts may be overtaxed. For example, the O/Ts may not notice an opportunity to give feedback to the training audience or the O/Ts may see an opportunity but are not prepared to give feedback—a crucial aspect of learning. Consequently, the training audience will miss a learning opportunity. Any one learning opportunity may not be that big of an issue, but when considered in light of the expense of holding the training exercises and the continued shrinking budgets, training efficiency is a concern (Oser et al., 2000). Oser et al. (2000) offer one approach to developing instructor support tools for the O/Ts.

Another need is instructor training. Currently, it may take up to 1 year for a new O/T to master the necessary skills for the best job performance (Sonalysts, 2002). It is likely that a significant portion of this learning curve is developing strategies to enable the new O/T to develop and maintain situational awareness of the scenario and training audience. One approach could be conducting a cognitive tasks analysis of the O/Ts aimed at eliciting the strategies the experts use to develop and maintain SA. Any methods revealed could, in turn, be taught to O/Ts in training.

SUMMARY AND CONCLUSION

As the United States' defense establishment continues to demand joint performance between the branches of the armed forces, the joint task force construct will continue to play an important role in accomplishing joint missions. Training the JTF HQ tends to be expensive and complicated, and relies heavily on the observer/trainers. Among other things, O/Ts have the complex and demanding job of developing and maintaining SA of the simulated training scenario, the training audience's performance, as well as the training audience's understanding of the training scenario. The SA of the O/Ts corresponds with Endsley's (1995) model of SA (e.g., perception, comprehension, and projection). Efforts to measure O/T SA and to develop tools to enable O/Ts to devote fewer cognitive resources to developing and maintaining SA are encouraged.

AUTHOR'S NOTE

The views presented herein are those of the authors and do not represent the official views of the organizations with which they are affiliated.

REFERENCES

Burns, J., Barnocky, J., Giebenrath, J., Grieve, D., & Blickensderfer, E. (2003) Employing cognitive task analysis to define intelligent agent system requirements. Proceedings of the 2003 Interservice/Industry Education and Training Conference. Arlington, VA: National Defense Industrial Association.

Endsley, M. R. (1995). Toward a theory of situation awareness in dynamic systems. Human Factors, 37(1), 32-64.

Oser, R. A., McCluskey, M. Blickensderfer, E., Campbell, G., Lyons, D. (2000) Intelligent agents to enhance learning in large scale modeling and simulation exercises. Proceedings of the 2000 Interservice/Industry Training, Simulation, and Education Conference. Arlington, VA: National Defense Industrial Association.

Sonalysts, Inc. (2002). Intelligent agents to enhance learning in large scale modeling and simulation exercises: Functional analysis and learning methodology report. Prepared for NAVAIR Orlando. Orlando, FL: Author.

COLLABORATION TOOLS FOR THE ARMY'S FUTURE FORCE

Cheryl A. Bolstad, Mica R. Endsley
SA Technologies

ABSTRACT

Collaboration tools are used to facilitate the communication and exchange of information among team members who are working together to complete a shared task.   The Army has under development a wide variety of tools for supporting collaboration. In addition, many commercial products have also been developed for supporting collaborative activities. Each of these tools offers very different types of capabilities, however, and little guidance exists as to which tools provide the highest levels of situation awareness (SA) and are appropriate for which types of collaborative tasks or situations relevant to Army Operations. An evaluation of these tools for Army command and control operations was conducted in a simulation exercise at Ft. Leavenworth. Overall, soldiers found to that face-to-face communication, a domain mapping tool and instant messaging were most effective for their tasks.

Key words: Collaboration Tools, Team Performance, Situation Awareness, Army

INTRODUCTION

In many complex systems, tasks will often need to be accomplished through teams.   Team members must continuously collaborate and share information in order to perform a common task. This dynamic process may be best exemplified by command and control (C^2) in the U.S. Army. During C^2 soldiers must continuously seek out new information, integrating it with existing information and share this information with relevant officers all for the purpose of creating, executing and modifying the Commander's plan. In current Army operations, this process is done while the majority of participants are geographically co-located. However, in the near future, the Army's envisions smaller teams working together in a distributed, asynchronous fashion. While this will give the Army more mobility as well as faster deployment times, it provides a challenge as to how these teams will continuously collaborate together from large distances.

One way to help coordinate and share information is through the use of collaboration tools (Bolstad & Endsley, 2003). The challenge is selecting the right tool for each task, as there are a variety of collaborative tools available. In the future, if soldiers are to function in a distributed fashion they will need collaborative tools and systems to exchange information and most importantly Situation Awareness (SA). By providing the soldier with the right collaborative tool at the right time he will be more likely create, maintain and share SA at a high level, which will be needed for distributed operations (Bolstad & Endsley, 2003).

Collaboration Taxonomy

To help determine which tool is best suited for specific tasks Bolstad and Endsley (2003) created a taxonomy of collaboration tools. The taxonomy describes the different types of collaboration techniques and tool characteristics that are needed to support the differing types of collaboration. The matrix consists of 13 major collaboration tool types (face-to-face, video conferencing, audio conferencing, telephone, net radio, chat/instant messaging, white board, file transfer, program sharing, email, groupware, bulletin board and domain specific tools) and four main content areas: collaboration characteristics (time, predictability, place and interaction), tool characteristics (recordable/traceable, identifiable, structured), information types supported (verbal, textual, spatial/graphical, emotional, photographic, video) and processes supported (planning, scheduling, tracking, brainstorming, document creation, data gathering, data distribution and shared SA). While the matrix is not exhaustive in its coverage of collaboration tools and collaboration characteristics, it does cover the majority of collaboration tasks that occur within the Army.

The matrix was color coded to show the level of support each tool provides for the various collaboration characteristics, tool types, information types and team processes. For example, the matrix section on collaboration processes shows that domain specific tools provide the highest level of support for shared SA, followed by face-to-face collaboration, video conferencing, audio conferencing, telephone and net radio (see Table 1).

Of interest during this experiment reported in this paper was to tool type Army officers selected when performing command and control tasks. When given a variety of collaboration tools, did the soldiers use the tools that best supported the processes they were doing (listed in Table 1). Specifically, did they use tools that best support shared SA.

Tool Category	Processes				
	Planning	Brain-Storming	Data Gathering	Data Distribution	Shared SA
Face-to-Face	Good	Good	Moderate	Moderate	Medium-High
Video Conferencing	Moderate	Limited	Limited	Good	Medium-High
Audio Conferencing	Moderate	Limited	Limited	Good	Medium-High
Telephone	Moderate	Limited	Limited	Good	Medium-High
Net Radio	Moderate	Limited	Limited	Good	Medium-High
Chat/Instant Messaging	Poor	Poor	Limited	Moderate	Moderately-Low
White Board	Moderate	Limited	Limited	Moderate	Moderate
File Transfer	Poor	Poor	Moderate	Moderately Good	Moderate
Program Sharing	Moderate	??	Low	Low	Low
Email	Low	Poor	Low	Moderately Good	Moderately-Low
Groupware	Poor	Moderate	Moderate	Low	Low
Bulletin Board	Poor	Moderate	Moderate	Low	Low
Domain Specific Tools	High	Limited	High	High	High

Table 1. Collaboration Tool and Team Processes

Experiment

A large simulation exercise was conducted at the Battle Command Battle Lab at Fort Leavenworth, KS. The study was conducted to determine which organizational structure best supports command and control in the future. During the exercise, soldiers were presented with a variety of collaborative tools for both military planning and execution. Soldiers were given several collaboration tools including: the Defense Collaborative Tool Suite (DCTS), group systems, MC2 (mapping tool) and Microsoft Word, Excel and Power Point. DCTS is a DOD (Department of Defense) collaboration tool. It is composed of multiple collaboration techniques including: online chat (instant messaging), shared white board, application sharing and file sharing.

METHOD

Participants

Forty-five participants, consisting of both active duty officers and retired officers familiar with Brigade level operations participated in this study.

Collaboration Tool Usage Measurement

Three sets of questionnaires on collaboration tool usage were created for this study: pre-test, during-test and post-test. The pre and post-test questionnaire were given to see if the participant's opinions on what tools work best for planning and execution changed during the exercise. The during-test questionnaire was designed to elicit what tools the soldiers were currently using to perform their jobs and which tools were most effective for these purposes.

PROCEDURE

Prior to participating in the exercise, participants were asked to fill out a pre-test questionnaire designed to determine their familiarity with the collaboration tools they would be using in the study. Participants then received one week of training on the new organizational structure and the positions they would be playing as well as the tasks they would be performing. Participants completed three days of simulated battle runs in which they planned then executed their course of action using these tools. The simulation consisted of the MC2 mapping system to displays the common operational picture (COP) and a separate display for collaboration tool usage (see Figure 1).

At random times throughout both planning and execution, activity was halted and the soldiers were asked to complete a 5-minute on-line questionnaire. In addition to collecting communication activity data and workload scores several questions were asked about collaboration tools used during the previous hour of the simulation. At completion of the exercise participants participated in an AAR (After Action Review) in which they completed the post-test questionnaire.

Figure 1. Exercise Set-Up

RESULTS

Pre-Test

The pre-test questionnaire asked participants how often they used currently available collaborative tools. Prior to the exercise, most participants were familiar (used at least once) with the tools to be used in this study.

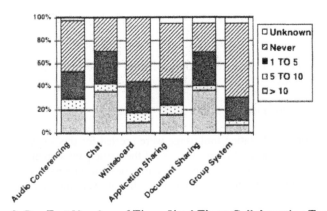

Figure 2. Pre-Test Number of Times Used These Collaboration Tools.

Participants were also asked to rank the tools they would use (when given a choice) for planning and execution. For planning purposes the top three tools were the COP, Microsoft Office Tools and Audio Conferencing. For execution the top three tools were network radio, COP and audio conferencing. These choices reflect currently available tools for command and control.

During-Test

At 16 times in the simulation the participants were given an on-line questionnaire and asked which tools they were currently using and how effective they were for their current activities.
Soldiers preferred to use slightly different tool sets for planning versus execution. Overall, soldiers reported using the mapping system (COP), chat, audio conferencing and instant messaging more frequently than the other collaboration tools (see Figure 3). However, they found face-to-face communication to be the COP, instant messaging and audio conferencing to be the most effective tools (see Figure 4).

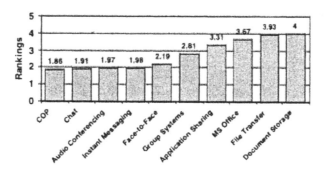

Figure 3. Overall Tool Frequency Rankings During Test

Post-Test

At the conclusion of the exercise the participants were asked to rate how likely they would be to use the specific collaborative tools in future command and control exercises. Using a scale from 1 (most likely) to 4 (not likely) the participants agreed almost unanimously that they would use face to face collaboration (M = 1.09) followed, by the COP (M = 1.26) and MS Office Products (M = 1.32) (see Figure 5).

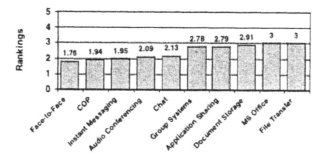

Figure 4. Overall Tool Effectiveness Rankings

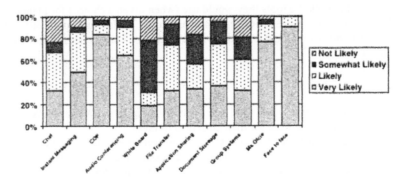

Figure 5. Likelihood Would Use Tools in Future Operations

CONCLUSIONS

Participants were given a variety of collaboration tools to use in this exercise. They preferred to use those tools that had the potential to provide the highest levels of SA (domain specific, face-to-face and audio conferencing). They also found these tools to be the most effective.

One surprising finding was the frequent usage of chat and instant messaging. This may be due to the constraints of the exercise or this tool may have been the substitute for electronic mail (email). In the post exercise discussions, email was one of the tools participants would have liked included in the tool suite.

ACKNOLOWDGEMENTS

Work on this paper was prepared through participation in the Advanced Decision Architectures Collaborative Technology Alliance sponsored by the U.S. Army Research Laboratory (ARL) under Cooperative Agreement DAAD19-01-2-0009. The views and conclusions contained herein, however, are those of the authors and should not be interpreted as representing the official policies, either expressed or implied of the ARL or the U. S. Government

REFERENCES

Bolstad, C. A., & Endsley, M. R. (2003). Tools for supporting team collaboration. Paper presented at the Human Factors and Ergonomics 47th Annual Meeting, Denver, Colorado.

EVALUATION OF TUNNEL CONCEPTS FOR ADVANCED AVIATION DISPLAYS

Lawrence J. Prinzel III, Lynda J. Kramer, Jarvis J. Arthur, Randall E. Bailey
NASA Langley Research Center, Hampton, VA, USA

ABSTRACT

Eight 757 commercial airline captains flew 22 approaches using the Reno Sparks 16R Visual Arrival simulated Cat IIIa conditions. Approaches were flown using a synthetic vision display that was chosen as an advanced aviation display to evaluate four tunnel or pathway concepts and compared their efficacy to a baseline condition without a tunnel. Two new "dynamic" tunnel concepts were developed and evaluated in addition to both a minimal and box tunnel concept. The results showed that the tunnel concepts significantly improved pilot performance and situation awareness and lowered workload compared to the baseline condition. The dynamic tunnel concepts were found to be the best candidates for advanced aviation displays. These results are discussed with implications for display design and future research.

Keywords: Synthetic Vision; Situation Awareness; Pathway Displays; Tunnel Displays; Highway-In-The-Sky

INTRODUCTION

Our society is highly dependent on air transportation. In the relatively short span of 100 years, we have progressed from flights of a few hundred feet to routine trips over oceans to distant parts of the world. Speed, altitude, and range all have increased a thousand-fold since that early December morning in 1903. As Leonardo da Vinci observed, "A bird is an instrument working according to mathematical law, which instrument is within the capacity of man to reproduce in its movements." Today, that dream has been realized. The sky is no longer the limit. Now, a new problem visits us. If air traffic demands does triple as predicted within the next 20 years, the relatively low accident rate of less than 2 accidents per million flights will become unacceptable (NASA, 2001). Dramatic steps, therefore, are needed to ensure the unquestioned safety for the traveling public that has made flying the safest mode of transportation.

The NASA Aviation Safety Program (AvSP), at NASA Langley Research Center, has taken on the challenge to "develop and demonstrate technologies that contribute to a reduction in the aviation fatal accident rate by a factor of 5 by year 2007" (NASA, 2001). This NASA Aerospace Technology Enterprise goal will be a difficult one to meet, and joint FAA and NASA research has been focused on several new technologies that together will help make it a reality.

NASA Synthetic Vision System

To help meet national aviation safety goals will require mitigating or eliminating the etiologies of accidents. A significant factor involved in many commercial and general aviation accidents is limited visibility. The ability of a pilot to ascertain critical information through visual perception of the outside environment can be limited by various weather phenomena, such as rain, fog, and snow. Since the beginning of flight, the aviation industry has developed various devices to overcome these low-visibility limitations. These include attitude indicators, navigation aids, Instrument Landing Systems (ILS), moving map displays, and Terrain Awareness Warning Systems (TAWS). All of the aircraft information display concepts developed to date, however, still require the pilot to continuously perform information acquisition and decoding to update and maintain their mental model in order to "stay ahead" of the aircraft when outside visibility is reduced. What this means is that pilots still have to interpret the "coded" (Theunissen, 1997) information and match it to the outside world.

AvSP initiated a new research project to develop technologies to help overcome safety problems associated with limited visibility. The NASA Synthetic Vision System (SVS) project is based on the premise that better pilot situation awareness during low visibility conditions can be achieved by reducing the steps required to build a mental model from disparate pieces of data through the presentation of how the outside world would look to the pilot if their visibility were not restricted. New technological developments in navigation performance, low-cost attitude and heading reference systems, computational capabilities, and graphical displays allow for the prospect of SVS displays for virtually all aircraft classes. SVS display concepts employ computer-generated terrain imagery, on-board databases, and precise position and navigational accuracy to create a three dimensional perspective presentation of the outside world, with necessary and sufficient information and realism, to enable operations equivalent to those of a bright, clear, sunny day regardless of the outside weather condition. The SVS concept includes the intuitive display of intended flight path by tunnel or pathway-in-the-sky presentations. When coupled with a synthetic view of the world, the spatially integrated depiction of the intended aircraft flight path and its relation to the world provides an intuitive, easily interpretable display of flight-critical information for the pilot. The safety outcome of SVS is a display that should help reduce, or even prevent, controlled-flight-into-terrain (CFIT), which is the single greatest contributing factor to fatal worldwide airline and general aviation accidents (Boeing, 1996; Prinzel et al., 2002; 2003; in press). Other safety benefits include reduced runway incursions and loss-of-control accidents (Williams et al., 2001) in addition to significant economic benefits (Hemm, 2000).

Advanced Pathway Displays

Although avionics have advanced significantly since Jimmy Doolittle flew the first "blind" flight in 1929, Theunissen (1997) noted that significant increases in aviation safety are unlikely to come by extrapolating from current display concepts. He further stated that, "new functionality and new technology cannot simply be layered onto previous design concepts, because the current system complexities are already too high. Better human-machine interfaces require a fundamentally new approach" (1997; p.7). Bennet and Flach (1994) argued that such an approach should not focus on development of "idiot-proof" systems because of the infinite potential problem space, but rather should provide the pilot information that would enable successful solution sets to be generated. These displays should present continuous information about spatial constraints rather than command changes to reduce error states, and should show error margins that depict the bounds that the pilot may safety operate in contrast to the compensatory control strategy required by current cockpit instruments. This can be accomplished through the use of "pathway" or "tunnel" displays. Several NASA projects, including SVS, are exploring the use of flight path depiction as key parts of the human-computer interface. Therefore, there is significant need and importance for research conducted toward tunnel concepts usable as part of these advanced aviation displays.

A considerable body of research exists demonstrating the effectiveness of pathway displays for horizontal and vertical guidance and enhancing situation awareness (e.g., Haskell & Wickens, 1993; Williams, 2002). Many of these studies, however, failed to emulate the flight conditions that tunnel displays are postulated to ameliorate (e.g., curved approaches). Rather, often they are conducted using part-task simulations under conditions of low workload (e.g., straight-in approaches). Moreover, the tunnels were presented alone supplemented only by minimal flight instrumentation. Therefore, little evidence is available to guide design for complex graphical displays, such as synthetic vision, when the tunnel interacts with other primary flight symbologies and graphical presentation.

Research Objective

The objective of the present study was to examine several tunnel concepts that have been investigated in past research to determine their efficacy for synthetic vision displays. Synthetic vision was chosen because it represents arguably the most complex graphical display currently being developed and, therefore, any research findings may better generalize to other advanced aviation displays. In addition, two new pathways were conceptualized and evaluated that theoretically represented the best combination of current tunnel formats. Together, four tunnel (box tunnel, minimal "crows feet", dynamic "crows feet", dynamic pathway) and baseline concepts were evaluated. Eight B-757 current major airline Captains flew the Reno, NV Sparks 16R visual arrival, curved approach under CAT IIIa instrument meteorological conditions (IMC); an approach of significant workload and difficulty under such conditions. The scenarios were chosen to best evaluate the four tunnel concepts, as part of the SVS display, under situations posited for a future commercial concept of operation for synthetic vision.

METHOD

Pilot Participants

Eight commercial pilots (ATP), who fly for major commercial airlines, participated in the experiment. All participants were HUD-qualified and were rated B-757 Captains. The HUD requirement was to ensure familiarity with a velocity vector and guidance symbology. All participants also had logged flight time in "glass cockpits" (e.g., A-320; MD-11) other than the B-757; therefore, all participants were familiar with a primary flight display (PFD).

Tunnel Concepts

Four tunnel (box, minimal, dynamic "crow's feet", dynamic pathway) and baseline (i.e., no tunnel) concepts were evaluated (see Figure 1). The "box" tunnel, a concept that is the subject of most of the tunnel research in the literature, consisted of a series of boxes connected at the corners to form a path within which the pilot flies. It was presented out to a length of 10 nm, with no fading. The minimal tunnel concept consisted of a series of "crows feet" presented in each corner of a tunnel segment (essentially a truncated box). The tunnel presentation was 5 tunnel segments per nautical mile (nm) with a total length of 3 nm, and faded gradually to invisibility over the last nautical mile. The third concept, dynamic "crows feet", allowed the "crows feet" to grow as a function of path error. Therefore, the pilots are given feedback as to where they are in the tunnel and if they are close to flying out of the tunnel. The idea of the dynamic tunnel was that if the pilot is flying in the center of the tunnel, there should be the smallest amount of clutter. However, if there exists appreciable path error, the tunnel walls would "grow" to help the pilot gauge where the boundaries of the tunnel are. This helps to overcome a frequent criticism of "low clutter" tunnels. The fourth concept, dynamic pathway, was a variation of the dynamic "crow's feet" concept in which the floor of the tunnel was presented at all times. For both the dynamic pathway and dynamic "crow's feet", when the pilot left the tunnel, the tunnel would change to a "trough" and resemble a box tunnel with the exception that the tunnel would open to "invite" the pilot back into the tunnel. All concepts and the baseline were paired with a navigation display with a Terrain Awareness Warning System (TAWS).

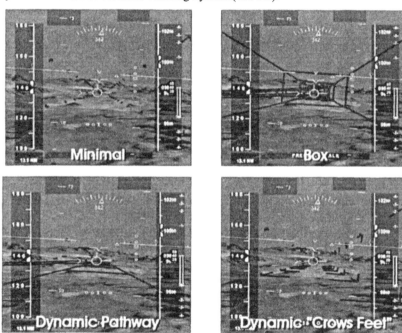

Figure 1. Four Tunnel Concepts

Experimental Task

Pilot participants were required to fly the Sparks Visual Arrival to Runway 16 at Reno airport (RNO). Twenty-two experimental runs were completed during the experimental session. The runs differed from each on the (1) initial starting position outside the tunnel, (2) the guidance symbology, and (3) task scenario. There were three initial starting positions that were randomly varied across trials to force the pilot to re-enter the tunnel on each run. The guidance symbology was also randomly assigned and factorially combined with the four tunnel concepts. However, these results are not discussed here and the results are confined only to the flight director "ball" that is standard on many current aviation displays. Finally, there were two scenarios required of the pilot participants. The first was the nominal Sparks 16R Visual Approach, but flown under IMC, and the second was a "cut-the-corner" scenario in which the pilot was instructed by Air Traffic Control (ATC) to leave the tunnel and fly "direct to" the McRAN waypoint 90 degrees opposite the KNB16 FMS waypoint. The latter scenario required the pilot to utilize the navigation display (i.e., using the predictor noodle to acquire the heading) and later to use the guidance symbology and velocity vector to re-enter the tunnel at the McRAN waypoint. Afterward, the pilot was cleared to continue the approach and land on runway 16R.

Simulation Facility

The experiment was conducted in the Visual Imaging Simulator for Transport Aircraft Systems (VISTAS) III simulator at NASA Langley Research Center. The single pilot fixed based simulator consists of a 144° by 30° Out-The-Window (OTW) scene, a simulated HUD, a large field head-down display (HDD) and pilot input controls. The OTW scene was used only during training. The pilot controls in the VISTAS III workstation are a left side arm controller, left/right throttle controls, rudder pedals, toe brakes, a PC track ball for display-related pilot inputs, and a voice recognition system (VRS). The VRS is a speaker-independent voice recognition system that provided a robust, rapidly reconfigurable pilot-vehicle interface. It was also used to provide automated alerts, warnings, and simulated ATC commands. The aircraft model was a B-757, and both the approach and departure speed targets were 138 knots. All scenarios were flown with moderate turbulence. Auto throttles were used, flaps were set to 30 degrees, and the landing gear was down.

RESULTS

After each run, pilots were administered a run questionnaire consisting of the USAF Revised Workload Estimation Scale (Ames & George, 1993), Situation Awareness Rating Technique (SART) (Taylor, 1990), and six Likert-type (7-point) questions specific to tunnel evaluation. Simple ANOVAs and Student-Newman-Keuls post-hoc tests were performed. Alpha was set at .05.

Mental Workload

There was a significant effect found for tunnel with respect to workload, $F(4,28) = 43.40$. The baseline condition (4.167) was rated significantly higher in workload than the four tunnel concepts. The minimal tunnel (3.167) was also rated significantly higher in workload than the box (2.583), dynamic pathway (2.542), and dynamic "crow's feet" (2.417), which did not differ from each other.

Situation Awareness

There was a significant effect found for tunnel with respect to the combined SART ratings, $F(4,28) = 11.41$. The no tunnel, baseline condition (3.417) was rated significantly lower in situation awareness (SA) than the four tunnel conditions. In addition, the minimal tunnel concept (5.083) was rated significantly lower than the box (7.167), dynamic pathway (7.458), and dynamic "crows feet" (7.542) which did not differ from each other.

Run Questionnaire

There was a significant effect found for several run questions asked. First, there was a significant effort found for SA, ("As I performed the task, my awareness of where I was in the tunnel was ___."), $F(3,21) = 22.07$. The minimal tunnel (2.833) was rated significantly lower in SA than the three other tunnel concepts. The dynamic pathway (5.00) was also rated significantly lower than the box (5.9167) and dynamic "crows feet" (6.0417), which did not differ from each other.

A second SA question asked concerned, "As I performed the task, my awareness of upcoming turns was ___." An ANOVA found a significant effect for tunnel, $F(2,21) = 5.06$. The minimal tunnel concept (3.292) was rated significantly lower than the dynamic "crow's feet" (5.208), dynamic pathway (5.208) and box (5.542) tunnel concepts.

A third question asked, "As I performed the task, my level of flight path control and performance was ___." A significant effect was found for display concepts (including baseline), $F(4,28) = 27.05$. The baseline condition (3.583) was rated significantly lower than the four tunnel concepts, which did not differ from each other.

A final question for tunnel evaluation was, "As I performed the task, my ability to intercept the path and re-enter the tunnel was ___". A significant effect was found for tunnel, $F(3,21) = 17.54$. Participants rated the minimal tunnel concept (3.667) significantly lower than the box dynamic pathway (5.083), dynamic "crow's feet" (5.333), and box tunnel (5.333) concepts. The three tunnel concepts were not statistically different from each other.

Flight Path Control

Flight path control was analyzed for the nominal task run for root-mean-squared error (RMSE). Because guidance symbology may confound flight path accuracy, the results were analyzed as symbology-tunnel combinations yielding six display concepts plus the baseline (i.e., no tunnel, ball symbology). An ANOVA found a significant effect for lateral RMSE across guidance symbology-tunnel combinations, $F(6,42) = 6.839$ (Figure 2). The baseline condition was found to be significantly worse for lateral flight path control (132.63 feet). No statistical differences were found for lateral RMSE between the three tunnel concepts regardless of the guidance symbology. No significant differences were found for vertical path error across the display concepts including the baseline condition ($\underline{p} > .05$).

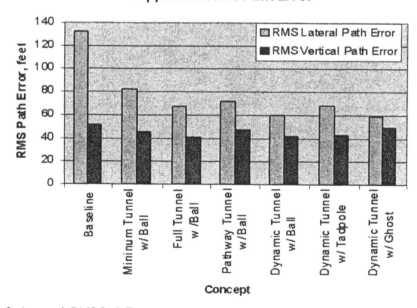

Figure 2. Approach RMS Path Error

Semi-Structured Interview

A semi-structured interview was conducted after the final experimental run. A number of Likert (1 to 7) questions were asked but space does not allow a detailed summary of the results. However, several interesting results were found. For example, although there was no significant difference in rating for effectiveness of tunnels for straight path segments, pilots rated the minimal tunnel concept (4.00) significantly less effective for curved path segments than the box (5.4), dynamic pathway (6.2), and dynamic "crows feet" (6.4), $F(3,28) = 10.09$.

Another interesting finding was that pilots rated the baseline (5.6) and minimal tunnel (4.5) concepts to have significantly more workload to intercept the path during the "cut-the-corner" scenario, $F(3,35) = 43.56$. There were no statistical differences between the box (3.0), dynamic pathway (1.9) and dynamic "crows feet" (1.8) concepts.

SA-SWORD

Overall, pilots ranked the dynamic "crow's feet" first in overall preference followed by dynamic pathway, box, and minimal tunnel. A distant fifth was the baseline condition which several pilots noted after flying the tunnel displays remarking, "how am I ever to go back to an EADI [electronic attitude direction indicator] after flying these displays?" An analysis of the results from the Situation Awareness Workload Dominance Scale (SA-SWORD (Vidulich & Hughes, 1991) confirmed this ranking. An ANOVA found a significant effect for tunnel, $F(4, 28)=84.369$ for the SA-SWORD paired comparison measure. Post hoc tests showed 4 distinct subgroups formed: 1) Dynamic; 2) Pathway; 3) Full and Minimum; and 4) Baseline. The Dynamic tunnel was ranked as having the greatest SA and Baseline (no tunnel) the worst. The ranking from highest SA to lowest was: Dynamic tunnel, pathway tunnel, full tunnel, minimum tunnel and baseline (no tunnel).

DISCUSSION

The results of the study indicated that all the tunnel concepts were better than having no tunnel at all. However, the minimal tunnel was found to be the least effective of the tunnel concepts in general. Although the "box" tunnel was effective, it had significant limitations in terms of excessive clutter while inside the tunnel. The dynamic pathway and dynamic "crows feet" tunnel concepts were the most effective, and were judged to be superior and similar in terms of situation awareness and workload. However, overall, the dynamic "crow's feet" tunnel was ranked the highest and is the recommended tunnel concept for future synthetic vision displays. These results can also be generalized to other advanced graphical aviation displays. Research is currently being conducted with head-up (Figure 3) and full-color, stereoscopic helmet-mounted displays to further evaluate these results.

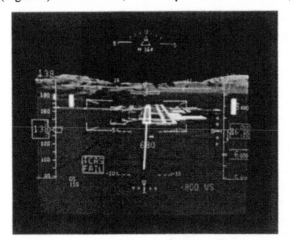 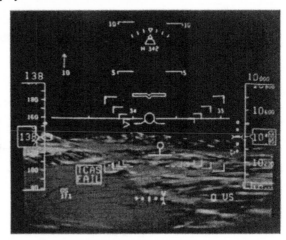

Figure 3. NASA Synthetic Vision Head-Up Display

REFERENCES

Haskell, I.D., & Wickens, C.D. (1993). Two- and three-dimensional displays for aviation: A theoretical and empirical comparison. International Journal of Aviation Psychology, 3, 87-109.

National Aeronautics and Space Administration (2001). Aerospace Technology Enterprise. Washington, D.C.: NASA.

Williams, D., Waller, M., Koelling, J., Burdette, D., Doyle, T., Capron, W., Barry, J., & Gifford, R. (2001). Concept of operations for commercial and business aircraft synthetic vision systems. NASA Langley Research Center: NASA Technical Memorandum TM-2001-211058.

Prinzel, L.J., Comstock, J.R., Glaab, L.J., Kramer, L.J., Arthur, J.J., & Barry, J.S. (in press). The efficacy of head-down and head-up synthetic vision display concepts for retro- and forward-fit of commercial aircraft. International Journal of Aviation Psychology.

Prinzel, L.J., Hughes, M.F., Arthur, J.J., Kramer, L.J., Glaab, L.J., Bailey, R.E., Parrish, R.V., & Uenking, M.D. (2003). Synthetic Vision CFIT Experiments for GA and Commercial Aircraft: "A Picture Is Worth A Thousand Lives". Proceedings of the Human Factors & Ergonomics Society, 47, 164-168

Prinzel, L.J., Kramer, L.J., Comstock, J.R., Bailey, R.E., Hughes, M.F., & Parrish, R.V. (2002). NASA synthetic vision EGE flight test. Proceedings of the Annual Human Factors and Ergonomics Meeting, 46, 135-139.

Williams, K.W. (2002). Impact of aviation highway-in-the-sky displays on pilot situation awareness. Human Factors, 44, 18-27.

Design Concepts for Distributed Work Systems:
One Brigade's Approach to Building Team Mental Models

Jodi Heintz Obradovich
Philip J. Smith
Cognitive Systems Engineering Laboratory
The Ohio State University

ABSTRACT

Research on teams engaged in problem-solving tasks suggests that they can generate representations of a problem that differ from those developed by an individual working alone, potentially providing richer or more effective insights into the problem. In this paper, we discuss issues surrounding the building of team mental models that were gained through a series of investigations that included field studies and structured interviews. The results of one U.S. Army Brigade process that enables the sharing of information and expert knowledge in the complex cognitive activity of planning for battlefield operations are presented. Design concepts to support distributed work and the building of common ground and team mental models are suggested.

Keywords: Collaborative planning; Distributed work systems; Teamwork; Team mental models; Common ground

INTRODUCTION

Research on teams engaged in complex problem solving and decision making suggests that teams can generate representations of a problem that differ from those developed by an individual working alone, potentially providing richer or more effective insights into the problem (Dunbar, 1998). This is possible because teams may bring multiple sources of knowledge and experience, a wider variety of perspectives, and the potential synergy associated with collaborative activity (Morgan & Lassiter, 1992)

Teams, however, also add complexities to the decision-making process not seen at the individual level. For example, within a team individual members may have unique information or perceptions about different task elements or cues, but those members may not share their unique information in group discussion (e.g., Stasser & Titus, 1987; Grigone & Hastie, 1993). Different areas of expertise are distributed among the team members so that even when they have access to the same information, they may evaluate it much differently and from different perspectives. Finally, the cognitive burden can become greater for the members of a team performing a decision-making task than it is for an individual decision maker. Team members must engage in three activities simultaneously. They must *recall* information (either from their memories or notes), must *exchange* that information, either by receiving or giving it to others in the group, and they must *process* that information, which involves the social and cognitive implications of that information and storing it in memory. Thus, it is possible that engaging in one of the activities interferes with a person's ability to engage fully in the other two (e.g., Lamm & Trommsdorff, 1973).

Other issues (e.g., trust in others, cooperation, coordination, and power or status differences among team members) also arise within teams (Guzzo, 1995; Wittenbaum & Stasser, 1996). Thus, understanding the process and means by which teams arrive at decisions requires going beyond a simple extension of individual decision-making practices. One needs to consider a number of factors unique to team decision making (e.g., group dynamics, interpersonal communication skills, conflict, competition, and hidden agendas). Also, because members of a team are individuals with different backgrounds, beliefs, and attitudes as well as different interpretations of events, plans and goals, the team must work to achieve a shared perspective or common ground (Clark, 1996).

One way of dealing with some of these issues that are central to successful teamwork during problem solving and decision making is to design tasks that help to ensure that individuals share their information and knowledge in an appropriate and efficient way. This paper describes a process called the Red Hat War Game that is used by one U.S. Army Brigade and illustrates a way in which one organization has incorporated into their planning process an event that enables the building of a team mental model by improving their information and knowledge sharing in a very goal-directed way. As the team members participate in this process, they are able to share different representations and insights into the critical elements of their planning and decision-making exercise, with each member bringing to bear his or her expertise and knowledge.

STUDY CONTEXT

The following sections of this paper are intended to help the readers better understand the context of U.S. Army decision-making process in which the Red Hat Wargame is embedded, so that they are able to understand the overall findings of this study. What is described below is the process defined in the U.S. Army field manuals. The Results section describes the addition to the process that one Army Brigade employs.

The Military Decision Making Process

The military decision-making process (MDMP) is the doctrinal analytical approach to problem solving and decision making that assists the commander and staff in developing estimates (significant facts, events, and conclusions based on analytical data) and a warfighting plan. The MDMP consists of seven steps that include receipt of mission, mission analysis, course of action (COA) development, COA analysis (war game), COA comparison, COA approval, and orders production.

Mission Analysis. It is during the Mission Analysis step (Step 2) to this process that possible threat COAs are determined based on evaluation of the battlefield environment, battlefield effects (e.g., terrain, weather, infrastructure, and demographics), and doctrinal threat depicting how the threat operates when unconstrained by the effects of the environment. One product of this step is the situation template (SITTEMP), which graphically depict expected threat dispositions. These templates are useful in depicting points at which the threat might adopt branches or sequels (alternative actions) to the main COA when the threat might be especially vulnerable, or other key points in the battle, such as actions that the threat might take against the friendly force.

War Game. Step 4 of the MDMP is the COA analysis, or war game. This phase identifies which COA accomplishes the mission with minimum casualties while positioning the force to retain the initiative for future operations. The war game is a disciplined process that attempts to visualize the flow of a battle. The process considers friendly dispositions, strengths, and weaknesses; enemy assets and probable COAs; and characteristics of the battlefield. It focuses the staff's attention on each phase of the operation, and is a repetitive process of action, reaction, and counteraction. The purpose of the wargaming effort is to stimulate ideas and provide insights to the staff that might not otherwise be discovered. One of the benefits of the war game is that it provides a common vision for the flow of the battle for all staff, enabling them to better anticipate events that occur during execution.

METHOD

A variety of methods were employed in order to arrive at an understanding of the impact of the process that one U.S. Army Brigade has incorporated into their planning and decision-making process. The investigators observed the Brigade as they conducted the Military Decision Making Process (MDMP) activity during a Warfighter Exercise and a National Training Center (NTC) rotation. Following the exercise, structured interviews with key Brigade officers were conducted in an effort to collect data to verify the investigator's understanding of the event and to provide further details of the Red Hat War Game process.

Following these interviews, the investigators described to U.S. Army officers from other Army units the Red Hat War Game process. These officers were asked for their thoughts and reactions concerning both positive and negative aspects and impacts of such a process. The investigators then re-interviewed some of the officers of the Brigade, sharing with them the reactions of the "non-Brigade" officers.

RESULTS

The results of the investigation reported here enable the researchers to arrive at design concepts that need to be considered when designing processes for the building of common ground and team mental models in the development of distributed work systems. (For a more complete description of design concepts for distributed work systems, see Obradovich & Smith, 2003).

Designing tasks to enable information and knowledge sharing

In one Army Brigade, the officers have incorporated into their planning standard operating procedures (PSOP) an additional step that they refer to as the "Red Hat War Game." The PSOP defines the purpose of this exercise as one "to refine and improve the ECOAs [Enemy Courses of Action] and ensure that the entire planning team is fully 'read-in' on these ECOAs" (Planning Standard Operating Procedures (PSOP), 2003, p. 81).

The Red Hat War Game is incorporated in the Receipt of Mission phase (step 1) of the MDMP. It follows the Staff Intelligence Preparation of the Battlefield (IPB), a systematic, continuous process of analyzing the threat and environment in a specific geographic area. The IPB process applies when rough ECOAs (Figure 3) and situation templates (SITTEMPS) are developed. Situation templates are graphic depictions of expected threat dispositions should he adopt a particular course of action. These templates are useful in depicting where the threat might adopt branches and sequels (FM34-130, Intelligence Preparation of the Battlefield, 1994). The participants in the Red Hat War Game include the duty Battle Staff representatives from all sections, units, and Battlefield Operating Systems (BOSs), which include intelligence, maneuver, fire support, air defense, mobility/countermobility/survivability, combat service support, and command and control (Figure 1).

The BOS experts bring their specialized knowledge of their particular BOS systems to the war game as they take on the role of their enemy counterparts ("Red Hats") and discuss how and when they would employ the available red assets to defeat the "generic" friendly Course of Action (COA) that has been developed for the particular scenario being planned. The BOS representatives play the red BOS commanders. They add graphics to the enemy SITTEMP as needed to include the necessary elements (e.g., unmanned aerial vehicles, named areas of interest, air avenues of approach, supply routes, locations of command and control).

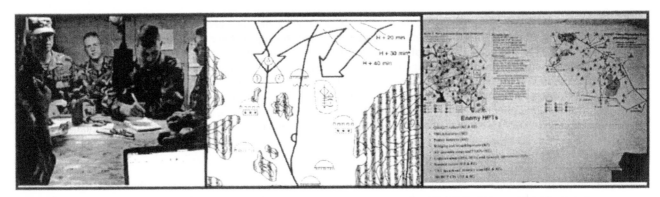

Figure 1. Officers during a Red   Figure 2. Situation Template   Figure 3. Enemy Courses of Action
Hat War Game   (SITTEMP)   (ECOAs)

The end state of the Red Hat War Game as defined in the PSOP is when "the Battle Staff has produced at least two fully developed ECOAs (Figure 3) to carry forward into wargaming and the [Operations] Order. Additionally, the Battle Staff has a common understanding of the ECOAs" (Planning Standard Operating Procedures (PSOP), 2003, p. 82).

This Red Hat Wargaming process allows the team to share different representations of and insights into the problem, which might not occur until much later, if at all, within the doctrinal MDMP process in which a single individual, the Assistant Chief of Staff (S2), is responsible for all matters concerning military intelligence, and security intelligence, including the development of the ECOAs and SITTEMPS that are used in the friendly wargaming step (Step 4) of the MDMP. This end result is emphasized in the following comments.

The Executive Officer (XO), who is the commander's principal assistant for directing, coordinating, supervising, and training the staff states that "...getting the Red Hat War Game and the IPB process out early allows you to save time later down the road because you're not waiting for the S2 to get all his stuff together."

The Assistant Chief of Staff (S3), the principal staff officer for all matters concerning training, operations and plans, and force development and modernization, suggests that "...when we get to the war game what should happen is the better Red Hat you do, the better course of action, the more detailed you are as we go through that three-step process, saves you time on that war game because as you look at the Red Hat and say, 'The dude is going to drop chemical on me, or we believe he's going to drop chemical at this target at me because my artillery will be positioned there.' Okay, when we get to the war game, your artillery better not be there, we better have put them somewhere else. When we come to the war game it's a non-event. Go ahead, drop it. I don't care. It's going somewhere where we're not. But, if you don't do that then the war game expands and you've just killed my artillery because he's 'chemed' and now all my force ratios are screwed up, so the nastier he gets the more you're forced to think about your own blue actions. I don't know of anyone else that does it that way."

Thus, by bringing together the various team members who have the necessary specialized knowledge and by giving them a task that necessitates the application of that knowledge to the planning process, the potential exists for developing comprehensive ECOAs and SITTEMPS that incorporate knowledge that might otherwise be left uncommunicated.

Potential for Groupthink?

During the interviews with Army officers from units who were unfamiliar with the Red Hat War Game, every participant raised concern that the Red Hat War Game process could lead to an environment conducive to groupthink. Janis (1972) defines groupthink as "a mode of thinking that people engage in when they are deeply involved in a cohesive in-group, when the members' strivings for unanimity override their motivation to realistically appraise alternative courses of action" (1972, p. 9). He suggests that groups who share a high degree of cohesiveness and 'esprit de corps' have a susceptibility to replacing independent critical thinking with groupthink, resulting in a failure to evaluate all their alternatives and options.

The Executive Officer (XO) of the Brigade, in response to the concerns regarding the potential for the Red Hat War Game to result in groupthink, states that "There is a potential for [groupthink], but I believe the expertise and involvement from the BOS representatives is worth the risk. The classic problem you face in any collaborative planning process is finding the 'sweet spot' where you optimize the positive contributions of a larger staff without creating a hive mind." This suggests that the value of involving members of the team with expertise in different aspects of the task may outweigh the risk of groupthink.

One method for countering the groupthink effect is to make each member of the group a "critical evaluator" (Janis, 1972). This Red Hat War Game represents an indirect method for introducing needed cognitive conflict (i.e., controversy over the best way to achieve the team's goal), as the ECOAs may bring into question aspects of the plan that have been developed for the "friendly" forces. This is something the literature suggests can improve decision-making effectiveness (Amason, 1996; Jehn, 1995). More specifically, "cognitive conflict stems from the existence of multiple plans or scenarios for achieving group goals," (DeVine, 1999, p. 612). This conflict increases the members' motivation to describe and justify their positions. The goal of using this method is to encourage the questioning of underlying assumptions and the consideration of alternatives.

Team mental model during battle execution

The S3 of this Brigade suggests that the "Red Hat War Game...really puts everyone in the same frame of mind...." The S2 states that "it gives the whole staff a pretty good feeling about what's going on in the battle. When they see this stuff, okay, if the enemy does this, it's the commander's decision point.... Everyone has a portion of the whole plan, including the enemy situation, and is very aware of what's going on." One planner/battle captain states: "For the operations guys, at least the battle captains, it gives them a better idea of what's going on as they start seeing the red icons start showing up [during the execution phase of the exercise]. They kind of have an idea of what the enemy is gonna do [because of the red hat war game] and whether or not that's actually happening. Besides just making it clear for them, it means they don't have to harass the S2 every two minutes on what does this mean. They can come up with the analysis on their own. It also, if we had time to get more detail, it would allow us to get a better "blue" plan just because we have something more specific to fight off of."

DESIGN CONCEPTS

The findings of this study lead the investigators to propose design concepts for distributed work systems as they apply to designing systems that enable the development of team mental models.

Distributed Work Systems – Design Concept 1. To deal with issues arising within decision-making teams, such as trust in others, cooperation, coordination, and power or status differences among members, assign tasks that help to ensure that individuals share their information and knowledge in appropriate and efficient ways.

Distributed Work Systems – Design Concept 2. Design and assign tasks that induce or influence the team members to engage in desirable behaviors and interactions, such as cognitive conflict, that are likely to improve decision-making effectiveness by encouraging the examination of underlying assumptions and the consideration of alternatives.

CONCLUSION

Problem solving and decision making in complex, cognitive tasks such as military battle planning events involve team members who have different information, knowledge, and expertise. As the team members share their unique expert knowledge, teams can potentially provide richer or more effective insights into a problem or decision than that of individuals working alone. One U. S. Army Brigade has expanded one step of the doctrinal military decision-making process to take advantage of the benefits that teamwork can provide. By conducting the Red Hat War Game, the process allows the building of a team mental model earlier in the decision making, allowing the opportunity for the sharing of information and expert knowledge to lead to an even more robust decision.

As a result of this field study during a Warfighter Exercise, an NTC rotation, and follow-on interviews, the investigators have arrived at design concepts to enable the building of team mental models in distributed work systems. The concepts included in this paper provide suggestions for process and interaction design.

ACKNOWLEDGEMENTS

This research was sponsored by the U. S. Army Research Laboratory under the Collaborative Technology Alliance Program, Cooperative Agreement DAAD19-01-2-0009.

REFERENCES

Amason, A.C. (1996). Distinguishing the effects of functional and dysfunctional conflict on strategic decision making: Resolving a paradox for top management teams. *Academy of Management Journal*, 39, 123-148.

Clark, H. H. (1996). Using language. Cambridge: University Press.

DeVine, D.J. (1999). Effects of cognitive ability, task knowledge, information sharing, and conflict on group decision-making effectiveness. *Small Group Research*, 30(5), 608-634.

Dunbar, K. (1998). Problem solving. In W. Bechtel & G. Graham (Eds.), A companion to cognitive science (p. 289-298). Malden, MA: Blackwell Publishers.

Grigone, D. & Hastie, R. (1993). The common knowledge effect: Information sharing and group judgment. *Journal of Personality and Social Psychology*, 65, 959-974.

Guzzo, R.A. (1995). Introduction: At the intersection of team effectiveness and decision making. In R.A. Guzzo, E. Salas & Associates (Eds.), Team effectiveness and decision making in organizations (pp. 1-8). San Francisco, CA: Jossey Bass Publishers.

Janis, I.L. (1972). Victims of groupthink. Boston: Houghton Mifflin.

Jehn, K.A. (1995). A multimethod examination of the benefits and detriments of intragroup conflict. *Administrative Science Quarterly*, 40, 256-282.

Lamm, H. & Trommsdorff, G. (1973). Group versus individual performance on tasks requiring ideational proficiency (brainstorming): A review. *European Journal of Social Psychology*, 3, 367-387.

Morgan, B.B. & Lassiter, D.L. (1992). Team composition and staffing. In R.W. Swezey & E. Salas (Ed.), Teams: Their training and performance (p. 75-100). Norwood, NJ: Ablex Publishing Corporation.

Obradovich, J.H. & Smith, P.J. (2003). Design Concepts for Distributed Work Systems. Technical Paper. Cognitive Systems Engineering. The Ohio State University.

Stasser, G. & Titus, W. (1987). Effects of information load and percentage of shared information during group discussion. *Journal of Personality and Social Psychology*, 53, 81-93.

Wittenbaum, G.M. & Stasser, G. (1996). Management of information in small groups. In J.L. Nye & A.M. Brower (Eds.), What's *social* about social cognition? Research on socially shared cognition in small groups. (p. 3-28). LEA.

INCREASING SITUATION AWARENESS OF DISMOUNTED SOLDIERS VIA DIRECTIONAL CUEING

**J. Christopher Brill, Richard D. Gilson, Mustapha Mouloua,
Peter A. Hancock, and Peter I. Terrence**
University of Central Florida

ABSTRACT

A current goal of the US Army's Land Warrior System is reliable communication of the presence and location of threats. To obtain the greatest benefit from such a system, it should be omnipresent, covert, and it should be usable in a variety of combat scenarios. The authors compared the relative benefits of 3-dimensional audio and wearable tactile display systems in meeting these demands. Based upon the literature, the authors have concluded that although 3-dimensional audio cueing might provide slightly better spatial resolution in one dimension, a tactile-based solution is ultimately of greater utility in all dimensions. Benefits of a tactile-based system include greater overall accuracy in directional cueing, less competition for cognitive-perceptual resources, and virtually silent operation.

Keywords: Touch; Tactile; Displays; Cueing; Situation Awareness; Alarms

INTRODUCTION

Getting situation-relevant information to dismounted soldiers is key to achieving victory on the battlefield. Indeed, the reliable communication of information regarding the location and severity of threats is part of the goal of the Land Warrior System currently in development by the US Army. The challenge in accomplishing this task is designing a system capable of providing information in two diametrically opposed scenarios. The first is full-fledged combat, a circumstance replete with a barrage of noise and context-irrelevant signals. The second is that of night covert operations, scenarios in which maintaining silence and the cover of darkness are mandatory for success. Despite the apparent disparities between these scenarios, the information most relevant to soldiers remains the same: locations of threats as well as assets. Due to the critical nature of threat information, it is an absolute necessity to present it through omnipresent communication channels.

At first glance, the two scenarios above might seem to require radically different solutions for displaying threat information to dismounted soldiers. Nevertheless, the authors propose a common solution that would effectively and covertly alert soldiers to the presence of threats while simultaneously cueing their approximate locations. Due to the constraints of the aforementioned scenarios, the solution cannot include visually based systems. Vision is not omnipresent; visual displays of alerts and alarms only "work" when the operator looks in their general direction. In addition, use of light-based systems during night operations negates the advantage gained through the use of night vision equipment. Therefore, the proposed system must appeal to one of two remaining omnipresent sensory systems through which one can derive directional information: audition or touch. However, a comparison of human perceptual and attentional capabilities reveals that, ultimately, a tactile display system may provide the best design solution.

Providing Directional Cueing Information

Auditory and tactile display systems are both capable of conveying the presence and the direction of threats and assets, each one with its own set of advantages and limitations. For example, several attempts have been made at providing 3-dimensional spatial information both aurally and tactually, but they have achieved limited success. Users of binaural 3-dimensional audio systems frequently experience front-back reversals, wherein sounds from behind the user are actually perceived as being in front. In addition, the ability of the auditory system to discriminate among sounds located at different elevations is poor. People often must tilt their heads to localize sounds, especially when their sources are at elevations greater than −13 to +20 degrees from the horizon (Buser & Imbert, 1992), although our ability to resolve sound locations in the horizontal plane is of greater accuracy (McKinley & Ericson, 1997).

As with 3-dimensional audio systems, some success has been obtained with tactile-based systems. Perhaps the most well known of these is the Tactile Situation Awareness System (TSAS), a wearable tactile display intended to provide spatial orientation cues (Rupert, 2000). To aid in the development of TSAS, Cholewiak, Collins, and Brill (2001) conducted a study to evaluate the spatial resolution for vibration applied to the torso. They used wearable displays consisting of eight small vibrating devices called tactors, spaced equidistant across the abdomen and arranged to represent the points of the compass (i.e., navel = "north," spine = "south"). The results showed that participants were very accurate in localizing stimuli applied to the naval and spine (nearly 100%), but accuracy was lower for localizing stimuli on the sides. In a follow-up experiment, the authors found that a six-tactor array improved accuracy over that of the eight-tactor array (97% versus 92%, respectively; Cholewiak, Brill, & Schwab, in press). It was also found that the ambiguities regarding localization of vibratory stimuli on the sides could be resolved by modulating vibration frequency. By providing unique sensations in the "east" and "west" positions, significant improvements in localization accuracy (to approximately 95%) were produced, even with an eight-tactor display. Although tactile displays might be somewhat restricted in terms of the number of loci that can be accurately resolved in the horizontal plane, the sense of touch boasts a significant advantage over audition in regards to accurately perceiving stimuli in the vertical plane and in circumventing the problem of front-back reversals.

Attention and Tactile Displays

Use of tactile communication systems might have additional advantages over auditory displays, particularly pertaining to the combat scenario. The literature suggests that tactile communication might avoid potential conflicts in sharing cognitive resources, a problem that could arise with auditory alarms (Wickens, 1984). Although Wickens' model of attention (1984) lacks an allocation of resources to the sense of touch, there is little ambiguity regarding the effects of resource sharing between tasks appealing to the same sensory modality. It is unlikely that soldiers will be able to send and receive verbal communications while simultaneously attending to an auditory alarm amidst the noise and stress of combat. Considering the likelihood of task saturation in the auditory channel, a tactile system holds promise not only because of its inherent qualities, but also because it should not interfere with vision or audition (Parkes & Coleman, 1990; Wickens, 1984; Wickens, Sandry, & Vidulich, 1983). Therefore, it is much more reasonable to suspect that soldiers will be able to receive and attend to tactile information (versus auditory information) due to the lack of competition for mental resources and in the relative absence of cross-sensory masking. As information received tactually should not compete with other signals for mental resources, its impact on mental workload is likely minimal.

A Case for a Covert Communications System

The concept of covert alarms refers to alarms that are not readily detectable by persons other than the intended recipient, which is the essence of tactile communication. Tactile alarms are silent in a world where noise means death. They require no light in worlds where sources of light make an individual a target. A comparison of the relative advantages and disadvantages of tactile and auditory threat cueing systems suggest that a tactile-based solution would best meet the criteria for utility across combat situations. The following points summarize the benefits of a tactile-based solution:

1) Tactile alarms are omni-directional and are especially effective given that the human sensory system is highly sensitive to tactile stimulation. Differential placement of tactile stimulators can provide a very useful low-bandwidth, silent, multi-source communication system.
2) Based upon data from Cholewiak, Collins, and Brill (2001), a tactile alarm system could provide directional information at loci separated by 45 degrees azimuth with good accuracy. This range could potentially be refined with modification of the stimulus parameters at critical loci (Cholewiak et al., in press) and some training. The system would circumvent the sensory limitations of binaural directional cueing. Limited directional information could also be presented in the vertical axis without the ambiguities or perceptual errors associated with 3-dimensional audio cues.
3) Multiple resource theories of attention (e.g., Wickens, 1984) suggest that it is easier to attend to signals appealing to different sensory modalities than multiple signals appealing to the same modality. On this basis, tactile alarms once again provide a significant advantage over auditory alarms wherein they theoretically tap into a different resource pool than that of traditional auditory or visual communication. Likewise, they are less likely to increase mental workload, as would auditory alarms.

CONCLUSION

The proposed system could establish a novel communication system for sending covert messages to soldiers in combat situations, especially during missions requiring stealth. By using tactile communication channels, the system offers a potential solution to the information overload problems associated with the technologically enhanced 21st century soldier.

REFERENCES

Buser, P. & Imbert, M. (1992). Audition. The MIT Press: Cambridge, MA.

Cholewiak, R. W., Brill, J. C., & Schwab, A. (in press). Vibrotactile localization on the abdomen: Effects of place and space. Perception and Psychophysics. Manuscript accepted for publication June 2003.

Cholewiak, R. W., Collins, A. A., & Brill, J. C. (2001). Vibrotactile spatial resolution in linear arrays. Abstracts of the Psychonomic Society: 42nd Annual Meeting, Orlando, FL.

McKinley, R. L., & Ericson, M. A. (1997). Flight demonstration of a 3-D auditory display. In Robert H. Gilkey and Timothy R. Anderson (Eds.) Binaural and spatial hearing in real and virtual environments (pp 683-699). Lawrence Erlbaum Associates, Inc: Hillsdale, NJ.

Parkes, A. M., & Coleman, N. (1990). Route guidance systems: A comparison of methods of presenting directional information to the driver. In E. J. Lovesey (Ed.), Contemporary ergonomics 1990 (pp. 480-485). London: Taylor & Francis.

Rupert, A. H. (2000). Tactile Situation Awareness System: Proprioceptive prostheses for sensory deficiencies. Aviation, Space, & Environmental Medicine, 71 (9, Sect 2, Suppl), A92-A99.

Wickens, C. D. (1984). Processing resources in attention. In R. Parasuraman and D. R. Davies (Eds.), Varieties of attention. Orlando, FL: Academic Press.

Wickens, C. D., Sandry, D., & Vidulich, M. (1983). Compatibility and resource competition between modalities of input, output, and central processing. Human Factors, 25, 227-248.

ASSESSING THE IMPACT OF A NEW AIR TRAFFIC CONTROL INSTRUCTION ON FLIGHT CREW ACTIVITY

Carine Hébraud
Sofréavia

Nayen Pène and Laurence Rognin
STERIA

Eric Hoffman and Karim Zeghal
Eurocontrol Experimental Centre

ABSTRACT

Airborne spacing for sequencing purposes was investigated from the flight deck perspective in a real time experiment. The objective was to assess the impact of initial conditions on the spacing task performance. Pilots' feedback was positive in terms of perceived benefits and task efficiency. The spacing task was achieved successfully despite a (still acceptable) workload increase. The initial spacing had no impact on flight crews' activity (assessed through manual speed adjustments). To broaden the activity analysis and to get an objective assessment of the impact of the spacing task on situation awareness, the next experiment will include the investigation of pilots' monitoring activity.

Keywords: Airborne spacing; Real-time experiment; Flight crew activity; Situation awareness

INTRODUCTION

The key driver of the study is to increase controller availability through a better allocation of spacing tasks between controller and flight crew. The principle of airborne spacing considered here is to provide the controller with a set of new spacing instructions for sequencing purposes. Through these new instructions, the flight crew is tasked to acquire and maintain a given spacing to a preceding aircraft (the target). This allocation of spacing tasks to flight crew – denoted airborne spacing – is expected to increase controller availability and to improve safety, which in turn could enable better efficiency and/or, depending on airspace constraints, more capacity. In addition, it is expected that flight crew would gain in awareness and anticipation by taking an active part in the management of their situation with respect to a designated traffic. The motivation is neither to "transfer problems" nor to "give more freedom" to flight crew, but really to identify a more effective task distribution beneficial to all parties. Airborne spacing assumes new surveillance capabilities (e.g. ADS-B) along with new airborne functions (ASAS).

STATE OF THE ART

Airborne spacing for arrival flows of aircraft was initially studied from a theoretical perspective through mathematical simulations, to understand the intrinsic dynamics of in-trail following aircraft and identify in particular possible oscillatory effects (Kelly & Abbott, 1984). Pilot perspective was also addressed through human-in-the-loop simulations (Pritchett & Yankovsky, 1998) and flight trials (Oseguera-Lohr, et al., 2002) essentially to assess feasibility. The ATC system perspective was considered through model-based simulations, to assess impact on arrival rate of aircraft (Hammer, 2000). Initial investigations were also performed with controllers in approach (Lee, et al., 2003). In order to get feedback on the use of spacing instructions for sequencing arrival flows, we carried out an initial air-ground experiment in 1999. Then, to assess the benefits and limits, two separate streams of air and ground experiments were conducted (Grimaud et al. 2001; Grimaud, et al., 2003). The air experiments provided positive feedback from flight crews. Despite a new task in the cockpit, which requires appropriate assistance to contain workload, pilots highlighted the positive aspects of getting in the loop, understanding their situation (through goal-oriented instructions), and gaining anticipation. Every crew successfully achieved the spacing task within the fixed tolerance.

OBJECTIVES

Beyond ensuring pilot effectiveness in performing the new spacing task (i.e. acquire and maintain the required spacing), it is essential to ensure that this new task fits into flight crew current activity. Introducing the spacing task has an impact on pilots in-flight operations, as it must be performed concurrently with the other tasks. The present experiment aims at investigating the impact on the spacing task performance of two different initial conditions (small versus large initial spacing value). As in previous experiments, it is expected that under airborne spacing flight crew workload is increasing with a higher demand on the pilot directly involved in monitoring and maintaining the situation. Moreover, the reduction of communications with ATC is expected to reduce communication load. Because time-based spacing task implies a time buffer allowing pilots to anticipate their actions according to a target's previous state, it is expected to be well accepted. Smaller initial spacing values are expected to induce a shorter "acquisition" phase and therefore more time spent maintaining the spacing. As previous experiments showed that it is more demanding to maintain rather than to acquire the spacing, smaller initial spacing values may be more costly in terms of speed adjustments.

METHOD

Participants

Six crews (12 airline pilots) participated. Four were captains and 8 first officers. The pilots ranged in age from 26 to 66 (mean age = 40,7). They had between 1 and 44 years (mean = 16,3) of experience flying in a commercial airline and between 1 and 7 years (mean = 4) of experience flying Airbus aircraft.

Equipment and Materials

Flights consisted of arrivals to Paris Orly and Charles De Gaulle from cruise to initial approach, and lasted about 35 minutes of flight time. Each flight was "inserted" in a previously recorded traffic with an operational controller, thus providing realistic voice communication (and party-line) along with a display of surrounding traffic (TCAS). The part-task cockpit simulator used is an Airbus A320 FMGS trainer (from FAROS) allowing to perform automatic flight, with pilot flying (PF) and pilot not flying (PNF) positions. Specific features have been developed to support the spacing task: new pages for data input on the Multi purpose Control Display Unit (MCDU) and new graphical indications on the Navigational Display (ND) to support monitoring tasks (Figure 1 and Figure 2). The target aircraft symbol and the reference line highlight the current spacing situation. The spacing scale indicates the current and required spacing, the spacing trend and closure rate, as well as the spacing tolerance margin. The predicted spacing indicates the position where the spacing will be acquired. The spacing scale indicates the current and required spacing, spacing trend and closure rate, and spacing tolerance. Moreover, depending on situations, specific advisory, caution or warning messages may be displayed (e.g. "accelerate", "slow down", "stabilise speed" or "unable spacing").

Procedure

Each session was planned to last 1.5 days. For each crew, the session programme covered a general briefing, training runs, 6 measured runs including NASA-TLX questionnaires and a debriefing. The 6 measured runs consisted in 2 runs without spacing task and 4 runs with time-based spacing (2 with a small initial spacing, the required spacing value minus 10% and 2 with a large initial spacing, the required spacing value plus 30%). In each condition, pilots flew one run as PF and the other one as PNF. The flight crew was tasked to perform a flight in automatic, together with usual tasks, namely communications with ATC, fuel check, ATIS, arrival preparation and briefing, and checklists. In addition to that, for runs including the spacing task, the crew was tasked a "merge" instruction, requiring to acquire and maintain a given spacing through manual speed adjustments. The task was composed of two successive phases: a "merge" phase during which the target and instructed aircraft are both converging to the merging waypoint followed by a "remain" phase, beyond the waypoint, during which both aircraft follow the same trajectory. In the "merge" instruction, the pilot was tasked to reach the required spacing by the time the target was over the merging point and then maintain it with a given spacing tolerance margin. In the scenarios, the required spacing was set at 90s +/-5s. Concerning the flight task distribution, it was suggested that the PNF would perform the input of data in the MCDU and that the PF would make the necessary speed adjustments to perform the spacing task. Both pilots would monitor the spacing. The target aircraft was under conventional control (i.e. not subject to airborne spacing).

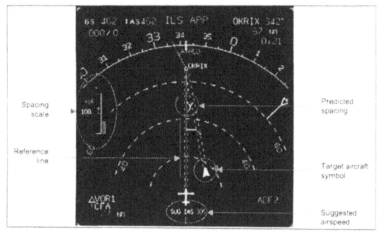

Figure 1. Spacing features on ND.

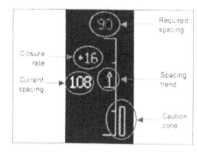

Figure 2. Spacing scale.

RESULTS

The impact of the spacing tasks on flight crew activity and effectiveness is assessed through objective data (speed adjustments and spacing deviation) and subjective data (observation, debriefing and questionnaire items).

Usefulness and usability

The main benefits of the spacing task perceived by the pilots are a better flight management (including an earlier preparation for the approach phase) due to a better anticipation of actions, less variation in trajectories due to less heading instructions, an accurate spacing control, and less communications with ATC due to less manoeuvring instructions. Pilots' feedback on usability of information displays was positive: graphical cues were appreciated and the dedicated input pages were well accepted. Suggestions were made to improve the suggested airspeed filter, which was felt too sensitive.

Workload

The pilots felt an increased but acceptable workload (especially for the PF). This feedback was confirmed by NASA-TLX results: mental and temporal demands remained at an acceptable level in all conditions for both PF and PNF even though it was globally slightly higher in runs including the spacing task. The real gain perceived concerned ATC communications: less frequent and less time-critical messages with the spacing task. This was confirmed through ground experiment.

Activity

For analysis purposes, the "merge" phase was split into two distinct phases: the "acquisition" phase and the "maintain" phase. On average, less than one speed action per minute was necessary to acquire and maintain the required spacing (0.7 in the large initial spacing condition and 0.8 in the small initial spacing condition). The analysis of the number of speed actions per minute in each spacing phase showed that the "remain" phase was the most demanding whereas the "acquisition" phase was the least demanding (Figure 3). Despite a larger number of speed actions during the "merge" phase when the initial spacing was small (i.e. when the "acquisition" phase was shorter), there was no correlation between the "acquisition" phase duration and the number of speed actions per minute performed during this phase. Indeed, a temporal analysis of speed actions (Figure 4) shows that speed actions are mainly triggered by changes on target state, which happen to occur during the "remain" phase (target speed reduction to 250 knot then to 220 knot and target descent to 3000 feet).

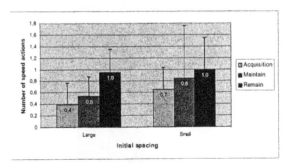

Figure 3. Average number of speed actions per minute.

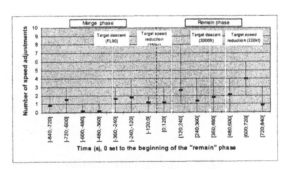

Figure 4. Example of temporal distribution (min, average, max) of speed actions (small initial spacing, Paris Orly).

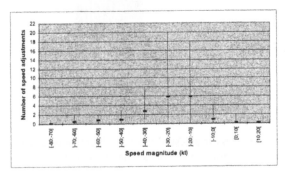

Figure 5. Distribution of speed magnitude.

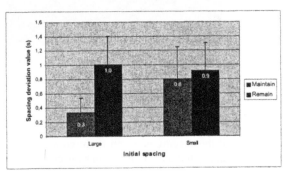

Figure 6. Average spacing deviation.

To go a step further, the magnitude of speed actions was analysed. Most speed actions (68%) were small adjustments comprised between −15kt and +5kt (Figure 5). This is a positive result as large speed changes could increase pilot workload, be detrimental to flight efficiency and may induce risk of oscillations for the following aircraft. However, too numerous speed actions could induce too much focus on speed resulting in excessive monitoring.

Effectiveness

Effectiveness was assessed through spacing accuracy. As the spacing deviation might be outside the spacing tolerance margin during the "acquisition" phase, the spacing accuracy was analysed during the "maintain" and "remain" phases. Results show that the average spacing deviation was 1 second or even below, which is far below the 5s spacing tolerance (Figure 6). In each run, the maximum spacing deviation was always below the spacing tolerance. Consequently, no case of loss of spacing occurred in this experiment.

CONCLUSION

The flight deck experiment enabled to confirm trends observed in previous experiments. It also allowed to assess that even though the initial spacing influenced the spacing acquisition duration, it had no impact on flight crews' activity (assessed through manual speed adjustments): less than one speed action per minute on average, most actions corresponding to small speed adjustments.

Beyond, monitoring task which became one major component of pilots' activity due to increased automation needs to be carefully addressed (Wickens et al. 1997). It is important to check whether spacing-related information and actions are not detrimental to flight crew situation awareness. Pilots expressed pros and cons. On the one hand, they thought that situation awareness was improved, as it was easier to understand the situation regarding the preceding aircraft. On the other hand, they were apprehensive to focus too much on the preceding aircraft to the detriment of primary flight parameters and other traffic.

To address this issue, the next step will consist of measuring pilots monitoring activity with an eye-tracking device. To get closer to current in-flight activity, an effort will be put on simulation realism with the use of a full flight simulator and scenario enriched with events occurring regularly during flights.

REFERENCES

Grimaud, I., Hoffman, E, Rognin, L. & Zeghal, K. (2001). Delegating upstream - Mapping where it happens. USA/Europe Air Traffic Management R&D Seminar, Santa Fe, USA.

Grimaud, I., Hoffman, E., Pene, N., Rognin, L. & Zeghal, K. (2003). Towards the use of spacing instruction. Assessing the impact of spacing tolerance on flight crew activity. AIAA Guidance, Navigation, and Control Conference, Austin, Texas.

Hammer, J. (2000). Preliminary analysis of an approach spacing application. FAA/Eurocontrol R&D Committee, Action Plan 1, ASAS Technical Interchange Meeting.

Kelly, J. R. & Abbott, T. S. (1984). In-trail spacing dynamics of multiple CDTI-equipped aircraft queues (NASA TM-85699). NASA.

Lee, P. U., Mercer, J. S., Martin, L., Prevot, T., Shelden, S., Verma, S., Smith, N., Battiste, V., Johnson, W., Mogford, R. & Palmer, E. (2003). Free maneuvering, trajectory negociation, and self-spacing concept in distributed air-ground traffic management. USA/Europe Air Traffic Management R&D Seminar, Budapest, Hungary.

Oseguera-Lohr, R. M., Lohr, G. W., Abbott, T. S. & Eischeid, T. M. (2002). Evaluation of operational procedures for using a time-based airborne interarrival spacing tool. Digital Avionics Systems Conference, Irvine, California.

Pritchett, A. R. & Yankovsky, L. J. (1998). Simultaneous design of Cockpit Display and Traffic Information & Air Traffic Management Procedures. SAE Transactions – Journal of Aerospace.

Wickens, C. D., Mavor, A. S. & McGee J. P. (1997). Flight to the Future: Human Factors in Air Traffic Control. National Academy Press.

ACCOMMODATING NAS USER GOALS AND CONSTRAINTS: CHOREOGRAPHED RESPONSES TO WEATHER EVENTS AT ARRIVAL AIRPORTS

Philip J. Smith, Amy L. Spencer, Steve Caisse, Carla Beck
Cognitive Systems Engineering, Inc.

Tony Andre
Interface Analysis Associates

Jimmy Krozel, Goli Davidson
Metron Aviation, Inc.

ABSTRACT

In this paper, a specific scenario is used to illustrate a concept of operations for dealing with weather events that reduce arrival rates into an airport, and to demonstrate the potential benefits. The primary focus of this concept of operations is the sharing of perspectives between traffic managers and NAS Users regarding priorities for flights that are already airborne at the time that a weather event impacts airport arrivals.

Keywords: Shared situation awareness; distributed work; air traffic management

INTRODUCTION

The focus of this paper is on how to better accommodate National Airspace System (NAS) User preferences and constraints for airborne flights approaching an arrival airport when weather constraints impact performance. In generic terms, this requires:

- Dealing with unexpected (or less than totally predictable) events that impact both airborne flights and departures that are still on the ground.
- Reasoning about the uncertainty associated with such an event in terms of its location, magnitude and duration.
- Identifying and evaluating alternative Traffic Flow Management (TFM) plans that integrate different TFM and Air Traffic Control (ATC) strategies and tactics in order to deal with the impact of weather constraints on traffic in terms of efficiency and safety as well as the impact on Users' business concerns.
- Implementing the selected TFM plan and adapting it as the event plays out.

Below, a concept of operations is outlined for tasks performed in a specific weather scenario at DFW and its surrounding airspace. Details on this scenario can be found in Spencer, et al., 2003, but in general terms this scenario involves an unforecast thunderstorm event which forms directly over DFW, effectively closing the airport at 2100Z for an uncertain amount of time – an estimated 45 to 75 minutes. Almost immediately, it is determined that the supercell is moving to the southeast and additional severe weather is beginning to form to the northeast. It is forecast that this weather will continue to impact both the northeast (BYP) and the southeast (CQY) cornerposts, closing those cornerposts beyond the duration of the airport closure.

At the time this event occurs the enroute DFW inventory consists of 120 aircraft evenly balanced over the four arrival cornerposts, UKW (Bowie), BYP (Bonham), CQY (Cedar Creek) and JEN (Glen Rose). At 2145Z the airport reopens, but conditions are IFR (Instrument Flight Rules) with a 60 AAR (Airport Arrival Rate). The reduced AAR is attributed to a two arrival runway configuration, 18R and 17C, with two minutes required ON separation.

The tasks required as part of this concept are listed below. Tasks 3-5 represent new concepts, and are therefore described in detail.

Task 1. Supercell detection and situation assessment by TFM.

Task 2. Handling of flights tactically until a TFM plan can be implemented.

Task 3. Developing and implementing a default TFM plan

Below we contrast our new concept with expected performance in the current NAS

Default Plan for the Current World.

In our depiction of the current world, it was assumed that the flights close to the airport at the time the weather event arises would be handled tactically. Those further from DFW, however, would be routed to holding stacks as shown in Figure 1. Based on the forecast that only UKW and JEN were likely to open soon, a total of 6 holding stacks would be filled near UKW and 6 near JEN.

Each holding stack can hold as many as 8 aircraft (from 10,000 feet to 17,000 feet). In our representation of the current world, these stacks were filled so that flights would be released to land according to a first come, first served rule under which those flights that were closest to DFW at the time the supercell arose would be placed lowest in the holding stacks closest to the airport. These flights would subsequently be cleared to land first once the airport reopened (assuming they didn't have to divert before the weather moved East). Note that this representation of performance in the current world did not take into account User priorities.

To assess performance, the 120 flights in the scenario were assigned fuel loads, and were randomly assigned to one of three priority categories, high (probability 0.2); medium (probability 0.4) and low (probability 0.4). An analysis of this depiction of the current world, in which User priorities for the flights were not considered, indicated that 12 high priority flights would have to be diverted (at a cost of $65,000 per flight), 21 medium priority flights would have to be diverted (at a cost of $25,000 per flight), and 16 low priority flights would have to be diverted (at a cost of $5,000 per flight). Thus the total estimated cost of diversions associated with this plan was $1,385,000. (See Spencer, et al., 2003 for additional details.)

Default Plan for the Future World.

Under our concept of operation, in the future world the default plan would take into consideration User preferences and constraints to the extent possible. This would apply to aircraft further from the airport, as it is assumed that the additional time would allow TFM to consider the priorities and constraints of NAS Users.

In order to develop this plan, certain "rules of the game" first would need to be established. First, within the constraint that safety is ensured, TFM would develop a default plan that maximized throughput without violating equity considerations across the affected NAS users. This initial plan would be developed using knowledge of NAS User preferences and constraints to the extent that they were automatically available by querying databases maintained by the Users, and would often be based on modifications of a predetermined default plan for this type of situation. This default plan will be modified as needed to handle minor changes in the routes necessary to avoid localized weather, and to route flights to accommodate priorities to the extent possible.

Note that this would require the development of a tool that allowed the dispatcher to provide information about the constraints or preferences associated with a flight *prior to the real-time development of a weather event* (often as part of the preflight planning or through automated computations). Note also that, for the development of the default plan, there would be no real-time involvement by dispatchers. Information about a User's preferences and constraints would be restricted to data available immediately to the TFM planning tool upon querying a database maintained and updated by the User. (Dispatchers and flight crews would, however, have an opportunity to request changes to the default plan once they received it.)

In this sample scenario, it is assumed that a pre-stored internal TFM play was available to deal with an unexpected closure of DFW due to weather, with the expectation that only UKW and JEN would be reopened first as the weather moved to the East. In this play:

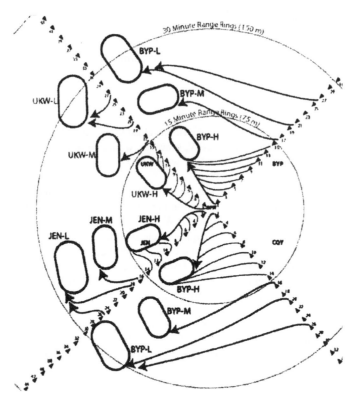

Figure 1. Flights routed (via specific transition points) to holding stacks.

- Flights already close to DFW when the weather arrives would be handled tactically, either diverting or being placed into the holding stacks at UKW or JEN that are closest to DFW (thus giving these flights the highest priority for landing once the airport reopens).
- To the extent feasible (in terms of ATC workload and constraints), flights that had not yet passed the transition points in the default plan would be put into either the high, medium or low priority holding stacks based on the priorities indicated in the NAS User databases. (For this initial analysis, it was assumed that all flights belonged to a single airline so that there were no equity issues.)
- To avoid complexity in the handling of aircraft by ATC, the pre-stored plan has 3 different transition points associated with the flow into BYP and 3 others associated with the flow into CQY. Flights from BYP destined for the high priority holding stack at UKW would transition at the point closest to DFW. Flights intended for the medium priority holding stack at UKW would transition at a point further out from DFW, and flights for the low priority stack would transition even further out from DFW. (See Figure 1.) The same approach would be used for flights that need to be moved from CQY to the holding stacks at JEN.
- Flights approaching DFW via UKW and JEN prior to the airport closure would be directed to the high, medium and low priority holding stacks as appropriate as they approach those holding fixes. (See Figure 1.)
- Flights would be put into each of the holding stacks such that the line-up from bottom to top reflected the prioritization of these flights (the assumption being that the stacks would be emptied from bottom to top once the airport reopens).
- Once the airport reopened, flights could be taken alternately from the pair of holding stacks at each of the two reopened arrival fixes (UKW and JEN) as appropriate to feed those two flows while accommodating priorities.

To build the default plan, using the pre-stored TFM play a decision support tool would:

- Assign each aircraft a spot in one of the holding stacks based on its requested priority as communicated by the NAS User database. If necessary, TFM could eliminate or move one or more of the holding stacks to deal with the weather constraints or use a tactic like vectoring instead of holding.

140

- Identify the route and altitude profile necessary to safely take that aircraft to its assigned place in a holding stack and display the proposed default plan to the traffic manager for modification (if necessary) and approval. The pilots and ATC could also modify this planned route as needed while enroute to deal with unanticipated developments.
-

Task 4. Disseminating and revising the default plan

In the depiction of the *future world*, after the TFM had reviewed and refined the default plan, appropriate information would be disseminated to ATC, dispatchers and the flight crews. The dispatchers and the flights crews might decide immediately to divert certain flights due to factors not considered by the TFM planning software. Such diversion decisions would allow other flights to move up in the holding stacks if the decisions were communicated to TFM early enough to modify the default plan.

The dispatchers, in consultation with the flight crews, might also choose to modify flight priorities based on consideration of factors not considered by the planning tool and the NAS User databases. By querying the planning tool, the dispatcher would be able to see what flights could feasibly be swapped to better accommodate these revised priorities. Assuming that such revisions were identified before the flights reached their transition points, with TFM approval, the planning tool would revise the default plan appropriately and disseminate the flight amendments as needed.

A dispatcher or pilot might also reject a flight amendment proposed as part of the default plan (because, for instance, he or she judges the reroute to be too close to the weather or an area of turbulence). In this case, ATC would handle that flight tactically.

For the assessment of this future concept of operations, flights were given the same random assigned to one of three priority categories, high (probability 0.2); medium (probability 0.4) and low (probability 0.4). However, because the assignment of locations in the holding stacks considered User priorities, when UKW and JEN reopened, a larger number of higher priority flights were accommodated.

Our analysis indicated that, in this depiction of the future world using our concept of operations, 1 high priority flight would be diverted (at a cost of $65,000 per flight), 13 medium priority flights would be diverted (at a cost of $25,000 per flight), and 33 low priority flights would be diverted (at a cost of $5,000 per flight). Thus the total estimated cost of diversions associated with this future plan is $555,000. Note that this contrasts with the estimated cost of diversions of $1,385,000 for this event using current TFM/ATC procedures. Thus, using these numbers this new set of tools and procedures is estimated to save $830,000 for this single weather event.

As stated earlier, our depiction of the current world assumed no communication of priorities from dispatch to TFM, and no tactical adjustments by the flight crews and ATC to further accommodate a limited number of high priority flights. Even if it was assumed that, through such labor-intensive manual processes, 6 of the high priority flights were accommodated in the depiction of the current world (at the expense of 6 low priority flights), the estimated savings for this single weather event is still $470,000.

MAINTAINING SAFETY NETS

The operational concept described in this paper maintains the basic definition of roles and responsibilities that exist today for controllers, traffic managers, pilots and dispatchers, along with the shared responsibilities and redundancies that such a distributed architecture provides in order to ensure safety. The strength of such a distributed architecture with overlapping spheres of responsibility is that it helps to make the system more resilient in the face of the slips and mistakes that any one person or system component could make.

In addition, the proposed concept would significantly improve information exchange among TFM, dispatch, controllers and flight crews, increasing access to critical information such as feasible hold times.

COGNITIVE COMPLEXITY AND WORKLOAD

The use of predefined plays with well-structured routes to deal with specific situations should help reduce workload and cognitive complexity. The worst case would be a situation where no predefined play applies, and where TFM, ATC, dispatch and the flight crews would have to deal with the situation tactically (and would therefore be unable to accommodate User preferences). In this case, traffic would be handled as it is today in such circumstances, so that in a relative sense there is no increase in complexity or workload under this worst case scenario.

Clearly, however, new tasks have been introduced for traffic managers and dispatchers in terms of generating, evaluating and refining the plans for handling the traffic for those cases where time permits the accommodation of User preferences, and these new tasks will therefore by definition increase workload. The cognitive demands of these tasks and their impacts on mental workload therefore require additional study.

In terms of flight crews, there will be some impact in the sense that more flights will now be potentially eligible for prioritization. Thus, more flight crews will be contacted by dispatch to discuss the proposed handling than is currently the case.

In terms of controllers, they would be given the route amendments for the flights just as they are today, and would have the same responsibilities for communicating with the pilots and ensuring safe separation. The primary issue regarding workload would therefore be whether there would be increased complexity or volume in handling traffic given the plans for accommodating User priorities.

The use of predefined plays should help in terms of controller workload in the sense that they will have previous experience with monitoring potential confliction points and with routing and merging specific flows. However, it is likely that additional tools and procedures will need to be developed to make it possible to share the workload among different sectors. This could require development of tools to support a limited form of dynamic resectorization and to help with the adaptive positioning of holding stacks. In addition, questions regarding the workload associated with taking flights into and out of multiple holding stacks need to be considered.

ACKNOWLEDGEMENTS

This work was funded under the VAMS program at NASA Ames Research Center.

REFERENCES

Spencer, A., Smith, P.J., Caisse, S., Beck, C., Andre, T., Krozel, J. and Davidson, G. (2003). Accommodating NAS User Goals And Constraints: Choreographed Responses to Weather Events at Arrival Airports. CSE Technical Report 2003-8, Columbus OH.

EVALUATION OF AN ONBOARD TAXI GUIDANCE SYSTEM

Jörn Jakobi, Bernd Lorenz, and Marcus Biella
German Aerospace Center (DLR)

ABSTRACT

In Europe, airports become more and more the bottlenecks compared to all flight phases of gate-to-gate flight operation. Because of their weather dependency, their strict time constraints (slots), their inflexible layout, etc., they often cannot cope with the traffic demand and thus cause traffic jams, delays, incidents or even accidents. This study supplements a series of prior and concurrent field trials testing the operational benefit of an Advanced Surface Movement Guidance and Control System (A-SMGCS). A-SMGCS comprises a range of new enabling technologies for both the flight deck and the air traffic control tower and is expected to significantly increase the planning and management of all aircraft and authorized vehicles on the movement area. Four commercial pilots performed a series of take-off and landing scenarios including extended taxi movements that were completed in a fixed-base cockpit simulator. The effectiveness of the DLR onboard guidance system TARMAC-AS is examined that combines flight deck to ground communication via data-link (DL) with an electronic moving map (EMM) to display airport surface traffic to the pilot crew. Evaluation was based on subjective questionnaires, route deviations, and visual scanning data based on eye-point-of-gaze measurements. Results support the notion that EMM + DL first, improve awareness of the global airport surface situation, second, lower the workload associated with R/T communication, third, allow for efficient taxi movements, and finally, provides important recommendations regarding operational HMI aspects and new procedures that has to be applied in the future.

Keywords: TARMAC-AS, Situation Awareness, Onboard Guidance, HDD, EMM, Data Link

INTRODUCTION

The permanent demand for more mobility and more life comfort causes continuously growing air traffic all over the world, especially in Europe with an average rate of 6% per year. However, the safety and demanding capacity of air traffic must be assured despite increasing traffic density. With this focus, the European airport system is becoming increasingly the major causing factor in the build-up of safety and capacity bottlenecks when compared to other phases of gate-to-gate flight operation. Because of their weather dependency, their strict time constraints for departures (slots), their inflexible layout, etc., airports often cannot cope with the traffic demand and thus cause traffic jams, delays, incidents or even accidents like the one that recently occurred at the airport of Linate near Milano that caused the loss of 114+4 people (Ranter, 2002). The current situation at highly congested airports drives an intense effort of airport traffic management organisations to implement an Advanced Surface Movement Guidance and Control System (A-SMGCS), which is outlined in the worldwide approved ICAO Manual on A-SMGCS (ICAO, 2003). An A-SMGCS comprises a suite of new enabling technologies and procedures for both the flight deck and the air traffic control tower and is expected to significantly increase the planning and management of all aircraft and authorized vehicles on the surface movement area interfacing with air traffic management (ATM) systems. New technology and operational procedures aim at achieving similar capacity of clear-weather also for low-visibility conditions without increasing controller or pilot workload or sacrificing safety. According to ICAO an A-SMGCS should support four primary functions that are: (1) surveillance, (2) routing, (3) guidance and (4) control.

The DLR-project TARMAC (Taxi And Ramp Management And Control) provides solutions for all four components. The *surveillance* requirement is met by TARMAC-CNS (Communication, Navigation, Surveillance) and provides an integrated multi-sensor and communication system for continuous automatic identification and positional tracking of all airport surface traffic. The *controlling* and *routing (planning)* function is provided by TARMAC-PL, the planning and controller machine interface, which assists the apron and tower controller to establish a co-ordinated and efficient runway occupancy planning by proposed route- and time information (Böhme, Anagnostakis, Clarke & Völckers, 2001). The present paper focuses on TARMAC-AS (Airborne System) (Härtl, 1997) that is interfaced with TARMAC-PL via data-link and accomplishes the planning and controlling needs of the pilot side. TARMAC-AS helps guiding the pilot to and from the runway, monitors own and other aircraft movements, issues warnings, and reduces voice communication. TARMAC-AS currently uses the existing navigation display for showing all relevant planning and guidance data on an Electronic Moving Map (EMM) including an onboard/ground data-link communication.

The potential advantage of these onboard guidance functions has been acknowledged for some years in DLR lab tests (Härtl, 1997) and could also be empirically demonstrated in different lab (Hooey, Foyle, & Andre, 2000) and field tests in the US, e.g. "SafeFlight 21" (Battiste & Johnson, 2000), as well as in Europe, e.g. lab and field test in the EU-sponsored project "BETA" (Wolfe, Wall, & Simpson, 2003, Klein & Jakobi, 2003). It seems generally accepted among system designers and pilots that an onboard guidance function can significantly contribute to an increase of the pilot's situation awareness that allows for more efficient ground movements by increasing taxi speed or reductions in route deviations and taxi conflicts in low visibility. However, procedurally, the guidance function is one of the most indefinite and less developed module of an A-SMGCS. Typical procedures have to be adapted or even newly developed. This, in particular, applies for procedures for using data link communication that has been only roughly specified up to now. Once this will be accomplished, an onboard guidance function can overcome its prototype status on its way to a mature, well-accepted, and certified system with standardised performance requirements and procedures.

The present study was carried out in an attempt to delineate the scope of the procedural issues involved in the use of an onboard guiding function. To this end, two two-man crews with four experienced commercial pilots performed a series of taxi-and-take-off as well as land-and-taxi scenarios under different conditions of visibility and traffic density, during which a range of human performance data was collected. Results were expected to inform us about procedural deficiencies with the existing prototype and to derive recommendations for operational procedures required for the implementation of this technology.

METHOD

Participants

Four male commercial flight crew members from Czech Airline (CSA) participated in the simulation flight trials. With CSA they flew mainly Boeing 737 but also ATR42/72. The tests were performed with two two-men crews whereas the roles of PF and PNF were changed after half of the test runs.

Equipment

The simulation trials were carried out in the DLR fix-based generic cockpit simulator that emulates the geometry and essential control and display functionality of an Airbus A320 cockpit. The outside view covers a range of 180° in the horizontal and 40° in vertical plane. During the taxiing phase the standard navigations display, which is not needed on ground, was used for the TARMAS-AS onboard guidance display. The display was presented at both the PNF position and the PF position and could be used by both independently. ATC instructions were given by a confederate controller of the ATC simulation unit either by voice or data link.

Experimental Procedures

Each of the two cockpit crews performed 16 test runs caused by a 2 x 2 x 2 x 2 complete within-subject experimental design. The four two-level factors were as follows: (1) There were two cockpit conditions, i.e. one equipped with TARMAC-AS Head Down Display (HDD), the other the standard NAV-display; (2) Visibility was either low or good); (3) Traffic density was either medium or high; and finally (4), Pilot role were either PF or PNF. In order to avoid recall effects, four different flight scenarios were used and balanced over all test runs, and additionally, were estranged by different airport traffic scenarios. Each test run was composed of an out- and inbound taxi scenario including a take-off and landing phase, respectively, and lasted approximately 25 minutes.

During all TARMAC-AS test conditions, ATC instructions were delivered by data link and were displayed alpha-numerically on the HDD. Time and safety critical clearances were complemented by additional voice messages. The PNF could accept or refuse them. After acknowledgment of a taxi clearance the route was indicated on the HDD and cleared sections beyond stop bars were highlighted in yellow colour and turned into green colour upon PNF acceptance. Restricted or still uncleared areas (RWYs, stop bars, etc.) were displayed in red colour. The crew could see own-ship position relative to the airport surface and also other traffic. Different modes and zoom levels could be chosen independently. Without TARMAC-AS support, the crew used standard paper charts and radio communication exclusively.

Measurements

The x-y position coordinates of the aircraft were recorded once per second. From these data, taxi speed, number and duration of stops, and route deviations were derived. Furthermore, duration of radio communication between ATC and Cockpit were recorded. The PNF's eye-point-of-gaze (EPOG) was measured using a video based system (IView^{TM}). Measurements were performed only during 8 of the overall 16 runs. Details will be given in the results section.

Additionally, the PF's and PNF's subjective situation awareness and workload were surveyed mid- and post-run. The 3D-SART (post-run) (Taylor, 1989) and the Simple Rating Scale for Situation Awareness (SRS-SA, [mid-run]) (McGuinnes, 1995) were used to assess SA, the Instantaneous Self Assessment (I.S.A. [mid-run]) (Tattersall & Foord, 1996) and the NASA-TLX (post-run) (Hart & Staveland, 1988) were used to assess the pilots' workload.

During a debriefing at the end of all test runs the crew members were asked for giving their statements concerning the TARMAC-AS's usability (System Usability Scale [SUS]) (Brooke, 1996) and their own acceptance to it. They were also requested to answer open questions related to design aspects and newly applied procedures.

RESULTS

All dependent variables were analysed in separate 2 x 2 x 2 x 2 (HDD x Visibility x Traffic x Role) analyses of variance (ANOVA) with repeated measurements on all independent factors.

Subjective SA and workload: The ANOVA revealed a significant effect of Visibility ($F_{(1,3)}$ = 16.1, p < .05) on average SRS-SA scores caused by higher SA ratings with good (M = 9.2) as compared to poor visibility (M = 8,5) on a scale reaching from 0 - 10. This effect was further qualified by a significant *EMM x Visibility* interaction effect ($F_{(1,3)}$ = 11.9, p < .05). As can be derived from figure 1, the interaction effect resulted from the fact that an SA advantage of using the EMM was only seen under poor visibility but not under good visibility. The post-run SART data showed similar results but did not become significant.

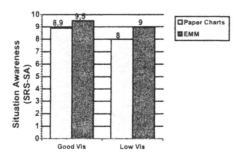

Figure 1: Situation Awareness by HDD and Visibility Conditions

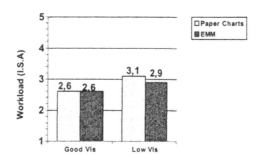

Figure 2: Workload by EMM and Visibility Conditions

The average mid- and post-run workload scores displayed an analogous pattern. A significant effect of *Visibility* ($F_{(1,3)}$ = 40.2, p < .05) and a significant *HDD x Visibility* interaction ($F_{(1,3)}$ = 20.1, p < .05) was found, both consistent in meaning to the SA results. Workload was rated generally lower in good visibility (M = 2.6) than in low visibility (M = 3.0) on a scale reaching from 1 - 5. With HDD use, there was no workload advantage against the paper chart when the visibility was good. As illustrated in figure 2, such a benefit occurred only when visibility was low. The post-run NASA-TLX data showed a similar pattern but did not become significant. No further effects became reliable for both the *workload* and the *situation awareness* data. In the debriefing, all four participants assessed the TARMAC-AS as very usable. No Pilot gave a rating below three in the 10-item system usability scale (SUS) scaling from one to five.

Communication: The ANOVA computed on the duration of voice communication involved the factors HDD, traffic density, and visibility. The factor pilot role was not considered, because always only one pilot communicates with ATC. Within the HDD condition, routine voice communication was replaced by data link. The analysis revealed that EMM plus data link reduced voice communication by a factor of four ($F_{(1,3)} = 31.04$, $p < .05$).

Surface movement: In 32 test runs only two deviations from the cleared route occurred, both without TARMAC-AS HDD support and in low visibility. The results obtained from the analysis of the taxi speed were similar to the pattern of WL and SA described above, although only the main effect of visibility became significant ($F_{(1,3)} = 9.9$, $p \leq .05$) in the expected direction. The observed higher average taxi speeds obtained with HDD could not be confirmed with sufficient statistical reliability ($F_{(1,3)} = 5.2$, $p > .05$). The HDD x Visibility differential pattern, depicted in figure 3, suggests an advantage of HDD, particularly in low visibility, however, this could also not be statistically confirmed ($F_{(1,3)} = 1,7$, $p > .05$).

Visual scanning: The eye-point-of-gaze measurement were taken from PNF only. EPOG measurements were performed during 8 of 16 runs crossing the conditions EMM vs. paper chart usage and low workload (good visibility/normal traffic) vs. high workload (low visibility/high traffic) analysed by a 2 * 2 ANOVA. This revealed a significant main effect due to HDD ($F_{(1,3)} = 12.7$, $p < .05$). The percentage of out-of-the-window gazes (OTW) decreased from 68.0% using paper chart to 33.7% using HDD. The impression that this difference was higher during the low workload condition as suggested by the pattern depicted in figure 4 could not be confirmed by significance of the EMM * WL interaction effect ($F_{(1,3)} < 1$) due to some erratic inter-individual differences.

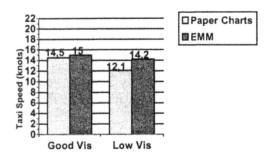 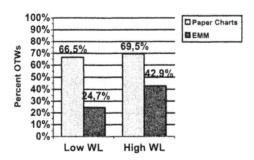

Figure 3: Taxi Speed by HDD and Visibility Conditions

Figure 4: Out the window gazes during a test scenario

TARMAC -AS usage: When using the TARMAC-AS HDD the PNF could choose the mode (3D-Perspective, ARC, NAV, or North Up) and the zoom level (50m till infinity). With 13 of 16 HDD test runs the 3D-Perspective Mode was used exclusively by using the closest zoom levels (50m/100m) predominately. The pilots explained this high preference for a 3D-perspective map by having a higher resolution in the area of highest interest closed to the aircraft, and a smaller resolution but good overview for the more remote areas of the a/c. A strenuous selecting of the best fitting zoom level is not further necessary. The auto zoom function that zooms out with growing speed (long straight ahead taxi ways, take-off) was also well accepted by the pilots.

The pilots further wished to get a taxi route cleared by voice segment for segment but the whole expected route should be transmitted by data link and should support voice clearances by green colouring of the cleared segments. An incoming data link message must always be accompanied with an alerting auditive signal to decrease undue head-down times.

After using touch pads, touch screen, track balls, and hard push buttons as input devices, the pilots preferred hard push buttons, as it is common standard in the cockpit. They argued that these buttons are very input failure-resistant and provide an excellent feedback to the user.

DISCUSSION

Situation awareness, workload, communication, taxi speed, taxi navigation errors, and visual scanning are important human-factors issues to be considered when A-SMGCS prototype tools are to be accommodated to operational procedures. The present study addresses these issues for the onboard guidance function TARMAC-AS, a module that represents the flight-deck contribution to enhanced airport surface operation. Despite of the low statistical power of the empirical data taken from a small sample of four professional airline pilots the findings are in good agreement with other empirical work (Hooey et al., 2000). This is particularly true for the subjective assessment of workload and SA, and, moreover, the post-session debriefing that will be discussed in the following.

SA and Workload: The results of this study could underline that an onboard guidance function (EMM +DL) contributes to safer and more efficient movements on the ground. "Workload" and "Situation Awareness" scores of PF and PNF showed a significant interaction between the use of TARMAC-AS and the visibility conditions. In good visibility there are only a small effect but in lower visibility conditions the use of TARMAC-AS showed a strong effect in increased SA and lowered WL scores. Thus, TARMAC-AS developed the operational benefit particularly under the conditions for which it is designed.

Data Link Communication: A further positive effect is the reduction of voice communication by support of data link communication. With current ATC procedures there are a lot of routine radio communications that are neither safety nor time critical but nevertheless, have to be performed via voice today, e.g. departure clearance, start-up and pushback clearance, or instructions for a frequency change. These routine communications burden the radio frequency very much and could replaced by data link communication. This can unload the radio frequency by more than half of time and could mitigate drawbacks of today's radio communication problems such as: misunderstandings (similar call-signs, language, accent, etc), read-back and hear-back errors, serial exchange of information, or the missing assistance in message compositions. DL could further help to visualise route information, could serve as a back up for voice communication, could enable further automation in data processing; and would allow the precise, concise and parallel exchange of information between ATC and the flight deck. In contradiction to the widespread opinion that DL will hinder the "party line" effect, it seems more appropriate to assume that by unburdening the radio frequency from routine information by DL, this information channel can be preserved for the most safety critical information that then has the potential of better alerting. Balancing these benefits of DL for nominal situations against the benefit of voice to communicate fast and flexibly during off-nominal situations along with non-verbal peripheral cues of the stress involved, will be a difficult procedural problem to be solved when DL is to be integrated. In future times, DL and R/T communication should migrate to a communication unit whereas advantages and disadvantages of both have to be considered and used in the most beneficial way. The parallel use of voice and DL in critical situations like "Take-Off" or "Landing" and the solely use of DL with routine information (see above) was a well-accepted procedure in this investigation.

Out Of the Window (OTW) Gazes: Consistent with a design philosophy also emphasized by Hooey et al. (2000) that an EMM should not prevent PF from eyes-out taxiing, the present study investigates the option of assigning PNF the role of EMM monitoring. With regard to airport surface awareness, Lasswell & Wickens (1995) as well as McCann, Andre, Begault, Foyle & Wenzel(1997) make a distinction between local and global awareness, which is of relevance here. Local awareness is developed and maintained by visual cues such as centrelines, taxiway signage, etc., that pilots use to control the aircraft in the immediate area. Global awareness correspond more to taxi navigation and include items such as cleared routes, other traffic on the airport surface etc. Eyes-out taxiing is mandatory for the maintenance of local awareness. The EMM should primarily support global awareness. The eye-point-of-gaze measurements, taken from PNF, confirm that the pilots in this role reduced their out-of-the-window (OTW) times markedly, in fact, down to two third of the time when they only had an airport paper chart. This shows again that maintenance of global awareness was the prevailing strategy of pilots in the role of PNF. Without knowing the visual scanning strategy of PF, and moreover, the communication between both pilots, it remains unclear how PF integrates all sources of information, i.e. outside scene, EMM, DL, and PF. Therefore, the potential risks of the OTW reductions seen in PNF are difficult to evaluate.

Taxi Speed: A relevant capacity factor with surface movement is the taxi speed: „...if RWY capacities are to be maintained and taxiways are not to become congested with aircraft, it will be important to maintain speeds similar to those normally used in good visibility." (ICAO, 2003, §3.5.4.2). The average taxi speed obtained in the present study point to the desired direction, i.e. showed the tendency that with support of an EMM (HDD) a higher taxi speed could be maintained especially when visibility is impaired. However, this effect was to weak to be confirmed with sufficient statistical confidence. McCann et al. (1997) also failed to find a significant speed effect of an EMM. However, supplemented by a Head Up Display (HUD), that was used by the PF only, they could show a significant effect. Following their distinction between local vs. global awareness mentioned above, McCann et al. (1997) suggest that the speed benefit is mainly a result of improved local SA and is mediated by "scene-linked" HUD symbology, such as runway cones marking the runway edges, overlaid to the airport surface including further information like speed advisories. To increase taxi speed, in particular, during low visibility condition it must be stated that a) EMM (HDD) should be supplemented by a HUD, b) Pilot/Driver must have trust that the system will prevent collisions, and c) the Pilot/Driver must understand how the automation behaves – exactly what the automation does, and why, and how.

Design and Concept Aspects: When using the TARMAC-AS HDD the pilots wished to get a taxi route cleared by voice, but segment for segment whereas the whole route shall be transmitted by data link and should support R/T instructions by green colouring of the cleared segments. An incoming Data Link Message should always be accompanied with an auditive signal to decrease head-down times. A second reason for an auditive signal was mentioned by the PFs: The PF wanted to know the source of a taxi instructions that he can distinguish between an nominal advisory of the PNF and an obligatory ATC instruction, since both instructions were told to him by the PNF who reads out the alphanumerical ATC instructions from the display. After using touch pads, touch screen, track balls, and hard push buttons as input devices, the pilots preferred hard push buttons, as these are common standard in the cockpit. The argued that these buttons are very input failure-resistant and provide an excellent feedback to the user.

CONCLUSIONS

Given the high degree of pilot appreciation and proven human performance benefits of onboard guidance systems such as TARMAC-AS or similar systems, the specification of standard operating procedures associated with their use have to be continued in order to avoid undue delays in the introduction of this technology. The modular approach of the TARMAC project matches well with the demand of a seamless integration of further enhancements (e.g. HUD, high-precision 4D-taxi guidance, link to automatic collaborative gate-to-gate system components, etc.) in a comprehensive and consistent data-linked A-SMGCS environment. Following a human-centered philosophy, the introduction of this technology should now proceed gradually and adequate attention should be paid to training demands. Careful monitoring of this design stage should prompt further human-in-the-loop simulation studies to refine design specifications that accommodate requirements derived during operational use.

REFERENCES

Battiste, V. & Johnson, N.H. (2002). An operation evaluation of ADS-B and CDTI during airport surface and final approach operations. Proceedings of the Human Factors and Ergonomics Society 46th Annual Meeting. Santa Monica, CA: HFES.

Böhme, D., Anagnostakis, I., Clarke, J.-P. & Völckers, U. (2001). Runway operations planning and control: sequencing and scheduling. Journal of Aircraft, 38, 988-997.

Brooke, J (1996). SUS: A 'quick and dirty' usability scale. In: W. Jordan, B. thomas, B.A. Weerdmeester (Eds.), Usability Evaluation in Industry. London, UK: Taylor and Francis.

Hart, S.G., Staveland, L.E.: Development of NASA-TLX (Task Load Index): Results of empirical and theoretical research. In P.A. Hancock & N. Meshkati. (Eds). Human mental workload, pp. 139-183. Amsterdam: North Holland.

Härtl, D. (1997): Investigations with an aircraft taxi assistance and guidance system in a future airport traffic Scenario. DLR Technical Report. Neubiberg: Universität der Bundeswehr.

Hooey, B. L., Foyle, D. C., & Andre, A. D. (2000). Integration of cockpit displays for surface operations: The final stage of a human-centred design approach. SAE Transactions: Journal of Aerospace, 109, 1053-1065.

ICAO (2003). Manual on advanced surface movement guidance and control systems ((A-SMGCS), AN-Conf/11-IP/4, Montreal 2003.

Klein, K. & Jakobi, J. (2003). BETA Recommendations Report. EC Growth Project BETA, Document 1999-RD.10804, D26 / 2003-05-07.

Lasswell, J.W. & Wickens, C.D. (1995). The effects of display location and dimensionality on taxi-way navigation. University of Illinois Institute of Aviation Technical Report (ARL-95-5/NASA-95-2. Savoy, IL: Aviation Research Laboratory.

McCann, R. S., Andre, A. D., Begault, D. R., Foyle, D. C., & Wenzel, E. M. (1997). Enhancing taxi performance under low visibility: Are moving maps enough? Proceedings of the 41st Annual Meeting of the Human Factors and Ergonomics Society, pp. 37-41, Santa Monica, CA: Human Factors and Ergonomics Society, 1997.

McGuinness, B. (1995). Situational awareness measurement in cockpit evaluation trials. Proceedings of the AGARD/AMP Symposium on Situation Awareness: Limitations and Enhancement in the Aviation Environment, Brussels, April 24-27. Seuilly-sur-Seine: NATO AGARD.

Ranter, H. (2002). Airliner Accident Statistics 2001: Statistical summary of fatal multi-engined airliner accidents in 2001. Aviation Safety Network, January, 2002.

Tattersall, A. J., & Foord, P. S (1996). An experimental evaluation of instantaneous self assessment as a measure of workload. Ergonomics, 39, 740-748.

Taylor, R.M. (1989). Situation awareness rating technology (SART): The development of a tool for aircrew systems design. Proceedings of the AGARD AMP Symposium on Situation Awareness in Aerospace Operations, CP478. Seuilly-sur-Seine: NATO AGARD.

Wolfe, A., Wall, V., Simpson, A., Gilbert, A. (2003). Analysis of results from BETA trials (phase 2). EC Growth Project BETA, Document 1999-RD.10804, 1999-RD.10804, D25II / 2002-12-24.

WHY SYSTEM-INTEGRATION TRAINING MATTERS IN NETWORK CENTRIC OPERATIONS

Brooke B. Schaab and J. Douglas Dressel
U.S. Army Research Institute for the Behavioral and Social Sciences

ABSTRACT

Observations in U.S. Army units suggested difficulties when unacquainted persons, each with different occupational skills, must collaborate at a distance, rather than face-to-face.
Researchers identified that there was a need to comprehend the interrelationships between different roles and functions. This research compared how training content influenced performance in these situations. Training content differed in that half the players were trained on their own intelligence assets (air **or** ground) and half were trained on both their own and their ally's assets (air **and** ground). Participants trained on both their own and their ally's assets were significantly more successful in locating the enemy SCUD launchers than those trained on their own assets only (F (1,52)=4.44, $p<.05$). When participants must collaborate by sharing uniquely acquired information, it is beneficial if all participants have an understanding of each others' roles and how they interrelate.

Keywords: Training; Digital systems training; Shared situational awareness

INTRODUCTION

The training side of the Army, in particular, needs to understand the dynamics of this new environment, where soldiers, from different locations and diverse military occupations, interact with their peers and leaders electronically. The purpose of ongoing U.S. Army Research Institute (ARI) research is to compare how training content influences performance in situations where unacquainted persons, each with different occupational skills, must collaborate at a distance, rather than face-to-face.

Observations and interviews of Army personnel incorporating digital systems into their units provided preliminary insights into this training issue of collaboration across systems (Schaab & Dressel, 2003). Classroom training on how to use your own digital systems is not enough. Soldiers require an understanding of how their system interacts with other systems, and they need to experience multiple training exercises, incorporating numerous scenarios, to develop an understanding of how to collaborate to achieve situational understanding. In one command center, soldiers actually placed two different digital systems side-by-side and cross trained each other to promote collaboration both face-to-face and with systems distributed in other command centers. They understood the need to comprehend the interrelationships between their roles and functions. Obviously, this becomes much more difficult when members are distributed.

METHOD

The game SCUDHunt was selected to study multiple training variables because it provides a simplified model of this interplay of shared awareness and communication, while permitting independent manipulation of variables thought to affect them. SCUDHunt requires participants to (1) collaborate from distributed locations and (2) share unique information from their intelligence assets for optimal game performance. The goal of the game is to gather intelligence to locate three SCUD missile launchers. The game thus provides a situation where the players must execute digital tasks to achieve a shared goal, while performing their tasks in geographically separate locations.

Participants and Procedures

Twenty-eight pairs of participants trained on the computer game SCUDHunt. Players controlled either ground assets (Human Intelligence, Communication Intelligence, SEALS, Special Operations) or air intelligence (Satellite, Unoccupied Aerial Vehicle, Manned Aircraft). Training content differed in that half the players were trained on their own intelligence assets (air **or** ground) and half were trained on both their own and their ally's assets (air **and** ground).

SCUDHunt requires players to deploy their assets to gather intelligence to locate three enemy SCUD launchers. Each member of a pair was at a different location when playing two games (each consisting of 5 turns or deployment of their assets) and each controlled different assets (e.g., air assets or assets on the ground). Communication pairs used either microphones/headsets or communicated using text chat.

A computer screen displayed the results or intelligence from all assets using a common operating picture seen by both players. Players shared information on where to deploy their assets and on the reliability of their assets. At the conclusion of each game, players presented independent strike plans indicating where they thought the SCUDs were located.

RESULTS

Performance did not differ between the two training methods during the first game. It is probable that participants were continuing to develop an understanding of how to play SCUDHunt during this first game. On the second game, participants trained on both their own and their ally's assets were significantly more successful in locating the enemy SCUD launchers than those trained on their own assets only ($F(1,52)=4.44, p<.05$).

CONCLUSIONS

When participants must collaborate by sharing uniquely acquired information, it is beneficial if all participants have an understanding of each others' roles and how they interrelate. When teams operate from a common perspective, they are able to coordinate their individual efforts (Salas, Stout, & Cannon-Bowers, 1994). Important aspects of collaboration are intertwined with issues of a shared understanding of the situation. Schrage (1990) found some prior shared situational awareness is essential for effective collaboration.

Military operations in the Information Age depend upon soldiers who are able to collaborate from dispersed locations. Training for these environments should include an understanding of how networks of systems interact to optimize performance. U.S. Army facilities supporting digital units have recognized this need and are including system integration training as part of their standard curriculum.

REFERENCES

Salas, E., Stout, R., & Cannon-Bowers, J. (1994). The role of shared mental models in developing shared situational awareness. In. R. Gilson, D. Garland, & J. Koonce (Eds.), Situational awareness in complex systems (p. 297-304). Dayton Beach, FL: Embry-Riddle Aeronautical University Press.

Schaab, B., & Dressel, J. D. (2003). Training the troops: What today's soldiers tell us about training for information-age digital competency. (Research Report 1805). U. S. Army Research Institute for the Behavioral and Social Sciences: Alexandria, VA.

Schrage, M. (1990). Shared minds: The new technologies of collaboration. New York: Random House.

SUPPORTING INTELLIGENCE ANALYSTS WITH CONTEXTUAL VISUALIZATION

Sarah Geitz
Micro Analysis and Design

ABSTRACT

Situational awareness of disparate activities within a global environment requires intuitive visualization techniques that display the context from which the information presented is derived. As computer networks have become an increasing part of the global communication infrastructure, the health and security of computer networks operations has become increasingly crucial in ensuring information superiority and national security. Clear avenues of communication guarantee the availability, integrity, and confidentiality of the information and information systems used in planning, directing, coordinating, and controlling forces in the accomplishment of the mission across the full spectrum of support to national security operations. While maintaining network health and security is a globally orchestrated coordinated effort, regional differences in network traffic, configuration, rule sets, and analysts practices exist. A case study is presented examining information assurance analysts' use of visualization tools at regional sites throughout the globe. The results of the study indicate the need for a method of displaying contextual indicators.

KEYWORDS: Visualization, context, information assurance, analysts, networks, intelligence, process

INTRODUCTION

As the information available to intelligence analysts continues to proliferate, their need for graphical visualization tools becomes more critical and urgent. As a general proposition, all effective intelligence information gathering and analysis, irrespective of whether it involves sophisticated graphical systems or simply pouring over the written or wireless communications of the past, requires effective tools or systems that:

(i)   detect patterns in behavior;
(ii)   track interactions between entities over time; and
(iii)   correlate statistical results. " [1]

These principles remain equally true for both traditional intelligence gathering methods and those of the computer age. Computer systems, individual user profficiencies on those systems and the myraid of programs and tools available for their use, have presented an ever increasing level of complexity in all three areas. This can be attributed partly to the flood of multimedia, multilingual and multi-channeled information collected and partly to the ongoing development analysis tools based on widely varying principles. The wealth of, numerousity and constant refinement of analytical tools and their lightening speed ability to massage data has increased the volume of intelligence information. Increased demands for the analysis, synthesis and coherent presentation of intelligence have also increased the problem of complexity without always bringing useful coherence to it. Precisley because there are so many (constantly updated) programs and software systems out there capable of meeting the three principles of intelligence gathering and analysis, the problem of "singing off the same song sheet" may become more acute.

Further, this issue may be especially pertinent to what should be seen as a fourth principle. In today's world of sophisticated technological visualization it is perhaps of equal importance to the long-recognized three,

(iv)   presentation and implementation - providing contextual indicators of the basis of the
        visualization.

The paramount concern here is verifying the data source and avenues it has traveled in its journey to the visualization tool to ensure that the commander fully comprehends both its value and to be able to place it in a meaningful context for his needs.

Tools developed using requirements defined by a limited number of users at a single location can result in data bias. Moreover, loss or distortion of data can occur when switching domains. The ability to successfully achieve the fourth principle of modern intelligence analysis - presentation, and implementation, providing contextual indicators of the basis of the visualization - may be especially affected by this. Consideration must be given to disparate regional needs, and for a variety of considerations such as target audience, user skills, information flow, workload, and business practices.

PROCESS OF ANALYSIS

The process of intelligence analysis consists of acquiring information from multiple sources, identifying and correlating evidence, interpreting the results then creating a "product". The "product" consists of materials that provide evidence for making decisions. The materials that provide evidence for making decisions must be put into a form that is clear, concise and readily understandable. The manual reformatting of information to fit each tool used is time consuming. Especially when large data sets are being evaluated appropriate evidence is converted into a graphical form for quicker, easier understanding. Today's visualization techniques offer many attractive methods to do this – however, they are complex, and can distract from the analytic thought process.

Traditional means of visualizing information such as pie-charts, x-y plots, or bar graphs do not map to the problems of visualizing ultra-complex data sets we see today or the live data that streams forth from sensor nets all over the world. Identifying and placing key intelligence components into visual context is elemental in establishing situational awareness. A combination of symbols, schematic diagrams, maps, charts, graphs and timelines can be used to visually depict almost any situation along with two and three dimensional models and animations.

Moreover the visual information needed by commanders and other decision makers to make battlefield decisions entails evaluating and applying this information to characteristics of the battlefield that will influence friendly and threat operations. These characteristics include establishing the limits of the area of interest, identifying gaps in current intelligence holdings, in-depth evaluation of effects on friendly and threat operations, such as terrain, weather, logistical infrastructure, and demographics. A solution to merging both multiple data type and multiple visualization types is being sought.

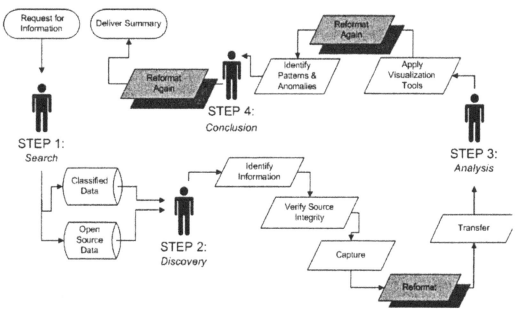

Figure 1. Generic Analysis Process Incorporating Visualization Tools

When information collected from disparate source domains using different systems is merged, a type of cultural impedance mismatch can occur. Each time information is passed on key elements of information may be lost resulting in a diluted picture. Even worse, if contextual information is lost the overall picture can become distorted. Setting software requirements based on individual users' requests and observations at one location may contribute to this problem. Differences in problem sets, the relative emphasis placed upon problem sets at different locations, and perhaps most importantly, individual differences in the ways users gather the data, analyze it, all ultimately can have effect upon the data used to produce visualizations.

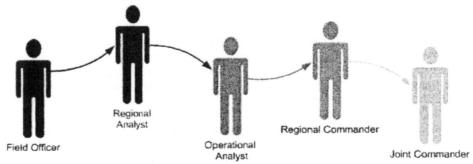

Figure 2. Information Dissolution

For software developers, identifying the appropriate data to populate these tools can be uncertain and difficult. When information collected from disparate source domains is merged, a type of cultural impedance mismatch may occur. Setting software requirements based on a limited number of individual users' requests and observations at one location may not match the needs of users at other locations due to differences in problem sets.

CASE STUDY: INFORMATION ASSURANCE ANALYSTS

The following is a case study documenting the development of a visualization tool for situational awareness for information assurance. They were observed over a period of nine months. During this time two tool studies were performed, the information presented here is the partial result of the second.

The analysts studied provide daily support to other commands in their mission to defend the DoD's computer and information networks. They serve as part of operational element for computer network defense conducting command and control protection operations to ensure the availability, integrity and confidentiality of the information and information systems used by commanders worldwide. Their role is to monitor the global picture, evaluate and to advise the six regional computer emergency response teams of potential intrusions and brief decision makers. The analysts operate efficiently to accomplish multiple goals. Added to emergency response, these analysts are tasked with performing in-depth analysis of incidents and intrusions and briefings on a daily basis.

BACKGROUND

The analysts described work in conjunction with six regional teams co-located globally. The regional teams respond to computer and network intrusions or incidents, perform vulnerability assessments and certification training as part of the computer defense. They communicate alerts and details of incidents and intrusions to a centralized command level. Much like firefighters or any other emergency response team, these analysts respond to events as they are identified. Since each event is unique, each event requires a unique response scenario. They also perform detective work in the form of, in-depth analysis of incidents, etc. Finally, they contribute information to a daily intelligence daily basis. The purpose of this brief is to provide commanders with current situational awareness. Much of the command level analyst's time is spent preparing Power Point slides for the daily intelligence briefs.

Visualization is important to establishing situational awareness for three major reasons. First, it allows analysts to rapidly examine patterns and anomalies in massive amounts of data. Second, provides a method for regional analysts to rapidly alerting the command level of source of intrusions. Third, it can provide a common method of viewing data emerging from disparate regional sites.

In late May of 2003 a visualization tool was simultaneously deployed at six regional theaters. Simultaneous deployment provided both a baseline for observing similarities and differences in analytical practices across the regional theaters as well as a baseline for establishing metrics. The visualization tool deployed was a generic graphing tool chosen for flexibility, ease of use and access to source code. It was deployed with the knowledge that further customization would be necessary.

In July 2003 questionnaires were sent to all regional theaters asking analysts to provide feedback on a recently deployed visualization tool. The questionnaires were part of a follow-up study designed in part to obtain a list of requirements. These requirements would be used in developing a customization plan for the recently deployed generic graphing tool. The more focused objective of the tool study questionnaire was to obtain feedback from analysts regarding the tools they were currently using, the tools they would like but did not have and to examine similarities and differences in analysts concerns across all theaters. The purpose of the questionnaire was additionally to identify information types, formats and practices. The resulting information was intended to feed into the development of consolidated global command view that would provide increased accuracy in the global situational awareness.

QUESTIONNAIRE

The questionnaire consisted of three parts. Parts one and two of the questionnaire elicited responses from analysts regarding the tools they had and the tools they used. Part three of the questionnaire referred to a list of the capabilities criteria. These criteria were derived from interviews, by observing analysts at the command level and from an earlier tool study performed at the command level. Numeric values were used to rate tools in the earlier tool study. Numeric values were not used this time due to the known time restraints being experienced by analysts. Additionally, the issue of combining data at different security levels was not addressed in this tool study.

Capabilities Criteria

- Easy to use
- Provides the capacity to place geo location related information on a map
- Has a short initial learning curve
- Produces meaningful visualizations
- Can be easily adjusted to look at multiple types of data and display all on one screen
- Can query for specific time frames: multiple days, one day, etc
- Can create & save filters for specific time frames: single or multiple
- Shows statistical information in the form of graphs and charts
- Provides multiple statistical views of the same data simultaneously
- Outputs data in a readily shareable format
- Reveals easily recognizable patterns
- Links entities to events over time
- Provides capacity to change data update frequency
- Looks at similarities in data, events, and entities over time
- Reveals new patterns for intrusion recognition, adaptive filtering and logging
- Can display events over time as thumbnail views
- Can display events over time as animated views
- Allows user to click on IP and drill down to all related material
- Can convert current view into a data sheet or build a data sheet view
- Reveals time based patterns for intrusions, adaptive filtering and logging
- Allows user to click on a hacker name and drill down to all related materials
- Can display and set alerts or alarms

No responses were received from theater 6, a current conflict zone. Individual responses were received from analysts in Theater 3, Theater 4 and Theater 2. One consolidated response representing the views of 19 analysts was received from Theater 1 and one consolidated response representing the views of 3 analysts was received from Theater 5.

All theaters were using the newly deployed generic graphing tool. Other responses varied by theater. Theater 2, Theater 3 and Theater 5 were more diverse in their tool use than Theater 4 and Theater 1. Theater 2 and theater 3 were both using web-based tools developed commercially and in house. They were additionally using an event correlation tool. Europe was also heavily using a statistical graphing tool.

ANALYSTS' TOOL PREFERENCE

Figure 3 documents the results of the first series of questions related to the tools the analysts currently used. This chart documents the types of tools used by analysts. The differing types of tools in use demonstrate diversity in analytic methods being practiced at different theaters. This could be in part due to differing network configurations, commanding officers, and individual analyst's backgrounds and interests. Only the recently deployed generic graphing tool was being used by all theaters.

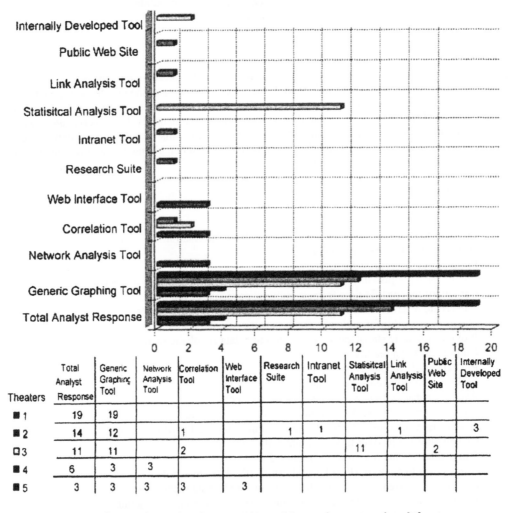

Theaters	Total Analyst Response	Generic Graphing Tool	Network Analysis Tool	Correlation Tool	Web Interface Tool	Research Suite	Intranet Tool	Statisitcal Analysis Tool	Link Analysis Tool	Public Web Site	Internally Developed Tool
■ 1	19	19									
■ 2	14	12		1		1	1		1		3
□ 3	11	11		2				11		2	
■ 4	6	3	3								
■ 5	3	3	3	3	3						

Figure 3. Comparison of tools currently used by analysts at regional theaters

156

TOOLS ANALYSTS WOULD LIKE TO HAVE

Again, responses varied by theater. Theater 3 and Theater 2 were interested in trying almost multiple tools while Theater 5 and Theater 1 were interested only in relationship mapping and intelligent query tools.

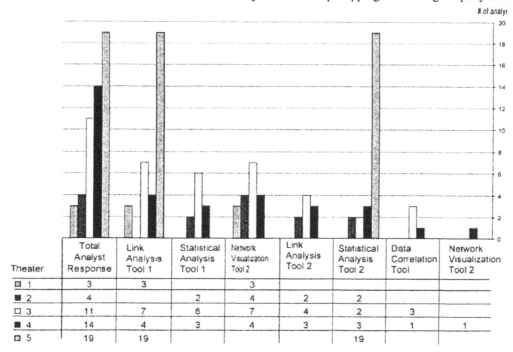

Theater	Total Analyst Response	Link Analysis Tool 1	Statistical Analysis Tool 1	Network Visualization Tool 2	Link Analysis Tool 2	Statistical Analysis Tool 2	Data Correlation Tool	Network Visualization Tool 2
1	3	3		3				
2	4		2	4	2	2		
3	11	7	6	7	4	2	3	
4	14	4	3	4	3	3	1	1
5	19	19				19		

Figure 4. Comparison of tools requested by analysts at regional theaters

CAPABILITIES CRITERIA

Analysts were asked to add to or adjust the criteria listed previously by providing comments. A synthesis of these comments is provided below.

Theater 1 Comments:

- Change this criteria (statement) from the following:
    - O Looks at similarities in data, events, and entities over time
    - *To this:*
    - O Looks at similarities and differences in data, events, and entities over time.

- Add-in/Plug-in for user-defined legends/notes (screen and print).

- (Tool should be) Compatible with industry standard report generators (e.g. Crystal Reports).

- (Tool should be) Comprehensive (and user friendly) documentation (installation manual, administrator's manual, database manual, operator's manual, etc.).

- Include the regional theaters in any design/evaluation of visualization products, particularly if the intent is to push it out to the field.

- Consider products with proven track record – we do not need to be the test bed for some new company trying to develop a product.

- Product needs to come with extensive support (24x7, levels 1,2,3, product upgrades/patches).

157

Theater 2 Comments:

- The biggest concern that needs to (be) considered (is) the amount of information overload ... Let's incorporate all these tools w/ the TRIAGE web client ... So it's a one-stop shop."

- (Requested a tool that) Can correlate data from several sources.

- The tools should be able to be integrated into the web project (being developed by a local analyst) in attempt to unify the triage processes.

- It's (referring to the recently deployed tool) visualization and querying capabilities are useful. If (it) can apply this "usefulness" against the multiple data sets relevant to each regional theater, then analysts can provide assessments more quickly by spending time looking at visualizations that come from data sets which have already gone through heavy analysis in terms of identifying relevant data and filtering out false positives.

Theater 3 Comments:

- (Requested) Extremely detailed documentation. There is little use trying to evaluate these packages without good documentation. I would suspect that the easier it is to set up and start using one these tools, the less powerful and useful it will be.

- (Requested) The ability to reach outside of the current dataset on the fly. I.E., if one is looking at just (one type of) data and notices a suspicious IP, they should be able to easily generate a new visualization that draws from multiple data sources (sites examples of data sources) without having to start from the beginning or closing the current visualization.

- If we get a new tool that requires specific hardware, it would be nice to receive the equipment to support it also.

Theater 4 Comments:

(The recently deployed tool) has already begun to make a positive impact by showing relationships much, much faster than any other methods I have seen. Please accept the following suggestions and questions for consideration:

- Name Resolution: Request look for a way to quickly provide name resolution information for multiple entries. For example, many (relevant) entities are not named. Many of the attacks we see are from multiple sources and looking up each one at a time (is there any place) ... to quickly grab and store it? Is tedious...

- Display Patterns: Request further refinement of display patterns. (Analyst then describes several methods of improving the current visualization and asks if it would be possible to have these ideas implemented.)

- Event Definition: What are the plans to update the event definitions? These will evolve as new ones are added. (What are your plans for adding) other sources?

- Legend: Is there any way to permanently remove the legend for the regional theaters? It takes up valuable space that could be used for the graph.

- Additional Hardware Interfaces: Does anyone have a recommendation for a plotter that can be used to show the bigger graphs? On a number of occasions, tracking of who connected to whom has resulted in absolutely huge graphs that become unreadable.

- Other: How do the command level and other regional theaters use (the newly deployed tool) to support their mission?

Theater 5 Comments:

- (Tool should) Display raw data on command.

- (Tool should be) Customizable to adapt to each regional theater's analysis methods.

CONCLUSION

These results indicate that the analysts were not only looking at different types of data in the various regional theaters, but they were looking at it through different lenses. Consequently, developing tools derived from requirements defined by limited number users at a single location can result in loss or distortion of information needed by analysts. Consideration must be given to disparate regional needs, and for conflicting considerations such as target audience, user skills, information flow, workload, and business practices. Tool use preference and perceived needs in different geographical theaters have shown a surprisingly large disparity in their respective data formats, functionalities and data use. Because of these variations, aggregating and correlating data from multiple sources for pattern recognition and trend analysis has proven difficult. Analysts tools must be not only be customizable to allow for rule or problem-based data selection, but also supply visual indicators regarding the context by which the information has been derived. For all of these reasons, it is not surprising that analysts perceive large gaps between the tools they have, the tools they use, and the tools they would need.

REFERENCE

Heuer, Richards, J., "Psychology of Intelligence Analysis", Center for the Study of Intelligence, Central Intelligence Agency, 1999. http://www.cia.gov/csi/books/19104/

MEASURING SIMULATION FIDELITY: A CONCEPTUAL STUDY

Dahai Liu, Dennis A. Vincenzi
Department of Human Factors and Systems
Embry-Riddle Aeronautical University

ABSTRACT

Fidelity is an important measure that can be used to evaluate the quality of human-in-the-loop simulation. Although the validity of the simulation is not necessarily related to its fidelity, appropriate levels of fidelity will facilitate transfer of training. Simulation fidelity and level of detail in a simulation model are major issues in the development of simulation models. Most applications of fidelity use a rather vague classification, such as high, medium and low. It can be argued that precise measurement of fidelity is required to gain more insight on simulation transfer of training, and fidelity can be quantitatively measured. Currently there is no standard quantification measurement of fidelity. This paper proposes a conceptual framework of fidelity assessment by integrating the current research results and using multi-layer methods (object, attributes and behavior). Mathematical model and assessment procedures are illustrated. Also the relationship between fidelity and human task performance were investigated. This framework shall serve as a springboard for future research on this subject.

Keywords: Fidelity, Quantification; Simulation; Transfer of training

Introduction

Simulation can be loosely defined as the attempted duplication of an environment. Technological advances have brought simulation closer to a perfect duplication of the real-world environment. Simulation is widely used in research, testing design, entertainment and training. Particularly for training, simulation is extremely beneficial in many situations. i.e., for pilot training for commercial airlines and the military, the reduction in time, fuel, maintenance, and wear and tear on the aircraft that flight simulation provides all translate into saving money. More importantly, simulation enables training when the real-world situation is dangerous and thus save lives. Mistakes made by the trainee in flight simulator while regrettable, are not life-threatening. The trainee can stop, rewind and try again. Through flight simulation, loss of life can be mitigated by giving inexperienced trainees exposure to these dangerous situations without actually placing them in harm's way.

The validity of simulation is largely based on the concept of transfer of training, that is, skills acquired in one situation are translated to another situation. In fact, the value of simulation depends upon transfer of training, especially for situations such as a space mission, in which real training is nearly impossible. Simulation can reduce or overcome this inability to undertake training. (Rolfe, 1998). Transfer of training from simulation can be either positive or negative, the ultimate goal is to facilitate positive transfer and avoid improper negative transfer. Three major factors will affect transfer of training: identical elements, stimulus and response, and the trainee (Throndike and Woodworth, 1901; Osgood, 1949; Carver, 1989; Cormier and Hagman, 1987).

It also can be argued that simulation quality plus human capabilities will ultimately determine the transfer of training efficiency. The key issue to the simulation quality or in the design of simulation is the "degree to which the training devices must duplicate the actual equipment" or environment, this degree of similarity is called simulation fidelity (Allen, 1986). The issue of fidelity needs to be addressed, not only because it is the most important factor to assess the simulation quality and validity, but also it is a critical factor to for cost-effective simulation devices design. Currently, fidelity or "level of details" continue to be the major issue in simulation development (Hughes and Rolek, 2003). Due to complex nature of simulation tasks, large numbers of objects and attributes and random human behaviors involved, quantification of simulation fidelity becomes the most challenging aspect of the fidelity measurement. Many researchers in simulation community have tried to develop the framework to standardize the fidelity definition and quantitative measurement. The most notable work is the framework developed by the Fidelity Definition and Metrics

Implementation Study Group (Gross, et al, 1999). Six major components of fidelity have been identified to characterize the simulation fidelity. These abstract defined components are *resolution, error, accuracy, sensitivity, precision and capacity*. A framework was established based on these six components and the semantic relationships between these components and other related concepts. The design requirements for fidelity can be defined by applying this framework. Schricker et al (2001) concluded that the main problems with how fidelity has been addressed in literature are 1) "No detailed definition; 2) Rampant subjectivity; 3)No method of quantifying the assignment of fidelity; and 4) No detailed example of a referent or detailed definition."

There are two major methods for fidelity measurement in the literature. The first is through mathematical measurement, that is, by calculating the number of identical elements shared between the real world and the simulation. The greater the number of shared identical elements, the higher the simulation fidelity. This is called the objective methods (Clark and Duncan, 1997; Gross and Freeman, 1997; Foster, 1997; Schricker, et al, 2001). Another way to measure fidelity is through trainees' performance matrix. By assessing a human's performance and then comparing it to the real world performance to measure the transfer of training, the fidelity can be measured indirectly (Mania, et al, 2003). This paper intends to review the previous work on fidelity definition and measurement, and propose a comprehensive conceptual model of fidelity, both mathematically and practically.

Definition of Fidelity

Many different definitions of fidelity exist. Many simulation professionals attempt to define fidelity comprehensively, while others argue that fidelity is a far too nebulous idea that can be even defined. This implies that efforts of defining fidelity are not being successful. (Schicker et al, 2001). The Fidelity Definition and Metrics Implementation Study Group (FDM-ISG) defines fidelity as "the degree to which a model or simulation reproduce the state and behavior of real world objects or perception of a real-world object, feature, condition or standard in a measurable or perceivable manner; a measure of the realism of a model or simulation; faithfulness. Fidelity should generally be described with respect to the measures, standards or perceptions used in assessing or stating it". (Gross et al, 1999). This definition gives a comprehensive overview of fidelity; it also implies that there are many ways to measure fidelity, objectively or subjectively. More specifically, fidelity should be defined on its simulated referent. It can be simply described "in terms of the extent to which a representation reproduces the attributes and behaviors of a referent." (Hughes and Rolek, 2002). A referent is "an entity or collection of entities and/or conditions – together with their attributes and behaviors –present within a given operational domain." (Hughes and Rolek, 2002). By using the concept of referent, the fidelity measurement can be simplified. As Schricker et al (2001) pointed that if one tried to consider fidelity issues on a real-world system, it will become far too intricate. Simulations are developed to represent a certain object/group of objects in a certain domain, it can be regarded as the simulated models of a certain referent of the reality. The relationships among real-world, referent and simulation models can be illustrated by Figure 1:

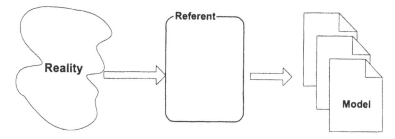

Figure 1 Relationship between referent and model (Modified) (Schricker et al, 2001)

For example, in the small aircraft aviation industry, one is particularly interested in studying the single pilot performance of a Cessna 172 (reality). A task-oriented partition and hierarchical layers of the cockpit objects would be the referent (display, radio, controls, pedals, chair, etc.); the models would be the computer simulated model to produce this referent such as Microsoft Flight Simulator.

In this paper, fidelity is defined based on the concept of referent, and for the purpose of measuring fidelity. Sublevel fidelity is also distinguished from different viewpoints: hardware/software elements viewpoints and human elements viewpoints. Simulation fidelity measures the degree to which a simulation model can accurately represent or re-produce a real-world referent. From the hardware/software elements of the model, fidelity can be further broken down into four basic categories: visual/auditory fidelity, physical fidelity, cognitive fidelity and motion fidelity; from the human performance aspects, simulation fidelity measures how well the training gained from the model can be transferred to the referent.

Visual/auditory fidelity can be thought of as the level of visual/auditory details that the simulation displays. For example, a simulated airport can include several elements or artifacts that could be found when directly viewing a real-world airport. The runways, lights, hangers, control towers, ground vehicles, natural surroundings, sirens, engine noises and other airplanes could be included in the simulations. Physical fidelity refers to how well the simulation represents the physical working environment, i.e. in flight simulation it refers to the cockpit environment and its various controls and instruments. Cognitive fidelity refers to the extent that the simulation environment engages the pilot cognitively (Kaiser and Schroeder, 2003). The cognitive engagements include the multi-tasking of communication, situational awareness, monitoring instruments and movement of the aircraft. The key to cognitive fidelity is to reproduce the flight elements to shape the mental model of the pilot. In other words, the simulation should produce enough stress for the trainee to gain the cognitive training experience. Motion fidelity is the degree to which the simulation can reproduce the motion felt (i.e., front, back, up, down, and side to side). Sense of motion may certainly facilitate the transfer of training, thus, a higher degree of fidelity may be achieved.

Measurements of Fidelity

Simulations are developed under the assumption that higher fidelity will always produce high simulation quality, thus facilitate the transfer of training. This assumption is not always true. Evidence indicates that transfer of training doesn't increase linearly as fidelity increases. As the "Alessi Hypothesis" (Alessi, 1988) states, there is a certain point at which adding more fidelity does not transfer training at the same rate as during early or beginning training. In other words, the law of diminishing returns holds true. This implies that implementing an "all you can afford" level of fidelity is not always the most cost-effective approach. To find the most appropriate level of fidelity needed for the simulation tasks, one needs to be able to assess the fidelity level. Research on simulation has been primarily focused on hardware and software development, which is targeted at "the ultimate display" to produce the real-time simulated environment. The question is what is the minimum fidelity that is required to achieve the required level of transfer of training? The importance of this fidelity measurement is also addressed by the FDM-ISG (Gross et al 1999) as "what aspect should be simulated and how to observe the simulation purpose and objectives best". This amount of fidelity requirements are essential for simulation system design, because the fidelity requirements will ultimately affect the simulation context, purpose and hardware/software requirement, and thus affect the trade-off results between cost and achieved transfer-of-training.

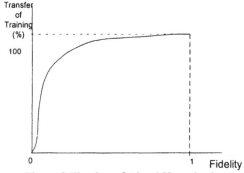

Figure 2 Illustion of Alessi Hypothesis

162

The Mathematical Model

Objective measurement of simulation fidelity tried to compare the simulated objects with the corresponding referent/real-world environment. The key of objective measurement is using mathematical methods to compare objects individually. Exact measure of realism is not feasible, "a goal which can never be accomplished" (Roza et al, 2001) because it is practically impossible to count everything, know everything about the reality/referent due to 1) the high degree of uncertainty, the overwhelming information involved and complicated attributes/behaviors associated and 2) human limitations on observing and explaining real world information. For years, researches on fidelity quantification focused on more the objective mathematical formulation. As Schricker et al (2001) summarized that for the quantification method, "the simpler it is, the less objective it becomes." A simple method worth to mention is the one proposed by Gross and Freeman (Schricker et al 2001), the measurement is based on four theorems:

I.) $0 \le F(A) \le 1$

II.) if $F(A) = 1$, then $A \equiv R$

III) $F(A) \ge F(Meta\ A)$

IV) $F(A) + F(B) = \min(F(A), F(B))$

Where A and B are models of interest, $F(A)$ is the fidelity of A, Meta A is a model of referent including A and R is the referent of A. The simple formula for determining the overall value of fidelity of a simulation system:

$$F_s = \sum F_i W_i$$

F_i is the fidelity of each referent characteristics and F_s is the fidelity of the entire simulation system. W_i is the relative importance rate of characteristics i. Obviously this formula contradicts Theorem IV above (Schricker et al 2001). The main reason for this contradiction is because it didn't define clearly the set, operation on the set and function.

Let set S defined as the following:

$S = \{A : A = meta_i R\}$ (R is the referent of the real world group of objects, S is the group of all possible simulation models of referent R), then the function of fidelity is defined on set S as

$F : S \rightarrow [0,1]$

It can be easily concluded that F is surjective, that is, each element of [0,1] is the image of at least one element in S. furthermore, we define the following operations

For $A \in S$ and $B \in S$, $A \oplus B = A \cup B$, (one can easily prove that $A + B$ is commutative and associative). Based on these notations, Gross and Freeman (1999)'s model can be modified as following: I, II and III are still true and IV becomes $\min(F(A), F(B)) \le F(A \oplus B) \le \max(F(A), F(B))$

Gross and Freeman (Schricker et al, 2001) stated that fidelity of any simulated system equal to the fidelity of the individual of the simulation of the lowest fidelity. That is not true intuitively, since if we adding low fidelity components (close to 0) to a high simulation model, it will certainly affect the overall fidelity, but it should not get close to zero. So it can be concluded that $F(A \oplus B) \ne F(A) + F(B)$ and $F(A \oplus B) \ne Min(F(A), F(B))$.

The simple formula $F_s = \sum F_i W_i$ still applies, for each model A, and $\sum W_i = 1$. This formula does not contradict with IV because these are factors to measure the fidelity and factor itself is not considered a model.

Procedure of Measurement

Fidelity can be measured directly by using the fidelity framework (Roza et al, 2001; Schricker et al 2001). The following Figure 3 illustrates a generic model of measurement framework:

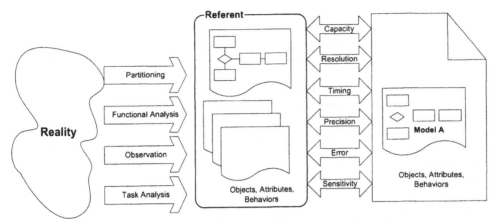

Figure 3 A Conceptual illustration of Measurement Procedure

By using this framework, all simulation task-critical objects can be identified as well their associated behaviors and attributes for the referent. Those are the target parameters. By comparing the level (percentage) of the corresponding objects from a simulation model, the fidelity can be estimated quantitatively. This framework is based on the assumption of Perato's Law (20 % of the elements contributes 80% of the training effects in simulation).

Indirect measurement of fidelity can be approximated by evaluation of human performance. It is assumed that the function of fidelity is bijective, that is, for one referent, two simulation models have the same transfer of training effect if and only if these two simulated models have the same fidelity. Since the ultimate goal of simulation is to transfer the skills gained to the real world situation and the objective measurement of fidelity are far more intrigue, the measurement of the human task performance would be a good metrics for any application that mainly targets transfer of training in the real world (Waller et al, 1998 and Mania et al, 2003). Although human performance assessment cannot give the quantitative answer of simulation fidelity, it can provide a relative efficiency of different simulated models for the same referent, and it is more intuitive and hands-on, this measurement is widely accepted and being used (Mania et al 2003).

Conclusion

In this paper, we briefly reviewed the concept of fidelity and it's measurement methods. Due to the complex nature of the simulated world plus the limitations of human cognitive abilities, it is not desirable to measure simulated objects directly. An abstract referent is required for fidelity measurement. Previous researches have attempted to formulate the assessment both mathematically and practically in an objective way. The mathematical model and generic procedural model proposed in this paper combined and integrated with the previous research results, provides a comprehensive overview on simulation fidelity definition and measurement, it shall serve as a springboard for the future efforts on this subject.

Nevertheless to say, the goal of fidelity assessment is to develop an objective measure and avoid subjectivity as much as possible. However, current available models cannot fully guarantee this goal. There are certain points that human subjectivity is inevitably involved, i.e, abstraction of the referent, evaluation of human performance, simulated objects/attributes/behaviors, human subjective justification are required. For the future research, a more rigorous set of measurement factors and automatic detecting devices are needed to eliminate this subjectivity. A limitation for the current models is that it is based on too many assumptions, the validation of those assumptions are also critical.

Technologies advance everyday to bring simulation to a more detailed level. This also indicates an urgent need for a standard theory/method for simulation assessment. It is a widespread belief that in the near future, fidelity quantification standard will be established.

References

Alessi, S.M. (1988). Fidelity in the Design of Instructional Simulations. *Journal of Computer-Based Instruction*, 15(2), 40-47

Allen, John A. (1986). Maintenance Training Simulator Fidelity and Individual Difference in Transfer of Training, *Human Factors*, 28(5), 497-509.

Carver, Cpt. T., (1991). Training Transfer: A Question of Quality, *The Royal Aeronautical Society Conference* p.11.1-1.6 London, UK, Nov. 1991

Cormier S. M. and Hagman J. D. (1987). Transfer of Learning. *Contemporary Research and Application.*, Academic Press, London.

Gross D. C. , Pace D., Harmoon, S., and Tucker, W. (1999), "Why Fidelity?", *Spring 1999 Simulation Interoperability Workshop*, Paper No. 99S-SIW-168.

Gross D. C and Freeman R. (1997). Measuring Fidelity Differentials in HLA Simulations. *Fall 1997 Simulation Interoperability Workshop*: Workshop Papers.

Hughes T. and Rolek E. (2003), Fidelity and Validity: Issues of Human Behavioral Representation Requirements Development, *Proceedings of the 2003 Winter Simulation Conference*, New Orleans, LA, Dec 2003.

Kaiser, Mary K. & Schroeder, Jeffery A., (2003). Flights of Fancy: The Art and Science of Flight Simulation, Principles and Practice of Aviation Psychology, *Human Factors in Transportation*, 435-471

Mania K. et al (2003), Fidelity Metrics for Virtual Environment Simulations Based on Spatial Memory Awareness States. *Presence, Teleoperators and Virtual Environments*, 12(3), 296-310

Osgood, C. E. (1949), The similarity paradox in human learning: a resolution. *Psychological Review*, 56, 132-143

Rolfe, J.M., (1991). Transfer of Training, *The Royal Aeronautical Society Conference* p.1-1.8 London, UK, Nov. 1991

Roza, M., (2000). Fidelity Considerations for Civil Aviation Distributed Simulations, AIAA 2000-4397, *AIAA Modeling and Simulation Technologies Conference and Exhibit*, Aug., 2000, Denver, Colorado.

Roza M. et al (2001), Defining, Specifying and Developing Fidelity Referents, *Proceedings of The 2001 European Simulation Interoperability Workshop*, Paper No. 008, London, UK, available at http://www.sisostds.org/doclib/doclib.cfm?SISO_RID_1003706.

Schricker B. C. et al (2001). Fidelity Evaluation Framework, *Proceedings of the IEEE 34th Annual Simulation Symposium*. Seattle, WA.

Thorndike E. L. and Woodworth R. S. (1901), The Influence of Improvement in One Mental Function upon the efficiency of other functions, *Psychological Review*, 8, 247-261.

Human Factors and Situational Awareness Issues in Fratricidal Air-to-Ground Attacks

Malcolm James Cook, Helen S.E. Thompson, Corinne S.G. Adams, Carol S. Angus, Gwen Hughes, Derek Carson
University of Abertay Dundee

ABSTRACT

In recent military operations advanced technology has increased the potency of coalition war fighters and some authors have high expectations for future technological developments (Hallion, 1997; Werrell, 2003), other are more conservative about the potential gains from technology (O'Hanlon, 2000; Cook et al., 2003; Cook, in press). There is increasing demand for faster sensor-to-shooter times to attack targets of opportunity because Time Sensitive Targeting (TST) is an operational requirement in modern warfare, which makes accurate situation awareness critical. Increasing the speed of response suggests a potential speed-accuracy trade-off and combat identification technologies are required to address this faster response. However, at the same time that sensors are improving the range of weaponry is being extended (Flack, 2002; Cook, in press) creating a capability gap. The key issue in situation awareness is the divergence of capability in targeting, related to coordinates using GPS guidance and the limited capability for identification at long-ranges in manned and unmanned platforms.

Keywords: Fratricide, Technology, Time-Sensitive-Targeting, Kill Chains, Errors

INTRODUCTION

> "Future targeting work will concentrate on improving precision and reducing the time taken to guide weapons onto targets fired from the sea and long-range, indirect land systems" (Barrie, 2003).

In recent military operations advanced technology has significantly increased the potency of U.S. and U.K. war fighters, with improved sensors and weapons resulting in significantly improved performance on ageing platforms. There are high expectations for future developments based on current performance (Hallion, 1997; Werrell, 2003) but there are some who are conservative about the potential gains resulting from new targeting technologies (O'Hanlon, 2000). Despite this concern there is increasing demand for faster sensor-to-shooter times and shorter kill-chains to attack fleeting targets of opportunity in recent campaigns. Time Sensitive Targeting (TST) is part of a move away from fixed Air Tasking Orders (ATO) that in itself is a reflection of operational needs in new theatres of action. The dynamic tasking reflects the high value attached to mobile or fleeting targets because the effectiveness of air operations in recent campaigns has frequently exhausted the fixed asset list, which in places like Afghanistan was relatively short. Even though the target density was sparse in Afghanistan many mistakes were still made (CDI, 2002). Increasing the speed of sensor-to-shooter action seems to suggest a speed-accuracy trade-off not unlike that associated with human performance and there are a number of technological fixes to address this. However, at the same time that sensors are improving the range of weaponry is being extended by specialist kits to extend the flight time of glide bombs, by increased operational altitudes to release weapons with greater potential energy and by the use of advanced stand-off weaponry with an internal propulsion system (Flack, 2002; Cook, in press). The key issue in situation awareness terms is the divergence of targeting, related to coordinates and the limited capability for identification at long-ranges. In addition, at short-range it is clear that the current sensors are not able to satisfactorily guarantee identification to the required level. Thus, it fratricide is more than a simple error that can easily be corrected with new identification systems that will be subject to failure in battlefield conditions.

The problem of friendly fire and the impact of such accidents on morale are well recognised and it has received attention from many authors in the media and the internet (Bickers, 1994; Leveson, Allen, and Storey, not known; Marcus, 2002; Nurenberg, 2002; Roberts, 2003). Personal accounts of war-fighting such as that from the first Gulf War, against Iraq by coalition forces, make frequent references to the risks of friendly fire and the actual cases that occurred (Gillespie, 2001), indicating the importance to the war fighter and the likely impact on their effectiveness. Advocates of new technology identify combat identification issues as highly significant in terms of improving military performance (Alexander, 2003; National Audit Office, 2002). It is worth considering the methods for improving the interface to automated and assisted target recognition systems to meet the new challenges while managing the risk of co-lateral damage and fratricide which has persisted in spite of the recognition of the problem in the first Gulf War (Koehler, 1992; Regan, 1995, 2002a, 2002b, National Audit Office, 2002). Recently the A-10 Warthog was given an approved life-extension program consisting of improved precision engagement capability, with a global positioning system (GPS), blue force tracking capability, and improved targeting pod (Hoyle, 2004). This is particularly poignant given the role of the aircraft in committing blue-on-blue engagements in the first Gulf War but that platform is not alone in its vulnerability to error. On the 26th February 1991 the Royal Regiment of Fusiliers travelling in Warrior armoured vehicles were attacked by an A-10 which fired maverick missiles at the vehicles even thought the vehicles were correctly marked and in their allocated area of operations. Thus, the A-10 pilot incorrectly identified the location, the vehicles and failed to make use of the markings. If the new variants of bombing and air-to-ground weapons are to become an effective weapon in future unmanned combat vehicles (UCAVS) then many of the same issues need resolved to answer the concerns expressed about bombing for many years (see Lindqvist, 2000). Human factors such as target diversity, stress, fatigue and problematic automation strategies are considered with regard to their impact on situational awareness and erroneous performance as suggested in Cook et al., (2003). The air-to-ground interface produces the second highest number of blue-on-blue attacks and during attack, which is a more likely strategy in asymmetric warfare by US and UK coalition forces, errors are more frequent (National Audit Office, 2002). It is not surprising to find that the vehicles that are found at the Forward Edge of the Battle Area, such as main battle tanks and armoured personnel carriers, are the one's most likely to be attacked because this is where the greatest confusion occurs with regard to place. It has been suggested that much of the current targeting is associated with place cues and not with identity cues (Cook, 2004), giving rise to the typical pattern of errors that are made.

Recently, it has been suggested that weapon systems can now reach much farther than sensors can be used to identify potential targets (Cook, in press). Even with the future sensors for offensive air systems, manned or unmanned, the issues are likely to remain the same (Cook, Angus, Adams, Findlay, McGow, Beath, Reeve, Shepherd, Beggan, Mollison, and Sinclair, 2003; O'Hanlon, 2000) because the problem is like many associated with human factors, in that errors are a concatenation of capability gaps and process failures resulting in catastrophe. A detailed examination of specific incidents like that associated with the Black Hawk Helicopter shoot down in Northern Iraq, during Operation Provide Comfort (Snook, 2000; Piper, 2000) suggests that organisational, technological and human issues contribute to the error chain, in much the same way that the same processes contribute to accidents according to Reason's popular model of organisational accidents (Reason,). In the UK, the National Audit Office (2002) has examined the need for combat identification processes and it has concluded that there is currently a significant risk that could be reduced by improvements in technology. In particular it was noted that Battlefield Target Identification and Identification Sensors were critical. However, the current solution has been to provide a piecemeal and quick-fix strategy based on thermal identification panels, glint tape, visual markings and coloured panels. The historical evidence suggests that this may not be enough because it has not proved satisfactory in the past and the NAO (2002) report supports this conclusion.

CAUSES OF FRIENDLY FIRE

At a recent industry forum a number of alternatives were proposed to improve combat identification and the strengths and weaknesses were considered. Schwartz (2004) has suggested that there are a number of panels, markers and identification schemes used by the coalition forces in Iraq, during the 2nd and most recent Gulf War. However, Nicols (2004) noted that the schemes had failed to be effective in some cases and there were still a lot of lessons to be learned from the current incidents where markings had been used. Wing Commander Chris Norton (2004) gave a user's perspective on the problem from the point of a serving pilot with a number of illustrations from the most recent conflict in Iraq. Wing Commander Norton indicated that on one occasion the same vehicles were attacked repeatedly because the battle damage assessment process could not identify evidence of their destruction. On another mission, aircraft were tasked with hitting locations where vehicles were identified but the targets were actually revetments dug in the shape of pairs of tank tracks. Finally, Wing Cmdr Norton gave an illustration where in Close-Air-Support (CAS) one of the most difficult types of cooperative engagement on a SAM site occurred but it was clear that this was the exception and not the rule. A key issue that frequently contributed to the targeting problems in recent conflicts was the quality of the imagery that was inadequate from the operational altitude of the aircraft at around 16,000 feet because the poor imagery made the targets difficult to identify. There is currently some dispute as to whether the thermal imaging sensors are inadequate or the displays on which the imagery is shown are ineffective, the result for the operator is the same. It was clear that the attempts to improve training using systems such as the ROC-V training system, described by Major Ray Compton, would not have dividends if the operational imagery was of such low quality. The critical point of the discussions was the use of place dominated and it was not identity that was used as a cue to targeting, which is in agreement with the interpretation put forward by Cook (2004).

THE KILL-CHAIN

The classical kill-chain contains a number of components which include the following steps outlined in Figure 1. The early stages of targeting aim to detect and identify the target. In theory the target would be tracked throughout the other stages because mobile high value assets will frequently be moved on the battlefield. Thus, place is not a good indicator of identity even though it sometimes has been used as such.

Nine of the critical steps in targeting
1) Detect 2) Identify 3) Assess 4) Apportion
5) Task 6) Acquire 7) Manoeuvre 8) Aim
9) Fire – the 10th step is the effect on the target.

Figure 1 Kill chain and targeting steps

The analysis of friendly fire incidents suggests that frequently the attacking aircraft, in an air-to-ground scenario, will have used the find and fix stages of the targeting process to determine if the potential target is a valid enemy asset. Thus, the initial stage of finding and fixing targets which is largely associated with the physical location needs to allow for easy segregation of enemy and friendly vehicles to prevent blue-on-blue engagements. This association of place with identity could be resolved with a network centric approach but it would need high levels of data integrity to prevent damaged friendly vehicles being identified as hostile. The segregation of enemy and friendly assets at long range is increasingly important because Synthetic Aperture Radar (SAR) enables detection at longer ranges and this could prime early weapon release with the longer range weapons. It is clear that a network centric fused multi-sensor image is required to release the potential benefits of the weapons and to prevent unnecessary own-force casualties. Careful analysis of the Black Hawk shoot down suggests that a *Big Picture* did exist but that procedural, organisational and technical failures prevented that picture from guiding the actions of the F-15 aircraft intercepting the helicopters. It is clear that large distinctive objects such as the Iraqi Scud Launcher shown in Figure 2 are relatively easy to identify in some circumstances but training is required when they are viewed from medium to high altitude with the rocket vertical.

Figure 2 An Al-Hussein Iraqi modified Scud Launcher.

EXPERIMENTAL ANALYSIS OF FRIENDLY FIRE

A series of short pilot experiments with experienced observers examined the effect of automated cues and aiding with threshold imagery simulating the various sensor options for future targeting systems. Examples of the simulated thermal images are shown below for the Warrior (UK) and BMP (Iraqi) vehicles. It was clear from this work on un-cued images and from previous experiments that the current sensor limits do not meet the future requirement for targeting at altitudes of 20,000 feet and above that altitude performance will fall further. Current technology developments are looking at targeting up to 40,000 feet to ensure that the platform is higher than the Surface-to-Air Missile (SAM) threat. Using simple geometry, where the weapon range forms the base of a triangle and altitude forms the vertical it is clear that the potential viewing ranges are of the order of 20-25 miles or more, even for short-range weapons at medium altitudes. This supports the reports of users such as Wing Commander Norton cited above, who feel that the task they are given in terms of identification is at or near the limits of what is possible, without further technology to increase the certainty of identification.

Figure 3 A Warrior (UK) armoured fighting vehicle and a BMP (Iraqi Operated) armored fighting vehicle.

When the use of vehicle markings, decoys and deception are considered with regard to targeting performance to ascertain the impact on effectiveness in a future campaign, against a sophisticated opposing force in a dynamic battlefield typical of current campaign, the conclusions are far worse. It is likely that combat identification based largely on radio frequency tags and other markings will fail to provide adequate protection. The experimental evidence suggests that at short-ranges performance improves for marked vehicles but as the range increases the dependence on the visibility or response of the tag is critical. This is reminiscent of the problems associated with intermittent IFF in the Black Hawk helicopter shoot down in Northern Iraq (Snook, 2000). However, UK forces lost a helicopter in the Falklands when the IFF was unresponsive and HMS Cardiff launched a SAM at the unidentified aircraft which was presumed hostile.

Only effective blue-force tracking with accurate GPS coordinates will significantly improve targeting performance if it is linked to weapon controls on-board the aircraft and prevents erroneous weapon release. The analysis of targeting errors suggests that no single system can afford protection against co-lateral damage or friendly fire because corroborative evidence is required to manage uncertainty and contradictions on the battlefield. The current and future combat identification systems must not fail to adequately embrace design principles outlined by Endlsey, Bolté, and Jones (2003) because they will not protect against uncertainty, decoys and deception. Thus, the phenomenon of fratricide on the battlefield will continue until the wider range of issues is addressed and the chain of events leading to fratricide is broken. If has been suggested that if a revolution in military affairs is to occur on the digitised battlefield then fratricide is one of the critical issues in enabling the warfighting (Owens, 2001) and that requires effective situation awareness.

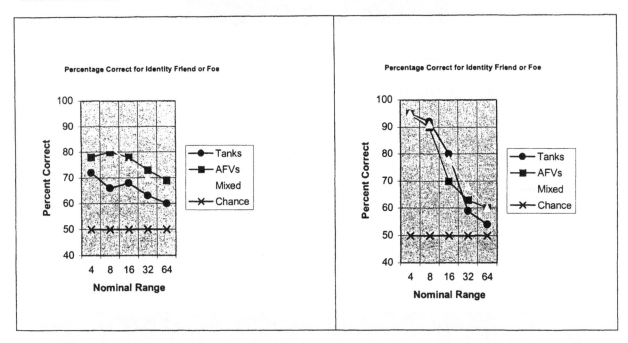

Figure 4 Graphs of Percent Correct Performance for Target Force Identity (Friend or Foe). Left hand graph illustrates performance without identification panels and the right hand illustrates performance with identification panels. The left hand side of the graph is short-range targets and the right hand side is long-range targets.

REFERENCES

Alexander, J.B. (2003) *Winning the war: Advanced weapons, strategies, and concepts for the post – 9/11 world*. New York: St Martin's Press.
Barrie, D. (2003) Reflective Mood. *Aviation Week and Space Technology*, July 14th, 40.
Bickers, Richard Townsend (1994) *Friendly fire: Accidents in Battle from Ancient Greece to the Gulf War*. London: Leo Cooper.
CDI (2002) Killing your own: The problem of friendly fire during the Afghan Campaign. Available at http://www.cdi.org/terrorism/ killing-pr.cfm
Cook M.J. (2004) Human factors of visual identification panels and automated RF IFF systems. Combat ID and IFF, 22nd-23rd March 2004, SMi Conferences, The Hatton, London.
Cook, M.J. (in press) Reaching out to touch someone. Defence Management Journal.
Cook, M.J., Angus, C.S., Adams, C.S.G., Findlay, P.C., McGow, F.J., Beath, F.F., Reeve, M.J., Shepherd, G., Beggan, C.D., Mollison, N., and Sinclair, P.M. (2003) Human factors of targeting and fratricide issues in multi-spectral targeting. *Time critical targets: Filling the capability gap*. MoD, Abbey Wood, Bristol (19th-20th November 2003): Published by Royal Aeronautical Society.
Compton, R. (2004) The ROC-V training system. Combat ID and IFF, 22nd-23rd March 2004, SMi Conferences, The Hatton, London.
Endlsey, M., Bolté, B., and Jones, D.G. (2003) *Designing for situation awareness: An approach to user-*

centred design. London: Taylor and Francis.

Flack, J. (2002) *NATO Air-launched weapons.* Sevenoaks: Crowood Press.

Hallion, R.P. (1997) Precision air attack in the modern era. In R.P. Hallion (Ed.) *Air power confronts an unstable world.* London: Brassey's Press.

Hoyle, C. (2004) Old hog.....new tricks. *Flight International,* 4927 (165), 30-31.

Koehler, A.C. (1992) Friendly Fire on Today's Battlefield. Available at http://www.globalsecurity.org/military/library/report/1992/KAC.htm

Lindqvist, S. (2000) *A history bombing.* London: Granta Books.

O'Hanlon, M. (2000) *Technological change and the future of warfare.* Washington D.C.: Brookings Institution Press.

Leveson, N.G., Allen, P., and Storey M-A. (not known) The analysis of friendly fire accident using a systems model of accidents. Available at http://sunnyday.mit.edu/accidents/issc-bl-2.pdf

Marcus, J. (2002) Analysis: 'Friendly Fire' danger. Available at http://news.bbc.co.uk/1/hi/world/americas/1937217.stm

National Audit Office (2002) *Ministry of Defence: Combat identification.* London: The Stationery Office.

Nurenberg, G. (2002) Killing friendly fire. Available at http://www.techtv.com/news/print/0,23102.3372908,00.html

Owens, B. (2001) *Lifting the fog of war.* London: John Hopkins University.

Piper, J.L. (2000) *A chain of events.* London: Brassey's.

Regan, G. (2002) *Backfire: A history of friendly fire from ancient warfare to the present day.* London: Robson Books.

Regan, G. (1993) *More Military Blunders.* London: Guinness Publishing.

Regan, G. (2002) *Air force blunders.* London: Carlton Books.

Roberts, H. (2003) Combat identification: The aims and realities. *Air International,* 64(6), 59-62.

Schwartz, D. (2004) The evolution of combat identification. Combat ID and IFF, 22nd-23rd March 2004, SMi Conferences, The Hatton, London.

Snook, S.A. (2000) *Friendly Fire.* Princeton University Press.

Werrell, K.P. (2003) *Chasing the silver bullet: U.S. Air Force weapons development from Vietnam to Desert Storm.* London: Smithsonian Press.

AIR TRAFFIC CONTROL

AN INTERPOLATION METHOD FOR RATING SEVERITY OF RUNWAY INCURSIONS

Thomas B. Sheridan

DOT/Volpe National Transportation Systems Center, Cambridge, MA

ABSTRACT

The FAA defines a runway incursion as: "Any occurrence at an airport [with an operating control tower] involving an aircraft, vehicle, person, or object on the ground that creates a collision hazard or results in a loss of separation with an aircraft taking off, intending to take off, landing, or intending to land." (FAA, 2002a).

A method for rating severity of runway incursions is presented. For each of a set of scenario classes covering different types of runway incursions, severity ratings are pre-assigned for combinations of closest horizontal or vertical proximity and minimum/maximum levels of pre-determined moderating factors. These values determine preset coefficients for a computerized algorithm, which is later used to determine the severity rating of each individual incursion and its particular reported variables.

Upon the occurrence of any runway incursion, analysts categorize the event with respect to the scenario and the levels of each of the several influencing factors. Closest horizontal or vertical proximity is estimated by the controller that observed the event. From this information, the computer determines the severity rating for that particular incursion.

Comparisons of calculations to ratings already made by the FAA are encouraging. All parameters of the algorithm including the "best" and "worst" ratings for each scenario and proximity, the factor definitions and the scaling of the factor influence, will be amenable to adjustment until validation of the model is complete.

Keywords: Air traffic control, Runway safety, Runway incursions, Severity rating, Scaling

INTRODUCTION

Severity of a runway incursion is defined here as the outcome of the incursion in terms of the closest proximity (horizontal or vertical) that an aircraft actually came, *or might easily have come*, to a collision with another aircraft, vehicle, or object on the runway. Factors that influence the probability of a *collision for a repetition of an incursion of similar circumstances* include: aircraft dimensions and performance characteristics, visibility, weather, airport geometry, and operator (controller, pilot or vehicle driver) responses. This rating is independent of events that occur after the time of closest proximity and, by FAA criteria, the number of people at risk.

Currently, reports of runway incursions caused by pilot or controller errors are filed by local FAA flight standards or air traffic control personnel, respectively. Figure 1 gives a de-identified example of a runway incursion report with airport, date, and particular aircraft de-identified. The reports of runway incursions are passed to a committee of subject matter experts (representing offices of Air Traffic, Flight Standards, Airports, and System Safety) in the FAA's Office of Runway Safety who read the reports, discuss the reported facts, and arrive at a consensus (or at least a majority vote) severity rating of A, B, C or D. The A rating is characterized by immediate need for extreme corrective action to avoid collision, B by significant potential for collision, C by ample time and distance to avoid collision, and D by little chance of collision while nevertheless meeting the definition of a runway incursion (see FAA 2002a for more extensive definitions of these grades).

Unfortunately the subjective rating method in current use has yielded inconsistent results with poor inter-rater reliability (Cardosi, 2003). While no rating system for runway incursions can be completely objective, it is hoped that by establishing *a priori* criteria and rules for translating factual data and quantitative estimates into ratings, and implementing the translation by computer, the new method will be more objective and more internally consistent than the current method (FAA, 2002b).

Aircraft #1, maintenance taxi requested taxi instructions to spot 53 for a gate 22 assignment. Ground control (GC) thought Aircraft #1 repositioning from Terminal D and did not realize it was at the southeast maintenance area. GC issued taxi instructions to "hold short of A." Aircraft #1 crossed Runway 35C when Local Control (LC) noticed the aircraft and asked GC if if was holding short of Runway 35L where Aircraft #2, was on departure roll. GC issued an immediate hold short clearance, which stopped Aircraft #1, but after the aircraft had already crossed the hold short lines for Runway 35L via Taxiway B. Aircraft #2 observed Aircraft #1 taxiing and aborted takeoff, stopping 300 feet short of Taxiway B.

Figure 1. Example of narrative from runway incursion report.

ASSUMPTIONS / DEFINITIONS

1. For purposes of calculation assume severity S is a continuous scale of 1 to 4. The conventional ratings "A, B, C and D" correspond to 4, 3, 2 and 1 respectively. In the new system we allow a "plus" adding 0.3 and a "minus" subtracting 0.3 from each numerical grade (e.g., B+ = 3.3, B– = 2.7). No A+ is considered; it is reserved for an actual crash.

2. Assume a set of independent incursion scenarios that broadly subsume all incursions, for example "Two landing aircraft on same runway (tail chase), one aircraft landed, one went around." Currently these are categorized under the following headings:
• Two landing aircraft
• One landing aircraft, one taxiing aircraft
• One landing aircraft, one aircraft taking off
• Two aircraft taking off
• One aircraft taking off, one taxiing
• (plus modifications of these when vehicles and/or pedestrians are involved)

To date, 52 such scenarios have been identified that specify the aircraft or vehicles, their status (e.g., taxiing, holding, taking-off, landing), and other descriptors of what actually happened at the time of the incident.

3. Assume a small set of closest horizontal or vertical proximities (CHP or CVP, respectively). In some scenarios, only one of these proximities will be appropriate; if both are appropriate, then the smaller proximity value is used.

4. Assume a small set of common scalable factors that further characterize each scenario (though not all are appropriate to every scenario). The factors are:
• Visibility/RVR/ceiling
• Takeoff or landing aircraft #1 (weight and thrust characteristics affecting takeoff and landing distances)
• Takeoff or landing aircraft #2 (unless second object is a vehicle or pedestrian)
• Controller erroneous communications or actions
• Pilot erroneous communications or actions
• Extraordinary remedial action taken by pilot

Each of these factors is scaled by a variable P from 0 to 10. P (for "potential") of 0 means there is no influence of that factor to make the severity of the given incursion greater than what is evident from the closest proximity alone, other conditions being "normal." P of 10 means there is maximum influence of that factor to make the severity of the given incursion greater than what is evident from the closest proximity alone with other conditions normal. The important idea here is that if all factors are ideal (i.e., visibility /ceiling is no problem, both aircraft are the smallest general aviation types (and hence, relatively slow, light-weight and highly maneuverable), no pilot-controller communication anomalies, and no extraordinary avoidance actions were taken by the pilot to brake, swerve, abort a takeoff or go around on a landing) then all Ps are therefore 0, and the severity of the runway incursion is adequately represented by the given CHP or CVP "best case." If, on the other hand, all Ps are 10 – visibility/ceiling are at their worst, both aircraft are large and heavy, pilot-controller communications are non-existent, and extreme avoidance actions are taken by the pilot – the resulting proximity of aircraft (or aircraft and other object) could easily have been much worse, so is represented by the given CHP or CVP "worst case." The greater each factor rating, the greater the expected variability of closest proximity for recurring runway incursions under the same conditions.

Selected points on each of the factor scales are labeled to indicate to a rater (person observing the runway incursion) what conditions for that factor are appropriate to each value of P. Page limitations prevent examples from being shown here. One may think of these scales as having enough such labeled points specified that the person doing the initial rating would be obliged to select the appropriate label for each factor. That would be an ideal in terms of reducing subjectivity and inter-rater variability. On the other hand, one might maintain that there will always be conditions that cannot be specified a priori by labels, so that the rater will necessarily have to select some P value in between the given labels. This is an issue that is not settled as of this writing.

As noted above, for different scenarios some relevant factors would be the same, while others would differ. For example, size of both landing aircraft in a tail-chase scenario are relevant because of potential closing speed in rollout of a large fast aircraft over a small slow one. However if one aircraft has stopped with its nose just over the hold short line, only the characteristics of the landing or takeoff aircraft are relevant.

Note that all of these factors are objective variables that, in principle, can be specified, though some factors, such as pilot-controller communications and extraordinary avoidance maneuvers, must be estimated. Such factors are comprised of actions that the pilot, controller, or vehicle driver, actually took. As such, they do not include what the pilot or controller might have seen or heard or thought (beyond what was realized in the actions taken), or what other events might have caused the incursion. *The model seeks to categorize severity, not determine cause.*

Some further examples may help to convey the idea of factor P ratings adding severity to the "best case" CHP or CVP. Suppose two aircraft landing head-on actually stopped 200 feet from one another in a perfect visibility situation. In a recurring perfect visibility incursion, this same closest proximity outcome has a higher chance of happening than in poor visibility where there is degraded information for all parties, and thus a greater chance of CHP being much closer. Similarly, if available response time for one pilot were extremely short (e.g., <5 seconds), then more variability would be expected in the distribution of recurring pilot responses (and hence, the severity of the outcome) than if the available response time were long. A final example is that of extraordinary avoidance response. If the incident involved no extraordinary avoidance responses, then the outcome defined by the other factors would be representative of the risk. However, if there were extraordinary avoidance responses, then the outcome could easily have been worse (based on the variability for repeated occurrences) than if the extraordinary maneuvers had not occurred. Thus, each such factor has the potential to make the rating of severity higher than it would be if it were defined solely by the closest proximity under the most favorable conditions. Thus, on a probabilistic basis, a greater P for any factor increases the severity rating relative to the closest proximity for the most favorable condition. However the combined influences can never push the severity rating beyond S_w.

HOW THE COMPUTER DETERMINES A SEVERITY RATING

This section describes how, given the scenario selection and factor ratings provided by the airport tower controllers and associated management, a computer can determine runway incursion severity. The steps are as follows:

Information permanently in the computer. Certain key severity ratings for each scenario must be preset into the computer. These form the basis of all severity calculations pertinent to that scenario. For every scenario a matrix as shown in Figure 2 needs to be specified, in this case for two aircraft taking off on intersecting runways.

On the vertical axis (leftmost column) we have several horizontal proximity values spaced along the runway (or in a different scenario the closest vertical proximity values where one aircraft flew over another aircraft or a vehicle already on the runway). For each closest proximity level there will be a "best possible" combination of all the factors (second column). Call this rating S_b for "S best." For the example in Figure

175

2 "S best" for 100 feet CHP is a B and occurs when all P values are 0, i.e. perfect visibility, two light GA aircraft, normal pilot-controller communications, and no special avoidance maneuver by either pilot.

Each cell in this second column must be rated A, A–, B+, B, B–, C+, C, C–, or D. For the current development all the tabled ratings were arrived at by consensus of panel of experts (consisting of a senior airline captain, a senior air traffic controller, and two senior air traffic human factors experts with pilot experience).

The third column, S_w for "S worst," is for the combined worst case of all the factors, when all P values are 10 (i.e., the worst visibility, two 747s, no pilot-controller communications, and extreme avoidance maneuvers. In Figure 2 for 100 feet CHP the combined worst case is an A.

Scenario #3: Two landing aircraft on intersecting runways, both landed, converging at CHP							
CLOSEST HORIZIONTAL PROXIMITY	COMBINED BEST CASE	COMBINED WORST CASE	GIVEN FACTOR IS WORST CASE. ALL OTHER FACTORS ARE BEST CASE				
			Visibility/ RVR/Ceiling	Information Comm.	Exceptional Actions	Takeoff A/C or A/C 1	Landing A/C or A/C 2
50	A (4)	A (4)					
100	B (3)	A (4)	A- (3.7)	A- (3.7)	A (4)	A- (3.7)	A- (3.7)
500	D (1)	A- (3.7)	A- (3.7)	B+ (3.3)	A- (3.7)	B- (2.7)	B- (2.7)
1000	D (1)	B (3.3)	C+ (2.7)	B (3)	B+ (3)	C (2)	C (2)
2000	D (1)	C (2)	C (2)	D+ (1.3)	C+ (2.3)	D+ (1.3)	D+ (1.3)
3500	D (1)	D (1)					

Figure 2. Example, given a scenario, of severity ratings for closest proximity and factor combinations

The remaining columns are labeled "Given factor is worst case. All other factors are best case." Those ratings mean that the particular factor labeled would have a P of 10 while all the other factors would have a P of 0. Call each of these ratings S_i, for the "i-th factor." By definition no S_i rating can be smaller than S_b or larger than S_w. When the CHP or CVP is great enough, "best" and "worst" are both D, so all S_i in between must be D.

Now we have all the information available in the tables from which to determine the severity S for any given scenario (and the associated table), a given closest proximity (any value, not just those in the table), and a given set of P values anywhere between 0 and 10. The question is by what algorithm to combine and interpolate between known information components. We are investigating several alternative algorithms. This is a challenge since there are two criteria to consider that can conflict with one another:

- Does the algorithm make logical use of all the components of information and not violate the assumptions implied above?, and
- Do the S values determined by the algorithm correspond to expert judgment over a reasonable sample of already rated runway incursions?

Calculating the S Given the Scenario Table and the P Values. For any given row in Figure 2 (a given CHP) a simplest method mathematically is to add to S_b a fraction of the remaining $(S_w–S_b)$ distance that is linearly weighted by the P values for each factor. That is, where the weighting fraction is the term in square brackets,

$$S = S_b + [\ _{i=1\ to\ N}\ P_i\ (S_i)\ /\ _{i=1\ to\ N}\ (S_i)]\ (S_w-S_b) \qquad (1)$$

It is important to note that, where P is scaled 0-10 for psychological reasons for the tower controller./ flight standards raters, in our calculations it is scaled 0-1 for all the equations.

One might argue that since D = 1 is really the bottom of the S scale, each S_i should start from 1, and thus the weighted fraction should be

$$S = S_b + [\sum_{i=1\ to\ N} P_i (S_i-1) / \sum_{i=1\ to\ N} (S_i-1)] (S_w-S_b) \qquad (2)$$

An alternative is to consider the S values as being in a multidimensional space of independent (and therefore geometrically orthogonal) factor influences. A hypothetical three-factor severity space (at any given closest horizontal or vertical proximity level) is illustrated in Figure 3. The ratings for any corresponding CHP row in Figure 2 would constitute three vertices of the space. Any combination of factor P values must lie within this space. If, for example CPH were 1000 feet in Figure 2 and we were only dealing with the first three factors, the best case vertex at P = 0, 0, 0 would have S=0, and the worst case vertex at P = 10, 10, 10 would have S =3.3. The vertices corresponding to the three "best case for that factor alone" would have S =3, 3 and 2.7 (ordered by size).

Superposed on Figure 3 are hypothetical (PS_i) vectors for each of the three factors (arrows along the edges of the small rectangle). The vector sum of these three orthogonal vectors is the diagonal of the small rectangle. This in relation to the longer diagonal in the large rectangle constitutes the vector fraction of (S_w-S_b), giving, in the general case,

$$S = S_b + [\sum_{i=1\ to\ N} P_i^2 S_i^2 / \sum_{i=1\ to\ N} S_i^2]^{0.5} (S_w-S_b) \qquad (3)$$

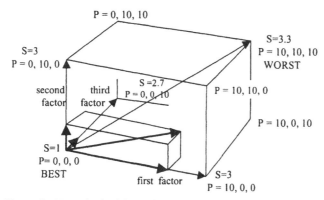

Figure 3. Hypothetical three-factor severity space. Vector fraction components in bold.

If the Si are based at 1 rather than 0 for the same reasons as given above for equation 2 we have

$$S = S_b + [\sum_{i=1\ to\ N} P_i^2 (S_i-1)^2 / \sum_{i=1\ to\ N} (S_i-1)^2]^{0.5} (S_w-S_b) \qquad (4)$$

The above four equations pose the problem that if one factor has a P weighting of 1 and others have P of 0, the calculated S will not equal the S_i for that factor as the scenario tables would imply. Instead S will be smaller because of the other factors' S_i values accumulated in the square bracketed denominator. A means to fix that is to treat the most heavily weighted "primary factor" (the factor having the greatest product P_iS_i (call those components P_1 and S_1) separately from the remaining factors by using an additional term $P_1(S_1-S_b)$. Then if the other P_iS_i are 0 and $P_1 = 1$ we get S = $S_b + (S_1-S_b) = S1$, as demanded by the assumptions that went into the prespecified table. Any remaining P_iS_i having value would then add their influence over a residual "potential S distance" (S_w-S_1) rather than (S_w-S_b) (This is like a physician rating the severity of a person's sickness primarily in terms of the major symptom he presents with, but augmenting the rating when other adverse health conditions are specified in the medical record.)

With this new twist we have two additional linear equations (depending on the origin of the S_i scale),

$$S = S_b + P_i(S_1-S_b) + [\ _{i=2\,to\,N}\,P_i\,S_i\ /\ _{i=2\,to\,N}\,S_i]\ (S_w-S_1) \tag{5}$$

$$S = S_b + P_i(S_1-S_b) + [\ _{i=2\,to\,N}\,P_i\,(S_i-1)\ /\ _{i=2\,to\,N}\,(S_i-1)]\ (S_w-S_1) \tag{6}$$

and two new vector equations (again depending on the origin of the S_i scale),

$$S = S_b + P_i(S_1-S_b) + [\ _{i=2\,to\,N}\,P_i^2\,S_i^2\ /\ _{i=2\,to\,N}\,S_i^2]^{0.5}\ (S_w-S_1) \tag{7}$$

$$S = S_b + P_i(S_1-S_b) + [\ _{i=2\,to\,N}\,P_i^2\,(S_i-1)^2\ /\ _{i=2\,to\,N}\,(S_i-1)^2]^{0.5}\ (S_w-S_1) \tag{8}$$

Figure 4 shows a scale of S, indicating by shaded portions of the scales the contributions to calculated S for equations 5-8 (above) and separately for equations 1-4 (below).

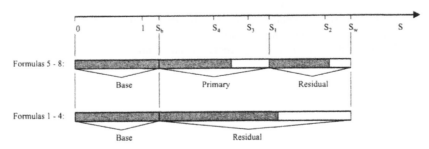

Figure 4. Components of S scales.

Finally, we wanted to compare equations 1-8 with an equation derived from conventional combinatorial statistics. If the factors can be assumed to be independent of one another, and if relative severity $(P_i\,S_i\ /\ S_w)$ can be assumed to be proportional to probability of failure with respect to that one factor, then probability of success with respect to that one factor is $[1-(P_i\,S_i\ /\ S_w)]$. The probability of success for all independent factors working together is the product of probabilities of individual factor successes, $_{all\,factors}\,[1-(P_i\,S_i\ /\ S_w)]$. Then the probability of failure of the combination is $\{1-\ _{all\,factors}\,[1-(P_i\,S_i\ /\ S_w)]\}$. This quantity multiplied by S_w with a scaling coefficient K added then becomes a final candidate formula for S,

$$S = K\{1-\ _{all\,factors}\,[1-(P_i\,S_i\ /\ S_w)]\}\ S_w \tag{9}$$

All nine formulas above have started with tabled S_b,, S_w, and S_i values from some one row (specified CHP or CVP) in the appropriate scenario table. What if the reported CHP or CVP (call it CP*) lies somewhere between the tabled values? In that case S value is determined by interpolation using the two CP values bracketing the reported value, CP_{lower} and CP_{higher}. Then

$$S(CP^*) = [(CP^*-CP_{lower})/(CP_{higher}-CP_{lower})]\ (S\ for\ CP_{higher}-S\ for\ CP_{lower}) \tag{10}$$

Latest experiments have suggested that equations 6, 8 and 9 are the best candidates for severity calculations.

VALIDATION RESULTS

Thus far, 55 official runaway incursion reports, already rated by FAA, have been coded and subjected to our severity rating calculations (all formulas, including some we have since rejected). Of those, 65% had comparable ratings (discrepancy less than 0.5), using the 1-4 numerical equivalents to D-A, and all with respect to an average of all the candidate formulas. As noted earlier, our goal was not to match the FAA ratings, but to provide a scheme with less variability and with defensible logic. Discussions were held with the FAA raters on incursions where discrepancies were near or exceeded 1, and we found significant disagreements even within the group of raters regarding those cases. Consider also that the tabled ABCD severity values were only an initial round, and that some formulas giving more extreme values have now been discarded. We fully expect to be able to "tune" our tabled severity ratings after further experience.

After more evaluation of which severity algorithms best match the FAA committee ratings, which ones are the outliers or show greatest variability etc., we plan to reduce the number of formulas, possibly to one, but maybe to two or three that can be averaged to form a final severity rating.

After some further development of the system mathematics and the software to make the user interface user-friendly, we expect to try the system out at one or more airports.

CONCLUSION

An objective method for rating the severity of runway incursions has been presented. The method requires subject matter experts to pre-assign severity ratings for various incursion scenarios, closest proximities, and best and worst combinations of situational factors. The observing tower controller and airport flight standards personnel estimate closest proximity and assign weightings to several situational factors. From this data a computer executes an interpolation algorithm to specify the final severity rating. Based on preliminary comparisons to the official FAA ratings produced by the Office of Runway Safety, it appears promising.

It is believed that this technique could be applied to rating severity of other "near miss" situations (e,g,, in highway, medical or national security contexts) where alternative scenarios and influencing factors could be identified, and ratings for each scenario could be pre-specified by subject matter experts for globally best and worst cases as well as "worst case for each factor acting alone."

REFERENCES

Cardosi, K.M. (2003). Volpe National Transportation Systems Center, personal communication.

Federal Aviation Administration's Office of Runway Safety (July 2002a). FAA Runway Safety Report: Runway Incursion Trends at Towered Airports in the United States. US Dept. of Transportation, p. B.1-2

Federal Aviation Administration's Office of Runway Safety (July 2002b). Runway Safety Blueprint 2002-2004. US Dept. of Transportation, p. 17.

ACKNOWLEDGEMENTS

The author gratefully acknowledges the contributions of the following co-workers: Dr. Kim Cardosi, Dr. Daniel Hannon, Matthew Isaacs, Stephanie Gray and Gina Melnik of Volpe Center; Capt. John Lauer of American Airlines; and Karen Pontius of FAA

INTERACTIONS BETWEEN CONVERGENCE ANGLE, TRAFFIC LOAD, AND ALTITUDE DISTRIBUTION IN AIR TRAFFIC CONTROL

Ashley Nunes & Brian J. Scholl
Yale University

ABSTRACT

Past research suggests that the ability of air traffic controllers to determine whether two target aircraft will pass too close to each other is mediated by the convergence angle between them: wider convergence angles are associated with impaired conflict detection (especially with high traffic loads), due to the greater required amount of visual scanning. We attempted to generalize these results in more ecologically valid displays (a) with broader altitude distributions than those used in previous studies; and (b) where controllers couldn't be certain that a conflict existed on every trial. Fourteen air traffic controllers performed a standard conflict detection task, during which both convergence angle and traffic load were systematically manipulated. Though we observed large effects of traffic load on both accuracy and response times, convergence angle did not affect performance, even at high loads. Thus convergence angle may play only a limited role in mediating controllers' conflict detection performance in many actual air traffic displays.

Keywords: air traffic control; visual scanning; convergence angle; conflict detection

INTRODUCTION

Air traffic controllers provide for the safe, orderly, and expeditious movement of traffic in the national airspace system. The provision of this service is highly dependent on the ability of the controller to extrapolate the trajectories of aircraft from their current positions to a future point and then to spatially determine whether or not their distance at the closest point of approach violates the minimum separation requirement. If it does, a conflict exists. A controller's conflict detection ability is in turn affected by a variety of factors that include (but are not limited to) traffic load, aircraft type, airspace geography, sector size, and convergence angle. Here we focus primarily on the role which the convergence angle between two aircraft may or may not play in mediating conflict detection.

The possible importance of convergence angle in this context is suggested by intuition, by previous research in other domains, and by anecdotal aspects of salient failures of conflict detection in the real world. Intuitively, it seems likely that a greater convergence angle between two aircraft will lead to greater difficulty in determining the likelihood of a conflict between them. This intuition is based primarily on the necessary step of scanning between the two aircraft in order to detect a conflict (e.g.. Bisseret, 1981): wider convergence angles will increase the time and distance of this scanning, and may often result in the encountering of more intervening distractor aircraft. As a result, it seems natural to expect that high convergence angles may lead to conflict detection impairments in terms of both response time and accuracy. Such predictions are also supported by empirical studies of the role of convergence angles in other contexts that needn't directly involve conflict detection. For example, wider convergence angles cause subjects to take longer when simply extrapolating trajectories (e.g. Smith, Ellis, & Lee, 1984).

This possible role of convergence angle in conflict detection is also suggested anecdotally. For example, in 1976, a British Trident collided with a DC-9 over Zagreb, Croatia killing 177 people. Although there were a variety of factors that contributed to this event, one of the primary causes was the controller's inability to detect the pending conflict between the two aircraft as they converged at 122°, until a mere 21 seconds before the collision — by which time it was too late. More recently, in January 2001, a Boeing 747 and a DC-10 belonging to Japan Airlines nearly collided over the sea off Yaizu City, Japan. A major contributing factor to the nearly fatal incident was the inability of the controller to notice the conflict between the aircraft as they were converging at an obtuse angle. Unfortunately this incident was repeated again in the summer of 2002 with fatal consequences when a Boeing 757 collided with a Tupolev-154 over Lake Constance, Germany, killing 71 people. As in the case of the Zagreb disaster, the controller only noticed the pending conflict, which occurred at an angle of 90° a mere 43 seconds before the collision. These sorts of anecdotes, in which conflicts involving large angles of convergence went unnoticed by controllers, highlight the need to consider conflict angle as a factor in the maintenance of overall system safety.

Past Empirical Investigations

Several previous empirical studies have supported the idea that convergence angle can mediate conflict detection. In one of the earliest studies, controllers were presented with images of two objects approaching an intersection at varying angles, and had to determine which object would reach the point first (Kimball, 1970). Performance worsened as angle increased, an effect, which was attributed to the increased visual scanning required between the two objects. Similar results were found in a second study, in which controllers solved a series of ATC problems presented on a radar screen (Enard, 1975 as reported by Bisseret, 1981). Each problem was presented using seven successive radar images simulating the aircrafts' approach minute by minute, and the displays involved convergence angles of 22°, 45°, and 87°. Again, in a conflict detection task, performance decreased as convergence angle increased. More recently, Remington et al. (2000) explored the roles of several variables on conflict detection in more cluttered ATC displays with many distractor aircraft, and again found that higher convergence angles impaired performance, especially (superadditively) with high traffic loads.

The Current Study

All of the evidence cited above highlights the importance of studying convergence angle as a critical variable, which may mediate ATC performance. Despite this previous work, we remain hesitant to fully accept that past results will scale up to real-world ATC contexts. Though past research has consistently improved in this regard (e.g. moving to actual conflict detection tasks, and then to cluttered displays with more than two aircraft), several factors remain unexplored. As such, the current study of the role of convergence angles in conflict detection differed from past research in several critical ways: **(a)** First, our study employed what is perhaps a more ecologically valid range of altitude distributions among the many aircraft present on each trial. Though Remington et al. (2000) — the most careful and revealing study of these factors to date — did use multiple distractor aircraft, many aircraft could occupy the same altitudes (with up to half of the aircraft sharing a single altitude on some trials, and even up to 5 aircraft per altitude in 'unrestricted' altitude conditions). In our study, in contrast, most aircraft were at different altitudes. **(b)** Second, our controllers had to detect on each trial *whether* a conflict was present, whereas the controllers in Remington et al. (2000) had to find the conflict that was present on every trial. Different expectations in this regard can give rise to importantly different scanning strategies, and we would argue that our task is more ecologically valid, since conflicts do not abound in every ATC episode in practice. **(c)** Finally, whereas the displays in previous studies used random speeds and distances, we held speed and time-to-conflict constant, in order to ensure that spurious combinations of these variables did not confound differences in convergence angle.

METHOD

Participants

14 air traffic control specialists (all male; mean age 40.2, range 31 – 57) from the Toronto Air Traffic Control Facility participated in the study, with union approval. All controllers were in possession of a valid ATCO license, enabling them to operate under both visual and instrument conditions and they were compensated monetarily for their participation in the study.

Task

The primary task of the controller was to make an assessment of conflict likelihood between a pair of aircraft present on the radar screen. To make the task more challenging, a (systematically varied) number of distractor aircraft were also present so that controllers had to first find the target pair amongst the distractors and then provide their assessment of conflict likelihood. The target aircraft pair was always traveling at the same altitude, whereas all distractors were traveling at different altitudes. All target aircraft traveled at the same speed and reached their point of closest approach approximately five minutes into the trial. The controller's task was to arrive at a conflict likelihood assessment as quickly as possible, without sacrificing accuracy. A conflict was defined as a situation where the aircraft came less than 5 niles from one another. Conversely, a non-conflict situation arose when the closest point of approach between the aircraft was greater than 5 miles. The distribution of conflict and non-conflict trials was equal.

Apparatus and Display

The ARTT Radar Simulation, manufactured and provided by Adacel Technologies, was used in the present study. The simulation was presented on a 15" monitor, and the airspace depicted was approximately 65 * 65 nautical miles. The aircraft themselves were presented as standard icons in the shape of asterisks, each of which had its own predictor line, history trail and data-tag (Figure 1). Collectively, the predictor line and history trail provided the controller with the current orientation of the aircraft, whereas the data-tag provided the controller with the aircraft's altitude, speed and destination information. In addition, the data-tag was presented in such a manner as to ensure that the controller's view of other traffic was not obstructed. The radar screen was updated once every six seconds and the target aircraft pair, which converged at the same, traveled a distance of approximately 23 miles to reach their closest point of approach. Although the selection of altitudes for distractor aircraft was completely random, a lower and upper limit of FL 180 and FL 420 were set respectively.

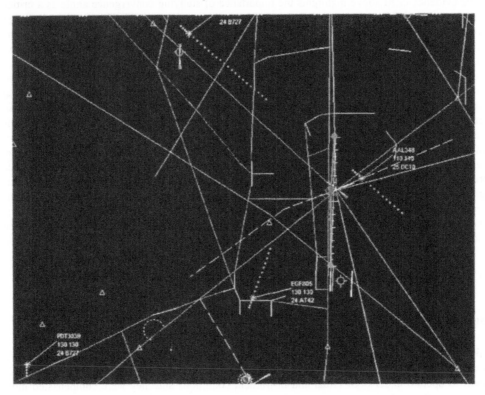

Figure 1: Screen Shot of Radar Display

Design and Analysis

Both traffic load and convergence angle were manipulated as independent variables in a fully-crossed within-subject design. Traffic load was varied across conflict trials in terms of the number of distractor aircraft present in addition to the two targets (2, 4, or 6). The two target aircraft on each conflict trial could converge at one of three angles (acute, right, and obtuse: 45°, 90° and 135°). Both response time (measured from the onset of the trial) and response accuracy (conflict present/absent) were recorded on each trial.

Procedure

Subjects were first familiarized with the task, displays, and conditions through verbal instructions and multiple practice trials (the results of which were not recorded). Each controller then completed 90 experimental trials, presented in two blocks of 45. Each trial began with the aircraft (targets and distractors), their associated data-tags, leader lines, and history trails being fully visible on the radar screen. The radar image was then updated once every 6 seconds during the trial until the controller made their response, which was a two-alternative forced-choice keypress indicating conflict presence for that trial.

RESULTS

Both response time and accuracy data are presented in Figures 2 and 3, respectively. Inspection of these graphs suggests that traffic load had a large effect on performance, but that convergence angle did not affect conflict detection. These impressions were borne out via separate two-way repeated-measures analyses of variance (ANOVAs) for each dependent measure, with convergence angle and traffic load as factors. The main effect of traffic load was highly significant for response time ($F(2,26) = 54.26$, $p < .001$) and marginally significant for accuracy ($F(2,26) = 2.54$, p = .098. As traffic load increased, conflict detection became much slower and marginally less accurate. (Subsequent planned comparisons for the accuracy data revealed that detection was significantly worse with four distractors, compared to two [$t(13) = 2.81$, p < .01] or six [$t(13) = 3.10$, p = .004). This confirms that our displays and design were sufficient to obtain differences in controller performance. Nevertheless, in stark contrast to previous studies, we observed no effect of convergence angle, for either response time ($F(2,26) = .244$, p = .785) or accuracy ($F(2,26) = .76$, p = .477). This was true even for high traffic loads: the interaction between convergence angle and traffic load failed to reach significance for both response time ($F(4,52) = 1.61$, p = .185) and accuracy ($F(4,52) = .33$, p = .856).

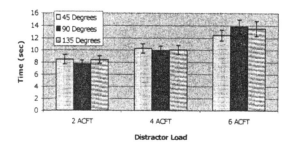

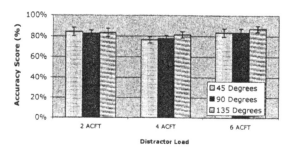

Fig 2: Controller response time across angle and load condition

Fig 3: Controller response accuracy across angle and load condition

183

DISCUSSION

The primary result of this study was the surprising resilience of controllers' conflict detection ability with wide convergence angles. Indeed, controllers were just as fast and accurate at detecting conflicts with the widest obtuse angle tested (135°) as they were with the most acute angle (45°). This pattern of results contrasts with both intuitive, anecdotal, and previous empirical reports, as discussed above, yet we are confident in it for several reasons: (a) First, the angular deviation in our convergence angles (90°) was considerable, and just as extreme as in past studies. (b) Second, our displays and design clearly had the ability to influence controllers' performance, as indicated in the expected highly robust effect of traffic load. (c) Third, previous reports suggested that effects of convergence angle were both large (up to 30 s in response time) and highly statistically significant (Remington et al., 2000), suggesting that an extreme amount of statistical power would not be necessary to observe them. (d) Fourth, we failed to find any effect of convergence angle even at high traffic loads, where such effects have previously been found to be especially pronounced (Remington et al., 2000). For all of these reasons, we think it is worth taking this result seriously, and considering why effects of convergence angle may arise in some designs but not others — and what implications this may have for the role of convergence angle in actual real-world ATC contexts.

Future research is clearly required to determine just when and why effects of convergence angle will arise in conflict detection. Yet, we can identify two issues that should be tackled in future work. First, we suggest that the precise nature of the altitude distribution among the distractor aircraft may be a critical understudied factor in mediating conflict detection strategies and performance. Whereas the distractor aircraft in previous studies tended to be distributed along only a few altitudes, which could overlap the targets (e.g. Remington et al., 2000), most of the aircraft in our study had different altitudes. This may be a critical factor in mediating any effects of 'visual scanning' between the two targets: when many distractor aircraft share the targets' altitude, such scanning may founder on intermediate distractors, which would not impede scanning if they all lied at different altitudes. This line of reasoning also explains why we may not have observed effects of convergence angle even at high traffic loads. The previously-reported super additive effects of these two variables (Remington et al., 2000) may also depend critically on the altitude distribution: a greater number of intervening aircraft at wide angles and high loads may not matter as much if few of those many distractors share the targets' altitude.

A second critical factor may be the controllers' certainty that a conflict exists on each trial. This type of ecologically invalid knowledge may engender importantly different scanning strategies — e.g. not terminating search early, or allocating extra time and attention to each distractor, which could give rise to (or exacerbate) the effects of variables such as convergence angle, which mediate the number of distractor aircraft between the targets. In contrast, the controllers in our study were not aware of the base rate of conflict likelihood and this type of search (for a situation which may or may not exist) may have led to the use of different search strategies, different termination criteria, etc. This may or may not be a more ecologically valid situation in the context of real-world ATC performance, but it seems clear that this is an important factor, which should also be considered and controlled in future studies.

We conclude that convergence-angle may not always mediate conflict detection to the degree that has been previously assumed, highlighting the need for future research to re-examine this issue. More generally, regardless of the particular variables being studied, future studies of conflict detection in air-traffic control should carefully consider and control the roles of previously underappreciated factors such as altitude distribution and conflict certainty.

ACKNOWLEDGEMENTS

We gratefully acknowledge Adacel Technologies for providing the simulation capability for the study. BJS was supported by NSF #0132444 and by internal funding from Yale University. AN was funded by the Natural Science and Engineering Research Council of Canada (NSERC) and the Canadian Bureau for International Education (CBIE). He is currently a graduate student at the University of Illinois at Urbana Champaign

REFERENCES

Bisseret, A (1981). Application of signal detection theory to decision making in supervisory control: The effects of the operator's experience. Ergonomics, 24 (2), 81 - 94.

Kimball, K. A. (1970). Estimation of intersection of two converging targets as a function of speed and angle of target movement. Perceptual & Motor Skills,30(1), 303-310.

Remington, R. W., Johnston, J. C., Ruthruff, E., Gold, M., & Romera, M. (2000). Visual search in complex displays: Factors affecting conflict detection by air traffic controllers. Human Factors, 42(3), 349 - 366.

Smith, J. D., Ellis, S. R., & Lee, E. C. (1984). Perceived threat and avoidance maneuvers in response to cockpit traffic displays. Human Factors, 26, 33 – 48.

AIR TRAFFIC CONTROLLER PERFORMANCE: CONSTRUCTS AND CONCEPTS CAN BE CONFUSING

Earl S. Stein Ph.D.
Federal Aviation Administration

ABSTRACT

Air traffic controllers do a demanding job under dynamic conditions. Over the years, researchers have built performance models that often blur the lines between the contributions of the operator and those of the system itself. Performance definitions and measurement continue to challenge us. In ATC we have carried on the aviation tradition using checklists and rating scales. These tools have face validity but may or may not be reliable. High fidelity, person-in-the-loop simulation created a host of objective, easily recorded measures. This generates a high volume of data. However, the variables are often intercorrelated. Some variables do focus on safety, and in aviation, safety is everything. However, controllers are good at what they do, so systems errors and a loss of separation are relatively rare events. This means that generally errors are not effective performance indicators, especially for research, where the goal is to find subtle differences induced by changes in procedure or technology. It is likely that questions related to controller performance and how it may be influenced by system changes will be around for a very long time.

Abstract: Performance, Air Traffic Control,

INTRODUCTION

Organizations and human factors professionals like to talk about performance as if it were a constant and easily defined concept. Given all the definitions researchers have offered, it is clear that we are really talking about a construct that varies with the situation and the system. Performance is whatever stakeholders say it is in a given situation. In air traffic control, the stakeholders are controllers and their supervisors. Over the years we have studied controller performance from many angles. Looking back on it, we often used mixed models that included the contributions of the controllers themselves and the system at large.

Air traffic controllers are complex human beings who have the skills, knowledge, and abilities to keep aircraft separated and on their planned routes. Overall their performance, by whatever definition, is exceptional. You do not hear much about it unless there is an incident or accident. Hundreds of thousands of operations, where nothing unusual happens, go on with out news note. Negative information about performance is more newsworthy. Performance is often used as an idealized abstraction. There are also many criteria, some of which may appear to work against each other. Two criteria frequently cited include safety and efficiency. Safety is pretty straight forward. Systems Safety Specialists will quickly say that there is no such thing as a perfectly safe system, and that increased safety carries a price. Efficiency in air traffic control has been reflected in our efforts to move more aircraft through the airspace with the shortest routes possible. Could safety and efficiency work against each other? The more a system is pushed to the edge, the less margin there may be for error. There could be a balancing activity between safety and other factors we would like to see in the system. One FAA supervisor, years ago, had a sign in his office which read, "Good? Fast? Cheap? Pick any two"!

Safety is still paramount, but we would like to maximize both safety and efficiency. Applying these goals as metrics has not been very useful in a research environment. Again we keep confusing the human and system componants of performance.

Sollenberger, Stein, and Gromelski (1997) stated that human performance is an essential component of overall system performance. When human beings are in the command and control loop, the decisions they make and how well they carry them out have a direct impact on the degree that the system can achieve its goals. System performance may be our ultimate goal, yet it is not the same thing as human operator performance that may add to or detract from it. System safety is most apparent when it breaks down and errors occur.

Some systems are more error tolerant and forgiving than others. Most systems do have some definition of minimum necessary performance for their operators, although they do not differentiate well when it comes to various levels of performance quality above the minimum level. For example, does the operator make errors of commission or omission? If there are no errors, then are there levels of performance above that error free point?

According to Pew, Miller, and Feehrer (1981), human errors are seldom the result of a single failure. Usually, they have secondary and other causes. A simple error can become more complex and can affect an entire system. Many complex systems have defenses against some errors but may fail to prevent a series of smaller errors.

When human error occurs, we look for responsibility or more simply blame. The operator is a viable target. Even when it is clear that the operator did something or failed to do something, it is not unusual for the system itself to make a contribution to the chain of events leading to the error. However, we tend to focus on the human culpability rather than on that of the system designers.

In air traffic control, there are actually some absolute standards for system errors such as minimal separation between aircraft under different conditions (FAA, 2002). A violation of an absolute criterion for error is a precise indicator of less-than-acceptable performance. Given the high number of operations controllers handle every year, documented errors number on the order of 1000 or so. Sanders and McCormick (1993) defined human error as an inappropriate or undesirable human decision or behavior that reduces or has the potential for reducing effectiveness, safety, or system performance. Counting errors simply does not work when you are trying to evaluate the impact of new technology or concepts. Generally, new systems do not introduce a marked increase or decrease in errors, given that their rate is already so low in the real world.

Truitt and Ahlstrom (2001), expressed their belief that human performance measurement was essential for long term moderization of the National Airspace System. Measuring performance and the performance itself are not the same thing. We assume a viable correspondence between the two. However, measurement can influence the outcome. Ever watch someone during a checkride? Is what they do and how well they do it exactly the same as under non-measurement conditions? Researchers have invested a great deal of time and effort trying to find effective measurement tools for air traffic control.

The FAA Human Factors Group at the William J. Hughes Technical Center (under one banner or another), has been doing air traffic controller research for well over twenty years. Research reports on this work are compiled on a CD ROM and available to anyone who requests them (Ahlstrom & Allendoerfer, 2003). Researchers at the Laboratory often discuss the human performance impact of new systems. We decided to put this to a test of sorts by looking at our own work as cataloged on our CD ROM.

We did a word search of 68 technical reports/notes that involved air traffic control questions. Surprisingly, only half of the reports made any mention of the phrase "Human Performance." We may have assumed it or perhaps phrased it differently. When we did use the phrase, it was usually in the introduction or executive summary. We seldom discussed it in the report, as the document dealt with whatever topic for which it was written. We mentioned "human performance" at the beginning of the report as an important issue that concerned us, either because we were trying to improve it or not get in its way by applying technology.

In the word search, we could have increased the reference count by dropping the word human and just using "performance" alone. That could have confused things further in that one of the points of this paper is that we often confound human performance with system variables. Under some conditions the humans may be doing their best, but are let down due to inadequate system design, inadequate maintenance, or simply because the system was beyond its useful life cycle and had not been replaced for some reason (often economics). The fire service C130 tanker that broke apart in midair is a case in point.

As one reviews all the work we have done over the past 20 years with controllers, we see performance related to humans or controllers mentioned at the beginning of the efforts. Then we stop discussing them. We shift to metrics which often are confounded, at least in part, by the system.

Controller performance most often stands out and alone when we are talking about observer ratings, with all their challenges regarding validity and reliability. We assume or imply what controllers have told us or would have, if asked, that they know what constitutes effective performance. That is why they can do or accept ratings on their three- point scale using FAA Form 3120-25 (FAA, 1998) and assume they are valid and reliable. They have subjective face validity. It is somewhat ironic that given the history of subjective rating in aviation, observer ratings often seem to have more meaning for pilots and controllers than more objective measures that can be collected in cockpits or radar control facilities.

This type of validity at times seems to have more merit than the use of operational definitions of performance. These require general agreement, are clear, concise and logically would be easier to build performance standards on. However, within the controller community, for example, operational definitions might reduce the mystique of what it takes to be a controller. While there is overlap and some agreement among controllers, there is often considerable disagreement about what really is good performance.

As researchers, we extol the virtues of measurement reliability and validity but often find ourselves back to ratings as the only common language with which we can communicate the issues related to performance. Most of the objective measures are not sensitive to change unless something meteoric happens. Mostly, as suggested earlier we are looking for subtle changes due to new technology or procedures. This search for appropriate metrics will no doubt continue unless we inadvertently stumble onto some new really new metrics.

Sollenberger, Stein and Gromelski (1997) developed a potentially better way of observing and rating controller performance. This began with identifying the dimensions that needed rating, starting with the FAA form, creating a rating system based on 8-point scales that emphasized writing down specific behaviors observed before rating, and testing the system using replays of simulations that had been accomplished in the laboratory. During actual ratings in a field facility, if the person being rated sees the supervisor writing, it is considered threatening, because supervisors generally do not catalog examples of behavior as a memory support for rating. They only annotate examples of less than effective behavior.

In the rating development work, the researchers assumed rater training would be a key element of behavioral observation and accurate rating. Initial trials with 10 supervisory controllers, all observing the same behavior, clearly showed that each brought his/her own internal criteria and experiences. They focused on different aspects of behavior and valued those aspects differently as well. Training trials involved open discussion of their differences as well as their common understanding. Inter-rater reliability increased steadily and stabilized. The weighted overall performance scores had a reliability of $r = .86$. Researchers had to make it clear, from the beginning that this rating system was for research only or the participants would not have been willing to use it.

Over the years we have used the rating form with subsequent improvements in multiple projects involving real-time simulation. Ratings have become a key element of our work along with a lengthy battery of automated systems measures. The objective automated measures may or may not reflect human performance but no doubt, do offer the potential for systems performance indicators. Buckley, DeBaryshe, Hitchner, and Kohn, (1983) referred to the automated data as Systems Effectiveness Measures. They developed, cataloged, and tested these measures using high fidelity person-in-loop simulation.

One of the down sides (and the strengths) of person-in-the-loop simulation, as well as new replay techniques we have for analyzing real facility information, is that both produce a large volume of data. You can analyze that data extensively with the modern software available. We tend to analyze and reanalyze the objective data streams with their massive amounts of information, because now we can. We have the software and the computer power to do it. If one analysis does not find some data for which we are searching, we may try another, perhaps more esoteric technique.

If you find yourself applying analyes you have not used before, that you found in the back pages of your statistical package manual, rethink what you may be doing. Is there such a strong need to find a significant difference or relationship? Will you have to write a three page explanation so that your peers can begin to understand the results? If the answer is yes, even if only admitted in private, review the original goals one more time.

New technology or procedures can produce performance changes which are very subtle and difficult to find. We need to keep in consciousness that an effect may actually be significant statistically and be meaningless in the real world. If the effect is small (see the literature on strength of association), it may actually not be a real world issue. Also an effect may be non significant (see the literature on sampling and sample size) and yet serve as a pointer or warning sign that further effort is necessary to ensure that the changes are not going to lower performance.

We want our systems to be all they can be, and we need them to contribute value for the investment of time and dollars that we have made or are considering. We also want systems which include humans to give the operator the best chance to perform, so he/she can help the system do what it is supposed to do.

System performance is the bottom line, and we hope that the human performance as an integrated element in the system makes a positive contribution. That is the reason why we keep people in the loop. A recent History Channel program, "Mailcall", covered the next generation of autonomous fighter aircraft being developed by Boeing. The aircraft mission is preprogrammed and they (the machines) could potentially fly it flawlessly, experiencing no fear or reservation. The military and corporate program managers, when asked whether this meant the end of fighter pilots, answered that there would always be a need for human pilots providing judgment and decision making capabilities. Even if someone could potentially automate a process like flying a fighter plane or working air traffic control, many feel the human operator will still be needed. People want certain activities, capabilities, and behaviors from the operator and accept less than perfect performance, by whatever standard, in order to achieve higher order goals.

What systems designers and users want is the human operator's flexibility and adaptability. Software and hardware have yet to catch up to the human brain. We need the system operated when there is incomplete data and judgment calls are required. We want an entity that can make value judgments when rule bases are exceeded. Further, we want to be able to trust the system operated by a human being with all his/her shortcomings and strengths. Ask yourself if you would get into an automated plane with no pilot or fly the airspace with no controllers, just machines making decisions that could and would affect your safety. Machines tend to degrade rapidly when something is wrong, and they can not feel remorse if they let you down. People trust pilots, for example, because the pilots share their fate if something goes wrong.

DISCUSION

As we progress into the front end of the 21st century, performance has become a mantra often without clear definitions. We have, in some respects, come full circle. We have both research metrics and the ability to break down air traffic events from taped recordings along the same or similar parameters. Yet for training and periodic evaluation of the controllers themselves, we still use simple over-the-shoulder ratings with 3-point scales. It is likely that the search for metrics that "truly" capture performance will continue indefinitely. That, at least, provides job security for those working on both the human side of events and those looking at systems variables using fast time models of airspace operations. As applied researchers, we need to use all the tools available to us to ensure that the performance implications of new technology are indentified. Further, we need to be sure we know what we mean by performance and whether it is the system or the operator's contributions we are measuring.

REFERENCES

Ahlstrom, V. & Allendoerfer, K. (2003). FAA NAS human factors group publications 1983-2003, 20 Years. (CD ROM). Atlantic City International Airport: Federal Aviation Administration, William J. Hughes Technical Center.

Buckley, E. P., DeBaryshe, B. D., Hitchner, N., & Kohn, P. (1983, April). Methods and measurements in real-time air traffic control system simulation. (DOT/FAA/CT-83/26). Atlantic City International Airport, NJ: Federal Aviation Administration, William J. Hughes Technical Center. (NTIS No. AD-A193 533/7/XAB).

Federal Aviation Administration. (1998, July). Air traffic technical training, 3120.4J. Washington, DC:Author.

Federal Aviation Administration. (2002). Air traffic control 7110.65N. Washington, DC:Author.

Pew, R. W., Miller, D. C., & Feehrer, C. E. (1981). Evaluation of proposed control room improvements through analysis of critical operator decisions (Report NP-1982). Palo Alto:Electric Power Research Institute.

Sanders, M.S. & McCormick, E. J. (1993). Human factors in engineering and design. New York: McGraw-Hill.

Sollenberger, R., Stein, E. S. & Gromelski, S. (1997, May). The development and evaluation of a behaviorally based rating form for the assessment of air traffic controller performance.(DOT/FAA/CT-TN96/16). Atlantic City International Airport, NJ:DOT/FAA William J. Hughes Technical Center.

Truitt, T. & Ahlstrom, V. (2001, March). In R. S. Jensen & L. Rakovan (Eds.) Situation awareness in airway facilities: effects of expertise in the transition to operations control centers. Proceedings of the eleventh international symposium on aviation psychology. Columbus, OH: Ohio State University.

USE OF DECISION SUPPORT TOOLS TO ASSIST ATC TRAFFIC MANAGEMENT COORDINATORS IN AIRPORT SURFACE MANAGEMENT

Amy Spencer, Philip J. Smith and Charles E. Billings
Cognitive Systems Engineering Laboratory

ABSTRACT

This paper discusses the roles and tasks of Air Traffic Control Tower Traffic Management Coordinators (TMCs), who coordinate the flow of surface traffic at major U.S. airports. It examines decision support tools designed to moderate often high workloads placed on TMCs and improve their situation awareness and efficiency. The paper results from several field and simulation studies of surface traffic management at large airports and extensive discussions and knowledge elicitation sessions with subject matter experts. The goals of the studies were to:

- Identify tasks involved in surface management at airports and gain insight into how and by whom these tasks are accomplished;
- Understand how decision support tools (DSTs) could assist TMCs and airline operations personnel in accomplishing surface management tasks;
- Suggest how decision support tools can best be structured to improve surface situation awareness and performance and decrease workload of air traffic control and airline personnel.

Keywords: Traffic Management Coordinator; Shared situation awareness; Distributed work

INTRODUCTION

To attain maximum efficiency in the operation of the National Airspace System (NAS), it is necessary to obtain significant improvements in collaborative decision making, which requires effective communication and coordination among FAA facilities and NAS users. An important aspect of NAS operations is the conduct and management of operations on the surfaces of airports.

Airport Control Tower Traffic Management Coordinators (TMCs) are in a sense the "glue" that ensures coordination of airport surface traffic; they also meet, wherever possible, the needs of users of the NAS: air carriers, the armed forces and individual pilots. Their roles include oversight, surveillance, decisions that affect NAS operations, and communication with users. One of the important tasks accomplished by TMCs is the coordination of surface traffic and flow management of aircraft arriving at or departing from their airport. TMCs do not primarily control individual aircraft movements (though they are experienced controllers); rather, their tasks are to maintain oversight of surface traffic as a whole, and to plan and direct the execution of strategies designed to enhance traffic movements on airport surfaces. The importance of this task is emphasized by the cost of even minor delays in traffic flow anywhere in the system; minutes saved in traffic throughput can save literally thousands or millions of dollars in operations costs over time.

Air Traffic Control Tower TMCs coordinate with personnel at Air Route Traffic Control Centers (ARTCCs), Terminal Radar Approach Controls (TRACONs) and Tower air traffic controllers (ATCs); they may also coordinate with users, including personnel within Airline Operations Centers (AOCs) and Ramp Control Administrators who are jointly responsible for expediting the flow of airline aircraft to and from their geographic areas of responsibility and the servicing of those aircraft between flights. These groups of experts control all aspects of airline and other aircraft operations.

We have focused on the surface movements of air traffic, which have been investigated in depth by NASA, the developer of a Surface Management System (SMS) designed to smooth and enhance traffic flows at major airports. The SMS is a suite of decision support tools designed to assist FAA and airline operations personnel to manage and execute surface operations more effectively. This management task requires the sharing of a very large amount of information about aircraft positions and intentions, airline objectives and FAA needs, all highly dynamic and all subject to rapid change, especially when weather, surface conditions or contingencies become potential or actual problems inhibiting airport traffic movements.

APPROACH

As indicated above, the people responsible for control of aircraft on airport surfaces are airport local and ground ATCs, managed by TMCs, Airline Operations Center personnel, ramp controllers and administrators. These experts have been studied by means of questionnaires, talk-throughs, direct observation in their workplaces, focus group activities, scenario walk-throughs, and simulation exercises using a full-task simulated airport traffic control tower. These activities have been augmented by researcher participation in collaborative decision making discussions and exercises, technical meetings and other similar activities. This paper presents a brief summary of the results of these investigations. It discusses the tasks performed, the interactions and coordination among operators, the information needed by them to perform, the need for shared situation awareness, and the ways in which surface management tools can assist human managers and operators to perform more effectively.

FINDINGS

Some over-arching findings about the human operators and their roles deserve mention before getting into the details of the studies.

- Airport tower traffic management coordinators must maintain a very high level of traffic situation awareness and must also share their insights in some form with all of the other persons involved in surface traffic movements. They will often find it necessary to modify or make new plans for surface movements in response to (or in anticipation of) changes in the environment, operational situation, operator needs, and unforeseen contingencies (e.g., airplane mechanical problems on the surface or in the local air traffic area).

- Nearly all of the information TMCs use for decision making is highly dynamic and there is a great deal of such information, requiring them to utilize many sources of visual, auditory and procedural information in their work. This often involves very heavy workload in very time-critical situations in which their decisions can literally "make or break" efficient traffic flow. Some of their data and information sources at present are rudimentary or the information is presented in ways that make it difficult to assimilate rapidly, or interpret effectively.

- Though the TMC is the coordinator and in many respects the manager of all surface movements at an airport, he depends on ATC's ability to move incoming aircraft expeditiously to airline surface areas, and on a predictable continuous feed of outgoing traffic from airlines and other operators. Airline Operations Centers and ramp control facility personnel are therefore critical to the TMC's ability to ensure system throughput. The information they have about FAA plans, and their awareness of the developing situation, often comes from FAA sources and the TMC, and without this flow of accurate timely information, they may be unable to make effective decisions and take actions that further the TMC's plans and support his/her needs.

- Because the information needed is distributed among various locations, functions and persons, and because it is highly dynamic, better means of information management and better decision support tools have the potential to appreciably improve the effectiveness of airport surface movements, and the effectiveness of the team of people who manage and execute surface movement operations. The focus of our research and of this paper is on decision support tools, such as NASA's SMS, that can assist TMCs, ATCs and airline personnel to operate on airport surfaces more efficiently and effectively.

Tasks that must be Performed; Interactions among Participants

The TMC's plans are executed by ATCs in the airport tower. The TMC must maintain surveillance of the movement strategies being used by the individual ATCs and must critique their strategy and actions when necessary or desirable to improve traffic flow (Spencer et al., 2002b). He or she will also maintain oversight of departure sequences and may suggest altering them. At multiple-runway airports, the TMC will also suggest or direct runway utilization decisions (specific runways for arrivals, departures or a mixture). During all of these activities, the TMC must maintain the "big picture" of the entire airport and its immediate surround; where actions by airport authorities or others are needed to improve traffic flows, he/she will request them or direct that they be performed. All the while, he or she is attempting to accommodate specific needs communicated to the tower by airlines and other operators.

To further the TMC's objectives, ATCs will move (actually, direct) aircraft that arrive at the airport or intend to depart from it in accordance with FAA policies and plans, surface constraints that they can see or that are communicated to them, requests by airlines, and their own decisions about the most effective ways to move individual aircraft. The TMC is observing their actions in real time and will often make suggestions either verbally or by re-ordering flight strips (if in use) to indicate desired sequences or locations.

Airline Operations Centers (Smith, Pear, 2002) are usually in contact with incoming company aircraft before they reach the airport; these aircraft are the input or "feed" they must accommodate by assigning movement paths in areas under their control, gates or positions at which they will be parked, unloaded, serviced, refueled and made ready for departure, and personnel and equipment to accomplish these tasks. Loaded aircraft must be moved to a departure position; their pilots or airline operations personnel must request and receive clearance for outbound aircraft to move onto tower-controlled surfaces of the airport. Special needs (e.g., priority cargo or passengers, requirements for particular runways or routings, mechanical problems, critical aircraft) must be identified and made known to the tower by airline operations personnel so the needs can be met during taxi-out.

Obviously, many or most of these specific tasks require communication among people located in many places on or off the airport. Some must be accomplished synchronously, by telephone or radio; others are performed asynchronously by computer, fax or teletype, but all of these means require that recipients attend to the content transmitted and consider how it impacts the flow of their other, continuous activities. As indicated above, the workload involved can be high on all system participants, and especially high on managers and coordinators, all of whom are multi-tasking most of the time.

Information Required for Effective Task Performance

Essentially, performance of the many tasks required for surface movement requires that the following information be known by, or immediately available, to someone in the task chain.

- The condition of the airport and surrounding airspace; constraints to air or surface movements
- The location, status and any problems of aircraft on the surface and surrounding airspace
- The intentions of pilots of individual aircraft and their companies; special needs of each
- Anticipated constraints on any part of the operation, as far in advance as possible
- Unanticipated constraints or problems as soon as they occur or can impact the system

In essence, these are the elements of high-level situation awareness in an aviation setting. In a system that may involve scores or hundreds of aircraft at, departing from or arriving into a major airport, the maintenance of situation awareness may be a staggering task, yet the lead managers, and especially the responsible TMC, are required to possess such situation awareness to a very high degree and to maintain it for long periods of time under rapidly-changing conditions, if their planning and decision making is to be fully effective.

Until this point in time, some of the information listed above has been available only in text form or not at all. Information relevant to particular decisions has been located in many repositories and locations, and the information is usually not integrated. The need for surface movement aids has been broadly recognized, leading NASA, among others, to implement programs to develop such aids.

The remainder of this paper deals with some findings obtained during the human factors evaluation of a Surface Movements System developed under NASA guidance. The NASA SMS is still in development and its characterization in this paper may not be representative of a final system, but the human factors implications of the work performed to date are still useful as guideposts to the needs of operators of the NAS for assistance and support with surface movements.

Decision Support Tools

Tools that are being developed to assist in the efficient use of resources on the airport surface must be designed to support and enhance shared situation awareness between ATC and operators. As stated above, an airport surface is a distributed work environment, and the decisions and actions of one entity can directly affect the decisions and actions of the others.

From an air carrier's perspective, many surface management tasks revolve around reducing taxi times for departing aircraft – longer taxi times mean greater cost to the company and, in the long run, this expense can be quite considerable. Therefore, any information provided to the carrier regarding airport operating conditions such as departure runway queue length and runway throughput will affect carrier departure management tasks. Since ATCs are responsible for the handling of aircraft on most active airport surfaces outside of the ramp areas, there are only a few decisions that a carrier can make in order to affect departing aircraft performance such as departure delays.

One such decision is aircraft push back timing (the point at which aircraft are pushed back from their parking gates). For example, with information regarding length of a runway departure queue, ramp tower personnel (Spencer et al., 2002a) can choose to hold aircraft that will depart from that runway at the parking gate (if that runway's queue is particularly long, due either to constraints effecting the runway, inefficient departure queue sequences, which can result from aircraft characteristics such as assigned departure fix or aircraft type, or simply due to the sheer number of active aircraft that must depart off that runway). By choosing to hold aircraft at the gate, carriers can reduce the cost associated with departure delays because, as one example, it is less expensive to delay an aircraft at the gate (with engines off) than to have an active (engines running) aircraft delayed somewhere else on the airport surface.

From an ATC perspective, if operators are making decisions without knowledge, or with incomplete knowledge, of surface constraints, it means that ATC may be burdened with the task of trying to efficiently handle aircraft that, for a variety of reasons, simply cannot be sequenced or handled in a way that will achieve maximum efficiency. Therefore, information, such as queue length, departure fix loading and predicted airport demand that can assist the carrier in making better departure management decisions such as aircraft pushback timing is desirable. These sorts of information can be made available on a continuous basis by a properly designed surface management tool.

The example provided above relates to departure management. Arrival management tasks can also be assisted through airport surface management decision support tools. One example identified in our various studies relates to better situation awareness regarding arrival times. Once an aircraft lands, there are many factors that can affect that aircraft's surface operations while en route to its parking gate. Factors such as runway crossing delays (due to a large number of flights arriving on that runway), taxiway queues, and the interactions of arrivals into and departures out of ramp areas can delay the arrival of aircraft. For example, without accurate information regarding an arriving aircraft's position on the airport surface and its operational intent, aircraft departing from a ramp area within which an arrival is scheduled to park can lead to a "nose-to-nose" event which can result in the necessity of tugs being dispatched to move one of the aircraft. This event can lead to delays in excess of 30 minutes.

Any number of contingencies can seriously affect surface management. One particularly difficult example is an airplane that becomes disabled because of a mechanical issue while in a departure queue. At many airports, that aircraft may block the queue until aircraft ahead have cleared the taxiway before it can be towed down the taxiway and runway to a turn-off point, then be towed back to its ramp or to a location where mechanical assistance is available. Runway and taxiway geometry can seriously handicap airport operations despite the best efforts of TMCs and ATCs, as can several other environmental factors. If this information is not rapidly communicated to other participants in the surface management process, they may continue to move aircraft onto the airport surfaces, creating gridlock and appreciably worsening the situation. The importance of *shared* situation awareness cannot be overstated. This is one of many cases in which a surface management information system can lighten the TMC's burden by permitting the rapid dissemination of time-critical information asynchronously to all potentially-affected users and operators.

SMS planning utilities can be most helpful to TMCs and others. An airport tower simulation study involved a change in runway usage from arrivals only to departures only during a push (a period of heavy arrival and departure traffic). TMCs using a prototype SMS were able to enter several proposed runway change times into the system's inputs and observe the projected results in terms of overall system throughput and delays, to compare the machine predictions with their own in real time. This feature was assessed as very helpful.

CONCLUSIONS

In general, these studies have found that effectively designed decision support tools are found to be useful by expert users, including information regarding aircraft state, position and movement, and the system as presented was very helpful in improving situation awareness. This is an important finding in view of the critical importance of maintenance of situation awareness for airport surface movements managers.

Despite the efforts of many in the aviation community, much important and potentially useful information that is known to certain system participants has not, thus far, been integrated into large information management systems whose outputs would benefit from better sources of information concerning system state, and especially system and participant intent. This is an extremely complex system now, and it will certainly become still more complex as a result of economic imperatives and improved automation. But it is quite possible that the greatest improvements in system effectiveness will come from greater emphasis on integration of the many information sources available within specific air carriers, other organizations and various FAA information sources. It is believed that further development of air traffic management systems should emphasize the integration problem, despite its difficulty and the rapid pace of information system development.

REFERENCES

Smith, P.J, Pear, C, Billings, C, and Spencer, A (2002). Support of Airline Operations Centers using the Surface Management System. Columbus, OH: Cognitive Systems Engineering Laboratory, The Ohio State University.

Spencer, A, Smith, P.J, Billings, C (2002a). Ramp Control Issues in the Design of a Surface Management System. Columbus, OH: Cognitive Systems Engineering Laboratory, The Ohio State University.

Spencer, A, Smith, P.J, Billings, C (2002b). Surface Management System—Simulation 2: Findings Regarding the TMC Position. Columbus, OH: Cognitive Systems Engineering Laboratory, The Ohio State University.

ON THE USE OF TRANSPARENT REAR PROJECTION SCREENS TO REDUCE HEAD-DOWN TIME IN THE AIR-TRAFFIC CONTROL TOWER

Norbert Fürstenau, Michael Rudolph, Markus Schmidt, Bernd Lorenz
German Aerospace Center (DLR), Institute of Flight Guidance

Thorsten Albrecht
Technical University of Braunschweig, Institute of Psychology

ABSTRACT

Initial results of a laboratory study on potential performance benefits of using a non-collimated transparent holographic rear-projection screen (HRPS) in a complex visual search task are reported. Such a head-up display may, in the future, support low-visibility airport surface operation of tower controllers. Using 18 participants, four display settings were studied that varied the location of a partial set of the task stimuli: (1) Foreground display on the HRPS; 2) integrated in the background display; 3) foreground display on a head-down monitor placed in the same line of view towards the background; 4) foreground display on a head-down monitor placed sideways with an angle of 45° to the line of view towards the background. A significant benefit in target detection time was observed only in the first three against the fourth setting. However, no differences were found within the first three settings. This finding is discussed in terms of the proximity-compatibility principle of display design, from which some suggestions for a follow-up study are derived.

Keywords: Transparent projection, head-down time, augmented vision, airport tower

INTRODUCTION

In meeting the demand for a more efficient use of airport resources there is an increasing trend of developing enabling technologies and decision-support tools (DST) to advance the efficiency of tower control, in particular, under conditions of low visibility. There is some concern that their use in the control tower may lead to increased head-down times drawing the controllers' attention away from monitoring the outside scene. Displaying information on head-mounted displays (HMD) or large transparent holographic rear projection screens (HRPS) instead of conventional head-down displays (HDD) may help to mitigate these potential problems. Large transparent screens may combine the benefit of both maintaining a high degree of eyes-out monitoring and providing a set of symbologies that are conformal to the airport surface traffic situation (e.g. connecting data-blocks or clearance status information to aircraft). If properly designed, such an augmented vision system will help the tower controller to become more independent of the weather condition in handling airport surface traffic (Fürstenau, 2002). The concept makes the assumption that superimposing two different visual domains can minimize the amount of visual scanning and head movement and facilitate a seamless transition of the controllers' attention between both domains.

A considerable amount of human factors research has been devoted to the application of HUD in aircraft cockpits, which has to be considered when designing augmented tower vision systems. As a conclusion of this research it seems generally accepted that the expectations that information presented on the HUD can be processed in parallel with information of the outside scene is a misconception of the perceptual and attention-related issues involved. Stuart, McAnally and Meehan (2001) analyzed the relevant literature to understand the effects of head-up displays (HUD) on visual attention. They state that neither of the two main assumptions in favor of HUD, i.e. improved divided attention between display and outside environment as well as reduced visual scanning requirement, has been convincingly demonstrated. They refer to experimental findings that show that potential disadvantages of these display systems stem from the same design feature that is claimed to confer the benefits: the spatial overlap of display information and far view. The overlap may lead to either perceptual or attentional interference between the two sources of information, corresponding to either masking of one source of information by the other, or attentional capture by one source so that important information from the other source does not reach the operators' conscious awareness. Concerning the perceptual aspects it is found that the major benefit of HUD´s may be due to collimation and superior symbology rather than the head-up presentation per se. Martin-Emerson and Wickens (1997) state that minimizing scanning between cockpit flight instruments and the far domain contributes substantially to the observed HUD performance advantage. Because large eye movements take only slightly longer than small movements (Stuart et al. 2001) this advantage is probably more due to attentional factors than to perceptual ones. Under expectation of important events to occur in the outside world (or background projection) the HUD or HRPS may allow for effective monitoring. This may not be the case if the far view events are unexpected (Fadden et al., 1998).

The task used in the present study, although of an abstract laboratory type, was designed to resemble a typical information processing demand of tower controllers: switching the focus of attention between the far view (e.g. aircraft location and identification) and near-view displays (flight plan and radar data) back and forth and combining information from both sources before decision making (clearance for runway crossing, takeoff, landing). In the first of two experiments three modes of presenting the near-view information were compared: (1) HDD, (2) HRPS, and (3) overlay projection to the far domain. Comparing the first two conditions may reveal the potential benefit of reduced head-down times for timely scanning the displays. The superiority of the last condition against HRPS may point to a crucial disadvantage of the latter, which is its lacking collimation. HRPS require the observer to switch between two different depths of focus associated with the near and the far visual domain. A sub-sample of participants participated in a subsequent experiment involving 6 sessions (one session per day) allowing more practice to develop. Only minor procedural changes were made except for a modification of the HDD condition to investigate the role of head movements. For that purpose the position of the HDD relative to the far-view projection was altered in such a way that switching the gaze between the near and far domain forced the participants to move their head both in the vertical and the horizontal plane.

METHOD

Task and Stimuli

Figure 1 depicts the display elements of the task. The participant had to look for a certain information (the 'code') in the background, which additionally contained a set of 24 further objects that differ as a function of shape (circles, squares and triangles) and color (black, white). This code had to be searched in the reference table in the foreground to obtain the verbal object specifications of the target. Finally, the participant had to decide whether or not the respective object was present in the background set of objects and then press the left mouse button if the target was present and the right button if not present. Response time and accuracy were measured. This task, essentially, required the participants to perform three subtasks in succession. First, they were to identify the code symbol, second substitute the code for a target symbol in a reference table, which also involved a transfer from a verbal to a visual target instantiation, and third search for the presence of the target. The 24 objects projected onto the background screen were randomly distributed in a 6x6 matrix, and the three-symbol code was presented randomly at

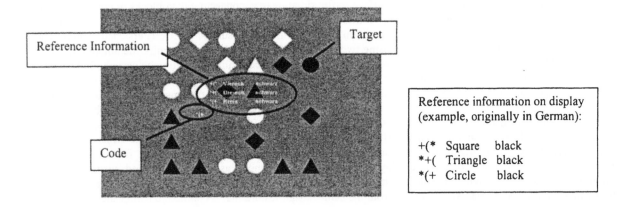

Figure 1: Screenshot of background projection stimulus with superimposed reference information. In this case the target had to be identified by the code defined by the sequence *(+ that correspond to the black circle according to the adjacent verbal object specification (in German: Kreis schwarz).

one of the remaining 12 free locations of the 6x6 stimulus matrix. Within a single stimulus, colors and object shapes were equally distributed, i.e. within the matrix, there were always 12 white and 12 black objects, and an equal number of eight circles, triangles, and squares. In half of the trials one target object was present, in the other half it was not present. Distractor objects were generated by the remaining five objects, each of them appearing at least once and at most seven times to create the full set of 24 objects. The code always consisted of three symbols, i.e. a parenthesis, a plus, and a star, in random order. The object size was 2.4° for circle and triangle and 2.7° for the square and the complete matrix size expanded a visual angle of 21.8° vertical and horizontal. The code symbol size was 0.5°. The size of the text elements of the reference table was 0.6° on the HDD and 0.9° on the HRPS. Background matrix and foreground reference table were presented simultaneously in each trial.

Apparatus

Participants sat in front of the display with a wide-angle projection in the background. Distance between eye and screen was 213 cm. HRPS display and background projection were in the horizontal line of sight with HRPS distance from the eye 90 cm. The large holographic rear projection screen (1 m width x 0.75m height) has been commercially available since a couple of years and is frequently used in advertisement applications. The compound structure with holographic foil laminated between two glass planes directs the light from a 1500 lm beamer positioned 36° out of the line of sight at the ceiling or bottom to the observer and serves for light collimation and at the same time suppressing light from the surrounding. This enhancement function allows the use as daylight projection system although in the present experiments the room was darkened. Notebook LCD HDD (15") was under the horizontal line of sight with vertical distance 50 cm (HRPS center – LCD center) and eye distance 60 cm. The display and projection resolutions were 1152 x 864 pixels in each case. The projections were controlled by two computers working in a client – server mode, with the server a notebook with 15 inch display, which served as HDD and the client a conventional desktop controlling simultaneously both the background projection and the HRPS projection.

Procedure

The experiment consisted of three blocks with 48 stimulus trials each, resulting in a total duration of about 24 min for the whole experiment. Each block corresponded to one of the three display modes. Variables object and target varied randomly within blocks. Each object became the target eight times for each of the two colors. For half of the 48 trials the target was present, which was balanced for sequence.

Stimuli were presented simultaneously with the reference information. Presentations were centered on the respective display. A fixation cross was displayed 1 s before stimulus display onset in the background center. The task of the participant was instructed as described above. Item presentation was machine-paced with a fixed inter-stimulus-interval (ISI) of 10 seconds. When no response occurred within the ISI an omission was recorded and the next trial presented.

Participants

18 Participants (15 DLR employees and 3 Psychology post-graduate students) took part without extra payment. 13 were male and 5 female, aged 21 to 60, and apart from the students all had a mathematical – technical profession.

RESULTS

Experiment 1

Only in 10 (0.4%) of the overall 2592 trials no response occurred within the 10-s response interval. These trials were excluded from the analysis. Overall performance accuracy was high (3.6%) and did not differ significantly between the three modes of presentation (chi^2 (df=2) = 0.89, p > .10). However, the frequency of false responses was influenced by the shape of the object (chi^2 (df=2) = 17.74, p < .001). In 52.2% of the false responses the target was a square compared to 30.4% when it was a triangle and 17.4% with circles as targets. Errors also occurred more often in terms of target rejections in target-present trials (72.8%) rather than erroneously accepting a target in target-absent trials (chi^2 (df=1) = 19.75, p < .001).

For the analysis of the reaction times, average scores for each participant and each of the 3x3x2 = 18 conditions were determined from correct responses only. These scores entered a three-way ANOVA with all factors varied within-subjects. Factors were Mode (HDD, HRPS, background projection), Object (circles, triangle, square) and Target (present, absent). Where appropriate, significance levels were adjusted using Greenhouse – Geisser corrected degrees of freedom, however, in the following the uncorrected number of degrees of freedom will be reported. Effects due to Mode were not reliable ($F < 1$). A reliable main effect of Object ($F(2,34) = 23.56$, $p < 0.001$) was found. Paired comparisons revealed that average responses to circle targets were about 350 ms faster than average responses to both triangle and square targets (p for both < 0.001), however there was no significant difference between square and triangle targets ($p > .10$). Target acceptances occurred about 800 ms faster than target rejections resulting in a highly reliable target main effect ($F(1, 17) = 94.74$, $p < 0.001$). An Object by Target interaction effects slightly failed to become reliable with sufficient statistical confidence ($F(2,34) = 3.07$, $p = .06$). This tendency resulted from triangle targets being faster accepted when present than squares, whereas triangles took longest to reject when absent.

Experiment 2

Inspection of the data obtained in experiment 1 revealed large individual differences and the existence of an ongoing learning progress during the experiment pointing to insufficient prior practice. Therefore, an extended follow-up experiment involving 6 sessions (one per day) was done with a sub sample of 6 participants (age range: 27 – 52, mean: 37.2, SD: 9.9). In experiment 2, the head-down monitor was placed sideways with an angle of 45 degrees to the line of view towards the background screen. This was considered to more realistically resemble the working condition in the ATC tower. The number of trials per block were increased from 48 to 60 and the ratio of present/absent trials was 40/60 instead of 50/50. In all other respects, experimental setup and procedure remained the same as in the previous experiment.

An overall of 6480 responses was collected. Only in 2 trials a response was omitted within the 10-s interval and only 86 (1.4 %) responses were wrong. This frequency was not affected by Mode, but was influenced by Object (chi^2 (df=2) = 7.44, $p < .05$) and Target (chi^2 (df=1) = 65.79, $p < .001$), both effects entirely consistent with the findings of experiment 1, i.e. errors occurred more frequently using squares as targets and false target rejection occurred more often than false target acceptances. The ANOVA computed for the correct RT data involved a further 6-level within-subject factor of Session. A reliable main effect of Mode ($F(2,10) = 30.50$, $p < .01$) was caused by an increase of 356 ms using HDD compared against HRPS ($p < .01$) and 402 ms compared against background projection ($p < .01$). The 50-ms advantage of background projection against HRPS was not statistically reliable ($p = .66$). A significant main effect of Object ($F(2,10) = 76.83$, $p < .001$) as well as a significant main effect of Target ($F(1,5) = 14.86$, $p < .05$) were consistent in meaning to the previous experiment, i.e. circles were on the average faster responded to in comparison to both triangles ($p < .01$) and squares ($p < .01$) while squares and triangles did not differ ($p > .05$) and target acceptances took less time then non-target rejections ($p < .01$). The main effect due to Session likewise became reliable ($F(5, 25) = 9.37$, $p < .01$). There was a gradual decrease in RT across sessions, however, none of the Bonferoni-adjusted paired comparisons reached the statistical significance ($p > .05$). The computation of polynomial contrasts revealed a significant linear trend ($F(1,5) = 12.81$, $p < .05$). A further reliable object by target interaction effect ($F(2,10) = 5.59$, $p < .05$) was observed. This was due to the fact that the RT advantage of circles even more expressed in rejection trials. Figure 2(right panel) illustrates this. The fact that in contrast to this, Mode and Target had an additive effect on average RT as illustrated in Figure 2(left panel), provides some indication as to the locus of the Mode effect. This will be discussed below.

DISCUSSION

The present study investigates visual attention issues of a large holographic 'see-through' rear-projection screen (HRPS). This technology may be used for air traffic controllers in the control tower to provide decision support information while at the same time enable a high level of eyes-out monitoring. The abstract experimental task forced the participants to switch their attention repeatedly between a near and a far visual domain.

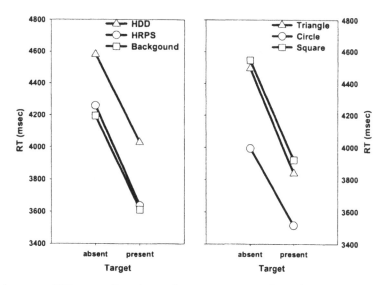

Figure 2: Average RT as a function of correct target detection (present) / rejection (absent) separated for Display Mode (left panel) and Object (right panel). Note that the effects of Display Mode and Target were additive, whereas an Object*Target interaction (p<.05) was found.

Near-view information was either presented head-down in the same line of view to the background (experiment 1) or with an angle of 45 degree sideways to it (experiment 2) and was compared to two head-up presentations, respectively: (1) HRPS and (2) overlay projection into the background. The latter had the advantage of presenting near and far view at the same focal distance, however, had the disadvantage of more perceptual masking and clutter. The latter condition was included to mimic the situation of a superimposition of the information set from the inside with an artificially reconstructed outside scene (Fürstenau, 2002).

The first experiment did not reveal any performance differences between presentation modes. In the second experiment, average RT was increased in HDD condition, whereas both head-up conditions did not differ. Performance accuracy was quite high and not affected by presentation mode in both experiments. This indicates that superimposition of display information with an uncollimated HRPS is not advantageous with respect to head-down times as compared to using HDD as long as the gaze transitions between HDD and the far domain occurs only in the vertical plane and requires comparatively little head movements. This observation is consistent with findings in the HUD literature reviewed by Stuart et al. (2001) that amplitude of eye movements is not an important factor for visual scanning efficiency, i.e. large movements take only slightly longer than small movements.

The task-immanent factors, i.e. type of object and the required response associated with target present vs. absent, displayed effects that are straightforward with reference to basic attention theory. The key element of the task was a conjunction search (Treisman, 1986) for a target object, i.e. a target was defined by two perceptual properties, color and shape. A conjunction search typically proceeds serially, and terminates upon target detection or when the last object is scanned in case the target is not present. The serial and self-terminating nature of target search is confirmed by the large RT differences between target acceptances and non-target rejections consistently observed in both experiments. On the contrary, single feature search may engage pre-attentive parallel processing taking advantage of perceptual pop-out effects. The RT advantage of using circles as targets leading to the reliable effect of Object can be explained by a certain degree of visual catch properties of circles contrasting them from triangles and squares. According to the feature integration theory of Treisman (1986) it can be argued that squares and triangles share single features (diagonal lines) giving rise to circles with a contrasting round shape to exhibit a pop-out effect to some extent. Evidence of a higher visual scanning rate caused by visual catch properties of circles is also supported by the fact that the RT difference between target acceptances and non-target rejections was reduced as compared to the other two shapes, which is suggested by the observed Object by Target interaction effect. It is interesting to note that the RT advantage of both HUD modes over the HDD mode observed in the second experiment was the same regardless of whether target acceptance or non-target rejection was required. The additivity of main effects due to both Object and Target support the conclusion that the HUD advantage was purely related to better sensory orientation resulting from eliminated head movements without having an influence on subsequent visual search or decision making processes.

The lacking sensitivity of the RT measurement to differences between both HUD conditions may be the result of attention effects operating in opposite direction. A disadvantage of HRPS is its lacking collimation. This requires adjustments to different focal distances when switching between both visual planes. However, the difference in the depth of focus becomes an advantage for stimulus processing. In fact, when participants attend to either the HRPS or the background scene one of the images will be blurred and less able to interfere with the other image, respectively. Such a masking of attention effects acting in opposite direction, although speculative based on the results of the present study, is partly a result of the specific serial attention demands of the experimental task that does not require capturing information from both visual domains in parallel. Therefore, visual elements of one subtask are irrelevant for the preceding as well as for the consecutive subtask and must be ignored. Based on the proximity-compatibility principle of display design (Wickens & Carswell, 1995) it can be stated that there is only a moderate proximity between these sub-tasks. Therefore, the potential for interference can be mitigated by appropriate separation of visual stimuli pertaining to the respective sub-task. However, many controller tasks require a true integration of inside and outside information, which is not well captured by the abstract task used here. To capture this aspect more appropriately, the experimental task has to be modified in such a way that elements of the near and the far visual domain are elements of an integration task that are ideally processed in parallel rather than being mere elements of a series of successive focused attention sub-tasks. This can be accomplished if the near field of view contains a cue that facilitates the search in the far field of view. Another issue that is not well captured in the present study using a static task is the potential disadvantage of HUD operation observed in a dynamic working environment where HUD reduced the probability of detecting unexpected events as has been observed during approach and landing simulations (Martin-Emerson & Wickens, 1997).

CONCLUSION

The findings of the present laboratory study provided some insight into human-factors related design issues of implementing the HRPS see-through technology as an interface for tower control. The mandate of maintaining a high degree of eyes-out airport surface monitoring must be weighed against potential costs of clutter caused by displaying too many items on such a device. In the abstract task used here, the predominant cognitive strategy that guided the visual search was serial in nature. In terms of the proximity-compatibility principle (Wickens & Carswell, 1995) the task proximity can be categorized as moderate. Therefore, a moderate level of display proximity that matches well with this task demand appeared to be a display arrangement that minimizes head movements, particularly in the horizontal plane. A see-through display is not superior to a HDD monitor that is properly aligned with the outside view. In a follow-up study the task demand will be modified so as to increase the level of task proximity to a true information integration task by using the cueing paradigm.

REFERENCES

Fadden, S., Ververs, P.M., Wickens, C.D. (1998). Costs and benefits of head-up display use: A meta-analytic approach. Proceedings of the 42nd Annual Meeting of the Human Factors and Ergonomics Society. Santa Monica, CA: Human Factors and Ergonomics Society.

Fürstenau, N. (2002). Perspectives of virtual reality for integration. Proceedings of the 12th Scientific Seminar of the DLR-Institute of Flight Guidance, October 30 – 31, 2002, Braunschweig, Germany.

Martin-Emerson, R. & Wickens, C.D. (1997). Superimposition, symbology, visual attention, and the head-up display, Human Factors, 39, 581-601.

Stuart, G.W., McAnally, K.I, & Meehan, J.W. (2001). Head-up displays and visual attention: integrating data and theory. Human Factors and Aerospace Safety, 1, 103 – 124.

Treisman, A. (1986). Properties, parts, and objects. In K.R. Boff, L. Kaufman & J.P. Thomas (Eds.), Handbook of perception and human performance (pp. 35/1 – 70). New-York: Wiley.

Wickens, C. D. & Carswell, C.M. (1995). The proximity-compatibility principle: Its psychological foundation and relevance to display design. Human Factors, 37, 473-494.

IMPLEMENTING VOICE AND DATALINK COMMANDS UNDER TASK INTERFERENCE DURING SIMULATED FLIGHT

Matthew R. Risser, Mark W. Scerbo, Carryl L. Baldwin
Department of Psychology, Old Dominion University, Norfolk, VA

Danielle S. McNamara
Department of Psychology, University of Memphis, Memphis, TN

ABSTRACT

Datalink is a text-based system with potential to address some of the problems associated with voice communications. Given the two communication technologies, the differences between processing speech and text are of concern. Moreover, the susceptibility of either format to interference during command processing is of primary interest. Participants responded to speech and text commands by setting controls during simulated flight while performing verbal, visual, and central executive interference tasks. The results demonstrate that longer message sets produce poorer performance and that performance suffers more under verbal and CE interference. These findings were obtained in the absence of a presentation format effect suggesting that both speech and text messages utilize an underlying verbal code and are therefore more susceptible to verbal interference. However, when control setting errors were made, more performance decrements were observed in the text condition during the presentation of both CE and visual interference.

Keywords: datalink, multiple resources, working memory, interference, speech, text

INTRODUCTION

Information between the flight deck and air traffic control (ATC) is typically communicated via voice. While maintaining communications with ATC, pilots must also perform their duties within the cockpit (e.g., scanning outside, monitoring displays, communicating with the aircrew, completing checklists, etc.). These tasks may be potential sources of interference that compete with the verbal ATC information. One way to address this issue is through datalink, a text-based system used to communicate information between ATC and the flight deck. Several investigators have begun to study datalink because the information processing characteristics of text and speech differ, which may ultimately affect pilot performance (Kerns, 1991, 1999; Navarro & Sikorski, 1999). Furthermore, speech and text message formats may also differ in their susceptibility to interference from other tasks performed concurrently (Risser, McNamara, Baldwin, Scerbo, & Barshi, 2002; Risser, Scerbo, Baldwin, & McNamara, 2003).

Recently, Scerbo, Risser, Baldwin, and McNamara (2003) examined the ability of individuals to implement speech and text commands of different length in the context of task interference containing either visual, verbal, or central executive (CE) working memory processes. We found that more errors were made in the context of central executive interference followed by verbal interference. More errors also occurred as message length increased. These results and those from our previous studies support Baddeley and Hitch's (1974) theory of working memory resources and the processing code dichotomy in Wickens' (1984) multiple resource theory. Specifically, these theories suggest that a decrease in performance can be expected when activities compete for the same resources.

One goal of the present study was to re-examine the results from our previous research (Risser et al., 2002; Risser et al., 2003; Scerbo et al., 2003) in a more ecologically valid environment using a flight simulator. Toward this end, we examined the impact of message length, presentation format (speech and text), and type of interference on the ability of individuals to set controls in a desktop flight simulator. As previously found, we expected that CE interference would have the most detrimental effect on performance followed by verbal and visual interference. The demands of the central executive processor require more working memory resources than either verbal or visual tasks according to Baddeley and Hitch's (1974) working memory model. Additionally, verbal interference was expected to impair performance more than visual interference because it shares a similar verbal code with the procedural ATC commands, as predicted by Wickens' (1984) multiple resource theory.

Risser et al. (2003) predicted that performance with the text format would be affected more by visual than verbal interference and that performance with the speech format would be affected more by verbal than visual interference. However, they did not observe these modality-dependent differences. Rather, they observed overall greater detriments from verbal interference. Nonetheless, it is possible that the additional visual complexity afforded by the flight simulator may render text presentation more susceptible to visual interference than the simple control panel used by Risser et al. One purpose of this study is to investigate that possibility. In addition, command presentation format used in the present experiment differed from that used in the previous studies. In the earlier experiments, the presentation of each word in either a word list (Risser et al., 2002) or a command set (Scerbo et al., 2003) alternated with a letter from the interference task. In the present study, command sets were presented as three-word sequences followed by the interference task. The change to a more natural, prosodic presentation was expected to facilitate chunking of information in memory and increase performance relative to the previous studies.

METHOD

Participants

Twenty-four participants (5 males and 19 females) whose ages ranged from 20 to 44 participated for extra credit in a psychology course. All had normal or corrected-to-normal vision and no reported auditory deficits. All participants were native speakers of English.

Stimuli

Flight Simulator. The primary task used X-Plane 6.70 that depicts a simulated 747-400 cockpit on an 18.1 inch screen during straight and level flight on autopilot. The participants were required to only manipulate the heading, speed, altitude, and radio frequency using the mouse.

Commands. Commands were presented as speech or text on a laptop with a 12 in screen. In the text condition, words were presented one at a time in the center of the screen. An 18-point MS sans serif font was used for the text commands and all text appeared in dark brown against a light gray background. In the speech condition, words were presented via computer speakers. They were digitally recorded in monophonic format at 22 KHz with 16-bit depth in a male voice. The words were presented at approximately 60 dBC measured from the position where participants would sit.

There were a total of 120 procedural commands comprised of three words in a verb-object-indirect object syntax, (e.g., "set heading 160"). Commands were presented in sets of two or three. There were twelve trials per command set presented in both speech and text formats. Participants were required to recall and execute as many commands as possible in the correct order. The commands were counterbalanced across command length and type of control. All trials for one presentation format (speech or text) were completed before beginning the trials in the other format. The order of speech and text trials alternated for each participant.

Interference. Three interference tasks were used as the secondary task: CE, verbal, and visual. In the CE task, participants were required to generate and call out letters at random. Participants were instructed not to use any type of strategy (i.e., spelling, grouping letters, etc.) and to maintain a pace of at least one letter per word. This was verified by the experimenter who recorded each letter as it was spoken by the participant. In the visual and verbal tasks, the letters were displayed on the screen after each 3-word command phrase. The letter sets were constructed to contain approximately equal numbers of targets and distractors. Letters were presented randomly and no more than two targets were presented sequentially. Participants responded by pressing the space bar whenever they detected a target. For the visual task, targets were letters containing a curved shape. For the verbal task, targets were letters containing the /ee/ sound. Interference tasks were presented with the same display characteristics as the commands.

Procedure

Participants were seated at a desk with both the flight simulator and laptop screen located about 3 ft. in front of them. The flight simulator screen was elevated about 8 in so that the laptop screen could be placed directly in front of it. Each command set was presented and immediately followed by three interference letters. Participants responded to the interference task as soon as it occurred. Immediately afterward, they executed the commands in X-Plane by setting the controls as accurately as possible in the order in which they were presented.

Design

A 2x2x2x4 repeated measures design was used in which the independent variables of presentation format (speech, text), command length (2 or 3), experimental trial block (first, second) interference task (verbal, visual, CE, and no interference) were combined factorially. Two dependent measures included the proportion of commands correctly set in the correct order (CSCO) and false alarms to other controls (FAOC). All participants performed four sets of three trials each, in which the four interference task conditions were presented in a counterbalanced order. The first block of trials was considered practice. Data from the remaining two blocks were analyzed.

RESULTS

The data were analyzed using a repeated-measures ANOVA with a criterion p value of .05 for statistical significance. Separate analyses were performed for the proportion of CSCO and FAOC. A Student Newman-Keuls post hoc comparison was used to analyze significant differences among means and interactions. Experimental block was included in all analyses; however, it resulted in no significant effects across trials. Due to space limitations, only data from the primary task are presented.

Message Length

A main effect for message length, $F(1, 23) = 93.71$, demonstrated more CSCO in the 2-command set ($M=.65$) compared to the 3-command set ($M=.46$). Conversely, there were fewer FAOC in the 2-command set ($M=.04$) compared to the 3-command set ($M=.09$), $F(1, 23) = 8.27$.

Interference Task

There was a main effect of interference for CSCO, $F(3, 69) = 55.94$, reflecting differences between visual ($M = .71$), control ($M = .66$), verbal ($M = .61$), and CE ($M = .23$) performance. Post hoc analyses demonstrated that CE interference resulted in fewer CSCO compared to all other conditions. Verbal interference resulted in worse performance than visual interference. However, the control condition did not differ from the visual or verbal interference conditions. The effect of interference on FAOC was also significant, $F(3, 69) = 4.31$. More errors were made on the CE task ($M =.12$) than the visual ($M = .05$), verbal ($M = .04$), and control ($M = .04$) tasks, which did not differ from one another.

Presentation Format

There was no significant difference between text and speech formats on CSCO. An effect of format for FAOC showed more errors were made when commands were presented as text ($M = .09$) compared to speech ($M = .04$), $F(1, 23) = 4.62$. Also, an interference task by format interaction for FAOC showed that more errors were made with visual and CE interference in the text condition compared to speech (see Figure 1), $F(3, 69) = 4.41$.

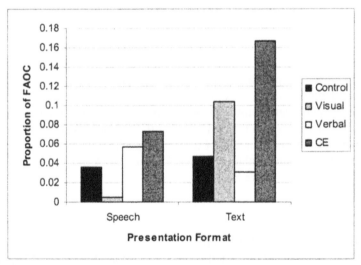

Figure 1. Proportion of false alarms to other controls (FAOC) resulting from a presentation format by interference task interaction.

DISCUSSION

The present study was designed to investigate participants' ability to correctly execute both speech and text commands during various types of interference in a simulated cockpit. In this experiment, as in others (Barshi, 1997; Scerbo et al., 2003), message length had an effect on performance whereby longer messages resulted in poorer performance. However, the effect of message length was not moderated by task interference as observed by Scerbo et al. (2003) who included a command set size of four. Thus, it is possible that any effects of task interference on message length were minimized in the present study because command set sizes of two and three were used. Also, the use of prosodic speech may have placed less demand on working memory because it facilitated the chunking of words into a single command, therefore, freeing up more resources for the interference tasks. In fact, a simple comparison of the means from this study and those of Scerbo et al. (2003) indicate a slight performance advantage under both visual and verbal interference for the more natural, prosodic command structure used in the present study.

As expected, CE interference resulted in the poorest CSCO performance followed by verbal interference. This result is consistent with Baddeley and Hitch's (1974) working memory model and replicates our previous findings (Risser et al., 2002; Risser et al., 2003; Scerbo et al., 2003). Additionally, verbal interference differed from visual interference regardless of presentation format for CSCO. This result can be explained by Wickens' (1984) multiple resource theory. Specifically, detriments in performance will be observed when resources use the same processing code. As we have found previously, we found here that verbal interference had a greater negative impact on performance than visual interference. We hypothesize that this result occurs for CSCO because both speech and text formats utilize a common underlying verbal code. Similarly, based on Baddeley and Hitch (1974) it can be predicted that performance will decrease because both the commands and verbal interference task use the phonological loop.

Presentation format (speech or text) did not result in a main effect on CSCO; however, there was an effect on the proportion of FAOC similar to Scerbo et al. (2003). There were more incorrect controls set in the text as compared to the speech condition. This may be due to a phonological recoding of text information, thereby placing a greater demand on working memory resources as suggested in Risser et al. (2002). The interaction of presentation format with interference task for the proportion of FAOC suggest that verbal interference had similar effects in both speech and text formats because of their underlying code. However, the CE and visual interference resulted in poorer performance when commands were presented as text rather than speech. This suggests that when errors are made in the text condition, supposedly during periods of high resource demands, CE interference is more problematic because greater demands are placed on working memory. On the other hand, the higher level of errors observed with visual interference during the text presentation may be the result of increased scanning requirements between the more visually complex flight simulator display and the datalink display. This additional source of interference is not present with the verbal task and speech commands because the participant can view the cockpit while listening to the information – an advantage for cross-modal displays (Wickens, 1991). Moreover, this additional requirement was not present in our previous experiments because all stimuli were presented on a single screen (Risser et al., 2002; Risser et al., 2003; Scerbo et al., 2003). Thus, this finding is consistent with that of others who studied datalink and "head down" time in the cockpit (Kerns, 1999; Navarro & Sikorski, 1999). Furthermore, it is also important to note that although an interaction was observed with the FAOC, very few of these responses occurred (i.e., under most conditions the proportions were less than .1). Thus, it may be premature to attribute too much meaning to a finding of this sort at this time.

The results from the present study demonstrate that longer message sets compromise the ability to recall and execute ATC-like commands in a simulated cockpit. Further, performance also suffers more under verbal and CE than visual interference when correctly setting the controls. These findings were obtained in the absence of a presentation format effect suggesting that both speech and text messages utilize an underlying verbal code and are therefore more susceptible to verbal interference. However, the interaction for FAOC suggests that more errors may occur during the presentation of text information, especially when there is a greater demand on working memory or additional visual scanning requirements. Collectively, the findings from this study and others (Risser et al., 2003; Scerbo et al., 2003) suggest that where datalink is concerned, changing the message format from speech to text should not have a detrimental effect on the ability to recall and correctly execute commands. Additionally, potential sources of task interference that involve verbal processing or the control of attention (e.g., task switching, decision making, etc.) may be a more serious problem (Baddeley, Chincotta, & Adlam, 2001). By contrast, when control setting errors are made in response to text compared to speech commands both visual and CE interference decrease performance even further. Moreover, because the results from the present study were obtained with a flight simulator they suggest that these effects may not be limited to simple laboratory tasks, but may be potentially observable on the flight deck. Consequently, pilots should take caution and consider the prioritization of their tasks in order to minimize interference with ATC information.

ACKNOWLEDGEMENTS

This research was supported in part by NASA Ames Research Center, grant NAG2-1481, to Old Dominion University. We are grateful to Andrea Gajeton for her help conducting the experiments and to Vasubabu Muppaneni for writing the computer programs.

REFERENCES

Baddeley, A., Chincotta, D., & Adlam, A. (2001). Working memory and the control of action: Evidence from task switching. *Journal of Experimental Psychology: General, 130*(4), 641-657.

Baddeley, A. D., & Hitch, G. (1974). Working memory. In G. H. Bower (Ed.), *Recent advances in learning and motivation* (Vol. 8, pp. 47-89). New York: Academic Press.

Barshi, I. (1997). *Effects of linguistic properties and message length on misunderstanding in aviation communication (Doctoral Dissertation).* University of Colorado, Boulder.

Kerns, K. (1991). Data-link communication between controllers and pilots: A review and synthesis of the simulation literature. *International Journal of Aviation Psychology, 1*(3), 181-204.

Kerns, K. (1999). Human factors in air traffic control/flight deck integration: Implications of data-link simulation research. In D. J. Garland, J. A. Wise & V. D. Hopkin (Eds.), *Handbook of Aviation Human Factors* (pp. 519-546). Mahwah, NJ: Lawrence Erlbaum Associates.

Navarro, C., & Sikorski, S. (1999). Datalink communication in flight deck operations: A synthesis of recent studies. *International Journal of Aviation Psychology, 9*(4), 361-376.

Risser, M. R., McNamara, D. S., Baldwin, C. L., Scerbo, M. W., & Barshi, I. (2002). Interference effects on the recall of words heard and read: Considerations for ATC communication. *Proceedings of the Human Factors and Ergonomics Society 46th Annual Meeting, Baltimore, MD*, 392-396.

Risser, M. R., Scerbo, M. W., Baldwin, C. L., & McNamara, D. S. (2003). ATC commands executed in speech and text formats: Effects of task interference. *Proceedings of the 12th Biennial International Symposium on Aviation Psychology, Dayton, OH*, 999-1004.

Scerbo, M. W., Risser, M. R., Baldwin, C. L., & McNamara, D. S. (2003). Task interference and message length on implementing speech and simulated data link commands. *Proceedings of the Human Factors and Ergonomics Society 47th Annual Meeting, Denver, CO*, 95-99.

Wickens, C. D. (1984). Processing resources in attention. In R. Parasuraman & R. Davies (Eds.), *Varieties of Attention* (pp. 63-101). New York: Academic Press.

Wickens, C. D. (1991). Processing resources and attention. In D. L. Damos (Ed.), *Multiple-task Performance* (pp. 3-34). London: Taylor and Francis.

TOWARD A NON-LINEAR APPROACH TO MODELING AIR TRAFFIC COMPLEXITY

Brian Hilburn
Center for Human Performance Research
The Hague, The Netherlands

Geraldine Flynn
EUROCONTROL Research Centre
Brétigny s/Orge , France

ABSTRACT

Air traffic complexity is thought to include those aspects of the static airspace and dynamic traffic pattern that contribute to an air traffic controller's workload, and is an important concept in evaluating ATM productivity, benchmarking cost effectiveness, and assessing the impact of new tools. Traditionally, standardized complexity indicators have relied on geometric aspects of the traffic flow, and/or observable controller behavior. In many cases, the best indicator has been the mere count of aircraft in an area of airspace. It is increasingly recognized, however, that such types of indicators do not always capture the richness of what makes some airspace more challenging (and ultimately capacity-limited). As part of its COmplexity and CApacity analysis (COCA) project, EUROCONTROL has therefore undertaken to construct a model of traffic complexity that better incorporates the cognitive aspects of air traffic control.

COCA is in the process of developing a model of cognitive complexity that promises to be unique in at least two respects. First, it is being built on an Information Processing model and sets out to elicit and refine complexity factors that relate directly to the perceptual and attentional aspects underlying cognitive complexity. Second, it is investigating the use of non-linear regression techniques to refine a generic complexity index for use across various types of airspace. Together it is hoped that this approach can strengthen current models of cognitive complexity, and benefit such modeling in air traffic control, as well as other complex human-machine systems.

Keywords: Air Traffic Control, ATC, Complexity, Workload, Neural Network

INTRODUCTION

The Merriam Webster dictionary defines "complexity" as the state of being "hard to separate, analyze, or solve...," and that would seem to agree with most people's intuition. Colloquially, the terms *complex* and *complicated* are often used interchangeably. From a systems perspective, however, the two can have quite different meanings. Cilliers (1998) noted that if a system consisting of a huge number of parts or elements (and therefore complicated) can be given a complete description, it is by definition not "complex." By this reasoning supercomputers and jumbo jets are complicated, but not complex. In a complex system, interaction between elements of the system is such that the nature of the whole cannot be determined by analysis of some subset. There are obvious examples of natural complex systems (e.g. the human brain), as well as complex human-machine systems (emergency management, C^3I, power generation systems (Worm, 2001; Perrow, 1999)), and their defining elements include:

- A large number of elements whose interaction defies analysis by traditional mathematical means;
- Dynamic interaction between elements, that involves transfer of energy and/or information;
- Redundancy that permits some subset of the system to carry out the function of the whole;
- Distributed cognition (Fields et al., 1998) characterized by localized autonomy and lack of information sharing between all elements; and
- Non-linear interactions between elements, which makes it possible for small perturbations to have large effects.

AIR TRAFFIC COMPLEXITY

In Air Traffic Control (ATC), complexity is thought to include those aspects of the static airspace and dynamic traffic pattern that contribute to an air traffic controller's workload, and is an important concept in evaluating ATM productivity, benchmarking cost effectiveness, and assessing the impact of new tools. Traditionally, standardized complexity indicators have relied on geometric aspects of the traffic flow, and/or observable controller behavior. In many cases, the best indicator has been the mere count of aircraft in an area of airspace. But clearly these do not always sufficiently capture the richness of what makes a given piece of airspace more challenging (and ultimately capacity-limited) than another. As part of its COmplexity and CApacity (COCA) project, EUROCONTROL has therefore undertaken to construct a model of traffic complexity that better incorporates the cognitive aspects of air traffic control.

The chief goal of COCA is to identify, develop and evaluate factors related to air traffic control complexity, and to validate and test complexity factors and identify those linked with controller workload and sector capacities. Within this broad goal, COCA has specifically set out to:
- Build a model of air traffic complexity;
- Apply this model to a comparison of complexity factors;
- Build a model of sector capacity; and
- Apply this model to sector classification.

It is commonly agreed in that air traffic complexity drives controller workload, which in turn is thought to ultimately limit sector capacity (Christien, Benkouar & Chaboud, 2003, Majumdar and Ochieng, 2000). Interestingly, the implicit intervening factor between workload and capacity—namely *controller error*—has thus far shown little relationship to traffic complexity (Stager & Hameluck, 1990; Gosling et al., 2002), although the data may be inadequate in this area (Rodgers, Mogford & Mogford, 1998). Research into the factors underlying ATC complexity has run a long, and still inconclusive, course. In fact, the earliest clear research reference to ATC complexity and associated factors dates back nearly 40 years (cf. Arad, 1964), nearly to the beginning of the ATC era itself.

The Role of Traffic Density

No single traffic characteristic has been as cited, studied and evaluated as has traffic density in terms of its influence on complexity and controller workload. Whereas traffic density is often used as the "best guess" measure of air traffic complexity, there are clearly cases in which it is insufficient. Anecdotal evidence suggests that controllers increasingly speak not of the difficulty of a given traffic density, but of the associated traffic complexity (Kirwan et al., 2001). Past attempts to assess complexity have generally relied on geometric relationships between aircraft (Histon et al, 2003), or on observable physical activity (Pawlak et al., 1996).

A simple diagram (below) illustrates how complexity can vary independent of traffic density. This diagram compares flight with (left) and without airway route structure (right (after van Gent et al, 1997)). Ten aircraft are presented in the same locations in each diagram. In the figure on the right, headings have been altered for four of the ten aircraft (assume, for the sake of simplicity, that all aircraft are level at the same altitude). It is obvious at a glance that the task of monitoring for conflicts and predicting where such conflicts might occur, is made more difficult if traffic flow is made only slightly less organized. This figure, by the way, also highlights one of the major potential cognitive hurdles to be overcome if mature free flight is to be achieved, namely, the removal of current day route structure would greatly increase the complexity of the controller's task and would, in particular, make it much more difficult to detect conflicts.

Figure 1. Traffic flows with route structure (left) and without (right). After van Gent et al. (1997)

It has been noted that traffic density is not only an important driver of complexity, but also correlates well with conflict rate. It does not, however, seem to correlate highly with the number or extent of altitude transitions (Chaboud et al, 2000). Further, a single indicator of density may not accurately capture the traffic pattern over time. Traffic volumes that fluctuate wildly over time (say, low routine traffic punctuated with one or two pronounced rushes per day) are more likely to generate conflicts (and appear complex to the controller) than is a sector of uniform traffic flow (Chaboud et al., 2000).

Cognitive Aspects of the Air Traffic Control Task

The obvious goals of the ATC system are to ensure adequate separation between aircraft, and to expeditiously move aircraft through airspace. In a sense, beyond adherence to the ICAO mandated separation standards, there are very few other constraints on how a controller should handle air traffic. ATC problems are often complex and ill-defined, in that ATC represents a large *solution space*– that is, ATC accommodates any number of successful strategies within the basic system constraints (Cardosi & Murphy, 1995). ATC represents a probabilistic environment, in which improper behavior does not necessarily lead to a negative outcome. Because many different strategies can be used to reach the same acceptable outcome, criterion measures of ATC performance have proven elusive.

Danaher (1980) noted that, in carrying out the functions of ATC, the controller must perform a variety of tasks. These include:
- Observing aircraft (either directly or via computer-generated displays);
- Operating display controls;
- Making data entries;
- Processing and updating flight progress information;
- Communicating with both aircraft and ground-based agents;
- Coordinating with co-workers; and
- Selecting/ revising plans and strategies.

These ATC tasks have obvious implications for such aspects of human performance as visual perception (Day, 1994), monitoring (Thackray & Touchstone, 1989), planning (Layton, Smith & McCoy, 1994), decision making (Amaldi, 1994), and memory (Stein, 1991).

While many other authors over the years have provided similar analyses of the tasks underlying ATC, a simple and more recent one is presented by Pawlak et al. (1996) who combined four major controller activities into a functional schematic, as shown below.

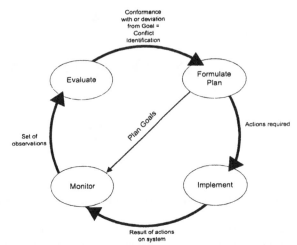

Figure 2. A model of the mental and physical processes required in ATC (after Pawlak et al., 1996)

Pawlak et al. (1996) defined four types of general tasks that controllers must perform. Of these, only the Implementation processes are observable (though the authors are careful to note that this is not always so—planned co-ordination can, in fact, be a form of implementation without observable action). Pawlak et al (1996) note that it is the other three processes—planning, monitoring, and evaluating—that combine to create mental effort for the controller.

A FUNCTIONAL MODEL OF ATC COMPLEXITY AND WORKLOAD

In the past, attempts to assess ATC workload have sometimes equated measures of direct task performance (such as time to perform discrete ATC tasks) with workload. Such observable workload (Cardosi & Murphy, 1995), however, provides only a partial picture of the workload experienced by a controller. For instance, a controller's observable performance cannot always convey the <u>cognitive</u> task demands—such as planning, decision making, and monitoring—imposed by ATC. Factors such as skill, training, experience, fatigue and other "stressors" all mediate the relationship between task demands and the workload experienced by a controller. Further, strategy plays an especially important part in determining a controller's workload. Notice that within very basic system demands, there are few constraints on how a controller should handle air traffic. As a result, the system can accommodate various control strategies without suffering a negative outcome (i.e., a loss of separation or, worse, a collision). How a controller chooses to prioritize tasks, or the compensatory strategies used to respond to workload fluctuations (e.g., shedding or deferring tasks, and deciding which tasks to handle first, or becoming more cautious in bad weather), all influence the controller's workload.

To help guide selection and refinement of the COCA cognitive complexity model, we first constructed a functional model of ATC cognitive processing that attempted to relate complexity, as an input tot he controller, and controller workload. This model distinguishes between task load (or system) factors external to the controller, and the controller's internal processes (Hilburn & Jorna, 2001). Task load consists of traffic complexity (which is driven by both airspace and traffic-related factors as well as by the demands of equipment, interface, and procedures (Mogford et al., 1995).

210

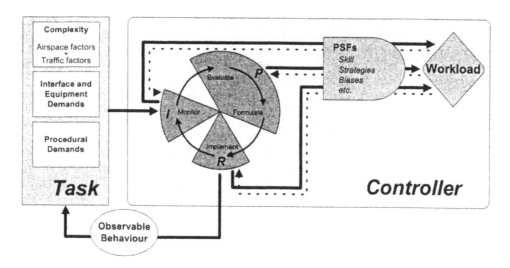

Figure 3. A Functional Model of Complexity and Workload in Air Traffic Control

According to this model, summed task load is the input to the controller. Controller activity (the "pinwheel" of the controller portion of the diagram) consists of four elements: Monitoring, Evaluating, Formulating decisions, and Implementing decisions (Pawlak et al., 1996). In fact, these activities map well onto the traditional view of human information processing which distinguishes between Input, Processing, and Response (abbreviated I, P and R, respectively, in the diagram).

Each cycle of this I-P-R pinwheel has one of two outcomes-- either overt action (in which the controller acts on the task load), or continuing the (non-observable) process of monitoring, evaluating, etc. "Implementation" in this sense can be deciding to postpone action (waiting to see what will happen). Again, observable activity does not capture all of a controller's processing.

Controller workload is a response to this information-processing pinwheel—the demands of monitoring, evaluating, etc. However, the response is not a direct one, rather it is mediated by Performance Shaping Factors (PSFs) such as skill, fatigue, age, training, proneness to anxiety, etc. that can influence the resulting workload. Notice also that the influence of PSFs runs downstream (dashed arrows), through the allocation of attention to monitoring, evaluating/formulating, or implementing. For example, a controller might defer routine housekeeping tasks (e.g., not sharing turbulence reports with pilots), or might combine tasks in parallel (e.g., through joint RT clearances). In this model, such adaptive strategies do nothing to moderate the complexity of the underlying task. This is an important element of the model, since it encompasses not only systematic biases (e.g. as in decision making and perceptual biases that can color monitoring and evaluation, as mentioned earlier) but also individual differences. PSFs are the noise in the complexity-task load-workload transform. The end result of this entire process is controller workload, which is a function of both task demands and the controller's internal and subjective response to those demands.

LESSONS LEARNED TO DATE

COCA is an ongoing project, and work is progressing in several parallel areas. On the basis of literature review and analytic (e.g., fast time modeling) work to date, a number of lessons can be drawn.

First, and perhaps foremost, is that no single indicator of air traffic complexity (or composite of indicators) applies equally well regardless of context. What works well in one setting might not work well in another site, or even at another time-of-day. Second, it is increasingly recognized that no linear combination of complexity indicators will adequately capture cognitive complexity of ATC in all contexts. Third, strictly geometrical approaches to capturing complexity (a number have been put forward) seem to have been beset with combinatorial problems in handling large numbers of aircraft (Durand & Granger, 2003). More critically (for the purposes of the current project), it seems that no geometric approach to date has fully captured the notion of complexity <u>as it is perceived by the</u>

controller. Work is ongoing (Histon et al, 2003; Davison et al., 2003) into the techniques that controllers use to derive underlying structure, and this appears promising.

Fourth, it appears that the study of air traffic complexity may be overly focused on understanding <u>high</u> complexity, to the detriment of the less complex situations. Operational ATC evidence would suggest that this is a dangerous oversight (in July of 2000, a high altitude mid-air collision occurred over Germany on a clear, quiet night). There is sufficient operational evidence (on the occurrence of ATC errors) as well as theoretical evidence (on human's poor monitoring performance and potentially-high workload under vigilance conditions (Parasuraman, 1987)) that <u>under</u> load might itself pose a serious threat to air safety. It seems therefore worthwhile to consider the range of possible conditions, including the potential impact of excessively <u>low</u> complexity on controller workload.

Finally, the majority of past research has used a linear approach to capturing airspace complexity. For example, linear regression approaches (Laudeman et al., 1998; Masalonis et al., 2003) attempt to combine factors using fixed regression weights. The main shortcoming of this approach is clear: The single resulting regression equation tends to apply only to the particular context (sector, time of day, even weather), and does not generalize well to other contexts. What is it that makes a given traffic pattern so complex? In one case it might be the pattern of altitude transitions, in another it might be military activity, or weather, that restricts full use of airspace and thus limits controller options. A number of alternatives to linear regression have been proposed (e.g., Maximum Likelihood Analysis, Time-series analysis, Genetic Algorithms).

Non-linear approaches, on the other hand, start from the recognition that complexity factors combine in a non-linear way. Though the same constellation of factors might well apply across contexts, the relative importance of each differs by context. Several non-linear approaches have been used to model airspace complexity. Among them are dynamical systems modeling using a non-linear extension of Kolmogorov entropy (Delahaye & Puechmorel, 2000).

The non-linear method that seems to have shown the most promise (or at least generated the most interest) is non-linear regression, typically by artificial neural networks (Chatterji and Sridhar, 2001; Majumdar & Ochieng, 2001). In practice, a neural network is trained to the general topology, and applies to "learning" new profiles (i.e., contexts). Sridhar (2000) reviewed work by NASA's Dynamic Density research team to investigate the use of neural network analysis of complexity factors. Training a neural net with samples of different complexity, they demonstrated 100% correct classification of the data.

This concept of non-linear regression has intuitive as well as theoretical appeal. It seems to fit well with what is known about naturalistic decision making (Klein, 1993), in particular that expertise in many fields is often more a process of pattern recognition than of action selection. In a variety of fields (whether it is fire control, trauma medicine, or air traffic control), once an expert recognizes / diagnoses a situation (hopefully correctly) the course of action is clear to that expert. Athenes et al (2002) noted just this about air traffic control.

CONCLUSIONS

The COCA project is in the process of developing a model of cognitive complexity that promises to be unique in at least two respects. First, it is being built on an Information Processing model and sets out to elicit and refine complexity factors that relate directly to the perceptual and attentional aspects underlying cognitive complexity. Second, it is investigating the use of non-linear regression techniques to refine a generic complexity index for use across various types of airspace. Together it is hoped that this approach can strengthen current models of cognitive complexity, and benefit such predictive modeling in air traffic control, as well as other complex human-machine systems.

REFERENCES

Amaldi, P. (1994). Cognitive processes during the management of real air traffic scenarios. Paper presented at the First Conference on Cognitive Science in Industry. September, 1994: Luxembourg.

Athènes, S., Averty, P., Puechmorel, S., Delahaye, D. & Collet, C. (2002). Complexity and Controller Workload: Trying to Bridge the Gap. In Proceedings of the 2002 International Conference on Human-Computer Interaction in Aeronautics (HCI-

Aero 2002). Cambridge, MA, USA: Massachusetts Institute of Technology.

Cardosi, K. M & Murphy, E.D. (1995). Human factors in the design and evaluation of air traffic control systems (DOT/FAA/RD-95/3). Cambridge, Massachusetts: U.S. Department of Transportation, Volpe Research Center.

Chaboud et al. (2000). Air Traffic Complexity: Potential Impacts on Workload and Cost. EEC Note 11/00. EUROCONTROL.Cilliers, P. (1998). Complexity and Postmodernism. London: Routledge.

Chatterji, G.B. & Sridhar, B. (2001). Measures for air traffic controller workload prediction. First AIAA Aircraft Technology, Integration and Operations Forum. Los Angeles, California.

Christien, R., Benkouar, A., Chaboud, T. & Loubieres, P. (2003). Air traffic complexity indicators & ATC sectors classification. Presented at ATM 2003.Budapest, 23-27 June, 2003.

Danaher, J.W. (1980). Human error in ATC system operations. Ergonomics, 22(5), 535-545.

Davison, H.J. et al. (2003). Impact of operating context on the use of structure in air trafficcontroller cognitive processes. Presented at the 5th Eurocontrol / FAA ATM R&D Seminar, Budapest, Hungary, 23rd - 27th June.

Day, P.O.. (1994). Air Traffic Systems Strategies Studies (ATSRATS) Interaction Index, Roke Manor Research Ltd.

Delahaye, D., & Puechmorel, S. (2000). Air traffic complexity: Towards intrinsic metrics. Presented at the 3rd FAA/EUROCONTROL ATM R&D Seminar. Naples Italy, 13-16 June.

Durand, N. & Granger, G. (2003). A traffic complexity approach through cluster analysis. Presented at ATM 2003.Budapest, 23-27 June, 2003.

Gent, R. van, Hoekstra, J.M. & Ruigrok, R.C.J. (1997). Free flight with airborne separation assurance. In Proceedings of the Confederation of European Aerospace Societies (CEAS) 10th European Aerospace Conference, 20-21 October 1997, Amsterdam, The Netherlands.

Hilburn, B. & Jorna, P. (2001). Workload and Air Traffic Control. In PA Hancock and PA Desmond (Eds.) Stress, Workload and Fatigue: Theory, Research and Practice. Hillsdale, New Jersey, USA: Erlbaum.

Histon, J.M., et al. (2003). Structural considerations and cognitive complexity in air traffic control. Presented at the 19th IEEE/AIAA Digital Avionics Systems Conference, Irvine, CA, October 2002.

Kirwan, B., Scaife, R. & Kennedy, R. (2001). Investigating Complexity Factors in UK Air Traffic Management. Human factors and Aerospace Safety, 1(2), June 2001.

Klein, G.A. (1993). A recognition-primed decision (RPD) model of rapid decision making. In G.A. Klein, J. Orasanu, R. Calderwood & C.E. Zsambok (Eds.), Decision making in action: Models and methods (pp. 138-147). New Jersey: Ablex Publishing.

Laudeman, I. et al. (1998). Dynamic Density: An Air Traffic Management Metric. Report NAS/TM-1998-112226. Ames Research Center, Moffett Field, California: NASA.

Layton, C., Smith, P.J. & McCoy, C.E. (1994). Design of a cooperative problem-solving system for en-route flight planning: an empirical evaluation.

Majumdar, A. & Ochieng, W.Y. (2000). The factors affecting air traffic controller workload: a multivariate analysis based upon simulation modelling of controller workload. Centre for Transport Studies, Imperial College, London.

Masalonis, A.J. et al. (2003). Dynamic density and complexity metrics for realtime traffic flow management. Presented at the 5th Eurocontrol / FAA ATM R&D Seminar, Hungary, 23rd - 27th June.

Mogford, R. H., Guttman, J. A., Morrow, S. L., & Kopardekar, P. (1995). The complexity construct in air traffic control: A review and synthesis of the literature (DOT/FAA/-CT TN95/22). Atlantic City, NJ: FAA.

Parasuraman, R. (1987). Human computer monitoring. Human Factors, 29(6), 695-706.

Pawlak, W.S., et al. (1996). A framework for the evaluation of air traffic control complexity. Presented at the AIAA National Conference.

Perrow, C. (1999). Normal Accidents: Living with High Risk Technologies. Princeton, NJ, USA: Princeton Press.

Rodgers, M.D., Mogford, R.H., & Mogford, L.S. (1998). The relationship of sector characteristics to operational errors. DOT/FAA/AM-98/14). Washington, DC: FAA.

Sridhar, B. (2000). Dynamic density and its application in traffic flow management. Presented at the Free Flight/DAG Workshop, NASA Ames, CA, 22-24 May.

Stager, P. & Hameluck, D. (1990). Ergonomics in air traffic control. Ergonomics, 33(4), 493-499.

Stein, E.S. (1991). Air traffic controller memory: a field study (DOT/FAA/CT-TN90/60). Atlantic City, New Jersey: FAA Technical Center.

Thackray, R.I. & Touchstone, R.M. (1989). Effects of high visual taskload on the behaviors involved in complex monitoring. Ergonomics, 32, 27-38.

Worm, A. (2001). On systems analysis and performance assessment in complex, high risk work environments. International Journal of Risk Assessment and management, 2(3/4).

A Quantitative Framework for the Development of a Computational Decision Support Tool for the Assessment of Pilots' Transformations Cost during Applications of Airborne Separation Assistance

Colin Goodchild and Pauline D. Yearwood

ATM Research Group
Department of Aerospace Engineering
University of Glasgow

ABSTRACT

One of the principal concerns with the introduction of airborne separation assistance authority and its applications, as proposed in future air traffic management, is the possibility of adverse changes on the cognitive and behaviour processes of the human operators, mainly air traffic controllers and pilots. The delegation processes of the four applications of airborne separation assistance - traffic situation awareness application, limited, extended and full delegation all have implications that reflect a significant change in the way that pilots and controllers will perform their respective tasks. In devolving to pilots more responsibility for maintaining safe separation it will be necessary to ensure that the changes do not increase pilots' demands beyond their human performance limit.

This paper describes the approach used in developing, expanding and creating the quantitative framework for the development of Multi-criteria Analysis for Pilot Evaluation, MpE a computational decision support tool. for the determination of the impact and consequential changes in pilot's operations during applications of airborne separation assistance. The implementation of the model is based on the expansion of the descriptors of change, termed *determinants* of MACE [(Muti-criteria Analysis for concept Evaluation, Eurocontrol 2000).

INTRODUCTION

The goal of Air Traffic Management (ATM), as defined in 1991 by the ICAO Special Committee on Future Air Navigation Systems (FANS), is "...to enable aircraft operators to meet their planned time of departure and arrival and adhere to their preferred flight profiles with minimum constraints without compromising agreed levels of safety" [1]. The key technologies required for the implementation of such an ATM system are Communications, Navigation and Surveillance (CNS), where, advances in these technologies and developments, involving their integration into systems architectures provide the information framework for a global ATM system.

The ASAS concept embodies the response of ICAO to the diverse emerging tools and procedures being developed to support a further engagement of the flight crew in separation assurance under the future ATM. Whereas there is evidence [2] to indicate ASAS applications for Autonomous Aircraft Operations (AAO), such as limited, extended and full delegation will result in result in reduce costs to airlines and higher workload savings for the ground environment, these applications also have the potential to increase the overall demands of the flight crew and air traffic controllers beyond their human performance limits. Pilots are observed to have an aircraft-centric view and are primarily concerned with traffic which impact their current or planned trajectories. Conversely, controllers are known to have a system centred, "big picture" view and are concerned with how the trajectories and total traffic flow will interact [3] and [4.].

Hence, the devolving to more responsibility for maintaining safe separation, as in the applications of limited, full and extended delegation may have a strong impact on the predictability of pilots' possible future action and trajectories; and on the availability and situation awareness of controllers. On one hand a very limited delegation would maintain a high level of predictability of aircraft behaviours and trajectories from a controller's point of view, with a counter part of limited gain in controller's workload. In which case, a more extended delegation leaves more autonomy to the pilot to manage the solution, with a risk of a possible reduction of predictability for the controllers.

As part of on-going research in the area of human factors in ATM, the University of Glasgow ATM research group has expanded and extensively modified the performance factors of a decision support tool. making it now applicable for the determination of the transformation cost in pilots. The transformation cost is defined as the increase in difficulty, how such difficulty scale and an assessment of which problems are most critical during a particular application.

The tool developed is Multi-criteria Analysis for Pilot Evaluation, MpE. This paper describes the approach used in the development of the quantitative framework of this tool, where the focus of the expansion has been on issues concerning problems such as mental representation of the changing situations and the context-dependent flexible coordination of concurrent cognitive tasks, which are inherent to dynamic situations during applications of situation awareness, limited, extended and full delegation of airborne separation assistance.

First a historical background of MpE is given. An illustration of its application with respect to the above four applications is also presented and the paper concludes with a discussion of results and discussion.mary,

BACKGROUND INFORMATION

Multi-criteria Analysis for Pilot Evaluation, MpE has been developed for the determination of the impact and consequential changes in pilots' operations during applications of airborne separation assistance. MpE incorporates the utilities of the decision support tool Muti-criteria Analysis for concept Evaluation, MACE [5] which forms part of the IMPACT Project [5] of tools, software and documents, conceived and produced by EUROCONTROL scientists and experts to analyst new air traffic management concepts.

MACE was designed specifically for air traffic controllers, however, by virtue of its operational principles of human performance and cognitive modelling it lends itself to easy manipulation for the design as other effective decision aids for the analysis of pilots' performance during airborne separation application, specifically limited, extended and full delegation.

The basic structural framework of MACE is one made up of five subject categories: project description, evaluation results, results improvement, determinants influence and simulation and two macros. The programme, use multi-criteria analysis techniques to compute a global score which is derived from the relationships between the indicators and sixteen criteria (expressions of human dimensions on the particular concept analyse) and interdependencies between these criteria.

The interdependencies between the criteria are typed and weight, and the comparison expressed as a distance between *Hell* and *Heaven* . This distance is a constant and results in the provision of only one location in the hyper-space leading to either *Hell* or *Heaven* where the closer to *Heaven* is interpreted as the easier to be learned and accepted, the closer to *Hell* the more difficult.

CONCEPT DEVELOPMENT AND EXPANSION

The quantitative framework of MpE is an expansion of the performance factors utilities of MACE, termed determinants which were extensively modified and expanded from their original forty (40) factors to eighty five (85) factors, incorporating the tasks required for the cockpit environment during each application.

The cognitive process was taken into account with regards the objective of the framework development, the ability of the programme to quantify the increase in difficulty, determine how such difficulty scales and assess which problems are most critical to pilots during the application of traffic situation awareness; limited, extended and full delegation. The core of the cognitive process is independent of the pilot's role and is based on the cognitive activities, derived from the original programme which are divided into the following five groups:

- Situational awareness, planning, and action.
- Knowledge, skills.
- Skills awareness, confidence and motivation.
- Workload, stress and fatigue.
- Human error.

The first step in the expansion was the re-classification of the two categories of the *determinants* technical and activity related categories. These were expanded as detailed in Tables 1 and 2.

Aviation Tasks	Communication Tasks
Navigation Tasks	Systems Management Tasks

Table 1. Technical Related Determinants

Assisted Tasks	Executed Tasks
Decision Tasks	

Table 2. Activity Related Determinants

Whereas the sixteen (16) interrelations of the *cognitive criteria* elements remained unchanged, it was deemed necessary to amend the list for the communication elements, Table.3.

COMMUNICATION FACTORS	
Air/Air Interaction	Pilot/Crew Interaction
Air/Ground Interaction	Pilot/System Interaction

Table 3. Criteria Expansion – Communication Factors

As some determinants were not deemed directly related to pilots' tasks, those not reclassified acted as external factors. The SHEL model interface [6] was used as guidance as the intension was to enable the programme to be as general and flexible as possible

Amendments were also made to the determinants influence elements where the addition of two other categories, simulation results and statistical analysts were created to display and analyse the results of simulations when used. Here, simulation results display the table of the simulation and results of the linear regression coefficients; and simulation analyst display all the analysis made to demonstrate the quality of the approximation with the regression.

OPERATIONAL EXAMPLE

To illustrates the functionality and capabilities of the extended quantitative framework, two thousand(2000) hypothetical simulations were conducted to assess applications of situation awareness; limited, extended and full delegation of airborne separation assistance.

First, the interdependencies between the criteria, were typed and weighted. Secondly, a relationship between Criteria and Determinants were derived to determine the acceptance level and the ability of the pilots with regard their new roles and as they relate to a particular application. This was derived through an equation provided by the program.

The value of heaven, $\delta_{projectP}^{heaven}$, identifies which Determinant scores have a strong impact, either positive or negative, and to obtain this value, a direct relationship, called h, between Determinants and $\delta_{projectP}^{heaven}$ was derived, again using an equation provided by the program. Then, using linear regression algorithm based on best square difference minimisation, a model also provided by the program was established:

ANALYASIS OF RESULTS

The results from the simulation are quite intriguing for of the 2000 simulations conducted for pilots, the regression coefficient   derived from the coefficient   ᵢ produced a value of: . = 0.956

This value represents a good indicator of the validity of the simulations as the square is nearer to 1. Table 4 details an overall summary of these simulations.

APPLICATION	DISTANCE TO HEAVEN	DISTANCE TO HELL	RESULTS
Situation Awareness	60.34	80.69	Very easy to accept and learn
Limited Delegation	58.29	82.79	Very easy to accept and learn
Extended Delegation	63.05	77.69	Easy to accept and learn
Full Delegation	64.45	76.27	Easy to accept and learn

Table 4. Summary of Simulation Results

Results for traffic situation awareness and limited delegation both revealed that these concepts will be very easy to learn and accept. Whereas the result, (60.34) for traffic situation can be attributed to the fact that core roles remain unmodified, the result of (58.29) for limited delegation, through indicating very easy acceptance, however indicates that such acceptance should be facilitated by the concept of flexible use of delegation where the levels of delegation correspond to incremental steps of practice, yielding to gradual confidence building. In addition this low rating suggests that pilots will very well tolerate limited delegation, a view supported by previous research.

An examination of the positive values of the *determinants* factors *zone of operation* (1.28, 1.28, 1.28) *and visual channel use* (1.43, 1.44, 1.44) revealed pilot's difficulty in all three delegation applications and support the view for the need of on board assistance tools such as autopilot target values or flight management system (FMA) trajectories for conflict detection and resolution, along with intent information about other traffic to reduce pilot workload.

Although the overall results indicated an easy acceptance level for extended delegation results from the simulation revealed that aircraft density at (1.44) will be a major problem for pilots. This is further substantiated by the noted increase in *distance to Heaven,* 63.05 from 58.29 as was recorded.

DISCUSSION

The following is a list of problems which were encountered during the use of the software which where highlight also detail recommendations for improvement.

MpE incorporates the utilities of multi-criteria analysis for concept evaluation (MACE) and as a result several problems were encountered when using the same ratings scale and measurements for pilots. The value scales embedded within the original software and which aid in quantifying the changes of the concepts introduced, through designed for an ATC environment, were designed specifically for controllers and found not applicable for pilots. While these value scales were adequate for the assessment of application of traffic situation awareness they were not fully inclusive and adequate for the applications of limited, full and extended delegations.

The cognitive components termed *criteria,* when used in MpE, did not accurately describe the activities of the concept being examined – the transformation cost of applications of traffic situation awareness, limited, extended and full delegation describe activities of a pilot's environment. Currently, differences exist between the tools with regards predictions and by extension influencing the human performance values output from the programme.

The structural differences that exist between the two programmes also appear to be a weak influence on the amount of workload that is experienced by each respective operator. The relative simplicity of the original MACE generating structure may be associated with the greater performance effects as predicted by MpE and require major re-programming. The more detailed the *determinant,* such as presented by MpE, combined with much larger interactive *criteria* may result in more accurate measure of both pilot's and air traffic controller's performances.

There is also the need for a broader performance rating scale or measurements within the programme. The user of both tools MACE and MpE, must make subjective judgement about future concepts and provide ratings/measurements to initially activate the programmes. Given this subjectivity and time-consuming nature of obtaining ratings, it would be desirable if the programme provided a broader range of ratings.

There was a great degree of consistency in the results across all the applications for pilots. The reason for this anomaly can only be speculated upon at the current time but it is likely that this anomaly occurred because of limitations in the contextual recognition of the software, as MpE was unable to determine the contextual differences associated with the different determinants.

This critical observation is indicative that more emphasis needs to be placed on accurately modelling the contextual properties of the pilot's environment and having the software tool recognize these contextual properties. Specifically, incorporating an accurate prioritisation and scheduling mechanism that is based on the contextual events in the virtual environment is required. Secondly, the fact that the simulation manipulations did not necessarily produced the expected effect or the effect that would have been expected of a human-in-the-loop experiment is a critical fact that needs to be addressed if the programme is to be introduced within the ATC environment.

CONCLUSIONS

The development of MpE to an extended framework of eighty-five *determinants* represent a comprehensive and psychometrically sound description of pilot's operational factors and as such render the software applicable for reliable pilot performance assessment during simulations of situation awareness application, limited, full and extended delegation for the determination of the effects of role transfer. The overall results, 4.11 from the increase in more active control responsibilities for the pilots may confirm the belief of Wickens et al [6], that such increase may lead to problems by increasing the operator demands beyond their human performance limits.

However, it should be noted that the application of the framework depended entirely on information provided by subject matter experts and literature review and as such was not tested, unlike the *determinants* used in the original software, MACE where some experiments have been conducted by Eurocontrol [5] in the ATC environment for controllers. In this regard, MpE if used in the pilots' environment the effectiveness of the expanded *determinants* need now to be evaluated through human-in the loop validation.

REFERENCES

[1] Galotti, V., 1997, *The Future Air Navigation System (FANS)*, England, Ashgate Publishing Limited.

[2] Allen, D. L., A. Haraldsdottir, R.W. Lawler, K.Pirotte,R..W. Schwab, April 1998, *The Economic Evaluation of CSN/ATM Transition*, CNS/ATM Projects, Boeing Commercial Airplane Group.

[3] Farley, T., and Hansman, R.J., " An Experimental Study of the Effect of Shared Information on Pilot/Controller Re-Route Negotiation," MIT International Centre of Air Transportation Report, ICAT-99-1, January 1999.

[4] Hansman, R.J., Endsley, M., Farley, T., Vigeant-Lanlois, L., and Amonlirdviman, K.] "The Effect of Shared Information on Pilot/Controller Situation Awareness and Re-Route Negotiation," FAA/European 2nd International Air Traffic Management R&D Seminar (ATM 98), Orlando, FL, December 1998.

[5] Eurocontrol, EOSAN. Multi-criteria Analysis for Concept Evaluation (MACE), EEC Report No.XX/99 IMPACT Project, (HRS-Z-05-IMPCT). Issued September 2000.

[6] Wickens, C., Mavor, A. Parasuraman R., and McGee, J. (1998). The Future of Air Traffic Control: Human Operators and Automation. National Academy Press, Washington, D.C.

STRESS, WORKLOAD AND FATIGUE

PILOT WORKLOAD PREDICTION:
NUMBER OF DISPLAY ELEMENTS (NUDES) AS A PREDICTOR

Harrie G.M. Bohnen and Antoine J.C. de Reus

National Aerospace Laboratory NLR, The Netherlands

ABSTRACT

Visual allocation of attention was used as a predictor of workload of military pilots. Pilots flew simulated missions with varying levels of task demand. They also performed a detection task and a memory task. The detection task involved visual sampling of display elements and responding to target symbols.

Missions that included the detection task were reported to be more effortful, but physiological indicators of mental effort did not confirm this. The number of display elements (7 or 28) had an effect on performance but no clear effect on perceived effort. Memory task and flight performance decreased slightly for the condition with 28 display elements.

The results suggested that pilots developed strategies to maximize mission performance and to avoid performance detriments for individual tasks. Efficient strategies can limit mental workload. It appears that predicting workload has more practical value when pilot task strategies are taken into account.

Keywords: Memory Task; Pilot Workload; Task Strategies; Visual Attention; Workload Prediction

INTRODUCTION

The ability to predict workload is an important step towards the optimal tuning of tasks to the capabilities of the military pilot, leading to better system performance and safety. The visual allocation of attention is one of the most important indicators of workload (e.g., see Moray, 1986). Therefore, an explorative study is performed towards the amount of information in the cockpit to be sampled as a predictor of workload.

In this study, the NUmber of Display ElementS (NUDES) defines the amount of information associated with a task. The NUDES on a cockpit display are manipulated in order to determine its effect on workload. For this purpose, a target Detection Task is used which requires the sampling of a number of display elements or symbols. The hypothesis is that pilots experience a higher workload in situations where more symbols need to be sampled. General task demands are not only manipulated by varying the NUDES, but also by the complexity of the flying task itself and by the addition of an auditory Continuous Memory Task (e.g., see Jorna, 1989). This way, the effect of NUDES is tested under different task load conditions.

METHOD

Participants

Seven male subjects participated in the study. All subjects had a background as F-16 pilot.

Apparatus

The study was performed at the National Aerospace Laboratory in Amsterdam, The Netherlands. A fighter mock-up with a simulated out-of-the-window view was used for the piloting task. The Memory Task was presented to the subject by means of a miniature headphone. A switch on the throttle (left hand) was used as response button. The Detection Task was presented on a head-down display in the mock-up. A switch on the stick (right hand) was used as response button.

Tasks

Flight conditions had a varying level of mental task demand. The first part of the mission consisted of six rate-one turns separated by straight legs. These rate-one turns were considered as simple flight maneuvers. The latter part of the mission consisted of a sequence of complex flight maneuvers.

The symbols (7 or 28 NUDES) for the Detection Task were presented on a fixed position on the screen. Four types of non-target symbols existed and one target symbol (Fig. 1). A symbol changed from non-target to target at random time intervals and at random positions. Only one symbol was the target symbol at any instance. Every 1.5 s one non-target symbol was replaced by another non-target. The first target symbol occurred within 15 s after the beginning of the task. The next target symbol was presented within 15 to 30 s (3 s steps) after the appearance of the previous one. The average interval was 22.5 s. The subjects had to detect the target symbols and to respond as soon as possible. The detected target was then reset to a non-target symbol. Target symbols that were not detected by the subjects automatically became non-target 15 s after their appearance.

To perform the Memory Task subjects had to remember two or four target letters. Thereafter, a series of letters was presented via the headset and subjects had to react to the target letters. Subjects also had to count how often they heard each target letter. After hearing a target letter three times, a specific response was required. The counting for that target letter then started again.

Figure 1. From left to right: the four non-target symbols and the target symbol.

Procedure

A within-subjects design was used with NUDES (0/7/28) and Memory Task loading (0/2/4) as factors. The order of presentation of NUDES was balanced as far as possible over subjects, while the order of the Memory Task was fixed: 0, 2, and 4. Rate-ones always preceded the complex flight maneuvers. In order to assess mental effort, heart rate data was collected using Vitaport. Visual sampling data were collected using a Gazetracker eye/head tracking system. All data were analyzed with the aid of Statistica.

RESULTS

Flight task performance

During rate-one maneuvering pilots had to keep their aircraft within 50 ft of the target altitude. Both the number of times and the percentage of time pilots exceeded this limit were analyzed (Fig. 2 and 3). Overall, especially the addition of the Memory Task (MT) increased the number and percentage of exceedings, $F(2,12)=5.52, p=.020$ respectively $F(2,12)=3.53, p=.062$. The addition of the Detection Task (DT) had a less prominent effect. A significant interaction effect between the two tasks (MT and DT) was found: in the highest workload condition (DT 28, MT 4) both measures decreased (exceeding number: $F(4,24)=2.51, p=.068$; exceeding percentage: $F(4,24)=4.05, p=.012$). This suggests a possible strategy shift.

The complex flight maneuvers involved more freedom for the pilots. Consequently flight task performance data for this mission part were not analyzed.

Detection Task performance

The percentages of correct responses (hits) for the DT and the reaction times related to those hits are displayed in Fig. 4 and 5. False alarms occurred very rarely. Looking at rate-ones only, no effect was found for the DT load (i.e. NUDES) on the percentage of hits, but the reaction times seemed to increase $F(1,6)=4.22, p=.086$. The addition of the MT had a minor influence on the percentage of hits $F(2,12)=2.67, p=.110$. The effect of NUDES on reaction time seemed reverse in the highest workload condition (DT 28, MT 4), though this did not reach significance.

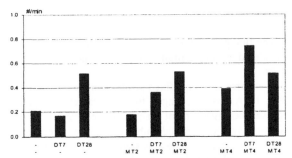

Figure 2. Average number of times the altitude limit was exceeded during rate-ones. DT = Detection Task (7/28 NUDES), MT = Memory Task (2/4 target letters).

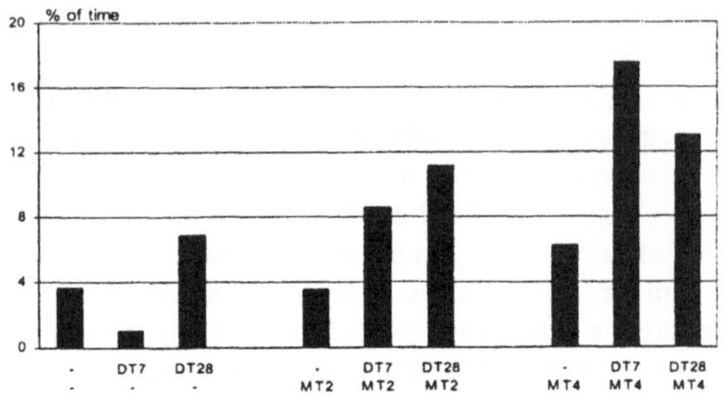

Figure 3. Percentage of time the altitude limit was exceeded during rate-ones.

During the complex maneuvers, trends of the NUDES were found on the percentage of hits, $F(1,6)=4.75, p=.072$. Comparing the complex maneuvers with the rate-ones without a MT produced a clear difference in the percentage of hits and the reaction time, $F(1,6)=9.18, p=.023$ respectively $F(1,6)=5.83, p=.052$. In other words, performance on the DT was affected by the complexity of the flight maneuvers.

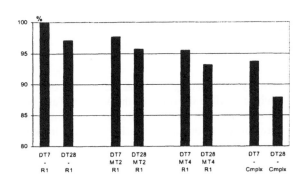

Figure 4. Percentage of hits in the DT (R1= rate ones; cmplx = complex maneuvering).

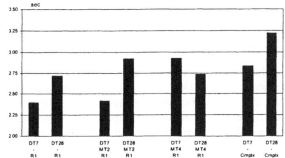

Figure 5. Reaction times to targets in the DT.

Memory Task performance

There were no false alarms during the Memory Task. In the MT with 2 target letters, hardly any mistakes were made with target letter detection (Fig. 6 and 7). Only when pilots had to remember and count 4 target letters, they started to make more mistakes $F(1,6)=3.98, p=.093$, though the largest effect was on reaction times $F(1,6)=12.02, p=.013$. The DT had a negative influence on reaction times, $F(2,12)=10.64, p=.002$. This effect was not significantly different for the two levels (7, 28) of the DT.

In the target letter counting subtask, a clear effect of the number of target letters was found on the percentage of hits and on the reaction times, $F(1,6)=8.78, p=.025$ respectively $F(1,6)=6.21, p=.047$. Also much more false alarms were produced with 4 target letters. The effect of the DT was not significant.

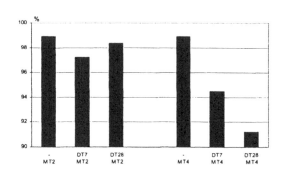

Figure 6. Percentage of hits of the MT.

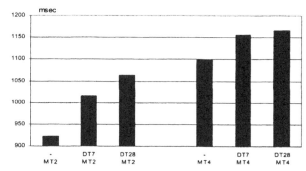

Figure 7. Reaction times to target letters in the MT.

Mental effort

The addition of the MT had a clear effect on heart rate during the rate-ones $F(2,12)=40.40,p<.001$ (Fig. 8). No selective effect of the DT was found on heart rate. When the complex maneuvers were compared to the rate-ones without the MT, a significant effect of flight task complexity was found $F(1,6)=28.18,p=.002$. No effect was found on heart rate variability.

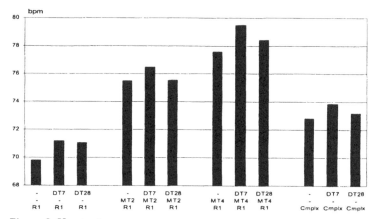

Figure 8. Heart rate

After each mission subjects used the Rating Scale Mental Effort (Zijlstra, 1993). Without the DT the mission is perceived as nearby "pretty effortful" (rating=70) while with the DT up to "very, very effortful" (rating=90/100), $F(2,12)=6.12,p=.015$. However, pilots did not perceive the DT with 28 NUDES as more effortful than with 7 NUDES. This may be because the difference is "drowned" in the perception of the mission as a whole.

Visual scanning

Looking at rate-ones only, a trend of the NUDES is found on the dwell time on the display where the DT was presented (Fig. 9). No effect of the MT was found, but an interaction with the detection task is suspected. Especially the DT with 28 NUDES seems to suffer from the addition of the MT, $F(2,12)=9.98$, $p=.003$. The time less spent at the DT display is spent on (the center of) the Head-Up-Display (HUD), interaction MT x DT: $F(2,12)=3.38,p=.068$. During complex maneuvering, more time is spent on the DT display as a function of the NUDES and less on the HUD, $F(1,6)=47.79,p<.001$ respectively $F(1,6)=12.42,p=.012$.

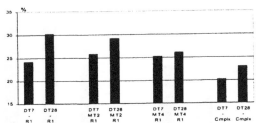
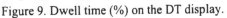
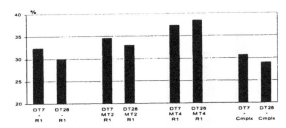

Figure 9. Dwell time (%) on the DT display.   Figure 10. Dwell time (%) on the HUD.

The NUDES greatly affected the mean fixation duration on the DT display: with 7 elements this was about 0.45 s, while with 28 elements this was about 0.60 s (rate-ones: F(1,6)=64.17,p<.001, complex maneuvering: F(1,6)=36.00,p=.001).

With 7 NUDES, pilots waited about 4 s before they re-fixated at the DT display. With 28 NUDES, this difference was about 5 s (rate-ones: F(1,6)=6.29,p=.046; complex maneuvering: F(1,6)=7.42,p=.034).

DISCUSSION

The results show that a mission that includes the Detection Task (DT) costs more mental effort. However, no difference was reported in the perceived effort between the two amounts of information to be sampled in the DT, that is 7 or 28 NUDES. This result was confirmed by the objective mental effort measures, heart rate and heart rate variability. This means that just adding the DT had an effect, regardless the amount of NUDES to be processed in that task. Subjects reacted more slowly to target symbols in case of 28 NUDES instead of 7, and they also missed more target symbols. The addition of the DT slightly affected flight performance. These changes in performance can indicate that subjects were not able to maintain performance because of limited resources, interference in visual processing, or changes in attention allocation. The latter suggests a change in task strategy to actively manage time and resources to accomplish the complete task (i.e., flying the mission and detecting critical symbol, accurately and on time). Strategy shifts can be seen as an index of increasing mental load, because pilots may change their strategy to keep workload at an acceptable level (e.g., see Hart, 1991).

Reaction time to the target symbols in the DT only increased for the high load condition (4 target letters) of the Memory Task (MT). The MT performance itself is slightly affected by the number of symbols in the DT. Flight performance also seems to decrease, although this effect is absent in the MT condition with a high load. This again might reflect a strategy-shift: performance on the MT is 'sacrificed' in order to maintain a minimal performance level on the other tasks.

Subjects rated the mission as somewhat above 'pretty effortful' while with the DT added to the mission it is perceived nearby 'very, very effortful'. The mission as a whole, which includes the MT and DT, can thus be described as highly demanding. No effects of the addition of the DT are found in the objective mental effort parameters. This can be caused by a ceiling-effect: the mental effort in the least demanding task situation, in which subjects had to fly and to perform the MT together, is already so high that an increase in resource allocation and hence mental effort is almost not possible anymore.

Effects on heart rate are only found when comparing rate-ones without a MT with complex maneuvers, which suggest an effect of flight maneuver complexity, and for the addition of the MT. As said before, adding the DT results in an increase in perceived effort and hence it is legitimate to state that those subjects had the willingness to spend resources in order to cope with the demands of the combined tasks. However, subjects were unable to cope with those demands, as was evidenced by a decreased performance on for example the MT. This can be another reason for not finding objective mental effort results (Aasman, Mulder, & Mulder, 1987).

The performance on the DT was lower during complex maneuvering than during rate-ones, regardless of the presence of the MT. During complex maneuvers pilots paid slightly less attention to the information presented on the DT display, but paid more attention to the outside world as flying the aircraft always gets the highest priority. Therefore it is not surprising that more targets are missed. The scanning measure that is most influenced by the number of display elements is the mean fixation duration on the DT display, leading to a longer total dwell time. However, the display is less often frequented, with more time between stares when more display elements are present. Furthermore, attention allocation policy can be affected by the NUDES, and has become less efficient, taking into account the performance decrease. Most interesting is that performing the detection task and the MT while flying rate-ones together results in larger dwell times at the central area of the Head-Up-Display (HUD). This can be seen as a simplification of the subject's sampling behavior in situations with a relatively high cognitive load. This decrease is in line with results of Spady and Harris (1983) who found that experienced pilots change scanning behavior in case of an increase in mental load.

Two amounts of visual information had to be processed in the DT (7/28 NUDES). The mental effort parameters did not show any difference for the two different amounts of visual load in this task. May, Kennedy, Williams, Durilap, and Brannan (1990) combined a simple visual task with a task in which subjects had to count a different amount of tones. Their results showed an effect of difficulty of counting on the scanning parameter, which is saccadic extent, used as an indication for mental workload. This suggests a mutual influence of a purely visual and a purely auditory task, both requiring minimal mental effort. In this experiment a slight effect of the amount of cognitive load in an auditory presented memory task (MT) on the duration and the time between stares for the target detection task is found. The fact that both tasks do influence each other can indicate that both tasks use the same cognitive resources that are limited. But considering the results of May, et al., (1990) this effect can also be caused by the fact that the MT load influences the subject's sampling behavior characteristics. This complicates the straight-forwardness of the working hypothesis used for the workload prediction as the level of cognitive load affects a subject's sampling behavior. Hence the assumed clear-cut relation between the predictor (NUDES) and the outcome variable (workload) might not exist.

CONCLUSION

How well do NUDES predict pilot workload? In this study NUDES clearly affect pilot performance measures, though the physiological measures of effort do not seem to be affected. In order to avoid too large performance decrements pilots develop strategies that serve to maximize the overall performance. As said before, research does suggest that a pilot's strategy selection can change workload, with efficient strategies leading to more balanced mental effort and performance. This study indicates that predicting workload by determining visual allocation of attention alone has less practical value than the capability to assess both task strategies (changes) and workload predictors together.

This study was specifically aimed at the effects of the number of display elements on workload disregarding the cognitive processes required after the perception of those display elements. The frequency of occurrence of critical symbols per time period was kept constant, and the number of cockpit displays itself is also not considered in this study. Predicting workload for actual mission segments, which require multiple task performance and hence multiple display visual sampling will result in more realistic predictor values. The information needed for those tasks is perceptually more complex and meaningful, requires higher order mental processing, and the task load varies over time in a natural way.

To determine the relation between the visual allocation of attention and workload in more detail, more workload scores must be set, preferably in realistic task situations. Definitely needed is a way to uncover pilot task strategies used for balancing workload and performance.

REFERENCES

Aasman, J., Mulder, G., Mulder, L.J.M. (1987). Operator effort and the measurement of heart-rate variability. Human Factors, 29(2), 161-170.

Hart, S. (1991). Pilots' workload coping strategies. AIAA/NASA/FAAMFS Conference on Challenges in Aviation Human Factors: The National Plan Tysons Corner, VA.

Jorna, P.G.A.M. (1989). Prediction of success in flight training by single-and dual-task performance. In: AGARD proceedings on "Human behaviour in high stress situations in aerospace operations". CP-458, Brussels.

May, J.G., Kennedy, R.S., Williams, M.C., Durilap, W.P., and Brannan, J.R. (1990). Eye movement indices of mental workload. Acta Psychologica, 75, 75-89.

Moray, N. (1986). Monitoring behaviour and supervisory control. In K.R. Boff, L. Katitman, and LP. Thomas (Eds.), Handbook of Perception and Human Performance. Vol II. Cognitive Processing and Performance (Chapter 40). New York: Wiley.

Spady, A.A., and Harris, R.L. jr and Sr. (1983). Summary of NASA Langley's Pilot Scanning Research. Second Aerospace Behavioral Engineering Technology Conference Proceedings, Society of Automotive Engineers.

Zijlstra, F.R.H. (1993). Efficiency of work behaviour. A design approach for modern tools. PhD thesis, Delft University of Technology, The Netherlands: Delft University Press.

MEASUREMENT OF STRESS AND MENTAL ACTIVITY
AMONG MARITIME CREW MEMBERS

Thomas Koester and Peter K. Sørensen
FORCE Technology

ABSTRACT

The stress level and communication of the deck crew on a ferry reflects the situational changes during the voyage. The – to some extend paradoxical – hypothesis is, that the phases of a voyage immediately before arrival to port are associated with higher levels of stress and mental activity as well as higher rates of actual and relevant communication than the final arrival phase of the voyage. The empirical findings from this paper supports the hypothesis, and the reasonable explanation could be, that the anticipation and preparation of the arrival and the resulting demand for situation awareness on level 3 is the generator of the observed high levels of stress in the phases before arrival. This knowledge could be valuable in the understanding of how the human factor contributes to the safety at sea, in the training of officers and in the design of procedures and equipment for the maritime domain.

Keywords: Stress, mental activity, situation awareness, psycho physiological measurements, maritime domain, behavior, communication.

INTRODUCTION

The work of maritime crewmembers on the bridge of a ship is characterized by variations in mental workload as well as corresponding variations in levels of stress and mental activity. Changes in situation over time require proper situation awareness and corresponding adjustments of communication and behavior. These changes of situation are often slow and predictable on longer voyages with only few arrivals to and departures from ports and with long distances over open sea without any interaction with other vessels. The changes will occur much more frequent and at a higher rate on short voyages in waters with heavy traffic and many arrivals and departures. A typical example is ferry routes ply between two harbors. These routes are often crossing a channel perpendicular to its main traffic routes e.g. The English Channel. Crossing of channels ad further to the rate of situation changes – especially in the case where the change is danger of collision with other vessels. Even though the work on ferries in tight schedules, under time pressure and commercial pressure could seem to be a stressful occupation, it is important to remember, that variations in stress level and mental activity with both high and low levels could be anticipated even on the busiest route. The measurements and analyses of these variations could be valuable in the understanding of how the human factor contributes to the overall safety in the maritime domain and the understanding of how the crew build and maintain situation awareness and adequate behavior and communication patterns. The available methods for measurement of stress and mental activity can basically be categorized in three groups: *Subjective methods* based on self reporting and/or questionnaires, *observational methods* based on the observation of crew communication and behavior and *psycho physiological methods* based on the measurement of physiological parameters such as galvanic skin response (GSR), heart rate (ECG/EKG) or electric activity in the brain (EEG). This paper describes how variations in stress level and level of mental activity could be analyzed and interpreted on the basis of measurements of brain wave activity (EEG). The special focus is the change in situation from being at open sea to the approach of the harbor and finally the arrival in the harbor, and the crew response to these changes of situation: The corresponding changes in level of stress and mental activity and changes in the communication pattern. The hypothesis is, that the phases of the voyage immediately before arrival can generate higher levels of stress, mental activity and communication than in the arrival phase when the vessel is maneuvered in the harbor basin although this final phase has the highest demand for manual control of the vessel. This mechanism can be explained on the basis of the three level model of situation awareness described by Endsley (2000a, 2000b), where the third level – which includes the anticipation of future events – could add further to the mental workload and the stress level of the crew.

METHOD

The electrical activity in the brain (electroencephalogram, EEG) can – according to Pettersen & Hoffmann (2002) – be expounded as a reflection of the mental state or activity of the person. The following frequency bands are used:

Frequency band	Frequency range	Mental state or activity
Delta	0.5-4 Hz	Sleep
Theta	4-8 Hz	Dreams
Alfa	8-13 Hz	Awake and alert
Beta-1	13-20 Hz	Mental activity, cognition, perception, attention
Beta-2	20-36 Hz	Stress, anxiety, fear

Equipment and Materials

EEG is measured by means of electrodes placed directly on the skin on the scull after certain predefined principles and standards e.g. the international 10-20 electrode system (Stern, Ray, & Quigley, 2001 pp. 82-84). The signals from the electrodes are amplified and the results are recorded electronically by means of analogue or digital equipment. The NERVUS system, designed for measurement of EEG (and other psycho physiological reactions such as electrocardiography (ECG/EKG), galvanic skin response (GSR) etc.), was used for data collection in the experiments described in this paper. The components of the equipment are an electrode cap designed for the international 10-20 system of placement of electrodes on the scull, a NERVUS amplifier with 16 channels and a cable connection to a computer with the NERVUS Monitor software for data capture and analysis. The EEG is measured by a sampling rate of 256 times per second, and the EEG spectrum is measured as 15 seconds averages according to the common standards (Stern, Ray, & Quigley, 2001; Fisch, 1999).

Procedure

The empirical studies included *on board measurements of EEG*, *simulator measurements of EEG* and *on board observations and registrations of crew communication*. The set of simulator measurements included two realistic scenarios in a full mission simulator, both arrivals to Rostock in Germany with the large car and passenger ferry M/S Color Festival. The on board measurements included three arrivals on the route between Rødby in Denmark and Puttgarden in Germany. The measurements were made on board the car and passenger ferry M/S Prins Richard. The on board observations and registration of crew communication were made on the car and passenger ferry M/S Prins Joachim on the route between Gedser in Denmark and Rostock in Germany. The routes and vessels in the study were selected due to the expected high rate of variations in stress and mental activity on this particular type of vessel and route and due to the fact that the routes were crossing a channel or operating in an area with heavy traffic further enhancing the above mentioned effect on stress and mental activity. The design of the study is quasi-experimental: Variations in EEG and crew communication are observed as reactions to variations in context, conditions and voyage as they occur in the real setting as well as in the simulator scenario and script.

Participants

The participants in the simulator experiments, as well as in the on board measurements and observations were all experienced captains and deck officers. The two participants in the simulator experiments had experience from the same route including the arrival to Rostock, and the vessel was – although not exactly the same – quite similar in maneuvering characteristics to the actual vessel usually sailed by the participant on the route. The participants in the on board measurements (one person) and observations (several persons) were all voluntary crewmembers with many years of experience from that exact route and vessel.

RESULTS AND DISCUSSION

The results obtained included – as mentioned – *on board measurements of EEG* made on board the ferry M/S Prins Richard, *simulator measurements of EEG* made in a maritime full mission simulator and *on board observations and registrations of crew communication* made on board the ferry M/S Prins Joachim. The measurements made on board the M/S Prins Richard were analyzed, and the average amount of Beta-2 activity in percent of all brain wave activity was calculated for one-minute intervals during the full duration of the voyage (46 minutes). The fine granularity of the analysis makes it possible to identify rapid variations in the Beta-2 level. The measurements made in the full mission simulator were also analyzed. This analysis included both the Beta-1 and the Beta-2 activity, and the average level was calculated for each of the following four phases of different length: *Open water* – from start to first VHF call to Rostock Vessel Traffic Service center, *approach* – from call to Rostock VTS to dredged channel, *channel* – in the dredged channel and *harbor* – inside harbor from passage of breakwater to arrival. The data material in the on board observations is collected as online registration of the crew communication. The communication is categorized according to three different types: Actual, relevant and general. The actual communication is important in the given situation e.g. related to navigation of the vessel, anti-collision work, alarms and management of critical situations. The relevant communication is not important in the given situation, but it is relevant in the overall maintenance of safe and efficient operation of the vessel. The general communication is not important in the given situation, and it is not directly related to the maintenance of safe and efficient operation of the vessel. Typical examples of general communication are private conversation between crewmembers about for example family matters, hobbies, vacation etc. or conversation about observations not directly related to the navigation of the vessel e.g. ongoing construction works on the shore or vessels at an adjacent shipyard in the harbor (Koester 2003a).

On board measurements of EEG

The results from the on board measurements on three voyages show similarities in four different phases of the voyage (see figure 1): *Departure* – first 15-25 minutes, *transit* – following 10-20 minutes, *approach* – 7-9 minutes before arrival and *arrival* – from 5-7 minutes before arrival until time of arrival. Rather high variations in Beta-2 activity for the first 15 to 25 minutes of the 46 minutes long voyage is seen in all three cases. The tasks performed in this period were typically related to the passage of the other ferry on the same route and the establishment of a proper situation awareness and overview of the traffic situation on the route ahead. The first 15-25 minutes of the voyage was in all three voyages followed by an equivalent period of about 10-20 minutes on open water with lower levels of Beta-2 activity.

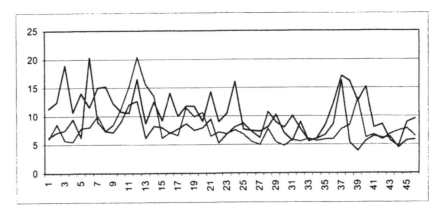

Figure 1: Variations in 1-minute averages of Beta-2 activity in percent of the total brain wave activity on three voyages with M/S Prins Richard. The x-axis is the time after departure in minutes.

After this phase of the voyage and 7-9 minutes before the time of arrival a sudden and significant increase in Beta-2 brain wave activity was found in two out of three voyages (*t*-test, first voyage $p=1.6*10^{-6}$ and second voyage $p=4.2*10^{-4}$). At this moment the vessel was in a position where it was approaching the harbor, but not yet in the harbor basin, and the crew was preparing for arrival. Eventually the level of Beta-2 decreases 5-7 minutes before arrival and remains at a rather low level until the time of arrival in the ferry berth (*t*-test, first voyage $p=2.8*10^{-4}$, second voyage $p=0.026$ and third voyage $p=0.0016$). The tasks performed in this last period includes manual control of the vessel by means of maneuvering handles and controls as well as communication with other crew members about tasks related to the vessels positioning in the ferry berth. Since Beta-2 activity reflects the level of stress, the increase in the approach phase could be interpreted as a short-term stress reaction related to the preparation and anticipation of the arrival. The decrease immediately after and 5-7 minutes before arrival indicates further, that the stress reaction more likely is a result from an increased demand for situation awareness on level 3 rather than a result from intense manual control of the vessel. Otherwise we would have expected a maintained high stress level until the moment of arrival rather than the actual observed decrease.

Simulator measurements of EEG

The results from the simulator experiments are not as significant as the on board measurements, but they exemplifies some interesting mechanisms in the variations of stress and mental activity. The results support in general the finding, that the stress level is higher before arrival – in the approach and channel phase – than when the vessel is maneuvered in the harbor basin. This is in contradiction to the fact, that the harbor phase is characterized by intense manual control of the vessel, and the expectation therefore would be higher levels of stress in that phase. Findings from the measurements of EEG in the first voyage in the simulator shows, that there is – although variations in mental activity are found inside each phase – no significant difference in mental activity (Beta-1 frequency band) between the four phases of the voyage, when they are compared. However, the stress level (Beta-2 frequency band) is significantly higher in the approach phase than in open water (t-test, $p<0.001$) and harbor (t-test, $p<0.05$). The stress level in the approach phase is also higher than in the channel, but this difference is not significant (t-test, $p=0.07$). See figure 2 left.

First simulator voyage   Second simulator voyage

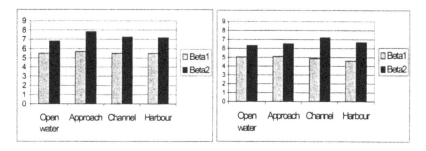

Figure 2: Average level of Beta-1 and Beta-2 activity in the four phases of the two simulated voyages. Levels show the average percentage of Beta-1 and Beta-2 activity of the total electrical activity in the brain.

These results support the findings from the onboard measurements. The increased stress level in the approach phase of the simulator voyages is equivalent to the increased stress level measured on board the M/S Prins Richard in the approach phase, and could therefore again be interpreted as a result from an increased demand for situation awareness on level 3 before entering the harbor (Koester 2003b). The other simulated arrival to Rostock illustrates a significant decrease in level of mental activity (Beta-1) in the harbor phase compared to the open water and approach phases of the voyage (t-test, $p<0.05$) – see figure 2 right. The harbor phase is characterized by this relatively low level of mental activity compared to the open water and approach phases even though the amount of alarms and radio communication is much higher, the task is difficult (maneuvering a large vessel alongside quay in narrow space) and requires intense manual control by means of maneuver handles. Since this is the last part of the voyage the anticipation and preparation of future events is assumed to be of less importance. The low level of mental activity could therefore – with respect to the other findings – be explained by a contextually related decrease in demand for situation awareness on level 3 (Koester 2003b).

On board observations and registrations of crew communication

The on board observations and registrations of crew communication illustrates an increase in actual and relevant communication and a decrease in general communication 20-30 minutes before arrival (see figure 3). The change in actual and relevant communication reflects the preparation and anticipation before the arrival. The decrease in general communication could be explained as an adaptation to a potential critical situation (the arrival) where a maximum of resources for actual and relevant communication is needed. The peak in communication before arrival supports the hypothesis and the findings from the measurements of EEG: The approach is – with respect to level of stress and mental activity as well as level of communication – much more demanding to the crew than the arrival it self (Koester 2003a).

CONCLUSIONS

It is possible to find examples from both the on board measurements, the simulator measurements and the on board observations supporting the hypothesis, that the phases of a voyage immediately before arrival to port are associated with higher levels of stress and mental activity as well as a higher rates of actual and relevant communication than the final arrival phase of the voyage. This hypothesis seems to be paradoxical with respect to the fact, that it is the last phase of the voyage, which has the highest demand for manual control of the vessel, and therefore would be expected to be the most stressful. A reasonable explanation could be, that the it is the anticipation and preparation of the arrival and the resulting demand for situation awareness on level 3 that generates the observed high levels of stress in the phases before arrival. An alternative explanation could be, that the communication could act as independent variable and the stress level could be the corresponding dependent variable, and that the observed increase in level of stress before the arrival simply could be a result from the change in communication pattern. It is, however, possible from on board measurements to argue against this alternative explanation. The increase in stress in the onboard measurements before arrival was observed even though the participating crewmember was alone on the bridge and no communication was observed at all.

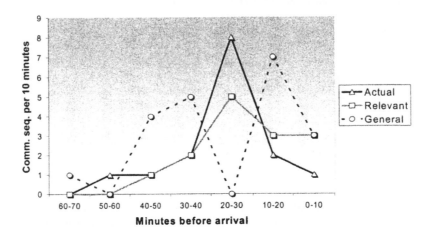

Figure 3: The variations in actual, relevant and general communication on a voyage with M/S Prins Joachim.

REFERENCES

Endsley, M.R. (2000a). Theoretical Underpinnings of Situation Awareness: A Critical Review. In M.R. Endsley & D.J. Garland (Ed.), Situation Awareness Analysis and Measurement (pp. 3-32). Mahwah, New Jersey: Lawrence Erlbaum Associates.

Endsley, M.R. (2000b). Direct Measurement of Situation Awareness: Validity and Use of SAGAT. In M.R. Endsley & D.J. Garland (Ed.), Situation Awareness Analysis and Measurement (pp. 147-173). Mahwah, New Jersey: Lawrence Erlbaum Associates.

Fisch, B.J. (1999). Fisch & Spehlmann's EEG Primer (3. rev. ed.). Amsterdam: Elsevier.

Pettersen, A.-H. & Hoffmann, E. (2002). Hjernebølgetræning af DAMP-børn. Psykolog Nyt 23. august 2002, pp. 3-9.

Stern, R.M., Ray, W.J. & Quigley, K.S. (2001). Psychophysiological Recording (2.ed.). Oxford: Oxford University Press.

Koester, T. (2003a). Situation Awareness and Situation Dependent Behaviour Adjustment in the Maritime Work Domain. Proceedings of the 10th International Conference on Human - Computer Interaction, Crete, Greece, June 22-27, 2003.

Koester, T. (2003b). Mental workload, psycho physiological stress reactions and situation awareness in the maritime full mission simulator. Paper presented at the Human Factors of Decision Making in Complex Systems conference, Dunblane, Great Britain, September 8-12, 2003.

THE PEACEKEEPER:
HOW THE ROLE OF THE MODERN SOLDIER HAS CHANGED
AND HOW THAT AFFECTS WORKLOAD

Mark E. Koltko-Rivera
Professional Services Group

P. A. Hancock
University of Central Florida and Institute for Simulation and Training

Joseph Dalton, H. C. Neil Ganey, Lauren M. Murphy
University of Central Florida

ABSTRACT

Our objective is to make human factors scientists aware of the need for research regarding military peacekeeping. Little research has focused on the soldier as peacekeeper, even though a growing percentage of U.S. soldiers' time is being spent in peacekeeping operations. The combat soldier faces a binary friend/foe discrimination task, and a mission involving the destruction of the enemy and the enemy's warfighting capacity, with relatively less restrictive rules of engagement. The peacekeeper soldier faces a fuzzy friend/foe/non-foe discrimination task, and a mission involving negotiation among disputing factions and preservation of life, with relatively more restrictive rules of engagement. Today's American military forces often must shift between both these roles, resulting in stress that impacts performance in either role. These two roles probably make different workload demands on their operators, suggesting a need for focused research on combat versus peacekeeper workload; some current research programs into these issues are outlined.

Keywords: peacekeeping, military training, workload

INTRODUCTION

> "We were taught how to sneak around these tanks quietly, surprise the enemy, and destroy him in combat. But here we are supposed to stay out of combat by being obvious. To me, it is like teaching a dog to walk backwards." (quote from O'Connor, 1996, p. A-3)

Around the world, various world organizations are banding together in efforts to promote and sustain peace. Over the last 53 years, the United Nations has entered into over 50 peacekeeping operations alone (United Nations Department of Public Information, 2001a). As the United States assumes an increasingly more prominent role in non-combat policing actions around the world, the tasks involved in that policing are falling to our military personnel. Since the end of the Cold War, U.S. presence in what are called Military Operations Other Than War (MOOTW) has increased. These operations are conducted under politically sensitive and complex circumstances. Whether we like it or not, we have become police officer to the world. We are now being called upon to help maintain order. "Peace operations are here to stay and the U.S. Army will be called upon to all corners of the globe to bring stability to chaos, order to anarchy, and peace to conflict" (United States Army Peacekeeping Institute [hereafter USAPI], 1996).

Soldiers are not just required to be warriors anymore. They must now be peacekeepers as well. This comes with a cost. Over 1,200 people have been killed while serving in peacekeeping missions for the United Nations (United Nations Department of Public Information, 2001b). The potential for violent death while peacekeeping means that peacekeeping missions expose soldiers to perhaps at least as much stress as warfighting—if not more so.

Peacekeeping missions are by no means new (Breed, 1998; Moskos, 1976; Segal, 1995). The U.S., however, has not participated in very many peacekeeping missions, due to its involvement in the Cold War (Franke, 2003). We are the new kid on the block of the peacekeeping arena.

What is getting trained?

The problem with this state of affairs is that the training that American soldiers receive is not conducive to peacekeeping actions. American soldiers are excellent warriors, known for their ability to complete their objectives in an efficient and effective manner. However, this does not translate into peacekeeping ability. As Possumato (1999) noted, "Army doctrine and training is focused on how to fight and win wars, not on how to keep peace" (pp. 1-2). A cursory analysis of the numbers of casualties that American troops have sustained since engaging in the first action in Iraq will show that, even though many deaths were incurred during the combat, the number killed while the soldiers have been acting as law enforcement or peacekeeping officers is much greater, almost two times more in hostile situations, almost three times more overall (Directorate for Information Operations and Reports, 2004). It may seem to the casual observer that there is a distinct disconnect here, inasmuch as American soldiers are incurring lethal casualties under supposedly peaceful conditions, when conditions "should be" safer. Part of the reason for this may be that peacekeeping is not seen by the U.S. Army as a separate mission, necessitating the inclusion of specialized preparation into current and future training programs (Possumato, 1999). Rather, peacekeeping is seen as a mission to be prepared for, "utilizing just enough and just in time procedures, as stated in FM 100-23" (Possumato, 1999, p. iii).

Given the large number of casualties currently being sustained by American troops in Iraq, this would seem to be a perilous procedure. Nonetheless, the American armed forces seems determined to continue in this path. Although consultants have cautioned the Army to not classify peacekeeping as "just extensions of what the Army does" (Possumato, 1999, p.10), and "in spite of the National Security Strategy's assertion that peacekeeping operations will be the most frequent challenge for the U.S. forces for the foreseeable future, BHAAR I (Boznia Herzegovina After Action Review) asserts that the Army still believes an ad hoc approach to training units for such missions is adequate to the task" (Possumato, 1999, p. 4).

An additional risk is that peacekeepers may lose the warfighting skills for which they had originally trained. As Sgt. Felipe Paul put it, "I'm a tanker [tank operator], that's what I do, been one for 14 years. But let me tell you, those skills are perishable. You got to use them, and all I'm doing here is checking people's driver's licenses" (quoted in O'Connor, 1996, p. A-3). As a tank commander said of his men, "my guys are great at driving three Bradleys (tanks) down a road in a straight line and setting up an unconcealed observation post, but when it comes to attacking a position, or holding a piece of terrain against an assault, that's where we'll need work" (Boccardi, quoted in O'Connor, 1996, p. A-3). These comments rings true with many Army officers, who acknowledge that peacekeeping troops will require re-training in their warfighting skills prior to their being sent to their next mission: "In a crisis we would still need about two months of retraining to get everyone coming back now ready" (Col. Goff, quoted in O'Connor, 1996, p. A-3).

The task of peacekeeping

Mission types engaged in by military units fall into several general categories. These categories are combat, peace support (which includes peacekeeping), and humanitarian efforts. With the increase in complexity that we have witnessed in contemporary operations, some missions contain aspects of more than one of those categories (Britt & Adler, 2003). Even within the category of peace support, there exist different functions. Peacekeeping missions, as the public understands them, support the building of peace in a region through non-violent aid. Peace enforcement, however, gives authorization for the use of force to encourage parties to sustain peace.

An example of a mission that had dynamic shifts in mission type was the Army operation in Mogadishu. The Army's presence in Somalia was to prevent the local warlords from intercepting aid that was being provided for the population of Mogadishu. This mission was drastically changed when the local militia attacked U.S. forces, using many different methods that the American soldiers were unaccustomed to, including surrounding themselves with women and children to serve as shields for them. The American forces were caught off guard by these tactics and were unprepared to meet them. "For the forces on the ground (in the Somalian conflict), transitioning between operational assignments meant continuous change in the mission and its objectives" (Franke, 2003, p. 33). As peacekeepers, soldiers must understand that, although they may be required to avoid the use of force as much as possible, they should be prepared to use all necessary force, should the tables turn for the worse. However, they also must understand how to use good judgment in the use of that force, given that they are there primarily to keep the peace. "Every [peacekeeping] soldier must be aware that the goal is to produce conditions that are conducive to peace and not to the destruction of an enemy" (Possumato, 1999, p. 5). Thus, peacekeepers are required to conduct a balancing act.

"The challenge of these missions lies not only in the fluid nature of the operational environment but also in the contrast between the goals of peacekeeping and the expectations and training of combat-ready military forces" (Britt & Adler, 2003, p.6). Britt and Adler (2003) have presented a framework of hypothesized factors affecting the performance of the peacekeeper, breaking the stressors experienced by the peacekeeper into three basic categories of stress: factors of the specific mission, factors relevant to the peacekeeper's unit, and factors relevant to each peacekeeper. Factors relevant to the mission include the rules of engagement, presence (or absence) of a peace treaty, and presence (or absence) of public support of the peace. Unit cohesion and morale and pre-deployment training would fall under factors relevant to the unit. These factors match up very closely to the concepts of environmental, internal, and task-based workload (Hockey & Hamilton, 1983), as they include aspects of the mission (task), their unit (environment), and themselves (internal).

The case for specialized peacekeepers

Some countries have recognized that what makes a good combat soldier is not necessarily what makes a good peacekeeper. These governments have therefore created separate forces for these roles (Wisher, 2003). Others, like the United States, select forces and give them pre-deployment training which, as stated earlier, may or may not conflict with the training that they have previously received from the military.

The missions engaged in by peacekeepers primarily differ from combat missions in the fact that there is no obvious enemy to focus on (Franke, 2003). Additionally, in many cases, peacekeepers lack the clear mission objectives and 'field of battle' that is customary to war. Warriors, operating under less restrictive rules of engagement, are able to prevail against clearly defined hostile forces, through the application of violence. Peacekeepers, however, must utilize diplomacy and avoid violence in the course of seeking peaceful resolutions to situations. Thus, we are presented with a case where soldiers are being tasked with jobs wherein they must assume different, even conflicting, roles (Diehl, 1988; Kutter, 1986).

In performing research on the peacekeeper, we would attempt to aid soldiers selected for MOOTW to maximize performance under dynamic conditions. We would seek ways to mitigate the stress, workload, and fatigue that is experienced by peacekeepers as they carry out their operation. It has been said that soldiers (as well as others who perform in extreme environments) experience hours of boredom interrupted by moments of terror. This is the case, not only for warriors, but for peacekeepers as well. A dynamic change in the state of a scenario (i.e., from peacekeeping to warfighting) may cause many operators to falter, as they struggle to adjust their schema of the situation to match with their current perceptions. As Castro (2003) suggests, we need to establish what the ideal states for optimal performance in peacekeeping missions are, in order to use them as criteria for treatment outcomes.

The tasks of the peacekeeper and the warrior may differ in terms of their somatic, cognitive, and affective features and are worthy of extensive research. The issue here, at an abstract level, involves differences in workload, which is the focus of the Workload Theory and Measurement research program within the Multiple University Research Initiative for Operator Performance Under Stress (MURI-OPUS) laboratory at the University of Central Florida (UCF; Koltko-Rivera et al., 2004). In addition to describing the difference between peacekeeper and warrior workload, we will seek methods to mitigate the stress and workload associated with the dynamic characteristics of the task that peacekeepers experience.

Other activities within the UCF MURI-OPUS laboratory are relevant to this task, as well. Galantino (2003) has described how the peacekeeper is made to change from a binary friend/foe mentality to a fuzzy friend/foe/non-foe classification model. This is directly related to the work that Peter Hancock and his colleagues at the UCF MURI-OPUS laboratory are doing, in developing fuzzy signal detection theory (Hancock, Masalonis, & Parasuraman, 2000; Parasuraman, Masalonis, & Hancock, 2000). By analyzing the choices these warriors *cum* peacekeepers are making, as well as measures of the workload that the soldiers are experiencing, we can determine the extent to which soldiers on peacekeeping missions are subjected to different workloads than their warfighting counterparts. This may provide compelling evidence for the peacekeeper position to be reassessed as a trained position within the U.S. armed forces.

In this paper, we have tried to bring to light a problem that American soldiers are facing in their roles as peacekeepers. We invite all human factors scientists to join with us in investigating the nature of the challenges they face, and in making recommendations to mitigate these stresses. Such research can help peacekeeping forces of all nations, and help to build a safer world.

ACKNOWLEDGEMENT

The views expressed in this work are those of the authors and do not necessarily reflect official Army policy. This work was supported by the Department of Defense Multidisciplinary University Research Initiative (MURI) program administered by the Army Research Office under grant DAAD19-01-1-0621.

REFERENCES

Breed, H. (1998). Treating the new world disorder. In H. J. Langholtz (Ed.), The psychology of peacekeeping. (pp. 111-128). Westport, CT: Praeger.

Britt, T.W., & Adler, A.B. (2003). The psychology of the peacekeeper: An introductory framework. In T.W. Britt and A.B. Adler (Eds.), The psychology of the peacekeeper (pp. 3-10). Westport, CT: Praeger.

Castro, C.A. (2003). Considerations when conducting psychological research during peacekeeping missions: The scientist and the commander. In T.W. Britt and A.B. Adler (Eds.), The psychology of the peacekeeper (pp. 11-28). Westport, CT: Praeger.

Diehl, P.F. (1993). International peacekeeping. Baltimore and London: Johns Hopkins University Press.

Directorate for Information Operations and Reports (2004) Operation Iraqi Freedom – Military Deaths. Retrieved February 1, 2004, from http://web1.whs.osd.mil/mmid/casualty/castop.htm

Franke, V.C. (2003). The social identity of peacekeeping. In T.W. Britt and A.B. Adler (Eds.), The psychology of the peacekeeper (pp. 31-52). Westport, CT: Praeger.

Galantino, M.G. (2003). Work motivation and the peacekeeper. In T.W. Britt and A.B. Adler (Eds.), The psychology of the peacekeeper (pp. 111-126). Westport, CT: Praeger.

Hancock, P.A., Masalonis, A.J., & Parasuraman, R. (2000). On the theory of fuzzy signal detection: Theoretical and practical considerations. Theoretical Issues in Ergonomic Science, 1, 207-230.

Hockey, G.R.J., & Hamilton, P. (1983) The cognitive patterning of stress states. In G.R.J. Hockey (Ed.) Stress and fatigue in human performance, pp. 331-362. New York: John Wiley and Sons.

Koltko-Rivera, M.E., Ganey, H.C.N., Dalton, J., & Hancock, P.A. (2004). Workload: A comprehensive model. Manuscript in preparation, University of Central Florida.

Kutter, W.D. (1986). Operational guidelines for U.S. peacekeeping commanders. Carlyle Barracks, PA: U.S. Army War College.

Moskos, C. (1976). Peace soldiers: The sociology of a United Nations military force. Chicago: University of Chicago Press.

O'Connor, M. (1996, December 13). Does keeping the peace spoil G.I.'s for war? New York Times, p. A-3.

Parasuraman, R., Masalonis, A.J., & Hancock, P.A. (2000). Fuzzy signal detection theory: Basic postulates and formulas for analyzing human and machine performance. Human Factors, 42, 636-659.

Possumato, D.P. (1999) Should the U.S. Army establish a peacekeeping training center? Carlyle Barracks, PA: U.S. Army War College.

Segal, D.R. (1995). Five phases of United Nations peacekeeping: An evolutionary typology. Journal of Political and Military Sociology, 23, 65-79.

United Nations Department of Public Information. (2001a). United Nations peace operations in 2001. Retrieved January 22, 2004, from http://www.un.org/Depts/dpko/dpko/pub/year_review01/index.html

United Nations Department of Public Information. (2001b). United Nations peacekeeping: In the service of peace. Retrieved January 22, 2004, from http://www.un.org/Depts/dpko/dpko/home_bottom.htm

United States Army Peacekeeping Institute (1996). Bosnia Herzgovina After Action Review I. Retrieved February 3, 2004, from http://www.fas.org/man/dod-101/ops/docs/bosrep2a.htm

Wisher, R.A. (2003. Task identification and skill deterioration in peacekeeping operations. In T.W. Britt and A.B. Adler (Eds.), The psychology of the peacekeeper (pp. 91-110). Westport, CT: Praeger.

Moderating Effects of Team Role on Workload Demands of Teams

Janie A. DeJoode and Olena Connor
New Mexico State University

Nancy J. Cooke
Arizona State University East

ABSTRACT

The purpose of this paper is two-fold. First, we present a way to measure workload demands on teams and second, we address how the effect of workload on teams differs from the effect on individuals within the team. Our research was conducted in the context of a simulated Uninhabited Air Vehicle (UAV) ground control station where 3-person teams were required to fly a simulated UAV for the purpose of taking reconnaissance photos. In two experiments, we have shown that workload demands differentially affect individual team member roles in our UAV team task. Consequently, measuring the effects of workload on teams by aggregating the effects of workload on individual roles may not be appropriate, particularly when teams are heterogeneous.

Keywords: Team workload, dual-task, subjective workload

INTRODUCTION

Team interactions in socio-technical environments are inherently complex with many factors such as task, coordination, and technology demands contributing to the workload that a team experiences. Consequences of team workload, such as ineffective teamwork or poor team situation awareness, in socio-technical environments can be catastrophic. Therefore, understanding team workload and how it differs from individual workload is essential to evading errors due to workload demands.

The effects of high workload on individuals have been well established in a wealth of research (Wickens, 2001; Bowers, Braun, & Morgan, 1997). This research has shown that task performance is hindered when there is an inadequate supply of resources available to the individual. Factors such as increased task difficulty and low operator skill consume more resources, thereby reducing an individual's ability to perform a task adequately. In order to adapt to high workload, individuals often temporarily terminate or indefinitely abandon certain tasks (Wickens & Hollands, 2000).

Three classes of measures have typically been used to examine the effects of workload at the individual level (Wickens & Holland, 2000). First, measures of performance serve as indices of workload under the dual-task paradigm. Under this paradigm, performance on the primary components of the task is distinguished from performance on the secondary, or concurrent, tasks. Second, workload can be measured by means of physiological indices such as an individual's heart rate variability or pupil diameter. Finally, subjective measures, such as the NASA Task Load Index (TLX) and the subjective workload assessment technique (SWAT) are used to assess an individual's experience of workload.

The effect of workload on teams has been explored to a lesser degree. Team workload has been described as the balance between the environmental demands imposed by the task and the team's resources (Bowers et al., 1997). When the demands exceed the team's resources, team coordination and performance decay. This added demand of teamwork, due to information sharing and coordination requirements, imposed on teams that is not required of individuals performing individual tasks, is the principal distinction between individual and team workload (Urban, Bowers, Monday, & Morgan, 1995).

Techniques for measuring the effects of workload on teams are scarce. In most cases, measures used to assess the effects of workload on individuals are adapted to be used at the team level. For example, the NASA TLX has been administered at the team level, requiring teams to rate their perception of the team's overall workload. Another technique that has been used to measure the effect of workload on teams is to simply aggregate the effects of workload on the individual team members (Bowers et al.).

Bowers et al. (1997) identify some of these gaps in the literature, by posing several research questions regarding workload in teams. Our research addresses two of these questions, namely 1) How are workload demands measured in teams and 2) How do the effects of workload on teams differ from those on individuals?

METHOD

This research was conducted in the context of two larger experiments that manipulated team dispersion and workload in order to examine the impact of these factors on team performance, process and cognition. The two experiments were basically replications with some minor differences in subject population and procedure described in what follows.

CERTT UAV Task

Our research was conducted in the Cognitive Engineering Research on Team Tasks (CERTT) Laboratory, where teams performed in a simulated Uninhabited Air Vehicle (UAV) ground control station. Our UAV team task is structured such that each team member receives unique, yet overlapping training and has a distinct role. Moreover, the three roles are interdependent in that coordination and information sharing among the team members is necessary in order to complete the reconnaissance mission successfully. The three roles include the Air Vehicle Operator (AVO), the Payload Operator (PLO), and the Data Exploitation, Mission Planning, and Communications (DEMPC) Operator. The AVO flies the UAV remotely, controlling heading, airspeed, altitude, and other UAV systems. The PLO adjusts camera settings, takes photographs, and monitors the sensors. The DEMPC is the mission navigator and is responsible for overseeing the mission. The team goal of each mission is to successfully photograph as many targets as possible in the shortest amount of time while following mission rules and avoiding system alarms and warnings.

Participants

Experiment 1 involved 13 mixed-gender and 7 same-gender teams. The subject population in Experiment 2 was more homogenous, consisting of 20 all-male teams. All participants were students at New Mexico State University who voluntarily participated for monetary compensation ($6.00 per hour).

Procedure

Ten of the 20 teams in each experiment were either in a co-located environment, where they could see each other and each other's displays or they were geographically distributed. In both experiments, each team completed four low workload missions in which the goal was to photograph nine targets, after which, workload was increased, requiring twenty targets to be photographed in the same time. Other mission parameters were also manipulated to increase the difficulty of the high workload mission (e.g., rate of fuel use, number of *ad hoc* targets called in by intelligence, etc.). Teams in Experiment 1 completed three high workload missions while Experiment 2 included only one high workload mission. The experimental design was a 2(dispersion, a between-subjects factor; co-located vs. distributed) x 2(workload, a repeated factor; low vs. high) mixed design.

Measures

In both experiments, the effects of increased workload were measured objectively utilizing a dual-task paradigm, in which performance was partitioned into primary and secondary task components. Primary and secondary task performance scores were calculated by subtracting points for penalties on particular components of the mission. For example, at the team level, primary task performance penalties can be incurred if the team fails to photograph necessary targets or if critical waypoints are not visited. Each component was weighted according to its importance to the mission goals. Furthermore, primary task performance and secondary task performance were standardized. The data presented here represent performance penalties in which high, positive numbers reflect a higher penalty (i.e., poorer performance) and low or negative numbers reflect low penalty (i.e., better performance). Primary task performance penalty components are different for the Team, AVO, PLO, and DEMPC. That is, the components on which each individual and the team can receive penalties are unique to each individual role and the team as a whole. However, secondary task performance penalty components include 1) time spent in warning state and 2) time spent in alarm state for all individuals as well as the team.

Subjective workload was measured using a modified version of the NASA Task Load Index (TLX). Participants rated workload on five subscales (mental demand, physical demand, temporal demand, performance demand, and team demand). The ratings on each subscale were weighted according to the extent to which each type of demand contributes to the workload in our task. These weights differ among the roles, as each type of demand does not necessarily contribute to each role's workload in the same manner. The sum of the weighted workload subscales yields an overall workload score for each role at each mission and ranges from 0 to 100. Large numbers on the subjective ratings scale reflect higher levels of perceived workload and small numbers are indicative of lower levels of perceived workload. We estimate the team's perception of workload with an average of individual scores.

RESULTS

In the interest of space and coherence, the results will be grouped by measure, rather than experiment. Also, we will report, but not discuss, the effects of dispersion as they are beyond the scope of this paper. Furthermore, due to the use of small sample (N = 20) in both experiments, extensive across-team variation, and an objective of identifying any potentially interesting effects at the expense of possible Type I errors, we considered -levels of ≤ .10 statistically detectable.

Effects of Workload on Dual-Task Performance

In both experiments, the analysis of dual task performance was performed at the team level as well as at each individual role level. These analyses examine the effects of workload and dispersion on dual task performance (made up of two components: primary and secondary task performance) using a doubly multivariate analysis of variance (MANOVA). Mission 4 and Mission 5 performance data were used as an estimate for low workload and high workload performance, respectively.

Experiment 1

At the team level, an interaction was found among task (primary/secondary) and dispersion, $F(1, 18) = 6.06, p = .02$, as well as between task and workload, $F(1, 18) = 12.25, p < .01$. The analysis of AVO performance revealed one significant interaction among task and dispersion, $F(1, 18) = 3.38, p = .08$. Finally, at the DEMPC level, there was a significant effect of workload, $F(1, 18) = 3.13, p = .09$, where dual task performance suffered in the high workload mission. In addition, an interaction among task and dispersion, $F(1, 18) = 4.40, p = .05$, as well as an interaction among task and workload, $F(1, 18) = 34.91, p < .01$, emerged. The remaining factors and interactions failed to reach significance.

Our remaining analyses focused on pin-pointing the source of the task by workload interactions found for the team and DEMPC levels. These interactions indicate that the workload manipulation differentially affected primary and secondary task performance for teams and DEMPCs. At the team level, *post-hoc* tests indicated that primary task performance suffered during high workload, $F(1,18) = 28.14, p < .01$, but secondary task performance remained relatively stable, $F(1,18) = 1.2, p = .28$, (see Figure 1). Similarly, DEMPCs accrued significantly more primary task performance penalties in high workload than in low workload, $F(1, 18) = 28.94, p < .01$, while their secondary task performance penalties for the most part remained constant across the levels of workload, $F(1,18) = .07, p = .79$.

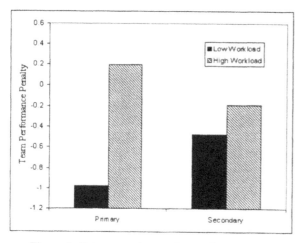

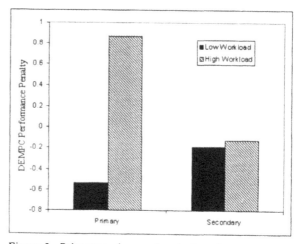

Figure 1. Primary and secondary task performance penalties for teams during low and high workload.

Figure 2. Primary and secondary task performance penalties for DEMPCs during low and high workload.

Experiment 2

Similar results were found Experiment 2. At the team level, a main effect of workload was found, $F(1, 18) = 27.95$, $p < .01$, as well as a significant interaction between task and workload, $F(1, 18) = 10.22, p < .01$. These two effects were also found at the PLO and DEMPC levels. For PLOs, analyses revealed a significant main effect of workload, $F(1, 18) = 21.82, p < .01$, and a moderately significant task by workload interaction, $F (1, 18) = 3.15, p = 09$. For DEMPCs, there was a main effect of workload was found, $F(1, 18) = 53.38, p < .01$, as well as an interaction between task and workload, $F(1, 18) = 26.57, p < .01$. In each case of a significant main effect of workload, performance penalties significantly increased during the high workload mission. No other effects were significant .

In examining the moderating effects of task (primary/secondary) on the relationship between our workload manipulation and performance, we discovered that for teams and DEMPCs, primary task performance penalties significantly increased during high workload $F (1, 18) = 18.84, p <. 01$ and $F(1,18) = 3.67, p = .06$, respectively, whereas secondary task performance penalties did not significantly change for teams or DEMPCs across the levels of workload, $F (1, 18) = .61, p = .44$ and $F(1,18) = .18, p = .67$, respectively. This finding is consistent with what was found in Experiment 1. However, as stated above, this experiment also produced and interaction between task and workload for PLOs. *Post hoc* tests showed that PLOs' incurred significantly more secondary task performance penalties during high workload, $F (1, 18) = 6.24, p = .02$, whereas the amount of primary task performance penalties acquired did not significantly change from low to high workload, $F (1, 18) = .91, p = .35$.

Effects of Workload on Perceived Workload

We examined subjective workload at the team level as well as at the individual role level. For the team level analysis, we used a repeated measures analysis of variance (ANOVA) to examine the effects of workload and dispersion on team subjective workload (an average of the individual ratings). For the individual level analysis, we also used a repeated measures ANOVA to examine the effects of workload, dispersion, and role (a between-subjects factor; AVO, PLO, DEMPC) on individual subjective workload. In the interest of capturing differences in perceived workload due to the workload manipulation, which occurred after teams reached asymptotic levels of performance (Mission 4), ratings taken after the final low workload mission (Mission 4) were used as an estimate for low workload and ratings taken after the first high workload mission (Mission 5) were used as an estimate for high workload.

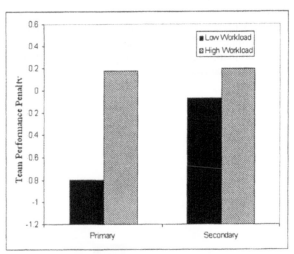

Figure 3. Primary and secondary task performance penalties for teams during low and high workload.

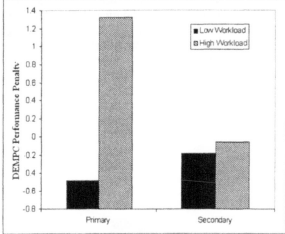

Figure 4. Primary and secondary task performance penalties for DEMPCs during low and high workload.

Experiment 1

At the team level, a significant effect of workload emerged such that there was a significant increase in the perception of workload in high workload, F (1, 18) = 17.13, $p < .01$. Neither the main effect of dispersion nor the interaction between dispersion and workload was significant. At the individual role level, a significant main effect of workload was found, where subjective ratings taken after the high workload mission were significantly higher. In addition, an interaction between workload and role emerged, suggesting that the workload manipulation differentially affected perceived workload for different team roles. No other factors or interactions reached significance. As post-hoc tests revealed, only PLOs and DEMPCs perceived significant increases in workload during Mission 5, F (1,19) = 4.22, $p = .05$ and $F(1,19) = 8.31, p = .01$, respectively (see Figure 5).

Experiment 2

As found in Experiment 1, teams perceived the increase in workload, F (1, 18) = 12.86, $p < .01$. Neither the main effect of dispersion nor the interaction between dispersion and workload was significant. At the individual role level, a significant main effect of workload was found, F (1, 54) = 16.27, $p < .01$, where subjective ratings taken after the high workload mission were significantly higher. In addition, a main effect of team member role was found, F (2, 54) = 2.61, $p = .08$, where DEMPCs' and AVOs' perceptions of workload were significantly higher than PLOs', $t(39) = -3.1, p<.01$ and $t(39) = 2.71, p = .01$, respectively. Finally, there was a significant interaction between role and dispersion, $F(2, 54) = 2.94, p = .06$.

DISCUSSION

This research has addressed two questions: 1) how can workload be measured in teams and 2) how do the effects of workload demands on teams differ from those on individuals? First, we used the dual-task paradigm to measure the effects of workload on team performance, as defined by a unique score specific to those tasks performed by the team as a whole, rather than by an aggregate of individual scores. Second, our analyses of workload effects on dual-task performance and subjective workload have shown that the relationship between individual and team workload in our UAV task depends on the role each team member is playing. Our initial analyses at the team level revealed that our workload manipulation 1) hindered teams' primary task performance and 2) was perceived by teams. However, analyses at the individual role level suggested that not all roles experienced and performed the mission in the same way. In our analyses of the effects of workload on dual-task performance, the detrimental effect of workload on primary task performance that was found at the team level only emerged for DEMPCs. Furthermore, as our analyses of subjective workload showed, not all team members experience workload to the same degree.

The fact that different team roles are affected differently by workload suggests that a simple aggregation of individual data in a heterogeneous team may not be a true reflection of the effects of workload on the team as a whole. Through utilization of appropriate measures and techniques, we can accurately identify how the effects of workload demands on teams differ from the effects on individuals. It is not until after we develop this accurate understanding of team workload that we can begin to take steps toward mitigating the negative effects of workload demands, through, for example, improvements in training programs and system design.

REFERENCES

Bowers, C. A. , Braun, C. C., & Morgan, Jr., B. B. (1997). Team workload: Its meaning and measurement. In M. T. Brannick, E. Salas, and C. Prince (Eds.), Team Performance Assessment and Measurement: Theory, Research, and Applications (pp. 85-105). Mahwah, New Jersey: Lawrence Erlbaum Associates, Inc.

Urban, J. M., Bowers, C.A., Monday, S. D., Morgan Jr., B. B. (1995). Workload, team structure, and communication in team performance. Military Psychology, 7(2), 123-139.

Wickens, C. D. (2001). Workload and Situation Awareness. In P. A. Hancock and P. A. Desmond (Eds.), Stress, Workload, and Fatigue (pp. 443-449). Mahwah, New Jersey: Lawrence Erlbaum Associates, Inc.

Wickens, C. D. and Hollands, J. G. (2000). Engineering Psychology and Human Performance, Third Edition. Upper Saddle River, New Jersey: Prentice-Hall, Inc.

USING A CHAT INTERFACE AS AN EMBEDDED SECONDARY TASKING TOOL

M.L. Cummings
Massachusetts Institute of Technology

Stephanie Guerlain
University of Virginia

ABSTRACT

Measurement of workload is a critical element of any research involving operator tasking in complex systems. One common method of measuring workload is through secondary tasking, which requires a subject to use spare mental capacity to attend to secondary tasking. Traditional secondary tasking testing can be intrusive and introduce an unrealistic artifact. However, embedded secondary tasks do not fundamentally change the task or task performance. This paper will discuss the use of a chat interface, resembling that of popular instant messaging programs, as an embedded secondary tasking measurement tool in the testing of supervisory control performance for monitoring and control of Tactical Tomahawk missiles. The use of the embedded chat tool to induce information-seeking secondary tasks yielded critical results needed for determination of operator workload. However one drawback discovered is that some subjects treated incoming instant messages as the primary task instead of the secondary, which degraded overall tasking performance.

KEYWORDS: workload, secondary tasking, embedded, chat, instant messaging

INTRODUCTION

Secondary tasking is a commonly used workload measurement tool which requires a subject, assigned a primary task, to use any spare mental capacity to attend to a secondary task. Measuring workload through primary tasking and other aggregate measures like operator utilization are important, but the use of secondary task measurements provides a more comprehensive workload analysis (Wickens & Hollands, 2000). Traditional secondary tasking such as tapping and time estimation tasks can be intrusive and introduce an unrealistic artifact during testing (Williges & Wierwille, 1979). However, embedded secondary tasks do not fundamentally change the task or task performance and provide more sensitive measurements because of their unobtrusiveness in a natural, ecologic setting (Shingledecker, 1987; Tsang & Wilson, 1997; Wickens & Hollands, 2000). When using any secondary tasking technique to measure workload, the secondary task should be a lower priority than the primary task, but for embedded secondary tasking, the lower priority task appears to be a part of the natural work domain. Some examples of embedded secondary tasks include monitoring subsystems for auditory alerts (Committee on Human Factors, 1997), and also radio communications for pilots (Shingledecker, 1987).

To measure workload through secondary tasking for a recently developed prototype for in-flight control of U.S. Navy's Tactical Tomahawk missiles (Figure 1), an embedded secondary tasking tool was created in the form of a communication window, otherwise known as a chat box. The dual display prototype, known as TTIMR (Tactical Tomahawk Interface for Monitoring and Retargeting), allows controllers the ability to monitor in-flight missiles using the map on the right, and also provides the ability to rapidly retarget missiles through the decision matrix display on the left. Possible reasons for retargeting a missile in-flight would include cases in which a target has moved or a more critical target 'emerges', such as when the radar of a surface-to-air missile site is activated. The chat box, which resembles popular instant messaging programs, is located on the left display and is expanded in Figure 2.

The chat box represents current technology in place on naval vessels, and is a natural embedded secondary task measurement tool since responding to communications is in theory secondary to the primary task of retargeting an in-flight missile. One important experimental design consideration for human subject testing is external validity, which is a measure of how well experimental results will generalize to an operational setting.

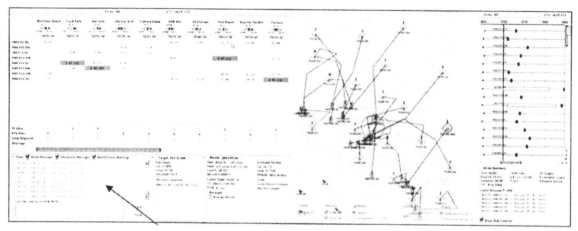

The Chat Box

Figure 1: The Tactical Tomahawk Interface for Monitoring and Retargeting

One way to strengthen external validity is to represent the operational environment as accurately as possible in an experimental setting (Adelman, 1991). The chat box feature is a familiar tool for naval personnel so its presence in the prototype helps to make an unfamiliar tool seem more realistic.

The chat box allows missile controllers to receive messages that contain basic information about missile status as well as instructions for action or queries for information from superiors. In human-in-the-loop experiments conducted with TTIMR, questions appeared to come from a higher authority and queried the subjects acting as controllers about past, present, and future elements of missile and target status. This type of secondary tasking which requires spatial reasoning is called a problem-solving secondary task (Gawron, 2000).

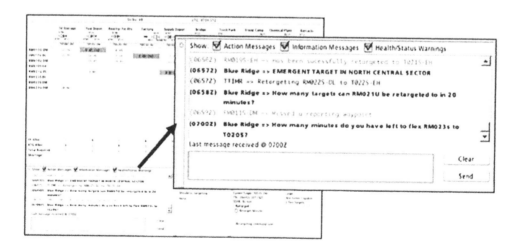

Figure 2: The TTIMR Chat Box

METHOD

When establishing requirements for manning for the operational Tactical Tomahawk system, the Navy's initial guess was that one operator could control at most four missiles (U.S. Navy, 2002). This number was not empirically determined and was only an initial guess. To further explore the validity of this requirement, an experiment was conducted that tested Navy subjects on their ability to successfully retarget in-flight missiles. Forty-two Navy personnel, both active duty and retired, participated as subjects. All subjects were volunteers with current or past Tomahawk experience recruited through contact with various naval organizations. In keeping with government regulations, subjects were not monetarily compensated.

Apparatus, Procedure, and Experimental Design

All subjects experienced two test sessions, which consisted of the launch of 8, 12, or 16 retargetable missiles. The number of missiles assigned to each subject was a between-subjects factor. Subjects were given a static brief, four at time, then split into two pairs to do both training and testing. All subjects received approximately three hours of training which included a slide presentation to explain the TTIMR prototype, two training sessions each lasting approximately 25 minutes, as well as observing an additional training session other than theirs. The rules for retargeting missiles were explained during all phases of training and reviewed before testing. The first training session consisted of a walkthrough of all screen elements and a demonstration of the retargeting process. Subjects were then presented with three different retargeting scenarios and if any mistakes were made, the program was paused to discuss the errors. The second training session mirrored an actual test session which will be detailed in the next section. The only difference between this second practice session and a test session was the possible pausing that took place in case of mistakes or questions. Subjects were thoroughly debriefed and all questions were addressed.

After training, all subjects were tested on two separate experimental sessions, with approximately a 25-minute break in between the two. Missile launch occurred in approximately the first 3.5 minutes in real time. After ~3.5 minutes, the strike went into a fast forward mode for approximately one minute, and then the clock and associated missile movement slowed down to real time. Approximately one minute after the resumption of real time, communications from the subject's 'superior' (the TSC – Tactical Strike Coordinator) were announced through the chat box. Subjects could see three types of messages in the chat box. The first were health and status reports from the missiles, which required no action. The second were information messages from either other ships in the strike or from the TSC. These messages provided general strike information and also required no action. The third type of message was an action message from the TSC, which required the operator to search for a piece of information available on the two screens and then type in one word responses. An action message was generated by the TSC approximately one minute prior to the arrival of an emergent event (of which there were four). Action messages were considered secondary tasking. Subjects were given clear instructions that their primary tasking was retargeting missiles and only when they were finished with the retargeting task or were idle, were they to attend to action communication messages.

Approximately two minutes from the resumption of real time, the first emergent target arrived. In every test session, this first emergent target arrival was considered practice and the associated metrics were not counted in any data analysis. In this practice emergent target scenario, only one possible candidate missile existed so the choice of which missile to retarget was obvious. Every time an emergent target arrived, thirty seconds later, the TSC queried the user with an action message. After the initial practice session, retargeting events arrived approximately two or four minutes apart. In every test session, the first retargeting scenario after the practice scenario was classified as an 'easy' scenario since a single emergent target arrived and only one candidate missile was presented in the decision matrix. The next retargeting scenario was considered of medium difficulty, and it required that a subject redirect a missile from its default target to another target in the strike (but not an emergent target) based on the instructions of the TSC. In the last scenario, known as the 'hard' scenario, subjects had to decide on a missile retargeting strategy based on the arrival of two emergent targets fifteen seconds apart. The arrival of the two emergent targets was considered a dual retargeting scenario because both targets were in competition for the same candidate missiles. In all scenarios, there was one correct answer according to the rules of engagement outlined during training. However, because the system presented all missiles which could physically reach a target, it was possible for a subject to retarget a missile that was not the best choice. The test sessions concluded when subjects retargeted a missile to both of the emergent targets and were no longer attempting to answer any action messages in the chat box.

RESULTS

Workload was measured via secondary tasking at six different points in each test session. The first, third, and fifth embedded tasks (via requests from the chat box) occurred during a monitoring period, with no other tasking. The second, fourth, and sixth embedded tasking requests occurred thirty seconds after a retargeting problem occurred. Figure 3 demonstrates that during the retargeting scenario embedded tasking, average time to respond increased for every scenario, indicating that secondary task performance degraded (points 2, 4, 6) and workload increased for the subjects during retargeting, as expected.

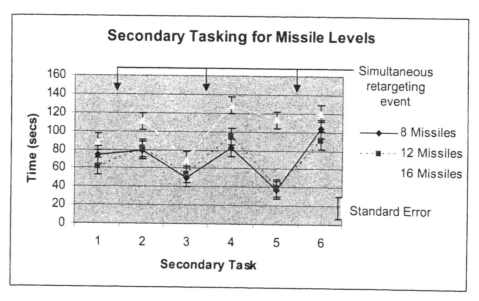

Figure 3: TTIMR Secondary Tasking

In addition to the secondary task performance degradation when coupled with a retargeting primary task, the secondary task times increased as the complexity of the scenarios increased. Points 2, 4, 6 coincide with the easy, medium, and hard retargeting scenarios so the reduction in spare mental capacity can be seen in comparison to the times. With approximately 120 seconds available for each secondary task, in general subjects with 8 and 12 missiles never exceeded this level while subjects controlling 16 missiles had no spare mental capacity for the medium and hard retargeting scenarios. This difference between the missile levels is quite obvious at all secondary tasking measurement points. The comparison of average secondary tasking for the three different missile levels in Figure 3 reveals the same trend that was statistically significant in the analysis of other performance metrics (Cummings, 2003) in that the decision times and overall performance scores for the 16 missile level was greater than for the 8 and 12 missile levels, which were very closely aligned.

CONCLUSION

The use of popular instant messaging chat interfaces can be an effective embedded secondary workload measurement tool when used in domains where chat-based communications are standard practice. As demonstrated in this research effort examining human supervisory control performance issues in the control of in-flight missiles, embedded secondary tasking workload measurements using the chat box showed a clear division in secondary task response times between different levels of controllable missiles. There is, however, one problematic drawback to using chat windows for secondary task testing, that of chat box fixation. Despite the training emphasis on only attending to the chat box when nothing else was happening, many subjects became fixated on the communications and would answer all queries before attending to the more pressing emergent target problems. All subjects were told repeatedly that retargeting situations were their primary priority tasking and that answering queries through the chat box was the least important of all tasks.

From the observer's standpoint, this over-attention to the chat box degraded the overall performance of the subjects, and from an operational standpoint, could have costly consequences. The overall performance scores of the subjects were correlated with binary fixation data (i.e. a person was considered fixated if they continued responding to an action communication message ten seconds after notification of an emergent target) with significant results, Pearson's correlation = -.292, p = .008, α = .05). These results demonstrate that the use of the chat box must be carefully planned and implemented as detailed instruction and training was not able to prevent some subjects from attending to the secondary tasking tool as if it was the primary task. However, the potential problems in using an embedded secondary tasking tool like chat are offset by the ecologic value of naturalistic workload measurement.

ACKNOWLEDGMENTS

This material is based upon work supported by the Naval Surface Warfare Center, Dahlgren Division through an ONR Future Naval Capabilities grant. Any opinions, findings, conclusions or recommendations expressed in this material are those of the authors and do not necessarily reflect the views of NSWC/DD or ONR.

REFERENCES

Adelman, L. (1991). Experiments, Quasi-Experiments, and Case Studies: A Review of Empirical Methods for Evaluating Decision Support Systems. IEEE Transactions on Systems, Man, and Cybernetics, 22(2), 293-301.

Committee on Human Factors. (1997). Tactical Display for Soldiers: Human Factors Considerations. Washington DC: National Academy Press.

Cummings, M. (2003). Designing Decision Support Systems for Revolutionary Command and Control Domains. University of Virginia, Charlottesville.

Gawron, V. J. (2000). Human Performance Measures Handbook. Mahwah, NJ: Lawrence Erlbaum Associates.

Shingledecker, C. A. (1987). In-flight workload assessment using embedded secondary radio communication tasks (282). Neuilly Sur Seine, France: Advisory group for Aerospace research and Development.

Tsang, P., & Wilson, G. F. (1997). Mental Workload. In G. Salvendy (Ed.), Handbook of Human Factors and Ergonomics (2nd ed., pp. 417-489). New York: John Wiley & Sons, Inc.

U.S. Navy. (2002). Tomahawk Weapons System (Baseline IV) Operational Requirements Document. Washington, D.C.: Department of Defense.

Wickens, C. D., & Hollands, J. G. (2000). Engineering Psychology and Human Performance (Third ed.). Upper Saddle River, NJ: Prentice-Hall Inc.

Williges, R. C., & Wierwille, W. W. (1979). Behavioral Measures of Aircrew Mental Workload. Human Factors, 21(5), 549-574.

EVALUATING THE EFFECT OF FATIGUE ON COGNITIVE AND VISUAL/PERCEPTUAL PERFORMANCE AT THE BEGINNING AND END OF EACH SHIFT IN A 12-HOUR FIVE-DAY ROTATING WORKWEEK

Othman Alkhouri
Ecole Superieure de Commerce de Lille

John A. Wise
Honeywell International

Steve Hall & Marvin L. Smith
Embry-Riddle University

ABSTRACT

The effect of cognitive and visual/perceptual fatigue on shift workers may not be the same for day-time workers since rotating shifts create enormous disruptions to the circadian rhythms of the workers. The purpose of this study was to measure the effect of fatigue on shift workers cognitive and visual/perceptual performance at the beginning and end of each shift during the workweek. The primary instrument used in this study was the Automated Performance Testing System (APTS), which is a human performance measuring system that contained eight various cognitive and temporal factors tests. The findings suggested that cognitive performance at the beginning of the shift was significantly higher than at the end of the shift.

Keywords: Fatigue, Cognitive Performance, Visual Performance, 12-Hour Shift, Five-Day Rotating Workweek, Automated Performance Testing System

INTRODUCTION

Safety of employees has become an important issue for researchers and corporations alike. The possibility of human error related accidents and the clear potential for additional mishaps in the future makes study of the effects of fatigue of major practical concern to the aviation industry in particular, and to other industries. Shiftwork disrupts and interferes with the biological and social rhythms; thus, forcing people to adapt to unusual working schedules. This disruption is mainly due to the fact that shift workers have to work when they should sleep and sleep when they should stay awake. In the normal day-work, night-sleep situation, people work when the circadian rhythm is high and sleep when it is low. According to Rosa and Colligan (1997), this schedule is best for performance, which means it is also best for safety.

When workers perform poorly, they are more likely to make errors that could lead to accidents or injuries. Shifts usually vary in duration from 4 to 12 hours, but it is uncommon to find shorter or longer ones as well. Twelve-hour shiftwork is becoming popular in various industries including the aviation/aerospace industry despite its possible contribution to fatigue and performance degradation. This can be due to the fact that workers do not mind putting up with fatigue and extended working hours to get more days off, which can be used to spend them with their families, go to school, or engage in recreational activities (Luna, 1996; Rosa & Colligan, 1997).

Monk (1990) discussed that it is always the maladjusted shift worker who is the agent of risk, rather than the work environment. These maladjusted shiftworkers can become agents of risk to themselves and others in a number of different ways (Monk, Folkard, & Wedderburn, 1996). The first way is through sleepiness at work, which can lead to various problems, such as missed signals, e.g., a red light, a dial going critical, or of inappropriate responses to correctly perceived signals. The second way in which maladjusted shiftworkers can become agents of risk is by being too upset and/or angry. Their anger may be either biological, i.e., circadian dysfunction, sleep loss, or social, i.e., an imminent divorce. Such mood changes can lead to a directly aggressive attitude toward the handling of dangerous machinery and to an absence of concern for the safety of others.

The third means by which shiftworkers can become agents of risk is through simple performance decrements. Although not subjectively sleepy, workers may be suffering circadian-related performance decrements that might lead to personal injury because of the critical nature of the work, e.g., welding, sawing, etc. One thing to consider here is that it is false, however, to think that shiftwork is necessarily accompanied by high risk, because virtually all safety and health aspects of shiftwork are primarily concerned with shiftworkers who are not coping for one reason or another, rather than the entire population of shiftworkers (Monk, 1990). In this study, it is hypothesized that shiftworkers are more fatigued at the end of the shift, whether day or night, than at the beginning of the shift.

METHOD

Participants

The participants were 12 airframe and powerplant maintenance technicians working a 12-hour, five-day rotating shift in the Gulf Aircraft Maintenance Company (GAMCO), which is located in Abu Dhabi, the capital city of the United Arab Emirates. The participants were from diverse cultures and ethnic origins. All participants were completely informed as to the purpose and length of the study and were given the choice to withdraw from the program only during the first week if they were not interested. None of the participants had prior experience with performance measurement systems. Withdrawal from the program was not permitted after the first week of the study by means of a memo issued by management for that purpose.

Instruments

The instrument that was used in this study was a performance measurement system known as, the Automated Performance Test System (APTS). The APTS battery employs various cognitive and temporal factors tests, which detects changes in performance and has the capability to perform in various field settings that might result from one or more environmental, physiological, chemical or psychological stressor conditions (Lane & Kennedy, 1988; Essex Corporation-Technical Manual, 1992). The cognitive performance battery had five tests: Code Substitution, Pattern Comparison, Manikin, Reaction Time, and Tapping. Each cognitive test took 100 seconds to run, except for tapping, which had two sessions, 20 seconds each. On the other hand, the temporal factors battery had three tests: Backward Masking, Visual Span, and Bistable Stroboscopic Motion. These tests measured visual/perceptual performance and were time-based tests; hence, they did not have time limitations. They were terminated as soon as the subject responded to a predetermined number of stimuli's.

Procedure

Each group of participants were briefed for one hour and subsequently taken through the APTS test battery. Participants were directed to respond quickly, accurately, and to the best of their abilities to the specific instructions for each test. Although the subjects were initially told to take at least seven practice trials since it was thought they would be sufficient for subjects to reach stability, which is the trial at which novelty effects are minimum; it was discovered later during the analysis stage that practice was a vivid element throughout the trials and that additional measures were required in order to compensate for its effects, which rendered the data not testable using the traditional t test method because of the improvements that were taking place as time progressed. The subjects were instructed to take the tests battery at the beginning, middle, and end of each shift in the workweek. Because there were only three computer terminals available, the subjects were told to come at specified time slots to minimize any interference and delays that might occur as a result of waiting for other subjects to get through the battery. The data collection from the APTS battery lasted for two-months, followed by the analysis stage, during which individual and group curves were plotted and examined to check performance trends, and in order to identify and isolate anomalous data points.

RESULTS

An Alpha (α) level of .10 was adopted for rejection of the null hypothesis in all statistical analysis. In order to compensate for the effect of practice, which was apparent throughout the trials for each test despite the various attempts to remove the element of practice through using the log function with the data points, a linear regression analysis was conducted with the logged trials being the independent variable, and the logged scores, whether number correct for cognitive tests or response time for temporal factors tests, being the dependent variable. A repeated-measures paired-sample t test was conducted to evaluate the hypothesis of the study. The large number of contrasts to be compared and the many cognitive and temporal tests within each contrast necessitated a composite for cognitive tests and another composite for temporal tests. The composites were computed as follows:

Cognitive Composite =

$$\frac{CS(Mean)}{CS(SD)} + \frac{PC(Mean)}{PC(SD)} + \frac{MK(Mean)}{MK(SD)} + \frac{RT(Mean)}{RT(SD)} + \frac{TP(Mean)}{TP(SD)}$$

Temporal Composite =

$$\frac{Mask(Mean)}{Mask(SD)} + \frac{VisSpan(Mean)}{VisSpan(SD)} + \frac{Strobe(Mean)}{Strobe(SD)}$$

Table 1. Contrasts comparing Beginning of shift Vs. End of shift.

Test	Beg Mean	End Mean	Difference Mean	Standard Deviation	Standard Error	t	p-value
CS	.0060	-.0176	.0236	.0397	.0120	1.969	.077
PC	.0292	.0218	.0074	.0440	.0133	.561	.587
MK	.0031	-.0337	.0369	.0434	.0131	2.816	.018
RT	.0161	-.0297	.0458	.0581	.0175	2.614	.026
TP	.0244	.0011	.0233	.0423	.0128	1.826	.098
Mask	.0686	-.0123	.0809	.1304	.0393	2.058	.067
VisSpan	.0053	-.0084	.0137	.0634	.0191	.716	.490
Strobe	-.0002	-.0097	.0094	.0416	.0125	.754	.468
Cognitive Composite	.3983	-.1783	.5765	.8236	.2483	2.322	.043
Temporal Composite	.2368	-.0960	.3328	.6418	.1935	1.720	.116

Note: DF = 10

The results indicated that the means for Code Substitution, Manikin, Reaction Time, Tapping, and Backward Masking at the beginning of the shift (Beg), whether day or night, were significantly higher than at the end of the shift (End). As shown in table 1, the cognitive composite mean at the beginning of the shift (Beg) ($\underline{M}$ = .3983, $\underline{SD}$ = 2.74) was significantly higher than at the end of the shift (End) ($\underline{M}$ = -.1783, $\underline{SD}$ = 2.87), $\underline{t}$ (10) = 2.322, $\underline{p}$ = .043. On the other hand, the temporal composite mean at the beginning of the shift (Beg) ($\underline{M}$ = .2368, $\underline{SD}$ = 1.42) was not significantly different from the temporal composite mean for the end of the shift (End) ($\underline{M}$ = -.0960, $\underline{SD}$ = 1.33), $\underline{t}$ (10) = 1.720, $\underline{p}$ = .116. Only one temporal factors test, i.e., Backward Masking, was significantly higher at the beginning of the shift (Beg) ($\underline{M}$ = .0686, $\underline{SD}$ = .2229) than at the end of the shift (End) ($\underline{M}$ = -.0123, $\underline{SD}$ = .1750), $\underline{t}$ (10) = 2.058, $\underline{p}$ = .067. Based on the outcome of table 1, the hypothesis was only accepted for the cognitive tests in the battery and rejected for the temporal factors tests.

DISCUSSION

The results suggested that shiftworkers were getting worse cognitively at the end of each shift with respect to the beginning of the shift. On the other hand, the visual/perceptual factors, which were measured by the temporal factors tests, did not indicate significant changes at the beginning and end of the shifts. This might have been caused either because there was no triggering effect for these tests on the outcome being measured or that there was no sufficient data points for these tests to capture significance. For most people, it would be common sense to assume that performance at the end of the shift is worse than the performance at the beginning of the shift in any typical workday in the workweek. Almost all cognitive tests showed significant p- values, with the exception of Pattern Comparison, and only one temporal factors test, i.e., Backward Masking, showed a significant p- value. The cognitive composite had a p- value equal to .043; while the temporal composite had a non-significant p- value equaled to .116. These findings suggested that fatigue takes its toll more cognitively than visually or perceptually by the end of the shift, regardless of the time of the shift, whether day or night.

CONCLUSION

The findings of this study suggested that cognitive performance at the end of the shift was significantly lower than performance at the beginning of the shift. On the other hand, visual/perceptual performance was not significantly different at the beginning and end of the shift. These findings serve to elicit the importance of scheduling tasks that require various levels of cognitive abilities at times at which subjects can be at their optimum cognitive performance levels. The application of human performance test batteries in this kind of studies has many implications in real life situations. These test batteries have the ability to sense the presence of a stressor over a wide dynamic range of the stressor, and are able to detect changes for a variety of different stressors. By having such properties, such systems will be able to identify potential hazardous subjects before their health and safety becomes impaired. This study points out to the need for long-term field studies in order to be able to draw unequivocal conclusions and make systematic assessments of extended work shifts.

ACKNOWLEDGEMENTS

The authors would like to recognize the efforts of both Bob Kennedy and Norm Lane (RSK Assessments, Inc.), who not only provided the use of the DELTA software, but without whose expertise the analysis would have taken much longer and would have yielded less interesting results.

REFERENCES

Lane, N. E., & Kennedy, R. S. (1988). Users manual for the U.S. army aeromedical research laboratory portable performance assessment battery. Essex Orlando Technical Report 88-5. Orlando, FL: Essex Corporation.

Rosa, R. R., & Colligan, M. J. (1997). Plain language about shiftwork. Cincinnati, Ohio: National Institute for Occupational Safety and Health, Division of Biomedical and Behavioral Science.

Luna, T. D. (1996). Shiftwork: Basic concern for commanders, supervisors, and flight surgeons. Brooks AFB, TX: Armstrong Laboratory, Crew Systems Directorate. Report No. AL/CF-TR-1996-0073.

Monk, T. (1990 April-June). Shiftworker performance. Occupational Medicine: State of the art reviews, 5(2), 183-198.

Monk, T. H., Folkard, S., & Wedderburn, A. I. (1996). Maintaining safety and high performance on shiftwork. Applied Ergonomics, 27(1), 17-23.

Essex Corporation (1992). DELTA: Human performance measurement system (Technical Manual) (2nd ed.). Orlando, FL: Essex Corporation.

AFFECT AS AN ASPECT OF WORKLOAD: WHY AND HOW TO ADDRESS AFFECT IN AUTOMATION AND SIMULATION STUDIES

H. C. Neil Ganey, Lauren M. Murphy, Joseph Dalton
University of Central Florida

Mark E. Koltko-Rivera
Professional Services Group

P. A. Hancock
University of Central Florida and Institute for Simulation and Training

ABSTRACT

Affect is a much-neglected moderator of workload and performance. Research literature demonstrating affect's influence on cognitive and physical tasks is summarized. In terms of cognitive performance, affect has been shown to influence memory function, decision making, problem solving, risk assessment, and performance on other cognitively loaded tasks. In terms of physical performance, affect has been shown to influence physical perceptions and interpersonal functioning, and to moderate performance on tasks that are heavily loaded for strenuous physical activity. Methodological suggestions are given regarding induction of affect in experimental studies, and assessment of affect. This paper presents the researcher in human performance, automation, and simulation with several resources: a rationale for including affect in the conceptualization of every study; a list of studies that demonstrate affect's role in moderating cognitive and physical performance; references to theoretical models for affect, performance, and workload; references for induction of effect; references for assessment of affect.

Keywords: Affect, mental workload, mood, performance

INTRODUCTION

Affect refers to emotion, including both the current emotional state of an operator, and the emotional traits (that is, the characteristic emotional dispositions) of that operator. Affect involves a subjective filter through which the operator evaluates external conditions. In this paper, we consider the role that affect plays in influencing mental workload and moderating performance. It is our position that (1) affect influences the physical and cognitive aspects of an operator confronting any task, (2) affect thus influences that operator's perception of workload, and (3) affect thus moderates performance on any given task. Thus, all human factors research, including research involving automation and simulation, should involve assessment of affect. To demonstrate the feasibility of this approach, we consider research regarding the influence of affect on cognitive and physical tasks. We then make methodological suggestions.

Affect has been largely ignored in human factors and ergonomics research, and this has been so from the earliest days of the field. Affect did not receive the slightest attention in the early magisterial reviews of the field published by Fitts (1963) and Taylor (1963), despite Taylor's long-ago plea:

> Learning and individual differences sometimes bring about greater changes in operator behavior than do the variables which are preferred by the . . . human engineer. If the engineering psychologist broadened his investigations to include a more deliberate study of social, motivational, individual-difference, and learning factors on psychomotor processes, the goal of proper man-machine system design might be served better. If this were done, conceivably interactions of great importance in optimizing systems – and no less important for psychological theory – would be discovered. (Taylor, 1963, p. 857)

However, it seems that most subsequent research has sided with Fitts, who implied that personality theory was of too little importance to consider at length in his review of engineering psychology (Fitts, 1963, p. 924). There are many possible reasons for this. Much of contemporary human factors and ergonomics psychology is grounded in cognitive psychology, which itself has been criticized for ignoring affect and motivation (Norman, 1980; Pervin & John, 2001). Affect may simply seem too "soft" for a psychological specialization that is rooted in engineering and hard science disciplines.

Nonetheless, abundant research demonstrates that affect influences performance on many tasks. (A theory of the neuropsychological basis of such findings has been proposed by Ashby, Isen, & Turken, 1999.) This has been demonstrated in research involving both cognitive and behavioral performance, often using experimental designs.

Cognitive Performance as Moderated by Affect

Affect influences memory function. Research using an "emotional Stroop task" paradigm demonstrated that, for many people, affect-laden terms delay responses (Williams, Mathews, & MacLeod, 1996). Overall, affective events – particularly negative events – were more recollected by participants, leading to a more rich experience of them in memory (Ochsner, 2000). Memory for incidents demonstrated a "weapon focus" effect, in which the presence in the incident of a weapon – an affect-laden stimulus that is no stranger to human factors research – inhibited memory for many other details of the incident (Loftus, Loftus, & Messo, 1987; Pickel, French, & Betts, 2003; Steblay, 1992). Memory also exhibits a mood-congruent bias: people with induced happy mood better remembered happy than sad materials, but people with induced sad mood better remember sad than happy materials (Mayer, McCormick, & Strong, 1995).

Affect also influences decision making and problem solving. Depending on other variables, experimentally induced positive affect promoted both risk-prone and risk-averse behavior (Arkes, Herren, & Isen, 1988; Isen & Geva, 1987; Isen, Nygren, & Ashby, 1988; Isen & Patrick, 1983); the same mood induction also increased creativity in problem solving (Estrada, Isen, & Young, 1994; Isen, Daubman, & Nowicki, 1987). In diagnosing liver disease, physicians with induced positive affect integrated diagnostic information quicker than controls; they also showed less distortion or inflexibility in their diagnostic reasoning (Estrada, Isen, & Young, 1997).

Assessments of future probabilities (i.e., risks) are affected by mood. Among healthy people, those with induced happy mood saw themselves as much more likely to experience positive health-related events in the future than those with induced sad moods (Salovey & Birnbaum, 1989). In terms of general life events, participants with induced happy mood reported higher likelihood of positive events occurring, and lower probabilities for negative events occurring, than control participants without induced mood; participants with induced sad mood showed just the opposite pattern, reporting lower likelihood of positive events occurring, and higher probabilities for negative events occurring, than controls (Wright & Bower, 1992; see also Johnson & Tversky, 1983).

Affect influences performance on other cognitively loaded tasks. Induced positive affect increased motivation for and performance on an anagram task (Erez & Isen, 2002). In a word sorting task, participants with induced positive affect used categories more inclusively than controls (Isen & Daubman, 1984). Induced positive mood influenced perceptions of task characteristics and task satisfaction (Kraiger, Billings, & Isen, 1989).

Additionally, affect's role as filter not only applies to external stimuli. Affect and time perception are also interlinked. We all know the saying that 'time flies when you're having fun.' We know this statement to be true, since research has found that positive mood states are associated with subjective underestimates of time passed, while negative affect leads people to report distensions in perceived time passed. (Hornik, 1992).

Finally, affect influences interpersonal functioning. Induced positive affect was associated with use of integrative (rather than contentious) solutions in bilateral negotiations (Carnevale & Isen, 1986).

Physical Performance as Moderated by Affect

Affect seems to moderate performance on tasks that are heavily loaded for strenuous physical activity, though there is a smaller literature on the topic. Among those attempting to qualify for national wrestling teams in the 1980 Olympics, pre-competition affect was a highly significant predictor of qualifying either for competition or for first alternate status in a given weight class; those wrestlers who so qualified showed lower scores for tension, depression, anger, fatigue, and confusion, while showing higher scores for vigor (Silva, Shultz, Haslam, Martin, & Murray, 1985). Though Lee (1990) found that pre-task mood state did not affect performance on a physical task, the performance was strongly affected by 'psyching up' behaviors, which are strikingly similar to induced affect. This is also in accord with the work of other researchers, who have found that successful elite athletes have positive affect and high levels of self-confidence, and tend to engage in positive self-talk, all prior to competition (Gould, Weiss, & Weinberg, 1981; Highlen & Bennett, 1979; Mahoney & Avner, 1977).

DISCUSSION

By this point, we believe that we have demonstrated that affect somehow moderates performance (a position we expand on in Koltko-Rivera, Ganey, Dalton, & Hancock, 2004a). Affect may do this by influencing three aspects of a task: (1) its perceived physical characteristics or demands, (2) its perceived cognitive characteristics or demands, and (3) its perceived affective characteristics. (These three types of characteristics define mental workload, that is, the subjective aspects of workload, in a model we are developing; Koltko-Rivera, Ganey, Dalton, & Hancock, 2004b). Thus, human factors scientists should include affect as a moderating variable in their research.

The researcher is always in need of solid theoretical frameworks. Two different types of theories about affect include (1) factorial approaches to personality in general, such as the Five Factor Model (McCrae & Costa, 1999), and (2) circumplex approaches to personality and emotion (Plutchik & Conte, 1997).

Two aspects of method deserve notice: the induction of mood for experimental studies, and the assessment of affect. Many of the studies described above induced mood in research participants; some of the methods used were evaluated by Isen and Gorgoglione (1983). In addition, contemporary simulation scientists have a distinct advantage over earlier researchers. With the advent of large-scale video screens, realistic computer graphics, and sophisticated game engines, the contemporary researcher can induce affect in ways that could only be dreamed of earlier. In terms of assessment, several instruments exist to assess affect, including multi-theoretical instruments (Matthews, Jones, & Chamberlain, 1990; Matthews et al., 1999), Five Factor model instruments (Costa & McCrae, 1992), and instruments appropriate for use in a circumplex model (see multiple chapters in Plutchik & Conte, 1997).

ACKNOWLEDGEMENT

The views expressed in this work are those of the authors and do not necessarily reflect official Army policy. This work was supported by the Department of Defense Multidisciplinary University Research Initiative (MURI) program administered by the Army Research Office under grant DAAD19-01-1-0621.

REFERENCES

Arkes, H.R., Herren, L.T., Isen, A.M. (1988). The role of potential loss in the influence of affect on risk-taking behavior. Organizational Behavior & Human Decision Processes, 42, 181-193.

Ashby, F.G., Isen, A.M., & Turken, A.U. (1999). A neuropsychological theory of positive affect and its influence on cognition. Psychological Review, 106, 529-550.

Carnevale, P.J., & Isen, A.M. (1986). The influence of positive affect and visual access on the discovery of integrative solutions in bilateral negotiation. Organizational Behavior & Human Decision Processes, 37, 1-13.

Costa, P.T., Jr., & McCrae, R.R. (1992). Revised NEO Personality Inventory (NEO PI-R) and NEO Five-Facator Inventory (NEO-FFI): Professional manual. Lutz, FL: Psychological Assessment Resources.

Erez, A., & Isen, A.M. (2002). The influence of positive affect on the components of expectancy motivation. Journal of Applied Psychology, 87 1055-1067.

Estrada, C.A., Isen, A.M., & Young, M.J. (1994). Positive affect improves creative problem solving and influences reported source of practice satisfaction in physicians. Motivation and Emotion, 18, 285-299.

Estrada, C.A., Isen, A.M., & Young, M.J. (1997). Positive affect facilitates integration of information and decreases anchoring in reasoning among physicians. Organizational Behavior & Human Decision Processes, 72, 117-135.

Fitts, P. M. (1963). Engineering psychology. In S. Koch (Ed.), Psychology: A study of a science: Vol. 5 (pp. 908-933). New York: McGraw-Hill.

Gould, D., Weiss, M., & Weinberg, R. (1981). Psychological characteristics of successful and nonsuccessful Big Ten wrestlers. Journal of Sport Psychology, 3, 69-81.

Highlen, P.S., & Bennett, B. (1979). Psychological characteristics of successful and nonsuccessful elite wrestlers: An exploratory study. Journal of Sport Psychology, 1, 123-137.

Hornik, J. (1992). Time estimation and orientation mediated by transient mood. Journal of Socio-Economics, 21, 209-227.

Isen, A.M., & Daubman, K.A. (1984). The influence of affect on categorization. Journal of Personality and Social Psychology, 47, 1206-1217.

Isen, A.M., Daubman, K.A., & Nowicki, G.P. (1987). Positive affect facilitates creative problem solving. Journal of Personality and Social Psychology, 52, 1122-1131.

Isen, A.M., & Geva, N. (1987). The influence of positive affect on acceptable level of risk: The person with a large canoe has a large worry. Organizational Behavior & Human Decision Processes, 39, 145-154.

Isen, A.M., & Gorgoglione, J.M. (1983). Some specific effects of four affect-induction procedures. Personality & Social Psychology Bulletin, 9, 136-143.

Isen, A.M., Nygren, T.E., & Ashby, F.G. (1988). Influence of positive affect on the subjective utility of gains and losses: It is just not worth the risk. Journal of Personality and Social Psychology, 55, 710-717.

Isen, A.M., & Patrick, R. (1983). The effect of positive feelings on risk taking: When the chips are down. Organizational Behavior & Human Decision Processes, 31, 194-202.

Johnson, E.J., & Tversky, A. (1983). Affect, generalization, and the perception of risk. Journal of Personality and Social Psychology, 45, 20-31.

Koltko-Rivera, M.E., Ganey, H.C.N., Dalton, J., & Hancock, P.A. (2004a). Human performance: A comprehensive strategy for research. Manuscript in preparation, University of Central Florida.

Koltko-Rivera, M.E., Ganey, H.C.N., Dalton, J., & Hancock, P.A. (2004b). Workload: A comprehensive model. Manuscript in preparation, University of Central Florida.

Kraiger, K., Billings, R.S., & Isen, A.M. (1989). The influence of positive affective states on task perceptions and satisfaction. Organizational Behavior & Human Decision Processes, 44, 12-25.

Lee, C. (1990). Psyching up for a muscular endurance task: Effects of image content on performance and mood state. Journal of Sport and Exercise Psychology, 12, 66-73.

Loftus, E. F., Loftus, G. R., & Messo, J. (1987). Some facts about "weapon focus." Law and Human Behavior, 11(1), 55-62.

Mahoney, M.J., & Avner, M. (1977). Psychology of the elite athlete: An exploratory study. Cognitive Therapy and Research, 1, 135-141.

Matthews, G., Jones, D.M., & Chamberlain, A.G. (1990). Refining the measurement of mood: The UWIST Mood Adjective Checklist. British Journal of Psychology, 81, 17-42.

Matthews, G., Joyner, L. Gilliland, K., Campbell, S., Huggins, J., & Falconer, S. (1999). Validation of a comprehensive stress state questionnaire: Towards a state "big three"? In I. Mervielde, I.J. Deary, F. DeFruyt, & F. Ostendorf, (Eds.), Personality psychology in Europe: Vol. 7 (pp. 335-350). Tilburg, The Netherlands: Tilburg University Press.

Mayer, J.D., McCormick, L.J., & Strong, S.E. (1995). Mood-congruent memory and natural mood: New evidence. Personality & Social Psychology Bulletin, 21, 736-746.

McCrae, R.R., & Costa, P.T., Jr. (1999). A five-factor theory of personality. In L.A. Pervin & O.P. John (Eds.), Handbook of personality: Theory and research (2nd ed., pp. 139-153). New York: Guilford.

Norman, D.A. (1980). Twelve issues for cognitive science. Cognitive Science, 4, 1-32.

Ochsner, K.N. (2000). Are affective events richly recollected or simply familiar? The experience and process of recognizing fellings past. Journal of Experimental Psychology: General, 129, 242-261.

Pervin, L.A., & John, O.P. (2001). Personality: Theory and research (8th ed.). New York: Wiley.

Pickel, K. L., French, T. A., & Betts, J. M. (2003). A cross-modal weapon focus effect: The influence of a weapon's presence on memory for auditory information. Memory, 11, 277-292.

Piedmont, R.L. (1998). The Revised NEO Personality Inventory: Clinical and research applications. New York: Kluwer/Plenum.

Plutchik, R., & Conte, H.R. (Eds.). (1997). Circumplex models of personality and emotions. Washington, DC: American Psychological Association.

Salovey, P., & Birnbaum, D. (1989). Influence of mood on health-relevant cognitions. Journal of Personality and Social Psychology, 57, 539-551.

Silva, J.M., Shultz, B.B., Haslam, R.W., Martin, T.P., & Murray, D.M. (1985). Discriminating characteristics of contestants at the United States Olympic Wrestling Trials. International Journal of Sport Psychology, 16, 79-102.

Taylor, F. V. (1963). Human engineering and psychology. In S. Koch (Ed.), Psychology: A study of a science: Vol. 5 (pp. 831-907). New York: McGraw-Hill.

Williams, J.M.G., Mathews, A., & MacLeod, C. (1996). The emotional Stroop task and psychopathology. Psychological Bulletin, 120, 3-24.

Wright, W.F., & Bower, G.H. (1992). Mood effects on subjective probability assessment. Organizational Behavior & Human Decision Processes, 52, 276-291.

TOWARD THE PERFECT OPERATION OF COMPLEX SYSTEMS

Michael Schrauf, Wilhelm Kincses
DaimlerChrysler AG Research & Technology, Stuttgart, Germany

Dylan Schmorrow,
DARPA, Arlington, VA, USA

Colby Raley
Strategic Analysis, Arlington, VA, USA

ABSTRACT

The aim of the studies was to develop a tool for evaluating the driver's workload based on scalp recorded event-related electrical brain activity (ERP). The implementation of the system is based on signal analysis of single stimulus evoked ERP variability. This variability is analyzed in driving tasks with different levels of complexity and used to infer changes in driver's cognitive state (workload). The ability to detect such changes has implications for the future design of advanced driver assistance systems (ADAS).

Keywords: Event-related potentials, ERP, DISTRONIC, driver assistance, electrical brain activity, EEG, information-processing, autonomous longitudinal control, temporal resolution

INTRODUCTION

In view of the fact that a large number of various assistance, comfort and multimedia systems will be integrated in cars of the future, it is of particular importance that the communication between these systems and driver does not diminish our high safety standards, but rather enhances driver safety. Cognitive load or workload can be defined as the portion of human cognitive resources engaged in performing a specific task. In order to assess the amount of cognitive load required to operate the vehicle while being assisted by the above mentioned systems it is important to find an objective, non-intrusive and online method to measure cognitive load.

Workload can be assessed by (a) subjective methods, (b) by measuring primary or secondary task performance or (c) by physiological techniques. Subjective methods, especially rating scales, which assess the operator's or observer's judgements of the task under consideration have several advantages but also several disadvantages as compared to approaches such as physiological techniques. From the numerous rating scales used in test and evaluation the following methods are commonly used for workload measurement: NASA-TLX (NASA Task Load Index), SWAT (Subjective Workload Assessment Techniques), MCH (Modified Cooper Harper Scale), SWORD (Subjective Workload Dominance Technique), Bedford Scale, and Zeis (Sequential Judgement Scale) (for a review see Hart & Wickens, 1990).

In general, subjective rating scales (especially if multidimensional ratings of workload are used, e.g. NASA-TLX, SWAT) have the advantage (a) of being applicable for a very broad range of tasks, (b) of having several subscales, (c) of having a high validity and (d) of fulfilling a satisfactory number of standards. However, especially in the case of multidimensional scales, the main disadvantage of subjective rating scales is that the more dimensions they have, the more difficult it is to rate while performing a task. Another disadvantage is the fact that subjective rating scales such as questionnaires are applicable just after task completion and are consequently not suited for online assessments. Furthermore, rating scales are likely to be influenced by characteristics of the respondents like biases, errors, negative memory effects, and pre-test attitudes (Dyer & Parker, 1975).

Brain imaging techniques have the advantage of measuring the mental state of a subject directly as compared to parameters obtained through variations in the autonomic nervous system. With respect to CNS (central nervous system) activity, workload can be detected from EEG recordings (Brookings et al., 1996) and derived measures such as ERPs. Through the use of complementary brain imaging techniques (MEG, fMRI), it is possible to understand in part brain activity during different stages of workload. Further EEG-based candidates of CNS activity measures are ERP components as well as EEG bandwidths which reflect arousal, attention and mental workload. ERPs in particular provide a sensitive index of workload that can be used in adaptive systems. Among ERP's, the most widely supported measures are based on the P3 and the N1 potentials of the brain (Donchin et al., 1986). Both the N1 and the P3 ERP measures have been determined to provide fairly sensitive measures of mental workload. The P3 has been shown to reflect primarily the allocation of perceptual-cognitive resources and not response-related processes (Donchin, 1987). The N1 brain potential has been found to reflect attentional resources associated with early information processing stages (Rugg & Coles, 1995). Most of the N1 and P3 studies of workload have examined dual-task performance. The amplitude of the P3 component to a secondary task of e.g. counting infrequent tones among more frequent tones (auditory oddball paradigm) decreases when combined with a primary task such as visual discrimination or psychomotor tracking. The P3 amplitude shows a dual-task decrement, i.e. it is reduced in amplitude when the eliciting task is combined with an additional task, e.g. visual or auditory distraction tasks. For applications such as the ones we intend to perform it is important to mention that motor tracking does not affect the amplitudes of the ERP components N1 and P3 caused by the secondary task (Israel et al., 1980a).

Consequently, ERP measures represent an ideal instrument for online-measuring of brain activity as a correlate of workload in order to assess the amount of brain resources engaged in operating a vehicle under different perceptual and cognitive conditions.

METHOD

Event-related potentials (ERP) data were analyzed for topographical differences of amplitude or latency in two conditions of a 2-tone auditory passive oddball paradigm. A standard (85%, 1kHz) and a deviant tone (15%, 2kHz) were used. Recordings were made from 32 sites (Electrocap, 10:20-system, impedance < 5kOhm, sampling rate 1kHz). Topographic maps were made using a horizontal and vertical linear interpolation. EOG artifact rejection was applied. Data were evaluated offline using a digital low-pass 25Hz filter (e.g. Polich, 1991). The experiment was performed on German public highways between Stuttgart and Düsseldorf (distance ca. 450 km). GPS data were recorded and synchronized with EEG-data for post-hoc analysis for post hoc analysis.

Experiment 1

In the first experiment, we compared two driving conditions: Driving sequences with and without DISTRONIC (Adaptive Cruise Control) were alternated every 30 minutes to minimize effects of sequence and attention. P3 characteristics of the ERPs were determined and averaged for each condition.

Experiment 2

In a second experiment, the driver was instructed to drive without the support of any driver assistance systems. The difficulty of driving conditions was supposed to be determined by the traffic situations defined by means of road characteristics such as highway exits, lane mergers, acceleration lanes, lateral acceleration in curves, number of traffic lanes and construction sights. To improve the temporal resolution of the studied workload assessment, we used the P3 time series to obtain context dependent measures. For this purpose we calculated the moving average of three successive P3 amplitudes and plotted the results in a roadmap (Fig. 4). Low P3 values (lowest quantil) were allocated to a high workload, medium values (mean high quantil) denote medium workload, and the larger values (upper quantil) denote the low workload category.

RESULTS

During early information-processing stages (< 100 ms, stimulus onset at 0 ms) no significant differences were found for either latencies or amplitudes between the driving conditions at all electrode sites.

Experiment 1

With the support of the DISTRONIC system, a trend of increased N1 amplitude was found at the central electrode positions (Fz, Cz, Pz). Clear differences appear both for latencies and amplitudes during mid-latency information-processing stages (i.e. P3 latencies decreased while amplitudes increased) as depicted in Fig. 1 and Fig. 2.

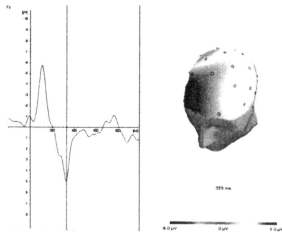 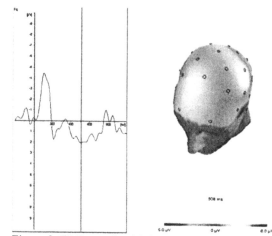

Figure 1. ERP map for driving with DISTRONIC: the curve shows the obtained potential variation at Fz (negativity up). A clear peak at 100 ms (N1) and at 330 ms (P3) can be seen. The map shows a clear positivity within the right hemisphere, especially at the frontal lobe.

Figure 2. ERP map for driving without DISTRONIC: the peak at 100 ms (N1) is about 25% lower in comparison to the "driving with DISTRONIC" condition. The map shows a broadened P3 starting at 400 ms (main peak at about 510 ms). No clear positivity can be seen.

Experiment 2

Under easy traffic conditions, a trend of increased N1 amplitude was found at the central electrode positions (Fz, Cz, Pz). Clear differences appear both for latencies and amplitudes during mid-latency information-processing stages (i.e. P3 latencies decreased while amplitudes increased) between easy and difficult driving situations. Results are depicted in Fig. 4.

CONCLUSION

Experiment 1

Results show that driver assistance systems such as DISTRONIC support the driver by decreasing driver's workload as measured by P3 variability (Fig. 3).

Experiment 2

Results show that ERP based workload measures such as the ones based on P3 variability are able to detect workload changes under different driving situations (Fig. 4).

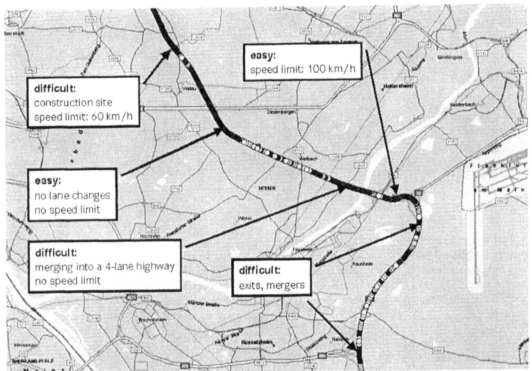

Figure 4. Workload measures during various driving situations. Each colored dot represents the moving average of three successive P3 amplitudes. Low P3 values (red, lowest quantil) were allocated to a high workload, medium values (yellow, mean high quantil) denote medium workload, and the larger values (green, upper quantil) denote the low workload category.

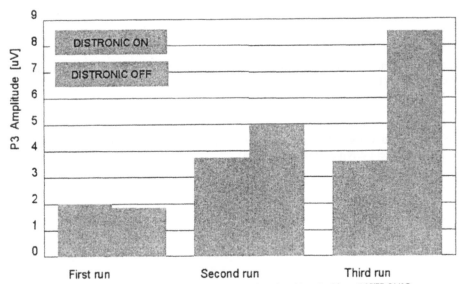

Figure 3. P3 averages recorded during successive sequences of driving (0,5 h each) with and without DISTRONIC.

APPLICATION

As an immediate application, P3 based workload measures can be used as indicators for assessing the impact of ADAS on driver's workload. The results show that this analysis makes it possible to relate in a meaningful way different workload levels to driving situations with different levels of difficulty.

REFERENCES

Brookings JB, Wilson GF & Swain CR (1996). Psychophysiological responses to changes in workload during simulated air traffic control. Biol Psychol, 42(3): 361-77.

Donchin E, Kramer A & Wickens C (1986). Applications of event-related brain potentials to problems in engineering psychology. In M.G.H. Coles, E. Donchin, & S. Porges (Eds.), Psychophysiology: Systems, Processes, and Applications, pp. 702-718. New York: Guilford Press.

Donchin E (1987).The P300 as a metric for mental workload. Electroencephalogr Clin Neurophysiol Suppl, 39: 338-43.

Dyer L & Parker DF (1975). Classifying outcomes in work motivation research: An examination of the intrinsic-extrinsic dichotomy. Journal of Applied Psychology, 60: 455-458.

Hart SG & Wickens C (1990). Workload assessment and prediction. In H. R. Booher (Ed.), MANPRINT, an approach to systems integration, pp. 257-296. New York: Van Nostrand Reinhold.

Israel JN, Chesney GL, Wickens CD & Donchin E (1980a). P300 tracking difficulty: evidence for multiple resources in dual-task performance. Psychophysiology, 17: 259-273.

Mathiak K, Hertrich I, Kincses WE, Rothe S, Lutzenberger W & Ackermann H (2002). Preattentive shift of covert selective attention in the auditory domain mediated by cross-modal interaction. Society for Neuroscience Abstracts.

Polich J (1991). P300 in clinical applications: Meaning, Method, and Measurement. Am J EEG Technol, 31: 201-231.

Rugg MD & Coles MGH (1995). Electrophysiology of Mind - Event-related brain potentials and Cognition, pp. 27-39. Oxford, UK: Oxford University Press.

DEMAND TRANSITIONS IN VIGILANCE:
EFFECTS ON PERFORMANCE EFFICIENCY AND STRESS

William S. Helton
Wilmington College

Tyler H. Shaw, Joel S. Warm, Gerald Matthews William N. Dember
University of Cincinnati

Peter A. Hancock
University of Central Florida

ABSTRACT

The National Research Council (Huey & Wickens, 1993) has identified transitions in task demand as an important dimension of human operator response. The effects of such demand transitions on vigilance performance have been explored in only two published studies (Krulewitz, Warm, & Wohl, 1975; Gluckman, Warm, Dember, & Rosa, 1993). The results of the first study suggested that the effects of transitions in task demand are characterized by simple psychophysical contrast. However, the latter study failed to confirm these results. The present study was designed to further explore whether demand transitions can be adequately described by a psychophysical contrast model. With that goal in mind, observers were shifted from a high salience (low demand) to a low salience (high demand) condition and vice-versa. Results failed to confirm the psychophysical contrast model. However, they did show that transitions in task demand have important implications for task-induced stress.

Key Words: Vigilance, Demand Transition, Stress

INTRODUCTION

 Laboratory studies of vigilance or sustained attention traditionally maintain a constant information-processing load throughout the experimental session (Davies & Parasuraman, 1982). However, the vigilance tasks encountered in many operational settings, such as air-traffic control, process control, and medical monitoring, can contain abrupt changes in the demands placed upon operators during a duty cycle. Consequently, the National Research Council (Huey & Wickens, 1993) has identified transitions in task demand as an important dimension for study in vigilance research.

Only two published investigations have focused upon this issue. One of these made use of changes in background event rate or the rate of repetition of stimulus events that need to be scanned in order to detect signals. Performance efficiency typically varies inversely with event rate (Warm & Jerison, 1984). Krulewitz, Warm, and Wohl (1975) found that observers shifted abruptly from a low to a high event rate during a vigil did more poorly than non-shifted controls on the high event rate. Those shifted in the high to low direction exceeded the performance of non-shifted controls on the low event rate. An outcome of this sort suggests that the effects of transitions in task demand are characterized by simple psychophysical contrast. However, a subsequent study by Gluckman, Warm, Dember, and Rosa (1993), using two different vigilance tasks to shift observers from single-task to dual-task monitoring and vice versa, produced performance changes that were devoid of contrast effects. In that study, the post-shift performances of the shifted groups equaled that of their non-shifted controls.

Gluckman et al. (1993) suggested that single-task and dual-task conditions in their study might have been perceived as so qualitatively different as to preclude any kind of direct contrast between them. Thus, contrast effects in demand transitions may be limited to changes in a single common dimension. In addition to event rate, performance efficiency in vigilance varies directly with signal salience (Warm & Jerison, 1984). Accordingly, this study was designed to determine whether contrast effects would be obtained when signal salience was shifted in high-to-low and low-to-high directions.

To date, studies of demand transitions have only examined effects on performance efficiency. However, vigilance tasks are stress-inducing, and the stress of sustained attention is closely tied to psychophysical demands (Galinsky, Rosa, Warm, & Dember, 1993; Hancock & Warm, 1989; Temple et al., 2000; Warm, 1993). Hence, a second goal for this study was to examine the effect of transitions in task demand on task-induced stress. Toward that end, the study made use of the Dundee Stress State Questionnaire (DSSQ; Matthews et al., 1999; 2002), an instrument that provides factor-analytically differentiated scales of *task engagement, distress, and worry*. Prior research has shown a vigilance signature in regard to the DSSQ – observers feel less task engaged and more distressed after a vigil than prior to its start (Grier, et al, 2003; Helton, Dember, Warm, & Matthews, 2000; Matthews, Joyner, Gilliland, Huggins, & Falconer, 1999; Matthews et al., 2002; Temple et al., 2000). The present study examined the effects of transitions in task demand on this pattern of stress response.

METHOD

Twenty observers (10 males and 10 females) were assigned at random to each of four conditions resulting from the factorial combination of signal salience (high and low salience signals) and switching (switch and no-switch). All observers participated in a 12-min vigil divided into six continuous 2-min periods. They inspected the repetitive presentation on a VDT of light gray capital letters consisting of an "O," a "D," and a "backwards D." The letters were exposed for 40 msec at a rate of 57.5 events/min against a visual mask consisting of unfilled circles on a white background. Critical signals for detection ($p = 0.20$/period of watch) were the appearance of the letter "O." Observers signified their detection of critical signals by pressing the key on a response pad. Prior to the main vigil, all participants were given a 2-min. period of practice to familiarize themselves with the vigilance task. In the high salience condition, the contrast between the letter stimuli and the background was 59 percent, as indexed by the Michaelson contrast ratio ([maximum luminance - minimum luminance / maximum luminance + minimum luminance] x 100; Coren, Ward, & Enns, 1999). In the low salience condition, the contrast between the letter stimuli and the background was 45 percent. Switch participants performed for 6 min at one salience level and then for 6 min at the other. This abbreviated vigilance task has been found to duplicate the general effects of signal salience and task-induced stress noted with more traditional long-duration tasks (Temple et al., 2000). The DSSQ was administered in two sessions: a pre-vigil questionnaire completed prior to the practice period and a post-vigil questionnaire completed after the vigil.

RESULTS

Signal Detections. Mean percentages of correct detections in all experimental conditions are presented in Figure 1. Separate split-plot analyses of variance (ANOVA) based on arcsin transformations of the detection scores were conducted on the pre-switch and post-switch segments of the vigil. The analysis of the pre-switch data revealed that signals were detected significantly more often in the high salience ($M = 98.5\%$) than in the low salience condition ($M = 95.5\%$), $F (1, 76) = 10.37$, $p<.01$, and that the overall level of signal detections declined significantly over time $F (1.7, 132) = 17.37$, $p<.001$. Moreover, the vigilance decrement was dependent upon signal salience, $F (1.7, 132) = 8.44$, $p<.001$. As can be seen in Figure 1, the decline in signal detections over time was more pronounced in the low-salience than in the high-salience condition. The analysis of the post-switch data revealed that signals were detected significantly more often in the high-salience ($M = 96.0\%$) than in the low-salience condition ($M = 85.9\%$), $F (1, 76) = 21.60$, $p <.001$. All other sources of variance in the ANOVA lacked statistical significance ($p>.05$). In these and all subsequent analyses, Box's epsilon was used when appropriate in computing degrees of freedom for the repeated measures factors to correct for violations of the sphericity assumption (Maxwell & Delaney 1990). False alarms were rare in this study; the overall mean false alarm rate was less than one percent. Consequently, false alarm data were not examined further.

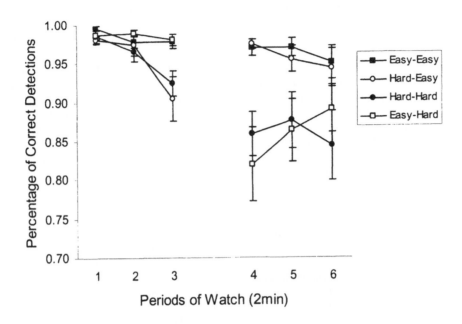

Figure 1. Mean percentages of correct detections for all experimental conditions (error bars are standard errors).

Stress. The DSSQ scale scores were standardized against normative data secured from a large British sample (Matthews et al., 1999), using the formula *(Raw score - Norm Group Factor Mean)/Norm Group Factor Standard Deviation.* Factor scores for Task Engagement, Distress and Worry were calculated using regression weights from the normative sample. Factor scores are distributed with a mean of 0 and a SD of 1, so that values calculated for a sample represent a deviation from normative values in standard deviation units. Change scores based on the DSSQ norms for the factors were determined for each observer using the formula *Normalized Post-Factor Score – Normalized Pre-Factor Score.* Separate 2X2 (salience) by (switch) ANOVAs were conducted on the change scores for each factor. The analysis of the Distress change scores revealed that the participants were significantly more distressed when switched ($M = 0.94$) than when not ($M = 0.49$), $F(1, 76) = 5.52$, $p<.05$, and the analysis of the Engagement change scores revealed a significant Salience x Switch interaction, $F(1, 76) = 9.73$, $p<.01$. All other sources of variance in these analyses lacked statistical significance ($p>.05$). The analysis for the Worry change scores revealed no significant results ($p>.05$). The change scores for the three factors are illustrated in Figure 2. Mean standardized change scores are displayed as departing from a standard score of 0 (i.e., no change). Error bars are *standard errors.* The profile of state change exhibited by the observers indicates that they were more distressed when switched then when task demands remained constant. It is also evident that the switched observers were less engaged than the non-switched controls on the easy task and more engaged than controls on the hard task. The observers' level of worry did not seem to be differentially affected by task switching. For both the hard and the easy tasks, the level of worry was lower post-switch than pre-switch. It is possible that this overall change in worry was due to the cessation of load uncertainty at the end of the experimental procedure, although space prevents us from a more detailed exposition on this interesting finding.

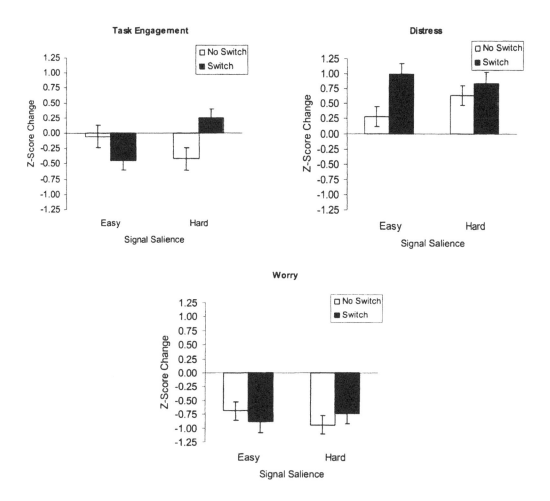

Figure 2. Standardized pre-post vigil change scores for the factors of the DSSQ in the easy (high salience) and hard (low salience) post-switch conditions for both switched and non-switched participants (error bars are 95% confidence intervals).

DISCUSSION

Consistent with the findings of Gluckman et al. (1993), the post-shift performance of shifted observers in this study simply equaled that of their non-shifted controls. Moreover, the effects of signal salience on performance efficiency in this study matched those of previous research with the abbreviated vigil and with long-duration vigils. As in these earlier investigations (Matthews et al., 2000; Temple et al. 2000; Warm, 1993), detection probability was poorer in the context of low- as compared to high-salience signals. Evidently, shifts in demand levels in vigilance do not necessarily produce contrast effects even when a single stimulus dimension is manipulated.

Although shifts in demand levels had no effect on performance efficiency, they had a notable effect upon observers self-reports of stress. Regardless of the direction of shift in task demand, shifted observers' were significantly more distressed at the end of the vigil than non-shifted controls. In addition, when observers were shifted from a low to a high salience condition, task engagement declined, whereas when they were shifted from a high to a low salience condition, task engagement was increased. Thus, the distress and task engagement dimensions of the DSSQ did not show similar results in regard to task switching. The presence of a distress/engagement dissociation in the present data provides further evidence for the utility of the multi-dimensional view of stress advocated by Matthews et al. (1999). The findings that transitions in task demand can produce increased feelings of distress, and in the case of shifts in the high-to-low demand direction (low to high salience), can also decrease task engagement may have long-term implications for employee well-being in operational settings. Accordingly, the results of this study underscore the National Research Council's view (Huey & Wickens, 1993) that workload transition is an important factor to consider in vigilance research.

ACKNOWLEDGEMENTS

This work was supported by the Department of Defense, Multi-University Research Initiative (MURI) program administered by the Army Research Office under Grant DAAD-19-01-1-0621, P.A. Hancock, Principal Investigator. The views expressed in this work are those of the authors and do not necessarily represented those of the United States Army.

REFERENCES

Coren, S., Ward, L.M., & Enns, J.T. (1999). *Sensation and perception (5th Ed.)*. Fort Worth, TX: Harcourt-Brace.

Davies, D.R., & Parasuraman, R. (1982). *The psychology of vigilance*. London: Academic Press.

Galinsky, T.L., Rosa, R.R., Warm, J.S., & Dember, W.N. (1993). Psychophysical determinants of stress in sustained attention. *Human Factors, 35*, 603-614.

Gluckman, J.P., Warm, J.S., Dember, W.N., & Rosa, R.R. (1993). Demand transitions and sustained attention. *The Journal of General Psychology, 120*, 323-337.

Grier, R.A., Warm, J.S., Dember, W.N., Matthews, G., Galinsky, T.L., Szalma, J.L., & Parasuraman, R. (2003). The vigilance decrement reflects limitations in effortful attention not mindlessness. *Human Factors, 45*, 349-359.

Hancock, P.A., & Warm, J.S. (1989). A dynamic model of stress and sustained attention. *Human Factors, 31*, 519-537.

Helton, W.S., Dember, W.N., Warm, J.S., & Matthews, G. (2000). Optimism, pessimism, and false failure feedback: Effects on vigilance performance. *Current Psychology, 18*, 311-325.

Huey, B.M., & Wickens, C.D. (Eds.) (1993). *Workload transitions: Implications for individual and team performance*. Washington D.C.: National Academy Press.

Krulewitz, J.E., Warm, J.S., & Wohl, T.H. (1975). Effects of shifts in the rate of repetitive stimulation on sustained attention. *Perception & Psychophysics, 18*, 245-249.

Matthews, G., Campbell, S.E., Falconer, S., Joyner, L.A., Huggins, J., Gilliland, K., Grier, R., & Warm, J.S. (2002). Fundamental dimensions of subjective state in performance settings: Task engagement, distress, and worry. *Emotion, 2*, 315-340.

Matthews, G., Joyner, L., Gilliland, K., Huggins, J., & Falconer, S. (1999). Validation of a comprehensive stress state questionnaire: Towards a state big three? In I. Merville, I.J. Deary, F. DeFruyt, and F. Ostendorf (Eds.), *Personality psychology in Europe* (Volume 7; pp. 335-350). Tilburg: Tilburg University Press.

Matthews, G., Davies, D.R., Westerman, S.J., & Stammers, R.B. (2000). *Human performance: Cognition, stress and individual differences*. East Sussex, UK: Psychology Press.

Maxwell, S.E., & Delaney, H.D. (1990). *Designing experiments and analyzing data: A model comparison perspective*. Belmont, CA: Wadsworth.

Temple, J.G., Warm, J.S., Dember, W.N., Jones, K.S., LaGrange, C.M., & Matthews, G. (2000) The effects of signal salience and caffeine on performance, workload and stress in an abbreviated vigilance task. *Human Factors, 42*, 183-194.

Warm, J.S. (1993). Vigilance and target detection. In B.M. Huey & C.D. Wickens (Eds.), *Workload transitions: Implications for individual and team performance* (pp. 139-170). Washington D.C.: National Academy Press.

Warm, J.S., & Jerison, H.J. (1984). The psychophysics of vigilance. In J.S. Warm (Ed.), *Sustained attention in human performance* (pp. 15-59). Chichester, UK: Wiley.

DECISION MAKING

DECISION QUALITY AND MISSION EFFECTIVENESS IN A SIMULATED COMMAND & CONTROL ENVIRONMENT

Scott M. Galster, Robert S. Bolia
Air Force Research Laboratory

ABSTRACT

The development of automated decision support systems requires a real-time metric of decision quality. Historical links between decision quality and mission effectiveness suggest that the former is predictive of the latter, and thus the outcome is what needs to be measured. The purpose of the present paper is to describe an experiment designed to separate the measurement of decision quality from that of mission effectiveness. Mission effectiveness and decision quality were examined using the RoboFlag simulation environment. Environmental uncertainty and knowledge of the opponent's strategies were manipulated factorially. Measures of mission effectiveness and decision quality were obtained along with subjective assessments of situation awareness and workload. Results are discussed in terms of decision quality as expressed by the tactics assigned to the operator's robots, and with respect to the mission outcome for each trial. Further, the number and appropriateness of re-tasking orders and the effects of unreliable information are addressed.

Keywords: Decision quality, decision making, mission effectiveness, situation awareness, automation, decision support systems

INTRODUCTION

Due to the advancement and proliferation of sensors, the amount of information available to the modern military decision maker is staggering. In order to cope with this influx, commanders may have to rely on automated decision support systems (DSS). One class of DSS will derive its input from sensors and other situational information, and produce a recommended course of action, which the operator will either accept or reject (see, for example, Taylor, Howells, & Watson, 2000). There are a number of difficulties with this type of system to which attention has been drawn before (Bolia, Vidulich, Nelson, & Cook, in press), including the potential for automation-induced complacency, disruption of traditional command structures, adversarial deception, and the difficulty in producing and evaluating decisions.

The development of such a DSS clearly requires a real-time metric of decision quality. Historical links between notions of decision quality and that of mission effectiveness imply that the former is predictive of the latter, and thus the outcome is what needs to be measured. This idea has been accepted by researchers studying strategic economic decision-making (Harrison & Pelletier, 1998), and appears to be taken for granted by scientists and engineers employing complex simulation as a vehicle for studying human performance. Yet, as Bolia and his colleagues have pointed out (Bolia, Nelson, Vidulich, & Taylor, 2004), there are at least two obstacles to this approach.

The first is its failure to provide a method for the explicit generation of the desired real-time measure. The DSS will likely need to be able to generate a plausible set of decisions, rank them according to quality, and recommend the best one to the operator. Relying on mission effectiveness – even if defined at a local level – may not afford the decision speed necessitated by high-tempo combat operations.

Second, military history is replete with examples in which doctrinally good decisions led to defeat, or bad decisions to victory. The Battle of Königgrätz, for example, was a landslide victory for Prussia, despite the fact that Moltke ordered the attack a day too early, a decision that could have cost Prussia the war (Wawro, 1996). Had the Austrians counterattacked in the morning, when Moltke's armies were not in contact with one another, they would likely have devastated the Elbe and First Armies, pivoting to defeat the Second Army in its turn. Benedek's refusal to order an attack – despite the pleas of his corps commanders – meant that the Austrians were sitting ducks when the Prussian Second Army finally arrived on their right flank. The result was a complete rout of Benedek's forces which quickly led Austria to sue for peace.

The example of Königgrätz raises two important points. First, a DSS based on doctrine would have recommended that Moltke postpone the attack for a day, which would have allowed Benedek and his army to slip across the Elbe and prevent the envelopment that subsequently occurred. Second, in adversarial situations, the outcome is affected as much or more by the decisions of a commander as it is by the decisions of his or her opponent. In this case, the victory was due less to the genius of Moltke than to the incompetence of Benedek.

Both of these points reveal the importance of context to the development of a usable DSS, and the difficulty of encoding such a context therein. The purpose of the present paper is to describe an empirical investigation designed to separate the measurement of decision quality from that of mission effectiveness using a system in which the appropriate context is available to the decision-maker.

METHOD

Participants

Eight males and four females ranging in age from 18-33 years ($M = 23.83$, $SE = 1.28$) served as paid participants.

Experimental Design

A within-subjects design was employed, with three robot-sensor Visual Range conditions (low, medium, high) combined factorially with three Opponent Postures (offense, defense, mixed) and participant Opponent Status Information (known, unknown). Additionally, for the condition in which participants were notified of the Opponent Posture (known), they were either informed reliably (75% of the time) or unreliably (25% of the time). Visual Range and Opponent Status Information were blocked factors and Opponent Postures were randomized with each block resulting in 6 blocks of 12 trials each.

Apparatus and Procedures

The experiment was conducted using the RoboFlag simulation environment, as it has previously been shown to be sensitive to the types of experimental manipulations previously described (Parasuraman, Galster, & Miller, 2003; Squire, Galster & Parasuraman, 2004). The RoboFlag simulation ran on three separate PCs communicating under TCP/IP protocol. The human operator utilized one PC while another ran the opposing team script and the third PC displayed a central processing executive (the "Arbiter") and collected the data. The RoboFlag simulation was modified to allow a single operator (blue team) to compete against an opponent (red team) operating under scripted procedures that simulated different opponent postures; offensive (all opponent players attack flag), defensive (all opponent players protect flag), and mixed (half opponent players attack flag, half protect flag). The field of engagement was divided into two halves, one for the blue team and one for the red, each with a designated flag and home area. Each trial had a simple objective: capture the opponent's flag and cross the mid-line into one's own half before the opponent can do the same before the time expired (60 s).

Each operator supervised six robots and did not receive strategy training or aid in the development of strategies or methods used to accomplished the game mission. To successfully complete the mission, the operator would be required to send some or all his or her robots to capture the opponent's flag, but simultaneously ensure that the opponent could not capture his or her flag. Teams started the engagement from their home area, and the trial began once the participant interface was viewable. The only control available to the operator was to put the robots on an offensive or defensive play.

The opponent's stance/position/configuration varied according to three available scripts: offensive, defensive, or mixed. In the offensive script (circle offensive play), all six red team robots attempted to win the game by capturing and returning to the mid-field line with the blue team's flag. In the defensive script, two different defensive configurations were established. The first used three red team robots to defend entrance to and access across the mid-line (patrol border); the other used the remaining three to defend against the penetration and possible exit from their flag area (circle defense). The mixed script distributed the team equally between offensive and defensive strategies (three robots on circle offense, three on patrol board). As previously described, participants were either informed or not informed of the Opponent Script prior to the initiation of each trial.

Participants were trained by showing them how plays were executed, how robots were selected and moved, as well as how the features of the interfaces showed different robot's status information, fuel, play, and status. Additionally, they were instructed that the only way a red team red robot could be seen is if they were within the visual range of the blue team robot, otherwise the red team robot was invisible to the blue team operator. They were shown how to retrieve the opponent flag, and given a chance to test out RoboFlag without an opponent. Prior to the training trials, participants were given written instruction based on the NASA-TLX (Hart & Staveland, 1988) and 3-D SART (Taylor, 1989) on how to evaluate and rate their perceived mental workload and situation awareness, respectively, after each trial. Participants completed one trial in each of the nine conditions (with knowledge of the condition) as training prior to the commencement of data collection trials.

RESULTS

Overall performance

The performance data were submitted to a 3 (offensive, defensive, mixed) Opponent Strategy × 3 (low, normal, high) Visual Range × 2 (known, unknown) Opponent Status Information Analysis of Variance (ANOVA). The overall performance metrics included the outcome of each game (won, lost or drawn) and the time elapsed for each game (mission completion time). The outcome measure was transformed such that a win was coded as +1, a draw was coded as 0, and a loss was coded as -1. The results of the ANOVA indicated that there was a significant 2-way interaction between the Visual Range and Opponent Status Information factors, $F(4,44) = 6.82$, $p < .01$, for the game outcome measure (see Figure 1). Participants held an advantage when they were playing against the red team that was on the offensive strategy. It is important to note that this did not necessarily mean that they won a greater percentage of the games because the averages could be brought down considerably with increasing numbers of draws. For example, participants could only win or draw when playing against the defensive red team strategy, they could not lose. However, the three conditions under the defense condition in Figure 1 reflect the influence the number of draws had on the number of wins. In this case, the advantage of the outcome was much lower because the participants played to a draw in a high percentage of the games.

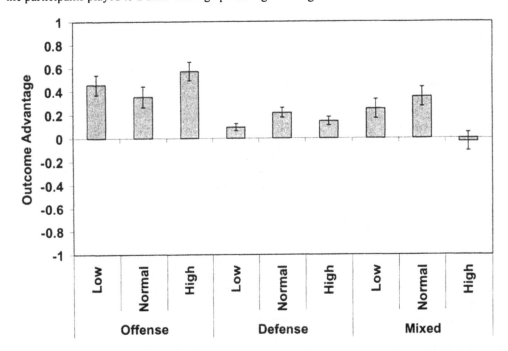

Figure 1. Transformed game outcome data as a function of Opponent Strategy and robot Visual Range.

A similar 3 × 3 × 2 ANOVA was conducted for the duration of each game, regardless of the game outcome. Game times were significantly different for the Visual Range, $F(2,22) = 4.59$, $p < .05$, and Opponent Strategy, $F(2,22) = 237.22$, $p < .01$, main effects. Regarding the Opponent Strategy, game times were shortest when the participant played against the offensive stance ($M = 34.18s$, $SE = 56s$) compared to when they played against the mixed posture ($M = 41.15s$, $SE = 0.78s$). The longest game times were those where the participant played against the defensive stance ($M = 56.09$, $SE = 0.56s$). These game times are similar to those found in previous experiments utilizing the RoboFlag simulation environment (Parasuraman, Galster, & Miller, 2003; Squire, Galster, & Parasuraman, in press).

Strategy utilization

As previously described, participants began each game either knowing or not knowing the status of the opponent strategy. At the start of each game, they assigned a strategy to their robots that would take advantage of the opponent strategy information, if it was available. The effectiveness of the strategy they originally chose is reflected in the number of strategy changes subsequently made throughout the rest of the game. This measure is indicative of the decision quality at the onset of each game. A high number of strategy changes indicate that the original strategy was inappropriate given the unfolding information available to the participants. The cumulative number of strategy changes were submitted to a 3 × 3 × 2 ANOVA analogous to that previously described. There was a significant difference in the 2-way interaction between the Opponent Strategy and the Opponent Strategy Information, $F(2,22)$ = 4.86, $p < .05$. This interaction, illustrated in Figure 2, shows that participants changed strategies more often when playing against the opponent in the defensive status. Further, the participants had to make more changes when they were not aware of the opponent strategy at the onset of the game. The number of strategy changes for the offensive and mixed condition are roughly equivalent and not dependent on whether the participant knew of the opponent strategy at the start of the game. When this information is compared to the data presented in Figure 1, one can see that the decision quality is separated from the outcome of the game. For example, considering the number of changes in the offensive and mixed conditions, one can see the clear difference in the outcome of the games for these two conditions. Given the same number of strategy changes, the participants won significantly more games when playing against the offensive strategy than they did when playing against the mixed strategy.

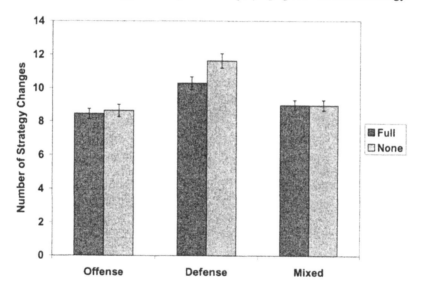

Figure 2. The number of strategy changes as a function of the amount of information the participant received about the opponent strategy.

Subjective Measures

The participants were queried for ratings of their mental workload and situation awareness after each block of trials they completed. The resulting data were submitted to a 3 (Visual Range) × 2 (Opponent Status Information) ANOVA. The results indicated that there were no significant differences for any of the factors regarding the situation awareness ratings ($p > .05$). The mental workload ratings did reveal a significant difference for the Opponent Status Information factor, $F(1,11) = 14.98$, $p < .01$. Participants rated their mental workload higher when they were not informed of the opponent strategy before the start of the game ($M = 48.89$, $SE = 4.03$) compared to the condition where they were informed of the opponent team strategy ($M = 42.31$, $SE = 3.88$).

DISCUSSION

The present study examined the differences in decision quality and mission effectiveness. The results indicated that the two do not necessarily follow a prescribed relationship and, in fact, have divergent associations. Decision quality for the differing opponent strategies, as measured here, resulted in game outcomes that were significantly different.

The RoboFlag simulation environment is not representative of the complexity of real-world decision-making, as is found in the battlefield or the operation of complex systems. It is, however, a useful tool to examine the differences in decision quality and the resultant mission (game) outcomes. It is clear that the number of strategy changes is not fully indicative of the variance seen in the game outcomes. Future work will examine the *appropriateness* of decisions given the amount of information available to the operator in addition to examining the number of strategy changes that were made. This information should provide a more meaningful measure of decision quality as it relates to the decision outcome. Notwithstanding, the present experiment served to initiate the examination of the differences between decision quality and the resulting effectiveness of those decisions.

ACKNOWLEDGMENTS

The authors gratefully acknowledge the technical contributions to this research of Matt Middendorf, of Middendorf Scientific Services, Inc., and Becky Brown, of Sytronics, Inc.

REFERENCES

Bolia, R. S., Nelson, W. T., Vidulich, M. A., & Taylor, R. M. (2004). From chess to Chancellorsville: Measuring decision quality in military commanders. In Proceedings of the Second Human Performance, Situation Awareness, and Automation Conference.

Bolia, R. S., Vidulich, M. A., Nelson, W. T., & Cook, M. J. (in press). A history lesson on the use of technology to support military decision-making and command & control. In M. J. Cook (ed.), Human factors of complex decision-making. Mahwah, NJ: Lawrence Erlbaum Associates.

Harrison, E. F., & Pelletier, M. A. (1998). Foundations of strategic decision effectiveness. Management Decision, 36, 147-159.

Hart, S. G., & Staveland, L. E. (1988). Development of NASA-TLX (Task Load Index): Results of empirical and theoretical research. In P. A. Hancock, & N. Meshkati (Eds.), Human mental workload. (pp. 139-183). North Holland: Elsevier Science Publishers.

Parasuraman, R., Galster, S.M., & Miller, C. (2003). Human control of multiple robots in the RoboFlag simulation environment. In Proceedings of the 2003 IEEE International Conference on Systems, Man & Cybernetics. Washington, DC: IEEE. (3232-3238).

Squire P.N., Galster, S.M., & Parasuraman, R. (2004). The effects of levels of automation in the human control of multiple robots in the RoboFlag simulation environment. In Proceedings of the Second Human Performance, Situation Awareness, and Automation Conference.

Taylor, R. M. (1989). Situational awareness rating technique (SART): The development of a tool for aircrew systems design. In Proceedings of the AGARD AMP Symposium on Situational Awareness in Aerospace Operations, CP478. Neuilly-sur-Seine, France: NATO AGARD.

Taylor, R. M., Howells, H., & Watson, D. (2000). The cognitive cockpit: Operational requirement and technical challenge. In P. T. McCabe, M. A. Hanson, & S. A. Robertson (Eds), Contemporary Ergonomics 2000 (pp. 55-59). London: Taylor & Francis.

Wawro, G. (1996). The Austro-Prussian war: Austria's war with Prussia and Italy in 1866. Cambridge, UK: Cambridge University Press.

FROM CHESS TO CHANCELLORSVILLE:
MEASURING DECISION QUALITY IN MILITARY COMMANDERS

Robert S. Bolia
W. Todd Nelson
Michael A. Vidulich
Air Force Research Laboratory
Wright-Patterson Air Force Base, OH
USA

Robert M. Taylor
Defence Science and Technology Laboratory
Farnborough, Hants
UK

ABSTRACT

The purpose of the present paper is to discuss the issues associated with measuring decision quality, both in the context of structured game environments, in which the moves of both players are severely constrained, and for the combat commander, who may exhibit more creativity in planning and executing a campaign. This discussion will also draw on evidence from the American Civil War Battle of Chancellorsville, in which one general broke two major rules of military doctrine – i.e., made doctrinally "bad" decisions – and still emerged victorious. The goal of the analysis is to guide the identification of candidate metrics of decision quality that are independent of mission effectiveness. It is proposed that this cannot be done in a manner that is free from the context in which the decision is being made, and that for decision support systems to work, a means of encoding this context needs to be developed.

Keywords: Decision Making, Decision Support, Situation Awareness, Context Sensitivity, Command & Control

Human life occurs only once, and the reason we cannot determine which of our decisions are good and which bad is that in a given situation we can make only one decision; we are not granted a second, third, or fourth life in which to compare various decisions.
– Milan Kundera, *The Unbearable Lightness of Being*

Advances in processing speed and information technology have afforded the ability, at least in principle, to construct real-time automated decision support systems to assist military commanders in making complex decisions, either in the context of planning or in the heat of battle (see, for example, Gollery, 2002; Taylor, Howells, & Watson, 2000). The capability of such automated systems to make or support decisions typically derives from artificially intelligent reasoning schemes that have been demonstrated to work in structured well-defined competitive environments, such as chess. One problem with introducing such "expert systems" into high-risk environments like combat is the lack of a framework in which to thoroughly evaluate their performance.

Before we proceed, we should define what we mean by the phrase "decision support system." For the purposes of this paper, a decision support system is an automated information system which provides one or more decisions to an operator, which he or she may exploit or reject as desired. There are clearly other classes of decision support systems – for example, maps – to which this argument does not apply. It should be noted, however, that while the discussion herein is framed in terms of decision support systems, the issue at hand is not the automated system itself but the ability to measure the quality or effectiveness of decisions, irrespective of whether they are made by humans or by machines.

To some extent the failure to discover an appropriate framework in which to effect such a measurement is due to the want of an appropriate baseline. After all, how do we identify a decision as "good" or "bad?" In chess, a good decision might be one that avoids checkmate, or affords the capture of an opponent's queen. In other words, the quality of the decision is measured by the quality of the immediate outcome. If the quality of the immediate outcome is measurable, the problem is solved. On the other hand, if there is no immediate outcome, or the immediate outcome is not itself measurable, then we are not any closer to a solution. In complex environments such as the battlefield, both situations are likely to occur.

One proposed strategy has been to verify the decision support system by presenting it with scenarios and presenting the same scenarios to human experts in the field, asking the latter what they would do under the circumstances. If the decisions agree, we might say that the decision support system works as well as the human. But this is really sidestepping the problem, since what we sought was not a system to mimic human performance – which is far from optimal (Kahneman, 2003) – but rather one which makes good decisions. Thus is the problem yet again transformed, resulting in still another question: how do we know when a decision, whether made by human or machine, is a good one? Tied up with this is the question of whether, given two decisions, it is always possible, assuming perfect information, to identify the better one.

Going back to the chess example, we have the idea of a decision being judged on its outcome. For moves made early in the match, the outcome may be far removed from the decision. This is therefore equivalent to equating decision quality with mission effectiveness, a case made by Harrison & Pelletier (1998), who suggest that the latter is predicted by the former. There are at least two problems with this method. One is that, in order for a decision support system to work, it needs to be able to evaluate the quality of a decision before recommending it to an operator. A chess program may be able to generate a list of all possible moves, but this is of little value to a player unless he or she has an idea of which moves are good ones. A good chess tutor or decision support system evaluates a number of moves and presents only the "best" move to the player.

Another problem with this approach is that it makes the tacit assumption that all decisions lead to the same outcome, but of course this is not the case. This can be seen even in the case of chess, since not only one's own but also the opponent's decisions must be taken into account. Thus what would be a good move against an inexperienced opponent might be a disastrous move against a master.

This assumption is avoided in chess programs by treating decisions as decision trees, and evaluating series of moves until one is found that leads to a favorable outcome, for example checkmate. But of course this still makes assumptions about the moves of one's opponent. In the end all one has is a chain of "if I make move x and she makes move y and I make move z and … then I will place her in checkmate." Consequently, I make move x. But if she makes move w instead of move y then perhaps move x was not the most appropriate move for me to have made in the first place. Anyway, the result may be different.

There is always a certain probability that a player will make a particular move from among a set of moves, but what is unknown is what that probability is. Certainly there are expectations that can be formulated about what an opponent will do, based on the opponent's previous behavior or on the structure of the game itself. In warfare, these same rules apply, but there are additional rules as well. For one thing, in war a general knows not only what doctrine says he should do in a particular situation but also that he is expected to do it. In this case, he might do something entirely different simply to throw his opponent off balance, even if it means doing something less tactically or doctrinally correct. This point is exemplified by the Israeli attack against the Egyptian Army in the Sinai during the Six-Day War of 1967. The Egyptians had prepared their defenses against an attack along the lines of that which had taken place in the Suez War nine years earlier, and were unprepared for attacks from other directions. This was because they assumed that the Israelis would stick to a proven plan rather than try something new. By doing the unexpected the Israeli forces took the Egyptians completely by surprise, and soundly defeated them (Herzog, 1984).

That the behavior of an opponent is not always easily predicted is also well illustrated by the Battle of Chancellorsville, fought 1-3 May 1863 (see Sears, 1986, for a detailed analysis of the campaign). Here the Confederate Army of Northern Virginia, numbering just over 60,000, divided its forces in the face of more than 120,000 Union troops of the Army of the Potomac, holding one flank in check while attacking the other. This action violated two major precepts of traditional doctrine: 1) the ratio of the attacking to defending forces should be at least three-to-one (this ratio would have been unfamiliar to Lee – Murdock (2002) suggests a later origin for this commonly cited force ratio – although he certainly would have been familiar with the concept of preponderance of force); and 2) one should not divide one's forces (Clausewitz, 2002; Sun Tzu, 1963). Despite the plan's apparent lack of regard for military theory, it worked, and worked well.

What does this say about Lee's plan of battle vs. that of Hooker? In fact, surprisingly little. From a doctrinal view point of, Hooker's was undoubtedly the superior plan, and would likely have worked had he been fighting anyone other than Lee. Indeed, the fact that Lee's plan worked at all was largely the result of a lack of flexibility in Hooker's own planning, and in Hooker's failure to execute the plan according to schedule. His failure to anticipate Lee's behavior was also an important factor.

Outnumbered two-to-one, Lee did not have many textbook options. As soon as Hooker crossed the Rappahannock Lee's position at Fredericksburg was essentially outflanked, and if he had retreated southward, Hooker could have devastated his army with a strike against his right. By dividing his army, Lee was doing the unpredictable, and counting on the element of surprise to increase his chances of victory. When Hooker's troops made contact with Lee's advance forces around Chancellorsville, the commander of the Army of the Potomac realized that his mental model of the situation was untenable, and fell back to a defensive position along the river. He suffered an utter loss of situation awareness, and never recovered his ability to react in the face of a fluidly changing situation. Lee's subsequent victory was due at least as much to Hooker's inability to make appropriate decisions as to his own plan of attack.

A study of Chancellorsville can tell us at least two things about decision quality. One is that doctrine is not always an appropriate baseline for judging the value of a decision. Another is that decision quality is not the same as mission effectiveness. The second lesson is at this point inextricably tied up with the first, since by doctrinal standards Hooker's plan was sound while Lee's was not.

This brings up the question of context. A decision might be judged good or bad based on doctrine *or* outcome given all of the relevant information, but if the decision maker did not have complete information, how do we judge the quality of the decision? As von Winterfeldt and Edwards (1986) have pointed out, "The quality of decisions really means the quality of the processes by which they are made, and that can be evaluated only on the basis of information available before their outcomes occur or become certain. Rational decisions are made and must be evaluated with foresight, not hindsight." One of the problems with using doctrine as a baseline against which to measure decision quality is that it is relatively context-free. Knowing nothing but the change in the disposition of forces, it is easy to say that Hooker had developed a meticulously detailed, well thought-out plan that took into account both the force ratio of his army to Lee's and the terrain over which the battle would take place. It is equally easy to say that Lee's plan to divide his forces was sheer madness. The context we're missing is Lee's realization that he was trapped, and that only by doing something entirely unexpected would he be able to stave off the wholesale destruction of his army. Fortunately for Lee, this context was also missed by Hooker, who as a result was unable to react appropriately.

It might be offered that Lee's decision and Hooker's reaction had more to do with Hooker's lack of knowledge about the disposition and movements of the Army of Northern Virginia than about Hooker's abilities as a general, and that, provided with an accurate situational picture, both he and Lee might have acted differently. On the other hand, there are examples of doctrinally unsound decisions leading to victory even in environments with more limited options, such as chess. Bobby Fischer's celebrated "queen sacrifice" against Donald Byrne in 1956 is but one example of this phenomenon (Fischer, 1972).

What makes the context so difficult to encode into a knowledge base that might be used to predict Lee's action is precisely that it is *Lee's* action and not that of some other general. The fact that Lee made the decision to divide his forces is more characteristic of Lee than it is of generals as a class, even when provided with the same situational data. Indeed, it is unlikely that Hooker would have made the same decision had the two commanders' roles been reversed. But except in protracted conflicts, there is rarely enough information available about the behavior of a particular commander to allow a system that takes such individual differences into account to be constructed.

One distinction we have failed to make in discussing the action at Chancellorsville is the difference between planning and reactive decision making. The former involves a detailed analysis of alternatives and is generally conducted prior to embarkation upon a campaign or battle, while the latter is more commonly associated with decisions made under time pressure, such as in the heat of battle – the *coup d'oeil* of Clausewitz. That these two types of decision making may be qualitatively different is implied by the Recognition Primed Decision (RPD) model of decision making, which suggests that expert decision makers under extreme time pressure do not make decisions by means of rational choice among alternatives, but rather by generating one or more sufficient solutions based on pattern matching or recognition priming (Klein, 1997). This is also hinted at by the contrast between Hooker's ability to develop a workable campaign plan and his abject helplessness when faced with enemy action which he had not been able to predict.

One corollary of the RPD model is that it might actually take longer for experts to make decisions using a decision support system than it would if they were operating on their own. Since experts are acknowledged to make good decisions anyway, any increase in decision time may not be associated with an appreciable increase in the quality of the decision. Further, one of the principal tenets of the RPD model is that speed of decision is often more important than quality of decision, implying that human experts may be able to make sufficient decisions faster than the decision aid. These propositions suggest that decision support systems, which may be useful for planning activities, may be inappropriate for real-time decision making.

After all this, are we any closer to knowing how to measure decision quality, or have our efforts been in vain? A little of both, perhaps. We have succeeded in clarifying some aspects of the problem. By identifying situations in which textbook decisions lead to defeat while apparently irrational decisions lead to victory, we have at least demonstrated that the problem of measuring decision quality may not be solved by transforming it into a problem of mission effectiveness. Simultaneously, we have shown that decision quality has little meaning independent of the context in which the decision is made. Finally, these claims as well as the RPD model of expert decision making indicate that the types of decisions that military commanders have to make in response to rapidly changing situations may not be well suited to decision aiding.

Of course, none of the arguments prove conclusively that it is impossible to measure decision quality. What they do insinuate is that, without a baseline against which to construct a metric, generic measures of decision quality are not likely to reveal themselves. On the other hand, context-sensitive measures are certainly possible, as exemplified by our analysis of the opposing commanders' decisions at Chancellorsville. The caveat here is that computers are not nearly as good at encoding context as humans – or, rather, humans have not been able to explicitly describe the means by which they encode context in a way that is convenient for assimilation by computers.

Despite these assertions, computers have been programmed to play chess at least as effectively as expert humans, and as such effective real-time decision support systems for the chess environment are possible. Yet the reason that chess programs work so well is not that they mimic the strategy or tactics of human masters, but that chess represents a constrained space that can be searched exhaustively (Russell & Norvig, 1995). The computer can then select the movement that will have the highest probability of leading to checkmate in the shortest number of moves. Chess masters, on the other hand, do not exhaustively search all possible chains of movements, or even a large number thereof. Instead, they generate one or more good options up front and evaluate their quality by means of mental simulation (Klein, 1997). The fact that computers and expert humans may arrive at the same move, or at least the same result, is an artifact of the structure of the game. The match context is automatically encoded based on the fact that the limited number of possible moves implies that all possible decision trees are derivable from the situation at any given time.

Even in chess, it isn't always clear what constitutes a good decision outside of the context of a particular match, and even then, a computer's assessment of a move's quality is based not on the local context but on the probability of its influencing the global outcome. But this probability is not available in combat situations, due at least in part to the inability to represent what Clausewitz would call friction, as well as a lack of knowledge about the nature and quality of the enemy's decisions, i.e., the context. Since usable decision aids require the ability to measure the quality of the decisions they recommend against other candidate decisions, good context-sensitive decision support systems for military commanders are likely to be a long way off.

ACKNOWLEDGMENTS

The authors would like to acknowledge Mark Draper and Scott Galster, of the Air Force Research Laboratory, for their helpful comments on an earlier draft of this work.

REFERENCES

Clausewitz, C. von. (2002). *Vom kriege*. Berlin: Ullstein.

Fischer, B. (1972). *My 60 memorable games*. New York: Simon & Schuster.

Gollery, S. J. (2002). Context building information-centric decision-support systems. *Proceedings of the 2002 Command and Control Research and Technology Symposium, Naval Postrgraduate School, Monterey, California, June 11-13, 2002*. Washington: Command & Control Research Program.

Harrison, E. F., & Pelletier, M. A. (1998). Foundations of strategic decision effectiveness. *Management decision, 36*, 147-159.

Herzog, C. (1984). *The Arab-Israeli wars.* New York: Vintage Books.

Kahneman, D. (2003). A perspective on judgment and choice. *American Psychologist, 58*, 697-720.

Klein, G. (1997). The recognition-primed decision model: Looking back, looking forward. In C. E. Zsambok & G. Klein (Eds.), *Naturalistic decision making*, pp. 285-292. Mahwah, NJ: Lawrence Erlbaum Associates.

Kundera, M. [trans. M. H. Heim] (1984). *The unbearable lightness of being.* New York: Harper & Row.

Murdock, P. (2002). Principles of war on the network-centric battlefield: Mass and economy of force. *Parameters, Spring 2002*, 86-95.

Russell, S., & Norvig, P. (1995). *Artificial intelligence: A modern approach.* Upper Saddle River, NJ: Prentice Hall.

Sears, S. W. (1996). *Chancellorsville.* Boston: Mariner Books.

Sun Tzu (1963). [trans. Samuel B. Griffith] *The art of war.* London: Oxford University Press.

Taylor, R. M., Howells, H., & Watson, D. (2000). The cognitive cockpit: Operational requirement and technical challenge. In P. T. McCabe, M. A. Hanson, & S. A. Robertson (Eds), *Contemporary Ergonomics 2000* (pp. 55-59). London: Taylor & Francis.

von Winterfeldt, D., & Edwards, W. (1986). *Decision analysis and behavioral research.* Cambridge, MA: Cambridge University Press.

METHODOLOGIES FOR EVALUATING DECISION QUALITY

P. Clark, S. Banbury, D. Richards & B. Dickson
Centre for Human Sciences, U.K.

ABSTRACT

The paper considers the quality of decision making undertaken by operators using decision aids within dynamic and uncertain situations, and proposes a number of novel approaches to its assessment. We argue that decision making should be evaluated both in the context of 'process' (i.e. *how* a decision was reached) and of 'outcome' (i.e. *what* decision was reached). Furthermore, we suggest that decision quality can be couched in terms of the quality of situation assessment processes undertaken in support of a decision (i.e. the decision 'substrate'), as well as the consistency and timeliness of the decision. The paper discusses a number of methodologies that show promise in evaluating these characteristics of decision making.

Keywords: Decision making; measures of effectiveness; uncertainty; decision aids.

INTRODUCTION

Success in modern warfare relies heavily on the war fighters' ability to out-think their opponent and gain, and maintain, the initiative. However, the factors that lead to the so-called 'fog of war', such as uncertainty, stress and the dynamic nature of modern warfare, can make these goals difficult to achieve.

The objective of the work outlined in this paper is to gain insight into the cognitive processes that underlie decision superiority, particularly in situations of uncertainty, and how they contribute to the effective use of decision aids. Decision aids have been developed to support and enhance operator decision making. Indeed, recent advancements in the quality and scope of these aids have led to their widespread adoption across the battlefield (e.g. automatic target recognition, automatic re-routing systems).

One problem about the use of decision aids is the requirement to present information about system reliability or data uncertainty. Unfortunately, directly informing operators about system reliability or data uncertainty will not necessarily produce the desired changes in the quality of their decision making. For example, a wide range of laboratory studies has demonstrated that humans exhibit systematic deficiencies in their decision making when presented with information about uncertainty (for a review see Kahneman, Slovic and Tversky, 1982).

Decision Quality: Outcome Vs. Process

The fact that operators have difficulty in making decisions when faced with uncertain information poses some serious problems to designers of decision aids that operate in uncertain environments and can at best provide 'most likely' advice to the operator. The paradox arises that, although designers strive to achieve transparency of systems in uncertain environments with some probabilistic label of 'success' or 'reliability', this strategy may not be appropriate if operators are indeed the fallible decision makers that the laboratory studies suggest they are. There is a need, therefore, to examine the quality of operator decision making using decision aids; particularly in situations of uncertainty. Although in these cases the decision aid provides a mechanism to overcome the systematic deficiencies in human decision making noted earlier, the fact that the aid is at best providing 'most likely' advice means that the operator is still required to critique its advice. If a sufficient level of systems transparency is provided to the operator, we should expect that the quality of decisions made using it would be improved. Ideally, an operator will follow its advice when it is correct, and ignore its advice when incorrect.

One difficulty with conducting research on operator performance using decision aids under conditions of uncertainty is deciding how 'performance' is defined. Indeed, the notion of what constitutes a 'correct' decision when faced with uncertainty is highly subjective and context-dependent. For example, how does one classify a decision that violates doctrine? Is it a 'good' or a 'bad' decision, even though it eventually turns out to be a 'correct' one (see Bolia, Nelson, Vidulich and Taylor's, 2004, discussion of the Battle of Chancellorsville)? Indeed, research has been dominated by assessing the quality of a decision by quantifying the value of the outcome for a given event. In many instances this will be a binary output in terms of a simple 'yes' or 'no', 'survived' or 'killed' outcome. Unfortunately, such a measure reveals little of the decision processes involved in arriving at a course of action. We should therefore consider decision making in the context of 'process' (i.e. *how* a decision was reached), rather than 'outcome' (i.e. *what* decision was reached). The following section discusses a number of methodologies that show promise in evaluating the quality of an operator's decision making, in addition to measuring its outcome.

Methodologies for Assessing Decision Quality

Experienced decision makers in domains such as fire-fighting and air traffic control appear to make recognition primed decisions (for a review see Zsambok and Klein, 1997). That is, they seem to do very little deliberate reasoning in order to compare options and weigh evidence. Rather, they appear to act intuitively, guided only by a match of the perceived situation to their previous experience and by adopting a strategy of 'satisficing' (i.e. a strategy that is satisfactory rather than optimal). Such a strategy is thought to be important when coping with situations in which a high degree of uncertainty exists (for a review see Kobus, Proctor & Holste, 2001).

A number of studies have shown that individuals have difficulty in expressing how they arrived at a decision as they develop expertise in a task (e.g. Johnson, 1983). The assessment of recognition-primed decision making, therefore, presents an enormous challenge, as directly questioning such individuals about the processes underlying their decision making can be exceptionally difficult and time-consuming. An alternative is to develop less direct measures of decision quality that do not rely on subjective assessments. The following section outlines a number of psychological and psycho-physiological methodologies that we feel have utility for relatively simplistic assessments of decision quality.

Decision Substrate

Inherent in the 'recognition-primed' accounts of decision making is the notion of pattern-matching the mental representation of the situation with past experience (for a discussion of the cognitive mechanisms that this process might entail, see Eriksson and Kintsch, 1995). Clearly, the quality of decision making is directly related to the quality of this mental representation of the situation, which in turn is directly related to the quality of the processes undertaken to acquire it. Indeed, Endsley (1995) distinguishes the term Situation Awareness (SA) as a state of knowledge from the processes used to achieve that state, and refers to the process of achieving, acquiring and maintaining SA as 'situation assessment'. Thus, one way of assessing decision quality is to assess the quality of the situation assessment processes underlying the formation of the decision (i.e. the decision 'substrate').

However, most of the existing measures of SA focus solely on measuring the level of SA in terms of 'product' (i.e. participants' awareness of key SA elements at one moment in time). Critically, they do not focus on the measurement of SA in terms of 'process' (i.e. the processes involved in situation assessment that produce a representation in memory, or product). In response to this, Banbury, Hoermann, Soll and Dudfield (under review) developed a more diagnostic measure to assess the efficacy of situation assessment processes. An exhaustive search of the cognitive factors thought to be important to situation assessment led to the development of the Factors Affecting Situation Awareness (FASA) questionnaire. The FASA questionnaire comprises 30 questions, divided into the following five sub-scales: *Attention Management* (participants' ability to attend to more than one task at a time and resume a task successfully after being interrupted); *Information Management* (participants' motivation to acquire appropriate information to make rational decisions); *Cognitive Efficiency* (participants' ability to ignore distractions and maintain SA despite external stressors); *Automaticity* (participants' experience of performing routine tasks in a highly practiced, automatic way), and *Inter-Personal Dynamics* (participants' knowledge of non-verbal communication and their views on what team membership entails). The scoring of the scale is designed so that, the higher the score, the more the participant is aware and in control of factors that could negatively affect the process of situation assessment. The content of the FASA scale is consistent with a number of studies using aviation accident and incident data (e.g. Shook, Coello, Bandiero, Endsley and Garland, 2000).

The FASA questionnaire was used in the assessment of a bespoke SA training program for commercial airline pilots by providing a more diagnostic measure of aircrews' acquisition and maintenance of SA (Hoermann,

Soll, Dudfield & Banbury, 2003). The results of the study demonstrate the validity of FASA to detect improvements to aircrew SA afforded by the training program. For example, the results showed no significant differences between the training groups at pre-training. However, following the training, participants who had received the bespoke training exhibited significantly higher ratings compared to pre-training (i.e. rated themselves to be more aware and in control of factors that could negatively affect the process of situation assessment), whereas those who had received the standard line-oriented flight training (LOFT) did not (Banbury, Hoermann, Soll and Dudfield, under review).

In assessing the efficiency of the overall decision-making process, it is also necessary to make judgments about the demands placed on the operator. Key factors that influence the ability to assimilate and process information may be described in terms of information quality and volume. These factors directly influence the amount of effort that must be invested to engage in decision-making activities. The 'effortfulness' of decision-making is commonly assessed using a number of well-validated subjective questionnaires. In addition, a system that interprets behavioral and physiological measures (e.g. electroencephalogram, galvanic skin response and heart rate) within a contextual model and derives high order estimates of cognitive–affective status can be used (e.g. a 'Cognition Monitor'; Pleydell-Pearce et al, 2000). These estimates are expressed as higher-state descriptors of executive load, visual load and alertness, as well as verbal and spatial load. This approach ensures that a fine-grained assessment can be made alongside a consideration of individual decision quality, as opposed to a global subjective rating aggregated over a period of time.

Thus, assessment of the quality of processes underlying situation assessment, or decision 'substrate', using the psychological and psycho-physiological methodologies described above should have utility for the evaluation of decision quality.

Decision Consistency

Previous research has demonstrated how the consistency of operator decision making (in this case military fast-jet pilots) can be affected by the manner in which information regarding the reliability of automatic target recognition aid was presented (Banbury, Selcon, Endsley, Gorton & Tatlock, 1998). The study required pilots to respond to a system-identified target with a "shoot/no shoot" decision and investigated whether the provision of an alternate option to the primary identification would affect the decision to shoot, especially if this secondary option was either another enemy aircraft or a friendly fighter. In addition, two different representations were evaluated: one in which the information was presented as system uncertainty, and one in which it was presented as system confidence. The results indicated that decision-making behavior changed when the system explicitly identified a friendly aircraft as the secondary target; prior willingness to fire on a target with a relatively high level of uncertainty disappeared. Clearly, pilots in this study showed inconsistent decision making between different display formats even though the underlying probabilities were identical.

The consistency of decision making is a useful insight into the decision quality, as it can be argued that differences of outcome from decisions based on the same data could indicate inappropriate or incorrect reasoning processes. We argue that operators who have made accurate situation assessments, and correct inferences based on these data, should reach the same outcome each and every time a similar decision is made. We also need to make the distinction between predictability and consistency; a consistent decision using the same data is not necessarily predictable. On the basis of these observations, we argue that measures of decision-making consistency across levels of data uncertainty or system reliability have potential utility for the evaluation of decision quality.

Decision Timeliness and Agility

In order for the operator to gain the advantage over opponents it is imperative that he (or she) 'out-thinks' them. In dynamic situations time is seen as being of high value, and can dictate not only the eventual outcome of the decision but also more importantly an individual's pattern of decision making. With the nature of modern warfare relying heavily on information quality and supremacy, it has become crucial that operators are able to adapt quickly to the changing context within which they may find themselves.

To use Boyd's (1987) characterization of the cognitive decision-making process (the OODA Loop) as an example, we argue that the opponent who can cycle through the loop faster, whilst making decisions that are more accurate, will gain increasing advantage with each cycle. By taking the initiative and forcing the opponent to adopt a reactive decision-making strategy, the war fighter is able to control his opponent's actions, and in doing so increase the likelihood of achieving the desired effect.

The speed of decision making can be couched in terms of decision 'timeliness' (e.g. a change of strategy at the appropriate time) and decision 'agility' (e.g. the ability to be adaptable to changing circumstances). For example, consider a pilot using an automatic re-routing decision aid, whereby the aid provides a number of candidate routes from which the pilot must choose. The routes that the system generates are based on a number of parameters (e.g. time on target, fuel and stealth) and will change as the mission progresses. For example, Figure 1 depicts the optimal choice of routes across the mission (A→B→C→D). The decision quality of the pilot can be assessed in terms of its timeliness (i.e. the time taken for the pilot to change to another route) and its agility (i.e. the match or mis-match with optimal route strategy).

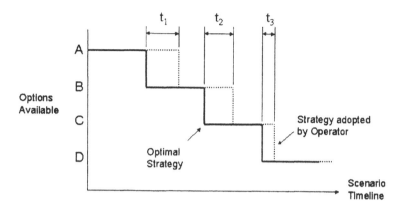

Figure 1: *Schematic of optimal choice of routes across a mission. Decision quality is assessed by examining differences between optimal route choice strategy and routes selected by participants in terms of 'timeliness' (t_1, t_2, t_3) and 'agility' (A →B →C →D)*

We are currently conducting a series of studies to examine decision quality of operators controlling several Uninhabited Combat Air Vehicles (UCAVs) on a strike mission. Operators will be assisted by an automatic re-routing decision aid that will suggest a number of alternative routes; one of which will be the optimal route. Decision quality will be assessed in line with the methodologies outlined above.

CONCLUSION

We have argued that there is a need to assess the quality of the processes undertaken to reach a decision, in addition to assessing the 'correctness' of the decision itself. We have also outlined a number of methodologies that have potential utility for measuring four dimensions of decision quality (i.e. the decision substrate, decision consistency, and decision timeliness and agility). Research currently in progress seeks to validate these methodological approaches in the context of the control of UCAVs assisted by an automatic re-routing decision aid.

ACKNOWLEDGEMENTS

This research is funded by the UK Ministry of Defence Applied Research Programme. The authors would like to thank Mr. Robert Taylor (Dstl, U.K.), Squadron Leader Charles 'Chaz' Kennett (Royal Air Force, U.K.), and Tom Hope (QinetiQ, U.K.) for their support, and Professor Eric Farmer (QinetiQ, U.K.) for his review of an earlier version of the manuscript.

REFERENCES

Banbury, S., Selcon, S., Endsley, M., Gorton, T., & Tatlock, K. (1998). Being uncertain about uncertainty: How the representation of system reliability affects pilot decision-making. In Proceedings of the 42nd Annual Human Factors and Ergonomics Society Conference. Santa Monica, CA: HFES

Banbury, S., Hoermann, H. J., Soll, H., & Dudfield, H. J. (under review). FASA: Development and validation of a novel measure to assess the effectiveness of commercial airline pilot situation awareness training. Manuscript submitted to International Journal of Aviation Psychology.

Bolia, R. S., Nelson, W. T., Vidulich, M. A., & Taylor, R.M. (2004). From chess to Chancellorsville: Measuring decision quality in military commanders. In Proceedings of the 2nd Human Performance, Situation Awareness & Automation (HPSAA) conference, Daytona Beach, FL.

Boyd, J. R. (1987). A discourse on winning and losing. Unpublished set of briefing slides available at Air University Library, Maxwell AFB, Alabama, May 1987.

Endsley, M. R. (1995). Toward a theory of situation awareness in dynamic systems. Human Factors, 37, 32–64.

Ericsson, K. A., & Kintsch, W. (1995). Long-term working memory. Psychological Review, 102, 211–245.

Hoermann, H. J., Soll, H., Dudfield, H. J. & Banbury, S. (2003). ESSAI — Training of situation awareness and threat management techniques. Results of an evaluation study. In Proceedings of the 12th International Symposium on Aviation Psychology. Dayton, USA.

Kahneman, D., Slovic, P., & Tversky, A. (1982). Judgment under uncertainty: Heuristics and biases. Cambridge University Press: New York, USA.

Kobus, D. A., Proctor, S., & Holste, S. (2001). Effects of experience and uncertainty during dynamic decision-making. International Journal of Industrial Ergonomics, 28, 275–290.

Pleydell-Pearce, K., Dickson, B. T. & Whitecross S. (2000). Cognition monitor: A system for real time pilot state assessment. In P. T. McCabe, M. A Hanson and S. A Robertson (Eds.), Contemporary Ergonomics 2000. London: Taylor and Francis.

Shook, R. W., Bandiero, M., Coello, J. P., Endsley, M. R., & Garland, D. G. (2000). Situation awareness problems in general aviation. In Proceedings of the 44th Annual Meeting of the Human Factors and Ergonomics Society. Santa Monica, CA: HFES.

Zsambok, C. E. & Klein, G. (1997). Naturalistic decision-making. Mahwah, N.J.: Lawrence Erlbaum Associates.

CHARACTERIZING DECISION MAKING IN NETWORK-CENTRIC COMMAND AND CONTROL APPLICATIONS: IMPLICATIONS OF PSYCHOLOGICAL RESEARCH

W. Todd Nelson, Robert S. Bolia, Michael A. Vidulich
Air Force Research Laboratory

ABSTRACT

Due to the dynamic and time-critical nature of military command and control (C2) operations, commanders and other operators are often required to execute complex decision making under conditions of significant uncertainty, risk, and time pressure. One of the key challenges in developing and designing future C2 systems will be to effectively characterize decision making in these environments. The importance of this characterization is further underscored by rapid advances in technology and the shift towards ubiquitous computing and network-centric operations. The purpose of this paper is to review some of the major theoretical perspectives gleaned from the psychology of decision making and to identify key factors and dimensions that may prove useful in the development of decision support systems in future network-centric C2 applications.

Keywords: Decision Making; Command and Control; Network-Centric Warfare

INTRODUCTION

Command and Control (C2), Decision Making and Decision Quality

As defined by U.S. Air Force doctrine, command and control (C2) refers to:

> The exercise of authority and direction by a properly designated commander over assigned and attached forces in the accomplishment of the mission. Command and control functions are performed through an arrangement of personnel, equipment, communications, facilities, and procedures employed by a commander in planning, directing, coordinating, and controlling forces and operations in the accomplishment of the mission. (United States Air Force, Air Force Doctrine Document 1, 1997, p. 79-80)

Military commanders and operators make decisions at all levels of the C2 chain – strategic, operational, and tactical – and across a broad range of activities such as planning and organizing, surveillance, threat detection and identification, target prosecution, and threat response. These decision makers are required to make high-stake decisions under non-optimal conditions characterized by time stress, incomplete and/or inaccurate information, rapidly changing situations, and uncertainty. Some situations afford more analytical decisions strategies, while others require that decision be made in a rapid and automatic fashion. As pointed out by Bryant, Webb, & McCann (2003), the need for decision making research in military C2 is well recognized, especially given the ever-increasing complexity, tempo, and risk associated with modern warfare. Along these lines, understanding how commanders and operators make good decisions, recognizing what constitutes a good decision, and measuring decision effectiveness will be essential to future C2 operations, and may be relevant to the development of decision effectiveness training and the design, development, and utilization of effective decision support systems.

Implications of Network-Centric Warfare on Decision Making

In the future, C2 will undoubtedly be affected by the move toward network-centric warfare (NCW), a concept of operations that relies upon a sophisticated information technology infrastructure comprising sensor, information, and engagement grids, which will enable novel styles of warfare characterized by "speed of command" and "self synchronization" (Cebrowski & Garstka, 1998). As noted by several researchers (Forgues, 2001; Kruzins & Scholz, 2001; Toomey, 2003; Vidulich et al., in press), *speed of command* is achieved through heightened shared situational awareness (SA) and real-time collaboration, which is expected to dramatically improve the speed and quality of military decisions. The concept of *self-synchronization* is also related to shared SA, since it requires that the commander's intent be preserved through all levels of command. In theory, *self synchronization* should radically reduce, if not eliminate, traditional operational decision cycles and provide relief from the decision and execution bottlenecks that have historically been characteristic of centralized C2, thus denying the opponent operational pauses and *locking out* their options (Forgues, 2001; Potok, Phillips, Pollock, & Loebl, 2003).

These concepts have several implications for decision making in future C2 operations. First, as compared to top-down hierarchical command structures, decision making will likely become more decentralized (see Dekker, 2003 for review). Second, shared SA in conjunction with effective engagement grids will provide a profusion of time critical targeting opportunities, which will require rapid decision making. Third, operators at all levels will be provided with an unprecedented view of the battlespace, including the ability to drill-up and drill-down to levels of description that may be inappropriate. Accordingly, deciding upon the most appropriate level at which to visualize the battlespace will be a continual challenge. Finally, as noted by Bolia, Vidulich, Nelson, & Cook (in press), the application of technological innovation in the absence of suitable tactics and doctrine is not sufficient for producing shared battlespace awareness and effective decision making. Rather, as military history has demonstrated, technological innovations often lead to undesirable effects including accidents, fratricide, or defeat.

DECISION MAKING: Review of Psychological Research

Decision making has been traditionally characterized as the act of choosing between alternatives under conditions of uncertainty (O'Hare, 2003). It may involve making estimates of frequency, predictions about the future, and selecting among numerous alternatives. There is a sizeable psychological literature on decision making, dating back to the 1950s, which includes several major theoretical perspectives, as well as hundreds of empirical studies. Of particular relevance for those studying decision making are the review chapters provided in the *Annual Review of Psychology*. The inaugural review, titled *Behavior Decision Making Theory*, was authored by Ward Edwards in 1961, and has been followed by twelve subsequent chapters. In addition, several domain-specific reviews of decision making have appeared in recent years – for example, a special edition of *Human Factors* (1996), edited by Salas and Cannon-Bowers, as well as a review chapter on *Aeronautical Decision Making* by O'Hare (2003).

O'Hare's treatment of Aeronautical Decision Making is unique in that he employs metaphors to describe the "decision maker," – e.g., the *Faulty Computer*, the *Rational Calculator*, the *Adaptive Decision Maker*, the *Character Detective*, the *Enquiring Expert*, and the *Organization Cog*. This approach provides a convenient pedagogical clustering of several major theoretical perspectives. For example, the *Faulty Computer* refers to the influential work of Kahneman and Tversky (Kahneman, Slovic, & Tversky, 1982) involving the effects of heuristics and biases in decision making. This perspective contends that the decision maker's judgments are guided by a relatively small number of heuristics, or *rules of thumb*, rather than by reasoning with probabilities, as would be prescribed by normative theories. Some of the major heuristics identified by this line of research include: *representativeness* – the belief that outcomes or samples that look random are more likely than those that appear systematic; *availability* – the notion that frequency or probability of an outcome varies directly with how easy it is to retrieve an example from memory; and *anchoring and adjustment* – a strategy by which the decision maker approximates, and then adjusts, an estimate based on additional information. Research on heuristics and biases has also led to the identification of other attributes of decision makers – namely, that they exhibit *overconfidence* in their decisions and that they are susceptible to a phenomenon called *entrapment*, in which the decision makers increase their commitment to an earlier decision or course of action. While much of this research points to the shortcomings of heuristics reasoning, recent research has emphasized that it generally promotes quick and accurate decisions, a finding that is consistent with research on expert decision making in natural environments (Klein, 1998).

According to Bryant et al. (2003), the study of decision making in military C2 has been approached from two major theoretical perspectives – the analytic approach and the Naturalistic Decision Making or Intuitive approach. The former involves normative models that describe how decisions should be made and assume that good decision making results from a rational/analytic process rooted in probability and logic. In other words, the decision maker acts like a *Rational Calculator*. Central to this perspective is the assumption that the goal of the decision maker is to optimize his or her decision given a specified set of dimensions – for example, cost and benefits – and that an exhaustive analysis of alternatives must be constructed and evaluated. According to Bryant et al. (2003), shortcomings of this perspective in military C2 include incomplete or ambiguous information, inadequate time for analysis, limited human knowledge and processing capacity, and the inability to specify probabilities associated with outcomes. Consequently, the analytic approach is considered to be inadequate for describing decision making in many complex, real-world environments, which according to some researchers (Cannon-Bowers, Salas, & Pruitt, 1996) has led to a paradigm shift in decision making research.

Naturalistic Decision Making (NDM) theories attempt to describe human decision making in complex, real-world environments, characterized by "how experienced people, working as individuals or groups in dynamic, uncertain, often fast-paced environments, identify and assess their situation, make decisions and take actions whose consequences are meaningful to them and to the larger organization in which they operate" (p.5, Zsambok, 1997). NDM is based on three fundamental principles, which posit that expert decision makers rely on: 1) holistic evaluation rather than reductionistic comparisons; 2) recognition-based processes to prime situational templates; and 3) the satisficing criterion, which suggests that speed of decision is preferred over decision optimization. NDM research has shown that, when confronted with novel situations, novices tend to create lists of alternative solutions and analyze the cost and benefits of each solution before proceeding. Experts, on the other hand, recognize something in the situation (even novel situations) as Gestalt, and have an almost instinctive knowledge of the appropriate response.

IMPLICATIONS FOR FUTURE C2 OPERATIONS

Research on NDM has several implications for this problem domain. First, given that NCW will require decentralized decision making, it will be necessary to have expert decision makers at all levels of the command structure who are able to quickly recognize a situation and make a satisficing decision. The speed of decision cycles required by many NCW operations, such as time-critical targeting, will not tolerate novice decision-making strategies that rely on slower, more deliberate analytic comparisons of alternatives. Second, given that research into NDM and the Recognition-primed Decision Model has afforded new insights into the way experts make decisions, does it tell us anything about how we might train novices to make decisions more like experts? Some researchers have investigated this possibility by providing military officers with context-independent "cognitive skills training" or "critical thinking training," both of which were associated with improved decision-making performance (Cohen, Freeman, & Thompson, 1997). These researchers have also developed an approach to training based on NDM. Their methodology includes: (a) engaging in deliberate practice; (b) obtaining accurate and diagnostic feedback; (c) building mental models; (d) developing metacognitive skills; and (e) becoming more mindful of opportunities for learning. Third, research from NDM has implications for the design and implementation of decision support systems (DSS). As Morrison and his colleagues (1998) have noted, decision making in operational settings mostly relies on NDM strategies, such as feature matching, and to a less extent on story generation and explanation-based reasoning. In the case of expert tactical decision makers, they noted that DSS designed to support "quick look" decision processes are perceived as especially effective if they allow rapid recognition of data patterns and require minimal interaction to extract meaningful data. This conclusion suggests that user-centered design approaches will likely be required to adequately specify operators' unique information requirements and decision processes.

Research on heuristics and biases also has several implications for decision making in future C2 operations. Clearly, strategic and tactical situation displays should be designed to diminish the tendency of decision makers to misuse *representative* and *availability* heuristics. These interfaces should also be designed to protect users from the powerful effects of *anchoring* and *framing*. It may be most beneficial to apply this design strategy to intelligent agents and DSS, which would be tasked to monitor and alert the operator of potential violations. More sophisticated agents would be designed to collaborate with the decision maker, protecting them from constructing "faulty realities" (Perrow, 1984), which, if progress unchallenged, may lead to disastrous outcomes (see Burns, 2000 for detailed analysis). The interaction between situation awareness, technology, and C2 has also been addressed, for the air battle management domain, by Vidulich and his colleagues (in press).

Decision making strategies in future C2 environments will most likely span a continuum from the analytic to the intuitive. Effective decision making will require technologies that support detailed analytic assessment for military planning, as well as those that enable rapid, time-critical decisions typical of tactical situations (the *coup d'oeil* of Clausewitz (2002)). Along these lines, Bryant et al. (2000), have proposed a model that synthesizes these two seemingly disparate approaches, noting that complex problem domains, such a C2, require a broad range of decision making strategies ranging from the analytic (e.g., exhaustive, optimizing, and compensatory), to the intuitive (e.g., non-compensatory, satisficing, non-exhaustive, and qualitative).

REFERENCES

Bolia, R. S., Vidulich, M. A., Nelson, W. T., & Cook, M. J. (in press). A history lesson on the use of technology to support military decision making and command & control. In M. J. Cook (Ed.), Human factors of complex decision-making. Mahwah, NJ: Lawrence Erlbaum Associates, Inc.

Bryant, D. J., Web, D. G., & McCann, C. (2003). Synthesizing two approaches to decision making in command and control. Canadian Military Journal, Spring, 29-34.

Burns, K. (2000). Mental models and normal errors in naturalistic decision making. Proceedings of the 5th Conference on Naturalistic Decision Making (pp. 1-17). Tammsvik, Sweden.

Cannon-Bowers, D., Salas, E., & Pruitt, J. S. (1996). Establishing the boundaries of a paradigm for decision-making research. Human Factors, 38, 193-205.

Cebrowski, A. K., & Garstka, J. J. (1998). Network-centric warfare: Its origins and future. Naval Institute Proceedings, January, 28-35.

Clausewitz, C. von (2002). Vom kriege. Berlin: Ullstein.

Cohen, M. S., Freeman, J. T., & Thompson, B. B. (1997). Training the naturalistic decision maker. In C. E. Zsambok & G. Klein (Eds.), Naturalistic decision making (pp. 257-268). Mahwah, NJ: Lawrence Erlbaum Associates.

Dekker, A. H. (2003). Centralisation and decentralization in network centric warfare. Journal of Battlefield Technology, 6(2), 1-6.

Forgues, P. (2001). Command in a network-centric war. Canadian Military Journal, Summer, 23-30.

Kahneman, D., Slovic, P., & Tversky, A. (1982). Judgment under uncertainty: Heuristics and biases. New York: Cambridge University Press.

Klein, G. (1998). Sources of power. Cambridge, MA: The MIT Press.

Kruzins, E. & Scholz, J. (2001). Australian perspectives on network centric warfare: Pragmatic approaches with limited resources. Australian Defence Force Journal, 150, 19-33.

Morrison, J. G., Kelly, R. T., Moore, R. A., & Hutchins, S. G. (1998). Implications of decision making research for decision support and displays. In J. A. Cannon-Bowers & E. Salas (Eds.), Making decisions under stress: Implications for individual and team training (pp. 375-406). Washington, DC: APA.

O'Hare, D. (2003). Aeronautical decision making: Metaphors, models, and methods. In P. S. Tsang & M. A. Vidulich (Eds.), Principles and practice of aviation psychology (pp. 201-237). Mahwah, NJ: Erlbaum.

Perrow, C. (1984). Normal accidents: Living with high-risk technologies. New York, NY: Basic Books.

Potok, T., Phillips, L., Pollock, R., & Loebl, A. (2003). Suitability of agent technology for military command and control in the future combat system environment. Proceedings of the 8th International Command and Control Research and Technology Symposium (pp. 1-22). Washington, DC: National Defense University.

Toomey, C. J. (2003). Army digitization: Making it ready for prime time. Parameters, Winter, 40-53.

United States Air Force (1997), Air Force Basic Doctrine: Air Force Doctrine Document 1, Headquarters Air Force Doctrine Center, Maxwell Air Force Base, Alabama.

Vidulich, M. A., Bolia, R. S., & Nelson, W. T. (in press). Technology, organization, and collaborative situation awareness in air battle management: Historical and theoretical perspectives. In S. Banbury (Ed.), A Cognitive Approach to Situation Awareness: Theory, Measures and Application. Aldershot, UK: Ashgate Publishing Ltd.

Zsambok, C. E. (1997). Naturalistic decision making: Where are we now? In C. E. Zsambok and G. Klein (Eds.), Naturalistic Decision Making (pp. 5). Mahwah, NJ: Lawrence Erlbaum Associates.

THE INVESTIGATION OF DECISION ERRORS IN AVIATION MISHAPS BY APPLYING THE HUMAN FACTORS ANALYSIS AND CLASSIFICATION SYSTEM (HFACS)

Wen-Chin Li[1], Tony Head[2], Fuh-Eau Wu[3], Szu-Yi Chen[4], & Chung-San Yu[5]
Cranfield University, Bedfordshire, U.K.[1], Cranfield University, Bedfordshire, U.K.[2],
Cheng-Shiu Institute of Technology, Kaohsiung, R.O.C.[3], Fooying University, Kaohsiung, R.O.C.[4],
Air Force Academy, Kaohsiung, R.O.C.[5]

ABSTRACT

The ability to make timely appropriate and effective decisions is an essential competence required of all fighter pilots, but until recently the training of decision-making remained unstructured and the quality of aeronautical decision-making (ADM) has been viewed as a by-product of flying experience in military aviation. This investigation applies the Human Factor Analysis and Classification System (HFACS) (Wiegmann & Shappell, 1997) and focuses only on those factors associated with decision errors. HFACS categorizes human error at four levels including (1) unsafe acts of operators, (2) preconditions for unsafe acts, (3) unsafe supervision, (4) organizational influences. The purpose of this study was to identify the role of decision errors in aviation mishaps in the R.O.C. Air Force. There were 1714 human causal factors associated with 519 aircrew-related accidents between 1978 and 2002. The overall analyses found that decision errors were implicated in 217 of the 519 (43%) accidents. The results indicate that 'inadequate supervision' was a key element of accidents which involved human error. 'Inadequate supervision' has significant association with the upper level of 'organizational influences' and the lower level of 'preconditions for unsafe acts' which have a significant association with 'decision errors'. In addition, the study findings highlighted critical safety issues in need of further research for developing the training of aeronautical decision-making in military operations.

Key Words: Aeronautical Decision-making (ADM), Accident Investigation, Human Errors, Human Factors Analysis and Classification System (HFACS)

INTRODUCTION

Flying a high-tech fighter with high stakes and under high G-force is not simply an issue of skilled psychomotor performance but is one of flight management and real-time decision-making. The pilots, in addition to carrying out routine tasks and making decisions, have to solve non-routine and ill-defined problems with only partial information available. Decision-making under such circumstances is therefore a complex task which involves situation assessment, choice amongst alternatives and risk assessment (Orasanu, 2001a). In many situations, information can be conflicting or have competing goals (e.g., trade-off between safety and mission success) that may be the result of personal biases or organisational values. Furthermore, in military aviation, a decision is often the pre-cursor to another decision or series of complicated decisions in order to achieve mission success.

In dynamic situations, the decision process of a pilot is confined by limited attention and working memory capacity. Direct attention is needed for recognizing and processing the flying environment to form decisions, selecting actions and making responses. Pilots are required to make rapid decisions that may result in incidents or accidents. An investigation of accidents for the last ten years (1993-2003) indicated that human factors were involved in 58% of all accidents in the ROC Air Force (western literature reviews report 65% to 85%, Hunter & Baker, 2000). Errors of judgment and poor aeronautical decision-making (ADM) were commonly reported. Concerning the nature of the military mission, pilots must perform a wide range of tasks in addition to flying the aircraft from one point to another point safely. A pilot's primary task is to deliver weapons, troops or equipment, and flying frequently becomes a secondary task. The military pilot must learn to make decisions related to mission performance as well as those decisions related to operate complex systems of the aircraft. There is a need for aeronautical decision-making to be trained more directly and incorporated into the tactical training programs in order to improve military aviation safety. However, there is no research on the contents of decision errors and the role of decision errors associated with accidents in the R.O.C. Air Force so far.

Literature Review

Aviation environments are complex and different factors such as problem types, aircraft types, flight phases, mission of operations, available time and resources, or involved risk may influence aeronautical decision-making. Aeronautical knowledge, skill, and judgment have always been regarded as the three basic qualities that pilots must possess (Diehl, 1991). The requisite knowledge and skills of flying have been taught in academic and line flight training and have subsequently been evaluated during pilot qualification. In contrast, ADM has usually been treated to be a gift that good pilots innately possess or an ability that is accumulated as a by-product of flying hours.

Decision-making in Aviation Operations

In military aviation, it may be a dynamic risky environment, however, pilots play the role as risk takers whose primary task is to minimize the risk by their skill and decision-making to perform the military missions safely. However, in 1977, Jensen reported that "51% of fatal general aviation accidents from 1970 through 1974 were associated with decisional errors". More recent studies (Jensen, 1997; Orasanu et al., 2001b) have also found that 'decision errors' is the major factor in aviation accidents. Orasanu and Fisher (1997) found that high performance pilots demonstrated greater situation awareness and the key cues for pilots' decision-making are time and risk. Cohen (1993) suggested that a decision bias is not a lack of knowledge or an inappropriate goal, but a systematic flaw in the internal relationship among a person's judgments and choices.

Pilots make important decisions frequently and these decisions may have a serious consequence. Some decisions are made with ambiguous information, under great risk, and with very limited time. Drillings & Serfaty (1997) suggested that naturalistic decision-making (NDM) has provided an alternative approach for understanding how pilots make decisions and for designing training interventions that will help pilots making decisions under uncertain, high pressure, high stakes, and in time-limited situations, compared with the research of classic decision-making. Kaempf & Orasanu (1997) advised that a critical component of pilot proficiency is the ability to make good decisions. However, Zakay (1993) found that practice on simulator, without time pressure, did not enhance pilot decision-making under time-limited situations. The authors pointed out that if decision-making is likely to be required under time pressure or other stressful conditions, training should also include task performance under those conditions. Orasanu and Connolly (1993) indicated that much errors of decision-making occur in an organizational context, and that the organization influences decisions both directly, by forming standard operating procedures and indirectly, by the organizational culture.

Human Factors Analysis and Classification System (HFACS)

The HFACS is a framework originally developed by Wiegmann & Shappell (1997) for the U.S. military aviation as a tool of investigating and analysing the human factors of accidents. Based upon Reason's (1990) model of latent and active failures, HFACS categorizes human error at four levels including: (1) 'unsafe acts of operators' (aircrew), (2) 'preconditions for unsafe acts', (3) 'unsafe supervision' and (4) 'organisational influences', with each one affecting the next lower level. Shappell and Wiegmann (2001a) reported that many accidents have roots of failure within the organisation, and it is the decisions made by those at the top levels that often affected middle levels of managers and supervisors to provide proper supervision to the operators. However, it is the frontline of operators who inherit all of the blame if accidents or incidents happen. Reason's (reference & year) model revolutionized the way that researchers viewed the human causes of accidents but, according to Shappell & Wiegmann (2001b), it did not provide the level of detail to apply the model in the aviation domain.

The HFACS framework bridges the gap between theory and practice by providing not only a theoretical tool for identifying and classifying the human causes of aviation accidents, but also practically applying it in the real world. To date, HFACS has been proved to be useful as both a data analysis framework and an accident investigation tool for military and civil aviation (Wiegmann & Shappell, 2003).

METHOD

<u>Data</u>: The data of military aviation accidents were obtained from R.O.C. Air Force between 1978 and 2002, and a total of 519 accidents happened within those 24 years. Each accident was examined to determine the extent to which HFACS causal categories contributed to the accident.

<u>Classification Framework</u>: The HFACS framework describes 18 causal categories within Reason's four levels of human failures (Shappell & Wiegmann, 1997). The first level of HFACS describes those unsafe acts of operators that can lead to an accident. The unsafe acts of operators include (1) 'decision errors', (2) 'skill-based errors', (3) 'perceptual errors' and (4) 'violations'. The second level of HFACS is preconditions of unsafe acts including (5) 'physical environment', (6) 'technological environment', (7) 'adverse mental states', (8) 'adverse physiological states', (9) 'physical/mental limitations', (10) 'crew resource management', and (11) 'personal readiness'. The third level of HFACS is unsafe supervision including (12) 'inadequate supervision', (13) 'planned inappropriate operation', (14) 'failure to correct problem', and (15) 'supervisory violation'. The fourth level of HFACS is organizational influences including (16) 'resource management', (17) 'organizational climate', and (18) 'organizational process' (Wiegmann & Shappell, 2003). Each of these 519 accidents was coded by a team consisting of two pilots and an aviation psychologist using the HFACS framework. To avoid over-representation by any single accident, each causal category was counted a maximum of one time per accident. In this way, the count acted as an indicator of presence or absence at each of 18 categories for a given accident.

<u>Statistical analysis</u>: This research applied Chi-square (χ) tests to measure the association between two nominal variables and providing empirical evidence for the theoretical models of HFACS. For further examination of proportional reduction in error (PRE), Lambda (λ) was applied to provide an estimate of the strength of association between two categorical variables, where one was the independent variable (IV) and the other the dependant variable (DV).

RESULTS

There are 1714 (100%) of human causal factors associated with 519 aircrew-related accidents that were accommodated using the HFACS. The overall analyses found that decision errors had been involved in 217 (43%) accidents.

The Association between Level-4 and Level-3

By applying Pearson's Chi-square to measure the association between Level-4 ('resource management', 'organizational climate', and 'organizational process') and Level-3 ('inadequate supervision', 'planned inappropriate operations', 'failed to correct a known problem', and 'supervisory violations') found that there were significant associations between 'resource management' and 'inadequate supervision' (χ^2=11.944, df=1, p<.001), 'organizational climate' and 'inadequate supervision' (χ^2=7.603, df=1, p<.006), 'organizational climate' and 'failed to correct problem' (χ^2=39.420, df=1, p<.000), 'organizational process' and 'inadequate supervision' (χ^2=7.603, df=1, p<.006), 'organizational process' and 'planned inappropriate operations' (χ^2=13.963, df=1, p<.000), 'organizational process' and 'failed to correct known problem' (χ^2=39.420, df=1, p<.000). There are two special associations of 'organizational climate' and 'supervisory violation' (χ^2=60.621, df=1, p<.000) as well as 'organizational process' and 'supervisory violation' (χ^2=45.885, df=1, p<.000) that have no association to level-2. However, further examination by applying Lambda to check the directional strength of association found that there were two significant associations between level-4 and level-3, including 'organizational climate' and 'inadequate supervision' (λ= .023, p<.014) as well as 'organizational process' and 'inadequate supervision' (λ= .286, p<.000).

The Association between Level-3 and Level-2

The results of the chi-square analysis demonstrated a significant association between Level-3 and Level-2 factors ('adverse mental states', 'adverse physiological states', 'physical/mental limitations', 'crew resource management', 'personal readiness', 'physical environment', and 'technology environment') namely 'inadequate supervision' and 'adverse mental states' (χ^2=29.089, df=1, p<.000), 'inadequate supervision' and 'physical/mental limitations' (χ^2=8.733, df=1, p<.003), 'inadequate supervision' and 'crew resource management' (χ^2=147.157, df=1, p<.000), 'inadequate supervision' and 'personal readiness' (χ^2=10.212, df=1, p<.001), 'planned inappropriate operations' and 'adverse mental states' (χ^2=5.655, df=1, p<.017), 'planned inappropriate operations' and 'crew resource management' (χ^2=11.184, df=1, p<.001), 'failed to correct a known problem' and 'adverse mental states' (χ^2=6.808, df=1, p<.009). There was a special association of 'inadequate supervision' and 'physical environment' (χ^2=4.769, df=1, p< .000) that has no association to 'decision errors'. However, further examination by applying Lambda to check the directional strength of association found that there was a significant association between the level-3 and level-2 factors 'inadequate supervision' and 'crew resource management' (λ= .287, p<.002).

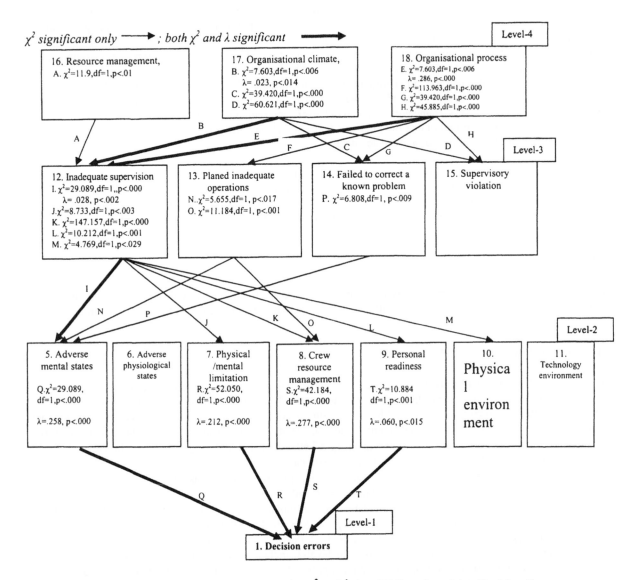

Figure-1: The Significant of Association for χ^2 and λ (p<.05) from Level-4 to Decision Errors
The Association between Level-2 and Decision Errors

The chi square analysis showed a significant association between Level-2 and 'decision errors' and included 'adverse mental states' and 'decision errors (χ^2=58.219, df=1, p<.000), 'physical/mental limitations' and 'decision errors' (χ^2=52.050, df=1, p<.000), 'crew resource management' and 'decision errors' (χ^2=42.184, df=1, p<.000), 'personal readiness' and 'decision errors' (χ^2 =10.884, df=1, p<.000). However, further examination by applying

Lambda to check the directional strength of association found that all of these four had significant associations between level-2 and level-1 which were 'adverse mental states' and 'decision errors' ($\lambda = .258$, p<.000), 'physical/mental limitations' and 'decision errors' ($\lambda = .212$, p<.000), 'crew resource management' and 'decision errors' ($\lambda = .277$, p<.000), and 'personal readiness' and 'decision errors' ($\lambda = .060$, p<.015).

DISCUSSION

This investigation focused on the role of decision errors in military aviation only. Decision errors involved 217 (43%) in 519 accidents within 24 years. The figure-1 shows that variables from level-4 to level-1 (Decision Errors) have significant association.

The Strength of Association between Organizational Influence and Unsafe Supervision

This investigation revealed that 'organizational climate' including aviation organizational structure, policies and culture as well as 'organizational process' including operational tempo, incentives, SOPs and safety program, can cause 'inadequate supervision' When 'organizational climate' and 'organizational process' are the independent variables (IV) and 'inadequate supervision' is the dependent variable (DV), the proportional reduction in error (PRE) was 2.3% (p<.014) and 28.6% (p<.000). For example, if commanding level do not discipline the chain-of-command, follow SOPs and train subordinates to cope with time pressure, the result will be the problems of a high probability of 'inadequate supervision' involved in accidents such as 'failed to provide guidance and training' for pilots to perform their tasks, and 'failed to track performance and qualifications' of pilots. Thus the organisation can have a strong influence upon the behaviour of its members.

The Strength of Association between Unsafe Supervision and Preconditions for Unsafe Acts

There was a strong association between 'inadequate supervision' and 'adverse mental states'. When 'inadequate supervision' was the IV and 'adverse mental states' is the DV, the proportional reduction in error (PRE) was 2.8% (p<.002). The explanation may be that if the supervisory officer failed to provide a reasonable schedule of missions for pilots having appropriate rest, or 'failed to track qualifications and performance' of pilots, then it has a high probability to cause accidents related to 'adverse mental states' such as loss of situation awareness, over-attention, distraction, or fatigue.

The Strength of Association between Preconditions for Unsafe Acts and Decision Errors

There were strong associations between 'adverse mental states', 'physical/mental limitation', 'crew resource management', 'personal readiness' and 'decision errors'. When those four factors were the IVs and 'decision errors' was the DV, the (PRE) was 25.8% (p<.000), 21.2% (p<.000), 27.7% (p<.000), and 6.0% (p<.015). The explanation could be that if loss of situation awareness, fatigue, over-workload, poor CRM, inappropriate operations, and burnout for holidays, then there is high probability that this will lead to accidents associated with 'decision errors' such as poor decisions, misdiagnosed emergencies, or inappropriate manoeuvres.

CONCLUSION

Individual factors such as workload, stress, situation awareness, attention, pressure, sensory limitations, age, g-force, oxygen deprivation, temperature, and many other factors all influence a pilot's performance. Social factors including crew communication, supervisory influences, and organisational culture also have an effect. This investigation has demonstrated that the HFACS framework originally developed for U.S.A. military aviation use, also can be used to identify the human factors issues associated with decision errors in the R.O.C. Air Force. Furthermore, the results of this study highlight the critical areas of human factors and decision error as a topic for further research. It is not surprising that 'decision errors' are associated with a large percentage of aircrew-related accidents. What is surprising is that accidents associated with 'decision errors' had a significant association with 'crew resource management' (level-2), 'inadequate supervision' (level-3), and 'organizational climate' and 'organizational process' (level-4). Especially, the factor of 'inadequate supervision', not only has significant association with upper level factors of 'organizational climate' and 'organizational process', but also has a significant relationship with lower level factors of 'adverse mental states', 'physical/mental limitation', 'crew resource management', and 'personal readiness', and all four factors have significant association with 'decision errors'. Therefore, fallible decisions of upper-level command can directly affect the middle level of supervisory practices, as well as creating 'preconditions for unsafe acts' and impaired performance of pilots, leading to 'decision errors'. Unfortunately, these 'organizational influences' often go unnoticed by accident investigators. Recently, aviation psychologists have investigated aeronautical decision-making, and the results suggested that ADM could be improved with training (Klein, 2000; Jensen et al., 2002). Therefore, the further research on decision-making in aviation needs to be focused on the links between different levels from organisational factors right down to individual operators. To improve aviation safety, the training program of decision-making for pilots needs to be developed to include not only the individual performance of pilots, but to aviation management to reduce the adverse effects of 'organizational influences'.

ACKNOWLEDGMENTS

This study was supported by Cranfield University for the presentation of this paper. We thank all colleagues and pilots who participated and contributed their expertise and knowledge to help this research.

REFERENCES

Cohen, M.S. (1993), 'Three Paradigm for Viewing Decision Biases', in Klein, G.A., Orasanu, J., Calderwood, R., and Zsambok, C.E. (Editor), Decision Making in Action: Models and Methods, Ablex, Norwood, New Jersey, pp. 36-50.

Diehl, A. (1989), 'Human Performance/System Safety Issues in Aircraft Accident Investigation and Prevention', in Jensen, R.S. (Editor), Fifth International Symposium on Aviation Psychology, Vol. 2, Columbus, Ohio, The Ohio State University, pp. 838-847.

Diehl, A. (1991), 'The Effectiveness of Training Programs for Preventing Aircrew Error ', in Jensen, R.S. (Editor), Sixth International Symposium on Aviation Psychology, Vol. 2, Columbus, Ohio, U.S.A., The Ohio State.

Dorneich, M.C., Whitlow, S.D., Miller, C.A., and Allen, J.A. (2001), ' Policy as an Interaction Method for Decision Support System', Proceedings of the Human Factors and Ergonomics Society 45th Annual Meeting, Vol. 1, Upper Midwest Chapter, Minneapolis/St. Paul, Minnesota, Human Factors and Ergonomics Society, Santa Monica, USA, pp. 326-30.

Drillings, M. and Serfaty, D. (1997), 'Naturalistic Decision Making in Command and Control', in Zsambok, C.E. and Klein, G. (Editor), Naturalistic Decision Making, Lawrence Erlbaum, Mahwah, pp. 71-80.

Hunter, D.R. and Baker, R.M. (2000), 'Reducing Accidents among General Aviation Pilots through a National Aviation Safety Program', in Hayward, B.J. and Lowe, A.R. (Editor), The Fourth Australian Aviation Psychology Symposium, Vol. 1, Ashgate, Aldershot, England,

Jensen, R.S. (1997), ' The Boundaries of Aviation Psychology, Human Factors, Aeronautical Decision Making, Situation Awareness, and Crew Resource Management', The International Journal of Aviation Psychology, Vol. 7, No. 4, pp. 259-268.

Jensen, R. and Hunter, D. (2002), General Aviation Aeronautical Decision-making, FAA, Washington, D.C.

Kaempf, G.L. and Orasanu, J. (1997), 'Current and Future Applications of Naturalistic Decision Making', in Zsambok, C.E. and Klein, G. (Editor), Naturalistic Decision Making, Lawrence Erlbaum, Mahwah, pp. 81-90.

Klein, G. (2000), 'Analysis of Situation Awareness from Critical Incident Reports', in Endsley, M.R. and Garland, D.J. (Editor), Situation Awareness Analysis and Measurement, Lawrence Erlbaum , London, pp. 51-71.

Li, W.C., Head, T., Wu, F.E., and Yu, C.S. (2003), 'The Investigation of Aeronautical Decision-making in Tactical Flight Training', in Jensen, R.S. (Editor), Twelfth International Symposium on Aviation Psychology, Dayton, Ohio, The Ohio State University, pp. 706-712.

Orasanu, J. and Connolly, T. (1993), 'The Reinvention of Decision Making', in Klein, G.A. , Orasanu, J., Calderwood, R., and Zsambok, C.E. (Editor), Decision Making in Action: Models and Methods, Ablex, Norwood, New Jersey, pp. 3-20.

Orasanu, J., Davison, J., Fischer, U., Cohen, M.S., Ciavarelli, A., and Slovic, P. (2001a), 'The Many Faces of Risk in Aviation Decision Making', Proceedings of the Human Factors and Ergonomics Society 45th Annual Meeting, Vol. 1, Upper Midwest Chapter, Minneapolis/St. Paul, Minnesota, Human Factors and

Ergonomics Society, Santa Monica, USA, pp. 307-310.

Orasanu, J., Davison, J., and Fischer, U. (2001b), 'The Role of Risk in Aviation Decision Making: How Pilots Perceive and Manage Flight Risks', Proceedings of the Human Factors and Ergonomics Society 45th Annual Meeting, Vol. 1, Upper Midwest Chapter, Minneapolis/St. Paul, Minnesota, Human Factors and Ergonomics Society, Santa Monica, USA, pp. 58-62.

Reason, J. (1990), Human Error, Cambridge University, New York.

Shappell, S.A. and Wiegmann, D.A. (2001a), 'Applying Reason: the human factors analysis and classification system (HFACS)', Human Factors and Aerospace Safety, Vol. 1, No. 1, pp. 59-86.

Shappell, S.A and Wiegman, D.A.. (2001b) 'Human Error Analysis of Commerical Aviation Accidents: Application of the Human Factors Analysis and Classification System', Aviation, Space, and Environmental Medicine, Vol. 72, No. 11, pp. 1006-1016.

Wiegmann, D.A. and Shappell, S.A. (1997) 'Human Factors Analysis of Postaccident Data: Applying Theoretical Taxonomies of Human Error', The International Journal of Aviation Psychology, Vol. 7, No. 1, pp. 67-81.

Wiegmann, D.A. and Shappell, S.A. (2001), 'Applying the Human Factors Analysis and Classification System to the Analysis of Commerical Aviation Accident Data', in Jensen, R.S. (Editor), Eleventh International Symposium on Aviation Psychology, Columbus, Ohio, The Ohio State University,

Wiegmann, D.A. and Shappell, S.A. (2003), A Human Error Approach to Aviation Accident Analysis: The Human Factors Analysis and Classification System, Ashgate, Aldershot, England.

Zakay, D. (1993), 'The Impact of Time Perception Processes on Decision Making under Time Stress', in Svenson, O. and Maule, A.J. (Editor), Time Pressure and Stress in Human Judgment and Decision Making, Plenum, New York, pp. 59-72.

DECISION SUPPORT FOR DECISION SUPERIORITY: CONTROL STRATEGIES FOR MULTIPLE UAVS

Thomas Hope, Richard Marston, Dale Richards
QinetiQ Ltd., UK

ABSTRACT.

We describe a problem that UAV operators of the future will face when responsible for groups of UAVs. To use the UAVs effectively, the operator must define missions which share targets effectively among available assets, as well as specifying the associated route plans – a difficult task even when the groups are comparatively small. We propose a solution in the form of a Decision Support System, which derives candidate solutions automatically and presents a ranked list for the mission manager to accept, reject, or augment as s/he sees fit. An initial version of the system will implement some simple methods for deriving the list of candidate solutions, which will support an experiment to gauge the effect on operator performance as well as providing the basis for future extensions.

Keywords: Decision Support, Situation Awareness, Automation, Task Allocation, Command & Control, UAV, Cooperative, Group Behaviour

INTRODUCTION

We are drowning in information but starved for knowledge

- John Naisbitt [1] -

The Information Age is upon us. Rapid advances in the tools and techniques of information technology have already changed the way that military forces (and their enemies) operate, and the pace of change will continue to grow. Just as the benefits of this change are increasingly evident, so too are the potential costs; more than ever before, we risk undermining our military forces by drowning them in information.

Unmanned Aerial Vehicles (UAVs) are at the sharp end of this dilemma. Advances in the technology that underpins UAV autonomy promise to reverse the current ratio (one to many) of UAVs to their human operators. This step, which recasts the role of the human operator as a mission manager with responsibility for a group of UAVs, is attractive because it realises the well recognised aspiration that UAVs should be the 'force multipliers' of the modern military [2]. Yet the opportunity also presents some significant challenges, because it defines a new and demanding role for the operators who manage these groups.

In some respects, this vision of the role of future UAV mission managers is analogous to the role currently played by the Forward Air Commander (FAC), who assigns new targets to teams of manned aircraft. But UAVs will not play exactly the same role as their manned equivalents, and the mission manager must take on some of the work traditionally performed by aircrew. In practice, this means taking on extra work and raises a very real risk of information overload. To manage this risk, we have begun to develop a real time Decision Support System (DSS), to assist the human operator in managing groups of UAVs.

Initial Problem Formulation

The current work addresses the way in which new tasks are allocated to particular UAVs. The mission manager (a human operator) is responsible for multiple aerial assets, which loiter over a hostile environment. Any or all of the UAVs might be tasked at any one time. As new targets appear in the Area of Interest, the mission manager must augment the current tasking, assigning a UAV to observe / engage it. In this context, a Composite Mission Plan (CMP) defines missions for some or all of the UAVs under the mission manager's control. Each mission defines an ordered list of targets that a particular UAV will observe / engage, as well as an appropriate route. Targets are assumed to be time-sensitive, so good CMPs make best use of the UAVs to engage as many of the targets as possible, as quickly as possible.

To support the way that operators augment a CMP to take account of new targets, we propose a DSS that offers some 'first cut' candidate solutions for the user to accept, reject or augment as they see fit. The quality of the support will consequently depend on the quality of these candidate solutions. Our goal is to design a DSS which identifies candidates and ranks them so that those near the top of the list are as close as possible to the solutions that an operator might prefer.

A Unified Approach

If our operator had access to manned aircraft, it would be appropriate to divide the responsibility for responding to new targets; as each new target appeared, the operator could make a broad assessment of the most suitable team to engage it, but leave the more detailed aspects of route planning to the aircrew themselves. With UAVs, the operator must solve both problems together.

Despite adding to the mission manager's workload, the unification of task allocation and more detailed mission planning is nevertheless an opportunity to make better task allocation decisions. When time is of the essence, the task should be given to the asset which can <u>reach the target</u> most quickly. This may not be the same as choosing the asset that is closest to the new target, since airspace restrictions or other threats might obstruct its path. It makes sense to inform the task allocation decision with knowledge of available routes.

Route planning is a core activity of the military mission planning community, but still adds a lot to the complexity of the task allocation problem. Electronic Mission Planning Systems (MPS) are an increasingly key component of mission planning processes throughout the modern military force, and an established source of decision support. Users expect these systems to automate many of the more mundane aspects of the process, like fuel-use calculations. More recent techniques offer the option of automatic route generation. Techniques like this, which support the rapid definition of candidate route plans, play a critical role in the way our system works.

Decisions in Context

A CMP is fundamentally a collection of routes, so is only as good as the routes that compose it. Typically, automatic route generation algorithms are pitched along the same lines as the DSS that this paper describes; they offer 'first cut' solutions for the human operator to amend. In our work, this input is not available until complete CMPs have been identified and ranked. CMPs must be constructed directly from the results of routing algorithms, so the quality of the ranked list that our system can define will depend on the quality of the automatically generated routes. Special attention must therefore be paid to ensure that the generated routes are as close as possible to those that a human expert might create. The problem is that different routes might be appropriate in different circumstances, depending on the tactical or even the strategic context; in some cases, the mission manager may be prepared to sacrifice a UAV to engage a target, while in others, the priority is reversed.

Our response to this issue has been to design a system which allows the mission manager to set high-level 'preferences', which constrain the kinds of routes that are likely to be generated. The system defines its 'decision context' in terms of two concepts – 'Effectiveness' and 'Survivability' – either of which may be emphasised at the expense of the other. A preference for Effectiveness implies a willingness to sacrifice assets if doing so might minimise the time to engage / observe targets, while an emphasis on Survivability implies that UAVs should not be risked if possible.

Multiple UAVs and Multiple Targets

A general formulation of our problem places the operator in charge of K UAVs, which must engage N targets. For the moment, we will assume that all targets are static, with known location and have equal priority, so that the goal is to minimise the time required to engage all targets.

Where $K = 1$, the best route plan takes the UAV on the shortest 'tour' of every target (a tour is a route that visits every target once) – an example of the ubiquitous 'Travelling Salesperson Problem' (TSP – see e.g. [3] for a definition). TSPs are 'NP-hard', which for our purposes means that algorithms which guarantee an optimal solution (a shortest tour) will tend to get very slow as the number of targets increases. A general definition of the characteristics of NP-hard problems can be found in [4].

When $K > 1$, the operator must decide how best to share the targets among the available UAVs, calculating the shortest, <u>cooperative</u> tour of the targets. This is akin to the 'Multiple Travelling Salesperson Problem' (MTSP), which is often explored in the context of logistics planning (e.g. [5]). That problem assumes that every 'salesperson' (UAV) starts at the same location. In our work, we want to allow our UAVs to be <u>distributed</u> around the area of interest, so our 'salespeople' must start at <u>different</u> locations. This extension might be called a 'Multiple Source Multiple Travelling Saleperson Problem' (MSMTSP).

For small **K** and small **N** (few UAVs and few targets), human operators might well be able to allocate their UAVs effectively. However, when either quantity increases the problem gets very difficult very quickly, because even small increases engender very large increases in the number of tasking options that might need to be considered. To express this relationship more formally, one first needs to count the number of ways of sharing **N** targets among **K** UAVs. A standard result in combinatorics (see e.g. [6]) tells us that this can be expressed as:

$$^{(N+K-1)}C_{(K-1)} = \frac{(N+K-1)!}{N! \cdot (K-1)!}$$

Then, since there are **N**! ways of ordering the targets within each 'target sharing combination', the final expression is:

$$\frac{N! \cdot (N+K-1)!}{N! \cdot (K-1)!} = \frac{(N+K-1)!}{(K-1)!}$$

In other words, when we have two UAVs and must engage three targets, there are 24 tasking options to consider; with four UAVs and five targets, there are 6,720 options. For five UAVs and ten targets, over 3 billion tasking options are available. The formal description also implies that the number of available tasking options is more sensitive to the number of active targets than it is to the number of available UAVs.

Many (perhaps most) of these options might be assumed away using heuristics. An example is the assumption that each new target will only demand changes to the mission plan of a single UAV; this might work in many cases, but may also be restrictive. In some circumstances, it may be desirable to respond to the appearance of a new target by sending a UAV which is already tasked – perhaps because it is already close to the new target. This choice will increase the time required to engage the UAV's other assigned targets, so it might also be sensible to re-assign those other targets to different UAVs. These and other 'cascade effects' will be missed if we restrict ourselves with the heuristic.

Implications

Remember that each CMP defines routes that take the UAVs to every current target, so it might be quite a challenge to define even a single CMP if time is limited, let alone the best one. In this context, the 'best' solution is a CMP which minimises the time to engage / observe all active targets. The implication is that an operator will struggle to make the best task allocation decisions, even when responsible for comparatively small groups. Some sort of decision support is clearly called for, to support the operator's role. As stated previously, our proposed solution is to design a system that derives a ranked list of possible CMPs, which the operator can accept, reject, or augment as they see fit. To meet this requirement, our system must derive candidate CMPs automatically and search the space of possible CMPs (the 'solution space') for the best candidates.

As indicated in the preceding section, the solution space will often be vast. Therefore, it will not normally be possible to search the space exhaustively. Further, it will be difficult to find search strategies that guarantee an optimal solution but still produce their result quickly. Remember that in practice, the goal is not to solve the problem but to support the operator. Our thesis is that this can be achieved with an approach that finds 'good', even if not optimal, candidate CMPs within the required time.

The MSMTSP has received little specific attention in the literature, but the related MTSP is rather more popular. For MTSPs and their more complex variants (of which the current problem is an example), many published approaches utilise some form of Genetic Algorithm (GA) to search the space of possible solutions (e.g. [7][8]) and our initial efforts follow that trend. There are few accepted principles for GA design [9], so our intention is to implement a variety of specific approaches, then select the best by means of empirical comparison.

Initially, we have focused on implementing the search as a simple 'Hill Climbing' algorithm. At each iteration, a small, random change is made to a current solution (the parent) to generate a new solution (the child). If the child is at least as good a solution as its parent, it survives to replace that parent. Then the process repeats. In the current context, a 'small, random change' implies a change to the way in which targets are shared between UAVs, or the order in which a particular UAV will visit its assigned targets.

Of course, it will be important to implement other approaches as well. Though clearly impractical as a real-time offering, a truly exhaustive search will guarantee an optimal solution; this will be a useful benchmark for the initial, empirical investigation of more pragmatic approaches. Similarly, we have implemented an exhaustive search that follows the heuristic mentioned in the previous section – shrinking the search space by ignoring cascade effects. It remains to be seen whether this heuristic's theoretical weaknesses will have a corresponding practical impact on the operator's performance.

Next Steps

This is a comparatively new project and there is still a lot to do. In the short term, we will run an initial experiment to assess the impact of our DSS on the way that human operators manage multiple UAVs to observe / engage static, ground-based targets with known location. The experiment will place its participants in control of a small group of simulated UAVs and deploy bespoke metrics to assess their 'decision effectiveness', given a variety of levels of decision support. As much as anything else, the experiment is useful as a catalyst for ongoing research into appropriate metrics for quantifying the benefit offered by DSS in general. A number of metrics are currently employed in the measurement of the cognitive attributes of performance, tracking both physiological and subjective correlates. The results will apply and support that research as well as provide the data that we need to inform extensions of our own DSS. Further analysis of the results may also reveal any consistent strategies (such as the heuristic described in section 5) employed by the participant when faced with decisions of this sort.

In the medium term, it will be important to extend the DSS to explore more operationally realistic scenarios. Firstly, it will be desirable to augment the system to cater for targets of non-uniform priority. It is pragmatic to assume that targets are static and have known location in the current work, but future versions of the system must certainly explore scenarios with mobile targets and targets of uncertain location. Other work at QinetiQ (e.g. [10]) will inform this extension. It will also be important to consider dynamic aspects of the environment, which might demand some change to the current CMP; examples are the inclusion of pop-up threats and unexpected lapses in UAV reliability. In parallel, we will hope to develop our mechanism for interpreting user preferences, basing extensions on (among other things) the feedback gained during the experiment described above.

DISCUSSION

We have defined a problem that UAV operators of the future will face, implying a requirement for DSS. Our initial work has focused on a simplified variant of the problem, assuming that targets are static and have known location. Our proposed solution uses automatic routing algorithms to support a process that searches the space of possible Composite Mission Plans and presents a ranked list of options to the operator. The initial system will support an experiment to assess the utility of decision support for operators responsible for small groups of UAVs, as well as providing a basis for further extensions that address more complex scenarios.

ACKNOWLEDGEMENTS

Thanks are due to Sqn. Ldr. Chaz Kennet, the military expert who has supported this work and shaped the problem that it addresses.

REFERENCES

J. Naisbitt & P. Aburdene, Megatrends 2000, William Morrow.

Vice Admiral Donald L. Pilling, US Navy Deputy Chief of Naval Operations Resources, Warfare Requirements and Assessments: Statement at the Congressional Hearings on Intelligence and Security, 1997. http://www.fas.org/irp/congress/1997_hr/h970409p.htm

Definition available from (among others) HyperDictionary: http://www.hyperdictionary.com/computing/travelling+salesman+problem

Definition available from (among others) HyperDictionary: http://www.hyperdictionary.com/computing/np-hard

S. Mitrović-Minić & R. Krishnamurti, "The Multiple Travelling Salesman Problem with Time Windows: Bounds for the Minimum Number of Vehicles," Technical Report, School of Computing Sciences, Simon Fraser University, November 2001. http://fas.sfu.ca/pub/cs/techreports/2002/CMPT2002-11.pdf

P. Griffiths & J. Harris, "Principles of Algebraic Geometry, " pg. 166.

D. B. Fogel, "A Parallel Processing Approach to a Multiple Travelling Salesman Problem using Evolutionary Programming," in the Proceedings of the Fourth annual Symposium on Parallel Processing,

S. R. Thangiah, K. E. Nygard & P. L. Juell, "GIDEON -- A genetic algorithm system for vehicle routing with time windows." In <u>Proceedings of the Seventh IEEE Conference on Artificial Intelligence Applications</u>, pg. 322-328, Miami Beach, Florida, February 1991.

S. J. Louis, "Genetic Algorithms as a Viable Computational Tool for Design", PhD thesis, Computer Science Department, University of Nevada, Reno, 1993.

M. Strens, "Machine Learning of Scheduling and Coordination Strategies in the Autonomous Command and Control of UAVs", Unpublished QinetiQ report.

DRIVER PERFORMANCE AND DISTRACTION

Assessing the Effects of Driver Sleepiness on Driving Performance using Combined Electrophysiological Monitoring and Real-time Computerized Driving Simulation: Normative Daytime Circadian Data

Henry J. Moller M.D., FRCP(C), DABSM
Leonid Kayumov Ph.D., DABSM
Eric L. Bulmash
Colin M. Shapiro M.B., B.(Ch.), Ph.D., FRCP(C)

Sleep Research and Human Performance Laboratory, Toronto Western Hospital
University Health Network, University of Toronto, Canada

ABSTRACT:

Driver sleepiness is a major public health issue. While medicolegal aspects of this issue are relevant to physicians, no accurate standardized hospital-based diagnostic instruments exist to assess impairment due to neurocognitive impairment. Our group has developed a normative data-base of driving performance and EEG-verified cognitive functioning during intentionally soporific standardized driving simulation testing sessions. To take into account circadian variation in performance, 30-minute simulations were repeated at two-hour intervals (i.e. at 10:00, 12:00, 14:00, 16:00).Measured variables include drivers' subjective ratings of mental status, EEG-verified "absence episodes" (AEs), and a variety of driving performance measures.

This normative data of combined simulated driving performance and EEG-monitoring shows significant fluctuations in reaction time, lane accuracy and intrusion of sleep-related EEG activity. Results from this database will serve as normative comparators to patients with a variety of neuropsychiatric conditions, allowing a more accurate prediction of potential crash risk by clinicians. By better understanding fluctuations in driver sleepiness and psychomotor performance, human performance researchers are in a position to better educate the public about cautionary measures to prevent vehicle accidents.

Key Words: Driving Safety, Driving Simulation, Sleep Disorders, EEG Monitoring

INTRODUCTION

Trends in sociodemographic population distribution, health patterns and technological advances are converging to create a challenge in human transportation safety (1). Medical professionals are placed in the difficult role of making objective assessments of driving safety in their patients, with decisions often carrying medicolegal weight (2). Yet much of the act of driving competency relates to a patient's subjective wellbeing, sensorimotor functioning, cognitive functioning and level of insight into any deficits. Selected medical and psychological tests are available, which can indirectly assess aspects of physical or mental functioning relevant to driving. Alternately, *in vivo* testing centres exist that can perform on-road testing. This method, while more ecologically valid, is often more costly, and more difficult to standardize. Our pilot research has aimed to evaluate the utility of a standardized computerized driving assessment device that is able to collect driving-related data in real-time during a standardized driving task. The aim of this device would be to balance ecological validity and cost-efficiency, essentially acting as a 'red-flag' for potential driving impairment, warranting more thorough naturalistic testing and/or licensing restrictions. While it is known that a wide variety of mental and physical conditions may affect fitness to drive, the chief focus will be from the perspective of a medical practitioner/researcher in the field of sleep disorders.

The adverse effect of sleepiness on driving ability has been well-documented, with some research suggesting that driving while excessively sleepy may make the driver more impaired than being under the influence of alcohol (3). Numerous sleep researchers have documented that circadian variations in sleepiness and alertness occur throughout the 24-hour period, with greatest proneness towards sleepiness occurring in the early AM morning period, as well as during the mid-afternoon 'siesta period' (4,5,6). Similarly, epidemiological reviews of traffic accidents have noted peaks in crashes thought to be related to sleepiness to occur at corresponding times of day and night (7,8). However, this issue has not been investigated in a controlled prospective manner, i.e. by investigating driving performance in correlation to neurophysiologically documented sleep proneness.   Concurrent to testing subjects' driving performance, we have used polysomnography measures including electroencephalography (EEG), electromyography (EMG) and electro-oculography (EOG) to record actual changes in levels of consciousness, ranging from fully alert wakefulness to impairments due to attention lapses, drowsiness and actual brief episodes of sleep intrusions into consciousness.

METHODS

Recruitment took place via advertisements in local newspapers and/or on hospital bulletin boards. Interested subjects were mailed a series of baseline questionnaires to assess study eligibility prior to a clinical screening interview. The questionnaire included the CES-D Depression Scale rating scores, Epworth Sleepiness Scale, Berlin Sleep Apnea Questionnaires, and ZOGIM Alertness Scale scores. The Previous Night Sleep Inventory (PNSI), a self-report sleep log assessing sleep latency, wakefulness and typical bed- and rise-times over the past two weeks was also completed. During the clinical interview, subjects were screened for eligibility and informed consent by a physician with expertise in sleep medicine. Informed consent was obtained from all participating subjects.

On the day of the clinical screening interview, patients undertook a 30 minute driving test in the driving simulator to become familiarized with the simulator and to control for possible learning effects. Subsequent testing for the purpose of the study took place in the form of 4 separate 30-minute standardized and supervised driving sessions occurring at 10:00, 12:00, 14:00 and 16:00.

Inclusion criteria: (screened for via sleep logs, questionnaires and clinical screening interview)

(1)   Age 18-65, male and female
(2)   Good physical and mental health
(3)   Valid Driver's License (verified by sleep lab staff)
(4)   Self-report of mean sleep onset latency of no more than 30 minutes (as defined by sleep logs) within the past two weeks.
(5)   Self-report of a mean sleep duration of no less than 6.5 hours (as defined by sleep logs) within the past two weeks.
(6)   Self-report of wakefulness, after initial sleep onset, of not more than 30 minutes.
(7)   Self-report of normal bedtime between 22:00-24:00, and normal sleep time between, and rise time between 7:00-9:00.

Exclusion criteria: Exclusion criteria for participation in this study were:
(1)   history of alcohol or substance abuse
(2)   major neurologic and psychiatric disorders
(3)   recent history (during the past 6 weeks) of medications likely to influence cognition or vigilance, such as sedatives, antipsychotics, stimulants.
(4)   history of past major medical condition
(5)   complaints of sleep disruption, excessive daytime sleepiness or impaired alertness within past 6 weeks.

Simulation/ Monitoring

A computerized simulated driving environment was used, consisting of a monotonous highway scenario, intended to provoke lapses in alertness, in combination with standard polysomnographic EEG/EMG/EOG set-up. (see Figures 1 & 2)

The York **Driving Simulator** (York Computer Technologies, Kingston, Ontario, Canada) was used to assess driving performance). The driving simulator consists of a personal computer, 15" monitor and peripheral steering wheel, accelerator and brake accessories. The simulator has been validated (9,10,11) as an effective and naturalistic research tool to measure psychomotor performance. The simulator presents a forward view from the driver's seat of a motorway road scene, with standard lane markings and signs signals appropriate to the road environment. The four-lane route has few turns, no stops signs or traffic lights, and posted speeds ranging from 70 to100 km/h. Following a single 10-15 minute practice session, subjects drove for 30 minutes following instructions Subjects were given standardized instructions to stay in the right hand lane, to avoid passing cars in the left lane, to obey all lane markings and speed signs and to keep both hands on steering wheel, while operating the pedals with the right foot only.

The simulator program samples a number of performance variables 10 times per second. These include reaction time for corrective steering maneuvers in response to "virtual wind gusts", mean velocity, mean variability road position, and a variable called "safe zone time", which is defined as the percentage of time the vehicle is traveling within 10 km/h of the posted speed limit, and within 1.3 meters of the centre of the right lane. Thus, at the end of a simulation run, a wide range of driving performance variables is available for the researcher. Other variables of interest, for example, mean ratio of accelerations versus decelerations or standard deviation of lane position (tendency to "weave") can ultimately be retrospectively accessed from the stored performance file.

Figure 1:
A subject's EEG activity is monitored during simulation are recorded

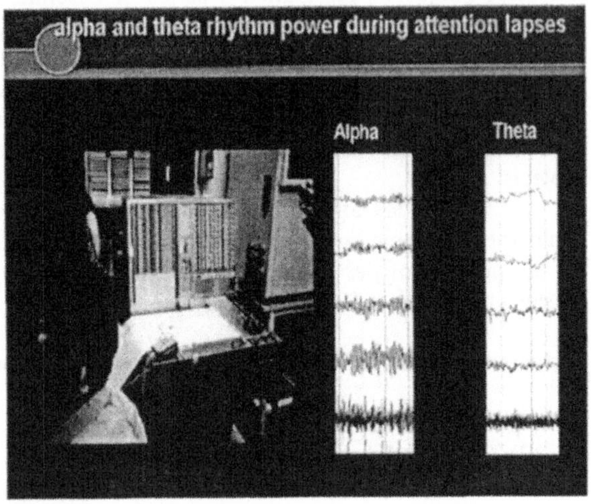

Figure 2:
Electrophysiological correlates of sleepiness

The **primary dependent performance outcome measures** included:

1) road position (expressed as a percentile, with the centre of the right lane being 25%, the centre lane 50% and the centre of the left lane 75%).
2) mean speed over the four 30 minute driving sessions.
3) mean speed deviation, calculated as the difference in km/h of speed of the vehicle
4) mean reaction time by driver to 'virtual windgusts' generated in standardized randomized fashion by the simulator.
5) off-road incidents, i.e. the number of times per testing session that the vehicle crashed.
6) drivers' subjective self-assessment ratings of levels of sleepiness, alertness and fatigue prior to each driving session, using visual analogue scales.
7) Occurrence of absence episodes was monitored using continuously recorded

EEG/EMG/EOG Polygraphic data during repeat driving task performance: recording involved a ground lead , 2 frontal leads (EEG), a right-sided para-ocular lead (EOG), and a submental lead (EMG).
Absence Episodes (AE's): were defined as :(a)occurrence of 15 to 30 seconds of any sleep stage by EEG/EMG/EOG criteria or (b)as intrusion of alpha- or theta EEG activity lasting more than 3 seconds but less than 15 seconds

RESULTS

Thirty individuals (20 male, 10 female) were included in the study with an average age of 31.7 +/- 11.5. Mean values of each variable at every time of simulation were attained and analyzed using a general linear model and paired sample *t* testing via SPSS

Over the span of four daytime testing sessions, the following mean performance measures were obtained: **Speed**: 89.2km/h ±4.1; **Speed Deviation**: 0.75km/h ± 0.39;

Road Position (RP): 29.0 ± 4.16; **Crash Rate:** 1.34 ± 1.16. On polygraphic monitoring, subjects experienced AEs with a mean frequency of 0.80 (s.d. 1.16, skewness 1.53). Circadian variation in test performance was noted with respect to RT (F=3.1, **p=.03**, df=3) and RP (F=3.8, **p=.01**, df=3), with significantly more accurate road position and quicker reaction times during the first driving session compared to subsequent trials. In terms of EEG-verified AEs, significant diurnal variation was observed: (F=3.4, **p=.04**, df=3) with a higher occurrence of "absences" on afternoon driving sessions. Drivers' Subjective ratings of sleepiness, alertness and fatigue showed virtually no diurnal variation on repeated assessment. Results are summarized in figures 3-7, stratified by circadian testing periods:

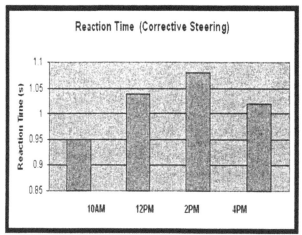

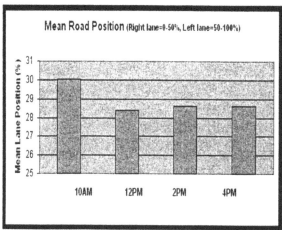

Figure 3:   **Figure 4:**

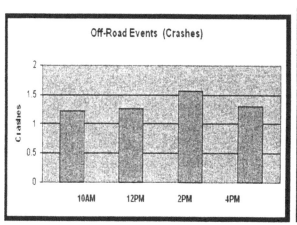

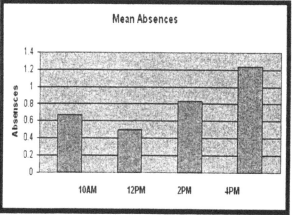

Figure 5:   **Figure 6:**

DISCUSSION

Excessive sleepiness is essentially a phenomenon that arises more readily due to a low level of external cues. This phenomenon is well-recognized in the sleep disorders literature; some examples of conditions that lead to excessive daytime sleepiness include sleep apnea, narcolepsy and chronic sleep deprivation. In disorders causing excessive sleepiness, sleep-related brain activity begins to intrude into wakeful consciousness; in the case of narcolepsy this may even include episodes of hallucinatory dreams. Thus, under certain conditions, the well-defined patterns of being awake and alert vs. drowsy and asleep can start to become more blurred (6,7). Traffic accidents due to impaired alertness are among the most dramatic adverse consequences of excessive daytime sleepiness.

In our normative subject group, reaction time was the performance variable that showed most significant diurnal variation throughout the day. While it remains possible that the 'novelty effect' of the first testing session of the day played as important a role as circadian factors, we have attempted to control for this by giving subjects a practice session. On polygraphic EEG testing, microsleeps or "absence episodes" showed a clear tendency to occur more readily on the last testing session. Although we would postulate primarily a circadian explanation for this phenomenon, it might also be argued that an element of 'task fatigue' played a role. Furthermore, compared to the first driving simulation test of the day, subjects' driving performance tended to become decreasingly conservative on subsequent driving sessions, with a trend towards increasing speed, speed variability and mean lane position towards the passing lane, although crash rates (which are events with a very low base rate) remained relatively constant throughout the day.

Our work with the simulator thus far has focused on the gathering of normative data from healthy individuals. This has allowed us to correlate changes in driving performance with brain-activity patterns associated with sleepiness. We believe that if this methodology is applied to patients with actual sleep disorders such as sleep apnea or sleep deprivation, the occurrence of absence episodes will be further provoked, and will show corresponding impairments on driving performance measures. Clinically, subjects usually perceive these types of episodes as brief periods of 'nodding off' or 'phasing out', often without even being aware of these lapses in consciousness. The lack of circadian variation of drivers' subjective ratings of their own sleepiness in contrast to the diurnal variation of EEG-data seems to confirm this. A previous pilot study by our group has found our driving simulator system more sensitive than conventional daytime polysomnography testing in assessing impairments in alertness relevant to driving in patients with clinically significant sleepiness (11).

There is clearly a significant medicolegal onus on the physician of the potential driver (2); in fact, physicians have been found negligent for failing to report medically impaired drivers causing harm in Canada, with courts emphasizing the doctor's responsibility not just to the individual patient, but to protect society at large as well. Not only does this responsibility put physicians in an awkward position towards the patient whom they often have known for years, but the actual task of detecting driving impairment in the office checkup is technically more difficult than law and policymakers might like to admit. From a clinician's perspective, the frustrating issue at hand is that there is no one clearly defined symptom or physical exam maneuver that can reliably screen for subtle impairments in the variety of facilities required to be intact for safe driving. While the ultimate 'red flag' would be a failed road test, this is more costly and time-consuming than our current health-care system allows for. The idea of an 'off-road' computerized screening test for medical fitness might serve as a cost-effective 'red flag' system that could be performed in a hospital laboratory, while still giving information relevant to performance on the road. The gold standard of driving assessment will likely always be a live driving assessment. In defense of simulated tests, one can make the valid argument that the actual *in vivo* road-test used to make licensing decisions is also only a 30-minute snapshot which can never truly test a potential driver under the variety of driving conditions he will eventually find himself.

There are broader sociopolitical issues that need to be considered in the context of computerized driving assessment methodologies. For now, it would appear that the detection of the distracted and sleepy driver is a feasible long-term goal to aim for, requiring continued input from medical and engineering/human factors researchers in collaboration with governmental/legislative authorities and the automotive industry.

REFERENCES

(1) Knipling RR & Wang J. Crashes and fatalities related to driver drowsiness/fatigue. Research Note Washington, D.C. : U.S. Department of Transportation, National Highway Traffic Safety Administration (2001)

(2) Determining Medical Fitness to Drive: A Guide for Physicians (6[th]ed), Canadian Medical Association (2000)

(3) Powell N, Schechtman K, Riley RW, Li K, Troell R, Guilleminault C. The road to danger: comparative risks of driving while sleepy. Laryngoscope (2001); 111; 887-93.

(4) Monk TH: The relationship of chronobiology to sleep schedules and demands. Work Stress 1990; 4(3):227-36

(5) Lenne MG, Triggs TJ, Redman JR. Time of day variations in driving performance. Accid Anal Prev 1997 29(4):431-7

(6) Shapiro CM, Kayumov I: "Sleepiness, fatigue and impaired alertness" Seminars in Neuropsychiatry 2000 (1), 2-5.

(7)Lyznicki JM: "Sleepiness, driving and motorvehicle crashes" JAMA 1998 (279); 1908-13.

(8) Smiley, A : Fatigue and Driving. Chapter 6 in: Human Factors in Traffic Safety , Lawyers & Judges Publishing Co.(2001)

(9) Arnedt JT, Acebo C, Seifer R, Carskadon MA. Assessment of a Simulated Driving Task for Sleep Research. Sleep (2001); 24S: A413.

(10) Arnedt JT, Wilde GJ, Munt PW, MacLean AW. Simulated driving performance following prolonged wakefulness and alcohol consumption: separate and contributions to impairment. Journal of Sleep Research (2000): 233-241.

(11) Moller H, Lowe A, Kayumov L, Hossain, N, Shapiro C. Can impaired alertness be detected more sensitively using a computerized driving simulator? Sleep (2002) 252-253

OLDER DRIVERS' REPORTED PERCEPTUAL LOSS CORRELATES WITH A DECREASE IN PERIPHERAL MOTION SENSITIVITY

Steven Henderson

Transportation Safety Board of Canada, Hull, Quebec, Canada

Don C. Donderi

McGill University, Montreal, Quebec, Canada

ABSTRACT

Eighteen older drivers (66 to 88 years old) and their passengers both reported on the drivers' performance using questionnaires that elicited responses related to attention and to speed and accuracy of object motion perception. The measure of reported perceptual loss was an equally weighted combination of standardized responses from the 17-item driver questionnaire and the 11-item passenger questionnaire. Peripheral stationary and drifting contrast sensitivity was determined for 0.4 cycles per degree sine wave gratings at fifteen degrees eccentricity. The temporal two-alternative forced choice staircase procedure consisted of randomly interleaved left and right visual field presentations.

The correlation between $\log_{10}$ motion contrast sensitivity and reported perceptual loss was -.63 ($p < .01$), between age and perceptual loss was .56 ($p < .05$), and between age and $\log_{10}$ motion contrast sensitivity was -.54 ($p < .05$). The partial correlation between $\log_{10}$ motion sensitivity and reported perceptual loss, independent of age, was -.47 ($p = .054$). We concluded that some age-related driving performance deficits are associated with reduced sensitivity to motion in the visual periphery.

Peripheral motion contrast sensitivity was discussed in relation to "useful field of view" (UFOV) measures of visual function, and offered as a primary deficit of high risk drivers with Alzheimer's disease.

This research was conducted at McGill University in partial fulfillment of the doctoral thesis requirement of the first author. Please note also that road safety is outside the mandate of the Transportation Safety Board of Canada.

Keywords: older drivers; contrast sensitivity; motion; vision test

INTRODUCTION

Drivers over sixty years of age are more likely to have fatal accidents than younger drivers, given equal mileage-estimated risk exposure (NHTSA, 2000; Yanik, 1986). Daytime fatality risk is higher than for for drivers over seventy-five than for any other age group (Massie, Campbell & Williams, 1995). Although physical frailty accounts for some of the fatality risk increase (Evans, Gerrish, & Taheri, 1998), older drivers are also more likely to be found at fault if they are involved in a multi-vehicle accident (Cooper, 1989; Stamatiadis & Deacon, 1995). However, this may reflect a bias of accident investigators or police to attribute fault to the older driver.

Mileage-based estimates of risk exposure can yield exaggerated accident risk estimates for older drivers (Janke, 1991). First, mileage estimates are usually based on self-reported data, which is likely to be inaccurate. Second, different driving environments expose drivers to widely differing levels of accident risk, and these differences are not captured in a mileage-based estimate. For example, accidents are much more likely to happen on urban roads than on limited-access highways, and older, low-mileage drivers drive proportionately more on urban roads than on limited-access highways.

Janke (1991) recommended that the indirect risk estimation technique of "induced exposure" be used to eliminate the bias inherent in mileage-based measures. This technique is based on the assumption that in a sample of two-vehicle accidents in which one driver was found to be completely at fault, the "innocent victims" comprise a random sample of drivers whose age distribution is a measure of relative risk exposure across groups. The accident responsibility ratio of a group is the ratio of at-fault accidents (the numerator) to not-at-fault accidents (the denominator). A ratio greater than 1 indicates that the group causes more than its expected share of two-vehicle accidents. Verhaegen, Toebat, and Delbeke (1988) analysed a sample of 660 two-vehicle accidents and found a responsibility ratio of 2.23 for drivers aged 60 to 69 years, and a ratio of 2.5 for drivers over 70 years of age.

Cooper (1989) derived accident responsibility ratios from a database of 14,063 accident-involved drivers in British Columbia in 1986. He reported ratios of 1.56 for age 71 to 75, 2.13 for age 76 to 80, 2.64 for age 81 to 85, and 5.67 for age 86 to 90. Stamatiadis and Deacon (1995) calculated accident responsibility ratios from a database of 144,410 two-vehicle accidents, and reported ratios of 1.55 for age 70 to 74, 2.24 for age 75 to 79, and 3.66 for drivers over 80 years of age. Cooper (1990) said that the ratio of responsible to not-responsible accidents by age showed "an exponential-looking increase in accident responsibility from age sixty-five up" (p. 95). The proportion of right of way (ROW) violations to total traffic convictions by age also follows a similar rising curve (Cooper, 1990).

The age-related increases in both ROW violations and accident responsibility may result from failures to detect other vehicles in the right-of-way. Accident characteristics support this hypothesis. Young drivers' accidents are mostly single-vehicle crashes. Older drivers' accidents most frequently involve an undetected crossing vehicle at an intersection (Viano, Culver, Evans, Frick, & Scott, 1990).

Verhaegen et al (1988) suggested that older drivers' high levels of accident responsibility indicate problems in perception and decision-making. However, many more of these accidents are due to failures of detection than to failures of decision. Summala and Mikkola (1994) found that only failures of attention increase with age, among the five largest categories of primary non-alcohol causal factors for 1357 fatal multi-vehicle accidents.

The demonstrated increase in driver accident responsibility with age may be caused by older drivers' reduced sensitivity to peripheral motion. In central vision, motion enhances the contrast sensitivity of low spatial frequency sine wave gratings, that is, below the CSF peak between 2 and 4 cycles/degree. Moving a grating across the visual field can increase the contrast sensitivity by a factor of 4 or more. Motion enhancement (the ratio of drifting to stationary contrast sensitivity) begins to fall off after about 60 years of age, and may have fallen by a factor of 2 by the age of 70 (Owsley, Sekuler, & Siemsen, 1983; Sekuler & Owsley, 1982).

If motion sensitivity in the peripheral visual field follows a time course similar to motion sensitivity in central vision, then some of the characteristic "failure of detection" accidents of older drivers may arise from a peripheral motion processing (PMP) deficit that reduces the power of a moving stimulus to attract visual attention (Steinman, Steinman, Trick, & Lehmkuhle, 1994) and to produce a reflexive saccadic eye movement towards it (Fuchs, Kaneko, & Scudder, 1985; Stein, 1984). According to this hypothesis, a PMP deficit reduces the salience of a moving object, thus disrupting the preattentive stage of scan-path generation and serial search.

We carried out a correlational test of the hypothesis that self and peer-reported perceptual loss in older drivers is related to a PMP deficit that reduces the ability of a moving stimulus to trigger reflexive visual attention. In other words, a measured decrease in PMP will increase reports of perceptual loss among susceptible older drivers. Because groups of older drivers are highly variable on both vision measures and driving performance measures, if there is such a correlation between a vision measure (PMP in this case) and driving performance, it will be strongest among older drivers (Shinar & Schieber, 1991). Another advantage of studying older drivers is that they have relatively few accidents involving alcohol (NHTSA, 2000).

METHOD

Participants

Participants (all licensed and active drivers) were 10 women and 8 men between 66 and 88 years of age (mean age = 74 years). All participants were English-speaking residents of Montreal and the surrounding suburbs, and were unpaid volunteers recruited through personal contacts among senior citizen's services and church groups.

Motion Processing Measure

Contrast sensitivity was determined for stationary sine wave gratings and for optimal velocity (Kelly, 1979) drifting sine wave gratings of 0.4 cycles per degree and 0.8 cycles per degree. The gratings moved across the oscilloscope face from the periphery towards the center of the visual field at a rate of 11 degrees per second for the 0.4 cycles per degree gratings and 5 degrees per second for the 0.8 cycles per degree gratings. The gratings were presented on two display monitors 57 cm distant from the head fixation point. The monitors were 10.2 cm wide by 8.2 cm high rectangular oscilloscope screens. The screens used a P31 fast phosphor (.038 msec decay constant), and they had no reference grids. They were centred at an eccentricity of 15 degrees visual angle (VA) to either side of an eye-level red LED fixation point. Each screen spanned from 10 degrees to 20 degrees visual eccentricity.

The contrast sensitivity of each peripheral field was determined using a temporal two-alternative forced choice staircase method. A single stimulus consisted of a vertical sine-wave grating presented in a raised cosine temporal window of 1.5 seconds duration, preceded and followed by a 0.5 second blank interval. During a trial, the participant looked directly ahead at a lit LED fixation point, and indicated whether a sine-wave grating stimulus appeared in the first or the second 2.5 second temporal interval (ie., "before or after the double beep" delimiting the intervals). Within a staircase, the contrast of the grating stimulus was increased on the next trial if the participant made an incorrect response, and decreased if the participant made five successive correct responses. To reduce the number of anticipatory eye movements, the left and right visual field staircases were randomly interleaved, so that the stimulus was presented randomly to the left or right visual field on any trial. If the experimenter, who was seated directly ahead of the participant, observed the participant to make an anticipatory eye movement, that trial was discarded before evaluation. The participant was blind to both the temporal (first or second) interval and the visual field side (left or right) in which the stimulus was to appear. The experimenter was blind to the temporal interval.

A block of trials continued for at least 20 trials within each staircase after the contrast has been alternately decreased and increased at least four times within both staircases, showing that the contrast thresholds has been bracketed, and the threshold for each block was the mean grating contrast of the final (at least 20) trials. This staircase procedure oscillates about the contrast yielding 89% correct responding (that is, where the probability of making five correct responses is equal to the probability of making an incorrect response on any of five consecutive trials, or where $p^5 = 5(1-p)$).

A series of training trials with very high-contrast gratings was used to familiarise participants with the task. The criterion to continue with the experiment was eight consecutive correct responses on the training trials, usually obtained within the first eight trials. As well, before beginning the forced choice staircases, initial grating contrast levels were determined using the method of ascending limits. For six randomly ordered (by side) test trials, the participant looked at the central red LED, and responded "left" or "right" as soon as a grating of gradually increasing contrast appeared on either the left or right oscilloscope screen. The response usually occurred within 10 seconds.

The experiment continued for four test trial blocks: two blocks per day on two separate days. A single test trial block continued until each of the left and right-side staircases had a total of 20 trials after four reversals of direction. A trial block usually took between 40 minutes and 1 hour. Stationary and moving gratings were tested in separate blocks. The stationary grating block always preceded the moving grating block. The 0.4 cycle per degree stimuli were tested in the two trial blocks on the first day, and the 0.8 cycles per degree stimuli were tested in the two trial blocks on the second day.

All participants were tested with both 0.4 and 0.8 cycles per degree grating stimuli, but only 0.4 cycles per degree gratings were used to estimate peripheral motion processing. With increasing eccentricity the contrast sensitivity peak is shifted to a lower spatial frequency relative to the contrast sensitivity peak of central vision (Kelly, 1984), so motion enhancement shifts to progressively lower spatial frequencies as eccentricity increases. Pilot testing of gratings presented at 15 degrees nominal eccentricity found motion enhancement ratios (MERs) of 3 to 4 for 0.4 cycles per degree gratings, comparable to central vision MERs for gratings of 1 cycles per degree (Sekuler & Owsley, 1982), while MERs were usually less than 2 for 0.8 cycles per degree gratings presented at that eccentricity. As the most sensitive assessment of peripheral motion contrast sensitivity should use the stimuli showing the greatest motion enhancement, only 0.4 cycles per degree grating stimuli were analysed.

Driving Performance Measures

Driving performance was assessed by a two-part (driver and passenger responses) driving perception questionnaire. Questions were designed to elicit information about the subjective effects of reduced detection distances and/or an increased probability of detection errors. The passenger, selected by the driver, sealed the completed passenger questionnaire into a supplied envelope before returning it to the driver, who brought both the driver's and the passenger's completed questionnaires to the vision test session.

The 17 driver questions related to perceptions of traffic speed (reduced motion sensitivity could lead to shorter detection distances and the assumption that traffic speed has increased), own driving speed relative to several standards (senior drivers are known to slow down in response to visual deficits, perhaps to reduce the pace of driving decisions), self-ratings of own driving performance relative to several standards, and self-report of how often they were surprised by a range of driving events.

The 11 passenger questions asked for judgements of average speed of the driver relative to city and highway traffic (slower means less safe), the driver's relative performance and safety, how often the passenger detected various situations before the driver, and the passenger's overall state of mind.

The 28 questions were combined by orienting the responses so that higher values reflected higher hypothetical risk, converting responses for each question to z-scores across drivers, then computing the average z-score for each driver. This procedure is equivalent to assigning equal weights in a regression equation, involves no capitalization on chance, and is unaffected by missing answers (Wainer, 1976).

The experimental hypothesis tested was that within a group of older drivers, peripheral motion contrast sensitivity would correlate significantly ($p < .05$) with accident risk as assessed by questionnaire scores.

RESULTS

Table 1
Pearson Product Correlations Between Age, Contrast Sensitivity, and Questionnaire Scores (N = 18)

	Age	Questionnaire scores	Driver questionnaire	Passenger questionnaire
Age	---	.56*	.50*	.43
Log_{10} contrast sensitivity (drifting)				
Right visual field	-.70**	-.55*	-.53*	-.39
Left visual field	-.37	-.64**	-.64**	-.42
Average across fields	-.54*	-.63**	-.62**	-.43
Log_{10} contrast sensitivity (stationary)				
Right visual field	-.34	-.04	-.08	.01
Left visual field	-.29	-.25	-.34	-.07
Average across fields	-.35	-.18	-.26	-.04

*$p < .05$. **$p < .01$.

Mean log_{10} contrast sensitivity was 1.68 ($sd = 0.17$, N = 18) for stationary 0.4 cycles per degree sine wave grating stimuli, and 2.15 ($sd = 0.18$, N = 18) for drifting grating stimuli.

Correlations of interest are shown in Table 1. The partial correlation between motion sensitivity and reported perceptual loss, independent of age, was -.47 ($p = .054$). In addition, driver and passenger questionnaire scores just failed to correlate significantly with each other ($r = .41$, $p < .1$).

DISCUSSION

Note particularly that the correlation between motion processing and questionnaire score is stronger than their correlations with age, indicating that peripheral motion sensitivity may therefore be used to screen drivers without regard for age, fulfilling the requirement that screening tests must not be age-based.

Although older drivers do compensate for age-related visual and driving deficits (Slzyk, Seiple, &Viana, 1995), they are poor at assessing their own visual processing skills and at detecting gradual visual losses occurring over time. They are unlikely to recognise the situations, intersections in particular, that are most dangerous for them (Holland, 1993). However, when informed of specific visual deficits by an eye care practitioner, older drivers willingly adopt compensatory strategies. Therefore, a two-tier strategy (Shinar & Schieber, 1991) for detecting and informing high-risk drivers about possible compensatory strategies for motion detection deficit might be an effective, inexpensive, and non-coercive method for reducing multi-vehicle accident rates. The driving perception questionnaire and motion processing tests of high scoring drivers would allow those with a peripheral motion detection deficit to be identified, informed of the deficit, told about particularly high-risk situations (left-turning or crossing traffic at intersections), and taught how to consciously scan the visual field at regular intervals and when approaching intersections, rather than to rely on a reduced or absent reflexive orienting response to movement. (Note that flight instructors spend significant time instructing their students to consciously scan the visual field outside the aircraft)

Ball, Owsley, and co-workers have proposed that the primary deficit causing driving performance decline is an age-related reduction in useful field of view (UFOV) (Ball & Owsley, 1991; Ball, Owsley, Sloane, Roenker, & Bruni, 1993; Ball & Rebok, 1994; Owsley, Ball, & Keeton, 1995; Owsley, Ball, Sloane, Roenker, & Bruni, 1991). UFOV test participants perform simultaneous peripheral target localisation and central target discrimination. Stimulus duration is shorter than saccade latency, preventing serial search of the visual field, so that processing of the test stimulus approximates processing of an image acquired during a single short fixation. Their apparatus, the Visual Attention Analyser, has three task sub-tests that assess duration threshold for central discrimination, concurrent central discrimination and peripheral localisation, and concurrent central discrimination and peripheral localisation in the presence of peripheral distractors. Visual Attention Analyser results significantly predict prior accident involvement.

Ball, Owsley, and their co-workers found that measures of peripheral light sensitivity (automated perimetry), letter acuity, and Pelli-Robson contrast sensitivity related only indirectly through UFOV to accident risk, and suggested that pure sensory measures do not improve the fit of the regression model over UFOV measures alone because they do not capture the complexity of the cluttered driving environment. Because they isolate measurements of sensory function from perceptual and cognitive influences, clinical ophthalmology tests (most particularly contrast sensitivity) typically assess only central vision, do not require concurrent use of central and peripheral vision, and incorporate no positional or temporal uncertainty in the test stimulus (Ball & Owsley, 1991; Ball et al., 1993; Owsley et al., 1991).

This may be why conventional sensory measures do not directly predict driving performance. However, the sensory measure of peripheral motion processing described above minimises perceptual and cognitive influences, uses peripheral vision during central fixation, and incorporates temporal and positional uncertainty into the test stimulus.

The PMP test and the UFOV test are complimentary measures of the visual attention required to drive safely. The (sensory) PMP test evaluates the power of motion to produce a saccade target (bottom-up scan-path generation), and the (attentional) UFOV test evaluates the extent of information available for visual search within a fixation. PMP and UFOV measures are not entirely independent, as the second sub-test of the UFOV test requires peripheral localisation of a solitary step-onset stimulus, a task that probably overlaps with motion detection under spatial uncertainty.

Scialfa, Thomas, and Joffe (1994) found that age-related shrinkage of UFOV increases the serial component of search tasks (parallel to serial compensation). Older participants increased visual search reaction time by requiring more saccades to identify search targets. Therefore, a relatively more sensitive PMP system and more accurate saccade generator will help compensate for UFOV shrinkage (due to age or stroke) and mitigate its impact on driving performance. Conversely, a large UFOV reduces the need for accurate saccades. Inclusion of the PMP test in a test battery could improve identification of high-risk drivers (reducing false positives), because it would help detect those drivers better able to compensate for a UFOV deficit

Estimates of increased crash risk for drivers with Alzheimer's disease (AD) compared to age-matched controls range from a factor of 5 (Friedland et al., 1988), to a factor of 2.5 (Tuokko, Tallman, Beattie, Cooper, & Weir, 1995). Although researchers have considered the elevated accident risk of AD patients to be a function of cognitive impairment (Fitten et al., 1995; Kraszniak, Keyl, & Albert, 1991; Parasuraman & Nestor, 1991; Tuokko et al., 1995), crashing and non-crashing AD drivers are not distinguishable by neuropsychological tests or by symptom severity at initial diagnosis (Lucas-Blaustein, Filipp, Dungan, & Tune, 1988; Tuokko et al., 1995). We contend for the following reasons that PMP deficit causes elevated accident risk in some AD drivers.

Visual deficits are now recognised by clinical researchers as a primary deficit of AD (Cronin-Golomb, 1995). One clinical subgroup of early AD patients displays Balint's syndrome (a visuospatial and motion processing deficit) as the first symptom of AD (Hof et al., 1993). Motion detection pathways, including middle temporal cortex, appear to be "dramatically affected in these cases" (p. 215).

Some mildly demented early AD patients show profound visual deficits for temporally modulated stimuli. Detection thresholds are higher for drifting or flickering sine wave gratings (Gilmore, Wenk, Naylor, & Koss, 1994;

Hutton, Morris, Elias, & Poston, 1993) and for 700 msec presentations of step-onset gratings (Cronin-Golomb et al., 1991; Nissen et al., 1985) relative to healthy age-matched controls. Some researchers have shown that correlated motion thresholds for random dot stimuli are more than double for AD patients (Gilmore et al., 1994; Silverman, Tran, Zimmerman, & Feldon, 1994; Trick & Silverman., 1991). However, Mendola, Cronin-Golomb, Corkin, and Growdon (1992, 1995) found no threshold increase using the correlated motion paradigm, perhaps because their stimuli could evoke correct "blindsight" responses from AD patients. This is made more plausible because Silverman et al. showed optokinetic nystagmus (OKN) for undetected random-dot motion, demonstrating relative sparing of accessory optic system processing in AD relative to cortical dysfunction. Increased visual evoked potential (VEP) latencies of P2 (indicating defective secondary visual processing), and temporal contrast sensitivity losses are also reported (Wright, Drasdo, & Harding, 1987).

If a sensory visual attention deficit is the cause of elevated crash risk in some early AD patients, then a variant of the motion processing test described above (perhaps modified into a spatial two-alternative task to eliminate any memory demand) could reliably distinguish between crashing and non-crashing AD drivers. If so, diagnosis of probable early Alzheimer's disease need not mean termination of a patient's right to drive, as early AD drivers with low risk of sensory attention deficit could continue to drive until precluded by later AD deficits.

The validity and reliability of peripheral motion processing measures and the driving perception questionnaire for predicting accident risk should be tested using accident data and driving simulator performance measures. We hope that further development of the forced-choice method and test equipment will likely reduce test time sufficiently to make motion processing assessment practical for driving examiners and motor vehicle insurance companies.

REFERENCES

Ball, K., & Owsley, C. (1991). Identifying correlates of accident involvement for the older driver. Human Factors, 33(5), 583-595.

Ball, K., Owsley, C., Sloane, M. E., Roenker, D. L., & Bruni, J. R. (1993). Visual attention problems as a predictor of vehicle crashes in older drivers. Investigative Ophthalmology & Visual Science, 34(11), 3110-3123.

Ball, K., & Rebok, G. (1994). Evaluating the driving ability of older adults. The Journal of Applied Gerontology, 13(1), 20-38.

Carsten, O. (1981). Use of the Nationwide Personal Transportation Study to calculate exposure. HSRI Research Review, 2, 6.

Cerelli, E. C. (1973). Driver exposure: the indirect approach for obtaining relative measures. Accident Analysis & Prevention, 5, 186-193.

Cooper, P. J. (1989). Differences in accident characteristics among elderly drivers and between elderly and middle-aged drivers. Proceedings of the 33rd Conference of the American Association for Automotive Medicine, 33, 153-167.

Cooper, P. J. (1990). Different ages, different risks: The realm of accident statistics. In J. P. Rothe (Ed.), The Safety of Elderly Drivers: Yesterday's Young in Today's Traffic, 85-133. New Brunswick: Transaction Publishers.

Cronim-Golomb, A. (1995). Vision in Alzheimer's disease. The Gerontologist, 35(3), 370-376.

Cronin-Golomb, A., Corkin, S., Rizzo, J. F., Cohen, J., Growdon, J. H., & Banks, K. S. (1991). Visual dysfunction in Alzheimer's disease: relation to normal aging. Annals of Neurology, 29, 41-52.

Cushman, W. B. (1992). A low-cost spatial contrast sensitivity display driver. Behavior Research Methods, Instruments, & Computers, 24(3), 461-463.

Fitten, L. J., Perryman, K. M., Wilkinson, C. J., Little, R. J., Burns, M. M., Pachana, N., Mervis, J. R., Malmgren, R., Siembieda, D. W., & Ganzell, S. (1995). Alzheimer and vascular dementias and driving: a prospective road and laboratory study. Journal of the American Medical Association, 273(17), 1360-1365.

Friedland, R. P., Koss, E., Kumar, A., Gaine, S., Metzler, D., Haxby, J. V., & Moore, A. (1988). Motor vehicle crashes in dementia of the Alzheimer type. Annals of Neurology, 24, 782-786.

Fuchs, A. F., Kaneko, C. R. S., & Scudder, C. A. (1985). Brainstem control of saccadic eye movements. Annual Review of Neuroscience, 8, 307-337.

Gilmore, G. C., Wenk, H. E., Naylor, L. A., & Koss, E. (1994). Motion perception and Alzheimer's disease. Journal of Gerontology: Psychological Sciences, 49(2), 52-57.

Hof, P. R., Archin, N., Osmand, A. P., Dougherty, J. H., Wells, C., Bouras, C., & Morrison, J. H. (1993). Posterior cortical atrophy in Alzheimer's disease: analysis of a new case and re-evaluation of a historical report. Acta Neuropathologica, 86(3), 215-223.

Holland, C. A. (1993). Self-bias in older drivers' judgements of accident likelihood. Accident Analysis and Prevention, 25(4), 431-441.

Hutton, J. T., Morris, J. L., Elias, J. W., & Poston, J. N. (1993). Contrast sensitivity dysfunction in Alzheimer's disease. Neurology, 43, 2328-2330.

Janke, M. K. (1991). Accidents, mileage and the exaggeration of risk. Accident Analysis & Prevention, 23(2/3), 183-188.

Kelly, D. H. (1984). Retinal inhomogeneity. I. Spatiotemporal contrast sensitivity. Journal of the Optical Society of America, A, 1(1), 107-113.

Kelly, D. H. (1979). Motion and vision. II. Stabilized spatio-temporal threshold surface. Journal of the Optical Society of America, 69, 1340-1349.

Kraszniak, A.W., Keyl. P. M., & Albert, M. S. (1991). Dementia and the older driver. Human Factors, 33(5), 527-537.

Lucas-Blaustein, M. J., Filipp, L., Dungan, C., & Tune, L. (1988). Driving in patients with dementia. Journal of the American Geriatrics Society, 36, 1087-1091.

Massie, D. L., Campbell, K. L., & Williams, A. F. (1995). Traffic accident involvement rates by driver age and gender. Accident Analysis and Prevention, 27(1), 73-87.

Mendola, J. D., Cronin-Golomb, A., Corkin, S., & Growdon, J. H. (1992). Vision in Alzheimer's disease: prevalence of deficit. Society for Neuroscience Abstracts, 18, 736.

Mendola, J. D., Cronin-Golomb, A., Corkin, S., & Growdon, J. H. (1995). Prevalence of visual deficits in Alzheimer's disease. Optometry and Vision Science, 72, 155-167.

National Highway Traffic Safety Administration (NHTSA) (2000). Traffic Safety Facts 2000: Older Population. DOT HS 809 328.

Nissen. M. J., Corkin, S., Buonanno, F. S., Growdon, J. H., Wray, S. H., & Bauer, J. (1985). Spatial vision in Alzheimer's disease: general findings and a case report. Archives of Neurology, 42, 667-671.

Owsley, C., Ball, K., & Keeton D. M. (1995). Relationship between visual sensitivity and target localization in older adults. Vision Research, 35(4), 579-587.

Owsley, C., Ball, K., Sloane, M. E., Roenker, D. L., & Bruni, J. R. (1991). Visual/cognitive correlates of vehicle accidents in older drivers. Psychology and Aging, 6(3), 403-415.

Owsley, C., Sekuler, R., & Siemsen, D. (1983). Contrast sensitivity throughout adulthood. Vision Research, 23(7), 689- 699.

Parasuraman, R., & Nestor, P.G. (1991). Attention and driving skills in aging and Alzheimer's disease. Human Factors, 33(5), 539-557.

Scialfa, C. T., Thomas, D. M., & Joffe, K. M. (1994). Age differences in the useful field of view: an eye movement analysis. Optometry and Vision Science, 71(12), 736-742.

Sekuler, R., & Owsley, C. (1982). The spatial vision of older humans. In R. Sekuler, D. Kline, & K. Dismukes (Eds.), Aging and Human Visual Function (pp. 185-202). New York: Alan R. Liss, Inc.

Shinar, D. & Schieber, F. (1991). Visual requirements for safety and mobility of older drivers. Human Factors, 33(5), 507-519.

Silverman, S. E., Tran, D. B., Zimmerman, K. M., & Feldon, S.E. (1994). Dissociation between the detection and perception of motion in Alzheimer's disease. Neurology, 44, 1814-1818.

Stamatiadis, N. & Deacon, J. A. (1995). Trends in highway safety: Effects of an aging population on accident propensity. Accident Analysis and Prevention, 27(4), 443-459.

Stein, B. E. (1984). Development of the superior colliculus. Annual Review of Neuroscience, 7, 95-125.

Steinman, S. B., Steinman, B. A., Trick, G. L., & Lehmkuhle, S. (1994). A sensory explanation for visual attention deficits in the elderly. Optometry and Vision Science, 71(12), 743-749.

Summala, H., & Mikkola, T. (1994). Fatal accidents among car and truck drivers: Effects of fatigue, age, and alcohol consumption. Human Factors, 36(2), 315-326.

Szlyk, J. P., Seiple, W., & Viana, M. (1995). Relative effects of age and compromised vision on driving performance. Human Factors, 37(2), 430-436.

Trick, G. L., & Silverman, S. E. (1991). Visual sensitivity to motion: Age-related changes and deficits in senile dementia of the Alzheimer type. Neurology, 41, 1437-1440.

Tuokko, H., Tallman, K., Beattie, B. L., Cooper, P., & Weir, J. (1995). An examination of driving records in a dementia clinic. Journal of Gerontology: Social Sciences, 50B(3), S173-S181.

Verhaegen, P. K., Toebat, K. L., & Delbeke, L. L. (1988). Safety of older drivers: A study of their overinvolvement ratio. Proceedings of the 32nd Conference of the Human Factors Society, 185-188.

Viano, D. C., Culver. C. C., Evans, L., Frick, M., & Scott, R. (1990). Involvement of older drivers in multi-vehicle side impact crashes. Accident Analysis & Prevention, 22(2), 177-188.

Wainer, H. (1976). Estimating coefficients in linear models: It don't make no nevermind. Psychological Bulletin, 83(2), 213-217.

Wright, C. E., Drasdo, N., & Harding, G. F. A. (1987). Pathology of the optic nerve and visual association areas: information given by the flash and pattern visual evoked potential, and the temporal and spatial contrast sensitivity function. Brain, 110, 107-120.

Yanik, A. J. (1986). What accident data reveal about elderly drivers. (SAE Technical Paper #851688). Warrendale, PA: Society of Automotive Engineers.

CROSS-CULTURAL ANALYSIS OF NAVIGATIONAL STRATEGY: FURTHER IMPLICATIONS FOR IRANS DESIGN

Ellen M. Carpenter and Carryl L. Baldwin
Old Dominion University

Hiroshi Furukawa
University of Tsukuba, JAPAN

ABSTRACT

As part of a cross-cultural validation study, 222 women and 82 men from the southeastern United States completed Japanese and American sense of direction and navigation (wayfinding) strategy scales. Factor analyses supported the idea that individual differences in orientation and wayfinding strategies are stable across cultures. Correlations between the two instruments suggested that they possess similar latent factor structures. In addition, gender differences consistently found in the American scale were also evidenced in the Japanese scale. Results are discussed in terms of their implications for designing effective in-vehicle route and navigation systems (IRANS) consistent with individual differences in navigational strategy.

Keywords: Navigational strategy; Wayfinding; IRANS; Cross-cultural

INTRODUCTION

An increasing number of vehicles across the globe are now equipped with in-vehicle routing and navigational systems (IRANS). IRANS are expected to reduce driver workload when navigating through unfamiliar or novel environments (Burnett, 2000). As the burden of wayfinding is shifted from human to machine, drivers should experience less frustration and anxiety about locating new destinations. This in turn may free up cognitive resources to attend to other vehicles, cyclists, and pedestrians, as well as road conditions and weather. All of these factors will function to increase the safety of vehicle operation. Burns (1997, cf. Burnett, 2000) has suggested that IRANS may also increase driver confidence, and ultimately the mobility of older and disabled individuals who may have been previously wary of traveling within novel environments.

A critical aspect of IRANS usability concerns its effectiveness, efficiency, and user satisfaction (ISO 9241-part11, 1997). The driver needs to reach the destination in a manner that minimizes mental workload and matches his/her needs, abilities, and preferences. The interaction between the driver's preferred navigational strategy and the IRANS interface, whether it is visual or auditory, is directly related to these criteria. Studies suggest that driver frustration (Baldwin & Reiss, 2000) and mental workload (Furukawa, Baldwin, & Carpenter, 2003) increase when route guidance systems do not match the driver's preferred navigational strategy.

Lawton (1994, 1996) provides strong evidence for individual differences in navigational strategy. Lawton's Wayfinding Strategy Scale measures to what degree individuals rely on route and orientation (hereafter referred to as "survey") strategies when driving new routes. An example of a route preferred navigational strategy is someone who relies heavily on "turn left", "turn right" directions, counting streets or traffic lights, and landmarks. A survey strategy navigator tends to focus on the use of cardinal directions (north, south, east, or west), mileage, using the sun to determine driving direction, and the relationship of the vehicle to the center of the city.

Significant gender differences in navigational strategy have been observed (e.g., Lawton, 1994, 1996; Dabbs, Chang, Strong, & Milun, 1997), with females reporting greater use of route strategies and males preferring survey strategies. Findings from Lawton (2001) also suggest that men and women differ in the spatial referents used in direction giving. Whereas women referred more often to buildings as landmarks, men referred more often to cardinal directions. However, referring to cardinal directions was greater for both men and women who lived in the Midwest/West than those living in the Northeast/South. This body of evidence suggests that the adaptability of IRANS may be driven by gender and geographical differences.

Very few studies have examined gender and navigational strategies across cultures. Lawton and Kalloi (2002) found that men in both Hungary and the United States reported greater preference for survey strategies. Women in both countries had higher route strategy scores, although the gender difference was significant only for the American sample.

Individual differences in preferred navigational strategy have also been documented in Japan. Takeuchi (1992) devised the Sense of Direction-Short Form questionnaire to address these differences. Like the Lawton Scale, the Takeuchi instrument has two factors, entitled "awareness of orientation" (AO) and "memory for usual spatial behavior" (MUSB). Translation of the items suggest that AO may be tapping into the same strategies as Lawton's survey factor, as several items refer to cardinal directions and visualizing the route as a map-like image. Similarly, MUSB may mirror Lawton's route factor, as it includes items about landmarks and left-right turn combinations. Therefore, the primary purpose of this study was to validate Takeuchi's Sense of Direction Questionnaire-Short Form on an American sample. Similar factor loadings would support the stability of individual differences in navigational strategies between the cultures and geographically diverse locations. A second goal was to examine the relationship between Takeuchi's and Lawton's scales in relation to gender. Finally, we sought to validate Lawton's Wayfinding Strategy Scale, used primarily in the midwestern part of the United States, on a sample located in the southeastern United States.

METHOD

Navigational strategy was assessed using Lawton's (1994) and Takeuchi's (1992) scales. Data were collected across two semesters at an urban, commuter university located in the southeastern United States.

Participants

The participants were 304 American students (222 women, 82 men) recruited from undergraduate psychology courses who received course credit for their participation. Their mean age was 21.7 years, $sd = 5.1$ years.

Materials and Procedures

The questionnaire administered consisted of 31 items, and was the aggregation of Takeuchi's 17-item Sense of Direction Questionnaire-Short Form (obtained from Takeuchi) and Lawton's 14-item Wayfinding Strategy Scale. In Takeuchi's scale, participants indicated, on a scale from 1 (strongly disagree) to 5 (strongly agree), how well the statements reflected their sense of direction and navigational ability. An average for the 6 items representing the awareness of orientation subscale was calculated and labeled AO. Likewise, the memory for usual spatial behavior (MUSB) subscale was calculated by averaging the responses to the 8 remaining items. (Three items that did not load on either factor in the Japanese sample were included in our questionnaire but not included in the subscale calculations). In Lawton's scale, participants rated how typical it was for them to use a particular navigational strategy. The scale ranged from 1 (not at all typical of me) to 5 (very typical of me). The five items representing survey strategies were averaged to calculate the survey (SURV) subscale. The remaining 9 items determined the route strategy (ROUTE) subscale.

Principal component analyses were run to determine if the present sample yielded the same factor structures as those from Takeuchi's and Lawton's original samples. Next, correlations were calculated among gender, AO, MUSB, SURV, and ROUTE.

RESULTS

Principal component analyses from the Takeuchi's Sense of Direction Questionnaire-Short Form indicated that our sample responded in a manner very similar to a recent Japanese wayfinding strategy study (Kato & Takeuchi, 2003). We found that only one item from the AO subscale did not load on that factor with our American sample (Table 1). Likewise, only one item from the MUSB subscale did not load in the same manner as the Japanese sample. The three items that failed to load on either factor for Kato & Takeuchi (2003) also did not load for the American sample. When forced into two factors, data from the present study explained only 39.9% of the total variance, as compared to 53.9% from the Kato & Takeuchi (2003) study.

Principal component analyses from Lawton's Navigational Strategy Scale indicated that our sample also responded in a manner very similar to the Lawton's Midwest sample from which the instrument was validated. Although our loadings were slightly smaller than Lawton's, 9 of the 10 survey strategy items loaded on that factor (Table 2). However, one item actually loaded on the route factor. Likewise, only one item from the route subscale did not load on that factor. When forced into two factors, data from the present study explained 36.7% of the total variance. Lawton (1994; 1996) did not report explained variance.

Table 1. American factor loadings for Awareness of Orientation (AO) and Memory for Usual Spatial Behavior (MUSB) subscales.

Item from Sense of Direction Questionnaire	AO	MUSB
Awareness of orientation		
I have become confused, as to cardinal directions, when I am in an unfamiliar place.	**.711**	**-.001**
When I get route information, I can make use of "left or right information, but I can't use cardinal directions.	**.709**	**-.021**
When traveling as a passenger, I have difficulty identifying which cardinal direction we are moving in.	**.701**	**.070**
I can make correct choices as to cardinal directions in an unfamiliar place.	.551	-.005
I can visualize the route as a map-like image.	.544	.172
I can't make out which direction my hotel room faces.	.528	.074
I can tell where I am on a map.	-.514	-.382
Memory for usual spatial behavior		
I have poor memory for landmarks.	.217	.706
I cannot remember landmarks found in the area where I have often been.	.006	.696
I can't use landmarks in wayfinding.	-.060	.664
I can't remember the different aspects of sceneries.	.110	.621
I often can't find the way even if given detailed verbal information on the route.	.213	.599
I can't verify landmarks in the turn of the route.	.090	.569
Did not load on either factor		
I have a lot of difficulties reaching the unknown place even after looking at a map.	.549	.411
I often (or easily) forget which direction I have turned.	.507	.419
I become totally confused as to the correct sequence of the return way as a consequence of a number of left-right turns in the route.	.482	.229
I feel anxious about my walking direction in an unfamiliar area.	.395	.152

Several significant correlations between the two instruments were observed (Table 3). As hypothesized, Takeuchi's awareness of orientation factor (AO) was correlated with Lawton's survey factor (SURV), with $r = .481$ ($p<.001$, two-tailed). Gender was weakly correlated with both of these factors, with $r = -.248$ ($p<.001$, two-tailed), indicating that males had a greater tendency than females to use these strategies. Takeuchi's memory for usual spatial behavior (MUSB) had a weak correlation with Lawton's route (ROUTE) strategy, with $r = .252$ ($p<.001$, two-tailed).

Table 2. Southeastern U.S. factor loadings for Survey Strategy (SURV) and Route Strategy (ROUTE) subscales.

Items from Wayfinding Strategy Scale	SURV	ROUTE
Survey Strategy		
I kept track of where I was in relation to the sun (or moon) in the sky as I went.	.690	-.003
As I drove, I made a mental note of the mileage I had traveled on different roads.	.661	.177
I kept track of the relationship between where I was and the center of town.	.620	.008
I kept track of the direction (north, south, east, or west) in which I was going.	.572	.013
I visualized a map or layout of the area in my mind as I drove.	.544	.310
Before starting, I asked for directions telling me whether to go east, west, north, or south at particular streets or landmarks.	.510	-.113
Before starting, I asked for directions telling how far to go in terms of mileage.	.481	.296
I referred to a published road map.	.470	-.053
I kept track of the relationship between where I was and the next place where I had to change direction.	.193	.553
Route Strategy		
I made a mental note of landmarks, such as buildings or natural features, that I passed along the way.	-.004	.746
Before starting, I asked for directions telling me whether to turn right or left at particular streets or landmarks.	.259	.683
As I drove, I made a mental note of the number of streets I passed before making each turn.	.138	.682
Before starting, I asked for directions telling me how many streets	-.141	.510
Did not load on either factor		
Before starting, I asked for a hand-drawn map of the area.	.117	.225

DISCUSSION

It appears that individual differences in sense of direction and navigational strategy among the Japanese are also evidenced in the American sample. The only item that did not load in a similar fashion referred to anxiety about walking direction in an unfamiliar area. It is possible that the translation did not quite capture the intended meaning, and may have been interpreted by some individuals in the present sample as referring to anxiety about personal safety, rather than walking direction, in an unfamiliar area.

As hypothesized, Takeuchi's awareness for orientation tapped into the same latent structure as Lawton's survey strategy. Takeuchi's memory for usual spatial behavior was weakly correlated with both of Lawton's factors. Consistent with prior research, males were more likely to report using survey strategies and possessing a greater awareness of orientation than females. Likewise, women reported using route strategies and having a greater memory for usual spatial behavior, both of which rely heavily on landmarks, although this trend was not significant. Previous research (Lawton, 2001) suggests that geographical location within the United States may influence navigational strategy, as inferred from what people use as referents in direction giving. However, the present study indicated stable individual differences between Lawton's original Midwest sample and our Southeast sample.

CONCLUSION

Individual differences in navigational strategy appear to be consistent across gender, geographical location with the United States, and cross-culturally. Regardless of the measurement instrument used, it is clear that individuals have preferred navigational strategies that can be classified along two dimensions – survey/cardinal directions and route/landmarks. It is imperative that these individual differences are reflected in the design on IRANS interfaces. Navigational information presented to drivers should meet their needs and preferences. Providing landmark information may not necessarily frustrate or influence the driving performance of a survey-oriented individual. However, presenting cardinal directions may actually increase the mental workload for a strongly route strategy person, as cognitive resources are expended in an effort to suppress superfluous, confusing information. Preliminary research by Baldwin & Reiss (2000) and Furukawa, Baldwin, & Carpenter (2003) support this hypothesis, and we will continue research in this area.

REFERENCES

Baldwin, C. L., & Reiss, R. (2000). Preferred navigational style assessment as a method of optimizing IRANS displays. Proceedings of the Fourth Conference on Automation Technology and Human Performance and the Third Conference on Situation Awareness in Complex Systems, Savannah, Georgia.

Burnett, G. (2000). 'Turn right at the traffic lights': The requirement for landmarks in vehicle navigation systems. Journal of Navigation, 53(3), 499-510.

Dobbs, J. M., Chang, E-L., Strong, R. A., & Milun, R. (1998). Spatial ability, navigational strategy, and geographic knowledge among men and women. Evolution and Human Behavior, 19, 89-98.

Furukawa, H., Baldwin, C. L., & Carpenter, E. M. (2004). Supporting drivers' area-learning task with visual geo-centered and audio ego-centered guidance: Interference or better performance? Proceedings of the HPSAA II Human Performance, Situation Awareness and Automation Technology Conference, Daytona Beach, Florida.

ISO (1997). Ergonomics requirements for office work with Visual Display Terminals (VDTs) (ISO 9241: Part 11 ISO/DIS 9241-11: Guidance on Usability). International Standards Organisation, Geneva, Switzerland.

Kato, Y., & Takeuchi, Y. (2003). Individual differences in wayfinding strategies. Journal of Environmental Psychology, 23(2), 171-188.

Lawton, C. A. (1994). Gender differences in way-finding strategies: Relationship to spatial abilities and anxiety. Sex Roles, 30(11/12), 765-779.

Lawton, C. A. (2001). Gender and regional differences in spatial referents used in direction giving. Sex Roles, 44, 321-388.

Lawton, C. A., & Kallai, J. (2002). Gender differences in wayfinding strategies and anxiety about wayfinding: A cross-cultural comparison. Sex Roles, 47(9/10), 389-401.

Aging and Driving Part I: Implications of Perceptual and Physical Changes

Janan Al-Awar Smither, Mustapha Mouloua, and Peter Hancock
University of Central Florida

Jacqueline Duley and Richard Adams
Booz Allen Hamilton

Kara Latorella,
NASA Langley

ABSTRACT

By the year 2030 one in every five Americans will be 65 years of age or older. Although future older adults are likely to be healthier and more active than their peers of today, age-related changes are inevitable and are bound to affect functional abilities especially as they relate to driving. With regard to physical changes, the driving task predominantly involves the execution of motor responses that are clearly subject to age-related declines. Furthermore, with age, a number of changes occur in the human eye that make the visual system operate less efficiently. In addition, declines in the performance of the auditory and vestibular systems and in spatial abilities also compromise driving and mobility. The present paper provides a review of age-related declines in physical and perceptual functioning and discusses their impact on the driving performance and safe mobility of older adults.

Key Words: Aging, Driving, Functional Capacity, Physical Capability, Perceptual Performance

INTRODUCTION

It is, at present, estimated that approximately 13% of the U.S. population is 65 years of age and older. This segment of the population is expected to compose 22% by the year 2030 (Berg & Cassells, 1990). Advances in healthcare, technology, and lifestyle however, suggest that the average older adult of the future will potentially have functional capacity that will exceed their modern day peers. Although future older adults are likely to be healthier and more active, age-related changes are inevitable and are bound to affect functional ability (Birren & Schaie, 1977) especially as they relate to driving.

Since driving is mainly an information processing activity, older drivers face more challenges than younger ones. Older drivers have more cashes than younger drivers because of sensory and decision-making processes. Younger drivers, on the other hand, have more crashes because of speed and risk taking (Cunningham and Brookbank, 1988; Verhaegen, Toebat, and Delbeke, 1988). Figure 1, which depicts the involvement, injury, and fatality rates by age group per vehicle miles of travel (VMT) shows how drivers over 75 are involved in more crashes than any other single age group.

Driving and Declines in Physical Functioning

Neuromuscular system changes that accompany aging affect motor performance capability (Vercruyssen, 1997). The driving task predominantly involves the execution of motor responses that are clearly subject to age-related declines (Vercruyssen, 1997). These declines include a general slowing down of behavior (Cerella, 1985), reduction in movement control, weakening in strength and flexibility, reductions in height and weight, and shorter arm and leg reach. In addition, joint pain and stiffness restrict head and body movement and mobility. These constraints on mobility serve to diminish older drivers' abilities to monitor lane position in heavy traffic, change lanes, view blind spots, view gauges, reach controls, and see over the steering wheel. Ultimately, such constraints reduce capacity to respond quickly to imminent danger. Older people also have problems raising their eyes and are slower to accomplish eye movements in order to fixate on objects that are moving around them. Often aging leads to substantial loss of peripheral information detection, which is vital for efficient and safe driving operations at busy intersections.

INVOLVEMENT, INJURY, and FATALITY RATES
(RATES per VEHICLE MILES of TRAVEL)

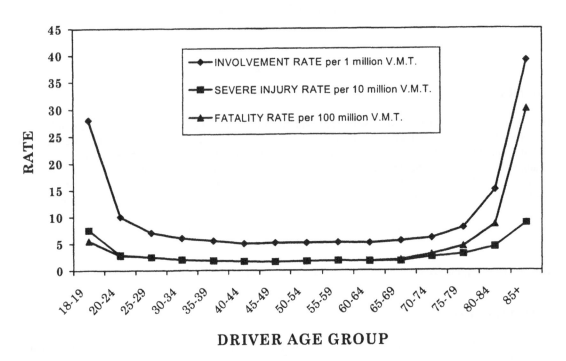

Figure 1: The involvement, injury, and fatality rates by age group per vehicle miles of travel (VMT)

Degraded sensory information due to aging affects reaction time when making perceptual discriminations such as road signs and signals. This effect is exacerbated further when coupled with other conditions such as poor visibility.

These findings have major implications for designing, and evaluating appropriate "standard" reaction times in traffic systems. Traffic situations that require scanning a multitude of visual information are difficult for older drivers, especially if they suffer declines in both static and dynamic visual acuity. Sources of this visual information include in-vehicle control panel displays, outside advertisement, directional signs, as well as the critical forward view of the roadway itself. Since we know that it would take an older driver 1.5 to 1.7 times longer on average than a younger driver to scan for information, it would be appropriate to place signs and signals well in advance of the necessary response to allow older drivers to plan and react safely and in a timely manner. Table 1 summarizes the documented motor related changes that have special implications for driving and aging.

Driving and Declines in Sensory and Perceptual Functioning

In terms of perceptual functioning, the driving task mainly involves vision. As we age, a number of changes occur in the human eye that make the visual system operate less efficiently (Owsley & Sloane, 1990). Normal age-related changes in vision are a result of structural changes which begin in the 40's, and retinal changes which begin in the 50's (Kline & Schieber, 1982).). Table 2, provides information on the range of visual deterioration with age and their implications for driving.

Few researchers have investigated the relationship between hearing ability and driving performance. Poser (1993) asserts that even complete and uncorrectable hearing loss is rarely considered a restriction for driving. One exploratory study, which examined the association between medical conditions, functional variables and at-fault collisions in a cohort of older drivers, included the two variables "hearing handicap" and "using a hearing aid" (Sims, Owsley, Allman, Ball, & Smoot, 1998). Such findings, however, indicated no significant relationships between either of these variables and crash history. An interesting investigation by Holland and Rabbitt (1992) though, suggests that older adults who are aware of declines in their sensory abilities (vision and/or hearing) are more likely to make adjustments in their road-use behaviors (e.g. restrict driving to daylight hours), and are also less likely to be involved in collisions.

Table 1. Implications of age-related motor changes on driving

Motor Function	Age-related Changes	Implications for Driving
Speed of response	Slower reaction time	Slower to respond to situation—e.g. break reaction time, changing lanes Affects ability to respond quickly to imminent danger
Movement control	Reduced control	Impacts safe driving in a timely fashion—takes longer to initiate movement and to carry it through
Strength and Flexibility	Weakens with aging	Affects ability to open and close vehicle doors, manipulate gauges and steering wheel etc.
Height and Weight	Reduction in both	Affects ability to see over the steering wheel, monitor lane position in heavy traffic, change lanes
Arms and Legs	Shorter reach	Affects ability to reach gauges
Joints	Pain and stiffness	Restricts head and body movement and mobility
Eye movements	Slow down	Slower to accomplish eye movements to fixate on objects that are moving around in the environment

General spatial abilities, which peak during the second or third decades of life, decline steadily in later life (Salthouse, 1982). These deficits cannot be attributed to the general slowing down of processing that accompanies aging, as they are apparent even when spatial ability tests are not time limited. Furthermore, tasks that require the older adult to integrate spatial information or to use working memory operations extensively show even more decline (Morrell & Echt, 1997; Salthouse, 1991). Cherry and Park (1993) found that familiarity and contextual cues, however, ameliorate the problems both younger and older adults have in spatial localization tasks.

As a result of declines in spatial ability, older adults experience difficulty with spatial relations and with mental rotation tasks. So, if an older adult is required to manipulate information displayed on one plane through another plane (e.g. use a mouse to control a cursor on the screen), he or she is likely to experience difficulty (Charness, Bosman, & Elliot, 1995). The same would hold true if an older adult is required to perform a task involving mental rotation. Examples of such tasks include localizing objects in 3-D space and interpreting information displayed in the rearview and side mirrors of a car. Older adults are also likely to have more difficulties in route finding and learning when information is displayed in a schematic as opposed to verbal form.

Table 2. Implications of age-related visual changes on driving

Visual Function	Age-related Changes	Implications for Driving
Static Visual Acuity	Decline from young adulthood on—Ave for >65 years is 20/70	Inability to see highway signs, dashboard information, etc. when stationary
Dynamic Visual Acuity	Declines steadily with age—more pronounced than static acuity	Inability to identify signs etc. when moving
Contrast Sensitivity	Lower sensitivities at some spatial frequencies	Impaired: 1. Identification of aspect ratios of objects and vehicles 2. Perception of road signs, 3. Distinction between symbols, faces, text, etc. 4. Perception of in-vehicle controls and gauges 5. Perception of the relative distance and speed of moving vehicles 6. Judgment under adverse weather and traffic conditions.
Dark Adaptation	Rate slows with age	Decreased ability to see under low levels of illumination and to recover from transient light adaptation
Accommodation	Decreased accommodative amplitude and increased latency	Poor recognition of dashboard information and difficulty in focusing on objects at different distances
Glare	Increased sensitivity and reduced tolerance	Impaired object detection and recognition with transient light adaptation
Color Vision	Impaired color discrimination especially in blue-green part of visual spectrum	Impaired information processing of color-coded highway and in-vehicle information
Motion-in-depth	Impaired ability to judge distance and speed of vehicle in front	Impaired gap judgment and more likely to rear-end vehicle
Gaze Stability	Lower pursuit gains	Impaired visual tracking of moving objects in vicinity
Critical Flicker Frequency	Thresholds show a steady decline	Persistence of low contrast images of vehicles and objects
Absolute Threshold	Sensitivity to light decreases by about 4% per year	Decreased ability to see under low levels of illumination

As with all other sensory abilities, older adults experience a decline in the sensitivity of skin and in the senses of smell and taste. These declines mean that older adults are less sensitive to temperature changes and extremes, to skin pressure, and to pain (Laux, 1995). Older adults also have more difficulty discriminating shapes and textures by touch and are also less likely to detect noxious gases and spoiled foods (Laux, 1995). These declines should be taken into account when developing systems that are likely to use tactile and/or olfaction input and output devices.

REFERENCES

Berg, R. L., & Cassells, J. S. (Eds.). (1990). *The second fifty years: Promoting health and preventing disability*, Washington, D.C.: National Academy Press.

Birren, J., & Schaie, W. (Eds.). (2001). *Handbook of the psychology of aging, 5th ed.* San Diego, Ca: Academic Press.

Cerella, J. (1985) Information processing rates in the elderly. *Psychological Bulletin, 98*. 67-83.

Charness, N., Bosman, E. A., & Elliot, R. G. (1995, August). *Senior-friendly input devices: is the pen mightier than the mouse?* Paper presented at the 103rd annual convention of the American Psychological Association, New York.

Cherry, K. E., & Park, D. C. (1993). Individual differences and contextual variables influence spatial memory in younger and older adults. *Psychology and Aging, 8*, 517-526.

Cunningham, W.R., & Brookbank, J.W. (1988). *Gerontology.* New York: Harper & Row.

Grafman (Eds.), *Handbook of neuropsychology* (Vol. 4, pp. 229-249). Amsterdam: Elsevier.

Holland, C.A., & Rabbitt, P.M.A. (1992). People's awareness of their age-related sensory and cognitive deficits and the implications for road safety. *Applied Cognitive Psychology, 6*, 217-231.

Kline, D., & Schieber, F. (1985). Vision and aging. In J. E. Birren & K. W. Schaie (Eds.), *Handbook of the Psychology of Aging* (2nd ed., pp.296-331). New York: Van Nostrand Reinhold.

Laux, L. (1995). Aging techniques. In J. Weimer (Ed.), *Research Techniques in Human Engineering.* Englewood Cliffs, NJ: Prentice Hall.

Poser, M.D. (1993). Automobile driving fitness and neurological impairment. *Journal of Neuropsychiatry, 5(3)*, 342-348.

Morrell, R. W., & Echt, K. V. (1997). Designing written instruction for older adults: Learning to use computers. .), *Handbook of human factors and the older adult.* San Diego, CA: Academic Press.

Owsley, C., & Sloane, M. E. (1990). Vision and aging. In F. Boller & J.

Sims, R.V., Owsley, C., Allman, R.M., Ball, K., & Smoot, T.M. (1998). A preliminary assessment of the medical and functional factors associated with vehicle crashes by older adults. *Journal of the American Geriatrics Society, 46(5)*, 556-561.

Salthouse, T. A., (1982). *Adult cognition: An experimental psychology of human aging*, New York: Springer-Verlag.

Salthouse, T. A. (1991). *Theoretical perspectives on cognitive aging.* Hillsdale, NJ: Erlbaum.

Vercruyssen, M. (1997). Movement control and speed of behavior. In A. D. Fisk and W. A. Rogers (Eds.), *Handbook of human factors and the older adult.* San Diego, CA: Academic Press.

Verhaegen, P.K. (1995). Liability of older drivers in collisions. *Ergonomics, 38 (3)*, 499-507.

Verhaegen, P.K., Toebat, K.L., & Delbeke, L. L. (1988). Safety of older drivers: A study in their over-involvement ratio. *Proceedings of the Human Factors Society-32 Annual Meeting*, 185-188.

Aging and Driving II: Implications of Cognitive Changes.

Mustapha Mouloua, Janan Smither, and Peter Hancock,
University of Central Florida;

Jacqueline Duley and Richard Adams,
Booz-Allan Hamilton;

Kara Latorella,
NASA Langley

ABSTRACT

In this paper, we review and discuss a number of age-related changes in cognitive capabilities and their implications on driving performance and safety. Previous research has shown that older drivers can exhibit performance degradation and a reduction in safety margin because of the relative decline in sensory/perceptual, cognitive abilities, as well as the slowing in motor response. We begin by reviewing and evaluating extant theories of cognitive change and the mechanisms that underlie such variation. Then we examine how these changes are manifested and influenced by advancing age. Third, we examine the impact of these age-related cognitive changes on driver performance. Finally, we outline the importance of these findings for intelligent transportation systems design, driver distraction and driver workload, and ultimately transportation safety in an aging society.

Key Words: Aging, Driving Performance, Cognitive Capabilities, Cognitive Changes, Safety, Intelligent Transportation Systems (ITS)

BACKGROUND

There are several reduced cognitive abilities that may affect driving performance of older drivers. First, it is noteworthy to mention that cognition does not act in isolation. There is a constant interaction between the physiological system in terms of visual information processing and cognitive performance. It is conceivable that older drivers who suffer from poor vision would ultimately have worse cognitive performance irrespective of the degree of age related cognitive declines. In other words, declines in physiological performance exacerbate the effects of aging on cognitive functioning. Brouwer (1993) contends that impairments that lie both on the level of receptor-effector organs and on the level of cognitive functioning, particularly attention, contribute to the problems older drivers encounter with the driving task. For example, perceptual, cognitive, and motor declines affect an older driver's ability to merge with traffic. On the perceptual level, older adults have difficulty seeing and determining the speed and distance of the traffic they need to merge with. On the motor level, they have difficulty turning their necks and looking back far enough to see that traffic. And, cognitively, they have difficulty maintaining all the information needed to make a decision about joining the flow of traffic because of declines in attention and working memory. When they eventually respond however, they are slower to do so than the situation requires.

Human Cognition and Driving

Clearly, cognitive performance is critical because driving requires the attentiveness of the individual to the driving environment (Transportation Research Board, 1988a, 1988b). Cognition is also fundamental to other phases of the task in that the driver, after perceiving the stimulus, needs to recognize it, make a choice of a response, and finally execute that response. Driving a modern automobile in light traffic on a clear day may not necessarily overtax many drivers. However, driving in heavy traffic at high speed at night on poorly marked roads or at complex intersections can exceed many drivers' abilities (Rinalducci, Smither and Bowers, 1993). This difficulty can be attributed to the decline in reserve capacity with aging. In other words, complex environments produce a need for more cognitive resources than usual. Younger adults are able to use "reserve capacity" to fulfill that need, however, that capacity diminishes with age and is not available in the same way for the older adult. This explains why an older driver has more difficulty in attending to the driving task and is slower at processing information, especially when required to make complex decisions. Older drivers also demonstrate slower motor responses (Rinalducci, Smither and Bowers, 1993). Thus, the older driver is at a disadvantage both perceptually and cognitively in dealing with complex traffic situations.

Darzentas, McDowell and Cooper (1980) reported that older drivers differed significantly in judging the length of gap acceptance as compared to younger drivers. In general, older drivers are more cautious about gap acceptance because they often exhibit slow maneuvers; gaps appear to be too short for them to execute comfortable maneuvers.

Spatial abilities are also affected by the aging process. Previous research has shown that age-related deficits in mental rotation tasks have detrimental impact on certain components of the driving task. Albert and Kaplan (1980) reported that older people tend to focus only one piece when asked to identify an object by mentally re-arranging several pieces. Thus, older drivers have major difficulties focusing on more than one source of traffic information in order to judge what a safe gap is at a busy intersection. Also, because older drivers tend to be very slow and not quite physically flexible when turning their bodies and heads when looking around, they often need to rely on mirrors (side and rear-view mirrors) to perceive the world around them. As a result, they have problems with perceiving and interpreting some of the mirrored scenes, as well as viewing moving vehicles in blind spots.

Traffic accidents caused by elderly drivers have been attributed by some investigators to neglect or inattention to relevant information from road signs and from other cars and pedestrians (Ponds, Brouwer, & Wolffelaar, 1988). McDowd and Birren (1990) discuss four commonly used categories of attention as they relate to age. These categories include (1) divided attention, (2) switching attention, (3) sustained attention, and (4) selective attention. Craik (1977), McDowd and Craik (1988), and McDowd and Birren (1990) suggest that there are age-related differences, especially when more complex tasks are employed. Brouwer (1993), Brouwer, Ickenroth, Van Wolffelaar, and Ponds, (1990), Brouwer, Waterink, Van Wolffelaar and Rothengatter (1991), and Brouwer and Van Zomeren (1992) have demonstrated that performance on divided attention tasks reveal age-related impairments and that the magnitude of the effect depends on the nature of the combined tasks. The above researchers were also able to demonstrate the effect in a combination of tasks in a dynamic driving simulator. Parasuraman and Nestor (1991), however, contend that the component of attention most implicated as a correlate of accident involvement in professional drivers is attention switching. These correlations were found in dichotic listening tasks and were higher for samples including older professional drivers than for samples including only younger subjects (Brouwer, 1993). Overall, levels of performance in a sustained attention or vigilance task seems to be lower for older as compared to younger adults, but there is little difference in the vigilance decrement. However, this does suggest that long stretches of highway or turnpike driving may place the older driver at risk. Rabbitt (1965) concluded that older adults are more distracted by irrelevant information than young adults. Plude and Hoyer (1985) suggest that age-related decrements in selective attention may be related to a decline in the ability to localize task-related information in the visual field. A reduced ability to demonstrate selective attention in a complex traffic situation could easily be a considerable hazard for the older driver. In other words, an older adult may be directing his or her attention to the wrong stimulus in the environment and therefore miss the cues indicating a potential hazardous situation. Ball and Owsley (1991) have developed a predictive model of overall and intersection accidents for older drivers using the factors of accidents, useful field of view (UFOV), visual function, eye health, and mental status. Mental status was assessed using the Mattis Organic Mental Status Syndrome Examination (MOMSEE). They found the best predictors of intersection accidents to be UFOV and mental status. It appears that declines in attention capacity result in an increase in intersection accidents among older drivers because there is too much to watch for from all directions.

INTELLIGENT TRANSPORTATION SYSTEMS

It is evident from the foregoing discussion that *average* aging is accompanied by deterioration in different cognitive capacities with individual differences exerting a significant influence on this pattern for any one individual. Further, it is clear that one disadvantage that accompanies aging is a differential disadvantage when dealing with complex, multi-dimensional, multi-task demands. The problem of the aging driver is thus exacerbated by the forthcoming introduction of intelligent transportation systems (ITS). These promise to introduce new functional capabilities into the vehicle but presently, only at the expense of elevated driver demands. Such innovations must be designed with the older driver in mind, otherwise these individuals who are barely competent now will obviously become a danger, and those of reasonable abilities will see an erosion of the margin of driver safety (Hancock, Lianeras, & Vercruyssen, 1999). ITS technology designs have to minimize distraction and suppress parallel or dual-task demands as much as possible. This will mean "locking-out" certain technical capacities while the vehicle is in motion, or passing legislation (as some states and countries have) to make such dual operations unlawful. However, the innovative designer can minimize the problems encountered by older drivers by a careful reading of the information presented in this article.

Table 1. Implications of age-related cognitive changes on driving

Cognitive Function	Age-related Changes	Implications for Driving
Reserve Capacity	Diminishes with aging	Declines in the ability to handle complex environments and situations—e.g. traffic congestion, busy intersections
Working Memory	Reduced storage capacity and processing efficiency	Ability to recall information about traffic environment is adversely affected Difficulty in storing new information and processing other information at the same time
Complex Judgment	Diminishes with aging	Difficulty in judging length of gap acceptance—problems in merging, lane changing, yielding right of way
Spatial Ability	Declines with aging	Major difficulty focusing on more than one source of traffic information—i.e. unable to maintain an accurate picture of the locations of objects and vehicles in environment
Mental Rotation	Declines in efficiency	Difficulty in interpreting information obtained from rear and side view mirrors
Divided Attention	Declines with aging	Impaired ability to control various devices at the same time—e.g. steering wheel, radio, phone etc.
Switching Attention	Declines with aging—appears to be most important	Switching attention from the various sources in the environment—e.g. rearview mirror to side mirrors to windshield to dashboard information etc.
Sustained Attention	Declines with aging	Problems with long stretches of highway
Selective Attention	Declines with aging	Problems screening out irrelevant information in a complex environment—e.g. which vehicle or object to pay attention to
Processing Speed	Overall slowing	Slower to detect , recognize, and respond to stimulus in environment

REFERENCES

Albert, M.S. and Kaplan, E. (1980) Organic Implications of Neuropsychological Deficits in the Elderly. In L.W. Poon, J.L. Fozard, L.S. Cermak, D. Arenberg and L.W. Thomson. (Eds) New Directions in Memory and Aging: Proceedings of the George Talland Memorial Conference. Hillsdale, N.J., Lawrence Erlbaum Assoc.

Ball, K., & Owsley, C. (1991). Identifying correlates of accident involvement for the older driver. Human Factors, 33(5), 583-595.

Brouwer, W.H. (1993). Older drivers and attentional demands: consequences for human factors research. In the Proceedings of the Human Factors and Ergonomics Society-Europe Chapter on Aging and Human Factors, (pp.93-106); Soesterberg, Netherlands.

Brouwer, W.H., Ickenroth, J., Van Wolffelaar, P.C., & Ponds, R.W. H. M. (1990). Divided attention in old age: difficulty integrating skills. In Drenth, P., Sergeant, J., & Takens, R. (Eds.), European Perspectives in Psychology, Vol. 2, (pp. 335-348); New York, John Wiley.

Brouwer, W.H., Waterink, W., Van Wolffelaar, P.C., & Rothengatter, J.A. (1991). Divided attention in experienced young and older drivers: lane tracking and visual analysis in a dynamic driving simulator. Human Factors, 33, 573-582.

Brouwer, W.H., & van Zomeren, Adriaan H. (1992). Assessment of attention. In Crawford, J. P., et al. (Eds.) A handbook of neuropsychological assessment, (pp. 241-266); Lawrence Erlbaum Associates, Inc. Hove, England UK.

Craik, F.I.M. (1977). Age differences in human memory. In J.E. Birren & K.W. Schaie (Eds.), Handbook of the psychology of aging (pp. 384-420). New York: Van Nostrand Reinhold.

Darzentas, J., McDowell, M.R.C. and Cooper, D.F. (1980) Minimum acceptable gaps and conflict involvement in a simple crossing maneuver. Traffic Engineering and Control, 21, 58-61.

Hancock, P.A., Lianeras, R.E., & Vercruyssen, M. (1999). Older drivers and smart cars: Is technology the answer? In: R. W. Cobb and J.F. Coughlin (Eds.). Are older a policy problem? The social construction of a public health issue. Johns Hopkins Press: Baltimore, MD.

McDowd, J.M., & Craik, F.I.M. (1988). Effects of aging and task difficulty on divided attention performance. Journal of Experimental Psychology: Human Perception and Performance, 14 (2), 267-280.

McDowd, J.M., & Birren, J.E. (1990). Aging and attentional processes. In Birren, J.E. & Schaie (Eds.) Handbook of the Psychology of Aging, 3rd edition (pp. 222-233). San Diego: Academic Press.

Parasuraman, R., & Nestor, P.G. (1991). Attention and driving skills in aging and Alzheimer's disease. Human Factors, 33, 539-557.

Plude, D.J., & Hoyer, W.J. (1985). Attention and performance: Identifying and localizing age deficits. In Charness, N. (Ed.), Aging and human performance. New York: John Wiley & Sons, Ltd., 47-99.Ponds, R.W.H.M., Brouwer, W.H., & Wolffelaar, P.C. van (1988). Age differences in divided attention in a simulated driving task. Journal of Gerontology, 43 (6), 151-156.

Rabbitt, P. (1965). An age-decrement in the ability to ignore irrelevant information. Journal of Gerontology, 20, 233-238.

Rinalducci, E.J., Smither, J.A., & Bowers, C. (1993) The effects of age on vehicular control and other technological applications. In Wise, J.A., Hopkin, V.D., & Stager, P. (Editors), Verification and Validation of Complex Systems: Additional Human Factors Issues. Daytona Beach, FL: Embry-Riddle University Press.

Transportation Research Board, National Research Council (1988a). Transportation in an aging society: Improving mobility and safety for older persons. Vol. 1. Committee report and recommendations. Transportation Research Board Research Report 218. Washington, D.C.: National Academy of Sciences Press.

Transportation Research Board, National Research Council (1988b). Transportation in an aging society: Improving mobility and safety for older persons. Vol. 2. Technical papers. Transportation Research Board Research Report 218. Washington, D.C.: National Academy of Sciences Press.

Printed and bound by CPI Group (UK) Ltd, Croydon, CR0 4YY

17/10/2024

01775694-0020